The Journals of David E. Lilienthal

VOLUME VII

UNFINISHED BUSINESS

A 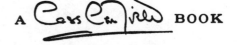 BOOK

Books by David E. Lilienthal

THE JOURNALS OF DAVID E. LILIENTHAL

VOLUME I THE TVA YEARS, 1939–1945

VOLUME II THE ATOMIC ENERGY YEARS, 1945–1950

VOLUME III THE VENTURESOME YEARS, 1950–1955

VOLUME IV THE ROAD TO CHANGE, 1955–1959

VOLUME V THE HARVEST YEARS, 1959–1963

VOLUME VI CREATIVITY AND CONFLICT, 1964–1967

MANAGEMENT: A HUMANIST ART

CHANGE, HOPE, AND THE BOMB

BIG BUSINESS: A NEW ERA

THIS I DO BELIEVE

TVA: DEMOCRACY ON THE MARCH

The Journals of David E. Lilienthal

VOLUME VII

UNFINISHED
BUSINESS
1968-1981

Edited by Helen M. Lilienthal

HARPER & ROW, PUBLISHERS, New York
Cambridge, Philadelphia, San Francisco, London
Mexico City, São Paulo, Sydney

F I R S T   E D I T I O N
Designer: Sidney Feinberg

Library of Congress Cataloging in Publication Data
(Revised for vol. 7)

Lilienthal, David Eli, 1899–
    The journals of David E. Lilienthal.

    Vol. 7 edited by Helen M. Lilienthal.
    Vol. 7 in series: A Cass Canfield book.
    CONTENTS: v. 1. The TVA years, 1939–1945.—v. 2. The atomic
energy years, 1945–1950.—[etc.]—v. 7. Unfinished business, 1968–1981.
    1. Lilienthal, David Eli, 1899–   . 2. Statesmen
—United States—Biography. I. Lilienthal, Helen M.
II. Title.
E748.L7A33   973.9′092′4   64–18056
ISBN 0–06–015182–X (vol. 7)

83 84 85 86 10 9 8 7 6 5 4 3 2 1

CONTENTS

[v]

A section of illustrations follows page 272.

PUBLISHER'S NOTE

With Volume VII, *Unfinished Business, 1968–1981,* Harper & Row completes the major publishing venture begun in 1964 with the appearance of the first two volumes of *The Journals of David E. Lilienthal.*

These seven volumes—covering more than four decades of Mr. Lilienthal's career—constitute an important historical record. It is doubtful whether any American of comparable stature in this century has written with greater frankness and feeling about the central issues and personalities of the times. Certainly few could approach his range of experience as an innovator of economic and social changes—changes which are vividly brought to life in these pages.

The Lilienthal *Journals* are above all the story of a man's life from day to day, and it is as a narrative—a human adventure—that we believe this work will endure. Its freshness, immediacy, and vigor were quickly recognized by readers of the early volumes. Its value as a prime historical source has also been established. The *Journals* are cited with increasing frequency by historians, biographers, and journalists.*

This is the extraordinary record of an extraordinary life. Mr. Lilienthal was a man of action, achievement, and controversy. He had strong convictions about social justice and freedom, and a tireless curiosity about the way people lived and worked all over the world.

Early volumes cover the period of his public service under Franklin D. Roosevelt and Harry Truman, when he became known first as the

---

*Mr. Lilienthal's papers, including the uncut journals in their entirety, are housed in Princeton University's Seeley G. Mudd Manuscript Library, together with the records of Development and Resources Corporation.

leader in the pioneering development of the Tennessee Valley Authority, widely regarded as the most lasting accomplishment of the New Deal, and then as the first Chairman of the U.S. Atomic Energy Commission in the fateful years of America's nuclear monopoly.

Subsequent *Journal* volumes record the broadening range and variety of his later activities: as a Wall Street entrepreneur; as a writer, lecturer, and business consultant; then as founder and chief executive officer of a unique private company—Development and Resources Corporation—that initiated economic development programs in five continents during the final quarter-century of Mr. Lilienthal's career.

This concluding volume of the *Journals* tells the story of the last years of Mr. Lilienthal's life, its pages enlivened by close-up views of many of the protagonists of yesterday's headlines—Lyndon Johnson, Robert McNamara, Richard Nixon, the Shah of Iran, and a crowd of others, all caught with a reporter's eye for detail and an insider's knowledge of the workings of power. Here is the record of the ending of American involvement in Vietnam, and of Mr. Lilienthal's participation in that tragic story. Here, too, is a bitter account of the political upheaval in Iran that drove the Shah from power, and abruptly ended the work of Mr. Lilienthal's company there. These are the endings; there are beginnings, too—new ideas, new enthusiasms, new possibilities for the future.

David E. Lilienthal died on January 14, 1981, at the age of 81. Among the many projects he left unfinished was the editing of this final volume of his *Journals,* a task which has been completed by his wife, Helen M. Lilienthal, with the assistance of their children, Nancy Lilienthal Bromberger and David E. Lilienthal, Jr., and Mr. Lilienthal's former secretary, Mildred Baron.

EDITOR'S NOTE

My husband began keeping a private journal in 1917, the year we first met, as undergraduates at DePauw University in Greencastle, Indiana. His early entries were handwritten in a bound notebook. There were few of them at first; most were year-end summaries, usually made at Christmastime. He wrote little during the twenties, when he was a young lawyer in Chicago with a growing reputation as an expert in public utility regulation. His journal-keeping became more frequent in 1931 at the outset of his public career (he was appointed to the Wisconsin Public Service Commission in that year, and in 1933 was named to the board of directors of the newly formed TVA).

The record of the 1930s is not, however, a full one. My husband set down many of the high points of the early years of the TVA—the White House meetings with Franklin D. Roosevelt, for example, and the battles fought and won against Wendell L. Willkie (over public power) and Harold Ickes (over TVA's independence)—but many other important events went unrecorded.

The year 1939 marks the beginning of the journals as a sustained narrative kept on virtually a daily basis. My husband wrote most entries in shorthand for a secretary to transcribe later. Some he composed himself on the typewriter; a few he wrote in longhand. He made journal entries at odd moments of his busy days, often jotting notes during conference breaks, or while travelling by plane or train. In these years, he had no idea that the journals would someday be published. He wrote them for himself as a means of expressing his anger or satisfaction at the events of the day; he thought, too, that they might be useful someday as a source for other writings.

When in the early 1960s he began reviewing his journals in order to prepare the first two volumes, he decided to let them stand as he had first written them. "If these Journals have a value," he wrote, "it is the value of a record made at the time, with instances of poor judgment, pettiness, vanity, and murky prose not edited and rewritten with the gift of hindsight, but remaining as originally set down years ago."

In this seventh volume, I have tried to follow this criterion. Space limitations have required substantial cutting of what my husband wrote in these years (much of the material eliminated concerns complex business matters of limited general interest). In what is included in this volume, I have made no changes except where the text would otherwise be unclear, and I have dropped those references to individuals (where no public issue was at stake) which it would have been in questionable taste to retain.

My husband had a strong sense of history and of his place in it; justly so, for he contributed much, not only to his own country but also to others. His pride in what he achieved is expressed in these pages, as is his chagrin at his mistakes and misjudgments.

He was often ahead of his time. Many of his ideas were later taken up by others (who not infrequently took credit for them). Many of his initiatives bore fruit in later years, his part in them forgotten or inadequately recognized. In the 1960s he was the first figure of any importance to warn of the unresolved dangers of atomic energy plants (at the same time accepting his share of responsibility for the planning stage of this program when he was AEC Chairman, 1946–50). He knew more of the human art of management, I believe, than did any other man, and gave freely of his ideas and experience to others. He was quicker than most to see the course events were taking, and what the future might hold (the term "multinational corporation" he coined in a 1960 speech). In recent years, he was the first to advocate reactivating the country's hundreds of abandoned small hydroelectric plants, a now thriving energy program of increasing importance.

He was a vigorous man, energetic and ebullient. For many years in Tennessee he rode his beloved horse, Mac. He was an enthusiastic sailor, swimmer, walker; he was dedicated to his garden. With advancing years, these activities were one by one denied him. In the last period of his life he suffered the frustrations of cataracts and the torments of arthritis (in 1980 he underwent a bilateral hip operation). He met these troubles as he had met so many others in his lifetime; he faced them, fought them, and won out.

His last years were clouded, too, by the overthrow of the monarchy in Iran, which brought to a tragic end the work of his company in a country he had known intimately for more than two decades. (His entries in this period, 1978–79, do not adequately reflect the bitterness he felt; so depressed was he by the events in Iran that for weeks at a time he would say nothing to me on the subject.)

His spirits were never daunted for long. His was an optimistic and activist nature. He was constantly developing new ideas and finding fresh outlets for his remarkable energies. Even in the depths of his physical ordeals and his despair over Iran, he was busy planning future work.

Of all his writings, the *Journals* were closest to his heart. In them, he showed himself most clearly as the man he was—a man of warmth, of conviction, of ideas passionately held and passionately acted on.

In a draft of what would have become his own preface to this volume, he wrote these words in 1979: "Now as I approach my eightieth birthday I reconfirm my belief in man's infinite potentialities for living and loving. I can say with a whole heart that I have lived the kind of life I most wanted, a life of taking chances, of not playing it safe, of being not merely an observer but a combatant in the arena of action."

—HELEN M. LILIENTHAL

The Journals of David E. Lilienthal

VOLUME VII

UNFINISHED BUSINESS

I

1968

Vacation in French Polynesia—Trip to Western Australia, Bangkok, and Iran—Exploring future of Roosevelt Island—Meeting with President Johnson—Trip to South Vietnam and Japan—White House dinner for Shah of Iran—African-American Institute dialogue in Nairobi—White House dinner for Prime Minister of Iran—Vacation in Grenada

JANUARY 1, 1968
BORA BORA, FRENCH POLYNESIA

I find it comes more natural for me to look ahead to a new year than to look back upon one that has gone. Every morning is a new beginning; the first day of a new calendar year underlines my eagerness to part the curtains of the future, whether that future is a new day or a new year.

I am deeply moved by what lies ahead. To find that my physical energies, my stamina, and my desire for the essence of living should be more powerful than ten years ago, than twenty years ago, makes my pulse thump.

JANUARY 2, 1968
BORA BORA

Sailing in a thirty-knot breeze—at least that—for two hours, in an outrigger canoe, was sheer physical ecstasy.

So long as I can have access to the sea, I have a source of physical pleasure and activity as great as any I have ever had.

JANUARY 11, 1968
PAPEETE, TAHITI

Thus ends what Helen described last evening as "the longest and most successful *vacation* you have ever had." True.

I didn't think I was capable of such a complete—almost complete—severing of the many skeins of concern, worry, intensity about my work, excitement about ideas.

In Papeete we visited the waterfront, where we saw some sea-beaten Pacific yachts and their non-stylish romantic crews. And the local general market: vegetables, fish. More important, saw the people who raise the food and buy it.

But it was not all swimming, long siestas, and wholehearted nothingness.

We had an opportunity to observe a French colonial possession, in transition. The transition that is going on in many parts of the world: Americanization is coming not through political means. It is through influence. The influence of American exuberance; affluence of our middle class; the appeal of American products, particularly popular music, electronic gadgets; the American passion for speed; informality of manners; and so on.

Political control doesn't mean as much in the modern world of swift communication and transport as this cultural (or anti-cultural!) influence.

JANUARY 13, 1968
NANDI, FIJI ISLANDS

My introduction to the Fiji Islands—a matter of a few hours—has not quite conformed to the "image" of Fiji I brought with me.

This continues to be a Crown Colony, a member in full standing of the Commonwealth. More than half the population is Indian, not Fijian. The Indian children play happily with the English children and the dark Fijians; a Fijian nanny looking after the lot.

JANUARY 14, 1968
SYDNEY, AUSTRALIA

As we touched down in a dither of fog and rain last night I couldn't take this as just another place on the "itinerary." For I had set foot on a "new" continent, for me the "last" continent, the only one I had not seen before.

FLYING TO PERTH, AUSTRALIA

People here look quite "different." Can't quite account for it. Is it an outdoor look?

This is just one more evidence of exuberance and vitality I have observed almost everywhere I go. (This is in such contrast with the doctrine preached day in and day out by the writing people, who put it down as a firm *fact* that the world is emotionally sick.)

Charles Court is one of the most sanguine and ebullient of practical men, the Minister of Development of Western Australia. "Dreamer with a shovel"—my phrase in my book about TVA.* Could he flourish, and be so widely respected if this vitality so evident in this wide, wide continent were not a reflection of a state of mind that is hopeful, not oppressed with a sick anxiety?

JANUARY 15, 1968
PERTH

A meeting last night with Charles Court at his home. For three hours he described to Gene O'Brien, Professor Ralph Grim,† and to me how he has gone about developing the mineral resources of this state, and what he wants to do to shape the future along lines of the regional integrated ideas I have been living and espousing now for so long. Court wants to develop diversity in the region, as an offset to the great power granted to the huge private mineral enterprises.

Tomorrow morning we start on what is scheduled as a three-day flight over the Ashburton/Pilbara region for which, so we are told, our services might be needed.

JANUARY 16, 1968
PORT HEDLAND, WESTERN AUSTRALIA

Writing these sketchy notes while sitting on the floor, my back against the wall, in my room at the Walkabout Motel. There isn't a chair.

A long flight in a Beechcraft over one of the most desolate, barren, godforsaken areas I have ever seen. Then, the excitement of seeing a major industrial development being born, the modern technical world

*TVA: Democracy on the March.
†O'Brien was chief engineer of Development and Resources Corporation; Grim was a consulting geologist. (It should be noted here that the *Journal* entries in Volume VII do not provide a complete or balanced account of the work of my husband's company. As its chief officer, he necessarily concentrated his energies on the larger and more demanding programs —Iran, Vietnam, Brazil—and on the exploration of new opportunities, as in this 1968 trip to Australia. His entries reflect these preoccupations; little appears, on the other hand, about some other D&R programs which required less of his personal attention—H.M.L.)

coming into being overnight. A great new port, new railroad lines being built by mechanical devices of the most efficient kind where two years ago there was nothing, not enough to sustain a flock of sheep.

All of this stems from the vast new iron mining activities up country.

Tonight Minister Court and his Chief Engineer, a delightful relaxed man, John Parker, told me that they, and the Premier, David Brand, want us to join in their work. The reasons they gave, the kind of role they described, remove the doubts I had yesterday. So it is up to us to work out an arrangement that will put D&R into development work in this remarkable Pacific continent-island.

How much in these matters depends upon personal impressions. "The Premier likes your presence," said Court. And illogical as it may be, it may be as good a reason as any why they feel they want us to contribute something—no one can be sure just what it will be—to the rapid transformation of this northern region.

JANUARY 17, 1968
PORT HEDLAND

From one extreme to another seems to be the theme of this vast wasteland of Western Australia, bleak, deserted, and really "outback"— and then in come the modern iron miners and the place jumps from nothing, almost literally, to the use of the most powerful machines we know.

After the long day yesterday, Court and I sat down together, in the open air under a full moon, and made a beginning on his ideas, and ours, about a role for D&R.

The theme he used was "regional development," about which they had a concept but we had the "vast experience."

Just what regional development means in this particular setting is quite different than in a truly and typical "underdeveloped country."

A big mining operation—one of the world's largest—is under way, is expanding; will move into processing of ore, moving the ore from the mines by new railroads, and then into the huge ore carriers, ships berthed at the giant port facilities here at Port Hedland.

All that is straightforward. D&R isn't needed for *that.* Water supply is already a sorely pressing problem, and the resources mighty slim. D&R with our special experience would have ideas about how to make the absurdly limited surface water go as far as possible.

Clearly one motivation for Court is to build on my reputation as a protection against the criticism that comes to anyone doing such a big public job as his. He was very frank about this.

They do need to have outside guidance and stimulation about making the most of the opportunity to develop the "forgotten land" of this part of Australia, he says.

But what strong motivation is there, what challenge is there in the job that would justify our sending some exceptional men to do our work out here?

This question brought the first response from Court that persuaded me—last night anyway—that he really understood the limitations under which he operated, and the vast opportunities for multiplying what could come out of this job. He spoke, for example, of the need, felt by the Premier, for planning for the whole state, including the Esperance area to the south, Perth, the Kimberleys.

10 P.M.
AT DAMPIER, ON THE NORTH AUSTRALIAN COAST

What a rugged day, temperature at noon a fierce 109°. A huge iron mine on the Hamersley Range; watching monster Marion shovels chew off a mountain of almost pure iron, being carried in trains sometimes a mile long into the hold of 100,000-ton ships at the new port of Dampier.

What was even more interesting was having "tea and cakes" at the Millstream Station, center of a *million-acre* sheep operation, in the way way back.

Topped off with an evening, at dinner, of the most delightful story-telling I believe I have ever heard. Sam Fletcher, a kind of aide to Minister Court, and Court himself, exchanging stories about the country horse races, political meetings in the outback, and finally stories of the war with the Japanese—they were fellow-officers.

Court himself is a special figure. Physically handsome, sandy hair, strong chin, the square shoulders and springy step of a soldier, looking at least ten years younger than his fifty-six years. Believes passionately in hard work. Has five sons, now all professional men, and each one, in his teens, has worked summers at the hardest kind of physical labor. (Come to think of it, so did I more than once in my own teens.)

JANUARY 18, 1968
PERTH

The third day of an intense trip and we stepped off the Beechcraft right into a nest of TV cameras. *And* a TV interview, followed by a separate press and radio interview. Mostly conducted by beardless and completely uninformed young men. About "your impressions" of the "project"—the stock question of the lazy reporter and equally lazy editor.

An hour after we landed I was busily engaged in this hotel room in doing a big drip-dry washing: pajamas, seersucker pants, etc., which are now slowly drying. Versatile man, the D&R Chairman of the Board.

JANUARY 19, 1968
FLYING TO SINGAPORE

Agreement reached with Court and Parker within ten minutes of my having presented our proposal this morning. Not a single word of disagreement.

Our real goal is to make a continuing place in Australian development. Parker said: "So, David, you have got a new glint in your eye because you have got a new challenge."

JANUARY 20, 1968
HOTEL SINGAPURA, SINGAPORE

While I doze and sun myself by the pool at this "enclave" hotel, it is of our week in Western Australia that I am thinking. Australia may be a Pacific nation to us Americans and once a stronghold for the British; it is also a symbol of American ideas, but in a Malayan setting, for there are several hundred million handsome, easygoing brown-skinned people that surround that doughty island-continent of Australia.

Less than five days after I landed in Western Australia I proffered a brief letter to Court and Parker outlining a program by which D&R would become general advisor to them on regional development.

Court read the page and a half letter, then read it again. He said the concept and the financial and other terms were acceptable. Half an hour later it was typed up, I signed it. D&R had made its beginning on another continent.

It would be wrong to overstate what this means. We have yet to prove ourselves; in a few months it may be clear to both that we don't have enough to contribute to make this truly the beginning of big things that both Court and I hope it will be, and think it will be.

But *how* do people reach a meeting of the minds and an agreement on goals and methods in so brief a time?

Some of Court's comments, after the arrangement had been agreed to, throw light on this. How do we of D&R, and in this case, particularly D.E.L., go about our profession as developers?

We have to have a prospective "client" who has already been influenced, long before we see him, by our way of thinking; which is essentially the TVA philosophy and approach to development. In Colombia it was Diego Garces, Castro, Eder; in Persia, of course, Ebtehaj; even in the

Ivory Coast the prestige of our regional ideas had somehow percolated to President Houphouet-Boigny. Here, clearly Court had thought about it a great deal, knew that he wanted our way of going at things, in a general sense.

Then too, Court wanted advisors who had a faith in the importance of private capital and private corporate methods in a major development task. This had been his approach with the iron mining companies who had been persuaded to provide the infrastructure of railroads, ports, towns, which may in other situations be the responsibility of a public body and public financing.

He had consulted Chase Manhattan and J. H. Whitney (particularly David Rockefeller and Benno Schmidt) about "who is the man and which is the firm best qualified to be our associates; what firm's recommendations would have the most influence on the actions of private investors?" They all said: "Get David Lilienthal and his organization."

"I ought to tell you," said Court, "that you are not the only firm that was considered for this important relationship. Two very well known American organizations sent men down here and pressed us hard. Gave us glossy brochures. It was what you call 'the hard sell.'

"But we have seen that kind of thing before; outfits that produce a fancy report, but there is *no meat* in it. And the men they sent we see right away are salesmen, not people who have *themselves* the qualifications or the records of accomplishment. And they oversell themselves. Besides, they are careful to make a proposition that is tilted toward their making studies and feasibility reports with an eye chiefly to ensuring that what they recommend will be something that *they will carry out.*

"Now, you went at it quite differently. The first question you had was whether you were qualified to do something that would advance our goals, and if you were not sure you could be effective in that way, you didn't want to undertake it at all. You showed all this week that you meant just that. You appreciated that we had well-qualified people here, and you didn't want to duplicate or supplant good people we have, just supplement them, and stimulate them with ideas they may have overlooked, or that have come to you out of your vast experience in America and all over the world. That impressed us a great deal.

"We found, by traveling with you, how quickly you get what it is all about here, in this new setting, in a place you have never seen before. Practically overnight you show that you understand things here in this new region that it would take a less experienced man months and years to catch on to.

"When you expressed such concern about keeping the cost of your service down, where it wouldn't be an embarrassment to me in my position, I believed every word of it. And you did; this proposal showed it.

"It was important in our thinking that the Premier took to you right away. In fact he was so enthusiastic about the impression you made on him—personally, not technically, because he doesn't really understand that part or try to follow it particularly—that he would have gone a lot farther in what you should be doing for us than I proposed to you. That will be very important as our relations grow and intensify, as I believe they will.

"The way you handled the press and TV showed that you understand, of course, how important it is that the public understand what we are trying to do. What you said to that young, ignorant TV interviewer, that the most serious obstacle to development of the northwest—as he put it to you before the cameras—was lack of public understanding of what development means and could mean. Not lack of water, or power, or financing, but that the public get some idea of what all of this is about. Well, that statement did it. You don't know as much about the facts of Western Australia as we do by a long way, but it is your experience and wisdom that we need."

Clark Clifford named as Secretary of Defense, so the Singapore papers report. The President picked this way of telling the world that come what may he is going to continue his commitment to a military road to some kind of settlement in Vietnam. Those of us who hoped that a new "fresh" mind would tackle this intractable and tragic stalemate won't get much comfort from this nomination.

JANUARY 22, 1968
BANGKOK, THAILAND

It seems we really started something in our U.S.–South Vietnam Joint Group Report of last November in recommending the establishment of a Vietnam Mekong Delta Authority that may mark the beginning of a working relation between Vietnam *and Cambodia* to do something about water control that may be of mutual benefit to both South Vietnam and Cambodia.‡

Bringing these two countries closer together is important at any time. But never more than now.

Tensions between South Vietnam and the U.S., and Cambodia, have been severe of late. The issue has been the tough one that Cambodia provides an involuntary "sanctuary" for North Vietnamese military forces, who can whack at allied troops and then dash across the Cambodian border and be free of pursuit.

‡The story of Development and Resources Corporation's postwar planning work in South Vietnam is told in Vol. VI of the *Journals, Creativity and Conflict.*

It fits my basic philosophy that we find a functional or physical development basis for better relations and perhaps cooperation. The fact that the best site for the control of the lower river is at Stung Treng, north of the *Cambodian* capital, is the key.

The four-nation Mekong River Committee met two weeks ago, here in Bangkok, and adopted a resolution showing great interest in the Joint Group's recommendation for a South Vietnam Mekong Delta Authority. The "dialogue" can now go forward *between Cambodia and Vietnam*. And this, in my opinion, will be more likely to be productive of results looking toward *international development of the river* than what has been going on here in Bangkok with the UN Mekong Committee over the past ten years, at great cost, with precious little to show for it.

7 P.M.

When I was shown into the U.S. Ambassador's office at eleven this morning, Leonard Unger was in full formal morning clothes: cutaway and striped pants.

I couldn't suppress an exclamation: mostly ambassadors appear in the same sloppy, badly wrinkled clothes everyone wears in these warm countries.

"It is the Shah's visit," he explained. "Have to be ready on a moment's notice to go off somewhere to some affair. The State Department doesn't have a uniform. So when I went to the airport yesterday at noon to be on hand as the Shah's plane arrived—along with the rest of the diplomatic corps—I had to be there in white tie and tails!"

The talk with him was very helpful, very much to the point, extraordinarily friendly. Particularly he wanted to relate our work in Iran, in transforming a poverty-stricken land and people, to things he believes Thailand needs, especially the group of young "up and coming" Thais who have ideas about the future of the country. "I wish you would definitely plan, next time you are here, to spend several days looking at this country and its development needs. You'll be surprised how much the Thais know about you, and how you function."

Thailand is moving ahead, economically; that is evident in Bangkok. But there are parts of the country—the rural areas particularly in the north—where much needs to be done, and he said he thought the way we go at it might be a great help. It is the rural north (where our American troops are, 50,000 of them by now!) where insurgency and trouble have appeared.

I told him about some of the recommendations of our Joint Report, chiefly those that had a bearing on the Mekong River and its relevance to *Cambodia*. And about how what we proposed by way of a Mekong

Delta Authority might shift the focus from tributary dams within those countries to seeing the river as a unity. We believed that the huge proposed power dam—Pa Mong—way up on the frontier of Thailand and Laos would have far less present relevance than the predominantly flood control Stung Treng in Cambodia.

JANUARY 23, 1968
FLYING FROM NEW DELHI TO TEHRAN

The only other passenger in first class is Bill Gaud, head of AID [Agency for International Development]. An unusually perceptive and straightforward man.

He was honest about Vietnam. On the whole picture he said, with a sad grin: "I honestly see no basis for optimism. I don't see that any progress has been made in the last year."

I was impressed that he was as conscious as I am of the importance of having the Vietnamese, not the Americans, make development decisions, do the work. "In some places this is happening," he said. "But up in Eye Corps area, near the DMZ, it is the damned Americans who do all the talking.

"[Ambassador] Ellsworth Bunker is fine. He sees things straight and he has some of the same doubts you and I have. It is not in his nature not to look hard at things and see them as they are."

JANUARY 24, 1968
TEHRAN, IRAN

The hard and exacting work of developing the new contractual and working basis seems almost to have been agreed upon between us and the Minister of Water and Power, Mansur Rouhani. For ten months John Oliver,§ O'Brien, and more recently Gerry Levin, a lawyer, have been plugging away, and have produced a document that is both a contract and an economic state paper.

The new arrangement defines what is to be expected of us in quite clear terms; the emphasis, of course, is on the Dez irrigation region, the enlarged area to which water will be brought within two and a half years.

JANUARY 25, 1968
TEHRAN

Dinner at the U.S. Embassy last night, very informal and therefore pleasant. Ambassador Meyer is a real Foreign Service pro. He is very

§President of D&R, 1964–69.

keen on the Shah, on his ability and achievements. To his mind there is only one explanation for the high standing of Iran these days, and that is the Shah's leadership, drive, and the way he does his homework.

JANUARY 26, 1968
TEHRAN

"Your name is very familiar to all Iranians; in fact, you are part Iranian. We may have to issue orders to the police not to grant you an exit visa so we can keep you here."

That was my greeting from Prime Minister Hoveyda as we came into his office.

For almost an hour he talked about his concept of the policies Iran should follow in development: give private enterprise plenty of leeway, *except* in the "service industries," oil, water, and power.

What Hoveyda said made great good sense; reminiscent of my interpretation of the New Deal (not what the centralists around F.D.R. thought), i.e., encourage private business except for the basic services, and if they got too rich, tax them.

"Too bad," said I, "that India hasn't learned something of the lesson of Iran and Australia's policies in these respects. They have natural resources aplenty."

"The trouble with India," said the Prime Minister, "is just too much London School of Economics."

That's one trouble; it is their susceptibility and the relish they have for finespun abstractions that make the London School theoreticians so appealing.

"My Cabinet is made up of young men who think the whole world depends upon *their* ministry. So they demand more and more for their part of the work. Twenty-seven Ministers, all of them pushing for more. Our Cabinet meetings! They are *passionate.* When I overrule them, they sit back and sulk. But I have to make allocations of what we have."

He chuckled; I never thought I would say that a Persian chuckled. But his sense of irony is very American.

Rouhani, who was with me, said, "I have to report to you that we have an agreement with Development and Resources to continue in the Khuzistan program in a number of fields [which he named] for an additional period of five years." So it does look clear that next Thursday—the contract having been translated into Farsi—I will sign in some kind of ceremony.

John Oliver is a generous fellow. He gives all the credit for the success of the negotiation to Gerald Levin, brought in by Burnett. Oliver thinks Gerry is a superlative negotiator, has an exceptionally good sense of the relation of figures, and is composed, whereas Burnett tends to press so hard that he often generates opposition. Oliver, if he were less secure, or vain, could have accepted my warm congratulations for the outcome without referring to Levin. But he isn't built that way.

People; they are mixtures, and you are lucky as a manager if you get a high average between weak and superior characteristics in the people you work with—*and in yourself.*

JANUARY 27, 1968
TEHRAN

"Chance, it was chance that was responsible for this great Khuzistan development."

Then Ebtehaj told again the story of our "chance" encounter at the Istanbul meeting of the World Bank in September, 1954.＜ "At that time I didn't have any particular business connection for you in mind, and you had never heard of the Khuzistan Region, of course. I just wanted you to come to Iran and take a look. I did send you an FAO [Food and Agriculture Organization of the UN] report about the Khuzistan lands—all negative —but that was about the only inkling you had.

"And then at the end of the first day's meeting in Tehran, when expert after expert, in my office, told you that Khuzistan was no good, my heart sank, *until* you said you didn't take too much stock in that kind of expert opinion; many of the same things had been said about the Tennessee Valley.

"I was told *not* to go to Istanbul. At that time the Council of Ministers had to approve before any important official could leave the country. The Ministers had denied permission for me to go to Istanbul. I was furious. I phoned the Prime Minister; told him that I was going without permission. And I did.

"If not, I would never have met you. There would not today be this project everyone in this country is so proud of, particularly those who opposed its beginning."

JANUARY 28, 1968
ANDIMESHK, IRAN

The flight this morning was through the snow-decked disdainful mountains, reaching out to us on all sides. Such magnificence in the sharp clear sunny light of an Iranian winter day. Ispahan, with its rectangular pattern, seen from the air, and here and there the gay colors of

＜Ebtehaj was then head of the Iranian Plan Organization.

a mosque, in that loveliest of all Persian cities. And on to Ahwaz, where we disembarked.

What a change in that once dusty little provincial town. Block after block of new buildings, elegant homes, a broad esplanade along the river and even a high-rise office building! But happily, along the busy streets and shops there is *still* the East, the turbaned men, the women in chadours. And the faces—wonderful faces of another world than the one I know.

To think that what I have done in stirring this country to develop this forgotten region should have made life so different for the dark faces we saw on the streets of Ahwaz; I who lived a life so remote from this town and these people who know virtually nothing about me.

When we reached the offices of the Khuzistan Water and Power Authority it was evident at once that the Managing Director, Dr. Iraj Vahidi, and those around him, so plainly attribute this to my ideas and belief in them and in the region, look to us for guidance, which they still need—more than my speeches about "working ourselves out of a job" would indicate.

The great excitement of the day, however, was driving down from Ahwaz, seeing the great stretches of beautiful land, now lush and green with winter wheat, land that has never before been farmed, because irrigation never reached it. But the Pahlavi Dam not far away, and the canals we are now digging, will bring water and life to these fertile lands. These are the lands—50,000 acres or more—that the Shah has directed be set aside for foreign development by American "agroindustry." This is the land which we hope foreign businessmen will see as an opportunity to begin a new chapter in Asia in the raising and processing of food.

JANUARY 29, 1968
ANDIMESHK

Andimeshk, until recently an ugly adobe-brick wide place in the road, now fine streets; a "suburb" of handsome houses fronting on wide paved streets, even paved sidewalks.

But in a walk through the old bazaar of Dezful, I found 17th, yes, 16th century Persia, hardly touched. Cobblestones in the winding little byways; sun-baked walls that must have been there for centuries. Four sturdy men sitting on the ground pounding a block of white-hot iron with great hammers swung over their heads and in perfect rhythm. An ass having a new set of plates fitted to his hooves, the hoof being cut down with a tool of a design of probably ten centuries ago.

And the faces! Men squatting in the sun, squinting up at the stranger, with sunken jaws, the Arab scarf wound around the head, looking as if they had been sitting in that very same spot in the sun since the days of the Sassanidae.

Dezful is reputed to be the oldest *continuously* occupied city in Persia, and perhaps in the world. Now in the main street a big new building housing the Bank Melli. And two big showrooms (not quite "stores") with electric ranges and refrigerators for sale. Even way back in the old bazaar, a street light, of sorts. Change, yes. But the backwaters, picturesque and in a way romantic, are still unchanged there; and in such a place as Dezful, probably will be for years to come.

When the big dam—only half an hour's drive away—was almost completed one of our D&R people talked to the "Mayor" of Dezful about the changes the new regulated flow of irrigation water and electricity would bring to this city. Knowing that Dezful has the reputation of being most "conservative," i.e., still dominated by mullahs and even strong touches of fanatic religious demonstrations at times, he said he was not expecting anything more than toleration.

The Mayor pulled his brown cloak around him and said: "This is fine. Perhaps this will awaken our younger people. This city has been asleep for thousands of years. It is time it woke up."

I was asked to speak to a joint meeting of Iranian KWPA staff and D&R people, at the office quarters in Dezful. A good-looking bunch. I recognized a good many men who had been on this project almost since the beginning. I said I would not reminisce, but speak about the future, not just the future of Khuzistan, but of Iran's new power in the world. I didn't mean military power, but in bringing about a real revolution, against the opposition of some of the strongest entrenched interests of Persia—the landowners, the political military, the mullahs, the sheiks, and the employers of labor.

I wanted to remind them that neither Khuzistan nor even Iran as a whole were more than part of a world undergoing great pain, turmoil, and swift change. I referred to other countries where we work, other continents, and the violence and the *hunger* that afflict so much of the world. "You are part of that world, here in Khuzistan, here in Persia, are part of it more than at any other time since Persia established itself as the first world empire thousands of years ago."

In my heavy gardening shoes I tramped happily through the fields of safflower, berseem clover, rich alfalfa (nine cuttings, and at least fifteen tons a hectare), this beautiful adornment of this once harsh and baked land. This was on the Safiabad Trial Farm, part of the Dez Pilot Irrigation Area which has demonstrated to the legion of Doubting Thomases what, properly handled, this land can do.

And particularly to the people of the interminable series of World

Bank Missions—what a low opinion of some of these kibitzers I have developed over the years during which they have been coming down here, filing their reports, and having the actual results make them out the theoretical dopes that some of them have proved themselves to be. The FAO team of experts who told Ebtehaj, solemnly, orally and in writing, that Khuzistan was no damn good and he should forget it.

My visit was conducted by our chief agricultural man, a Dr. Pollard, formerly of the University of Utah at Logan. His respect for the Persians, and particularly the village people who come in to help on the farm, or who farm their own land in the Pilot Area, endeared him to me. However good a man may be technically, if he is scornful and lacking in understanding of these people, he might better stay in his research or teaching or experiment station work back home.

JANUARY 31, 1968
ANDIMESHK

It is at this time that I begin to get uneasy about *really* how taut a ship it is. A job of this kind can be impressive to the tourist-type visitor, even more so to the "big shot" down for a look, from the central headquarters.

So, yesterday, I asked to see the construction schedule chart before we went out to see the sights.

Unhappily I found on a major piece of work that an Iranian contractor (who had won the award for a sector of the diversion dam and canal) was so far behind schedule, and had so little idea of how to get the work done, that the representations we had made as to when water deliveries would start on part of the project simply could not be fulfilled. I was furious.

When D&R was awarding the contracts, and providing discipline on the schedules by withholding the funds to the contractors, this didn't happen, and wouldn't happen today if that were the system. But with my insistence that the Iranians run the job, through KWPA (the creation of which I promoted), D&R can't do much of anything about such a situation directly. But we can certainly yell like hell, we can certainly advise Rouhani and the Shah if necessary that unless such a situation is corrected the representations to the agribusiness people can't be met.

10 P.M.
TEHRAN

Seeing at first hand the results Oliver gets by his own distinctive methods has erased the reservations about his ability for this work, reservations which have sometimes been considerable.

By his just plain good horse sense he removed the last obstacle to an agreement with KWPA which might have upset all the last ten months' work in Iran, and came out with a favorable contract and a great measure of good will toward us by the Iranians from top to bottom. When it comes to dealing with people "man to man," Oliver is quite superior.

Neither he nor the other men in D&R will ever make much money. This bothers me.

"Forget it, Dave," John said. "You have a way somehow of making any enterprise you touch exciting for the rest of us. You have given us the opportunity to enjoy the kind of work that makes life good for us. And we are not needing money all that much." Then he said something that honestly brought the tears unashamedly to my eyes: "You give us the excitement that makes the nitty gritty work we must do worthwhile."

FEBRUARY 2, 1968
FLYING TO ROME

In six weeks I have visited islands of the South Pacific; crossed Australia and explored remote areas of that still hardly populated continent; on to Malaya and Thailand; to the newly awakened center of the ancient Persian Empire; across Mesopotamia; looked down, as we do at this moment, upon the great brown lizards of the Apennines with their hump backs now dusted with snow; in an hour in Rome; and by Monday or Tuesday, will have completed the circling of the earth.

Could Homer have dreamed up a story more fantastic? And though not full of privation and bloodshed, it was a trip for a purpose, a voyage through devilishly tricky political waters, on a course that has not been charted—indeed, part of my purpose is to chart it for others who will follow.

This *same morning* I was in the heart of the Middle East, women in their chadours, mullahs in dark brown cloaks and white turbans, and the fields in mid-winter.

A long way—and not in miles alone—in a single day.

FEBRUARY 3, 1968
FLORENCE, ITALY

The Rapido pulled into Firenze; I got out of the car. Striding toward me, two figures. A huge long-legged, bearded man; by his side a blond-thatched pale boy, the long legs of a yearling colt. David put his great arms around me, I felt that half-grey beard against my face. David 3d clung to me, the sweetest of smiles in a sensitive face, the voice still that of a child, the body halfway between child and adult.

FEBRUARY 4, 1968
ON THE RAPIDO RETURNING TO ROME

David looked somber as he saw me aboard, and I was sad. He is *such* a man, faces up so gamely and clear-eyed to his problems, has learned so much about himself, that I admire him enormously. And we do communicate: a long conversation this morning—we *shared* the talk, which is the essence of good conversation. It happened to be about how a solitary worker—a writer—functions; and I compared it to the way I must function, who am constantly in the midst of people and the complexities and subtleties of other people's personalities.

I want David to like me, to love me. But it would be more of a price than I am willing to pay for having him like his father, that his father would abdicate his own ideas and convictions—or as in the case of Vietnam, his half convictions, half doubts—in order to keep the peace with his son.

FEBRUARY 5, 1968
FLYING THE ATLANTIC

I must face up to this question:
Can my explicit effort to make the long-term development program essentially a Vietnamese rather than an American effort stand up to the facts that these Viet Cong forays of the past days display?
Any man with a sanguine, optimistic nature, such as mine, is always on the edge of seeing plus factors that don't really exist.

FEBRUARY 7, 1968
NEW YORK

Several of the basic assumptions underlying our long-term development ideas and program for Vietnam have been cracked wide open. I kept saying that postwar development studies could be made now that would be relevant to the country when the war is definitely over.

During the night it came over me that I ought seriously to consider whether I have any business in an enterprise based on so many assumptions of policy and of fact that, if not destroyed by the recent Tet offensive, are crumbling.

FEBRUARY 13, 1968
NEW YORK

What should be "done" with Welfare [later Roosevelt] Island?

This was the subject of a Mayor's Committee luncheon meeting this noon.

What pleased me was to hear so much disillusion and skepticism about planners and their lengthy, beautifully bound reports and surveys, culling facts and lots of words, but leaving it there, with nothing recommended and a mountain of words producing not even a mouse of action. To have D&R compared with all of these, favorably, is satisfying. And deserved.

The first question I asked was: why do *anything* with Welfare Island; what public interest would be served by doing something about it? The assumption is that those who ask such a question are reactionary. But it did precipitate just the kind of discussion I find clears the air.

Those at the meeting included Mrs. Vincent Astor, a lively red-headed woman with a delightful voice and manner; Augie Heckscher, looking shaggy and far less tense than when he was directing the Twentieth Century Fund; Marcia Davenport, the novelist; and Ellmore Patterson of Morgan Guaranty, a very sensible sounding man.

But the star was a slender intense man, with the imagination of a poet, Philip Johnson, one of America's leading architects. He thought Welfare Island could be used to intensify the already overwhelming problems of New York, *or* in a way to change their course. I added: a demonstration, it could be, on a manageable scale, of what a piece of New York could be like without high-rise apartments and automobiles.

FEBRUARY 15, 1968
NEW YORK

A five-minute phone conversation yesterday noon and D&R had another assignment, this time not 10,000 miles away, in an underdeveloped country, but almost in "walking distance": the development of Welfare Island in the East River.

The first phase of this job calls for imagination and the kind of across-the-board approach to a development problem that is distinctive with D&R.

My cousin Beatrice Tobey and her husband, Barney, asked me to go with them to see Melvyn Douglas in a new play, *Spofford.* We enjoyed the play, which is 90% Douglas. What a superb pro he is: the character he plays he *is.* We went backstage afterward; it was surprising to me to see that he wasn't *in fact* the canny old country coot he had been for more than two hours—in the play—but the sophisticated and gracious Melvyn Douglas I knew well years ago.

FEBRUARY 18, 1968
AT HOME, 88 BATTLE ROAD
PRINCETON, NEW JERSEY

Everyone's mind seems to be made up about the American commitment in Vietnam. "Mind" is hardly the word, either. Everyone's *emotions* have been committed.

All this is reflected in the newspaper reporting and the pictures. The Viet Cong slaughter of hundreds of civilians never is depicted.

In social gatherings to utter one good word for the President of the U.S. and particularly the Secretary of State is to put an end to sociability and make the whole session a wild name-calling.

There is one thing I could say: millions, in South Vietnam and in the North, have been made homeless, uprooted. However the war proceeds, these people can't just be left without any help, without any compassion.

This is more than a war refugee issue: it is one of the main moral issues in the world today. These suffering human beings will be there, whichever way the war goes. How do they get fed, resettled, how does a new Vietnam, *North and South,* meet the long-term as well as the crisis needs of these people?

"Do you approve of your government's policy in Vietnam?" That's the question. At a dinner party tonight I answered that it wasn't a matter of approving or not approving; I was taking responsibility to try to make our being in Vietnam better for the Vietnamese, in any way I could.

Said my questioner: "Well, anyway, you take responsibility; that's what lots of people don't."

To take responsibility for your opinion and do something about it, even if the opinion turns out, by hindsight, to be wrong ("wrong"—what does that word really mean in this context?) is at least not a cheap sounding-off of an empty, albeit heated "opinion."

FEBRUARY 22, 1968
PRINCETON

In this morning's *New York Times* a front-page story reporting *military* weaknesses at Khe Sanh, in minute detail. (Depth of trenches; inadequacy of bunkers; lack of helicopters.) This story is relevant to what the *Times'* story calls an "imminent" attack on a garrison of American Marines now under enemy guns at Khe Sanh.

How can anyone square this with any notion of patriotism? Or excuse this on the ground of "dissent" from the policy of our being involved in Vietnam?

If the battles now "imminent" should take place, and our men are badly hit in their defensive positions, who can tell how many Americans may die or be wounded because of those stories, how much the attackers are helped by those detailed stories. And what public interest—what "right to know"—is impaired by *not* publishing such military information?

Yesterday morning John Burnett spent with the Jamaica, Long Island, community development group: all Negroes except one. At noon he came into my office with the glint of satisfaction—and victory—lighting up his face. They had accepted the D&R proposal for development of their urban community just as it stood. "I liked those fellows; they are good." And he liked to see the way the new work in the urban field that he heads is making steady progress.

MARCH 4, 1968
NEW YORK

"Joe" Fowler* is now the Secretary of the Treasury. At the very vortex, day by day, of one of the most severe financial storms in recent history, he gives the impression of confidence and of being on top of his job, easily one of the most responsible posts in the world.

"If I had a nerve in my body this would have gotten me down a long time ago," he said.

"At the Cabinet meeting where I reported on my end-of-the-year visit to Vietnam," I said, "you had said you would like to talk to me about the relation of long-time economic development of Southeast Asia and the Asian Development Bank, of which as Secretary you are the key figure.

"The Mekong River is the most important single economic and symbolic factor in the long-term development of Vietnam, and of Southeast Asia as part of that development. I have found that so far there has not been a practical overall look at the river, to get some order of priorities. The UN Mekong Committee has been working out there in Bangkok for ten years and has spent $115,000,000—mostly on a whole series of investigations and surveys. In Thailand the U.S. Bureau of Reclamation is spending a lot of money on a detailed and conventional study of a single project—a study so detailed that it has been going on for almost ten years, and has another five years ahead of it.

"A quick, crisp look at the whole river system hasn't been done. What has been going on more nearly resembles the old Rivers and Harbors pork barrel approach: a tributary dam for each of the Southeast Asian countries, to keep each one happy."

Said Fowler: "I have said to Zagorin, the U.S. Executive Director of

*Henry H. Fowler had been a member of TVA's legal staff in the 1930s.

the Asian Bank, and to Takeshi Watanabe, the Japanese who is its President: the U.S. wants the Mekong River development to be a major item in the Asian Development Bank program. We don't want South Vietnam to be a continuing responsibility of the U.S. The Mekong River, being regional, should be a major item for the Bank as a regional and international agency."

Jim Grant is a rugged fellow. Quickly he had settled into the reality of what "has happened to us" in Vietnam: a grave defeat, a shaking of most of the favorable assumptions of progress.

"We have to revise our AID program greatly," Grant said. "But I don't want you to make any drastic contractions in your *long-range* program."

"The top priority," I said, "in my mind, is maintaining and strengthening the Joint Group activity. This joint activity *with the Vietnamese* was the heart of our work, was distinctive. It is *relevant* to the future as no amount of technical studies or economic reports could be."

He understood this, and completely agreed.

Don MacDonald is here, looking pretty shaken and worn. He asked to see me alone for a moment. "I want to say this: Now at least we know what none of us realized before: this is war.

"And since this is war, much of what we in AID are doing is *irrelevant.*

"I came here prepared to suggest that we cut back AID out there almost to nothing. I see that this was too drastic. I agree that the Joint Group work is crucial, if you can build it into something that the Vietnamese recognize as their own—which is what you have been trying to do, with considerable success so far."

MARCH 5, 1968
NEW YORK

A colloquy in the Carlton lobby, Washington.
Senator Paul Douglas: "David, I'm enjoying reading your diaries. Paul Poynter sent them to me. Very exciting they are too."
Jim Rowe: "Senator, how do you find time to read these days?"
Douglas: "I have insomnia."
A new angle for Harper's sales department: To insomniacs. This will while away the long night. To others. These *Journals* are so exciting they won't put you to sleep.

Jim Grant reported that before the Joint Group settled on new quarters, Thuc or one of his people consulted an astrologer: considered routine.

MARCH 9, 1968
NEW YORK

Why is it I notice and record tiny irrelevant details? That at the big square conference table of Education and World Affairs, Bob McNamara wore short sox of the early 20th century *and* garters.

I have written this journal in all sorts of places and under all conditions—which accounts for the kind of prose I often find in the typed version as it comes back from my secretary. But this, I think, is the first time I have tried to write in a taxi lurching its way down Third Avenue.

MARCH 10, 1968
PRINCETON

Have just come back from a walk with Eddie Greenbaum, through a misty-moisty half-rain. As counsel for the present Mrs. Rockefeller in her effort (unsuccessful) to get custody of her children, he saw Nelson under conditions of what Eddie, this morning, called "synthetic intimacy" which a lawyer develops with a client.

While the custody trial was going on, Eddie spent a couple of weeks living with the Rockefellers in their New York apartment; Nelson would come in to talk to him, after Eddie had turned in for the night. At that time Eddie was certain Nelson would not want to run again for President because it was such an abhorrent thought to the woman he loved so much. But time has passed; unless Nelson makes a strong effort to get the nomination, it will be Nixon.

A very human personal relationship may once more prove to be a decisive factor in the course of our national life.

MARCH 13, 1968
NEW YORK

A total immersion today in our involvement in America's top problem at home—her cities. And the range? From the grubby down-at-the-heels Negro community (200,000 people) of South Jamaica, Long Island, to "what to do about Welfare Island," with some of the New York elite hearing D&R's first report on that new undertaking of ours.

The five Negroes in the office of the Jamaica Community Development Corporation were among the most impressive men, in such an undertaking, I have ever met. Articulate, intelligent, action-minded, and cultivated. That's quite a lot to say about any group.

MARCH 16, 1968
NASSAU

Here for the Education and World Affairs "retreat," a fancy word for a meeting.

We sometimes hear it said that if only "the best minds" in America could be brought together and "thought through" our problems, *then* we would make real headway.

Well, gathered in a room in this hotel were many of those "best minds." Certainly not the least informed nor least experienced nor least prestigious men. I have less confidence in the ability to achieve progress through an elite than some people, but still, it is worth a good try, if we don't expect more than any group of thinking men can do.

A better pair of intelligences than Bob McNamara and John Gardner would be difficult to find. Doug Knight, the president of Duke, a singularly articulate clear-headed younger man. John Rockefeller 3d; where could you find a better informed or more disinterested or sensitive man? And John Hannah of Michigan State, as wise a man as there is in America, a steady, emotionally balanced man. Frank McCulloch of Time-Life, with his talent for sensing the soft spots in any euphoric illusions about American strength. Herman Wells of Indiana, as keen a judge of the peculiar mixture of logic, reason, *and* emotional bias which is American life and the ambiance in which important decisions are made in our country.

This is not the whole list (and I do add something of a different sort) but if there is anything in the "best mind" theory, this would be a pretty good place to start.

The discussion that opened this morning began with the "crisis" in the diminution of support for "international study" in the universities and soon widened into a gloomy picture of the American position in the world.

The session was chaired by President Grayson Kirk of Columbia. His quick resumé of university education for international understanding had unique perspective.

Frank McCulloch gave us a gloomy picture of America's prospects in the world. We are declining in every way, in every sphere. The hungry people of the world increase and become increasingly angry. We have lived too long on illusions, that we are liked, or feared; that we know more than other peoples.

A happy beginning.

Ed Mason of Harvard, always with a critical stance, about how well the universities *perform* in the international field. John Gardner, fresh from his baptism of government administrative experience as Secretary

of Health, Education, and Welfare, added a similar note. Are the universities producing what is useful?

McNamara put it: the university community should be helping the
Joint Chiefs. But both in Defense and elsewhere in government the social
scientists have "turned their back on government" instead of helping.

McNamara, his eager, snub-nosed face dark as leather from skiing
at Aspen, looked ruefully, but with a fetching grin, at the university
people around the table. I could see he had the debacle of Operation
Camelot in his mind—the investigation by social scientists into "public
attitudes" in Chile—which became a scandal way out of proportion to the
facts.

At the conclusion of the session I was called on: "I have learned that
one doesn't lightly disagree with Frank McCulloch when he is being
pessimistic; I recall that three years ago, at one of our EWA meetings—
he was then stationed in Hong Kong—he said the most gloomy things
about the prospects of military victory in Vietnam, that it would take
years and years, and a million men. That seemed just a journalist's way
of shocking us then; today it doesn't come too far from the current American 'military judgment.'

"But there is one area in which American influence and power—
which he says have eroded—continue rapidly to grow. That area is
American private business. American multinational business is growing
in power and influence throughout the world. Look how American capital and business management have become powerful even in Eastern
Europe and the Far East.

"All I am saying is that the most internationalized institution in the
world is to be found not in government or the universities but in business.
And I would add, as a corrective to the things being said here, that *all*
research and teaching and education about 'international affairs' does
not take place in the universities; much of it takes place in American
business operating the world over.

"American business needs what the universities produce in the area
of international research and education. Just as government does. They
should be the best customers of what the universities produce in this
area. But they are not.

"Here—between the university and multinational business—is a
great gap. It needs to be closed. And it can't be unless the universities
know about the *world economy* that is growing up rapidly due to American multinational business."

The central topic of this "retreat," we were reminded, was how the
academic community—the universities, or "the Academy"—could become involved in the Vietnam issue. That the Academy was indeed estranged from the government, bitterly and vocally and highly emotionally estranged, had been evident for a long time.

The afternoon was wearing along. Someone suggested that two men who had the closest direct involvement with Vietnam sat at the table. We should call on Bob McNamara and David Lilienthal.

McNamara came to bat without any of the worn-down look or heavy sense of angst that so impressed me when I sat next to him at the Cabinet table some weeks ago.

"There is no military solution for Vietnam. The nation hasn't accepted that fact." What McNamara meant, exactly, by saying—for the first time explicitly, in public—that there was no military solution wasn't too clear.

"As to communication between government and the academic community, there isn't any."

He cited the case of "one of my closest friends, a uniquely great scientist, who recently resigned from a critical technical project that could be almost decisive for the Defense Department, because he was passionately opposed to the continuation of the war." It became apparent he was referring to Professor George Kistiakowsky.

"There is almost a sit-down strike by the academic community refusing to work with the government because of their disagreement about Vietnam."

Then, his voice ringing out and the room very still, he looked across the table at me: "What would have happened if David Lilienthal had said to the President, when he asked Dave to provide his services and that of his organization, that he wouldn't do so because there was some facet of our policy in Vietnam he didn't agree with? I don't know how Dave feels about all facets of that policy, and I never asked him and I doubt if the President did. But when the President said he was needed and his organization was needed, Dave went ahead at a very considerable inconvenience to him, tackling a very tough job.

"But much of the academic community doesn't act that way. How can we get the Academy involved with and for their country in a time of crisis such as exists today if they refuse to have anything to do with their government?"

John Hannah, sitting next to me, turned, looked at me with that half-smile of his. "Dave, you haven't said a word all afternoon. Why don't you tell us about your long-term development work?"

I launched into what was much on my mind. I was told afterward that my voice boomed, that I showed great feeling, that my voice was "disturbing, in a good sense."

All I do remember was that what I said seemed without coherence, but that I had put feeling into it.

"Why is it," I asked, "even when disagreeing completely on many questions, as a people, we can be rational and reasonable and without runaway emotions? Yet about Vietnam our emotions get the better of us, so that it is hardly possible these days for people to discuss Vietnam, or any phase of it, without bitterness against those we disagree with, and with intense flaring burning emotional outbursts? Why?"

I spoke about what a wonderful people the Vietnamese were, that the agony of Vietnam we hear about is not simply the agony of American division and confusion and dismay about our own involvement; the great agony is the one the South Vietnamese, North Vietnamese, all, are going through.

"I plead with you to think of Vietnam as people, poor people who are suffering, and who have suffered greatly, and must go on suffering. And let that temper your own emotional state."

When I stopped talking, the place was very quiet. Then we adjourned, and a file of people came up to me.

It isn't what I said; it was the passionate appeal that we try to disagree without hating each other, without gorge rising, without estrangement among us, that seemed to have struck some kind of note. Fellow-trustees and their wives stood around afterward and talked about the "why" that I had raised, why this particular issue unleashed such unrestrained emotions among a reasonable and rational people accustomed to disagreement. In their minds I hope was this thought: that the academic community has been the most unrestrained in these emotional outbursts, yet it is precisely the universities and colleges who stand for reason and rationality.

MARCH 18, 1968
NASSAU

Day before yesterday John and Blanchette Rockefeller invited Helen and me to lunch. At John's suggestion—it being very noisy with music out on the terrace—we lunched at a Howard Johnson's here in the hotel. After much deliberation they ordered hamburgers, we, food of equal elegance. I had known how perfectly natural it is for this "scion of immense wealth" to pay no attention to "side," and of his complete lack of interest in food, for that matter. Going to a Howard Johnson's as lunch guests of the Rockefellers seemed the most natural thing in the world.

He is such an intense, *serious* man. He peers at you, in the way he has of half leaning toward you as if what he is saying is for your ears alone, and she is so refreshingly just herself that I always feel, with them, that the usual thing said, i.e., that "the very rich" are different people from the rest of us, just isn't true.

Today Helen and I lunched with Sol and Tony Linowitz.† What a sharp intelligent eye that man has; and with it a real passion for public

†Sol Linowitz was U.S. Ambassador to the Organization of American States, 1966–69.

service and idealism. He spent last evening with McNamara. "My guess —it is a pure guess—is that he is thinking about coming out for [Robert] Kennedy," he said.

I looked shocked, I guess. This didn't support my thesis of McNamara's almost excessive loyalty to President Johnson, even where he differed with him.

MARCH 19, 1968
NASSAU

The business meeting of EWA yesterday morning included one performance that was excellence itself. The President, Bill Marvel, summarized brilliantly the two days of discussion that preceded.

Many of the points he laid before the board dealt with one aspect or another of Vietnam and the consequences of that divisive issue in the estrangement of the academic community from government.

I thought to myself that if an institution largely made up of university presidents or academic people found that Vietnam was, in several ways, a devouring consuming issue even in *their* world, how right it was that I hadn't shied off getting myself, a former public servant and a liberal, deeply involved, not to say tortured, by that issue, in my work and that of D&R.

I thought to myself: This is not an issue that you could possibly have sat out. Vietnam is at the center of all American problems.

Keith Glennan said to me: "Dave, when I was first appointed to the AEC, I asked you, 'What is your advice to a neophyte in this atomic energy business, just fresh from the hinterland, coming in the AEC?' You answered in four words: 'Resign and go home.' Remember?"

After dinner Sol Linowitz insisted that we visit the huge gambling casino on Paradise Island (once called Hog Island). I was astounded at what I saw. I have seen the great unwashed en masse; this was a spectacle of the great very much washed, the affluent, with nothing better to do than stand around tables tossing counters on to colored squares. On one dice turn the winner took off a stake that Sol said represented $5000 in winnings. The faces of the players, older men and women mostly (the stakes too high for the young, perhaps), were studies in concentration, but without any emotion displayed, when the wheel stopped turning and one fellow won and the other lost.

McNamara, walking with me, tall and smiling, along the edge of these crowds, was recognized from time to time, and a buzz would go up and spread like a wave through that part of the crowd. None of us played, which relieved me, not for puritanic reasons but because of the bad publicity, especially for McNamara, gambling while the fighting was going on, in a bitter and detested war which he headed for so long.

Linowitz is greatly troubled by the atmosphere in Washington about the war; worst of all, Sol feels, a rigidness, an inflexibility, particularly in Dean Rusk, but also the President. "The only thing that is being done that contains the germ of hope and affirmation about the future, something to give the Vietnamese some encouragement about their future, is your work," he said.

"Why is it you don't speak up about it? You have the credibility; people, more people than you would believe, have trust in you. You certainly should tell the President what you have told me about how you are again setting out to do constructive things—such as the Mekong River."

But it isn't that simple, pleasant as it is to hear such comment from so bright and earnest—and worried—a man. The President obviously is completely persuaded that only by punishing "the enemy" in a military way can this be brought to some settlement.

I would guess that it is the whiplash of his bitter critics, particularly the Kennedy onslaught, that is in the center of his mind.

MARCH 21, 1968
NEW YORK

Letters in today from Tom Mead, head of our Saigon office. Full of confidence and of ideas. "I'm inclined to question all the common, ready-made assumptions, one of which is that since the Tet attacks progress [in development] is unthinkable."

MARCH 22, 1968
ON THE TRAIN TO PRINCETON

Went to a luncheon meeting with Gene Black. What an expansive-seeming man he is, with that ineffable grin and capacity to make fun of himself. We hadn't seen each other for a couple years.

Gene gave a blow-by-blow account of his "mauling" by the Senate Committee on Foreign Relations a few weeks ago. He was appearing in his capacity as the President's Special Advisor on Southeast Asian economic development. He asked the Committee to endorse a bill to provide funds for the Asian Development Bank, which almost single-handedly he had created. But it has no money. The President had started it off by a declaration—in a speech—of a billion-dollar contribution from the U.S. But it needed money for operations.

The Senate Committee would have none of it. Except for Wayne Morse, who is against everything, and Albert Gore, who is against everything that Johnson wants, whatever it is, other Senators favored the idea behind the bill—but no money for *anything about Asia* so long as the Vietnam war goes on.

"Gore got really personal and nasty," said Gene, not accustomed (as I was when a public servant) to such rough handling. This was a new experience for the former head of the World Bank, respected all over the world, but now abused by a country-music politico from the state— Tennessee—that gave the world a great internationalist and statesman, Cordell Hull.

"I wanted to get you into that Mekong River picture from the start," said Gene. "Your idea of a quick survey to see if what the U.S. Mekong Committee is doing needs adjustment. But how can this happen? Cambodia has resigned from the Committee, and doesn't belong to either the World Bank or the Asian Development Bank. Not only where the money comes from for what you suggest, in this memo, needs doing, but unless Cambodia wants this, we're stymied."

When the day comes that a political settlement of the war between North Vietnam and South Vietnam is finally reached—as it must some-day—it will be of the greatest importance that there be a multinational reality—the Mekong River—as an active symbol of the *future* to begin the process of tying the nations of Southeast Asia together by more than mere political ties.

MARCH 23, 1968
PRINCETON

Cass Canfield, without doubt the dean of American publishers, his reading glasses perched almost on the end of his nose, looked intently at my memorandum about Volume IV of the *Journals,* and grunted, almost to himself: "Exciting."

This remarkable man can say "exciting" in the most unexciting tone imaginable. In fact, if I didn't know his manner so well, didn't know how many writers and public men he has energized and stimulated, I would have thought that I had misheard him.

I spoke of the *current* importance of what I wrote in the period of the volume, which is 1955–1959. For I feel sure that economic development overseas, now at the lowest point in its history, in this country certainly, is due for some searching re-examination. This also is keyed to Bob McNamara succeeding two bankers as head of the World Bank; it will probably mean the consideration of a new approach to the vexing and frightfully important (and frightening) problem of the poor getting poorer while the developed countries get better off.

When has there been a time of more excitement, more events to stir one's imagination, or anger, or appetite for life?

The political Presidential campaign boiling. The war, with General Westmoreland removed in Clark Clifford's first move as Defense Secretary toward a re-examination of the poor showing on the balance sheet of military *results*; the Civil Disorders report, the greatest denunciation of the whole of American society in my memory; the youth revolt, not only on the campuses but in their non-disguised contempt for previously "accepted" standards of behavior, accepted but hardly lived up to, particularly the sanctimonious ones about the relations between men and women; the threat to the dollar; and so on and on. All at one time.

But the big event is that today I saw the gleam of a lilac bud, tiny but definitely pale green, and the coy phallus of a crocus in the debris of my garden, a golden spray, a burst of gold of Japonica. And glory of glories, the tiny steel-grey button of a columbine, defying the zero blasts of last winter, and proving that life is impossible wholly to destroy, or even long to discourage.

MARCH 24, 1968
PRINCETON

What is the measure of progress in economic development in the poorer countries? An article in *Business Week,* reporting on the Harvard Advisory Service, repeats the old economists' song: it is increased GNP, the economists' god. If that increases—and they say it has, markedly— then the less developed countries are going good.

The total productivity may have increased, but does that mean that the social problem of disparity of income *within* the less developed country has improved? American GNP has increased and increased, hiding the fact that the distress and profound dissatisfaction among the poor, and particularly the black poor, have increased. In fact, the increase of overall and total affluence may actually stimulate dissatisfaction and revolt among the non-affluent.

MARCH 26, 1968
NEW YORK

John Oliver bounced into my office this noon, a jubilant, mischievous look on his face, tossed down a four-page green copy of a memorandum. "You can be the first to congratulate me on that document."

And after I read it, I did. It was a faithful rendition of the laying down of the law I went through with him yesterday morning. The memorandum embraces the ideas, the goals, the methods, and the tone of prudence without sacrifice of steam and enthusiasm that I think should guide this, or any other outfit of our kind. For the first time I think I got over to the management that the cost side of an enterprise is just as important to watch, to work at, to be ingenious about, as the revenue side.

Now, will we live up to it? And for how long?

I didn't found D&R to run a tax-exempt non-profit foundation, which has no real trouble about costs. Nor a government agency. I want to build into this public service enterprise a *discipline* that is one of the advantages of a private undertaking.

MARCH 30, 1968
PENN STATION, NEW YORK

This brown paper sack is all the paper I have at the moment. But I am so fascinated by the variety of life that I simply must write down what I feel.

I walked along Ninth Avenue, a street that is as picturesque as any foreign bazaar or open market: vegetables, dried cod, looking like cord wood, dried bay leaves and other herbs, in big open gunny sacks. And the people!

Isn't it this constant contrast, this exotic unbelievable *mix* that makes American life so utterly enchanting—and sometimes makes me furious with those who are so gloomy about their country?

MARCH 31, 1968
PRINCETON

"The country is without a President," I said to Helen as we heard President Johnson conclude his long TV "report" by saying that the divisions within the country were so great that he could not engage in a political campaign: "I will not seek nor will I accept the nomination of my party for the Presidency."

Will there now be some semblance of fairness to a man who has fallen in a battle for his country, as he saw it? Will this crisis—it is nothing less than that—close the ranks, and even close some of the ugly, bitter mouths that have been making for his destruction?

Helen asked: "Does he mean it?" I think he does. By removing himself he has removed what the petition signers, et al., have claimed is the only real issue: get rid of L.B.J. Now they will find that all the country's troubles won't magically disappear with the disappearance of L.B.J.

The President put his country ahead of his personal ambition and personal pride. What finer thing could be said of anyone?

APRIL 4, 1968
PRINCETON

With Helen to an Archeology Society lecture by Dr. Cuyler Young, Jr. He talked about the beginning of "urban" life in Mesopotamia. Anything since several thousand years B.C. had no chance of getting into that lecture. But it was about a part of the world I have come to know quite well.

Particularly interesting to me was the change in culture and in the way men organize themselves that comes with a change—or advance— in some technique, such as the method of building a structure.

"Too bad," said Dr. Young, "that before D&R went into Khuzistan we didn't have a team of archeologists spend some years digging the place up, for the changes D&R brought are so rapid and complete that the archeologist will have little now to work on." I sympathize with that viewpoint, but at the same time find it, to a "developer," somewhat amusing.

Turned on the radio a moment ago, interested to learn about the President's efforts toward a cease-fire, when I heard a voice saying that someone—I didn't catch who—died in the emergency room very shortly after he was struck with a shotgun wound in the head. Only when I heard President Johnson's voice, reading a message of sorrow, did I breathe more easily; it was not the President.

But the killing of Martin Luther King in Memphis presages in a terrible way the beginning of what may be a bloody, ugly period of American life that may make last summer's disorders pale.

APRIL 8, 1968
NEW YORK

Not surprising—as I hear from Saigon—there is unease among the Vietnamese that the Americans are preparing a Munich, deciding *for the Vietnamese* the terms of their surrender to the Communists.

This is going to be a rocky period. Trying to make peace is tough at best, but when it is someone else's peace you're making—not too exaggerated a way of putting it for these circumstances—it becomes most difficult, unless you are a Chamberlain. And these days so many Americans—writers, pundits, Senators, newspaper editors—are more than a little Chamberlainish.

APRIL 9, 1968
WALDORF ASTORIA, NEW YORK

The grand ballroom saw something quite wonderful last night: a Freedom House award for "Don Pablo" Casals. A memorable emotion-stirring event.

What made it an extraordinary event was the figure of the indomitable little man (ninety-two, I believe) who had gone into exile rather than live under Franco, and the "musical tribute" paid him, the playing of Bach's Triple Concerto by a group of musicians, each a concert musician himself, played with love and gusto. I could see the Maestro, sitting not far from my own seat on the dais, terribly intent, waving his hand gently as if he were leading, as he watched the performers, many of them his musical children. Have rarely seen the ballroom more jammed, to the crystal rafters. When they broke into applause at the end of the first movement, the old master held up his hand as if to shush them.

So bent is he that, standing, he is almost parallel to the floor and seemingly frail; but his face is unwrinkled, stern, strong, and when he spoke, his voice was strong, full of emotion but clear. No wavering old man's voice at all. And those marvelous hands, with which he gestured, raising them up while he looked at us of the audience as if we were also his pupils—as, indeed, as an example for us of courage, we were.

10:30 A.M.

Phoned Ambassador Bill Leonhart that I believe this is a time when the U.S. should give positive reaffirmation of its intention to help in a very substantial way in the rehabilitation and development of Vietnam in the postwar period. We will be soon ready with suggestions of things to *do*.

Feel strongly about this; otherwise the evidences of anti-American feeling now so apparent in the Viet side of the Joint Group may be a symptom of anti-American emotion that could make the forthcoming talks with Hanoi tenfold more difficult.

Visit with Mrs. Eugenie Anderson.‡ She expressed the shock about the President's refusal to be a candidate that must have been felt by many other Democrats. (I myself didn't feel that way.) "I felt when I heard his statement that it is too much like an abdication to take very easily."

I said I thought Humphrey should announce his candidacy soon; otherwise the Kennedy apparatus will run right over him as it did in 1960.

‡An influential Minnesota Democrat, former Ambassador to Denmark.

Being "statesmanlike" with the Kennedys is to be the nice guy that gets the air.

APRIL 10, 1968
NEW YORK

The most dramatic illustration of the fallacy of the gloom theory of life occurred not long ago at the meeting of the group to discuss formation of Development House, to study and come up with ideas about the future of economic development overseas.

The two most sage and sophisticated men in the group, Pete Collado of Standard of New Jersey and Gene Black of Chase, looked as if they had lost their last dime. To them it was clear that there could not be a worse time than right now to launch anything new: bad state of feeling in the Congress, the international monetary situation, the limitation on export of capital, the ugly political mood of the country, etc., etc.

That was Saturday afternoon. Then Sunday night in the final hundred seconds of his telecast the President said he was not a candidate. Everything changed. Monday the stock market went through the roof, the biggest, most ebullient day in terms of volume in the history of the exchange. Gloom changed 180° to overoptimism, almost as silly as the excessive gloom of two days earlier. Then Thursday came, another wave of excessive gloom and despair: the assassination of Dr. Martin Luther King and the outbreak of riots, robbery, burnings in the cities of Chicago, Baltimore, Washington.

The time for gloom and doom on the one hand and for euphoria and throwing your hat in the air on the other simply can't be any single day or event. As one person who has been through these things again and again, I am able to understand this and to behave accordingly.

It isn't easy for the average private citizen to insulate himself from this fantastic volatility of feeling and the spread of fear or euphoria that TV coverage and today's circulation-hungry journalism have added to the usual volatility of American public opinion.

Met yesterday with the absurdly successful and tough-minded Texas investment banker Benno Schmidt and two City Commissioners about what to do with Welfare Island. Our D&R group had pulled together a proposal for the next steps, plus a plan for moving toward action. Benno said this is just what they needed, the writing was clear, the presentation, with maps, illuminating. The City Commissioners were equally impressed.

Schmidt said, "I read this three times, carefully, and it is just right —raises the right questions, has the relevant facts. We go on from here."

A visit in my office today with William Randolph Hearst, Jr., with two of his newspaper editors in tow. The President had said to them: "About land reform in Vietnam, go see David Lilienthal." So here they are.

But before we could get to that Hearst had a good time kidding about how unmercifully the Hearst papers had hit out at me on the TVA— "creeping, bolting Socialism and all that sort of thing." I really liked him, with his impulse to kid me and himself. He seemed to be genuinely interested in my version of "land reform." This is not just dividing up land or giving title to a little piece of land to a peasant. It should be more basic than that.

I thought land reform had become a political slogan without much real meaning, or a social worker do-gooder idea. The first and basic question was how to increase the *productivity* of the land. Chopping it up into little pieces, with poor peasants owning them, might simply mean that the peasant was condemned to subsistence farming on that little plot that he owned—hardly a progressive doctrine—or he was forced to try to farm the uneconomic land he *owned* by running a losing race with the money lender in the next town. Which is the way much politically inspired "land reform" works out.

I think that before we got through they came to realize that "land reform" isn't as simple as the critics, in and out of Congress, say it is.

I saw Zero Mostel in one of the wackiest movies imaginable: *The Producers.* What a zany clown he is, what an artist of facial expression, how he can prance around with that huge corpus. Great fun.

APRIL 16, 1968
WATERGATE HOTEL, WASHINGTON

"When the President finished his TV talk Sunday night before last, the postwar period began. From that time on the Vietnam war began a completely new stage, and our Joint Development Group's work and particularly D&R's part in it, took on urgency."

This is the way I began what I had to say to Jim Grant of AID as we opened a two-and-a-half hour session with him, the quite soothing Roy Wehrle, and the big Chuck Cooper.

"When the pictures come out in the Saigon papers of the U.S. negotiators on one side of the table and, on the other side, the North Vietnamese enemies, it will mean one thing to most South Vietnamese: 'They are talking about what to do *with us.*' We of the U.S.," I said, "better have some reassurance ready for them before that happens, particular things that show we are standing by them, the South Vietnamese."

"This last year," Grant said, "you have made good progress, establishing relations with the Vietnamese. Now we should be getting some additional specific programs from you, if in fact the postwar period is on us, with the beginning of talks between the U.S. and the North Vietnamese."

I made the point that whether these talks make any headway or not, the very initiation of them in itself marks a whole new chapter in this long, ugly, agonizing war, a new kind for the U.S., perhaps for the world. And a new dimension to the concept of planning for a peace that will be no peace (in the old-fashioned early 20th century sense) after a war that is no war, in the long established notion of what a war between two opposing camps is.

When I went to see Katzenbach [Acting Secretary of State] I told him I thought that the postwar development, in as specific detailed terms as possible, should be part of the negotiations which are about to begin. "I have said that, in effect, three times today," he replied.

I described our ideas about the Mekong and what it could do *for Cambodia* as well as Vietnam, the whole bit.

"Dean [Rusk] is always talking about building peace. But what you are describing is the only way to build peace—not by treaties and that sort of thing. Dave Lilienthal's work is more important than what the boys in the Pentagon are doing, and is more important than what Averell [Harriman] will be saying at the Paris talks. This is exciting."

More than once North Vietnam came into Katzenbach's comments. "Too bad the Mekong River doesn't go through North Vietnam. But it goes on up *into China.*"

APRIL 17, 1968
WATERGATE HOTEL, WASHINGTON

The view of the Potomac from my balcony, in the morning light of early spring, is opulent, European opulence. Super-luxury living structures line this new waterfront: here are the new rich of this new city that once was the sleepy roost of sleepier civil servants, and retired dowager relicts, a city where nothing much really happened except the concerns of a government center that the rest of the country could pretty well forget about, and mostly did.

Yet only a matter of days ago troops of the U.S. were standing guard over this city, the smog of fires set by violent black men drifted over this scene of almost European decadence.

I realize how much there is to do and what soggy conditions I must operate in. The principle I have erected almost into an eleventh commandment is: we must do this as a *joint* enterprise with a group of Vietnamese, uneasy, only moderately competent, and mostly men who must moonlight, the pay they get so meager that we can't be too indignant if they only give the work a part of their time.

AT THE NATIONAL AIRPORT

A quick visit with Sol Linowitz, always a delight. What a savvy fellow he is, just by being himself. Told him I had, finally, taken his judgment seriously (given on the beach at the Nassau meeting) that I have "credibility" in the Vietnam situation. He said, "You are the only one who still has—and you should speak up, and act accordingly.

"Remember," he said, "you're not a schnorrer—do you know what that means? Beggar. When I had my first run-in with the President he was arguing vigorously about something I didn't agree with, and I said, 'Mr. President, when you got me, you got *all* of me; not just the part that goes [here he nodded his head] yes, yes, but also the part that goes [here he shook his head] and says no.' You, Dave, are also in that happy position, and people know it."

APRIL 28, 1968
PRINCETON

Now I am expected to go to Saigon about the "postwar" and long-term development of that country, and somehow work with the Vietnam Government as if nothing much had happened.

But the feeling of "withdrawal" rather than negotiation is definitely in the air, and no amount of rhetoric *alone* by the President can change it.

The last time I went to Saigon I made a big point of trying to get the non-military side of this conflict into a position of high priority. In that I failed—except for some pleasant words.

APRIL 30, 1968
WASHINGTON

I stepped into the President's office about 5:45. My first impression was that I was talking to an *ex*-President. The paraphernalia of the Presidency was all there, as before. But I felt that here is a man who is not living in the *present* tense.

The President was standing reading a piece of paper, completely absorbed. He looked up, with that eyebrow-raised look he has, gave me a big hello. He moved over to his rocker, pointed to a seat on the sofa, me maneuvering in order not to walk in front of him.

With the picture taking going on, the President leans way over, *acts* in fact. With his face so close to mine I found it awkward for conversation. Not for him: he was in his whirlwind mood.

"When I saw your name on the appointment list I thought [here he gave me that "us fellows" look that is in contrast to the patrician, almost patronizing "good fellowship" of F.D.R., or the hard-bitten genuine ruralism of that great old boy H.S.T.], Dave and I come from the same period; we have and always have had the same interests: conservation; REAs; rivers; all those things that came out of TVA."

He screwed himself up in his rocker with the big headrest jammed against his head (a head that is much greyer than when I last saw him, but his color excellent—looks like a healthy man).

[I am copying my shorthand notes made immediately after this Oval Office session.]

"Dave, you and I are alike; we began at the same time. We were both radical—but prudent. You have to be prudent [I thought, What a strange word to use in this connection] for people to believe in you. You and I are no Birchers, but we're cautious, sometimes even suspicious. Pretty much alike.

"Now about your idea—they've told me about it, your talks with Nick [Katzenbach] of having parallel negotiations going on, one about military matters and the other about development. That's what I was talking about in my speech at Johns Hopkins and it still stands. Develop that Mekong, make it do for Southeast Asia what the TVA did for the Tennessee Valley. No matter what, old man Mekong he just keeps rolling along."

He looked out in space, stood up, Rostow§ came in, a paper in his hand for the President to read. "I have been telling Dave we ought to have a Johnson Plan, like the Marshall Plan was for Europe. And get it on a film and show those people what it could mean for the poor farmer, like you did that picture of the river for TVA. You got to show some imagination, Dave; the trouble with us is we're getting old, need to use imagination."

After which I went on my way through that door again.

Our conversation was disjointed, and for a couple of hours afterward I felt I didn't get my point over—and no wonder; he was talking about every sort of thing. But as I reflected I realized he *had* the point. It was just that he didn't think the negotiations themselves would go far enough or fast enough for the development idea to be coupled with them.

I'm not convinced of that. In any case, a couple of days later I wrote the President a letter about a speech I'm to make in Tokyo which had been written, of course, many days before he made his pitch about stir-

§Walt W. Rostow, Special Assistant to the President.

ring up the people of Southeast Asia to see graphically what peace and development could do for them.

The things the President said that were important were momentarily overshadowed by President Johnson himself, the person, by the massive energy, the torrent of words, the windmill gestures, the showmanship that is part of him.

MAY 1, 1968
WASHINGTON

A long talk with Clark Clifford. His office in the Pentagon has a great view of the river and Washington but is so noisy from jets roaring by from the airport that it was hardly a place for contemplation. Clifford showed that he was *sure* that now this country had a *policy* about Vietnam, for the first time. Wherever that policy led, however tough and hard it would require us to be, it was clear in his mind what we had to do.

"Thus far," he said, "it has been *our* war. Now more and more it has got to be *their* war. They've been put on notice that all the Asians that have been depending on Uncle Sam to fight for them have got to defend themselves."

I said, "The whole basis of our development work has been built upon the proposition that the Vietnamese wanted political independence— didn't want any foreigners to run them, neither French, nor North Vietnamese, nor Americans. To be politically independent I felt—and so told them—they had to be *economically* independent, had to stand on their own. Our studies made it plain that, once the war is over, they could be. Many of them, of all classes, are actually affluent. They have great resources but also more foreign exchange than any but a few countries we have worked in.

"After the President's speech curtailing the bombing and calling for a negotiated end to the fighting, I heard reports that the Vietnamese were very uneasy—understandable, of course. What should I say that is relevant to that unease?"

"The President's TV speech of four weeks ago," said Clark, "was a war speech a week before he made it, a report on the war. When he made it, it began as a peace speech. Unilateral curtailment of bombing; no substantial increase in U.S. troop levels. Then his statement that he didn't choose to run . . . I learned of that only a half-hour before he made the speech.

"Now, of course, there has been a drumfire from the military. They say the North Vietnamese will step up their shipment of men and arms into South Vietnam. And they have.

"So *then* Hanoi responded that they would talk.

"The North Vietnamese are completely tired of this war, too."

I have no doubt that this is true. Sooner or later they will find the right time to try to obtain their objectives by some means other than fighting.

I wanted his opinion about the *present* military situation. So I led into it by going back to my most recent trip to Saigon. "This was in late November. I was quite discouraged while I was out there when I saw how *cocky* our people were about how things stood, both the civilians and some of the generals. It's a bad business to be so sure that things were all that good."

"Well," he said, "you weren't wrong in your reservations, were you?"

He talked at length about the Tet offensive, and the North Vietnamese ability to launch an offensive against thirty-seven cities, and in Saigon itself.

"They failed to hold any of these places, and the populace didn't greet them with roses of welcome. But the psychological damage within the U.S. was terrible, terrible.

"The military around here keep after me, but as long as I am here and for what it is worth, I think our course is the only one open to us."

MAY 3, 1968
KENNEDY AIRPORT, NEW YORK

When, at 4 o'clock last Wednesday, I was ushered into the Secretary of State's imposing big office, Dean [Rusk] said, "Hope you don't mind my not wearing my coat." I made some inane remark about "shirt-sleeve diplomacy," as he motioned me to a seat on the far side of his office.

He knew I was soon to go to Saigon; was glad of a chance to make a few points that I might want to have in mind when I see Thieu and Ky as well as the American Mission.

"In the first place you should know, when you get out there, that the extent of Hanoi's response has been greatly exaggerated. All they said was that they would establish contact to discuss our terminating all military activities. That's a long way from negotiations about peace.

"We are still locked up about a place for talks. We'll get a site; but right now we're far apart even on that.

"There is no sign that they really want to talk about stopping the fighting—not yet. The shipment of men and arms from the North into the South goes on at a much greater pace since we offered to curtail our bombing.

"Right now you shouldn't give them the impression out there—because there's no evidence of it—that it's about over. Certainly this President isn't going to let them go down the drain. And any new President won't either; things look different when you're making speeches to get you into office, but to have the responsibilities of the Presidency itself is quite a different thing. *Any* President will refuse to just walk out on Vietnam. After all, we have lost 20,000 Americans, dead. No one, whoever he is, can be President and just toss all that away."

He settled back in his chair, and apparently wanted to talk in a personal way.

"You know, Dave, I'm really a kind of do-gooder; I always have been. You know that. But all I have had has been one crisis after another in this job. Seven years of them, one after another, beginning with the Berlin crisis in 1961."

"You know my admiration for your great integrity and singleness of purpose. And your incredible stamina," I said.

"Well, this job has made an old man of me." He didn't say this in the least in a self-pitying or dramatic way. But I felt a good deal of shame that some of my countrymen should be so cruel and personally venomous about him, without a bit of responsibility for anything they say.

MAY 4, 1968
FLYING TO TOKYO

The event that on last Wednesday afternoon Dean Rusk felt was not just around the corner was in twenty-four hours an actual fact: an agreement on a place and time for the initial discussions with North Vietnam.

A week from now the newspapers and TV of South Vietnam—and of the world—will show pictures of the leaders of *North* Vietnam sitting across a table in Paris from two Americans, "negotiating" the fate of *South* Vietnam.

The agreement on Paris as the site for these talks brought back to mind what the President said to me last Tuesday when he went into one of his windmill dramatic acts.

"They wanted to meet in Warsaw. I won't have that; I won't have a place where our friends of South Vietnam can't be present, and that is what would happen in Communist Warsaw. And as I told that Chief Rabbi the other day, complaining that I hadn't agreed to go to Warsaw, they wouldn't allow any Jews there; Tad Szulc of the *New York Times* couldn't be there because he is a Jew.

"How would it be if I were told—no Negroes can be present, no brown people?" As he roared this out, he flung his hand to the right and the left —Hanoi brushing off Negroes over here, brown people over there.

Well, the President won the first round, the site of talks.

MAY 6, 1968
SAIGON

The boom of artillery shakes the place, and at times it does seem to be right next door.

My D&R colleagues here, Tom Mead, Nick Philip, O'Brien, didn't really expect my plane to land, and when it did, didn't think I would be on it. They had a "very lively" time of it here last night.

I'm off to sleep.

11:30 P.M.

"To sleep," did I say? An hour ago the "crunch" sound of a tank cannon seemingly right outside twice awakened me. I padded to the third floor, and there we watched the sky filled with flares, dropped by parachutes, lighting up a wide quarter not far away, on the edge of the city. Fighter bombers came darting in, striking the area under the lighted sky. Two shells that must have been mortars tossed toward us, whanged away, setting the windows shivering.

So if this isn't war, it is a good facsimile of same. And this whole eruption of aircraft, the bum, bum, bum of cannon, crackle of small arms fire—all may be due to a small number of VC in this kind of warfare.

How can we do very much in a country that is, by this night's measure, still so far from anything resembling "postwar" or "long-term" development?

MAY 7, 1968
7 A.M.
SAIGON

Ten minutes ago: the most violent percussion yet, seeming to be next door, set this concrete building trembling. But even before the curfew was over at seven, down the abandoned streets came the accustomed swarm of bicycles and scooters.

Down that alley I can see very young children, in their Catholic school dress, playing games. I guess after twenty years you get used to these things.

5 P.M.

We saw Ellsworth Bunker for forty-five minutes or so. He seemed as composed and relaxed as ever. Not much impressed, outwardly, by the last few days of fighting—or whatever this kind of violence should be called.

I said that in November, when we submitted a preliminary report to President Thieu and Vice President Ky, they and their new Cabinet had seemed to be very much interested in economic matters.

"If there isn't a strong and continuing interest, in the Vietnam Government, in development, there is little justification for our being around here," I said, to sum it up.

Ellsworth said, looking down and weighing his words carefully, "I don't think there is any cause for discouragement. They are uneasy about what may come out of the talks to which they are not direct parties; that's natural. At first they were—well—very upset and hurt. But they have been reassured by things the President has said. Thieu is planning a trip to the U.S., probably in June, to see the President."

MAY 8, 1968
SAIGON

About dawn what sounded like an ammunition dump going up, and over the airport a dazzle of many flares. But nothing like the show of the night before.

The appearance of Saigon has certainly changed completely since I was here in November. Truckloads of soldiers in battle dress just went dashing by, followed by a medical ambulance. Armed men *everywhere,* whereas before a pretty girl would be sitting in a sentry box chatting with a soldier who stood outside, chivalrously, so she could be in the shade.

MAY 9, 1968
12:45 A.M.
SAIGON

Is this whole American effort to sustain Vietnam through its agonies just a massive kind of self-deception? Does a country which has accepted, or had imposed upon it, the great dogmas of democracy—the consent of the governed, voting, legislative bodies to persuade or placate, the whole democratic bit—have a chance over the long run against the discipline and ruthlessness of its competitors, the Communist North Vietnamese and the two nations that support it so lavishly, China and Russia?

8 A.M.

Very much steamed up about some way to turn all this planning exercise into concrete specific things.

What about a sawmill, now hardly running, near Saigon, or a veneer plant? How to get the logs? What stands in the way, our forester Henry Kernan says, are the French-type multiplicity of regulations, taxes in the field, permits—the classic and outworn concept of the forester role, the "don't touch that tree" style.

The broad textbook generalizations that the development planners and economists use drive me absolutely nuts. They never get down to cases. It is always way up there, and people of that kind love to debate general propositions and general principles. I find this tiresome and futile.

"Give me a case"—something that can be weighed by a business-man's mind.

5:30 P.M.

I had promised before I left home that I would not do anything foolish, would not deliberately go into a war zone.

Well, I sure am in a war zone, with fighting going on in large units a half mile away. The reports are that it will be hot and heavy tonight. The VC—two divisions—are gathered in formation along the port, preventing loading, shooting the place up, and trying to force an entry into the city from that direction. The Chinese section is on fire.

MAY 10, 1968
10:45
SAIGON

Have just come from an hour with President Thieu at the Independence Palace.

In his manner, Thieu exuded confidence. Spoke in excellent, easy English, compared to his reliance solely on Vietnamese last November. He followed the discussion, and at times led it with an assurance and a *grasp* of the administrative side of not too simple a subject.

The peace talks begin today in Paris. He evidently had it much in mind. If there is uneasiness, he certainly didn't show it.

The President said he intended to create a National Planning Council, persons of Cabinet rank. The President would be the Chairman.

The President favored the ideas we had about the Mekong Delta; he was much concerned with "the whole country; it is important that something be planned and done for the Highlands and the coastal region of Central Vietnam."

I told him both the central and the northern part were regions of our studies and plans. We emphasized the Delta at this time because that was an area where early results could be shown, and because it was one of the greatest assets of the country. But to get results there was need for an agency that would have responsibility for action.

"How soon could such an authority actually begin work?" the President asked.

"The work has already begun," I said, "in studies that would lay the foundation for design of structures, such as dikes. We believe that in a few months surveyors could go into the field to get the information required for design and for construction."

MAY 12, 1968
TOKYO

A potluck lunch with Ambassador Alexis Johnson at the Embassy Residence. Two-and-a-half hours of as interesting and relevant and realistic talk as I have ever had—on almost any complicated subject—followed. A man with the Ambassador's experience and judgment is one of the great assets of any country, and particularly ours.

Johnson was wearing a pale yellow shirt and a flamboyant necktie. "Excuse this garb; I just feel I ought to let myself go now and then," he said with a half-grin.

No single individual has been closer to the *beginnings* of our major involvement in Vietnam.

So closely is Johnson's name identified with Vietnam that two years ago, when he was nominated for a Rockefeller Public Service Award— I was then on the selection committee—it was strongly argued against him that he was not a proper person for such an award because he had been for so long associated with "our policy in Vietnam." This got Bob Murphy's Irish up (member of the award committee) and the award to Johnson went through. That was a prelude to the ensuing blackballing among academics and intellectuals of *everyone* who had anything to do with the Vietnam war or policies.

A sharp look of pain crossed Johnson's face as he said, "I really think that in the perspective of history the American press and television bear much of the responsibility for the ugly defeatism and lack of understanding about Southeast Asia."

Johnson spoke at length, with the assurance of a man who knows, about the relations between Japanese business and businessmen, and their government, even about their temperament.

"The Japanese may give the impression of being an unemotional people. Their demeanor, their facial expressions. But don't believe it. Underneath they are intensely emotional, even sentimental."

Mr. Yutaka Tsuji, the British-speaking head of the *Asahi* newspaper's symposium project, took me for a "conversation" with Takeshi

Watanabe, head of the Asian Development Bank. At the *Asahi* newspaper office (circulation six million!), Watanabe, very dignified, was seated in a big overstuffed white chair. At a long table along the whole side of the room nine young men, staff members of the foreign news department, a microphone all set up.

The "conversation" went fine because Watanabe is such a friendly, relaxed man.

Tsuji said he was the reporter assigned to cover my arrival at Tokyo airport in 1951 when Helen and I came to Japan as General MacArthur's guests.

Said Tsuji tonight: "I ran a picture of these two people, looking at each other lovingly. The headline was: After All These Years of Married Life the Husband Has Kept One Secret, but Only One, from His Wife: the Secret of the Atomic Bomb."

MAY 13, 1968
TOKYO

I alternate, in my mind, between saying that America has taken a strong turn toward isolation—or a *return* to isolation. Or (more characteristic of me) of believing that we shall continue to bear more than our share of world responsibilities.

In the taped interview with Watanabe before our little gallery of "journalists" I warned that it must not be assumed that America would not draw back into its shell and let Asia handle its own problems. The bugaboo of "stopping Communism" no longer had the same appeal to fear.

But I don't fully believe this.

6:30 P.M.
ON THE "SUPER LIMITED EXPRESS" TRAIN, TWO HOURS OUT OF TOKYO

What an impressive country, flying through it on this train that makes our railroad system seem something out of the 19th century—which it practically is.

10 P.M.
TAWARAYA INN, KYOTO

I never realized what a great invention is the chair—any chair. This inn is that delightful change I have wanted, and after these recent hectic days a change I can certainly use. But after eating a meal with my legs under me, on the floor, the muscles begin to put on a protest demonstration.

The room "maid" is a grinning little old lady. She couldn't be pleasanter, nor more amused, watching me trying to manage my chopsticks. She brought in a gold-covered guest book, and turned it to a faint scrawl: "With gratitude and affection, Robert Oppenheimer." The owner knew that I was Robert's friend; I suppose this accounts for my being asked to write under his name—which gave me a pang. I wrote, "Here one feels keenly that all men can indeed be brothers." This I did feel, strongly; but it is in this country where Oppenheimer's work—far from his intention —was to destroy 80,000 people in a flash of time, and set off a world-wide chain reaction the end of which we know not.

There were in this golden book—actually a series of heavy cardboard sheets joined together—a number of interesting signatures. A big full two-page drawing by Ben Shahn. And one very recent one:

John D. Rockefeller IV
Sharon Percy Rockefeller

One of many honeymooners, but not the least well known.

MAY 14, 1968
KYOTO

An overpowering sense of *disengagement* was sweetest when from someplace back of me came a tottering old man (though only seventy-six), cropped hair, shrewd knowing eyes, supported entirely by two strapping young, handsome girls, looking at the old boy with such love and high respect. He was the abbot of the monastery, confined to bed; but when he heard of the "famous visitor"—my companion, Morino of the *Asahi* organization, must have given me quite a buildup—he insisted on coming out to greet me.

"Thoreau," said the very frail old abbot, waving his thin arm and long graceful fingers at the dark green bank of cedars; they enclosed completely the little ancient temple where we were having green tea in great bowls, with sweet cakes.

Other-worldly was this word "Thoreau" in the midst of a day so remote from the super-modern Japan we saw this morning in Kyoto, and in Tokyo. A far-away feeling, a sense of tranquillity and serenity compounded of all we had seen: the great gorge of the Takao Valley; the absurdly erect and skinny cedars, some of them one hundred feet tall with little tufts at their top. The cedars pass through the shadow and light of tiny maple leaves. The roof and some of the timbers of this very old monastery—Kozanji—are eight hundred years old.

My legs had become stiff as boards, trying to keep them under me. The old man sank to his knees, drew his legs under him like a gazelle. How do they do it?

The abbot said to Morino that I had a German name. He explained that he had taught philosophy in Germany before the war, for a time. Then I heard the word "pragmatism" in a long Japanese sentence. "John Dewey," I said; he nodded.

By saying "Thoreau" I saw he meant that in this temple, high in the woods, he too had thrown off civilization, as did Thoreau.

While again having tea, one of the young women, accompanied by an older woman, asked me to write my name and some comment in a big guest book, using a paint brush.

What you lose in comfort in such an old inn as Tawaraya you make up in knowing that you are really in another country, and not just in still another Hilton or Intercontinental Hotel.

All day long I have not laid eyes on even one American or European, not one. Strange, for this is the tourist season and Kyoto is a great showplace. Morino and I walked for an hour or more through the crowded business shopping center, went to a restaurant, and visited a park, a lovely, dreamlike place of shadows and incredible coverings of moss. Many Japanese tourists, and solemn young honeymooning Japanese couples. "This is the marriage season," says my companion.

MAY 16, 1968
KYOTO

The avidity with which I go on looking at everything! Morino seemed far more tired last night, at the end of twelve hours of gadding about, than I did.

First, the hollyhock festival. I stood on the curb observing this yesterday, with what seemed like a million young black-haired bright-eyed Japanese school children, and assorted adults and babies.

The procession from the Imperial Palace was not the half-phony kind put on for American tourists in so many places. Dating back to the 6th century, the odd but credible dress of the courtiers and warriors, the stern officers riding horses, the huge carriage—Gosho-Gurumo—with its eight-foot-high wheels bound in brass, dripping with wisteria, in which royal personages once rode in this festival, drawn creakingly by an unhappy ox decorated like a Sicilian pony, the ladies walking along with make-up so thick that their chalk-white faces seemed like masks.

The anachronisms were mighty few. There is here an anomaly, the *contrast* between the respect for the "traditions" of Japan and their observance, and the mad whirl of ultramodernity and a furious pace of technical and industrial advance (progress).

At the shrines and temples and gardens, both the young and elderly Japanese utterly absorbed and entranced in these evidences of an ancient way of life. Yet they themselves (the kimonoed ladies as well as the mini-skirted or blue-jeaned young ones) have the look of alert *people on the move.* As indeed they are.

At noon an enormous Japanese meal at a little restaurant in the area where the geisha artists live—one could read their names on the door posts of their apartments.

Morino asked if I would like to see Japanese classical dancing and music: the last performance of the year.

It was two hours of sheer delight. Crowded to suffocation, where we sat. Some of the performance was graceful, some of it slapstick, some of it a very sentimental love story, a tribute to wifely faithfulness. The concluding number as colorful as anything I have ever seen.

Then wandering along the busy night streets, and an hour's massage of my sore muscles by a young farmer-type very businesslike girl, and I had completed the destruction of the tradition that I am not the sightseeing type.

MAY 17, 1968
KYOTO

The president of the Agricultural Workers Union of a village I visited yesterday, near Nara—himself a farmer—and the exquisitely beautiful temples and figures and statues I saw nearby, each *within an hour of each other.* This is the kind of contrast that moves me more than I can say. For the union leader and his enormous gold-covered teeth, and the farmer and his pink-cheeked wife whose home I visited have a link, a *continuity* with these magnificent 7th century buildings and the works of art they house.

About forty families in this village. The couple we visited live well, and work very hard—four women picking the strawberries ten hours a day during the April-till-July harvest. Then the fields are plowed up and turned into flat little flooded rectangles, rice seed planted under mats till the green shoots announce that another stint of hard work is ahead—the stooping process of planting the shoots in the water of the paddy. And on and on.

But what independent, handsome people these farmers are. The agricultural union man is their protection, his union warehouses the crop of berries, markets them at the best time; supplies of fertilizer, etc., are purchased for the union group.

Farming is becoming less and less attractive to the younger people, says Morino, and housing developments near the cities are purchasing farm land at prices the farmers can't resist.

MAY 20, 1968
TOKYO

Paris is wracked by the clashes between the police and the anti-government demonstrators; the masterful DeGaulle who so recently lectured President Johnson on how to run a country is having tumultuous "last days." The Great Charles' sympathies are with the North Vietnamese; this may be one of the reasons they chose to hold these "peace" sessions in Paris.

I *did* walk out on the *Asahi* newspaper's symposium. I just couldn't stand any more academic generalizations and abstractions from the "participants," most of whom are professors. They write about "the development process," which they definitely don't understand—because they have retreated into the easier world of analyzing and classifying, and reciting their little analyses to inexperienced student minds.

Two American businessmen are participating in this arid symposium. Their explanation for participating was that though the Japanese and Asian businessmen are hard-headed, their intellectuals are looked up to for their opinions on *any* subject, and the farther away from reality the better.

MAY 23, 1968
FLYING TO NEW YORK FROM SAN FRANCISCO

Ambassador Johnson could not have been more helpful in what I was trying to do in Japan.

On Monday he gave a "working" dinner in my honor which included two very able and *wary* permanent secretaries (as the British phrase has it) from Foreign Affairs and from Finance, Haruki Mori and Yusuke Kashiwagi.

Johnson was disappointed that they didn't "open up" more, particularly on what Japan would do to carry part of the financial and other load of "economic aid" (as he put it) for underdeveloped Asian countries. But I thought they exhibited the kind of caution that non-policy professionals usually do, particularly in the presence of a new and somewhat notorious outsider.

Kiichiro Satoh, the Chairman of the Mitsui Bank, was a personage in a muted and very Japanese way.

As I expounded on the opportunities of private business and private banking, as distinguished from out-and-out gifts to underdeveloped Asian countries, he began to open up, like a shriveled lotus. He shook my hand several times, as we parted after the party. The light in his eye, in place of the very wary look of an hour before, made me feel I had instilled some confidence in him in my direction.

After dinner Johnson was full of reminiscences.

"General Maxwell Taylor had resigned as Chief of Staff because of the Dulles 'massive retaliation' threat. Kennedy brought Taylor back to the White House as a kind of overall military advisor.

"President Johnson called Taylor and me in; said he wanted both of us to be on the job in Vietnam—this would be about 1964 or so. Taylor would succeed Lodge as Ambassador, but he wanted me there, too. 'How?' I asked. 'As Deputy Ambassador?'

"President Johnson said 'fine'—and that has been a title that has been going ever since."

The Ambassador continued: "I knew Taylor since we were both students in the Japanese language course in 1936, and we could work together, whatever the titles.

"I was in on the important decisions, and agreed with them. The bombing of North Vietnam, the dispatch of large numbers of troops—the whole set of decisions. Sometimes I have some tremors of conscience about what has happened, since—but I was there, and I am responsible, and I think at the end it will be seen we did the only thing that could be done."

MAY 26, 1968
PRINCETON

Up at 5 A.M. for a walk in the cool air, the eastern sky aglow, and the birds, more confident of the future than most of us mortals these days, uttering their chorus of greeting to the new day. In our garden one rhododendron standing twelve feet high, a solid pyramid of bloom. The world seems a good one, in contrast to my so-what attitude of yesterday. I'm recovering from the fatigue and the dizzying effect of jet travel, the long trip across the Pacific and the continent.

Some of the Japanese I got to know deserve a portrait in the gallery of people I keep adding to in my wanderings.

Mitsutoshi Morino, for example. A member of the newspaper *Asahi*'s Cultural Project staff, designated to be my guide and mentor in Kyoto. I found him a delightful companion, always smiling and cheerful, constantly trying to find places about Kyoto that would fit, literally, the specifications that had been given him: "Mr. L. likes gardens; he likes the countryside; he wants to visit a farming village; he says he wants to see some temples." And so I did.

Morino was a source of great interest for me, and not a little amusement. His knowledge of roses, their names, culture. He is head of the Japanese Rose Society, edits their journal. Yet he has never actually raised a rose.

He took a liking to me—as I did to him. "You are my fawthah," he said, with that big grin. Then I asked about his father.

"My father was a general, in the Japanese artillery. He was sent to China, was there for five years." The rest of the story I never got.

Tetsuya Senga, head of the Federation of Economic Organizations of Japan, was another fascinating personage. Senga is a skinny man of about fifty, alert, much less cautious than I would have expected (and found, among government representatives who were much younger and more sophisticated).

The big economic issue in Japan right now is "aid" and business activity by the Japanese Government and business in Indonesia. The Diet is completing legislation providing funds, etc., for this purpose.

But the Indonesians don't yet know enough about how to run a government, or business, to make the Japanese feel very secure about how to become active in that country.

So I described—as an analogy—the Industrial and Mining Development Bank of Iran, and how D&R's activity had provided an economic and physical base for American investments in Iran, with greater assurance that they would be dealing with Iranians of the Industrial Bank who had some operating experience.

MAY 30, 1968
NEW YORK

About the "future" of the Joint Development Group, with new events, I reacted as I would like to think I do when I am at my most effective. "Don't try to plan things too precisely; think about various alternatives, yes; but let events unfold; the essence of the Joint Development Group is in its form, as a Viet-American private non-governmental group. The function can be carried out in many ways."

JUNE 2, 1968
PRINCETON

I was a radical in my youth; I'm still a radical in my not-youth. I was an idealist in my young manhood; I am even more of an idealist today.

More because I know now the obstacles to sustaining ideals in the face of realities to be overcome.

Where came the notion, espoused by many these days, that because some men dry up emotionally (physically too—maybe that's the reason for the emotional drought), *all* men who are *young* are speaking the language of the future, and those no longer young are of the past?

Who will listen these days to one who has not only seen the glory of conflict, but of overcoming doubts and fears *by doing something about them?*

JUNE 3, 1968
NEW YORK

I have something I want terribly to say and to write that will explain and make contagious the sense I have—almost of exultation—about the state of the country. So far from being "rotten to the core," "sick," as those of little comprehension (or violent partisanship) are describing it, I honestly believe this to be one of the two or three healthiest (not happiest; I didn't say happy, but healthy) periods I can remember.

JUNE 5, 1968
7:40 A.M.
PRINCETON

Half an hour ago, coming awake, I turned on my tiny radio expecting to hear how the primary in California turned out. The most incredible words: "The bullet is lodged in the brain, but he is reported as breathing well...." It was seconds later before I learned with horror: Senator Robert Kennedy shot, in the early morning, and in very critical condition.

My first impression: when you stir up hatred and intense emotion, about a political issue, or virulence against one political personage, Lyndon Johnson, you light a fire that will spark hatred and then violence in many unbalanced minds. When a man of superior intellect will say, as one did last summer, that "Johnson is just like Hitler," when people who are good allow themselves to become so inflamed as they have about the Vietnam war and those who supported it, what can you expect but that less clear heads may do terrible, terrible things?

Assassination of a leader with a gun is a horrible thing. But assassination of a man's character is no less bad, and the two kinds of assassination are not unrelated.

5:30 P.M.

Jim Perkins, president of Cornell University, as he greeted me at the Century this noon, had little of the insouciance so characteristic of him. "I have been sitting on a powder keg these past two months," he said.

"The hours we spent with the heads of the SDS [Students for a Democratic Society]—almost every day. And when a white student got on the roof of a fraternity house with a rifle and began firing at black students —blanks, as it turned out—I thought to myself: My God, any one thing could set this whole place ablaze!"

The dark cloud of the shooting of Senator Kennedy hung over us, as we sat talking, in the art gallery of the Century. Back of us were four of Beatrice Tobey's posters, very attractive in an exhibition of *New Yorker* covers. Gay as these made that room, it was in contrast to the somber feeling that spreads everywhere over this one of a series of wanton acts of violence.

The wave upon wave of the consequences of the shooting of Senator Kennedy—how widely they may spread: the negotiations in Paris, the war in Vietnam, and, of course, the election of a President.

In the dark cavern of the Century, I saw a face once so familiar: Lewis Strauss.◄ I strode over to greet him; we both overdid the cordiality a bit, I suppose, as men do who once were close friends, then estranged, but whose manners are good.

"Do you know, Dave, in Washington they have already forgotten AEC?"

Said I: "Too bad, for both of us, they didn't forget it *sooner.*" Lewis laughed explosively, and out came that phrase so familiar in the days when we were great friends: "I'll have to remember that; that's one for the books."

How many episodes of his life and mine have been "one for the books."

JUNE 7, 1968
NEW YORK

Around St. Patrick's Cathedral a great throng, lined up against the wooden police barricades, great searchlights blazing, a policeman every few feet, and pouring out of the side door of the Cathedral a steady stream of people. They had been standing in line for hours and hours to walk through the church and past the closed coffin of Robert Kennedy.

At first, with all the floodlights and the dignitaries to be gaped at, I thought: My God, can't we even mourn without turning it into a movie premiere? But that wasn't a fair comment; there were people drawn partly by curiosity, of course. But it was a solemn and a sad mob.

◄AEC Chairman, 1953–58.

Had received a telegram from "the Kennedy Family." "You are invited to attend the high requiem mass Saturday at St. Patrick's Cathedral." It will be "the thing to do" to come. The place will be filled with the powerful—and the peewees—of public and private life, bowing or shaking hands with each other, at one of these "reunions" called a big public funeral. I feel the quiet and reverential service for F.D.R. in the East Room of the White House is more in keeping. But styles differ; I guess that is all one should say.

JUNE 9, 1968
PRINCETON

Yesterday was an emotion-charged day, from early morning, when I reached St. Patrick's Cathedral, until almost eleven at night, when we sat at the television here at home and looked into the dark night in Washington at the graveside.

[The following notes were written on the pages of the little booklet handed to each mourner, mostly while I was watching this most impressive ceremony.]

Along the side walls within the Cathedral are perhaps a dozen TV sets, so those with "poor seats" can see what is going on. High up, near the choir loft at the back, a huge TV camera pointed, like a small cannon, toward the high altar. Near the altar, a huge scaffold, and on it many cameramen, hanging out over the side, some with still cameras, others with portable TV cameras.

Then the "dignitaries":

The first man to enter the Cathedral through the bronze doors was McNamara; early—8:30.

Rostow wanders in, looking *very* alone.

I said to myself: These people, the last of the Kennedy Cambridge group—Schlesinger, Galbraith—as they come in, they are now part of a *past political generation!*

Above, in the great arch, the American flag and opposite the Vatican flag.

Large Negro group, some in wild-colored sport clothes—led by the movie star Belafonte.

Even in the midst of this crowd: a sense of mortality.

"There's McCarthy—Gene," an excited whisper.

Salinger, with his boylike pout. Nixon, very somber; back of me a whisper from the two young political workers, "Yeah—Dirty Dick."

The white head of Chief Justice Warren.

The President, down the aisle, slowly, the Secret Service all around.

Well, the full cast is here, and now the ceremonial on the altar begins.

Peals of the organ. Processional down the main aisle of many Catholic ecclesiasts, dark hoods, red and pink and lavender. Some Greek Orthodox prelates in black.

The ceremony begins; great surprise to see the stalwart figure and hear the resounding voice of Ted Kennedy making a speech. Admire his fortitude—and the speech, long quote from brother Robert, a great statement.

President stands while the Archbishop addresses him—two Secret Service men also standing several rows behind.

On the scaffold, on the right wall, the lights and cameras. A cameraman with his shirt tail out.

In the midst of modernity, the ancient rituals and substantiations of the Communion.

The slow procession down the main center aisle—brother Ted with the eldest son of Bobby, then the flag-covered coffin. As it passed me (I was close to the aisle), I found myself dropping my head at the sight of the flag—THE flag. Then the widow, the startled look through the black veil, and then the *little* children, and Jacqueline holding John Jr.'s hand fiercely. The little children—somehow *they* broke me up.

Helen is not given to encomiums, for me or anyone else.

But quietly she said: "There were some things in the speech of Robert Kennedy that Edward Kennedy quoted, in the service yesterday, that you could have written, that you have said in almost those words."

What were they?

". . . youth [is] not a time of life but a state of mind, a temper of the will, a quality of imagination, a predominance of courage over timidity, of the appetite for adventure over the love of ease."

And later on:

"Some men see things as they are and say 'why?' I dream things that never were and say 'why not?' "

JUNE 11, 1968
WASHINGTON

The staff meeting I have been clamoring for came off and was, for me, a great source of excitement and satisfaction. The group included some more or less "juniors." These are the ones who give me the most satisfaction in this company because they perk up when I come up with unconventional ideas whereas the older ones look weary. I don't much blame them. They have their hands full handling all my *old* ideas, much less adding some of my new ones.

A "grim picture" is the way Ambassador Bill Leonhart summed up the Vietnam story today. I have just walked back across Lafayette Park from his office in the Old State Building.

And grim it is. Not one flicker of progress in Paris. Stop all bombing and get out. "Reciprocity" is a dirty word in Hanoi's vocabulary.

So the postwar work seems much farther away from reality than it did when the agreement was made to meet in Paris. Some of my ideas about an economic trade-off certainly would make no impression whatever while Hanoi is so sure it will drive us out of the country. As a conciliatory move, give them rice? They expect to *take* the rice, and the people too.

JUNE 12, 1968
EN ROUTE TO PRINCETON

At the State Dinner for the Shah of Iran, the President greeted me in the reception line heartily. How skilled are people like Mrs. Johnson who have spent a life in the public arena about personal references, such as she and the President made to almost every one of the non-governmental guests.

In what I fear was a pretty self-conscious way, I thanked the Shah for giving his "gracious permission" to dedicate the next volume of my *Journals* to him. In the most natural, unkinglike way—he does have a warm personal touch—he said it was he who wished to thank me.

During the period just before the food was served the President showed good, even high spirits, and sat munching salted nuts, hunching over his plate. Margaret Truman Daniel, who sat on my right, remarked on the new big plates (the ones on which no food is served, just for decoration I guess they are). An old-fashioned eagle around the border, etc. The President leaned way over to show her, with a long arm, the bluebonnets on the rim, the Texas flower. Quite proud he was of this.

Margaret Daniel is one of those really rare people who makes everyone feel completely at ease, tells a story with a wry humor, a light in her eye, a toss of the head. Delightful. I was lucky to be sitting between her and the President. For she told stories about the White House—the domestic side—and L.B.J., crouched way over the table as is his table style, would grin and match them.

His comments to her about "your daddy" were so warmly affectionate. "That trip he took to Key West, I believe it did him a world of good; he ought to get away more." Well, Margaret said they had the four grandsons along, and "Anyone who can stand that bunch for a week can't be sick, that's for sure. They wear us out, but not Daddy.

"Fact is," she said, ruminating a bit, "he just plain doesn't like to travel. Uses his age as an excuse. But he just *likes* being at home in Independence. 'I like it here; why should I go somewhere else?' "

The President's face was full of grin-wrinkles, amused. *He* is hardly a stay-at-home!

"I came up to the family rooms a while ago and there were three strange women; I asked Bird: 'What's all this?' She said these were three girls she had gone to college with, and she had promised herself she would have them to the White House and never had. When I may have grumped up a bit, Bird said—get this, Margaret—she said, 'If Bess Truman could have her bridge group to the White House every blessed week, I guess I can have some old college friends in once in five years.' "

Margaret talked very interestingly about the White House as a place to live—and with a sly wink made it plain it was something you could do better without. "Each President," she said, "is supposed to supply his own china; that explains this Texas bluebonnet plate we have here. Fortunately for us Mrs. Roosevelt *left* a lot of china, so we didn't have so much of a problem." I liked the little domestic touch.

"How do the grandsons take the business of having a grandfather who was President of the United States?" I asked.

"Well, like the grandchildren of any well-known man, it is something of a problem. But we try to play it down, of course. Only one time I made a botch of it. We had Adlai Stevenson's grandson visiting us. Something came up about President Truman. To play it down, I said to the boys, 'Oh, anyone can have a grandfather who becomes President,' until I suddenly realized this wasn't exactly the thing to say to a grandson of Adlai's!"

I sent warm greetings back to President Truman. "Oh, he will be so pleased that I saw you, and sat next to you," Margaret said.

"It isn't just that I respect President Truman; I really came to love the man," I told her. And this sentiment I believe is shared by many of the men who got to work with him.

The dinner over, the lectern placed before the President, a waiter tapped on a glass, and the President rose. "I am told we have had two hundred Heads of State as our guests in this room in the past five years. None have we welcomed with greater affection and pride than the statesman from Iran who is our guest tonight; and there is another statesman here tonight who has helped both Iran and his own country, and many countries throughout the world, who has honored me by sitting here at my table, Mr. David Lilienthal."

I gulped; then was so pleased that Helen was there to hear this, as well as a reference to me by the Shah when he later made his soft-voiced response.

The President went on in a gracious toast, and the Shah responded. As the Shah sat down the President leaned over, reached out for my hand, pressed it hard in that big fist, and grinning, said:

"Dave, there's no charge for the commercial"—and a mischievous grin, as if to say: That ought to make you feel good, being singled out by the President at a State Dinner.

It did.

I thought Helen had a good time at the party. (Of course, we sat at separate round tables, as is the custom.) Having said our goodbyes to many people, and to Mrs. Johnson, at Helen's suggestion we walked out through the front portico, into a lovely warm night, the fountain playing, across Lafayette Park back to our suite at the Hay Adams. A good evening, and how glad I was that I am now in the kind of public service as a private citizen where I can pretty much control my time and ration my frustrations.

JUNE 16, 1968
PRINCETON

I strongly believe in the mixing up in staff meetings of men of different responsibilities—engineers, economists, urban problem people—and ages.

Resistance to a mixed staff meeting is part of a philosophy and custom I had to fight even in TVA. I don't believe in funneling things to the decision-maker through one senior man. Today I was able to break out of this circle. A mixed staff is the way the "top man" gets cross-fertilization of ideas and personalities. Also, it encourages younger men to speak up—as Wood Tate did at our Monday meeting; critical of me, as it happens, but that made it all the better.

It is as easy for the top men to be fooled by the apparent acquiescence of their staffs as it is to be their prisoner.

An exciting event early in the week. A young man from Cali, a Dr. Scarpetta, telling me his concept of a new foundation* based on Universidad del Valle in Colombia. The basic idea fits my notions about management as expressed in my little book on management as a "humanist art." It is to be directed toward the management of multinational enterprises, and to training for them.

I agreed to go on the foundation's board of trustees, with two of my most trusted and beloved Cali friends, Manuel Carvajal and Dr. Gabriel

*Fund for Multinational Education.

Velasquez, and volunteered to provide some "seed money" to get things
under way. When he said it would speed things up if they had $20,000
right now for the formation period, I said he could count on me for
$25,000.

JUNE 17, 1968
NEW YORK

Such a pleasant, happy visit with Mehdi Samii this noon. He is a very
companionable man, for all his high talents as a banker, *the* central
banker for one of the fastest growing countries, Iran.

He agreed that the White House function last week pleased the Shah.
"I have never seen the Shah so relaxed. After the dinner people would
approach him and he would open a conversation with them in the most
informal way." Mehdi gave me that big smile of his—he is one of the few
Persians I know who smiles broadly, and with his entire countenance,
eyes included, and it is a good thing to see.

"Sometimes I find it difficult, when I'm with His Majesty, not to put
out an arm and put it across his shoulder, as one would to a friend, he
is that informal at times. And then I realize that this isn't the thing to do,
not at all. But it is good to feel that way about him," Mehdi said.

He told me that the Prime Minister had sent Khodadad Farmanfarmaian to Europe on a hopeless kind of mission. The Prime Minister
wanted to see if some of the almost 30,000 Iranians educated abroad
could not be persuaded to come back to Iran. Almost nothing came of this.

JUNE 21, 1968
NEW YORK

The meeting of the board of directors of the Bedford-Stuyvesant Cor-
poration† yesterday afternoon—concerned with the improvement of a
Brooklyn black ghetto—to my eyes was less a business meeting than a
tableau of sorts.

The setting: the board of directors' room on the 35th floor of the CBS
building; the corridors hung with vast splashes of paint on canvas, of the
most expensive ultramodern abstract painters.

André Meyer, with whom I drove to the meeting, said: "I don't understand this kind of painting," he who owns one of the great collections of
Postimpressionists.

Around a large oval table sat some of the new rich (a great improvement over the old rich, I think): William Paley of CBS, sandy-haired, and

†For the origins and early work of this enterprise, see *Journals,* Vol. VI, *Creativity and
Conflict,* pp. 325, 425–426, 443–444, 466–467, 496–498.

a face that doesn't look as if it had been used; Tom Watson, very tall, erect, iron-grey hair, no longer showing the effect of waiting till his domineering father died to let him run IBM; two very competent leaders, Frank Thomas and Judge Jones, of the B-S Restoration Corporation, the community organization; James F. Oates, Jr., head of Equitable Life, looking soft and bemused; André Meyer, head of Lazard Frères, tired but following everything, and occasionally exchanging glances with me as I showed signs of being bored by some of the vapid little speeches. Douglas Dillon, easily the most impressive man, presiding, and doing it beautifully, with his slow, deliberate way of speaking, a bright eye, a gift of understatement. Benno Schmidt, with his raucous, very slow voice, repeating himself a couple times in every comment he made, and then cautiously saying that he had a footnote: that his firm, J. H. Whitney & Co. was contributing $100,000 to the B-S work. Roswell Gilpatric, as sharp and alive and disciplined a face as I know of. And by way of contrast, Senator Jack Javits, behaving like a Southern Senator of the old school in everything except appearance and New York accent. Making speeches about what as a Senator he could do to get "dough," in contrast with the quiet assurance of the other men, who have done things in quite a different field.

We began by standing, silently, heads bowed, in memory "of our late colleague," Senator Kennedy. A brief understated tribute, in the best of taste, by Dillon: it was Senator Kennedy's idea, this enterprise, and it was his enthusiasm and determination that brought it into being.

John Doar, a big man, wavy hair, reported, as one of the executives. A good number of specific things *had* been done, by way of a home mortgage "pool," restoration of an old broken down dairy, etc. André has been giving of his time—not just that of his organization, and not only the $50,000 he gave—to get things done of a kind that move things along. André isn't much on rhetoric, but he does have the kind of judgment that an operating organization needs.

B-S, unlike the many Urban Coalition groups being organized, is manned to do particular things in a particular place. Whether it can provide a "universal pattern for the whole country," as Javits kept saying, I doubt. The energy and judgment as well as the big amounts of money this group is putting up make it doubtful if another such example could be found.

JUNE 23, 1968
PRINCETON

I just came in from three hours of as happy a way of pouring out my energy as there is. Digging, dividing, transplanting, mixing humus and cow manure with a soupçon of lime and a touch of 5-10-5 fertilizer.

A fan letter—an exuberant one—from a lady in McHenry, Illinois, received yesterday, said: Do you still garden? (She had read about this in my *Journals.*) She has a "big idea" about peace: no man should be given great power unless he is a gardener; such a man won't blow up the world because he will want to see how his garden comes out next year.

Friday morning a professional visit with Dr. Dana Atchley. He had just been given two great honors: the new medical building at Columbia Presbyterian is to be named The Dana W. Atchley Pavilion, and he is receiving the Kober Medal for distinction as a physician, an award from the Association of American Physicians—the aristocrats among the practitioners and the teachers of clinical medicine.

Dana knows me like a book. "I am *not* going to humor you by taking *your* blood pressure. You have never had anything wrong with your heart; your blood pressure record is like that of a kid. I can learn more about your blood pressure and your heart by looking at you this way, and talking with you about the state of the world, than I could learn from an electrocardiogram."

There is a physician who knows his patient.

Reading the transcript of Humphrey's interview in the *Times,* set out in full this morning, this sentence: "Most all political developments follow functional activities." That use of the term "functional" is almost a trademark with me; I hope he understands what it means—what it means to me, at least.

I recall that Senator Joe Clark, when we were both on vacation at Bora Bora in January, thought I was "too idealistic," relying on that idea. Political arrangements must come first to attain peace; he thought this was obvious, but I disagreed.

Speaking of Joe Clark: we had a pleasant dinner together Wednesday evening. He talked about his political problems in the forthcoming fight to hold his Pennsylvania seat in the Senate. "This is my third time around the track, and in twelve years you pick up a lot of scar tissue. My public relations advisors tell me it will cost a million dollars to put on a campaign. Well, that's just out of the question."

I told him I intended to contribute to his campaign. One important reason is that I think we have got to get over this business of making Vietnam the *only* issue of public policy; a man with Clark's great record as a public servant should be returned to the Senate even though I think on Vietnam he has been pretty extreme in some of his positions.

JUNE 24, 1968
PRINCETON

A long day today with the Education and World Affairs Board, and a gathering of the heads of a number of Standing Committees, men of distinction from many universities. It was a good, stimulating meeting. A Dr. Snyder of the University of California did a bit that should have been taped, a good-natured satire on academic long-worded double talk. Exposure to these really superior intellects is a wholesome thing for me —now and then, especially *then*.

I realize all over again that I was *so* right not electing to try an academic career. Studies, studies, studies; but when Peck's Bad Boy (i.e., D.E.L.) prods them on what action might happen as a result of these studies, except to provide fodder for even more research projects by faculty members, the answers are lacking.

JUNE 25, 1968
PRINCETON

Yesterday's report from Landrum Bolling, former president of Earlham College, was as good as I would have expected. He spoke of the caliber of present day students. They are much more "socially aware" than any student group he has known.

But, said Bolling, these young people have been exposed to television, the first full generation who have. And they think they *know* because of what they have *seen*. They *know* about Africa, they have seen it on TV.

There is among them a "latent anti-intellectualism" and an extraordinary kind of innocence. "Students come to college these days thinking they know pretty much everything about two subjects: sex and international affairs. As a matter of fact, they are about *the most innocent generation* we have ever had in these two subjects."

Lunched with Cass Canfield today.

I talked to him about David, as a writer. How different his life is from mine. He has to dig everything out of himself; I live mostly on my stimulation, or frustration, even anger and rowing, with other people.

"Yes," Cass said contemplatively. "Yes, it is a lonely life being a writer, no doubt about it. I sat at a dinner party in London years ago, at the right of Max Beerbohm. I said to him: 'Of the twenty people around this table I know only a half dozen. Tell me what the others do for a living.' 'Well,' he said, 'you pick out the ones that look depressed and you can be sure they are writers.' "

JULY 1, 1968
MARTHA'S VINEYARD

Only an hour ago an indigo sea carried me away from the imaginary world of fact to the real world of a summer's day. I walked the paths of Cedar Tree Neck, and from the top of the cliffs felt myself swept under in the watery blue, as now I am by the green waves of woodlands. Neither on the Neck nor here any sign of other human beings.

Much as I depend upon people for my interest in life, this kind of solitary recess is such a balm; all my senses are strangely heightened by the very fact of isolation, of being quite, quite alone, no sound but the wind through the treetops, or the shore, carrying the waves forward to break in a sound that is not really a sound—rather an emanation.

JULY 3, 1968
MARTHA'S VINEYARD

Doctors sometimes use the expression: "the threshold of pain." A man is said to have a "low" threshold of pain, for example.

Resentment, frustration, and similar emotional pains or lesions also have their thresholds. These powerful emotions can be brushed back, contained, kept outside the realm of consciousness, outside one's conduct and behavior; and then something ticks them off, some tiny flash, some seemingly irrelevant word or gesture or glance—and resentment or hatred or repugnance or remorse takes over.

What a dark unknown, the unlighted forest of emotion!

It has become the "modern, enlightened view" that suppressing these resentments is wrong; grudges, a sense of injustice or ill will, and the rest, should be ventilated. Where they involve other people— here's the rub—the targets of these emotional dissents should be "told off."

Nate Greene, who considered himself a modern sophisticate, certainly an intelligent one, once denounced me as a "resentment collector." But whether I collected resentments (a charge probably true enough), my rule, almost without exception, was to keep them within myself. I believed the real therapy for rational or irrational resentment was to "work it out within yourself." In my kind of life—with plenty of occasions for a feeling of being unjustly treated, in full public view—I hold on, keep all this within me.

Acceptance of reality—isn't that the course for me? Neither explosions of wrath nor bewailing injustice nor pouring out resentment— "ventilating" it—or just keeping it bottled up. Someplace between these extremes, working it out within myself—a torturing kind of discipline— is, I feel, for me the only avenue open.

JULY 4, 1968
MARTHA'S VINEYARD

The last man on earth; a world that had been evacuated of all its people. What would it be like?

That is the sensation this afternoon has given me. The air still; not a leaf stirs. A soft pale blueness over everything. I walked through the heavy, untouched Cedar Tree Neck area. The path was soggy, many years of leaf-decay underfoot. Not a sound. Even the tiny black stream in the woods moved in its darkness silently. And when I broke out into the sand dunes, both the Sound and the mirrorlike wood-fringed fresh lake were soundless.

JULY 5, 1968
MARTHA'S VINEYARD

The young people of today—how much they are on my mind. For a couple years now I have been saying to all who would listen that this is one good, lively generation. Then, more recently, a few show a true rebellion against the hypocrisy of their elders, against the emptiness of spending one's life standing on the General Electric escalator until after thirty years you are a vice president.

What this generation seems not to have is the slightest knowledge of the history of revolt in this country, particularly in the twenties and thirties. The poor dears, with their long hair and their happy "dissent," seem to think they have invented rebellion of thought, of action, of political thinking, of disdain for the Establishment. But while you can forge history, and rewrite it (unhappily, this is the full-time vocation of many professional intellectuals these days), you are ignorant of it *at your peril*. It is the young generation's ignorance of the noble rebels who have only recently left the stage of life that bothers me.

Bitterness against the Establishment? Can anything written or said by Paul Goodman or the other voices of the rebellious, disenchanted, alienated generation compare in violence and disdain, even despair, with Edgar Lee Masters, or Clarence Darrow, or John Altgeld? There have been wave upon wave of such free spirits, saying the very things that these articulate young ones spit out with such scorn and sense of having invented something *new* in an America of rebels.

JULY 8, 1968
MARTHA'S VINEYARD

To feel utterly well, physically vigorous, and seemingly untiring, to sleep deeply and long, to plunge into the very cold Sound and then swim underwater with a long hard breast stroke, to swing an axe and watch the bite of my big saw until a 12-inch scrub oak topples, to drip sweat, to stretch out in the sun, naked, and feel that special kind of animal warming only the sun can give—in short, to be a healthy animal: all this earthy happiness is still mine to enjoy. So the chant: "Happy Birthday" has special meaning.

Doesn't a completely functioning body, rested, happy in a muscular way, take over the mind and even the more introspective emotions; put them in their place, secondary to the healthy body? The body *in charge* may be the way it should be. With "modern" over-intellectualized man this is rarely true.

In any case, the body of D.E.L. is definitely in charge today, on this blowy, sunny isolated hilltop, on my 69th birthday.

JULY 9, 1968
MARTHA'S VINEYARD

Just returned from nine ecstatic hours of sailing in a galloping breeze, at times reaching twenty knots. In Erford Burt's 27-foot Bristol, he and I were driven by a cocky wind and swells deep and then high across the Sound, through the tricky water of Woods Hole, into Buzzards Bay, and into the arms of historic New Bedford Harbor. It was from this wide harbor that hundreds of whalers set off for the distant Pacific. I could imagine that harbor filled with scores of full-rigged ships more than a century ago, ready to hunt the whale.

JULY 11, 1968
MARTHA'S VINEYARD

How little that is useful or even relevant to the crisis problems of our cities comes out of the many university centers of urban studies. How remote are their "studies" from the concerns that are bugging mayors and businessmen alike.

Isn't it possible to revive the kind of interaction between people in the universities and those in active political life, a cross-fertilization, that made Madison in the thirties a place of fertility in social action? It was this informal working alliance between the University of Wisconsin academic community and the state government experts and legislators that brought forth such Wisconsin innovations as unemployment insurance and social security, tax reform, etc.

Later some of these same men—Art Altmeyer, for example, at the University and Harold Groves in the legislature—who gave Wisconsin these advances in solid social reform provided momentum for the Federal programs for these same objectives, on a national basis, the essence of the New Deal.

But the universities today, over the United States (including Wisconsin, I fear) have since withdrawn to the remotest corner of their own academic towers. They move in on the Government to get funding, and utter cries of anguish if the funds aren't forthcoming, "with no strings." The gap—indeed it has become a chasm—between the academic world and Government has widened. All of this made more profound by a kind of disdain, even bitter antagonism, from the academics toward all things governmental.

I was on the deck, sandpapering an old bench we have just acquired. Helen knocked sharply on the window. Exasperated. "Can't you ever just do nothing *at all?*"

It's true; this is the most difficult thing of all for me, doing "absolutely nothing." I had climbed up into some tall trees, cutting out the tops for the view, dragging the heavy decapitated arms away, doing a lot of physically hard chores (which are a delight). She was right; I should just stop.

The question is not, really: can't you do nothing, but *why* do you keep at it until the sweat pours off you in cascades, and you drive on, from one activity to another, physical or otherwise? Why? Why? What goes on? What is the source of this extraordinary obsession to be "doing something all the time"?

JULY 18, 1968
MARTHA'S VINEYARD

"What do you think of that Tom-m-m? Would you believe he is seventy-nine years old?" This was Rita Benton (at the supermarket this morning) beaming on a wiry-looking Tom, and herself looking like some modern statue of Mother Earth.

"Tom, do you ever paint portraits? I'd like Helen to sit for a portrait —she has refused for thirty-five years—but maybe she would if it were Tom Benton."

"No, Dave, I don't try commercial art any more. I tried one of Harry Truman, and the whole family would gather around, and the assistants and the secretaries, and they didn't like this and that—mostly because I painted him wrinkles and warts and all. No, I've given that up."

Long phone conversation yesterday with Nick Philip [of D&R]. As is my custom, I soliloquized. This is a process by which I walk through a problem and reach a conclusion. A verbal walk is what it is. Going from one step to the next, or pulling back from a path that seems wrong, and moving on in a different direction. So often these verbal walks end up by my deciding that *nothing* should be done, or nothing done now.

My technique of weighing a problem, and possible conclusions step by step, has been long in developing. For me this cautious, self-testing of the ice goes against what I think is my basic temperament. My first reaction is an emotional one, and the response inside me (and usually verbally as well) is definitely impulsive. "Do something" is my impulse. Do it now, right away, before the opposing views get set.

Then I settle back and become an almost entirely different actor. Is this the best time to take such a position? Are you sure enough of the facts? (Rarely does this have as much of a bearing as one might suppose; where my instinct or my nose for a situation and for personalities is really working—it often does—an elaboration of the facts rarely adds much; mostly it protects one against being caught off base by some minor error or omission of fact; rarely is it decisive.)

Many executives go through something like this process, where the responsibility is clearly on them to decide, rather than "refer for further study." But I doubt whether it is common for them to do the analysis as I do, by a formal step by step walk through the options and alternatives they see open.

JULY 21, 1968
MARTHA'S VINEYARD

Tom Mead recently wrote Nick Philip a letter from Saigon that is a classic as an exposé of the kind of editorialized reporting that goes on, and the *actual facts* of the situation in Vietnam:

> Your letter—and others I have had from family and friends— reveals that there is once again some anxiety over our well-being out here. Last week's *Time* Magazine has the rockets "raining down" on Saigon. It neatly sums up the entire situation as "Saigon's nightmare."
> The facts are these. Rockets have been used by the V.C. for some months. Only an occasional rocket has fallen in the center of the City. There have been shellings, on a small scale of the port area, and [a] suburb, but in the last two weeks, these have diminished.
> There have been some civilian casualties and some damage to property, but on the whole, on a city the size of Saigon and so spread out, the effect is negligible.
> The life of the city during this time has been practically normal. Streets are crowded and shops open. Our curfew is now a reasonable

9.00 PM to 6.00 AM, so we can go out to dine. Washington D.C.'s curfew was only half an hour shorter this week.

The people of Saigon are pretty well unperturbed by this.

JULY 24, 1968
WASHINGTON

A taxing day in discussions with Grant and Leonhart of AID.

Several times during the discussions I spoke explicitly about the injection of the military establishment, i.e., the Department of Defense, into economic development and so-called counter-insurgency matters by the use of "social scientists."

My question is why in the hell the military should have anything to do with economic development in other people's countries, under whatever guise—counter-insurgency or what not?

AUGUST 6, 1968
NEW YORK

In ten days we are "due" to deliver to Western Australia a "report" for a program for the development of Ashburton/Pilbara, and Western Australia.

I thought the idea of a "report" was the wrong note. It implies a completed full-fashioned set of ideas, rather than a basis for an *interchange* of ideas between ourselves and Minister Court.

This noon I dictated and dispatched a very informal letter—lengthy —to Minister Court. I hope it will serve as a new way of going at such a "non-report."

I am fed up to here seeing able, quick-witted men such as we have in D&R follow the conventional "consultants" pattern of a "report" (usually elaborately bound, and almost invariably dull and without spirit) as if so living, moving, and human a situation as development could be packaged in that time-worn way.

It is a matter of *style,* in the broadest sense, that I am seeking, a new style more nearly representing the unconventional approach to human affairs (called "development") that we here are fashioning year by year.

How unbelievably dull, and *irrelevant,* the TV pictures from the Republican convention at Miami. Heavy-jowled patriarchs there to design the New Politics, a guide for Youth! Miami, the ignoramus' capital of the world, now the biggest ho-hum spectacle in years. The TV and press feel they have been *personally* affronted because "there is no drama" (meaning fights).

Whatever may be said about us "Dimmicrats," they usually run their shows to suit not the media but their own bellicose, bickering over-dramaticized souls.

AUGUST 10, 1968
MARTHA'S VINEYARD

The "convention" of the Republicans was well named: as conventional as if this were 1910 or 1920.

Nixon playing the piano and singing "Home on the Range" with a big new smile and the same old ideas. Maybe he is right, that the country really *wants* a Harding-return-to-normalcy. It isn't what it will *get* with Nixon.

Water in motion—now *there* is something full of magic. I stood on the sand of Cedar Tree Neck this noon—not a soul to be seen in that whole half circle—and watched, absolutely fascinated, as the water of the Sound gently poured over a misshapen boulder near the shore: poured over it, then swirled at both edges of the rock into two tiny whirlpools, then dove down under the next tiny wavelet, and again the pure silver, as if a thing alive, again streamed over the surface of the rock.

The natural world is one such mysterious sensation after another.

AUGUST 11, 1968
MARTHA'S VINEYARD

"Cherish" is the word that came to me again and again during this miracle of a morning. "Cherish" every such hour, drink it in, record it on that tape recorder in your head—the one that is directly connected with your heart and spirit.

Cherish: what a great word, a tender word, a mature man's word.

I know no one who is more eager and, yes, *determined* to live. Yet I am rational enough to know, and now and then actively to realize, that one day the books will be closed on me and my life. It is not sad, because this realization—not an apprehension (not now, at least)—makes stronger within me the concept of *cherishing* the moments as they come.

Cherish beautiful days; cherish ideas. Above all cherish people, individuals, the strong, the beautiful, the weak, the interesting, the sated. But particularly cherish those few who have my intensity about life and what one should do with it. This latter impulse isn't a "disposition in anticipation of death" (to paraphrase an old legal expression).

My whole story, from early youth, is a preoccupation, often terribly self-conscious and tiresome to others, with trying to have a goal, a purpose, and driving toward it.

At the country store—Alley's in West Tisbury—a pudgy little girl wearing an outsize sweatshirt reaching down to her knees; across the back, in huge pink block letters:

I LOVE MANKIND
IT'S PEOPLE I CAN'T STAND

In attacking the "urban problem" is the answer found by doing something about the cities? Isn't it equally relevant to ask *where the people come from* who produce urban congestion—and why?

And by the by, whatever happened to the *hobo* of my youth? The hobo in Valparaiso, Indiana, wasn't looking for work, he wasn't "unemployed" in the present-day sense. He was on the move because he didn't want a job and liked living from hand to mouth; dressing in rags didn't bother him. He wasn't "alienated," he was a happy man because he had no responsibilities and no fixed abode, and didn't have to wash. Hooking a ride on a freight car was his preferred mode of moving from place to place.

The hobo has reappeared, after a long absence. He is the present-day hippie. Male and female this time around; he is more of an institution than the hobo. But it's much the same style. Every society *needs* their gypsies and hobos and hippies.

AUGUST 13, 1968
MARTHA'S VINEYARD

My chief innovative idea (if it should stand up to a closer look) was how Western Australia development finances might be raised. Why shouldn't the bonds, or even the debentures or common stock of a development fund not be made attractive to the private capital markets, not only of Australia but particularly of Japan and the U.S.? This would give Japan, now getting a windfall from purchase of Australian iron ore, a further stake in the development of the region from which these great and essential ores come. Since cordial political relations between Japan and Australia are important, even vital to Japan, why should not Japan be persuaded to invest in the general development of Australia through the securities of such a fund?

The most important concepts, I thought, were: 1) that the development of the Ashburton/Pilbara region—our original assignment—must be seen in the full context of Western Australia as a whole, and while a good place to begin thinking regionally, this must soon be viewed as part of the overall development future of the entire Commonwealth. 2) The increasingly closer reciprocal relationship between Australia and the U.S. is an important factor in considering a ten-year look-ahead.

AUGUST 16, 1968
MARTHA'S VINEYARD

We live in the sky here; these high wide windows; our little house is mostly windows. As Barney Tobey said when he and Beatrice were here this summer: "You bring the outdoors inside." How much we miss, even in Princeton, not seeing the *whole* sky, as we do here, from early morning until the burnished glow of the western sky, the sun down, but its mark of glory lingering on and on.

AUGUST 17, 1968
MARTHA'S VINEYARD

This morning a deep all-embracing fog. All the once familiar objects are transformed by this mantle of other-worldliness. The gulls rise in alarm, but they are no longer gulls but creatures of the opaque air.

It is on such a morning that the moors and the cliffs of Cedar Tree Neck move me most deeply. Something elemental about that greyness; the great boulders symbolize the immutability of Nature, of God, and there I stand, so full of busy-ness and self-importance in my work, so full of myself and my plans for this country or that: how absurd I am, against that setting.

But it is the *beauty* of such a morning by the Sound that shakes me most. The marshmallows now in a burst of pale pink, their faces delicate on those long slender necks rising from the wetland near the little wooden footbridge; spots of scarlet here and there in the leaves, and the plumes of sumac, the softness of the green.

AUGUST 20, 1968
NEW YORK

A letter in from the newspaperman of *Asahi Shimbun,* Mitsutoshi Morino, who "adopted" me as his "father" last May. His letter begins:

"Dear Mr. Lilienthal, my respectful beloved father:" And went on, "Since August 1, you have been a grandchild of a girl as you adopted me as a son in Japan. . . . She is so cute and has 2.580 kilogram by weight."

The Metropolitan has an extraordinary exhibit of French Impressionist paintings, loaned by private owners in the New York area. What a treasure of art there is in this city. A whole group of Claude Monets, inimitable and delicate; half a dozen or more Pierre Bonnards, bold, the composition striking, some of them with the air and light *moving* through the whole picture, somewhat the way the wind moves through the treetops at "Topside" so that one is stirred and freshened by the lights and spaces Bonnard has produced.

It was all memorable. To lose oneself in contemplation of beauty and deep feeling is to find oneself.

How unutterably sad. Just turned on the TV: the Communists have moved their troops into Czechoslovakia.

Where now are those pundits who told us that the Cold War is over, that the Soviets are transformed? Will we hear any admissions of error from them? Of course not.

AUGUST 28, 1968
MARTHA'S VINEYARD

It is difficult, yes, impossible, to maintain a sense of perspective, much less humor, while watching and listening to the reporting of the Democratic convention, as off and on we have been since noon today.

What has so angered me is not the result of the voting on the so-called Vietnam plank. There was a 1 to 1½ vote favoring a plank that made much sense, though I would have been better satisfied if it had been more explicit in disavowing confidence in the results one can hope for from the military operations of our forces.

My heated and humorless state of mind is outrage at the partisan and snide way in which the media reporters have injected themselves into the most sensitive parts of the workings of a political convention in which they are neither candidates nor delegates.

At one point, while the chairman was speaking in support of a ruling he had made, the TV camera switched to Brinkley, who gave his own interpretation of what that ruling should have been. Brinkley actually participated in the debate, and from his point of far greater vantage than that of the elected delegates who were earnestly presenting their various views about the Vietnam plank. This, and the cynical comments made throughout, seems to me the sort of thing that should not go on under the guise and cloak of news reporting on the publicly-owned airwaves.

This convention, despite the snide remarks, gave everyone a full opportunity to say his say about the Vietnam war. It was the *only* issue that was debated, as if only this was important. The debate this afternoon was presented by people from both sides of the issue, and for the most part with dignity and without long boring rhetorical flourishes.

AUGUST 31, 1968
MARTHA'S VINEYARD

Dinner at Katharine Cornell's place here. Lynn Fontanne, jaunty but definitely an old lady. And Alfred Lunt, a black patch over one eye, very erect but grey, following his wife through the room, with that mark of respect and affection that has lasted so many, many years, on stage and off.

Kit's close friend, Nancy Hamilton, was sparkling; such a lively and talented woman.

Kit was quite subdued. Her reserves of energy are low; illness has changed her. Two years ago her life was in the balance; now she is slowly regaining strength. That romantically handsome figure that moved so many of us when she was the unquestioned star of stars has lost some of the proud erectness that was so characteristic of her stage presence. She is still smiling and warm, but the exuberance is missing—naturally enough.

What a beautiful woman she is. Neither illness nor anxiety can rob her of the light that shines from her eyes, the noble structure of her great forehead.

SEPTEMBER 1, 1968
FLYING TO NEW YORK

David Schwartz and his new wife are vacationing in Edgartown, and we went in for a drink with them. I have great respect for Dave, as a public servant.

He was Justice Reed's secretary, received the Rockefeller Public Service Award, has given up a lucrative private practice to become Commissioner of the U.S. Court of Claims. When he was counsel for D&R, it was his collaboration with me in 1960 on my idea about what I called the "multinational corporation" that made it possible to get my paper for a Carnegie Tech Symposium written, and my ideas and terminology (i.e., "multinational" corporation rather than "international") put into permanent written form.

David's wife has a nineteen-year-old daughter, a student at Radcliffe, who was not only in the demonstration at the Democratic convention in Chicago, but was one of its many organizers. This brought us closer to the harsher realities of the day: on the one hand well-organized "demonstrations" including force, as a political implement, and on the other, the issue of "police brutality," raised so sharply by the efforts of the Chicago police to keep that organized mob (or "peaceful" marchers) from storming the Democratic convention and taking over the streets of Chicago.

Schwartz was greatly disturbed by the things he had learned, at first hand, about the "demonstration." He was convinced that the "kids" were being used by a group of revolutionaries, out to batter down American society by violent guerrilla and terrorist means.

"I was a radical when I was young, too; but we knew what we wanted. We were Socialists; we had a program for the improvement of society, and what we did by way of 'protest' was to work to bring about changes we believed in.

"The kids themselves don't know what they want. They have no program they are fighting *for.*"

II P.M.

In my middle age I have not been one who envied the young. A time of inner confusion, of trying to find out who in the hell you are.

I look with anything but envy on the current crop, the spectacular ones especially, with their long hair (both sexes), tattered clothes, exhibitionist garb.

But I changed my mind tonight, a good deal. Spent several hours in Greenwich Village, on a holiday evening. The Village is the Holy City of the very self-conscious young. They were out in full force. (Not all really terribly young, I should add.)

In Washington Square Park they were having such a good time. It was the ability to let yourself go, and to have the extra energy to strum a guitar with such violence, or neck madly and horizontally in the glare of a street light with people going by in droves; to feel that you are the center of the universe for a few precious moments; to have no responsibilities, no problems that skitter across your mind, as they do mine even when I am off duty.

These are people having fun of the kind that only the young, a certain kind of young at least, can have. And *that* I did envy—and, I confess, admired and half-coveted.

So they do go without washing their feet, sit around for hours whanging those guitars, and all the rest. So they are full of catch phrases about "the Establishment" and tearing down the "power structure." So they don't have a *cause,* any sense of what they would do to make things better, as I did as a young rebel and radical—well, let them have fun.

They are young, and look as if they don't expect being young would last but a few moments, so make the best of it. They don't know that some of us no longer "young" can be truly young almost forever; *if* we have the knack.

SEPTEMBER 2, 1968
NEW YORK

Standing at the curb on Fifth Avenue at 45th I saw some of the most vivid pictures of America as it is in this great city. It was the Labor Day parade, and it was full of excitement, every kind of face, occupation, manner, language and color—and "place of origin." To witness this Americana was a great experience.

For what must have been an hour they marched, in column after column, the International Ladies' Garment Workers. Local 23, the "Blouse, Skirt and Sports Wear." Local 23 is their college, their affiliation, the center of their special kind of social cohesion and loyalty. And so on down the list, including Degraders and Refurbers. These are people who only a bit more than a generation ago were unmercifully "sweated"; now they are a recognized part of a major industry.

The snappy drum and bugle corps, probably high school bands from nearby towns; young girls in spangled uniforms, in such contrast to the Middle European union members, or to the Chinese and Puerto Rican union locals, swarms of them, mostly with small children along.

The marchers weren't the only excitement. A number of long-haired and usually spectacled young people, from Columbia University, I guessed, gathered in groups and began yelling "Peace Now" and some raucous sounds about "Hump" (as the signs called Humphrey). I could hear them excitedly discussing where they should stand to insure getting the police to run them off, but the police didn't find them interesting. That is, until the burly Steel and Iron Workers, Local 40 ("Life begins at 40," they said), came along. Then the steel workers broke over the police barricades and gave the protesters what they wanted, some excitement. The police gathered in a hurry, led by a captain. I moved over to get my quota of excitement too, and a stern-looking quiet-spoken captain of police said to me: "Move along now, Mac; get out of the way before you get hurt."

In the midst of one of the parading groups a baby stroller being pushed by Mama, and a big fat two-year-old asleep in the midst of the drumming.

Such a fascinating array of occupations: Bartenders' Union, any number of locals of various butchers' unions, all carrying signs: "Don't Buy California Grapes; Help the Farm Workers' Union Organize the Grape Pickers." And some Mexicans, dark and handsome men and women, carrying a flag with the Mexican eagle on it, looking as if they thought this parade was some kind of dream.

Have just seen a TV half-hour. CBS: *On the Road* with Charles Kuralt. It makes up for much of the scurvy that infects so much of TV. It was about the *good* there is in this country, little glimpses of places, people, events that are familiar to me, but known to so few people in the over-intellectualized, over-rarified, over-sensationalized media. I kept saying to myself as the picture went on in Indiana small towns, in Vermont, Tarpon Springs, and so on: "How right, how right."

It is the people who hate themselves, who have messed up their own lives, who are the ones who hate this magnificent country, a place and a people without parallel.

SEPTEMBER 5, 1968
NEW YORK

With the excuse—or the deadline—of the speech I am to make to the American Management Association September 26th, I have been tossing some ideas back and forth on the theme of the management of change.

We have a need for a new style of manager at a time when change is not only in the air but is an acute necessity.

We hear a lot of talk about change, but mostly it comes from articulate and thoughtful journalists, theoreticians in the universities and the "think tanks," the compilers of "surveys," the TV commentators, and so on.

The people who know best *how* change comes about are the people who are in charge of change; they are the do-ers, the people who lead a managerial life.

The prime characteristic of the managerial life is that men who effect change in that role have to be accountable for the course they elect to take in the change process. They can't just gabble about change, "protest and demonstrate" about it, write surveys about it, point out the number of "options" that we have. They have to *take a stand* about what they believe should be done and go ahead and do it (or have it done) and face up to the consequences. If it works, it is fine; if it doesn't, they get their blocks knocked off.

It is the special genius of this country to get things done, do things, not just stand there splitting ideological hairs. It has been the do-er and doing impulse that have built the country. The vitality of a *doing* people has attracted the envy and the admiration of the world. Almost any other part of the world beats us when it comes to abstractions, but many of them are unable to get beyond the abstract stage into making things happen, which is another way of saying making for change.

But this ability to get things done, to *do,* rather than simply *talk* about doing, is inadequate for today's needs. For the managerial life to fulfill its function in the process of change, the manager has got to be far more than just a do-er.

For one thing, he has got to be more aware of *why* he is doing what he is doing. He has got to be more of a philosopher in that he sees the meaning of things as well as being able to get things done. He has got to be much more articulate, be capable of explaining what he is doing and why he is doing it. He has got to be much more sensitive to the needs for change in a longer-range view than at any time in the past.

Perhaps the most tragic of illustrations of the inadequacy of just mere ability to get things done is the mounting cost of armament, much of it obsolete before it is completed, which has no "military" function, ironically, because it is so fantastically destructive and is so increasingly costly as to bankrupt or impoverish even so rich a country as this—and our Soviet antagonists.

I have less than admiration for the "sayers," but they do have the most influence in our country because they are so extraordinarily articulate. And when what they say or preach or "forecast" turns out to be wrong, they are not accountable or responsible. They can write their editorial columns, make their TV comment, issue their surveys, do their operations analyses, and if this product doesn't make practical, operational sense, they may be scolded but nobody really holds them accountable.

In contrast to the sayers, the do-ers, the managers, the people who lead lives of action seem to be temperamentally inarticulate, both in government and business, where it seems to them too risky to say much about what they are doing, so they simply go ahead and do it.

SEPTEMBER 7, 1968
NEW YORK

I wonder whether there has ever been a time when so much attention was paid to young people, or to certain kinds of young people? Not long ago it was the teenagers; now they still are called "the kids" but many of them are in their early twenties.

Last night I went to what is called "the East Village," a few blocks east of the Greenwich Village area. What I saw is the lower depths of the youth movement of today. These are not derelicts such as we used to see on lower Bowery and Skid Row—the down and outers.

On the streets and in the doorways of slums youths are smoking marijuana and panhandling or just sitting on the sidewalks. The long hair, the frayed dirty clothes, the look of refugees.

They are getting money from somewhere: the gear they wear, the high cost of drugs, the whole atmosphere is more that of remittance men between checks from home. Many of their parents are glad to settle for not having anything to do with their East Village young ones—except to send that check.

Went into a favorite dance spot for young people: the Electric Circus. These young people were different from those sprawling in the streets. A wild effect from stroboscopic lights. Most of them looked like the gawky post-adolescents at a Michigan City high school dance of fifty years ago, except for their clothes. No drunkenness—maybe that comes later though. The place keeps open until 4 A.M.

Another observation of the young. Went to a reshowing of an ancient favorite of mine: W. C. Fields and Mae West in *My Little Chickadee.* The audience—this was a place on 72nd Street—was mostly young people, mostly boys, or young men. Everywhere around me and through the audience they shrieked and guffawed over the same gags that used to put me in the aisles thirty or more years ago. They were absolutely delighted with the broad antics, which in this picture are anything but "sophisticated." I would have supposed that Fields and Mae West would not seem funny to this avant-garde generation.

You can't be all that worldly wise to be able to howl over these comics from a thousand years ago!

Yesterday completed a week of intensive discussions and thinking about the next stage of our development work program for the whole country of Vietnam, the product and summing up of eighteen months' work.

It went very well.

Nick Philip made most of the difference. He is a production man. The more I work with him the more I can communicate with a minimum of words. He concentrates on a sticky point, sets out what needs to be done, or I need to decide or do something about, and leaves out the usual spatter of words. We don't hash and rehash things that are obvious, or that have been decided before, or about which nothing can any longer be done.

He has something of Gordon Clapp's‡ analytical ability but less philosophical—which means less words need to be spent getting to the vitals of a matter. To him I am just another ordinary mortal, not a super-guy, so he can dissent from me without difficulty, and agree without overpraise.

‡TVA Chairman, 1946–54; co-founder in 1955 and President of Development and Resources Corporation until his death in 1963.

SEPTEMBER 8, 1968
PRINCETON

A phone talk this morning with Beatrice [Tobey]. I said something about having too many things to do, or things I very much wanted to do, including a book I'd like to write. But where will I find the time?

"You don't know how lucky you are," she said. "Don't you realize that most men [she didn't say "at your time of life"] are not asking themselves 'How can I do all the things I terribly want to do,' but 'What should I do with myself?' "

The American Management speech, much in my mind these days, serves as a focus for my fury about the *onlookers* in life (that isn't my word: I stole it from a friend, but it says it). Are we as a people more and more becoming voyeurs, getting our kicks from watching, a peephole society?

Suppose tomorrow we closed the hospitals and medical schools and doctors' offices, and turned all these people into diagnosticians; every doctor concentrating on what is *wrong* with the sick people; no one doing a thing about therapy, about cures, no one willing to do more than analyze, collect facts, doing studies about illness, but staying clear of the patient, of doing anything about curing people.

Isn't that what so many of these political and economic analysts, surveyors, institutions for the study of this and that, are doing about society? All observers, all diagnosticians, no doctors.

Having a delightful time reading Jonathan Daniels' latest book: *Washington Quadrille.* He inscribed a copy for me with a line that pleased me very much, I must say: "Great workman and witness of our time."

SEPTEMBER 10, 1968
NEW YORK

At lunch today with a most impressive young man, physically and in demeanor, LeRoy Bowser. His crinkled hair is sprinkled with grey but his huge bushy mustache coal black, his skin the color of chocolate.

LeRoy was full of stories about how the black people of Jamaica, in Long Island, were learning how to get things done, making mistakes, shouting at each other in these large community or board meetings they enjoy, but sticking to a principle I have given many of the years of my life to articulate and give substance to in human affairs—

that is, the strength must come from the individuals, the people directly involved in building a community or a community function. Not from the outside, not from "experts," not out of a book or survey. I hope he will write some of those stories; they are classic. He tells of the foibles with a huge chuckle that makes his grenadier's mustache tremble.

As I left my office this evening, I felt: You, David Lilienthal, are having a good time. I couldn't help sticking my chest out a bit and squaring my shoulders, saying to myself: You don't just work here for someone else; you made this happen; you made something come into being out of your head and your drive and your imagination that didn't exist before. And it is not just a book or a manifesto or a theory, or an inchoate idea; it is something you can see, and feel its reality.

SEPTEMBER 11, 1968
NEW YORK

Sat next to Professor Archie Cox of the Harvard Law School, who has been holding public hearings about the violent student uprising of last spring at Columbia.

I tried to learn from him something of these student leaders of the Students for Democratic Society—the SDS.

One thing he said I fastened on to: "Sometimes during the hearings a group would get into an argument among themselves—so they hardly knew we others were there—about revolutionary theory." In great and precious detail, I gather.

Reminded me of my years, in my early teens, reading Emma Goldman and attending one, perhaps several, anarchist meetings in Chicago. At those meetings I recall that the emphasis was on the finer points of tactical theory. Cox explained that it was arguments about this same sort of thing that these present-day student amateur revolutionaries enjoyed most of all and that splintered the firebrands into all sorts of intellectual groups.

Interested in what Elmo Roper—a shrewd and experienced man— said to me about Gene McCarthy. "I have known him for a good many years. A Jesuit, yes; he believed he could become President completely on his own. So vain you might say he is a mystic about himself. I don't believe he will endorse Humphrey any more than he was willing to join forces with Kennedy though their ideas were about the same. Extraordinarily monumental ego."

SEPTEMBER 12, 1968
FLYING TO WASHINGTON

Newspapermen and TV people tend to have a disease of their occupation, like silicosis among quarry workers. It is chronic cynicism.

SEPTEMBER 13, 1968
WASHINGTON

For the first time since I have had anything to do with the World Bank I came out of Bob McNamara's office feeling that here was a man who had an affirmative, a positive feeling about development.

The banker posture, saying "No" and *looking* "No" before anyone has even begun to talk about a country's needs, has given way, under McNamara, not only to the outlook of a manager but also to a man with genuine *enthusiasm* about a country.

This was noticeably true when he spoke of Indonesia.

"Do you know, David, that in twenty-two years this Bank has never made a loan or done anything at all about Indonesia, a country of 122 million people?

"I went out there and found a top group of good people—it is a thin group and there is little talent below the top, but still . . .

"What they need more than money is some philosophical support and that is the kind of thing you can give them."

But it was Vietnam I wanted to talk about. I said: "As you well know, we have been working for one and a half years on a long-term program for Vietnam. Thuc§ and I want to look ahead to the postwar period of reconstruction. In that process the consultative or consortium method and leadership the World Bank has developed may be the best way to move ahead on the reconstruction task."

When I used the word "reconstruction," giving it strong emphasis deliberately, he grinned, picked it up.

"Yes, this may be the very place where the 'reconstruction' part of the Bank's name, and function, should come into use."

Then he talked at some length about how important it was that the "image" of the Bank, as being dominated by U.S. policy and personnel, be changed, and the international side emphasized.

"The cancellation by the Bank, at the direction of Dulles, of the Aswan Dam loan left a big dent in the picture of a truly international body.

"In view of my association with the war in Vietnam [what a mountainous understatement *that is*] and some of the episodes of the past, to

§Vu Quoc Thuc, chief of South Vietnam's long-range economic planning.

have a World Bank man physically in Vietnam, or any impression that the Bank is now considering financing undertakings in Vietnam, would be a mistake.

"You say you insist on doing these things with the Vietnamese; it is a big part of the job. When you leave they will be better able to carry on."

I underscored the point: "To have the patience and forebearance, to wait until the fellow in whose country you are working works things out in *his* way.

"I didn't welcome the President's insistence that I take on this Vietnam responsibility, as you well know," I said. "I became almost spoiled by the Iran experience. For there, after many ups and downs, we did find that there were some very able Iranians who could and did take over one responsibility after another fairly quickly.

"But in Southeast Asia it isn't likely to happen quite that readily— certainly with a war on top of all the other difficulties. I think Vietnam has taught me, and most of the rest of us, a quality of patience; we must try to stick, stubbornly, to the concept of not doing the job ourselves."

Said McNamara: "That's the way, though; that is the way it should have been done before. I think that is the basic *weakness* in our position out there."

But my guess is that the "weakness" he had in mind—one of them surely—was in the military field. God knows he should know.

10 P.M.
PRINCETON

"What a guy. What an imagination, what a sardonic intelligence."

Those words are me about our writer son, having just finished reading the title story in David's new volume of short stories, *Time Out*. Is the hand and head that produced such a witty and elaborate commentary on phoniness the same person who looks out on me, here in my bedroom, from those pictures of a boy blowing a saxophone or boxing with his father? No longer the long-legged boy who robbed the refrigerator to build those huge six-layer sandwiches.

SEPTEMBER 21, 1968
PRINCETON

Running a company—or sitting on top of it and absorbing the inevitable bumps—is a seven-day-a-week occupation.

Yesterday I intended to banish D&R from my thoughts, after an over-stimulated ten days. But I spent a couple hours on the phone. The important thing seems to be to *expect* that there is no such thing as complete insulation from an enterprise (and a "cause") that means as much to me as D&R does.

SEPTEMBER 27, 1968
PRINCETON

To a full Waldorf ballroom yesterday morning I delivered myself of my latest thinking about change and about leadership.◖

What appealed to me most at the gathering was the extemporaneous response of a remarkable young man, Hodding Carter III of Greenville, Mississippi. He was given the Appley Youth Leadership Award and it was to this award that he responded.

Tall, young, slender, aristocratic in bearing—his family have been leaders in the Delta of Mississippi for generations. A superb speaker in the modern style. He graduated summa cum laude from Princeton and went back to Greenville and to Mississippi when he could have had almost any job in the U.S. in the cities. He did the hard work of building a Democratic Party of black and white people.

One younger member of the panel asked: "How can you be optimistic when all about us we see these dreadful things?" I thought to myself: Young Carter is the answer to why I feel optimistic. It only takes a few such extraordinary people, just a few, to turn this ranting and confusion and ugliness that is so characteristic of the young these days, and the *not* young, into something *great,* the greatest, in fact.

SEPTEMBER 29, 1968
PRINCETON

Physically the Hackensack Meadows are a soggy, stinking marsh-land spreading over northeast New Jersey only a few miles from the Hudson River and New York City. They are a classic example of the difficulty of getting things done, in a democracy, as I discovered (all over again) during a two-day conference on the subject held here at Princeton.

Making these perhaps 20,000 acres of polluted, garbage-strewn rat-infested land available for use, in a uniquely strategic location, is no insuperable engineering problem. These acres could be "dried out" by physical methods that are well known, and at a reasonable cost.

But these marshes are far more than a physical problem of reclamation, turning acres now unused into land of fabulous value: $50,000 an *acre* or more.

The area is part of two major New Jersey counties, Bergen and Hud-

◖American Management Association meeting.

son. Within those counties are a number of municipal corporations, which means mayors and councils. Three hundred years of history overlay them, too, direct grants of title from the British Crown, a constitutional provision that gives a state education fund prior rights to any sales or use of such of these lands as are riparian; for the marshes are tidal.

The only problem worth considering is how to persuade the mayors and the legislators coming from those counties and municipalities that a *regional* approach to the development of these acres is the only way they can be developed for the public interest (i.e., location of industry, clearing up of pollution, housing, etc.).

For a century people have been trying to find an answer to the Hackensack Meadows; in the last fifteen years these efforts have produced a stack of reports, surveys, engineering studies, economic studies "this high," said Fairleigh Dickinson, Jr., a sponsor of legislation to set up a regional agency.

All of the studies and reports, I thought, were based on old-fashioned and outmoded ideas—i.e., treating the reclamation of the Meadows as an ordinary "flood control" project by which to get Federal funds via the pork barrel route of the Corps of Engineers.

I said, with not a little vehemence, that there are new things stirring in this country, new ideas about how to combine private capital and public benefits, and these are the tools I think must be adapted to such a problem. When that happens the recalcitrant mayors will look at this differently, the legislature likewise. And yet until the second day of the conference here, when I exploded with a declaration for "optimism and the new ideas of how we are going to rebuild the cities of this country within a generation," no one there had referred to these new ways.

Glad I attended this meeting, for it exposed me to a real-life situation, not a report, a survey, the kind of statement of a problem in terms too precise to be real, to be believable. "Individuals—back of everything are individuals," said a New Jersey poet I quote so often: Whitman. When you think of development as what can be made appealing to individuals, you have made the problem complex, true; but when you turn the problem into numbers or engineering or Socialist terms, you have made it simpler but totally unreal.

OCTOBER 2, 1968
PRINCETON

Reading the daily papers these days, you might think the U.S. is on the edge of revolution and civil war. Or if you were to watch some of the staged TV scenes of "protest demonstrations" presented as "news."

Then comes the first day of the World Series and you know it is the same U.S. it has always been. Almost 60,000 peaceful citizens crowding into Busch Stadium, twenty-five million TV viewers practically holding their breath. Why? To see if that great big handsome pitcher, Bob Gibson, can break the record for strikeouts in a World Series game. (He did.)

But will the "social history of our time" that men are now gathering on little index cards, and will someday write dull books about, have much to say about how relaxed, inside, a people must be to drop everything in the middle of "a life or death political campaign" to listen to or watch eighteen grown men play a game with a ball?

OCTOBER 6, 1968
CAMBRIDGE, MASSACHUSETTS

Yesterday I drifted through the waters of nostalgia—the 45th reunion of my Harvard Law class—and not a maudlin thought nor sodden, introspective inward look.

Went to a fascinating class in Evidence, finding the third-year men far from the wizards I thought they would be.

Heard a teaching fellow, Ferren, talk about the new interests of law students in being a part of the action: not just old-fashioned Legal Aid, but becoming part of activist *causes.* Then to a luncheon meeting; the new dean, Bok, young and handsome, telling about the future of the School, in the present day world. Bok is a modern man, none of the Frankfurter Anglophilian adoration of the upper class English.

Almost 60% of the students at the School now say they *do not intend to practice law.* There is a wave of idealism, and a skepticism about the virtue of becoming a corporate lawyer or simply making money. This is the way I was, as a student in the School, of course. But how many members of my 1923 class shared that view? Now, praise be, I would not be alone were I a student in 1968.

The evening dinner meeting was given over largely to speeches; one of them by Ken Keating, now a judge of the Court of Appeals of New York, and Robert Williamson, the sober tall *very* Down-East Chief Justice of the Supreme Judicial Court of Maine.

I am sure, as Jack Spalding, now a justice of the Massachusetts Supreme Judicial Court, who presided, said, that Keating has made a good judge, though he never had served as a trial judge. "The important issues that come to the appellate courts these days are only occasionally common-law cases; mostly they are in the field of public law and public policy. So a man with broad legislative experience, such as Ken has had as a Senator, is particularly qualified as a judge. The courts more and more are deciding issues between different departments of the state government where a man without legislative or executive public office experience hasn't much to offer by way of judgment."

An interesting point, I thought.

Keating regaled us with his "research." He had collected news stories of what was going on in the U.S. and the world in the spring of *1923*. His point—and the news stories he cited of 1923 confirmed it—was that many of the events of those days forty-five years ago were of a piece with much of what is going on today. Though in retrospect those days seem quiet to today's younger people, they were not actually too dissimilar from 1968. We worked through those "crises"; we have yet to do that with our contemporary ones.

As part of the reunion, members of the Harvard Law School 1923 class were asked to say how the world looks to them forty-five years after.

A noted Philadelphia lawyer, one of the few black members of the class, Raymond Pace Alexander, pointed out the complete lack of dialogue between Negro and white students in the 20's, remarking that "this failure to know the Negro student, his feeling of deprivation, the depth of the trauma to him in being an outcast, ignored, a student by 'sufferance' only, a second-class citizen, has contributed vastly to the greatest problem that America faces today—that of racism. Your children and grandchildren today condemn such attitudes and they are the hope of America for the future."

At the reunion I was repeatedly referred to as the leading member of that class. That was ironic. I was, as a student, the one "least likely" to receive that accolade: my diffidence, my lack of self-confidence as a student (well justified it was, too!) until my third year, the glamour of my brilliant or aggressive or much better prepared fellow-classmates, my radical views compared to most of the fellow-classmen who were preparing, hard, to become members of the Establishment, and did!

Jack Spalding in introducing me at the dinner said: "He has always been about thirty years ahead in his ideas, and the rest of the country has had to catch up with him, as it has. Though some of his ideas seemed to us advanced and even radical, they became accepted."

In the cold grey dawn of today to record these things seems grossly immodest. But there is a point to them beyond the satisfaction I get from hearing such pleasant, friendly statements from men who were forty-five years ago, and still are, arch-conservatives, among the pillars of our society.

The lesson is: don't underestimate *any* young person who is full of feeling and conviction, no matter how way-out his ideas may be; don't underestimate the quiet fellow in the back row who never "volunteered" an answer—which is the way Felix Frankfurter years later remembered me, as a student.

The *New York Times* today strongly endorses Humphrey for President in a long editorial.

On the same page a sad and almost memorial column about President Johnson by Scotty Reston.

L.B.J. had been so pressed on all sides on the one issue—"stopping the bombing." I am sure that Ellsworth Bunker strongly supported my efforts to get economic ideas emphasized because of his lack of confidence in the straight-line military thesis.

Spent an hour with Ambassador Bill Leonhart last Friday afternoon. "The negotiations in Paris are completely stalled," said Leonhart, "completely. Until Hanoi is willing to recognize Saigon, nothing in the way of economic development affecting both countries is possible."

OCTOBER 13, 1968
PRINCETON

A party of D&R staff and their wives here yesterday afternoon confirmed my conviction that this is one of the most alive groups of men I have ever worked with, and that covers some darn good men.

Seeing them in the relaxed atmosphere of our garden and living room made them seem more like *separate individuals* than when they poke their heads into the door of my office to take something up with me.

I have never run so informal an organization as this one, almost casual are the relations, the laughter in the halls. I think I contribute something to this tone. Particularly is it an achievement, this casualness and lack of jurisdictional friction, when the organization has grown to its present size.

As I looked out on this group, chatting away merrily, and thought of the considerable number of distinctive individuals now part of D&R, I was struck by how I have adjusted to the pressure of responsibility I feel toward them and their careers, their living plans, their home locations, the whole tangle of individual problems that "founding" this company has produced.

Planted several hundred spring bulbs these past two days: Darwin tulips, the early April kind, crocuses, winter aconite, snowdrops, and so on.

How many years I have done this; how many very early springs I have peeked hopefully to see if the first green sabers are venturing through the cold, almost half frozen soil. The happy anticipation of the leaves, the bud, then the tall queenly stalk; or some of the earliest little fellows, sometimes finding them in the snow.

OCTOBER 15, 1968
NEW YORK

To walk down Madison Avenue at this hour—goin'-home time—is to swim against a solid people-torrent of such a variety as I daresay doesn't exist in any other place on earth.

Throngs packed together, as in many other cities. But the faces in this unbelievable city are *all different.* Odd faces of quite old people; the handsome new class of elegant black young men; the diminutive chunky men and oblong women with an Eastern Europe background; the putty-faced prematurely resigned and slumped men; the spruce, brisk "executive" type with that squash-court spring in their walk. And of course the girls, mostly flashing thighs, so pleased with themselves and the looks they get. How sprightly they are with their saucy looks, and the wild colors they wear.

A little chat with Paul Hoffman.* He always makes one feel that he is truly interested in the man he is talking to. How rare that is, and so genuine. When I mentioned the Mekong UN task, and that we were being asked to assist the UN Bangkok staff, he said, soberly, as if it were near the top of his mind: "The staff performance there is in serious trouble."

OCTOBER 19, 1968
PRINCETON

Helen immured herself in my study all last week, and is down there now, working on the index. To provide a set of guides through the jungle of such a journal as Volume IV is a chore that is extraordinary. For the journal text touches on so *many* subjects, is in *no order* whatever, of course, but just as the events or reflections happen.

OCTOBER 21, 1968
NEW YORK

The substance of the meeting of the Bedford-Stuyvesant Corporation was very encouraging. Genuine specific progress is rolling up. Not just rhetoric but a block rehabilitated, a site selected for a big central market. A good staff.

The board and the head of the black organization, Frank Thomas, and the others, with Doar's leadership, have done a good workmanlike job. But the millions from the Federal Government and the grants from

*Administrator of the UN Development Programme, 1966–72.

rich people and organizations make this possible in this one place. Could it be even remotely duplicated? I doubt it.

NOVEMBER 6, 1968
NEW YORK

The "new leadership" that was going to unite this country actually divided the millions of voters as nearly in half as it is mathematically possible to do.

The Presidency is now in hands that bring dismay to many of us, and the country is more divided than ever on the race issue.

Humphrey showed the *stoutness* of heart that few men possess. I honor such a man. He had what it takes to make a great leader.

NOVEMBER 8, 1968
NEW YORK

A bit of conversation with an impressively tall younger man, Dean Acheson's son, David.

I said: "Your father used to say—to my dismay—that he would never write a memoir, or an account of his career in State. I hope he has gotten over that nonsense."

"He certainly has; the book is finished and will be ready in a few months. This is how I got him over that business of not writing about his public life and his memoirs. I said: 'If you don't write it, someone else will. Do you want to wait until Adolf Berle does?'

"That *did* it," said David, with a grin.

It's a wise son who knows his father.

NOVEMBER 14, 1968
NEW YORK

Gerry Levin reports from Tehran that he is making headway toward a better financial basis with Iran to replace that system of advance payments I devised when we began out there, and that stood us in such good stead for all those years. In fact, that advance idea protected us with the working capital which made the first ten or eleven years of this operation financially successful and stable.

NOVEMBER 19, 1968
NAIROBI, KENYA

The President of Kenya, Mzee Jomo Kenyatta, opened the three-day talkfest this morning.† Down the central aisle in the National Theatre he picked his way, waving a long straw-colored fly whisk, carrying a big gold-headed cane, saluting the applause of the audience. A grizzled man, with the enormous broad shoulders of a farmer (which he is).

He read something prepared for him that was in the best tradition of nothingness appropriate to a welcoming talk, read it very slowly, almost haltingly and completely without expression. (I suspected that he couldn't see the script clearly. He didn't wear glasses, not to spoil the image of the old rebel.)

I was told that when he speaks to his people in Swahili, his voice is more of a roar, that he berates them, scolds and inspires. But this morning was the performance of a ceremonial officer, which is the function he performed.

Kenyatta is one of the new independent Africa's authentic heroes, the first to organize a fight against the British, and particularly to use terrorist methods (Mau Mau) against the planters. Giving up the uplands of Kenya, where the British landowners lived the lives of Long Island tycoons, was the loss of a prize of great value.

The day's discussions were spirited, and far more candid than I would have expected. Mostly this was candor against Americans, in which two leading American Negroes joined in criticism of American racism.

I found it a bit difficult to control my expression when the presiding officer, the Prime Minister of Somaliland (a Moslem) referred to America's Founding Fathers and their eloquent declarations for freedom and justice, but did not mention that many of those Founders were owners of black slaves. And when the Algerian delegate, the most radical of all, spoke feelingly of how all Africans (including Algerians, of course) loved each other as brothers *and always had.*

That it was Africans, white and black, who sold their beloved black brothers into slavery was not recalled. Naturally. Nor would it have advanced the cause of "understanding" very much to have reminded them.

NOVEMBER 21, 1968
NAIROBI

Three solid days of Dialogue.

The directing committee of this conference asked me to "sum up" the conference in our final session. I quote from some of the points I made in this summing up:

†A conference, or "dialogue," sponsored by the African-American Institute, with some forty participants, half from African countries, half from the U.S.

"Our stance here," I said, "has been toward the future in our discussions. Toward the next three decades, the years between 1968 and the year 2000.

"What I see in Africa makes me feel I have been here before. I have seen this accumulation of problems, inertia, skepticism, and have seen that this mountain of difficulties can be moved, and has been moved.

"I recall the dismay I felt when fourteen years ago we first went to Iran to help develop the bleak Khuzistan area. While there were some very talented Iranians, their numbers were few. I found this discouraging and said so to a great Frenchman, Jean Monnet, on my return from the first trip to Iran. He said something I have never forgotten.

" 'David, it does not take many talented and tough people, particularly young people, to make such a change as is being envisaged for Iran. Indeed, it makes the problem of overcoming inertia easier rather than more difficult. When the matrix of progress has been fashioned by the few, the followers need to be numerous, but they come, in number. But to have to deal with large numbers at the time patterns and leadership are being fashioned would make the job almost beyond managing. So don't grieve over the limited number.' "

At this point I turned to the chair that had been occupied by a quite beautiful young Congolese woman, Madame Lihau-Kanza. She is the first woman university graduate in all of the Congo. In the discussions, she was forceful, candid, full of fire to the point of belligerence, and with not a trace of speaking only from the "woman's point of view."

I said that had the younger Belgians, some of whom I knew quite well, been able to encourage and identify even a dozen men and women of that caliber and the independence and the eloquence and the education of Madame Lihau-Kanza, the whole story of that country could be quite different.‡

"The future belongs to those people in the world with the greatest upward swing of vitality and endurance, and adaptability to their environment. The future depends upon the spunk of the young people.

"As to Africa, with few exceptions, the African peoples in terms of vitality and endurance and ability to live with their environment seem to me clearly on the way up. It is hard to see this for many of us because our view is blurred by the fact that they have so far to go by our own standards. It is blurred by the constant repetition in our ears of the term 'tribal' as if the tribe was a peculiar African institution synonymous with primitive, brutal, retrogressive. I dissent from this view. Africa is a continent of increasing vitality, now freshly released to find its way not into a Western type of civilization but into a kind of life new to Africa, new to the world.

‡See the *Journals*, Vol. V, *The Harvest Years*, pages 80–83.

"In my personal view development is not 'to be planned,' nor priorities set nor methods prescribed by those outsiders who provide the assistance.

"I stress the need, by Africans and Americans and the World Bank and other UN aiders, to recognize and encourage the great indigenous talents and energy in these underdeveloped countries. I urge that we depend more on human spontaneity, on incentives, and less on 'principles and planning' or the models of economists and their abstractions.

"A further and a crucial issue here was population control. I found it ominous that to a man the Africans who expressed themselves here either disagreed that there was a need for population control or believed that increases in population were essential, whereas those on the American side rather assumed the desirability of family planning, population control, a major world issue, would be accepted. Beneath this complete gap of agreement I strongly sensed a feeling among the Africans that white people were pressing for population control because of their fear of what a preponderance of black and other colored people would do to the whites in the world. This to me is an alarming symptom.

"Understanding what America is like was as limited and imperfect as my understanding of what Africa is like, though I too have been exposed at firsthand to Africa."

I made reference to "the need for a new theme, a new thesis for assistance and a new mechanism for assistance from the developed to the developing countries."

As I concluded my remarks, critical of planning and of economists as being abstract and detached, Dr. Edward Hamilton asked to be heard in disagreement. Since he is director of the staff of the World Bank–Pearson study group on the future of economic development, his comments took on special importance. He began by saying, "I recognize that one cannot successfully argue with poetry." He felt that in opposing the current concepts of planning and the relevance of statistical methods I was calling for a new look at aid before having all the facts.

I acknowledged that the task of development was in fact an act of faith, an expression of basic values. This being true, it is not an unfair characterization of what I was saying that Ed Hamilton should describe it as poetry. But one does not apologize for faith nor its expression if it appears to be "poetry."

The most important fact of the world today, I said, is this emotional change in values and in people's assessment of themselves and their potentials. Therefore to rely too much upon statistics, figures, numbers, which are a residue of the past, rather than a prediction of future probabilities, seems to me as inappropriate as to use mechanical devices of another age and time.

On this, of course, we heard much from the two "militant" black Americans, Bayard Rustin of CORE, and Dr. Charles Hamilton of Roosevelt University (co-author, with Stokely Carmichael, of *Black Power*). Hamilton said: "If I understand Mr. Lilienthal, he was talking about what we call in the black militant movement the involvement of people in their own destiny, among the black population of America. If that is what he says comes to, and I think it does as to the underdeveloped countries, then I want to be recorded very much in agreement with him."

Some of the African representatives, including those from the Mediterranean countries of Algeria, Morocco, and Tunisia, added their bit. The non-Negro Americans said very little; the criticism of American race relations was on a well-worn script, and actually no more violent than the facts called for.

Then Minister Diawara of the Republic of the Ivory Coast asked to be heard.

"The racial issue," he said, "is *not* basic. Racial problems exist everywhere.

"America is 90% white. Africa is 90% black. So talking about the racial question as you have been, you are just going round and round.

"But the relations between the U.S. and Africa go well beyond racial problems.

"You ask here: How can we interest the American public more in Africa? Well, the lack of interest in Africa is common throughout the world.

"So, we have achieved independence. That is a very great deal. What more can we do? If interest in Africa by outside powers is diminishing, perhaps that is a good thing, if you think about the former colonialism."

NOVEMBER 23, 1968
LAKE MANYARA, TANZANIA

Out there beyond the darkness and the utter quiet—a night you can almost touch—is a vast expanse of forest and marsh and plain through which elephants snort and blow, the arrowlike impala tuck under them their slender graceful little legs, rhinos bed down and all manner of nocturnal wild beasts are on the prowl.

Helen and I flew from Nairobi to this beautiful lodge perched on the very edge of a cliff overlooking the great Rift and Lake Manyara. Rimmed by mountains smoky in blue haze. A great afternoon we have had. The high points: a huge lumbering bull elephant who didn't care for our nearness to his harem, and lowered his head, flapped his great ear-wings, and started for our Land-Rover; a pair of tiny fuzzy leopard cubs followed attentively by their unbelievably beautiful mother, who shep-

herded them across the path and up an incline, looking at us contemptu-
ously—and the flight, no less, of countless incredibly graceful impala.

NOVEMBER 25, 1968
KEEKOROK LODGE, KENYA

Memorable days on the Serengeti plains, yesterday and today. To see
this world possessed still by the animals and birds, a world that is still
new and young, as it was in the beginning. How moving this can be:
animals who are neither afraid nor seemingly aware of humans who
looked at them close by.

It made *all* the difference that we were accompanied by Mr. and Mrs.
John Owen on this journey into the world of lions, leopards, elephants,
giraffe, wildebeeste, gazelle, warthogs, hyenas, cheetahs, rhinos, and
birds of a hundred kinds. For the fact that there is this huge area of
Serengeti hardly touched by any outside force is due largely to the absorbing diligence of this big earnest committed Englishman.

Owen's job is a distinguished one in Africa: director of the Tanzanian
National Parks, by appointment of the African government headed by
President Nyerere. He speaks with great deliberation, and with the assurance of a man who has but one great purpose in life, to preserve the
ecology of this park region (the size of Belgium) and to somehow find the
money to support this work.

The high point came yesterday afternoon. Driving with the Owens,
their daughter Jill, and a remarkable black warden, we sighted a sleepy
old lion near the track, and perhaps a dozen rods beyond him, along a
little stream, a pride: four lionesses with their cubs, a dozen of them. The
family scene, the male utterly indifferent and aloof, the females being
chewed by their cubs, pawing and licking each other. No notice of us, less
than fifty feet away.

The variety of sights almost too many to describe: a rhino, standing
as still and inert as a prehistoric fossil, and prehistoric is the way she
looked, being suckled by her calf, a funny-looking creature, without
horns, burrowing its way into the source of food, looking like Piglet in the
Milne stories. We might just as well have been a rock for all the attention
the mother rhino paid us.

NOVEMBER 27, 1968
NAIROBI

The dialogue with African and American leaders was one purpose of
this expedition, and a most unusual occasion it was. But it was the visit
to the big-game parks that made our trip a unique experience.

On our visit to the Serengeti plains we were with the two most knowledgeable men in East Africa, so far as big game are concerned—i.e., wild
and free animals: Myles Turner and his chief, John Owen.

Turner, born in Africa, for ten years or more was the outstanding
professional white hunter, particularly of lion. "I would go out with rich
men, usually American and usually very rich, who wanted the ultimate
in a hunting experience: shooting lion, rhino, elephant, leopard, buffalo.
But I got disgusted with slaughtering these beasts and became a conservationist." Now he is Owen's chief deputy.

"It's hard to believe how competitive these men were. They would
come out here, at great expense, two or three in a party. And they would
get into the most awful arguments about who killed the biggest buffalo.
Sometimes they became bitter enemies, refusing to go back together in
the same plane or ship."

I said in the summer we lived on Martha's Vineyard Island, in New
England. Turner's face lighted up: "Martha's Vineyard, New Bedford,
Nantucket—that's the place where most of the *original* big-game hunters came from. The sperm whale is the biggest, fiercest animal in the
world, and those who hunted him in those little whaleboats, they really
took their lives in their hands."

To hear a man who was famous all through Africa for his courage
and skill hunting lions and leopards and charging elephants talk this
way about those hapless young New England farm boys—in terms of big
game hunters—I found fascinating. Turner has a big collection of books
in his little house nearby about every side of the pursuit of the sperm
whale.

NOVEMBER 28, 1968
10:30 P.M.
NAIROBI AIRPORT

The entire waiting hall of the airport was completely jammed with
Indians, as we were unloaded from our bus.

Of every kind and description: an elderly Sikh with a dazzlingly
white full beard, smiling benignly on a very young English girl who was
talking with him. A dignified old lady, a silver disc in her nose, carrying
two huge packages and an umbrella. Lovely young girls, their faces eager
and smiling as often they are not among Indian maidens. Some of the
women wore garments heavily encrusted with gold and silver. All in all,
an affluent crowd.

All of which reminded me again of how pervasive is the Indian
mercantile presence in Kenya. It seems that almost every store is run by

these dark bright-looking people. And on the campus of the University College many earnest Indian faces.

I saw no evidence that the English were hated by the black Kenyans, as so often whites in America are despised as "whities" these latter days. Whether there will be a reaction against the Indians, all of whom seem comfortable and many obviously well-heeled, it's hard for me to tell, but I suspect it will happen.

NOVEMBER 29, 1968
LONDON

Sad news from home. The only child of my first cousin Aline Szold Sholes, Terry van Mourick, and her husband Larry, killed in a casual commuter air trip, they who had taken every conceivable risky adventure, across Asian deserts in their Land-Rover, and flying the Andes in their own small plane. The kind of young people whose luck meant that everything they touched turned out famously. Random is the word for good fortune, random the word for the spear that strikes down the "lucky."

DECEMBER 7, 1968
PRINCETON

At the White House dinner for the Prime Minister of Iran last Thursday, I was seated, again, at the President's table. The President was affability itself. There really isn't anything else ahead for him to strive for, and his demeanor showed it.

Helen was seated at one of the little tables between Chief Justice Warren and Mrs. Rusk. Helen said to the Chief Justice: "This will be our last White House dinner—for at least four years." In his solemn courtly way he said, with a grin: "The last for me, too." Mrs. Rusk smiled in her quiet way, as if to say: "For us, too." (And what a relief that part must be for her.)

After the dinner and the usual exchange of toasts, and a ballet in the East Room, we stood around visiting. Dean Rusk greeted me—as he did many others—unperturbably as if he had not been the subject of as ugly and sadistic attacks as I can remember—except, of course, for the press bushwhacking of the President.

The Vice President was on hand, and as bouncy and gay as a man could be. To me he said: "Well, we gave them something to think about, didn't we?" Beamed and greeted one and all with the natural warmth that will not be found in the White House after January 20, I fear.

DECEMBER 18, 1968
NEW YORK

More and more public recognition is being given to D&R as the prototype of something that lies ahead on the American scene. (As a mark of how at last D&R is being understood—or described—in terms of its uniqueness, there is an article based on an interview with me in the current *Columbia Journal of World Business.* And a footnote added this year to the 1961 *New Yorker* profile of me written by John Brooks some years ago, now published in a book called *Business Adventures.*)

DECEMBER 23, 1968
SPICE ISLAND INN
GRAND ANSE BEACH
MORNE ROUGE
GRENADA, BRITISH WEST INDIES

(That is about the most elaborate heading I've ever committed to these journals; but it fascinates me that so isolated and simple a spot should have such an imposing address.)

Such a setting, a caricature of do-nothingness, does, however, encourage a tendency never very far removed from the surface with me, of self-examination of the most intimate kind. Happily, I think, my intense and outward-directed work does not often permit this. It is a kind of luxury, an extravagance, this business of looking inside oneself excessively.

DECEMBER 25, 1968
GRENADA

No amount of sweating and groaning by the non-pro writer—which I am—can take the place of that daily intense living with words and the expression of thoughts and emotions in phrases and sentences, of a professional writer.

David's writing illustrates the point. A recent review of his short stories speaks of the economy of his writing, never an extra word and yet the words he uses create the mood he seeks.

None of this characterizes my own journal writing, nor my letters. When I record ideas or describe events, I rarely show any sign of compactness. The style is more nearly that of conversation, my kind of conversation, when I am ruminating or groping for words to describe or surround an idea.

Exploration by words, speaking to myself, as I do, is a chief function of my journal, and is part of my working style. That I can't fit it also into a more readable and muscular writing style is unfortunate perhaps, for a reader, but not, necessarily, for me, for whom the words are written.

DECEMBER 27, 1968
GRENADA

Negotiation—with which I have been much concerned most of my life—is a little-understood art. Because it is an art that deals with the subtleties of the relations between human beings, few people ever comprehend it, or master it. It is as far removed from "splitting the difference," or taking advantage of another's weakness, or the bluffing of poker, as can be imagined—but that is the way "negotiation" is too commonly conceived.

DECEMBER 30, 1968
GRENADA

What manner of year was 1968?
For me a happy year. It certainly wasn't a happy year for the world. But a time of movement, of change, of vitality. This I say despite the continuing tragedy in Vietnam. That nightmare of bloodshed, frustration, bitterness is not something remote from my personal and professional life during 1968. Most of my energies and personal emotional expenditures concerned our role in trying to move that horror into more hopeful waters.

DECEMBER 31, 1968
GRENADA

Midnight, and ships' whistles blowing, fireworks lighting up the harbor of St. George across the bay.
Overwhelmed with a vague enveloping sadness, as slate-grey as the moonlight on the sand and surf. Why?
I have enough good sense to know that such tragic moods are transient, that acute, agonizing frustrations are part of a full life, that the fantasies of the imagination are part of the unreal world within you, that to realize that there are things that are beyond one's grasp does not mean one doesn't reach, and in the reaching feel both rapture and pain.
Is it a more vivid realization, at the end of a year and the beginning of another, that there isn't much more time to reach out for more of the profound and fulfilling experiences of life? Does this sadness that almost overwhelms me arise from a realization, from so experienced a man as

I am, that one does not get all that one wants—much less feels he deserves —of life; that "adjustment" and "compromise" are not just words one sings out to the impatient young, but are part of the rules of life that you yourself must bow to? Even you, who have had—and are now having— so much more than most of your fellows?

II

1969

~~◁◊▷~~

Trip to South Vietnam and presentation of Joint Group
Report on economic development to President Thieu—
Meeting with President Nixon and presentation of Joint
Group Report—Visit to Iran and Ivory Coast

JANUARY 20, 1969
NEW YORK

So now it is "President" Nixon.

I heard some of the inauguration ceremonies this noon, including the
rich baritone revivalist speech of Billy Graham, the Protestant vicar of
God.

President Nixon's inaugural address was much in the words of Graham. This is still pretty much a small-town country. So invoking God's
name and his authority in every other sentence still goes well.

I'm way over my head in Vietnam as our Development Report approaches completion. Never has there been drawn in so short a time so
broad a picture of a country that is in such agony and disruption.

Instead of a postwar development report in Vietnamese, then translated into English, there will be two reports, one in Vietnamese, the
other in English. *But*—and this is quite remarkable—the reports will
reach the same conclusions but without identical language. Our reports
will not be simply an attempt at a literal translation of the Vietnamese
—or the other way around.

This seems to me a mark of advance when an American group is
working with a foreign group on the development of their country.

JANUARY 26, 1969
PRINCETON

It is only rarely that Helen expresses herself about my work. I know why: home is a refuge from the strains and the excitements of that work. Helen notices my concern about D&R, of course, without speaking of it.

This morning, reading my inner mind I suppose, that I might well be considering finding a terminal point in this kind of work, she said: "Dave, I don't think you would be happy just being a consultant, or working only part time. You need to be in the middle of things; it would probably be harder on your health than the way you're living and working now."

JANUARY 31, 1969
NEW YORK

Bob Murphy* is a craggy, loose-limbed man, with a great smile. But don't be misled: when he is aroused or disturbed—as he was several times in our conversation at lunch this noon—those blue "smiling Irish eyes" can be the blue of ice.

I said I was through the first 300 days of Harrison Salisbury's new book, *The 900 Days—The Siege of Leningrad.* "Hitler could have taken Leningrad almost any time he wanted to, in an early stage of the war," said Bob. "But he couldn't make the final decision. Shows how one-man control can be fatal."

When Murphy spoke of Ellsworth Bunker the admiration showed strongly in his lined face. "What a man, and at seventy-four, and taking on a new wife at the same time. He may look starchy, you know; no expression in his face. But he has got what it takes. Patience. And more patience."

Murphy leaned over the table, his eyes like points of laser light. "No victory! What kind of a war where you don't want victory?" He was disgusted. He was referring to the war in Vietnam, of course.

He certainly has no soft illusions about the North Vietnamese leadership. "The worst terrorist crew in recent history," he said. "Forty-two thousand slaughtered, men, women and children."

FEBRUARY 5, 1969
NEW YORK

Just back from a 5-to-9:15 session at the Council on Foreign Relations, on our Vietnam postwar reconstruction program.

*Diplomat, former Under Secretary of State.

It was an intent, responsive audience (one of the most difficult, admittedly, in New York) and the questions and the discussion around the big dinner table very helpful. They took our program in utter seriousness, and responded to my enthusiasm, warmth, and humor.

"We're not accustomed to such down-to-earth practical talks," said Henry Wriston, the patriarch of the Council, as we left. So my ebullience and sometimes graphic and simple illustrations and occasional tough language helped rather than stood between me and this sophisticated group.

I confess I was reassured. That I can hold and move an audience of sophisticates and "experts" too, and do this for hours on end, and come out of it as fresh and untired as I am tonight answers some of those vagrant self-whispers about "age," or flagging energy. It just isn't so, and I should remember it the next time this myth creeps up on me, as of course it will from time to time.

Among the guests at the Council was Harrison Salisbury, the only man in the group who had been in *North* Vietnam. Before the meeting I told him that his book, *900 Days,* had kept me awake nights, it was so absorbing. He replied, in that quiet, almost abstracted way he has: "Well, you paid me back for whatever sleep you lost. I was up half the night last night with the fourth volume of your *Journals.* The story of the jailing of Ebtehaj—and the rest. Iran is a Hairbreadth Harry story; you wonder how it is all coming out." I wonder too.

FEBRUARY 6, 1969
NEW YORK

Lunch yesterday with John Rockefeller 3d.

John's gentle and considerate manner is one of several rare personal gifts he has. He has the ultimate secret: to be interested in *other* people, plus an utter simplicity of manner.

I talked to him about the need for population control in Vietnam, inquiring whether the Population Council could assist those in Vietnam who agreed with us on this: that unless the rate of population growth is slowed down, the economic advances we can see ahead for them will be wiped out.

How he got on the question of age I forget; perhaps it was our common concern about John Gunther's ill health.

In his earnest way John expressed his conviction that one should go straight ahead using the energy and strength he has, and not try to conserve his health by limiting his activities simply in order to conserve health.

He spoke of his father, John D., Jr. As he grew older he became concerned about how to conserve his health. So he withdrew from outside activities, saw fewer people. "That isn't the way I see it, for myself," said John. And it is clear that he is actually branching out into more public activities and more public appearances. This latter comes hard for so reserved and modest a man.

FEBRUARY 9, 1969
PRINCETON

A great snowfall is like a child's magic words: abracadabra. The familiar disappears, whish; a whole new world takes its place. As if this were the first day of the world; not a mark of man's imprint anywhere.

A cozy feeling too. Here I am in a house secure against the storm outside, a wood fire laid, books to read, the woman I chose as far back as my college days to spend my life with, and many warm and loving friends.

FEBRUARY 12, 1969
PRINCETON

The appointment of John Hannah as head of AID is one of those great breaks that you hope might happen, but know would be too good to be real. On the overall concept I so deeply believe in, his appointment gives a chance to return to first principles.

The thesis I outlined in the [1964] lecture at Columbia (later published as *The Road to Change*) has found its way into legislation, if not into managerial reality, as yet. John Hannah's heading AID brings that reality closer.

The legislative statement of my thesis, and the one I repeated at Nairobi, and which Congressman F. Bradford Morse referred to as "the Lilienthal concept," is expressed in Title IX, an addition to the Foreign Assistance Act of 1966.†

FEBRUARY 20, 1969
WASHINGTON

I walked down the long, long corridor on the seventh floor of the State Department. Dean Rusk, for the first time in seven or eight years, is no longer sitting in that office, nor Katzenbach. But what else has changed? Little.

†The provision was sponsored by Morse, later UN Under Secretary General for Political and General Assembly Affairs.

Alexis Johnson, now Under Secretary of State for Political Affairs, came out to pick me up, in the waiting room, stooped, very Scandinavian in appearance.

I said I wanted the new Nixon Administration to know that, although a private citizen, I had plans to present formally a thousand-page post-war development report and program to the Head of State of another country. I hoped this wouldn't present a serious protocol issue.

The report, with its tone of optimism about Vietnam's economic future, could have considerable "psychological impact" in Vietnam and here, of the right kinds, said Secretary Johnson. So it was important to present it publicly so it would get the maximum public attention.

I said that our study indicated that after the war Vietnam could make a much quicker recovery than people supposed, quicker than Korea, for example. "That confirms my hunch," said Johnson. "Your estimate of the people is about like mine; they have a lot of recuperative power—bounce, you might say."

FEBRUARY 22, 1969
PRINCETON

Last evening a letter came in asking me to write my recollections of the wreck of the Hagenbeck Wallace Circus train in the summer of 1918. Scores of circus people were burned to death when a freight train crashed into their sleeping cars, outside Gary, Indiana. I was a cub reporter (age eighteen) on the *Gary Tribune* and was the first newspaper "man" to cover the disaster.

Janette and John Wheeler in for a late afternoon visit. A handsome woman, with dark, candid eyes, and a straightforward demeanor to go with those honest eyes. With obvious affection, she calls this genius "Johnny." He looks like a man who might indeed be called Johnny: gentle of voice, informal, and almost self-deprecating of manner. Yet within that head one of the most soaring, imaginative mentalities of our time. The whole world of scientists listens to this mild-mannered, modest man, when he speaks of the most basic of concepts, relativity and "gravitational physics."

Wheeler spoke most interestingly of their visit last summer to Russia, to Tiflis, for an international scientific conference. A scientist colleague, Andrei Sakharov, published an essay last summer calling for greater intellectual freedom; Wheeler thought this particularly significant.

"As a scientist, I need to keep in touch with their work in relativity, for they are doing good work. Most of the papers were very good. But some were duds, given by men who had some political connection, or they would never have been on the program.

"The Russian scientists in this meeting were greatly interested in our national election. This was before the election, you understand. 'You must elect a strong President,' they said, earnestly. 'You must have a strong President to offset the weakness in the Soviet leadership.'" And they favored Nixon. I can understand that. Nixon did give the impression during the campaign of being a strong man—in Russian eyes and by their standards—compared to Humphrey, whose demeanor and divided following must not have given an impression of a "strong" man.

FEBRUARY 23, 1969
PRINCETON

Last evening Helen looked up from her reading: "Listen to this. Xerxes commenting on his cautious uncle's advice." Then she read me this from Herodotus, *Histories:*

"There is good sense, Xerxes announced, in everything you have said; nevertheless you ought not . . . think of every accident that might possibly overtake us. If upon the proposal of a plan you are always to weigh equally all possible chances, you would never do anything. I would much rather take a risk and bear my share of the consequences, than be safe from all sort of disaster simply because I was too scared to act at all. . . .

"Certainty, surely, commonly is beyond human grasp. But however this may be . . . profit comes to those who are willing to act, not to the over-cautious and hesitant."

FEBRUARY 25, 1969
NEW YORK

The largest crowd I have ever seen at the Council on Foreign Relations, to hear Averell Harriman give a non-report on the Paris non-Peace talks. He was in fine form, vigorous, handled questions very well, by which I mean he told us damn little that one couldn't have read in the newspaper reports or columnist speculation. But a forceful articulate talk just the same.

That Harriman is more critical of the Saigon Government than of the North Vietnamese was to be expected, a reflection of Ave's frustration. That he blamed American "pressure" (i.e., stepped-up military activity) as responsible for North Vietnamese military activity was unconvincing but at least was candid.

Jack McCloy was asked to sum up what Harriman had said: "Ave says we shouldn't cut and run, but get the hell out of there as fast as we can."

Harriman has a great deal of friendly confidence in the Russians, based, I suppose, on his many negotiations with them in years gone by. I suppose that is why he gives the Russians so much "credit" for getting Hanoi to agree to a negotiation at all, when neither Peking nor Saigon wanted any such thing. Was this such a help, I wonder? Hasn't the Paris negotiation given the Communists, the world around, a beautiful front showcase for arousing anti-American sentiment? Ave thinks the North Vietnamese did "withdraw" large segments of troops. Withdraw them to where? It's like saying that a man has "withdrawn" from New York when he takes a commuter train to Newark, a half-hour away, where he can return anytime he feels like it.

A big warm smile on Cass Canfield's face. "I've just read a full-page review of your new *Journals* [Vol. IV] to appear in next Sunday's *Times*. A good one; a 'selling' review. And a review is in type for next week in *Newsweek,* and *Time* magazine." Hard to believe that something I wrote so long ago will now see the light of day, and actually be reviewed in a serious way as a "current item."

MARCH 1, 1969
PRINCETON

"The decision-making process": this expression is one of the latest fads. Especially among those who pour facts into a *machine,* a computer, under the illusion that what comes out are decisions.

The presentation of "options" they regard as the decision-making process! But it is *weighing,* in one's head, what action one will take, and does take—*that* is decision-making, not the dangling before the acting man's eyes the many possible options that are "open" to him.

MARCH 2, 1969
PRINCETON

John Brooks' review of the *Journals* in this morning's Sunday *Times* book section is mighty satisfying, I must say. And Harper's ad quite striking in appearance.

An hour and a half with André Meyer.

André was relaxed, friendly, excessively generous toward me, clearly wanting to find some way to be helpful, extravagant in his praise for the "good" we had done. And clear-headed, straightforward, realistic, and *right,* in his appraisal of the D&R future, and what in his opinion it would take to get on a "practical," earning basis.

André believes we have taken on too many different activities, too many to be successfully managed under a single management. We must consider "lopping off" such things as urban development.

I think the whole D&R concept depends upon a wide range of inter-related capabilities. But we may have overdone not only the rapidity with which we have expanded, but the diversity of undertakings.

MARCH 4, 1969
NEW YORK

Just came from a visit, at dinner, with my grandson Mike. Such an extraordinarily handsome young man (except longish hair). So happy to see me.

Yes, he said, he *had* been "heavy on marijuana, LSD, and so on" when he was in Europe, in fact began it on the Vineyard. Nine out of ten of the people in the East Village, where he lives, near the Bowery, are "druggies." But not he, since he had found "Meher Baba, who is God." He is ecstatic, in the most earnest, persuasive way, about the "new life" of Baba. So for an hour he talked about Baba and Indian philosophy.

"Grandfather, you *must* come to a meeting, right now, or later. Grandfather [looking at me with such touching earnestness], it will change your whole life."

"But Mike," I said, "I don't *want* my life changed. I'm a happy, fulfilled man."

MARCH 9, 1969
PRINCETON

Dean Rusk, private citizen, at dinner at the Goheens‡ last evening, looked composed, but no more so than when one met him in his office, fending off the wave upon wave of crises that were his lot for *eight* years; earnest about public issues and folksy about lesser things.

He did talk to me, to one side, about Vietnam. "What about interesting the *North* Vietnamese in some kind of economic development assistance? I know they even tried to steal some 'miracle rice.' Why not inject postwar development into the discussions with them?"

I said I had tried this idea out months ago, was told: No, the time isn't right.

"I'll talk to [Secretary of State] Bill Rogers about it, will do it Monday.

‡Robert F. Goheen was president of Princeton University, 1957–72.

You'll find that the farther down the line you are in the Department, the more timid they are.

"The Russians did underwrite the understanding with Hanoi about the conditions under which the bombing of the North was to be suspended. Just no question about that. So they may be willing to do something about this present military activity."

Eddie Greenbaum and I took quite a walk, the day being a smiling one, the sky sharp and blue against the snowbanks.

He had finished reading Volume IV of the *Journals*. "You said a good word for some real drips," he said, chuckling. "Your trouble is, I guess, that you like about everyone."

"Not everyone. I said some critical things about one of your friends, Lewis Strauss."

Eddie then told me how it happened that Lewis had resigned as President of the Institute of Advanced Study, a post he has held all through the time when the AEC, under Lewis' chairmanship, was persecuting Robert Oppenheimer, then Director of the Institute.

How he came to resign? When the Chairman of the Institute Trustees died recently Lewis asked to see Eddie, a trustee. Wanted Eddie to propose him as Chairman, while he continued to hold the office of President. Eddie said he thought there was something strange about a man wanting to be both Chairman *and* President. Whereupon Lewis became angry, "in fact *very* angry," stormed out of Eddie's office, and resigned as President. Thereby probably losing the Institute a large contribution for the new school of social sciences they have planned.

MARCH 13, 1969
NEW YORK

A weird and personally distasteful experience last evening: to the Beaumont Theatre to see a performance called *In the Matter of J. Robert Oppenheimer.* I say "personally distasteful" because it relived for me that half-nightmare of security phobia throughout my term as Chairman of AEC, and the later ugly persecution of Robert Oppenheimer,§ pursued under cover of official secrecy.

A personally unhappy evening, but a surprisingly good construction of a drama out of facts still fresh in people's minds.

What obtruded into my consciousness wasn't so much agony over what was being done to Robert, or to our standards of decency. Mine was also a personal, subjective reaction: that I had to apply these measures of *false* security, myself, as head of AEC; I who didn't believe in the

§See *Journals,* Vol. III, *The Venturesome Years.*

effectiveness for security of this cloak and dagger crap, nor in judging a man by what some anonymous informant told some thin-minded FBI or AEC agent.

Yesterday was a particularly bright spot: the D&R training program for Peace Corps volunteers is a reality. This is something that John Burnett has built, and it is good.

MARCH 20, 1969
ON THE TRAIN TO PRINCETON FROM WASHINGTON

It was a good, very satisfying meeting with the new Secretary of State. One measure: he took me to the door of that office where I have been so often, under Marshall, Acheson, Rusk, and as he opened his door for me to leave he said: "It is a great thing that you have been willing to undertake this difficult job for us." Which is almost exactly what my "Democratic" friend, Dean Rusk, said at our last meeting in that self-same room.

The seriousness, even the patent eagerness which Rogers attached to the possibilities in our economic development approach to Vietnam impressed me: did he think that here, perhaps, was one new approach that just might ease the criticism, even help change American public opinion, which is his chief concern?

It was taken for granted that we continue to do what we are doing.

MARCH 22, 1969
PRINCETON

Two streams of life and of work converge, join, in turbulence into a single stream. This is the essence of my story in these past few weeks.

The two separate life streams: the first, the preoccupation, the worries, the motivations that dominate a man who is responsible for conducting a private for-profit business; the second stream, the larger scope of thought, the sometimes shaking, sleepless-night concerns of a major public responsibility, the Vietnam reconstruction task.

The powerful eddies and swirling waters, when two streams are forced to join, to converge, by the power of gravity; this occurred most dramatically in the past several weeks, since I concluded that I must take over the actual direct management of D&R because of the mounting financial—i.e., private business—pressures of D&R.

And at this very time of a D&R reorganization the profound public obligations I have assumed stood out in startling relief to my private corporate obligations. My meeting with Secretary Rogers day before yesterday demonstrated how completely I had again assumed, private citizen or no, almost as heavy a public responsibility as at any time in those nineteen years when I was in fact a full-time public servant.

This weekend the President, meeting with Ellsworth Bunker, Rogers, and Kissinger,◖ will be seeking some new route, or even a temporary gambit, that will give the country hope that the Vietnam war's end may be approaching.

There is mounting criticism of the Nixon Administration that the pledge to end the war is not being fulfilled. Some of this criticism is petulant and unworthy of grown men—e.g., Senator McGovern's statements of the past few days. How deeply felt it is through the country it is hard to say.

To keep the two streams—public and private—in balance as they converge was the burden of a perceptive little talk Helen gave me, here in the upstairs living room, while I was having my breakfast before a fire.

"Dave, are you going to put so much importance on the financial and business side, important as it is, that the really distinctive thing about D&R may be endangered? If in your efforts, through your new General Manager Levin, to strengthen the faltering financial picture you call for the resignation of men who built D&R around a public concept, you may produce a financial success, but what will you have accomplished for D&R's main purpose?"

I was glad of this reaction, from one who doesn't have the details and, therefore, can exercise a fresh judgment, and one I respect. (As John Brooks said in his review of Volume IV, she is, indeed, a person who is "uncannily understanding.")

Helen says very little about it, but she is somewhat concerned about the risks to my personal safety in the forthcoming trip to Vietnam. Myself, I don't think much of it. What I haven't told her is what I worked out with Rogers: that I shall visit several parts of the country outside Saigon, chiefly the northern provinces (Hue and Danang, the latter under a good deal of enemy fire these days) as well as the Central Highlands and a couple places in the Delta.

The purpose is to be able to come back, in reporting to President Nixon, with the credentials of an on-the-spot observer. This does somewhat increase the hazard to me, compared to going only to Saigon, and particularly since the enemy offensive is still going quite strong.

The revolt against making major "defense" decisions *in secret* reached a climax yesterday, in the Senate hearings—televised, of course! —on Secretary of Defense Laird's espousal of the anti-ballistic missile deployment issue.

◖Henry A. Kissinger was then Nixon's Assistant for National Security Affairs.

Which makes more relevant today my position of years ago (as televised last Sunday on a *Speaking Freely* interview on NBC) that the question of a crash program for the H-bomb should have been discussed in public, not in secret, as it was.*

Here are excerpts from my remarks, in the course of the Newman interview, on that issue:

> Mr. Lilienthal: . . . At the time I was Chairman of the Atomic Energy Commission, and responsible for weapons, I fought as hard as I could—in secret because it was highly classified at the time— against starting another wave [of new kinds of atomic weapons], the so-called H-bomb. Now we're going through another cycle [the anti-ballistic missile]. This is part of the fallacy of believing that weapons will solve *any*thing.
>
> Economic, human development *will* solve a great many things. That's one of the reasons I find the task in Vietnam . . . a heartening one. I think with the economic development and prosperity of that area, and of North Vietnam, we will find we have brought more peace than all the billions we're spending on weapons.
>
> Mr. Newman: . . . You were talking about the development of the hydrogen bomb; you said you fought against it in secret because it was highly classified at the time but shouldn't have been. Why shouldn't it have been?
>
> Mr. Lilienthal: Because the H-bomb [would speed up that form of world suicide we call the atomic arms race, and that] involves the fate of practically every human being. An issue of that kind certainly should not be decided by four or five people in secret. . . . I think issues of that kind should be debated the way the anti-ballistic missile is [being today]. . . . The H-bomb should have been discussed openly.

Secretary Rogers asked me the other day: "What is the thrust of your report on economic postwar development in Vietnam?"

The main thrust of this Joint Report is that the economic future of Vietnam should be in the hands of the Vietnamese. The virtue of a *joint* study and report is that it better assures that economic development will in fact be "Vietnamized."

MARCH 27, 1969
PRINCETON

I am back in public service, and up to my eyes, or so it would seem, and at the highest and most sensitive levels.

I vaguely realized, all along, I suppose, that public service—of high

*See *Journals,* Vol. II, *The Atomic Energy Years,* December 1949 and January 1950.

visibility—was what the Vietnam work involved. This is underlined now that, as a private citizen, I plan a trip to Saigon to put a big report about the future of another country into the hands of the head of that other country. This is topped off with the decision by the Secretary of State, and the new President, that the report should also be presented by me to President Nixon, in a simple White House performance, for the purpose of getting the American President identified with our work, on even more than an equal basis with the President to whom it is directed, President Thieu.

MARCH 30, 1969
PRINCETON

It is the cynical attitude that so prevails in American life today that bothers me most. And which I must seek to dispel. If I can make it clear that this Vietnam report and our work out there is a serious attempt to do something constructive toward peace, and by no means a "gimmick," then that will be more important than any judgment about the "soundness" of the economic policies, etc., recommended.

It is quite possible—so I hope—that our report, coming at this time, can turn the hearts of the people of Vietnam, North and South, to the future of "that country," and by "that country" I mean the whole of Vietnam. This is the way Professor Thuc thinks of Vietnam—not just North and South, but the whole country.

Is it at all possible to get such a notion accepted even in small part? I'll try damned hard.

There may well be many more of us who believe this than we realize.

APRIL 2, 1969
PRINCETON

I quote from part of a letter to our writer son David:

I know how far down the scale is the kind of life I lead compared to [yours as] an artist. It is the stimulation of ideas and events and balancing of risks that stir me—*from the outside.* But if I had to sit here before this typewriter and in this big house with only myself, I'd dry up and have little to write about and little to say. You [writers and artists] have a touch of a holy fire, you and those others, few they are, who fashion life out of themselves, sculpting out living things and feelings with the most difficult and most wonderful of tools, words.

APRIL 6, 1969
PRINCETON

"Conservation" is a noble cause. But it is always in danger of becoming a mindless cult.

In all the years that I have observed—and indeed, been part of—practical conservation (TVA was certainly such a pioneering effort) I have never known a time when the thinking about it has been more fuzzy and emotional than it is today.

The cultist conservationists organize, petition, emote about *any* "change in the natural environment," anything that "upsets the ecological balance of nature."

Pollution is bad. But it is man who changes the environment—and he, man, is a part of nature's environment, he is part of the balance of nature.

Man's *behavior,* his way of *satisfying his needs,* are just as much a part of the balance of nature as are the acts of jungle predators (the lion, the cheetah).

Man is not a thing apart from nature, nor is his behavior—rational, irrational, predatory, benevolent, cruel at times—something apart from the cycle of nature.

We must take into account man's needs, his efforts to cope with his environment, not as something simply to "protest" about, but as the very heart of the problem of adjusting to and obeying nature, of which man's behavior is just as much a part as are the migratory instincts of the birds.

APRIL 11, 1969
PRINCETON

To some people the tools of their trade, of their life's work, are a canvas, a block of stone, a drafting board for an architect, a roll of paper for a writer. It is through these inanimate things they express themselves.

With me—as an architect said to me yesterday—the tools are the people I work with and through, *and for.*

APRIL 20, 1969
FLYING AN HOUR OUT OF TOKYO,
HEADING FOR SAIGON,
VIA HONG KONG

A three-hour dinner of at least a dozen separate courses last night in Tokyo. Seated on the floor, of course. Four of us, Nick Philip and I, and across the little table, Tsuji, head of the Cultural Department of the great newspaper *Asahi Shimbun* and a quite young lady, an assistant, and a very knowledgeable, serious one too.

This long procession of Japanese food was served us by three matrons, who filed in and out of the sliding panels with dishes only one of which I had ever seen before in Japanese cooking. The most delightful part of this cavalcade of food was the complete lack of hurry, or sense of time.

Tsuji, who I should say is fifty, is not characteristically Japanese in appearance. His English is very British. His sense of drama and his candor, in that little room, was something I didn't see in my earlier meetings with him where others had been present.

"When I was a young man," he said, "and through the beginnings of World War II, my faith was a simple one. Like all other Japanese I worked hard—we all worked very hard. We did this because of a faith, a faith in the Emperor and in our country. When I saw the flag of Japan" —at this he played out the part, looking upward as if the flag were being raised there in that little plain room—"or when the national anthem was played, tears would come from my eyes, down my cheeks. That flag, the Emperor, my country—that was the heart and soul of my faith. Then we were defeated. We were betrayed."

He turned to the young lady at his right.

"You are of another generation. You do not have these same memories. What does it mean to you when you see the flag, when you hear the national anthem? Do tears come to your eyes, does it make your heart beat faster?"

She took this question with calmness. "No, no. I feel that it is a beautiful flag, that the music is beautiful. But that is all. It is a beautiful color as it moves in the breeze. That is all."

Tsuji resumed. "You see? That is what another generation feels, most of them. And it is no longer for me a cause of tears of feeling when I see the flag. And my feeling about the Emperor is the one that most Japanese now feel, I am sure. What is that feeling? Is the Emperor still the center of our faith? We pity him. We pity the Emperor.

"So what is to take the place of that faith in our country? What is it now that makes us work so hard? Japanese work very hard." Then suddenly he talked about Israel. "I visited a kibbutz in Israel. Many young Japanese were working in that kibbutz. I asked them about it. They say the Israelis work very hard because on both sides of them are hostile Arabs who would destroy them. So they have the feeling about Israel that we of my generation had before the war was lost, before we were betrayed, before the Emperor became a cause of pity, not veneration."

APRIL 21, 1969
5 A.M.
SAIGON

I am staying at the beautiful villa some French "exploiter of the Indo-Chinese" built for himself perhaps thirty-five years ago. Now it is the official residence of Donald MacDonald, head of the AID Mission here, and I am his official guest.

What a contrast between those Europeans who "made a good thing" of this quite rich country and the American "proconsuls" who, instead of taking treasure *out,* have brought it in, by the billions of dollars. What a travesty. For the Americans are less respected than the French who lived on this country.

Here there is the same kind of wrangle and clash of personal ambitions among the Vietnamese with whom I must deal in the next week as one finds almost everywhere where change is the order of the day. Added to which, war.

I doubt most seriously that either the Vietnamese *or* AID, here or in Washington, are *able* to make a decision that will stick. So the danger is that a hiatus of indecision will develop. A chasm of time during which nothing will happen, threatening all the good work we have done.

We tackle problems, not groan over them.

If indeed the Vietnam catastrophe is the most important single event of our life, then I shouldn't find the difficulties of helping with it too great or frustrating. What the hell have I lived through troubles for if not to face up to big ones, not slink away from them?

APRIL 22, 1969
SAIGON

Ellsworth Bunker's warmth and openness with me this morning is a personal reflection of the progress he must feel Vietnam has made in recent months—militarily; in the political leadership of Thieu; in the molasses-in-January progress (but progress) in the political settlement discussions.

"What is your inclination, Dave, about continuing with the postwar development work after the end of your present contract?" asked Bunker.

I said that we had one clear option: we could "honorably" withdraw at the end of our contract period December 31, 1969. But if the work is as important as I think it is, and if the Government of Vietnam made it possible for us to do a reasonably good job by organizing itself on the development side, then I would be prepared to continue.

This unique development task, of great magnitude and vast political and human consequences, is not something to be abandoned by me, or by

D&R, for less than the most compelling of practical reasons, reasons that show that the work simply cannot be done.

The Ambassador spoke with refreshing candor about how much more the Vietnamese were contributing to the fighting of the war than a year ago. "We were remiss," he said, using that quaint word. "We were remiss in arming them with obsolete rifles until very recently.

"The problem is finding ways of buying time; time is what is needed."

APRIL 24, 1969
DANANG

This morning I heard of a brand-new tax gimmick. I remarked on the large number of American visitors who had to be accommodated, "briefed," taken around. "Especially Generals," said my AID "guide."

"If an American officer spends five days a year as an observer in another country than the one in which he is stationed, he gets a large tax deduction [exemption] running into a substantial proportion of his annual pay. So the Generals come here in droves, spend their five days, sleep through briefings, and make a good thing of it."

APRIL 27, 1969
SAIGON

Don MacDonald knocked at my door late yesterday afternoon, after he and I had returned from a trip to the Mekong Delta. Said he with a flourish:

"Lilienthal and MacDonald Lost and Abducted. Presumed to Be in Cambodian Prison Camp.

"That," said he, in the low register of his voice, "that is the kind of headline I thought of when you and I were abandoned, you might say, by everyone, out in the middle of the Bassac River."

Abandoned we were, by a complex masterpiece of non-planning of trip logistics that had the makings of an Asian Mack Sennett amphibious comedy. But it "made" the trip, risky as it actually was, I suppose, though we were in what is known as the "most relatively secure" province, to use the jargon of pacification.

What happened? We visited a farming showplace, a big one, in An Giang Province, were "briefed" about the AID farm program in as dull and non-brief a performance as I can remember, then went by dusty bumpy road to two villages, Phu Hoa, and Hue Duc, along the Bassac River and canals.

The "Itinerary for Lilienthal Party" then called for "boat trip to Long Xuyen" (pronounced Sween).

At the airfield we had been met by an armed escort, helmets, side arms, motorcycles, plus a jeepload of police, sirening our way, waving aside peasants in conical hats—to my dismay and irritation. All of this manpower was a recognition that even in a "relatively" secure country-side, armed protection was prudent.

So into a police launch our party went for the "boat trip." A big gleaming 75-h.p. Chrysler outboard to propel this big launch. A half-hour later, the power motor sputtered. The native boatman looked resigned, the American advisor not surprised. "The spark plugs get fouled up several times on such a trip." But, said the boatman, by a gesture, no wrench to open the plugs. So we drifted, in a furious sun, the boat sucked into the oozy mud of the river's edge. Half an hour later we moved again. And a further half an hour later the motor began to buck, and died.

All the while the little waggle-tail canoe-like water taxis, loaded with festive passengers—Saturday was a national holiday—went zooming by, propelled, *not* by 75-h.p. American outboards but by little milk-shake-sized propellors at the end of a long shaft; *they* had no spark plug trouble.

After another hour of drift, we bumped into some shore rocks at Long Xuyen, got out—and no one in sight. The grand police escort, the jeep of soldiers ordered to guard us against the VC or whatnot with their very lives, and the others who had accompanied us—where in the hell were they? We soon attracted a crowd of smiling, grinning, giggling women and jubilant children. But of course, no one understood our English, nor our gestures. Lost.

Our schedule for return to Saigon badly bent, the police finally found us.

But this all added to a sense of reality: the smiling friendly people, the grubby street. We saw the life of these amphibious people pretty much as it looks to them. They live a life that is half of the time in the water, partly to frolic (as with the innumerable brown little kids), to wash madame's long black hair, to get water for the meals, the preparation and eating of which we saw so plainly.

This was hardly a daredevil "adventure." But it was such a relief after the almost endless meetings with Ministers and newspaper interviews and discussions about postwar development.

At Hue Duc the newly *elected* village Councilmen greeted us, with the village Chief, a square-built sobersides of a man of about thirty, in a black jacket, just back from a several weeks school for village administration.

He, and about 1200 other village officials, were graduated April 21 in a ceremony addressed by President Thieu, at Vung Tau. A newspaperman, David Hoffman of the *Washington Post*, told me just this morning that Thieu's extemporaneous speech was one of the greatest things he had ever read from a Vietnamese leader. It wasn't covered by the American press—there were only Vietnamese correspondents there—but I have a translation I have just read; it is a great statement on decentralization.

Seeing that young village leader, a scowling, serious man, gave me a sense of observing the beginnings of democracy at the place it is always most needed—in the *local* communities.

The village Councilmen were dressed in their best: long black tunics, with some decoration but quite severe. Most of them were or seemed old. Partly because they had lost most of their teeth so their faces were concave. Several with Ho Chi Minh type chin whiskers, sparse, yellowed; like a bunch of movie set extras, they seemed.

What of the *future* of D&R in Vietnam? It was an answer to this question that my presence here was intended to crystallize, if not completely settle.

It did neither.

We are agreed with MacDonald about the work for the balance of 1969. I made plain that since AID could not express a formal intention that we carry on work in 1970 and 1971, we must begin, therefore, to phase out, assign no more people for the work, and prepare for an orderly withdrawal before the end of the year.

With the Joint Group at an end, who succeeds to the functions of postwar development? I believe it should be the various and appropriate Ministries: Public Works, Economics, etc.

APRIL 29, 1969
AN HOUR OR SO OUT OF HONG KONG

Ellsworth Bunker is without any doubt one of the most extraordinary men I have ever known. Extraordinary in personality, in endurance, and in a mysterious, inexplicable genius for influencing people and shaping them. And in that process affecting the course of great events. Don Mac-Donald literally worships the man.

The metamorphosis of General Thieu into President Thieu, a political leader and thinker, within less than two years is perhaps Bunker's greatest achievement. It could be that the emergence of Thieu as a distinctive Asian democrat could be one of the most important consequences of this war.

There are so many sides to Bunker—as there are to most men of special talents in public and private affairs. His ability to freeze, to be apparently completely passive and poker-faced, and then suddenly he can throw back his head in a characteristic way and laugh heartily. And a sense of humor that he rarely loses, in a job that is far from amusing, a job that has many frustrations. To say nothing of weariness and boredom—with the constant string of visitors from the States whom he must wine and dine.

I had said to Bunker I wished he hadn't broken up his whole day by attending my medal-awarding followed later by the delivery of our report to the President.

He laughed that little laugh of his, neither a chuckle nor a full-scale laugh: "Oh Dave, we have been friends a long time; I wouldn't have missed this for anything. But I do spend a good deal of time with visitors, you're right about that." Then he gave me the number of visitors, mostly members of Congress, in a single month. "And each one, of course, feels he should be given plenty of time, and wining and dining. It is all to the good; they come out here, mostly, with their minds made up from what they have read, but after seeing the real situation, at firsthand, it changes most of them. So it is more than worthwhile. But it does keep me going, particularly now that I need to keep in close touch with President Nixon and General Abrams and Paris too." But a man less sorry for himself— as I feared he was just a tiny bit last May—I have never seen.

A stalwart public servant.

Bunker made a very wise comment that applies to any negotiation: "You can't negotiate—you shouldn't negotiate—against a time deadline. That *stiffens the backs* of the other side, every time." And why not?

APRIL 30, 1969
FLYING HOME FROM HONOLULU

At 5 o'clock yesterday Bunker and I led a big group into the Presidential hall, in the Palace. I was motioned to a big overstuffed chair to the left of the President's seat, Bunker on the right, and lined up in parallel rows about thirty people; to my left the Vietnamese who had been part of the Joint Group, on the right an American delegation. Directly opposite the President's seat, a remarkable pair of huge matched elephant tusks, set upright in an ebony standard.

When the President arrived, in swarmed a dozen cameramen; as has become standard practice everywhere in the U.S., but with this important difference: here these cameramen didn't act as if events of all kinds, formal, tragic, violent, or private, were performed solely for the purpose of being photographed or filmed by them. They took their pictures, and then were shooed out.

Professor Thuc, assisted by some huskier fellow, placed on a table before President Thieu the report, in Vietnamese, beautifully bound in leather, together with a great stack of the working papers; also a copy in the English version.

Then Professor Thuc made a lengthy and excited speech in Vietnamese. Thieu himself, in a most composed way, summarized in English some (perhaps most) of what had been said between Thuc and himself.

That part was over. Then he turned to me. The lines of care showing more by far than a year ago, and the unusual patch of grey hair at his crown had now turned to a pure white.

He thanked me for "your cooperation. We want that cooperation of Development and Resources to continue, to go right on, for many years, in fact, while these programs are carried out." He particularly stressed the development of the fertile Delta of the Mekong River, and said of that undertaking, "of course" that would go forward. "But also in the Eye Corps and the coastal area of Two Corps."

I thought it was time to say some things that were on my mind.

I stressed that the report was only a beginning, not a specific national plan, but a framework for policies and programs, as we said in the report. But it would be just a lot of dead pages, only words, unless it was turned into reality by action by the Vietnamese people.

I went on: "All through this lengthy report you will find a theme of permitting and encouraging *private* activity by farmers and businessmen, getting rid of unnecessary limitations upon the *spontaneity* of the Vietnamese people. But most of all, the report, throughout, stresses the strengthening of *local* government and local activity, in the villages and hamlets.

"I have just read a translation of your remarkable extemporaneous speech at Vung Tau, where you expressed your views to the village officials, on their graduation from a training course in local government. Particularly I was impressed with the strong statement on decentralization, that these elected village leaders must have authority to carry out their increased responsibilities, as part of your policy of building upon the Vietnamese tradition of village government."

MAY 3, 1969
PRINCETON

From the time I saw the gleam of the dogwood of Princeton at about noon, everything except the garden receded. I did the very kind of heavy digging, lifting, wheelbarrowing, and so on that I definitely know I should *not* do the very first day, after the super-sedentary life one leads in twenty thousand miles of flying, and days of "conferring." But the muscle soreness is pleasurable: reminds me that I am a male who loves to use his whole body and not just his brain.

MAY 10, 1969
PRINCETON

The dinner at the Iranian Embassy was a bore. But I had a good talk with the Secretary of State, in whose honor the dinner was given by Ambassador Hushang Ansary, and his unbelievably handsome young wife.

My initial admiring impression of Rogers was confirmed. A man of unusual warmth and humor. The test of a man in public life is: can you, from the altitude of great position, make fun of yourself, and make it believable that you really are amused at your shortcomings? He did. He was introduced as being "calm." "No, I'm not really calm; I'm *numb*. I had no idea of what I was getting into."

During the period after the dinner, Dean Rusk and I were chatting with a fellow-guest, a big professional football player. Said this big guy, "Yes, you're right, football is tougher than it used to be. You have to think. You have to think while you are being kicked in the head." Dean said to me: "Just like being Secretary of State." How right he was.

Senator George Aiken still beaming. He had just made a speech, considered critical of President Nixon's Vietnam progress toward what they call "peace" (meaning, actually, getting the hell out of Vietnam no matter how or what the consequences). He was very warm and friendly.

"About this postwar development thing you are doing," he said, "the *sooner* it is postwar the better. The Mekong River; we would support that and all the rest once we get rid of the war. Three billion a day: let's spend one billion of it on ourselves, put a billion away, and then we can well afford the rest for rebuilding. And we ought to include North Vietnam in that too."

MAY 13, 1969
NEW YORK

Sunday morning's *Times* carried, as its top story (page one, right-hand column) a long story from Saigon on our postwar report.

The lead was actually one that I had hoped someone would use: that the cost of redevelopment of Vietnam for a decade was about the cost of *one month* of war: a dramatic statement that should have some appeal.

MAY 16, 1969
WASHINGTON

I won't pretend to myself that I wasn't disappointed this morning: very little in the press about the delivery of our report to the President yesterday.

The reasons are plain enough: the "story" had been told, extensively, in the press for weeks; so it is certainly no longer news, nor was anything I said to the reporters afterwards particularly newsworthy.

Until yesterday I had never "laid eyes" on our President. What *physical* impression did he make on one new beholder?

A big head for an only medium-sized body. A hearty handshake, great personal courtesy. A way of sitting low in the chair at his desk, so that I was surprised at how little of him "showed." Very dark and very large eyes, an impression I never get in seeing him on TV. It is the *pupils* that are so large and dark, when he looks at you hard and intently.

The Oval Room, center of power in this shaken-up world, I could hardly recognize. It is so spare, almost as if he had just arrived and most of the furniture was still in the moving van. His big walnut desk is without gadgets, and only a few sheets of paper, at which he glanced (a briefing paper about the report) when he asked questions, with only slight interest.

Back of him were two gaudy-colored paintings of the White House grounds, tulips and azaleas. Two couches, facing each other, beside the fireplace clear across the room from his desk, a fire burning merrily. Even the fire, in that cheerless room, seemed somehow made of plastic.

My impression of that room was that it was almost empty. One reason for this uncharitable view is the contrast with the last time I was there, something over a year ago, when I reported to L.B.J.

President Johnson had filled the room with his overwhelming size, energy, and restlessness. The place was then cluttered with furniture, with telephone devices, even with a teletypewriter clacking away in the corner. When L.B.J. telephoned, he punched buttons and sat with his elbows jammed on his knees, looking fierce and speaking fiercely.

By comparison, a calm man in an almost empty room. But Nixon is by no means an empty man. My heart went out to him, I confess; such burdens as he has.

When I grow a bit bored—or even just a little sorry for myself—I catch myself at once: I am not cut out to be an outside observer, through print and words, sitting in the bleachers while history unfolds. This Vietnam assignment, with all its frustrations and limitations and wear and tear, has opened the door for me into a whole new area of public affairs, and life-and-death issues of *real* people. President Nixon wasn't someone in a news story yesterday; he was a real human being I watched in action, at what he described in his speech the other night might be a "turning point" in the world's single most critical problem, the Vietnam war.

What he had said the night before was still in the President's mind. "I worked for weeks on that statement; every word was carefully chosen.

I don't like to *read* a speech but this was one where the greatest care had to be taken against a poorly chosen extemporaneous word."

The single phone on his left, where I sat at his desk, rang. He picked up the receiver, put it down. He rose. Would I excuse him for a moment? And left, instead of asking us to leave, or taking the call as L.B.J. would have, at a phone at a remote part of the big room. When he returned, in a few moments, I rose; the President smiling, then looking very sober. "You have heard about Fortas.† I have just phoned him my *personal* regrets." The cloud stayed over his face.

The President leaned back, looked at the two big reports (the English and the Vietnamese), and asked: "Should we have a picture of you giving the report to me?" Pushed a button, and shortly the doors flew open and in rushed the White House camera corps, the big floodlights over them. Several of them recognized me, yelled, "Hi, Mr. Lilienthal," and I hi-ed back.

So we stood up, the President directing the scenario, holding the big report in his hands, smiling at the cameras, saying *sotto voce*, "We should talk to each other." I was clumsy as hell; should have handed the volumes to him, but soon they called time, out went the floodlights and men, and we resumed our seats.

"I haven't read the full report, but I have a summary. As I understand, you find that for $3 billion the country can be reconstructed in a decade? That would be one-tenth the cost of a year of war."

I said, "The figure we used was 2.5 billion, or about the cost, for ten years of reconstruction, of one month of the war."

He gave me a sharp look, thought, I surmised, that "one month of war for ten years of reconstruction" was a good political gambit—as I do.

"I want to ask another question: What did you find about the spirit of the people? That's almost the essential."

So I expressed my now familiar views about how hard-working, quick to learn, resolute, etc., they are.

The President picked this up: "They are a tough people, no doubt. That's why they fight so hard; against each other too. They could probably lick anyone in Southeast Asia, Laos, Cambodia, maybe even the Thais."

Sizing me up, sideways, the President asked:

"What comes next? Are you going to continue on this job?"

I said, "Thieu and some of his Cabinet have asked our company to continue. We haven't yet worked things out with AID, but are talking about it."

I had already been in the Oval Office about forty-five minutes, twice

†Abe Fortas had just resigned from the Supreme Court in the wake of conflict of interest charges.

as long as had been allotted us. The President rose, shook my hand firmly, then putting his left hand over our clasped hands, said something about appreciating our work, and I left.

Out in the crowded lobby, electric cables spread all over making a shambles of what, in 1935, as I so well remember in the F.D.R. days, had been a sedate place.

I moved toward the north exit of the west offices, and was soon caught in a tangle of reporters. Now outside, where five TV cameras were lined up alongside a battery of mikes, reporters' questions were put: What would be the effect on your recommendations and findings of a wholly different kind of government in Vietnam?

I answered that, short of an out and out takeover "by China or the North Vietnamese on a Communist basis," the exact kind of government that evolved didn't much affect the recommendations: the land is there, the people, the rivers, the need for food—little would be affected by some other government in Vietnam. A complete Communist regime wouldn't, of course, follow our recommendations about an open economy and reliance on the private as well as the public sector.

Is the report "realistic?"

But what is *realistic*? The land is real; the people are real; their need for food and a sense of hope for their daily living is real. The farm women I saw in the open market in Danang a couple weeks ago raise their garden truck or chickens, plod their way to market to sell them, the fishermen go out into the Bassac River to catch fish. Those things will go on, whatever goes on in the negotiations or even on the battlefield. Those things are real. Rice will be grown, fish will be caught, people will brew their tea. These things don't stop because economists or intellectuals or newspapermen or politicians are trying to find a "settlement" of a power struggle.

MAY 18, 1969
PRINCETON

Last evening dinner at Bill Marvel's. The other guests, Professor James Billington and his tall, slender, refreshingly natural wife, and Professor Morroe Berger and his wife, huge dark eyes, a Levantine countenance, a good sense of humor.

Billington is one of my favorite people of the Princeton faculty. He wields a verbal snickersnee of wit and irony that slices off stuffy heads before one's very eyes. Tall, pale blue eyes, very youthful in appearance, one of the best prose stylists in academic life, witness his great volume about Russian (*not* Soviet) cultural history, *The Icon and the Axe;* witness his article in *Life* magazine kidding the pants *and* shorts off the international gathering of brains recently held here in Princeton, and copiously and solemnly written about in the *Times.*

Now he is considering a commission from *Life* to do a think-piece about the "social responsibility" of business toward the black urban areas. I commented that this has gone through the fizz stage of rhetoric and big-name committees; they didn't really know what they were going *to do,* after organizing these coalitions. Billington said that those businessmen he had interviewed so far seemed to bear out my comment; "It is significant that most of those assigned to this 'social business' turn out to be advertising vice presidents or agencies."

MAY 19, 1969
NEW YORK

This noon I lunched with a new member of the Nixon team, Glenn Olds, Ambassador to the UN in its economic affairs. He said he saw no evidence that anyone, except Kissinger, feels that there must be some sign of hope and affirmation or the political future of Nixon will be very sour.

He said, "I see no one who is trying to present the whole picture of the Pacific, of which the Vietnamese war is just a cruel fragment.

"If the opportunity to lift people's sights to the future, which is what the D&R report was aimed at, is lost in drooling about magic rice seed or digging wells, then a great opportunity will be lost."

The UN [Economic] Development Programme is one of Olds' major responsibilities; he spoke with the utmost candor about the future of that instrumentality.

Paul Hoffman, its present head, was a great figure in the Marshall Plan days, and ten years ago in the UN picture. But his vigor is gone, and his imagination and drive.

Can the World Bank fill the need for an integrated overall look at the development needs of the world, or of Southeast Asia? As I see it, after long exposure in Colombia and Iran, the Bank approach just doesn't include much else than *project feasibility,* which is a wholly inadequate concept. And then there will be the World Bank's Pearson Commission Report. I see little hope there. The report will complain that the rich countries don't contribute as much of their GNP as they should, will provide statistical stuff from a stable of analysis boys, but no inspiration.

Olds is a bright-eyed, earnest man. But he will be so overwhelmed with the duties at UN, and so far removed, I fear, from the seats of authority in Washington, that if he can inject a note of boldness and movement it will be a miracle indeed.

His close relations with Henry Kissinger may help. He said that it was he, as a "talent scout" for Nixon, who recommended Kissinger.

MAY 24, 1969
PRINCETON

During the past two years I have been contributing to that side of our D&R work that was my part of the chore, chiefly dealing with new business, immediate or long-range, and producing leadership and ideas for the Vietnam assignment. I should not have had to dig into the details of financial management, as I had to do for two days this week.

MAY 27, 1969
NEW YORK

This week I must face up to the closing out of the Urban Development Department. Which means people. It means a great disappointment to a brilliant and most likeable man, John Burnett, who has pounded himself to pieces to make this program work—which it did for a time. And Ronald Zweig, who hasn't been able to do more than assure us that "down the road" urban development will be one of the most important of D&R's roles. Which it might be. But this small company can't stand the losses while that is happening.

So I must face the music again, take the pain (for that is just what it is) and not temporize.

MAY 28, 1969
NEW YORK

"A conscience." No one has ever *seen* a conscience; but it is at least as real, to a man with responsibilities, as an item on a balance sheet, or an engineer's slide rule.

What to do about closing out the urban development work is a case where conscience—what is the right thing to do?—is at the very center of the managerial decision.

John Burnett has greatly helped to build up the training work. He negotiated the Peace Corps training contracts, threw his enthusiasm into the concept.

As I talked to John, a painful task for me, he was composed, fair, proud, his emotions of disappointment, perhaps even of shock, well in hand.

From now on I shall not look backward to question whether this was the right thing to do. It is done, and that must be that.

As Wendell Willkie told me years ago, when we in TVA were buying his Tennessee Electric Company, "Someday *you* may have to cut back on a good going organization, then you'll know how *I* feel these days, damn you."

So I do.

But I have no second thoughts at all about the wisdom of D&R, a small undercapitalized private firm, getting out of the urban development "business." It is not yet tenable as a private business; it is still mostly platform rhetoric, and for D&R prohibitively expensive rhetoric.

MAY 30, 1969
PRINCETON

A letter from AID's Mendenhall aroused me. AID now proposing to determine what D&R and the Vietnam Government's program should be. The American AID group has become so unpopular in Vietnam, and so terribly mistrusted.

Once you start backpedaling and showing that you can be pushed around by an old-line bureaucrat such as AID's Joe Mendenhall, you get pushed even further. A draft of a letter to Mendenhall, prepared for [Nick] Philip to sign, caving in to AID's views, would have made us out traitors to the representations we have been making to the Vietnamese these past two and a half years.

As I went out of my office, Miss Baron looked up at me with a note of concern I can't remember seeing on her face before. "Oh, Mr. Lilienthal, you are responsible. You aren't going to let that letter go out, surely?"

Of course, she was right, with the rightness of feminine instinct so often closer to the mark than technical judgment.

I rewrote the latter part of that letter so it was a far way from the marshmallow acquiescence of the many earlier drafts.

It is true that one "can't go home again." But it is also true that no man built the way I am inside can dodge his responsibility to himself and to those who trust him by any phony rationalization.

Never have we had a more magnificent rose border, eighty-five, all suddenly in bloom. The first bloom is rarely the best, but this year they have surpassed themselves.

Has there ever been a time when jingo-type oratory, or extravagant praise or awe of the military, has been at a lower ebb? The Pentagon, powerful as it is with almost half of our national budget to spend, and in the midst of a war, is certainly on the defensive on big things—i.e., the war in Vietnam or the anti-ballistic missile. A good sign, too. I sympathize with the commander in the field under the current barrage of criticism from Senators about just how to conduct a particular military campaign. He is responsible for his troops. He knows full well, in the dark of the night, how terrible it would be should he make a bloodstained mistake, and then be brutally crucified by the after-the-fact wiseacres.

Yet no public figure—civilian or military—should be above criticism, such as one finds every day in the press.

JUNE 8, 1969
PRINCETON

Another very early morning gardening foray, before coffee, widening two other borders.

Yesterday afternoon, a glorious day indeed, to the Greenbaums for an unusual cocktail party. Dottsie had set up, all about their lovely rolling lawn, dozens of her sculptures, all the way from the great lead bas-reliefs to tiny little bronze figures.

JUNE 10, 1969
NEW YORK

It is an eager work-life I lead. Even the troubles are lively ones, those which call on my background of experience. No amount of imagination about the future can take the place of the reality of the *now.*

A cable from Fred Moore [of D&R] in Perth: Minister Court agrees that D&R assume an advisory role for the whole of Western Australia, including planning of the electric power system.

The downs are tough, but the ups can be terrific.

A friendly note from Henry Kissinger, received yesterday. He invites us to continue to press our ideas, quite in contrast with what has actually been happening in AID since I got back from Saigon.

JUNE 18, 1969
NEW YORK

Today I felt we were going places, my own role well played: leading a small staff discussion, asking the questions that memoranda leave unasked, and in the face-to-face discussion that only staff discussions can provide, getting answers, or exposing, sometimes brutally, the fact that only the surface has been touched, the essence not explored and dug into. I enjoyed these sessions, tough as they were.

The subject: what do we do to make something besides talk-talk happen in Australia?

Spent over an hour with a most formal little man, Dr. Baker, from the University of Texas "oral history" project. The subject: your recollections of "Mr." Johnson, as he insisted on calling L.B.J. Complete with a very fancy tape recorder.

As he packed up, he said, "Oral history has become something of a fad." I agreed. "In fact, for those of us who still work hard, and think, mistakenly perhaps, that we are *making* history, the time spent on this rash of oral history recording may prevent history being made."

JUNE 19, 1969
NEW YORK

Tuesday noon—the 17th—to a small luncheon for President Lleras Restrepo of Colombia. Held at the palatial, utterly elegant headquarters of the Center for Inter-American Relations.

The President is a diminutive man, but in some mysterious way he has great stature. Tough, stubborn, and highly intelligent.

Dave Bell,‡ looking taller and almost transparent, so thin he is, remarked to me that here, in Lleras, was a good economist who was also a good politician. I agreed. But added that I was still looking for an economist who was a good economist.

A bit shocked by Lauris Norstad's appearance: he was co-host of the luncheon; now chairman of Owens-Corning Fiberglas, largely a public relations post, though the General is capable enough to run almost anything. So *frail*-looking; my best recollection of him, during my AEC days particularly, was that of a wiry, sturdy man. I couldn't help wondering what he thought of the crashed illusion that air power was about all we needed in our world-wide military establishment.

JUNE 24, 1969
PRINCETON

When I see ugly events and ugly issues dealt with in a cheap way by cheap people my faith is sustained by observing good people, staunch, considerate, devoted to great issues and the broadest concerns. It lifts my heart to see how *many* such good individuals there are.

In Washington yesterday, meeting with the Education and World Affairs trustees in the National Academy of Sciences Building.

‡Former head of AID.

I sat next to John Hannah at the great oval table of the Academy's boardroom. He told of what he must put up with in the daily appearances before Congressman Otto Passman's Subcommittee dealing with the AID appropriation request. What a way to treat a really noble man. A record of devotion to the best in his country's life. At an age and with an earned prestige that would entitle him to leave to someone else this dirty job of pulling AID through its worst hours. He faces it all with outward equanimity, without a single sharp word about either Passman or the incredible and foolish complexity of the government establishment.

"A bureaucracy is never efficient," he said in a soft voice, "and when bureaucracy is under attack it is even less efficient. So many, so unbelievably many, who have to be consulted at every step, who feel they must review everything that is done.

"Passman spends most of the hours of each of these long sessions telling dirty stories, or anecdotes about Louisiana. And most of it he directs should be off the record, not in the transcript of the sessions."

I got the definite impression that Hannah believes a Vietnam pullout —fancy journalistic word for humiliating surrender—has been decided upon by this Administration.

I felt much the same way, though for different reasons, about Bob Goheen. We came back to Princeton together. Had to wait for hours at the airport.

In those hours Goheen's character and good manners shone like a light. Considerate, completely unstuffy (after all, he is the successful president of a great and ancient university), with humor and good nature and an interest in other people.

We should measure our faith in mankind by such examples as Hannah and Goheen, not by the cheap ones, the bitter and cowardly and completely unworthy men.

McNamara stayed throughout the long EWA session, and made some good sensible contributions: about the troubles the foundations have with the Ways and Means Committee, about the unwisdom of having the EWA "retreat" held at some vacation resort, as recommended by [Bill] Marvel and [Herman] Wells. "If we have thirty members by that time, and their wives, that's sixty people at foundation expense going off to St. Croix. I question the wisdom of this."

How right he is. "The foundation life" that I have been making fun about may be coming to a close. And so with the non-profit research outfits, Rand, Hudson Institute, etc., etc., for they too live on tax exemptions, since they have, by their definition, no taxable income—i.e., non-profit.

I talked to McNamara about the Vietnam Delta.

In response to my description of what the Vietnamese appear to think (or AID wants them to think) the World Bank will do about D&R's appraisal report on the Mekong Delta, McNamara said, "The World Bank is certainly not going to get into this. It must be through the UN. The World Bank must be very careful about this, as we are an international agency, and particularly with my background in connection with the war."

JULY 1, 1969
NEW YORK

As I reflect on the improvement in D&R since Gerald Levin became General Manager, it is an impressive picture. It is good to see how much toughness and hard work have done to begin the process of straightening us out.

JULY 13, 1969
MARTHA'S VINEYARD

Last night a hard driving rain. Bartok never orchestrated a more dramatic percussion selection, with the spirited drumbeat of the rain amplified by the roof, a roof that was like a drumhead. The bass timpani of the thunder, the swish of the lashing treetops was the string section. Cozy and comforting to hear this music through the night, waking long enough from time to time to muse and dream with one's eyes wide open.

The evidence that Scotty Reston is correct is all about us. Our values don't come from the home, the church, the universities—as we have been constantly told. They come chiefly, says Scotty, from the press and TV.

Day before yesterday, full of a revelation I wanted desperately to share with someone, I wrote to my son:

> What I have discovered, between my sixtieth and seventieth birthdays . . . will only seem relevant to you a decade or so from now.
> What I have found is simple, and utterly complex and mystical too. . . . The wrinkles deepen but the heart and the spirit can be as intense and enveloping as ever. The *capacity* to give, to love, to dream dreams and have visions, to respond to others and to cause others to respond to you, is still there, unquenchable, if given a chance . . . the emanations of the heart and the emotions are not functions of years. . . . This enduring capacity to feel intensely and live intensely carries with it at times the price tag of pain and frustration; there are no highs without lows. But the sustaining article of

my faith, now confirmed by [still another] decade of my own experience, is that in the world of feeling, of imagination, of daring and challenge and creation, man need not be a hostage of the calendar; an aging body [need not] mean an aging heart and spirit.

JULY 19, 1969
MARTHA'S VINEYARD

Sailed alone yesterday, a happy easy sail, learning to manage the new rig of the jib sheet: jam-type cams instead of the cleats. No matter how awkward and amateurish one is—this describes me as a single-hand sailor still—making some headway in learning how to manage new gear, or rearranged gear, gives a satisfaction that is laughable, in retrospect, but delicious at the time. Pleasure is to be found in the most prosaic acts; if, I suppose one should add, if one is the kind who is sufficiently aware to sense pleasure when it happens, in little things and in profoundly moving occurrences as well.

JULY 20, 1969
FLYING FROM THE VINEYARD TO NEW YORK

About nine last night I saw my granddaughter Pam's bright golden head and wide-bottom pants coming up through the woods below "Topside." She had come from Edgartown, and, in true Vineyard summer custom, was given a "hitch" in the last part of the trip. I was taken aback: a girl walking the highway alone at night. She thought nothing of it.

But she was full of news. Senator Ted Kennedy had had an accident in driving on Chappaquiddick almost twenty-four hours ago—after midnight Saturday night. Said Pam, quite excited: "His secretary, who had passed out, was drowned as the car went off a rickety bridge. Edgartown is swarming with reporters and TV cameramen. And everyone is talking about scandal."

Martha's Vineyard is in the national news, and on so sad a note.

The memorial service for "Miss Emma" Daggett last evening was a New England story out of another time, but not another place. The place: the little church on a country road in the Lambert's Cove area.

Miss Emma was as energetic a woman as I have ever known, wearer of curious hats that sat way on top of her piled-up hair, bright eyes, back as straight as the backs of the uncomfortable pews in which we sat to hear a conventional eulogy for an unconventional eccentric woman of great ability and power.

As I looked at the fading and, in some cases, very old friends in the pews, I thought that a casting director had selected us.

Across the aisle from me an old man, cheeks sunken, nose now a beak, leaning on his cane as he sat there. He probably remembered Emma when she was a bustling girl, brought up in that combination farmhouse and fisherman's dwelling on Cedar Tree Neck, or a young woman who thought nothing of walking four miles to the Lambert's Cove church where we were meeting, and four miles back. She became an outstanding teacher of art in a New Jersey region within sight of New York City.

Filling the silences was the steady tick-tock, tick-tock of a clock. Too dramatic even for Hollywood, that touch of the seconds that were being counted, seconds and minutes that would never come again, for all of us, but particularly for that fine parchment face across the aisle. Tick-tock —I can hear the ominous warning sound even now, up here in this plane scooting cityward through the overcast.

JULY 21, 1969
NEW YORK

Surely the world will never be quite the same, after what I saw at midnight, on the TV set in this little hotel room, lying back comfortably in my bed and watching the astronauts climbing out of their spacecraft, and listening to the conversations that went on across 240,000 miles of space.

Two ghostly figures bouncing about on the moon. They were there because getting there was something men wanted so badly that there was no stopping it. It could not be stopped by all the skepticism, lethargy, ugliness, faintheartedness, jealousies emotions so familiar to human-kind.

True, solving human problems is much more difficult. But back of this achievement of last night is a human problem. The human problem is to find goals sufficiently clear and desirable and understandable so that we humans will drive to them, overcoming everything else.

Last night at a D&R party, the wife of a new engineering staff member said to me: "Mr. Lilienthal, do you really believe what you have written and we have all read, that man has infinite capabilities; do you really have all that faith in human beings?" (A question I have often been asked.)

"I really do," I said. And what is going on in the heavens tonight is one piece of supporting evidence.

JULY 24, 1969
NEW YORK

An hour-and-a-half staff meeting this morning, to hear about two of our less-known activities. Jack Swift gave a quite exciting—and beautifully organized—description of the work we have been carrying on in Nicaragua, now in its third year. The purpose, with Nicaraguans, is to examine, inventory, and classify the land resources as a basis for a new tax system, to examine the land and water and forestry resources preparatory to "doing something with the facts"—which is the way the quite intelligent Nicaraguan Government describes their part of the effort. A good story.

Then a jaunt to Afghanistan. An irrigation project, still in its early stages, in the fabled Hindu Kush mountain area.

Yesterday, luncheon with the alert investment banker Ferd Eberstadt and his partner Bob Zeller. Eberstadt hasn't lost any of his dry humor, nor his zest about business, even now when the market has been "behaving poorly."

I owe Ferd Eberstadt a great deal. Much of what I learned about private industry and responsible finance, after I left public service, I learned from working with him and tenacious Howard Kniffin of Lazard Frères. Together we transformed a puny, ailing minerals separation patent enterprise into a major industry, which formed the basis of my private fortune.§

Said Helen last week: "You are the greatest fellow for not letting well enough alone." Truer words were never spoken about me, whether on some trifling matter around the house or on a serious question of directions or conduct of my life or work.

Ho Chi Minh has once more rejected all the recent American-sponsored proposals such as: an election under international supervision, agreement to permit Viet Cong participation in the election, approval of the withdrawal process of American troops. Result: Hanoi is more than ever sure that they can achieve a complete military victory, if they continue the war.

§See *Journals*, Vol. III, *The Venturesome Years*, indexed under "Minerals Separation North American Corporation" and "Minerals & Chemicals Corporation of America."

JULY 26, 1969
PRINCETON

Senator Ted Kennedy's appearance on TV last evening on the Chappaquiddick tragedy was human drama at its peak. This was no virtuoso performance by a man not to be believed, such as candidate Nixon's [1952] TV defense of his election "fund" in which "my little dog Checkers" is the drooly part one remembers. This last night was a man in deep trouble, and my heart went out to him.

AUGUST 5, 1969
MARTHA'S VINEYARD

Today and yesterday Helen and I plugging away, at the long table, reviewing the huge stacks of manuscript—the transcribed entries—for the upcoming Volume V of the *Journals.* We have developed a style of working together that I find "efficient." We both now know our respective roles; therefore decisions can be made quickly and without false motion; more important, we each *identify* questions, about taste, length, clarity, etc.

Long "unstructured" conversation the other day with samples of today's "rebellious" young. But such intelligent, thoughtful young. Grandson Mike the most appealing. Most interesting of all, Anne Shattuck. An alert face, not conventionally pretty but arresting. Diminutive, but very sure of herself.

Mike has a single note: Baba and India. He is very vague in expressing himself on any other subject. Anne is apparently his special friend. Which is a comment on both of them. For she is as smart and precise as one could expect of a much older person—to my surprise she says she is sixteen.

Says Anne, because of Baba they have a philosophy of love for everybody and everything to take the place of "polluting our bodies" with drugs in order to reach out for wider things.

"I was very, very shy," said Anne. "Then I found Baba, and realized that I wanted to reach out to other people and they would not reject me. I speak now to everyone."

Why the "revolt"? I asked. "Boredom?" Pam said: "Yes, boredom. All of us found that we didn't have responsibilities, things that were expected of us. Our parents did everything for us. And the idea of making it big, competing, all that sort of thing, we just don't want. We want to live simply. We don't want lots of money or to have all kinds of material things."

I found them refreshing. And tried not to worry too much about how long this would last, or what comes next.

AUGUST 28, 1969
MARTHA'S VINEYARD

A Vineyard summer quite different from any of the twenty that preceded it. The reason: our exposure, at close range, to members of the most distinctive new generation of young people that anyone alive can remember. Articulate and with a strong sense of entity.

Different, but by no means uniform. Pamela, big blonde, half child, half grown woman, differs from her dreamy, vague brother Mike. Mike borrowed our sleeping bag, and with his Irish Setter puppy, heads for the woods and sleeps out. His friend Joe is returning to Spain to become a guitarist, he says, and to "find a little piece of land where I can raise things." Mike and Joe continue to paint houses, but making silver ornaments and leather things is Mike's idea of how he will support himself. "I tell them," says Pam, "that there is no market for what they are going to make. And they will be surrounded by freaks; but what we all want is to get away from American freaks." (She defined freaks for us. They are the bushy-haired beats and hippies.)

The evening TV newscasts begin with a view outside the Edgartown courthouse: the preliminaries of the inquest into the Kennedy-Kopechne tragedy. This is becoming a media circus. The atmosphere even here is not that of an isolated place.

If the enemies of the Kennedy political establishment haven't already destroyed the last of the tribe, they propose to finish the job with this inquest.

AUGUST 31, 1969
MARTHA'S VINEYARD

I had a spirited little visit with Kingman Brewster, president of Yale. A brawny man who can kid himself, and does. "We were once on opposite sides," he remarked, "on the antitrust issue. I taught antitrust law at Harvard; was later in the Antitrust Division of the Justice Department. In the Law School your book *Big Business*◖ we found was to be taken very seriously, a real contribution. You made out a strong case that bigness was both beneficial and inevitable."

I broke in: "Events, since I wrote that book, have established that I was only 50% right. Bigness beneficial? *Not* proved. Inevitable: proved."

◖*Big Business: A New Era.* New York: Harper & Row, 1952.

In his booming voice Roger Baldwin told of a meeting with Mike on Baldwin Beach on the south shore. Roger was most enthusiastic about Mike, with his shoulder-length hair and his hippie appearance. "Mike, what are you looking for?" Said Mike: "I am looking for God." This didn't take Roger aback. "Mike, isn't that what all of us are looking for, each in his own way?" "But," said Mike, "I have *found* God." "Great," says Roger.

A brief visit with Scotty Reston. Tilting a bottle of beer to his lips, he looked like a man at ease.

"How sets the world, Dave?" I opined, "Better." "I guess so," said this unusual man, a mixture of restrained optimist and dour skeptic. Said I: "I hear you are leaving New York, going back to Washington to live."

Through carefully selected words and a strained tired look in his face, he spoke of the impossibility of doing all that he had been doing as executive editor of the *Times.* "Keeping up with all the daily stories, writing a column, and listening to people in the organization you have to deal with—you can't refuse to see them about their gripes, or just give them ten minutes; it means too much to them."

As I know all too well, the administrator's life is not an easy one. Especially for anyone who, seated at his typewriter, can tell us exactly what we should be doing in Vietnam or what is wrong with Johnson, or Nixon, or whoever.

I am ashamed that I get some morbid satisfaction out of seeing a distinguished writer struggling with the kind of personnel problems that are at the heart of management.

SEPTEMBER 1, 1969
NEW YORK

A Massachusetts Supreme Court judge has ordered the Kennedy case delayed until it can be determined—I assume—whether any man can be heard, in fairness, with three hundred newspapermen and TV cameras trying the case in public.

The common law and our Constitution were designed to protect the personal liberties of the rich and powerful as well as the poor—we should never forget that.

SEPTEMBER 5, 1969
FLYING TO THE VINEYARD

An East Tennessee old-home reunion with John Harper, president of Alcoa. We reminisced about the agreement that beady-eyed Arthur

V. Davis, founder of the aluminum industry, and yours truly, for TVA, negotiated back in the thirties. "That is the most complex contract I have ever seen in my life. I never could really understand it. All I know is that we never had to refer to the contract; we let the operating boys of Alcoa and TVA run the two hydro systems in the best way for all parties. Our relations with TVA have always been very good, and still are."

SEPTEMBER 6, 1969
MARTHA'S VINEYARD

I was so impressed with Mike last evening. Not only his extraordinarily good manners and charm and grace. But he is genuine. His verbal renunciation of what he calls "material things" he lives out.

Sunday he went into a little church at Lambert's Cove in his overalls and long hair. "The organist gave me a big warm smile of welcome. They gave me a seat in the front pew, with my dog. Everyone was so nice; shook hands with me after the service, asked me to come again. I would go this Sunday, but my clothes—I don't have any city clothes." I said I thought church was a place where city clothes didn't really matter.

I wonder if Mike hasn't got something that the more ambitious, competitive, earthy people have lost; perhaps we're all the poorer for having lost that otherworldly simplicity.

SEPTEMBER 15, 1969
NEW YORK

Was there ever an elaborate fancy-dress costume party such as I saw yesterday afternoon in Central Park? Literally "thousands" of young people vying with each other for costumes that have no relation to anything I know about: hair bushed out to the size of a huge pumpkin, Red Indian headdress on ordinary American faces, broad flat hats, dazzling colored pants. The feeling I had was that these thousands of young people are at the *end* of some kind of period, not the beginning, that the frenzy can't last in this grotesque form.

SEPTEMBER 24, 1969
FLYING FROM LOS ANGELES TO NEW YORK

I spent much of yesterday at the D&R camp at Hemet, California. There D&R is in charge of the training of a group of Peace Corps volunteers. The camp is a former labor camp; crude and simple but not ostentatiously so. The countryside and the conditions at Hemet are intended to be as nearly as possible a replica of conditions in the parts of central India where these forty or so young men will teach Indian villagers what the "teachers" are now in the process of learning: raising poultry, handling calves, repairing and operating farm machinery, etc.

What makes this all distinctive, different entirely from university agriculture extension courses, is that the men are learning Hindi, or other Indian languages. For weeks they go through an intensive and ingenious course of learning to speak and understand the words and phrases that will enable them to teach basic agricultural skills to Indians, in their own language.

How deadly in earnest *these* young people are. They work fourteen hours a day. And no nonsense. I watched them during a four-hour period, when they must not use *any* English, go through a scenario of discussion of the virtues or otherwise of a white leghorn chicken, as if they were sellers and buyers of such a chicken in an Indian village—all in Hindi. Eight weeks ago when they started the D&R training course, half of these young people, sweating over an irrigation pump or a tractor or a calf, had had no rural experience and, of course, no Hindi.

The average age of these alert hard-working "young people" at our camp at Hemet was not far off the age of the 400,000 who sat in the mud and feces at the rock festival at Woodstock, finding that rock music and odd costumes better expressed their attitude toward the world.

SEPTEMBER 28, 1969
PRINCETON

Yesterday heavy gardening; providing a fit place for some new iris. A good day it was, beautiful, with a touch of autumn in the crisp air. And the night before, a long, long sleep.

Why, then, today do I have this low and dispirited feeling?

Some of us, I opine, are strangely built. The exuberant reviews of Alexander Kendrick's biography of Ed Murrow reminded me that I am by no means the only individual—Ed was certainly one—who has streaks of glumness, when all the facts say "what a lucky and favored man you are."

Ed Murrow paced within the cell of his temperament, battling fiercely at the walls that didn't exist, cursing the locked door that was never locked. He knew all the great ones of the world; he had a beautiful wife with great talent and warmth; he had enormous influence on people and events. And, of course, no financial problems.

Yet he had periods when, for no explainable reason, he was very much in the dumps—about the world, yes, but also about Ed Murrow.

Does it really help, when such a mood crosses the path of such as me, to recite all the many reasons why I should not only be "happy," but even elated, by the cards life has dealt me?

I *know in my mind* how fortunate is my life: I sit here in the garden Helen and I have created and nurtured, and know that this is good. I am breathless with the wonder of the bronze-colored dogwood as I walked this morning on the Institute Common. My friends are many and interesting and miss no opportunity to tell me of their admiration for what I stand for, or to express affection by the very tone of their address.

"Try it on; how can you be so positive that you can't get into it?" Helen speaking. So I put on my tailcoat (over the pink plaid sport shirt I was wearing). Well, I'm bigger across the shoulders; all that exercise, you know. But of course the pants—my middle will never get into it. But damned if I not only got into the pants, but the waistband was too loose by an inch or more. I looked into the inside pocket and read: "The Willard Shop, Nov. 10, 1950." Good grief, twenty years ago.

OCTOBER 3, 1969
PENN STATION, NEW YORK

Penn railroad station is designed for everything but *people*. I'm writing these notes while sitting on my up-ended dispatch case. Nowhere else to sit; people standing all around, and the rush hasn't yet begun.

Gave a small luncheon for Professor Thuc, just arrived from Saigon. Thuc gave us a picture of how he thinks we should judge the American intervention. "Americans should understand that they have won a great military or logistic victory. In 1965 the Communists were in a position to take over the whole country. Now they have had to fall back on guerrilla warfare. That is what your military victory compelled them to do.

"In the guerrilla kind of fighting, the first phase, now the *present* phase, there is no need for large numbers of American troops. What can they do? Nothing much. Of course, your own generals didn't understand this. But it is more than time for withdrawal of American troops."

"What has been the reception of your report in Washington?" Osborn Elliott* asked me.

I said that the Secretary of State had put considerable importance on it. A similar word from Kissinger.

"Then, no word; no declaration from the White House of postwar and peaceful development as a major policy course. Nothing has happened on the American scene—that is, Washington—since mid-May."

*Editor-in-chief, *Newsweek* magazine.

This puzzled Elliott. "I guessed that Nixon would grab your report, make a big thing of the opportunity to talk about peace in development terms, future of the people, and so on.

"But Nixon hasn't been doing anything about *anything* for months, and this is just part of the way he is non-leading."

OCTOBER 4, 1969
PRINCETON

At a shindig Thursday night Mac Bundy† said, "I have rarely known a time when there was as great a gap between the realities of Vietnam and public opinion about it. What we have now in Washington is what we had in a way under Ike: a non-government."

Non-government, with *this* President, is probably close to what he wants; and wants with all his considerable political senses alert and functioning. L.B.J. rushed the issues, rushed the public, and that worked well for a long time. But not in the final crunch. Nixon may not be "drifting," as Ike probably did by temperament and in his naiveté about the political process; Nixon may well have decided that non-government is the best line.

But where does that leave the country, about Vietnam—and everything?

OCTOBER 5, 1969
PRINCETON

How good it is to have friends who have a wide range of interests. Bill Dix, Princeton University librarian, for instance. He knows about books, in *every* dimension. His eyes sparkle when the subject is turned to the implication of books. The way growth in an interest in having books had much to do with a transformation in the life of Indonesia; or how the Franklin publishing enterprise in Iran had an important economic consequence. Books were needed for the literacy program; this led to an increase in the market for white paper, and that led to the use of bagasse —by-product of our cane sugar operation at Haft Tapeh—the papermill now being constructed.

OCTOBER 8, 1969
NEW YORK

It is clear to me that the postwar development effort has little effective support from the Government of Vietnam. If one believes, as I do and

†President of the Ford Foundation.

have said so often, that more and more of the responsibility for the fighting *and* for development and planning should be on the Vietnamese, then we should withdraw.

In my mind, this particular show is over. It is a great personal relief. And with good reason. The almost three years we have put in on this task have been emotionally wearing in the extreme. I have diverted from D&R's other important opportunities and tasks most of my energy and a large share of my time, for despite a good staff, the responsibility has been on me. It has been a disturbing experience, in a deteriorating set of circumstances.

This is not to say that I regret at all that we undertook the job, nor that it wasn't a memorable experience. But enough is enough. This gives me, and D&R, an "honorable" exit. I only wish my country had an equally "honorable" peace ahead, instead of a humiliating and cruel defeat, with consequences throughout the world that are terrible to contemplate.

OCTOBER 14, 1969
NEW YORK

Dinner with Dana Atchley. I asked him to tell me about the classes of fourth-year medical students he teaches twice a week.

The classes, he said, consist of students who present an "appraisal" of a particular patient. "I tell them I am not interested in disease, nor a diagnosis, but in the human being. Do you know how well, or poorly, a patient can manage to do his job in life, how well he can live with that ailment? Shouldn't you as a physician not just analyze what causes the pain in an angina patient's chest? Everyone with any common sense knows it is that the arteries don't carry enough blood when he needs it. That kind of diagnosis is easy and irrelevant. What kind of work does he have to do and how well can he perform it within the limits of this physical condition? That's what the doctor should know about, and try to be helpful about.

"All this scientific training and equipment is draining the common sense out of our generation of physicians. When God made the world, He gave many people brains and brilliance and all that; but He short-changed most people on just plain common sense."

The *Times* Friday last (October 10) had a seven-column half-page story, "A Plan for Welfare Island Is Unveiled." This is the plan D&R's staff developed and presented last February.

D&R's part in that project has never once been mentioned in any of the press reports about Welfare Island. Not even a minor reference.

The book Dean Acheson vowed he would never write has been published and with a fanfare of publicity.‡

What Dean said about the intellectuals warmed my heart, since more and more I feel as he does, perhaps with even greater cause: "The intellectual, strictly channeled into one discipline, wants to run them all."

OCTOBER 16, 1969
NEW YORK

I told McGeorge Bundy we were going to close out our Vietnam development planning work in April.

"That would be unthinkable," Bundy said, "just when it is important and timely that you are there. Why, the war is almost over; now is the time when the development planning becomes most important."

OCTOBER 19, 1969
PRINCETON

Talked by phone with Augie Heckscher§ Friday to alert him to the forthcoming report D&R is making on New York City's power supply. Augie's special interest would be in what we say about the new high priority that electric power companies must give to the effect on "human environment" in producing power in an urban setting particularly.

I asked him how he felt about the Welfare Island plan, which appears to be moving toward reality. He said, "It is exactly what D&R and the Citizens Committee recommended last February. It is very sensitive and imaginative, as one would expect from the very beginning of your connection with the problem when our Committee first met at River House many months ago."

Last Monday, after a lunch with the *New York Times* staff, I had a half-hour or so with Seymour Topping, recently made assistant managing editor.

"Nothing of a development kind in Vietnam, such as you have been working on, will happen," he said, "until there has been a political settlement, after the pulling out of all American troops. Nothing can happen until a replacement by a Cabinet of a leftist kind. Those who had anything to do with the Thieu regime—I mean Americans and Vietnamese both—will have no standing whatever with the leftist government that must succeed the Thieu operations."

‡*Present at the Creation.* New York: W. W. Norton & Co., 1969.
§Commissioner of Parks, New York City.

OCTOBER 25, 1969
FLORENCE, ITALY

We flew from Rome to Pisa, after the air journey across the Atlantic Friday night, and to our surprise and delight not only were we met by David, but by Davey, a wriggling and sturdy Margy, and Peggy, now grey but sleek.

This villa, their home, in the little town of Settignano, perches on the edge of a hill looking over the city of Florence. An old house, stone stairways, great baronial rooms, heavy walnut carved furniture in the living rooms, great high decorated ceilings. On the top floor, with huge windows, David's study, with all of Florence below.

OCTOBER 29, 1969
HERAKLION, CRETE

The island of Crete and the island of Manhattan are not the same. But David Lilienthal doesn't change much, it would seem.

The Minoans were every bit wonderful, and the rubble of Knossos *should* have elicited from me the appropriate ohs and ahs. They didn't. I marveled at my spouse's stamina. She was seeing this palace the second time (earlier with Nancy) and yet her zest seemed greater than if this were the first time. I was just plain bored, but trying to be "cooperative."

Off on a hillside I saw a man outside a small house wielding some great sledge, whanging it on stone. "What energy!" said I, out of my lethargy.

Helen hardly glanced that way. "Oh, that's outside the palace area."

I said, "He's *alive.*"

This may not be a fair assessment on my part. But that comment pretty well sums up my general attitude about antiquities; for human beings now alive I have enormous and increasing interest.

This morning we saw plenty of Cretans who are very much alive. And to what purpose? Well, that's something else. We stood, in streets absolutely packed and jammed with people as they celebrated the Greek victory over the Italians twenty-nine years ago. Troops and a small-town band; but the feature was a proud and *endless* parade of children and youths.

OCTOBER 31, 1969
AT THE ATHENS AIRPORT
WAITING FOR THE FLIGHT TO TEHRAN

When Helen asked me, "What did you most enjoy about Crete?," traitor to "culture" though it makes me, I had to answer: the hour at noontime yesterday looking out on the quiet, enfolding bay at Minos Beach, the sun so warm, the sky dazzling, no walking around through the rubble of long-past structures. I am not much of a tourist; the starts and stops, the going from plane to train to bus to hotel, the digging out of tickets and passports and baggage checks, wearies me.

Other than the joy of seeing David and his family, the second most enjoyable event of the trip so far was the impromptu walk I took last night through the streets of Heraklion.

The people are so full of bounce, a handsome well-fed lot, all of them short, some alarmingly so, but mostly beaming and earnest as they went about the business of buying and selling. On the well-lighted streets of this middle-sized city, or down the dark lanes branching from the main drags, the only people who weren't in motion were the old men sitting in the coffee shops. They are the very symbol of inertia and repose and of just sitting as a way of life.

Little shops six feet wide selling nothing but buttons; windows awash with silks and shelves stacked high with goods; men pounding tin into shapes; fruit and beautiful vegetables, such as cauliflower the size of the harvest moon. A pert little local gal in a leather suit, the skirt almost to her sassy rump, sashaying through the crowd, attracting no particular attention from the men, but a huge farmer-type older woman stops, views the retreating waggle, turns back with a look of amazement and disdain, her mouth drawn into a thin and ominous line.

NOVEMBER 4, 1969
TEHRAN

An hour this morning with Amir Abbas Hoveyda, the Prime Minister of this nation of twenty-seven million people, a nation with a multitude of troublesome problems. A more relaxed, informal, and person-to-person individual it would be impossible to find. A striking-looking man, of below average height, twinkling brown eyes, an impressive dome of a baldish head, and conversational ease and versatility.

Slouched in a low chair, he puffed at a smallish pipe and made me feel at once that he enjoyed my visit.

He began by talking about my *Journals.* If I ever had any doubt that keeping these journals is worth the effort—even this writing, tonight, after quite a day—it was dispelled by his opening remarks.

"I have read your *Journals.* You are quite evidently a calm man. You are not only a man of action—as everyone in Iran knows—but a writer." He paused to make sure I realized that the latter accomplishment impressed him fully as much, perhaps more, than the former.

"You know, you discovered Khuzistan for us Iranians. We didn't know about it. You are the Columbus of Iran, just as another Columbus discovered your country. Your country was there all the time but Columbus discovered it. Khuzistan was there all the time but you found it.

"There are three kinds of men who come here for business purposes. You are the third kind: you know about management and business but you understand our people because at heart you are a philosopher, so you can understand people in a strange country. Your name is not only known throughout this country, but we like you."

I sat there like a schoolboy who had expected to have the principal tell him what's what, and then this: from a Prime Minister. It was "we like you" that flabbergasted me.

He talked about his own job and how he handles it.

"I came to this task with no particular background of experience; I was a minor official for a time. I have a large Cabinet of young Ministers each of whom is certain that *his* Ministry is all that counts, his Ministry is the one that should get whatever it wants. When people ask me how I manage to make my decisions, I say—half joking, of course—'I listen to all of them while they fight with each other about their ideas. Then I do just the contrary of what they recommended!'"

When he talked about the Shah, his eyes glowed. "I am devoted to this man. He knows *everything.* When I go to see him I carry my little black book of facts in my pocket, for when he asks a question of fact you had *better* know the answer, and I have it in my book, for I am not good at carrying figures in my head. He will ask: what is the average rainfall in Fars? I will venture some figure. No, the Shah will say, that is a bit high —or low. He knows every detail about this country. A remarkable man."

I thought to myself that the same could be said for the Prime Minister.

NOVEMBER 5, 1969
FLYING BY CHARTERED PLANE TO KHUZISTAN

The audience, a half-hour, with the Shah yesterday noon was one of the most decisive and impressive of a long series.

The Shah can be one of the most informal of men, with whom I have at times felt completely at ease. No dropping of an innate dignity or reserve, but also no feeling "I am in the presence of a monarch."

But when he is surrounded by the physical trappings of a sovereign, it takes some doing to treat him as just another intelligent and personable "old friend"—his phrase about me at the White House dinner a couple years ago—and despite years of friendly meetings under all kinds of circumstances.

The Palace of Saadabad is almost under the shoulder of the mountains. In I went, through the great iron gates, for the long walk on a graveled path, through an avenue of noble trees, fountains, and reflecting pools, and the rose garden I remember so well from a previous visit. About every fifty feet a couple officers, who stiffened into a salute as I came abreast. Then a graceful, full arm gesture, with nodded head, indicating where I was to go, until finally I reached the marble steps.

From there on, as I entered the Palace, the splendor of kingship was almost overwhelming; hard to remember that the setting was simply the "residence" of another man, with the same number of arms and legs as myself or any other human being. These surroundings of elegance are one of the implicit ways in which power is maintained.

As alone as a man can feel, I walked through the great hall, passing a phalanx of liveried men, in pale blue with gold buttons, or morning tailcoats, waving me on with those gestures that remind one of willow trees yielding before a breeze. My steps resounded on the pink marble floor. On left and right, great rose-colored marble columns, big as great oaks. Finally I was motioned to a small room, looking out on the reflecting pool. Through windows the snow-covered Zagros Mountains, a jagged line, haughty and unrelated to men, under the intense blue of the desert sky.

The ceiling at least thirty feet high; a great chandelier; a gleaming carved walnut desk, a dark green sofa, flowery carpets everywhere. On the desk two pens, among the gold ornaments, each pen topped by a feather, one red, one gold. The window was open, and a too-cool wind chilled me; at the altitude of this Palace my lightweight suit wasn't enough to keep me warm. So I turned the gold-plated device and closed the window, wondering if some sharpshooter off among the trees might not sound an alarm.

My audience had been set for twelve noon. At five minutes before twelve, a young man in full morning dress came in with the inevitable tea in a gold-circled cup. At exactly twelve, I was motioned into the hall, and through great doors into a huge room. At the other side of the room a grey-haired middle-aged man in a dark suit came toward me with outstretched hand. The Shah motioned me to a seat beside him, and began to talk—the usual, "how are you, how long have you been in Iran," etc.

When I said I would be going to Khuzistan tomorrow, he brought out a pair of dark glasses, though there was no bright light in the room, and said, "Yes, I'm going to Khuzistan tomorrow as well, to inaugurate a petrochemical plant. But it goes much too slowly; much too slowly. We should be much farther along. We can produce chemicals, for fertilizers and plastics, that could compete for international markets on both sides of us. But the development of the land goes much too slowly."

He said he was more than ever committed to the idea of large-scale farming and the industrial processing that should go with it. He gave me credit for pressing for the greatest productivity of the land, and the utilization of Khuzistan's products by processing and marketing. Looking very much concerned, he said, "Yes, that is the road we have determined on. But it is not going fast enough.

"The land is the most important of all assets for us," he said, "that remarkable vast area of Khuzistan. Oil; yes, oil is a great source of revenue. But it will not last forever. Twenty years, fifty years, who knows. One day it will be gone. But the land will be there."

I spoke of the concept which Gordon [Clapp] and I presented to him years ago: exchange the proceeds of an exhaustible resource, oil and gas, for the development of an inexhaustible one, the water and the land.

"I understand," I said, "that your trip to Washington was a considerable success." "Yes," he said rather wearily, "there is no problem between our two *states*. The problem is better understanding between our two peoples."

All through the audience, he kept interjecting what has become familiar in these relations with the King: a great regard and respect, generously and warmly expressed, for me as a person devoted to the welfare of Iran, and certainly not "just another contractor." "A unique relationship," he said.

5:30 P.M.
D&R GUEST HOUSE, ANDIMESHK

A heartening look at what has happened on this vast desert: to think that an idea, a conviction, some toughness and drive, brought about this transformation, and put new light in the eyes of these handsome people.

To the great dam, down the cascading road through those magical tunnels; the great cloud of spray as the spillways poured out the water that has gone through the four turbines; a scamper with a diminutive Iranian agricultural worker—a longtime friend—to see the alfalfa on the trial farm. Said he, "The best quality alfalfa and the most productive in the world; better than California."

A one-and-a-half hour flight in a huge Iranian Army copter, over the lake and back into the upper reservoir. What a cruel landscape those gorges are, so deep and narrow and devilish.

NOVEMBER 7, 1969
ANDIMESHK

What lies immediately ahead, on the time schedule, is the arrival from Tehran of the Big Money Man, Robert McNamara, and a flock of

Ministers. In two helicopters they will see the Dez Project, and particularly the Haft Tapeh "integrated agricultural complex," as it is now being rather loftily and most proudly referred to by the more sophisticated Persians. Only a few years ago it was the cane sugar Lilienthal Folly.

Then dropping into the trial farm at Safiabad—50,000 acres of luscious green. Leo Anderson's◄ and his Iranian associates' best job, I think.

The Shah expressed impatience with the slow pace of agricultural development by large-scale farming, which has now become his fixed policy. The organic sickness of the Iranian bureaucracy: their inability or unwillingness to take action so that things can move is largely responsible for this.

What stunned me yesterday was to find that only vague plans were referred to for building village centers for the peasants who will be moved from the lands to be used for large-scale farms. To move these people off their land before alternatives are actually in being and before the new proprietors are established will indeed produce problems.

The human needs of these people must be given the highest priority. If large-scale operation will result in increased productivity, and if the people of this country, all down the line, will share in that increase, individual preferences or even hardships are a part of the price of this kind of transformation.

Out of my TVA experience come many analogies: when a new dam's gates were closed and the water rose, East Tennessee farmers who had lived on their own land, and their grandfathers' before them, had to move. Their farms, and their families' graves would be under one hundred feet of water. But since the building of these TVA dams was part of the rebuilding of the life of the people of the region, the individual farmer's unhappiness wasn't allowed to stop the bringing of benefit to a whole region. TVA did something about this human problem: long before the water began to rise alternatives were developed by TVA's assistant "county agents." The displaced farmers weren't just handed their money for their land and told to shift for themselves.

NOVEMBER 8, 1969
ISPAHAN

Attended a luncheon given by the University of Ispahan's new young chancellor for the McNamaras. McNamara is famous for his machine-gun volley of questions, questions, questions, calling for numbers and percentages.

◄Former D&R chief representative in Iran.

"I'm on my way to the Ivory Coast from here," I said.

"Yes, I know about what you are doing. President Houphouet-Boigny told me of the problem of moving 90,000 villagers and I asked him who was assisting in this work. When he said David and his firm were engaged to do this I was very pleased, for it is not just an economic but a social problem of great difficulty."

Leaning forward across the table and talking directly to the young crew-cut pipe-smoking chancellor, Dr. Montamedii, McNamara said: "David's firm has the responsibility to plan the resettlement of 90,000 villagers who will be forced to leave their ancestral homes in the Ivory Coast because of the construction of a big dam on the Bandama River."

The chancellor looked hard at me. "Ninety thousand—that is a prodigious human problem. They are probably like the villagers in our country. They feel themselves a part of the land."

I said, "It is not a question where you just send in an experienced land buyer; we learned that in the TVA. The men we sent to work this out with the to-be-displaced farmers had to sit down and get acquainted. Efficiency isn't the whole thing; it is a job that calls for compassion and patience."

McNamara picked this up. "Not just saying: 'Here is the appraisal of the land, and here is the money.' "

NOVEMBER 9, 1969
ISPAHAN

I ought to record something of the pleasure and delight we have had in revisiting this jewel of a city. Didn't Sacheverell Sitwell, in his poetic book *Honeycombs and Arabesque,* call it the most beautiful city in the world?

Of all the efforts to reproduce an ancient exotic atmosphere and style in modern terms, I feel that this hotel, the Shah Abbas, is the only fully successful one. An ancient Persian caravanserai was on this site, and its plan, a hollow square, has been maintained. From each room, one looks out on a garden of roses and a reflecting pool. In this quadrangle years ago the merchants using the caravan route parked their camels and stored their goods, where they could keep an eye on them against robbers. The lacework of doorways to each apartment is without a blemish of tawdry showiness.

The great mosques of Ispahan are as beautiful as tradition depicts them. The majestic Palace of the great Shah Abbas, its slender pillars upholding the platform where he watched polo games being played in the open square.

Yesterday we wandered through the musty, covered bazaar, examining objects also "covered," with dust, and observing the lupine faces of the haggling merchants. Big-eyed alert-looking young boys rush by carrying trays of steaming tea; half the men seem to be squatting over brass or silver, tap, tap, tapping designs. The whole place is about as quiet as my Whitehall Street office these months of incessant building all around us.

NOVEMBER II, 1969
TEHRAN

Dinner last evening was a delightful interlude in the high-pressure life of the last eleven days. A family meal with Ahmad Ahmadi, his American wife, and their three beautiful young children.

Ahmadi was one of D&R's first staff men active in the early D&R days, in agriculture. A big, bulky Persian with a reflective mind; now, Deputy Minister for Natural Resources (which includes fisheries).

The *Journals* have fascinated him; he spoke of them again last night. "After reading some of those entries I have often thought about the contrast between autobiography and a journal such as you have written. I admire the fact that you have let the record stand more or less as it was at the time. A memoir or autobiography tells what a man thinks about what has happened in his life but only at one moment of time; he rewrites his whole life in the light of the values he has at the time he writes, usually long, long after most of the events and ideas that have shaped him.

"But you chose to let the man tell of his values and ideas and hopes as a process of change. A man isn't the same throughout his life; it is the way he changes and becomes many men that is fascinating to me and that doesn't appear in a memoir or autobiography.

"Not always true, of course. I have read all of Gide's journals, in the original French. He doesn't change throughout his life; same man. That is in contrast to your *Journals,* which show the evolution of a man."

Yesterday's meeting with Mehdi Samii revealed again how charming and warm he is. A good friend.

I noted Samii considers himself someone who should express disagreement to the Shah, and occasionally to me, when he feels it is essential. As guardian of the development funds, he really *must* do this, for the King wants to do everything, and do it now, whether Iran has the revenues or not.

Ebtehaj says that the Shah loads too many "jobs of all kinds" on Samii. He had the chief responsibilities for the elaborate coronation arrangements of last year, including negotiations with Van Cleef and Arpels, the great jewelers, in the design of the very brilliant new crown for the Empress.

I said, with indignation, that the agricultural budget had not yet been approved, though we were halfway or more through the current year; this required D&R to carry almost $400,000 of expenditures on their behalf, some of them due over a period of eighteen months!

"D&R will just stop providing services that Iran says it can't afford to buy. But we need a decision and I propose that we have it now."

My guess is that within ten days or less we will get that approval and the overdue funds will begin to flow. If not, I can't at this moment predict *what* will happen about D&R's posture here.

What Samii wanted to talk about was his concern about large-scale agribusiness.

"This has the seeds of great trouble for this country," he said. "There are places where if we moved farmers off the land they own and put it into an agricultural corporation to be managed as a consolidated operation, there would be great social unrest.

"In parts of Khuzistan, where the conditions are good for large-scale farming, where the peasants own very little really, this might work. But to start this all over Iran would put an intolerable burden on our funds —for they will need much money for services, credit, management, and so forth." I agreed.

To my mind, the most sensitive of all the questions about our efforts to increase agricultural productivity and its marketing and industrial components (or consequences) continues to be: what about the people, the peasants?

What we now propose in Persia is to provide *consolidated* or large-scale agriculture in lieu of small and inadequate tracts that resulted largely from the mistaken (I think) and fervid slogans of the "land reform" legislation of only a few years ago. I said we knew this approach was an experimental one; that it should be undertaken much as the pilot area in the Dez was, with a few prototypes.

Helen and I have just returned from a party which an innocent-looking, printed card described as a dinner in honor of Mr. and Mrs. David E. Lilienthal given by Mr. and Mrs. Ebtehaj at their home.

But such a "home": a palace in splendor and size. And such a party: nearly one hundred and fifty people at a sit-down dinner. As to the regal splendor of the house itself, I can only quote Mr. Arbuthnot, who said, "It boggles." "What boggles?" "The mind."

The Minister of Finance, Jamshid Amouzegar, a tense, aquiline, youngish man, rushed to me to tell me of a comment by His Majesty at a luncheon yesterday at the Palace given by the King for Bob McNamara. "Have you heard what was said?" No, I hadn't. "Well, I found it very moving; I have never heard the Shah say anything so warm and heartfelt about *anyone;* it just isn't his nature to pay compliments."

Reza Ansari, formerly Minister of the Interior, a great friend, brilliant co-architect of the Khuzistan undertaking, has been appointed by the Shah to be the "personal representative" of the King's twin sister, the Princess Ashraf. He is to be her administrative officer in charge of a wide range of charitable and educational activities in which the Royal Family is involved and the Princess and the Shah deeply concerned.

Reza said to me, "I want your help and your drive and your ideas."

Uppermost in his mind was the establishment of a new university, named after one of the oldest educational institutions in Persia, Jondi Shapur.

Reza's idea—and the Princess's—is that Jondi Shapur be located in the heart of Khuzistan, on a hundred-hectare tract. It should be primarily an agricultural college, "the largest and the best in Iran." Reza wants help in interesting a "well-known American of great reputation to advise on how to go about making this a great university."

What I thought most important was having such a college or university in the heart of the "new agribusiness center of the world," next door to our trial farm at Safiabad. "Not the old conventional agricultural training of the land-grant colleges, but a new kind of education and of research related to the future transformation of agriculture into a link between the land, the people, and technology," said I, with an assurance, that, afterward, I thought pretty cocky.

NOVEMBER 12, 1969
ROME AIRPORT, TAKING OFF FOR PARIS

Hold everything about serious issues: surrounded by a flock of photographers, Gina Lollobrigida has just come aboard, accompanied by what the columnists call "her constant companion, a Mr. Kauffman." She I recognize. Such eyes, encircled by eyelashes out to here. And the husky voice of the slightly dated but still very considerably stacked movie actress. A good, spirited one, too, as I remember her last film.

NOVEMBER 13, 1969
PARIS, LE BOURGET AIRPORT, AWAITING PLANE TO IVORY COAST

On our way through Paris we met with our French partners—the initials are OTAM—in the Ivory Coast village relocation project. OTAM spelled out is L'Omnium Technique d'Aménagement.

We were met by a most British gal from their Paris office who said Mr. Pick, an OTAM partner, would take us to dinner. I assumed we would go around the corner to some little bistro on the Rue Montelambert for a quickie. Instead of which, Pick and his wife, and an associate, M. Prud'homme, and his wife, arrived at 8:30. After a leisurely drink, we were taken to Maxim's, that famous and wickedly expensive restaurant.

Despite the most ugly possible decor, Maxim's *was* impressive, for one reason: the Duke and Duchess of Windsor a couple tables away. With them a noisy, raucous, bald American businessman and his repulsively shrill wife, she complete with last year's wig.

EN ROUTE TO THE IVORY COAST

Below us, under a still burnished sun, the sands of the great Sahara of Mauritania, tawny wavelets of a quiet sea. Soon the westernmost bulge of Africa.

On this plane eleven severe, even stern, men, all dressed exactly alike, in dark grey jackets, high at the neck, big outside pockets; over the left breast a round red badge, with the profile of a corpulent man who has changed our contemporary world, Chairman Mao. They are completely silent, at least in the presence of the other passengers.

These are the very first Communist Chinese I have seen. It is not my imagination only, for Helen too said they gave her a bit of a chill—something about the impassive look on their faces.

NOVEMBER 14, 1969
YAMOUSSOUKRO, IVORY COAST

In New York several weeks ago Minister Diawara exacted a promise from me that I would come to the Ivory Coast on this special and particular date, the 14th of November. *Not* the 13th, nor the 15th, nor later, in January. On that date the President of the Republic would be presiding over a nationwide celebration of the beginning of construction of the Kossou Dam.

We got to this town on this day—the President's home town, his country palace being close by—by a dash from Iran. But when we drove up to the access road to be present at the celebration, the road was barred by half-hysterical Italian workers of the firm of Impregilo, the constructors, and a hundred local police. The hysteria because the President was about to set off a blast of dynamite, which had nothing whatever to do with the dam construction but was a good show.

NOVEMBER 16, 1969
ABIDJAN, IVORY COAST

On the long drive back from Yamoussoukro through the dense dust of the back roads we passed through a village all decorated with crude arches to greet the President et al. as they went on to the Kossou damsite. Their dancing made a gay and lively tableau.

I asked that we stop at a small village where the market was in full swing. I learn a good deal by such simple markets. The quantity of *plastic* materials—containers, sandals, etc.—continues to increase. The steaming big kettles of food, much of it made from cassava; the little babies on their mothers' backs, their heads lolling in sleep, and with baby brother obviously on the way in the bulge in front; these are conventional enough. What fascinated me in this market were stacks of many-colored bits of glass. These were identified as Venetian glass beads of perhaps the 17th century, produced in quantities for trade with the natives, at a time when many of them were selling other "natives" as slaves. And great heaps of whitened cowry shells, once almost the sole currency. *And* a whole stack of faded blue jeans.

The Kossou Dam is being paid for by America and Italy. Half by the Export-Import Bank—Kaiser Engineering having talked that bank into the loan, after the World Bank took a negative view of its economics. The other half by Italy, for Impregilo, the same Italian construction consortium that built the Pahlavi Dam for us on the Dez.

When I returned yesterday afternoon Helen had read a letter from my cousin Bernardine and sadly said I should read it now. My heart has been chilled and desperately hurt ever since. Bernardine's only child, Rosemary, had killed herself.

Bernardine has been a part of my life, one of its most important influences, since I was a boy of thirteen and she a rebellious young woman of eighteen (but more experienced of life's intensities and crises than most women of thirty).

Poor dead Rosemary. For fifteen years or more, an alcoholic, a recluse. Her story made all the more tragic by the contrast with her gaiety as a child, and as a glamorous young woman. One of New York's most sought-after photographers' models, her head sculptured by Epstein, her swains rich playboys. And then the great love affair with John Meston, who became a most successful TV writer (*Gunsmoke* made him a millionaire). Their divorce, and then down and down. Many attempts at suicide, now a "successful" one.

NOVEMBER 18, 1969
ABIDJAN

Helen and I have just dined with the President of the Ivory Coast, Houphouet-Boigny, at his elegant residence. "Not the Palace," he said; "we like this quiet place better." Quiet it is, but as grand as can be imagined. The other guests were the President of the Bandama Valley Authority, Aoussou Koffi, and Len Langeland of D&R, who interpreted (and extrapolated too, I have no doubt) and did it beautifully.

When our car arrived the President stepped out to greet us, a short, quiet, and very neat man, with a sad face, heavy eyelids as if he were quite tired, a face that occasionally broke out into a charming, twinkling laugh.

Dining on dishes embossed in gold. Helen remarked afterward: "Quite a long way from the bush" (where we were so recently).

I reported to the President the points I had made this afternoon in a two-hour session with Koffi and his staff about the Kossou Dam project relocation problems. These are very grave, large in scale (from 90,000 to 120,000 people to relocate, in a hurry, for the water behind the dam now being constructed will rise within a couple years).

The President said, "I was in Washington when President Kennedy was alive—and we still mourn for him—I told him I had discussed development with Mr. Lilienthal. President Kennedy said, 'Mr. Lilienthal is himself a development program.' "

He explained that his wife was in Paris seeing her doctor. Helen, at his right, said, "My husband has told me how beautiful your wife is." He smirked, as any well-brought-up husband will when his spouse is so spoken of.

Dinner over, we again sat in the large drawing room. The President signaled to a retainer, who returned with a dark oblong box which he handed to Helen and, with a small-boy smile, helped her open it. Inside, a heavy rather ornate gold bracelet. "As a souvenir," he said, "from the Ivory Coast."

In the wide glass-enclosed foyer, a gleaming Venus de Milo, half life-size, on a pedestal, standing alone; as white as the whitest alabaster. When you are sure of yourself, in a black republic, you don't need to insist that the Venus should be black or brown, she can be white.

An appealing figure, the President. The country has certainly progressed in an extraordinary way under him. The word is that he can pour it on when things don't go to suit him. But none of the flamboyance of Kenyatta or Nkrumah, none whatever. What is the source of his extraordinary authority in the country?

NOVEMBER 19, 1969
FLYING TO DAKAR

A "working session" had been scheduled by Aoussou Koffi for 4 o'-
clock, yesterday, my last day in the Ivory Coast. I knew that the Authority's staff "advisors" from several French companies, and from D&R and
OTAM, would be present.

Koffi had met with all of his advisors, last night, and said his own
staff were "all a bunch of idiots—we had done nothing, nothing, nothing."

So, in this atmosphere, I went to the table at Koffi's left. Koffi began
with a warm personal comment about me. What impressed him were two
things about Mr. Lilienthal: first, that TVA "should be centered about
man"; and second, that Mr. Lilienthal was glad that he was thought of
as Chairman of TVA rather than head of the atom bomb project.

Koffi invited me to say what I thought should be done about the
Bandama River Valley, the Kossou "barrage," the problem of relocation
of the people which is required by the rising water of the barrage, and
the prospects of the entire region.

With such an assignment, I said I have for so long been scornful of
perfectionist "experts." What I believed came out of long experience and
strong feeling about the "study" phobia (and of all the members of
the study tribe, the precise, over-logical French types are about the
worst).

That a dam should be built on this site, that the people living in the
area to be flooded should be resettled has been settled; for the dam was
now under construction. Finding new homes for 90,000, perhaps 120,000
people and scores of villages, an enormous task, had to be done. Time did
not permit minute and over-detailed studies.

"First things first. We are dealing not with an academic exercise or
theory, but with some hard facts, and with little time to meet one of the
largest movements of people in my knowledge," I said.

I had some definite proposals to make:

"First, begin now with the task of moving the people, their resettlement; do not wait out the nine-month period of study provided by our
contract and the contractual scope of work. Revise that schedule completely, so that by January 1, or February 1 at the latest, the first villages
will be moved to areas on the perimeter; set as a goal the movement of
not less than four villages by March; this will be a considerable fraction
of the 10,000 people who will have to be resettled by March 1971. The dam
will not be completed until 1974, but the water level by March 1971 will
be quite high.

"The first resettlement should be before the waters have risen because villagers will become fearful if they begin to see the waters rise while they are still in their villages. The emotional problem can only be met, in part, by the earliest kind of action.

"I propose that the Authority prepare an early pilot demonstration of how the resettlement of *all* will be carried out. The mistakes in the first effort can be observed and perhaps corrected as to later resettlement.

"I particularly advise against too great precision. Peasants are far more adaptable, have far more ability to adjust and work out their problems, than experts generally give them credit for.

"In these demonstrations some of the benefits of moving to new locations can be demonstrated. For example, provide the village with electricity, long before power from the dam is available, by a small portable generator, perhaps. And similarly, provide fertilizer.

"Some of the village people, particularly the younger ones, should be told about the opportunities for settling in the almost unoccupied southwest, where D&R years ago made a careful study of the possibilities of that large area. The villagers should be given a choice, to the fullest possible extent, of staying within the same area—i.e., the Kossou perimeter—or given incentives to settle in the southwest.

"In resettling emphasize the human and emotional side, not the scientific, that is, the precise kind of land—which is what most of the work in the past six weeks has been concerned with."

One man pointed to an area on the map: in this area to be flooded many of the people depend upon their coffee trees. It takes at least four years for a coffee tree to bear. In the meantime these people in their new land would suffer a complete lack of income. Would you say they must be content with that loss?

"Some of the adjustments will be harsh perhaps. There are ways to ameliorate these losses. I would strongly advise against providing people in that situation with a subsidy, for subsidies have a way of becoming permanent, and the burden on the country would be very great. Find a temporary amelioration—many such suggest themselves to your mind, I am sure, as to mine."

There were a number of questions from the "staff" people. The questions asking for answers which gave me the opportunity to bear down on my instinct against overplanning, overprecision in dealing with human problems, emotional problems.

Koffi wrote furiously throughout the perhaps fifteen minutes I talked, in a schoolboy's kind of notebook. When I said that this line of ideas required a change in the schedule of studies, and toward action, his very black, stocky face literally beamed with approval.

"Give action the top priority; but don't forget the economic development plan we must develop."

Then Koffi commented: "You have lighted a lantern for us all." And the meeting was over.

We are now about to leave Dakar for a long, eight-hour nonstop flight to New York.

An hour out across the Atlantic ocean, a sad piece of news, in leafing through *Time.* Ferd Eberstadt dead, suddenly, of a heart attack. A dear friend, a distinctive personality, salty, fun to be with, a great man to work with as I did during the Minerals Separation North American Corporation mergers. I talked to him by phone just before leaving. Lucky though: he died still working, with his business boots on. Me too, I hope.

DECEMBER 3, 1969
NEW YORK

The official historians of the AEC have just published the second volume, titled *Atomic Shield,* covering the beginning days of the AEC and for the succeeding six years.

I have read their account of most of the period when I was the luck-less character trying, as I used to say, "to replace the front wheel of a bicycle while riding it downhill lickity split."

Part of the history is a recitation of the technical problems and ad-ministrative moves that filled that period.

But it is mostly an emotional and dramatic account, written more in the style of a novel than of a staid official history of a government agency. Since they had Volume II of my *Journals (The Atomic Energy Years)* to draw upon, and those recounted, from day to day, my emotional state, of discouragement, disappointment, anger, despair almost, and occasional exulting, much of the account is in that frame: how I felt, as well as what I and the others did.

When I had scanned through this official account of ups and downs, me trying with a five-man group to manage the big decrepit organization, the Manhattan Project, which we had inherited, with kibitzers on every hand, most of them arrogant and ignorant (the effrontery, for example, of the scientific geniuses of the General Advisory Committee, Oppen-heimer the worst of the lot, telling me—an experienced manager—how to manage a large organization!!), I closed the book and said to myself: Only an absolute fool would have tried this AEC job at all, and only a lunatic would have remained on that job for more than a fortnight.

But I did stay on. And as my term ended, the authors of the history made a summing-up: understanding and generous, not for what I did but the spunk I showed in trying to hold to standards in which I believed, against the waves of chaos, secrecy-hysteria, and irresponsible kibitzing, the lot of anyone who tries to run a complex public job in a democratic way.

DECEMBER 8, 1969
NEW YORK

Sitting across from me, as Chairman of the Fund for Multinational Management Education, was Peter Drucker, the famous management expert.

He has built a great reputation about management by the only sure road to such a reputation open to such as he: by *writing* about it, brilliantly, but never putting his precepts to the sweaty test of actual management responsibility.

Strangely enough, the man at that round table of the Fund's board meeting who shows more of the creative sense for what management is all about is a physician. Gabriel Velasquez, of Cali, Colombia. As he talked about putting together all the elements of a community that must go into a health-care program—a subject on which he and his friends in Cali have been working for ten years—I heard the voice of a man who knows how to think and to perform in a modern management sense.

Gabriel, talking about the Cauca Valley, said, to an inquirer: "Yes, it is called CVC, outside the *Valle;* but we still call it Plan Lilienthal."

DECEMBER 9, 1969
NEW YORK

At lunch Jim Conant, looking quite fit, and full of himself, leaned over to me and launched right in: "What did you think of the Philip Stern book about the Oppenheimer case? Before you comment, let me tell you what I think. It is a story of a man that too many people wanted to assassinate, and so they assassinated him. His character anyway. It's a better way than other countries have of disposing of unwanted people, I guess. But Stern presented this story as if this was the normal, usual kind of security investigation, when you and I know it wasn't."

I said I thought the Stern book stuck to the record of the case itself. I agreed it would have given more perspective, would have heightened the effect, if he had spent more space describing the kind of investigation procedure the first Commission set up. "Can you imagine," said I, "given the kind of security regulations we of that AEC established—designed for us by Justice Owen Roberts—that we could have tolerated a cross-examination of Oppenheimer by a *prosecutor* for the later Commission—without an opportunity for the guy being investigated or his counsel being permitted to see the records?"

Jim said he had finished an autobiography. "I give the background of the bomb project that is too often missed. To read some of these things you would think that Oppie built the bomb all by himself. Actually, if you pick one man, it should be Vannevar Bush. *He* had the responsibility."

DECEMBER 15, 1969
NEW YORK

One measure of a man is how he spends his spare time. Mine, I spend, lavishly and with delight, on books and manure. Came back home from the Princeton University Store the other day with almost a hundred dollars' worth of books, then on to Obal's for ten bags of cow manure; had five bags spread over the border, just before a snowfall. I gloat as I think of that manure slowly decomposing during the winter, making the garden soil even more delectable than it was, which was considerable.

DECEMBER 25, 1969
CHRISTMAS DAY
PRINCETON

How can anyone's mind be grooved with mundane worries about his business when the skies on a Christmas day benignly cover the familiar realities with the soothing, gentle cloak of snow? Snow: what greater proof that the Lord dearly loves the earth. And that in spite of the occasional lunacy of its stiff-necked human and animal inhabitants.

I have been admonished, with affection, to lay aside serious thoughts. So I try to think about the garden. Happily, I got it tucked in snug and warm at just the right time—that is, when the ground was for the first time frozen solid. So the roses are heeled up with soil, topped off with a blanket of salt hay. How comforting that is to see.

I took two walks today. How lucky to live an *alternating* life; the human, or inhumane, jamming and excitement of New York City, particularly at Christmas time, and then the outdoor cathedral of open spaces amid which we live on Battle Road.

DECEMBER 31, 1969
PRINCETON

More than at any time I can readily remember I feel that the *end* of a year is not so much an end as a beginning.

Surely a beginning of a new setting for my work. The very discussions of an "alliance" or merger with some large corporate partner injects a note of a new beginning, of starting on an unfamiliar road, risky, not a straight clear road, but with turns and dips unknown. Because it is not familiar and repetitious and comfortable, it will add to the zest of my work and my spirits, and will take me out of the old ways.

My work is by no means the whole of my life. Perhaps less the whole of my life than for many who have reached my age and station and security.

For the new year I feel eager and confident about the more personal side of living. There will be downs and dumps ahead; I am that kind of person. But I view the prospect with a certain joy and fullness of heart. I have learned much about living this last year, and not all of that learning process has been pleasant. But the lessons have not been in vain.

I do not this night feel reflective enough to record a year's-end summary, a custom that goes back many years in the history of these journals. I am too eager, curious and confident about meeting the new year's events to be in a mood for looking back.

III

1970

◦◦◦◦◦◦

Vacation in Guadeloupe—Meetings about proposed
Jondi Shapur University in Iran—DePauw University
Commencement—Trip to Iran

Must D&R "affiliate" with some big outfit? What will happen to this
brave experiment, D&R? What about the magic?

The evidence that D&R does have "magic" comes in all the time. Yet
are we now deliberately seeking to turn this enterprise over to the hands
of probably first-rate businessmen—but third-rate poets of change?

JANUARY 12, 1970
NEW YORK

Sol Linowitz and I had a long visit with André Meyer this morning.
I wanted these two to get together, as two friends, both men with exceptional minds and creative imaginations.

As Sol began talking with André I could see that it wasn't just lack
of financial figures in our presentation to them about D&R that bothered
them. André said, "It will be very difficult to find even two or three men
in a big organization that will understand your unique D&R company.
And they wouldn't have anyone in their big company who could supply
that top management you feel you need. Such men are more than rare;
maybe they don't exist."

Said Sol: "What would concern me most would be if your hotshot

[165]

brainy business advisors found a big company chief who would want David as a flower to wear in his buttonhole, to improve his image."

The first ten minutes between these two great business brains was entirely given over to Jackie Kennedy, André with a dreamy look on his face. How did high-society glamour get into what I assumed would be a discussion between two business geniuses?

We are all human; some humans are just more so than others.

JANUARY 23, 1970
PRINCETON

On the American public scene one should never be surprised at any-thing. Not even when a stuffy, conservative President stands up before a joint session of Congress in the robes—and words—of Gifford Pinchot, Teddy and Franklin Roosevelt, Adlai Stevenson, and Ken Galbraith.

That is approximately what happened yesterday in Nixon's magnifi-cent rhetorical appeal for the preservation of our natural resources and an expression of doubt that *growth* was what America needed, rather than quality.

It is niggardly to ask whether he really means it, or to ask where Nixon was when a beleaguered TVA was in the midst of an overall restoration of a worn-out Valley, or when the cities went completely out of control and into the hands of the real-estate interests. It is enough that last night, as President, he stated the case for a new America.

I tried to say this in my "toward a greater America" speech twenty years ago. This theme is recurrent, this impulse to save and restore. What has been lacking in recent years has been to take the rhetoric seriously, *to do something* about these goals.

When I wrote a letter, in mid-December, to Secretary Rogers sug-gesting a public statement by the President or the Secretary about postwar reconstruction in Vietnam, I didn't really believe anything whatsoever could come of it; lost in the maze of an overburdened State Department.

As it turns out I was quite wrong, and the "arrow I shot into the air" had some effect.

This morning a letter from the Secretary. I quote here one para-graph:

> The subject of postwar reconstruction in Southeast Asia is re-ceiving considerable attention now in the Administration. In this respect, the report of the Development and Resources Corporation and its Vietnamese counterpart on the postwar development of Viet-Nam has been extremely useful.

FEBRUARY 1, 1970
PRINCETON

Our dinner party was to welcome two new neighbors on Battle Road, Walton Butterworth and his wife Virginia. Walton has had a long and exciting career in the Foreign Service.

Another guest, Eugene Wigner. Tiny, bubbling, intense. One of the great scientists of the century, aware of how relatively little judgment he has, or knowledge of public affairs, and yet wanting so badly to do something about political issues that greatly disturb him.

George Kennan was in a warm and outgoing mood. He talked easily about the illusion that being a scholar, sequestered in the cloistered calm of Princeton and the Institute (my characterization, *not* his) would give him plenty of time to himself and his scholarly interests.

"After a few months I began to miss the operational side of life that I had become accustomed to in the Foreign Service. The stimulation of having things to do that I had to do.

"The only time I have to do my writing now is on the weekends. All sorts of people come to see me here," he said, "who think my reputation, deserved or not, means that I have something to say about *current* public issues. If you want to do scholarly work, you can't do it in your home base, which is what Princeton is for me."

FEBRUARY 3, 1970
NEW YORK

Today a choice, priceless letter, written in his distinctive longhand, from Dean Acheson, from Antigua in the Caribbean.

An excerpt:

As I think about the flow of affairs, I am impressed with old Lord Salisbury's point of view—if you are not going to do anything about a matter, hold your tongue about it—"I am not in favor," he said, "of a policy of scold." Another wise thought of his was that the world was happier when the ruling classes in every country could speak no language but their own. Even happier, perhaps, when they spoke little of that. What would you think of a State of the Union message which said only—"It stinks"?

That sounds like Cal Coolidge, which shows what the tropics do to me.

FEBRUARY 15, 1970
CLEARWATER, FLORIDA

How lucky I am that I have a brother who to me is a reminder of how close a blood relation can be. That is Ted to me. It also gives me a sense of the closeness that can exist between men of completely different intellectual and life experience.

Visiting Ted at this "retirement village" I have also had a picture of how it would be if *all younger people disappeared,* and the world were left to the over-middle-aged, affluent but not quite rich. As I studied some of them at a huge eating place yesterday, the men looked like boys who had just been told that "there is no school today."

FEBRUARY 24, 1970
NEW YORK

For a long period I have been severely skeptical that a recession (or depression) of consequence is possible because inflation—i.e., expectations of rising prices in the future—prevents it. This time I'm not so sure. We all may well have a couple years of squeezing, with unemployment of 5% or more. That isn't a "panic" by pre–New Deal standards, but it will be something less than fun just the same.

FEBRUARY 26, 1970
NEW YORK

I wonder if I actually welcome trouble, vicissitudes, and crises. I suffer, goodness knows; but "the abyss" has some kind of fascination of its own. I have learned so many times that it is out of close shaves in my work that I learn, that my ideas fall into place, that my perspective lengthens.

MARCH 2, 1970
GUADELOUPE, FRENCH WEST INDIES

Is it an illusion, the assumption I hold, that I *need* a high level of stimulation to be happy and functioning as a man?

Isn't there *also* a time in the life of a very active, restless, egocentric man, as I am, when he can settle back and contemplate what he has accomplished, reflect upon what he has been up to over the years, speculate about where the world is going? In short, what his whole life has meant.

It is the *"has* meant"—the past tense—that has bothered me most, that I have been most unwilling to face. Is there any other kind of life than that of battling, raising ned, insisting on schedules and deadlines, being critical of others and myself?

MARCH 6, 1970
GUADELOUPE

To our joy, our daughter Nancy is with us here on Guadeloupe. Said Helen: "Nancy has a great capacity for enjoyment."

As her father, I am reassured deeply. For a well-educated young woman to spend most of her time herding her two big sons, running a household, ministering to a professionally critical philosopher husband —i.e., one whose profession is ideas—this is indeed a strenuous life.

MARCH 9, 1970
GUADELOUPE

Yesterday Nancy and I walked to a nearby cemetery. Perched on the ridge overlooking the sea is a random assortment of the most imaginably elaborate homes for the dead, the mausoleums of the well-to-do of what long ago was a very prosperous town. What made it fascinating were the plastic floral "pieces"—huge, complicated, and startlingly lifelike too, adorning everyone.

MARCH 13, 1970
GUADELOUPE

The latest word about our work for Vietnam brings to a close a chapter of my work that as a citizen I couldn't avoid taking on, that I gave all I had to making reasonably successful, if "success" is a word that can be applied to *anything* about Vietnam.

My colleagues are persuaded, as I am, that our corporate development (i.e., "new business") expenditures are inappropriate for a company of our kind.

MARCH 14, 1970
GUADELOUPE

A spirited and satisfactory letter from Beatrice Tobey. Mostly about David Ely's latest book, *Poor Devils.* Barney and she gave it very high praise; likewise its author, the "gutsy, talented, and exciting son . . . you and Helen spawned."

There was a New York touch in the letter too: "Did you see the eclipse? [Total, of the sun.] We saw it in Central Park, surrounded by thousands of hippies, who looked quite surrealistic in that silvery twilight. It was eerie, and I almost believed a bearded pot smoker who kept shouting that it was the end of the world."

It has been a *good* holiday.

We are on a ridge, with trees and grass below our two rooms in the very end of the hotel, and farther below us an inlet of the sea. The waves break ceaselessly against the boulders, with a rhythm like a heartbeat, and a sound that most of the time is a swish, gentle and soothing.

The meals are uniformly splendid French cuisine. "To the French," the bouncy young maître told me, "food is *important*. Meals are important to us, not just to fill the stomach, a time to enjoy and to relax."

MARCH 16, 1970
NEW YORK

As Reza Ansari and I came from the Century dining room, who should greet me but Bob Goheen, president of Princeton, and Kingman Brewster, president of Yale. I introduced Reza to them and explained we had been discussing the establishment of a "brand-new university in Iran" on which he wanted advice from American university leaders.

Said Brewster, a bit on the sour side, "Why a new university? There are a considerable number of old ones in this country that could be had for practically nothing." Presidents of Princeton and Yale, at one time! Reza was impressed.

Reza told me a fantastic story of "troubles with students" now going on in Iran. And showed great concern—as well he might—about the future that this student violence portends. His concern *must* have been based not so much on these "demonstrations" as in using them as a prop for the idea of a new Iranian university. And back of the new university was an idea that shocked me at first.

"Who runs Iran today?" he asked. "It is the Government; and who is the Government? It is the men, like myself, 80% of them anyway, who got their training in American universities. The kind of country Iran now is is because of the fact of American education and American books translated into Farsi used in the Iran universities.

"But what about the *next* ten years? The men being educated in the Iran universities should be using books that have the imprint of Western ideas too; but that may not be the way it will go. This eruption among the students—it was so serious that the Shah ordered the universities closed —shows, I think, that the Communist-Mossadegh influence is still around.

"The Shah divorced Soraya and married Farah, the present Queen. Then the Shah did something without precedent: he changed the Constitution to make the Queen the Regent in the event of his death.

"Now, with Princess Ashraf's initiative and support, Jondi Shapur is to be more than just another new university. Jondi Shapur may be an effort to create a new kind of education, different from that going on in the universities in Iran today."

I spoke of the analogy of the creation of the Weizmann Institute in Palestine. It was conceived as a center for modern technical and cultural training, bringing to all Palestinians, Arab and Jew, the products of European and American traditions and learning, an intellectual oasis for the development of the Middle East.

Similarly Jondi Shapur could extend its influence beyond Iran, throughout the Middle East, I thought.

Would I get together a panel of American university people of the "highest calibre" to meet with the Princess Ashraf, this week or next? I suggested that he ask Doug Knight (now of RCA) to act as the catalyst or arranger of such a meeting.

MARCH 21, 1970
PRINCETON

To a meeting at the Woodrow Wilson School, the participants being students from many colleges and (about equal in numbers) businessmen. The subject, of course: the "sins" of business, pro and con. The young people continue to be harsh and unrelenting, the businessmen present defensive.

Joe Barr, now president of a big bank in Washington, D.C., made a spirited talk. Mostly he drew upon his own experience as a Congressman from Indiana and as Under Secretary, later, briefly, Secretary of the Treasury.

A sample gem:

"After the Cuban crisis debacle, Jack Kennedy said to us at a high-level meeting: 'We have got to take people's minds off Cuba, so let's go to the moon.' A twenty-five-billion-dollar distraction." A wave of incredulity swept the audience. "I know that's the way it was; I was *there.*"

MARCH 26, 1970
NEW YORK

Her Highness, the Princess Ashraf, is not only small, but diminutive and dainty. But the strength of the woman, and the quickness—i.e., perception, the ability to go right to the heart of a question—is a rare quality in anyone.

The occasion for these comments is the meeting with her this noon, and luncheon at her New York residence. The subject: the proposed new university, Jondi Shapur. The other American guests were Doug Knight;

Jim Killian, Chairman of the Corporation of MIT; Professor Maurice Peterson, an agricultural expert of Davis, California; and two Iranians, Reza Ansari and the head of the Ministry of Higher Education, Rhnama.

The Minister of Education went off in a rhapsody about what this university could be thirty years from now, a center of culture for the entire Middle East. The Princess stepped in, with a smile: "Yes, but first, what will it mean to my country?"

I put in my non-royal oar to similar effect: "If we don't have things going in thirty months, there may be nothing apparent in thirty years."

APRIL 12, 1970
PRINCETON

I shouted up the study stairs to Helen: "It doesn't take an army. It takes one good man."

The "man" I was talking about was Joe Sir, the merchant-statesman of Fayetteville, Tennessee.

Without Sir's persistent campaigning on the issue, the present TVA board wouldn't have changed its position—as I have just learned it has —for the one I openly favored back in 1960 and 1961, about the necessity of developing the tributary streams.

APRIL 19, 1970
PRINCETON

Wednesday noon a long luncheon meeting, with Rodman Rockefeller, Nelson's eldest son, and President of International Basic Economy Corporation (IBEC).

Rockefeller is very tall, his hair streaked with grey and worn long, a good strong voice, rather high-pitched, eyes set close together in a long narrow face. Greatly interested in the details of the unusual company— IBEC—his father established some twenty years ago.

Nelson set out to establish through IBEC that improving the way of living of ordinary people, in Latin America particularly, could be done through private profit-making business, in the production and especially the distribution of food, which in this case has meant supermarkets, and later large-scale growing of poultry and expertise in poultry genetics.

I explained to Rodman that I had suggested we get acquainted because the stated overall objectives of IBEC and D&R appear much the same. "Though, of course, IBEC is a huge undertaking, very large, and D&R by comparison is quite small."

I suggested that there might be areas where D&R has expertise that could be usefully employed by IBEC. I kept away from any thought that there might be an "affiliation."

Two aspects of D&R particularly interested Rockefeller, who had apparently been doing some studying about D&R. One was our "regional approach"; the other was the interaction of one aspect of development upon every other—what we call the unified approach, what they said was "integration."

Rockefeller looked thoughtful as he said: "We haven't gone at our efforts in that way; particularly we have, I think, tended to neglect the regional approach, and that has been a weakness."

MAY 2, 1970
PRINCETON

The fullness of spring today! And in Princeton this is as near Paradise as mortals are vouchsafed. After an overlong cold, wet pre-spring, a prolongation really of winter, the garden has opened its heart to a summer sun—80°. The flowering dogwood and magnolias and the ruddy early crab (the malus), the peony stalks reaching up and up—the whole orchestra of growth, so moving.

A sad note, a frustrating note for me: because of a strained neck vertebra, I continue to wear this damned foam-rubber collar, and am under instructions *not* to do any gardening. A dire sentence. Helen has taken over the garden, putting in plants by the dozens.

Yesterday, out here, dictated a draft of the DePauw Commencement speech I'm to give in three weeks.

The speech's theme is a radical one, one I have been thinking about for a long time: that a period such as ours today, a period of conflict, of tension, of shaking up, of examining anew every institution, is indeed a great time to be alive. Because it means we must be functioning, thinking, and doing.

MAY 8, 1970
NEW YORK

Dean Acheson, private citizen, said last evening, his voice still drifting off in a high note at the end of his sentences. "It wasn't enough for the Nixon Administration to be able to evoke emotion in order to provide leadership in a government; you have to know how to 'manage' a government." (I pricked up my ears at his use of one of my favorite words about change—i.e., the need to know how to lead it and how to manage it.) "Jack

Kennedy didn't know the first thing about how to run a country, and neither did the people he had around him."

About the "disorders" among students at his beloved Yale, Dean said, his mustache fairly quivering, "You can't stay ahead of the young; while you are trying to be popular with them one day, the next day they have gone around three corners ahead of you."

MAY 11, 1970
NEW YORK

Our granddaughter Pamela's visit in Princeton was enchanting. How good to have a young person around, in the relaxed, natural atmosphere of a home where she feels loved, not bossed or lectured or told what to do and not to do.

We talked and talked, Pam and I, mostly she. This time she was most articulate. Far from my counseling her, on how she should live, *she* got after me, in the sweetest way, about my mending *my* ways. By which she means: "Grandfather, why do you have to work so hard? Can't you get other people to do what you are doing? Why don't you set aside part of every day for fun, and doing nothing, or play, instead of pounding away all week and then doing the same on the weekend?"

MAY 12, 1970
NEW YORK

The men I see from the window of my office on Whitehall across the way are building two more great iron skeletons. They have been having *their* say, *their* protest, *their* dissent. Friday they set out to tell the young "protesters" what they thought—and the way they did it was with their fists and their boots, smashing into the "kids" with brutality. The construction workers' way of "expressing" themselves is about in the same category as that of the kids, with their rock throwing, and taunting the police with provocative obscenities.

MAY 25, 1970
CRAWFORDSVILLE, INDIANA

My 50th Reunion, and the Commencement address I labored over so much, have come and gone. I went through the usual low period, feeling that all that time and effort and straining to make a worthwhile speech are wasted. Followed almost always by a sense of satisfaction, of something boldly spoken and done as well as I know how. What is life about anyway, if one is willing to do only those chores that have been measured out carefully, calling for no more effort than the foreseeable results warrant?

What wasn't a gesture was the radical tone of my speech, in the heart of the most conservative part of the most conservative region in America.

The faces of the students were hard to decipher. In the front row among the graduates, two beautiful golden-haired girls, who had sensibly removed their slippers and were cooling their toes in the grass. I assumed, I hope correctly, their minds were far, far away from the serious "problems" and "challenging questions" I was talking about. But the men, some of them, looked at me quizzically—is this old geezer saying what I *think* he is saying?

Was reassured this morning, though. A tall, earnest-looking man said he had a daughter in the graduating class, and she was "inspired," she told her father. "I think we parents are doing a better job than we used to; maybe our children forced us into it, but that's not so bad. My daughter told me that her brother went to Washington to tell our Michigan Senator just how he felt. Our son was afraid I would strongly disapprove, and didn't want to tell me what he had done. It's pretty bad when our children are afraid of us for doing what is right."

So I get evidence that words, if they grow out of having "been there," may be more effective and useful than I imply.

Was this because I sensed that so radical a declaration as my speech would be resisted, or not understood, or was it that I was, unconsciously, trying to identify myself with the rebels of the younger generation, or to demonstrate my own gusto and relish that we had a chance to revitalize dead institutions or my eagerness to cut myself off from the noisy student sloganeers?

The strongest impression I had in looking at that sampling of students is that puzzled look. "Say, this is what *we* are saying; so how come that old boy is saying it?"

NOON

FLYING TO NEW YORK FROM INDIANA

Had an impromptu visit this morning with the new president of Wabash College, Thaddeus Seymour. It was more than a visit, sitting there in the lobby of the handsome Wabash College library: it was a rare experience. A huge young man with an outgoing manner, a shrewd but not calculating look, obviously one who considers education the most important task he could possibly be committed to—and this he expressed more by his manner than by a single self-serving phrase. He will give those eight hundred young men at Wabash the best kind of leadership—leadership by example.

His warmth of feeling about the Middle West, and particularly Indiana, greatly impressed me. (Seymour is one of those few people who can say that they were born on the island of Manhattan.) Bit by bit I'm changing my own picture of Indiana from one of being somewhat defensive about coming from the Middle West.

"The change of tempo here in Indiana is just right, I think," Seymour said. "I find there is much more to Indiana than I knew. In fact, I'm glad that Wabash is considered an Indiana college, rather than a national one."

I reflected on this very perceptive shorthand way of saying something basic. The draining to the Eastern Seaboard of the brains and energy of the middle country has bothered me for a long time. Particularly since I might be said to be one of the prime examples of the hegira, the exodus from middle America to the metropolis. Not entirely, though: I went from a small town to Chicago; before I found myself in New York I had worked on behalf of state government in Wisconsin, and of the South in the Tennessee Valley.

Part of the joy of this trip was the visit Sunday evening with Helen's longtime friends, Esther Roach and her sister, Gladys Otto. Who stole the show, for me, was the girls' mother, Dolly. Her approaching birthday is her 95th. A wisp of a tiny woman, but such a personality! How conscious she is of the presence of a *man*—as it happens, a most impressionable man when women are concerned. A little coquette, I thought. And a charming one. What spunk. And endurance. She sat up through the several hours of visit we had at dinner and afterward, without any sign of fatigue, hearing every syllable, putting in an occasional sharp comment. As I said goodbye I leaned way over and kissed her hand as if she were an elderly queen. But the feminine radiance from this very old lady really called for a sturdy masculine embrace.

JUNE 12, 1970
PRINCETON

"General Greenbaum died in his sleep at 1:30 this morning."

Dr. Haynes told me, "He had lost all enjoyment of life so it would be hypocritical of me to say that I am sorry." How greatly I will miss the vigorous-minded gentle friend whose "Sunday companionship" I had come to depend on so much, and relish.

Both Helen and I think mostly about Dorothea—"Dottsie." She is a strong and doughty person, but after a lifetime with so distinctive a personality as Eddie, one does not just go on as if nothing much has happened.

Helen and I were so pleased that at considerable cost of effort and courage, the General came to our garden party a few weeks ago. Seated in a chair in our living room, he greeted the many Princeton people who admired him. It is a pleasant memory of Eddie Greenbaum.

A phone call from Senator Albert Gore. "Dave, I want you to raise some money for my campaign, there in New York. The Nixon and Wallace people are out to get my scalp."

"Why should people be for you?"

"Wa-a-l, against the Vietnam war, you know, and my opposition to Nixon's nominee for the Supreme Court, Carswell—that was really a civil rights fight." I said I would co-sponsor some "receptions" for him for fund raising, beginning next week.

My chief reason for trying to help Albert is that he is one of the young generation of politicos who stood up for TVA, and fought McKellar and the old way in Tennessee politics generally. The way in which he expressed his views in opposition to Johnson on the war I thought, at the time, extreme. But I do believe that in choosing whom to support in public matters one should not insist that the man's views and votes and position on every issue be exactly as you yourself see them. The perfectionist is the dogmatist.

JUNE 15, 1970
NEW YORK

There are many, many good people in this world: I pass them on the streets, in the subway, every day. But of great men who have left their mark of greatness on the world there are mighty few.

Spent an hour this late afternoon with one of these rare spirits, David Morse. For twenty-two years he has been head of unquestionably the most effective international UN agency, the International Labour Organisation, operating out of Geneva. I can't remember when an institution has ever received a Nobel Prize, and yet this is what happened last year, a tribute to this remarkable man's guiding hand, organizational genius, and warm personality.

He is a slender figure of a man, baldish, uses his eyes to emphasize and underline points, much as Felix Frankfurter did. In some ways he reminds me of Felix, in manner, in the bounce of his mind. But a steadier and a far more sagacious man, I would say.

When I was in TVA, David, then a quite young man, was chief counsel of the Petroleum Labor Policy Board. The chairman of the board, Billie Leiserson, "seconded" Morse to TVA to help us work out collective bargaining and grievance procedures with the large labor force of TVA. Morse made a great impression on me for his understanding of my point that TVA would be judged as much by the effectiveness and democracy of its collective dealings with labor as by the grandeur of its dams or the innovations of its power operations.

Then, when I was AEC Chairman, we had a serious problem with labor relations. Each of our contractors—the work was almost entirely done through large companies—had different concepts of labor relations. Some very bad.

David, who was by then Under Secretary of Labor, brought together a group of advisors: George H. Taylor, professor of industrial relations at the University of Pennsylvania; Lloyd K. Garrison; as well as himself.

This was the beginning of the structure of AEC labor relations under the most difficult possible circumstances. But we went at this problem in a sensitive—and successful—way.

JULY 4, 1970
MARTHA'S VINEYARD

The "young" people are very much in evidence on this island. They arrive with sleeping bags and primitive tents to camp out in the woods and to be driven off by the police. Pam, speaking very slowly and gently, says the people of the island are "hostile to anyone who is young." The people of the island point to the vandalism of the past couple years, the "scruffy and dirty appearance" of many of the young, the weird appearance of many, the men with their hair frizzed out, the girls in the most shabby clothes they can find. "No Bare Feet" is a sign one sees on almost every store.

Here on this hilltop, shrouded in a deep and mysterious fog, Helen and I are isolated from all this. We seem as remote as if this were a retreat in the Himalayas.

The big news is Leona Baumgartner Elias' recent marriage to Alex Langmuir. Day before yesterday we went to a party in honor of the newly married at Joe and Trudi Lash's, overlooking Menemsha bight.

Leona *looked* as a bride should look; stars in her eyes, her hair crowned with a tiara of island leaves. Langmuir is a tall man, also in his middle sixties, a world-famous expert in epidemics.

I love Leona so, both for her toughness of fibre and for her femininity, which she sustains despite having administered big public health jobs where she was the boss over many men—quite a trick that is.

JULY 8, 1970
MARTHA'S VINEYARD

Now I'm seventy-one. The old phrase was: after seventy he's living on borrowed time. But it is also the accepted folklore about age that one does not himself sense that he is "old." Not even when he notices how many men of very active lives, his contemporaries, marched steadily across the obit page within the year past.

JULY 10, 1970
MARTHA'S VINEYARD

Day before yesterday, July 8, Scotty Reston's mile-long Continental came rolling up our hill. I was at the bottom of our deck to greet him. He hardly looked at me; opened the car door, scurried out and started toward the path to our guest house, saying, over his shoulder: "Hi, my friend. Do you know you have a wild turkey or a pheasant or something here?" And then we both watched our avian conversation piece, the brilliantly colored ring-necked pheasant—whom we call Phineas—who has adopted us. He was definitely posing, showing off his profile, his scarlet neck and purple head resplendent in the late afternoon sun. Having made his vain point, he resumed eating cracked corn and seeds of grass.

"The most influential newspaperman in America today" climbed our steps, and we settled down for almost two hours of talk. I soon learned that this was an "interview." I assumed it was not for the *Times* but for the *Gazette,* which has become not only his and Sally's "property" but a source of great satisfaction.

Show me a newspaperman who has never had this fantasy: to run a "country newspaper." Of course the *Vineyard Gazette* is in many ways remote from the conventional "small-town newspaper" which I knew or worked on as a reporter in my youth: the *Valparaiso Vidette,* the *Michigan City News,* the Mattoon whatever it was called. But not different in every way, for the personals, dear to the heart of small-town subscribers, are the same.

What distinguishes the *Gazette* is the quality of its editorship, and that means Henry Beetle Hough. And now, of its publisher, Reston. Its subscribers are also the sophisticated or the literary or famous people who come to this island in the summer season.

As Scotty saw the big birthday greeting card Helen had put at my place at lunch, he said: "Is this your birthday? Just 'interviewed' Nelson [Rockefeller] and this is his birthday too. When I took some pictures of Nelson with this Polaroid of mine, Happy said: 'After all these years of having his picture taken, Nelson is always self-conscious,' and he agreed.

It goes back to the time he went off to enter Dartmouth; his father said, 'If I ever see your picture in the newspapers while you are a student up there, I'll cut off your semester's allowance.' Happy insisted this left a mark on him about picture taking ever since."

A big notebook on his lap, Scotty began talking to me about why I was optimistic. "I feel that way too," he said, with a stern, intent frown of concentration. "But it's a feeling, an emotion. I just don't believe, inside me, that this country is falling apart, that it is 'disintegrating,' as John Gardner said in his Illinois Legislature speech the other day. Your optimism speech at DePauw didn't get any newspaper coverage to speak of, while John's story of doom was front page in the *Times.*"

"A gloomy prediction of catastrophe always gets top billing in the news and on TV. The same with stories of violence and so on. Something optimistic or what might be called 'good news' just isn't news," I said.

Scotty interrupted to agree, and to explain why this was pretty largely true.

"Most reporters," he said, "began covering police courts; in my case, sports. That meant they went to the police headquarters for their stories, looked at the blotter of arrests, and there was their story. Of course, the arrests were about violence. I think that is changing; it is changing because more and more reporters are coming straight to the city room from Harvard or wherever, and they have the background to understand more complicated subjects; in fact, many of them are more qualified than the Foreign Service or government people they cover. When I took over the news of the *Times* a while back, I named a man to be the 'good news' editor; there are always plenty of good things going on."

Getting back to my reasons for optimism, besides this feeling inside of me, I said that just to have a feeling, a conviction about America, "that's not good enough, that kind of emotional reaction. It's up to those of us who feel strongly that way to point to the evidence, to have reasons as well as feeling."

"Your reason," Scotty said, "is that you see the country in turmoil, but you believe that out of turmoil good things come, greater strength."

I said I would prefer another word but would settle for "turmoil." The opposite of such turbulence and controversy and even violence is a prescription for staleness and absence of creativeness. That we have had before, and aplenty. "Remember the silent generation of college students not so long ago; that was something to be worried about, because nothing good comes out of bland acquiescence, the opposite of what we have today, what you called 'turmoil.' "

Without disagreeing, he brought me back to the reason I find that the upset conditions in the country are actually signs of health "provided,"

I put in, "we are on the way to something affirmative, to a better way. The turmoil, to be a cause for optimism, must be part of that process—which is what I tried to say in that DePauw Commencement speech this spring."

One of my deepest instincts is that when you talk about the state of the nation or the development of a nation, you must relate this to the way individuals grow and develop.

The growth and development of an individual's potential depends to a great extent upon the trials and frustrations and unhappiness he goes through. Not only the development of his potentials, but his individual pleasure and satisfaction, the highest of which is overcoming harassing obstacles on the way. The "turmoil" of the individual is not the end result, but there must be opposition and even failure and certainly pain of various kinds to produce one of the highest forms of satisfaction, which is achievement.

"You said that you were remaking your company. In what way?"

I said it had grown too large, too many people. That means problems, and less "fun" for me. Less originality. More repetition, and there is nothing I care less about in my work than repetition.

JULY 14, 1970
NEW YORK

I sauntered along the quay, the wind blowing strong and fresh from the harbor. The big fireboat snug against the Marine Fire Department headquarters; in the dimming sunlight, the crew members in a cluster on the afterdeck. What do firemen, marine or otherwise, *talk* about during the many hours that they just sit and wait for payday?

To the nearby Seamen's Institute for dinner, and a good one: fresh whole mackerel, lentil soup as thick as brown pitch, and toasted coconut pie. Seamen's fare indeed! Wandered around the lobby of the hotel for seamen, looking at mementos and pictures of seven-masted schooners, but actually looking at the men, fresh off the merchant ships. One quiet-faced, subdued, hollow-chested little man had pornographic tattoos from wrist to elbow. On the bulletin board of "This Week's Activities," for the seamen, three *separate* lines announcing Alcoholics Anonymous meetings, and one of Alcoholic Assistants, whatever that is.

Outside, the towers of lower Manhattan: One Whitehall, our own quite new building now dwarfed by the new ugly monsters recently built, hardly finished, cutting off a large part of my wonderful view of the harbor. Off in the mid-distance, lights gleaming in the heart of a dark and towering phalanx, high against the sky, the first of the twin towers of the New York Port Authority building.

JULY 19, 1970
MARTHA'S VINEYARD

Joe and Claire Flom arrived by plane early Friday morning and the four of us have had an active and a happy time ever since. Not all vacationing, but a good combination of work and non-work.

Joe Flom—forty-three?—is out of a tradition that is probably passing. His parents immigrants to America (as were mine), he brought up in Brooklyn. "They were very poor," said his chic, tall, dark-haired wife Claire. With determination enough for a dozen, he put himself through City College, by working nights and studying on the long subway ride between Brooklyn and City College. At the Harvard Law School he had the special distinction of being on the *Law Review.* Now recognized as perhaps the leading American lawyer in the field of corporate acquisitions and mergers. A once familiar American saga, Joe's career.

JULY 24, 1970
MARTHA'S VINEYARD

The radio reports that the largest unit in the Con Ed New York City power generating system—called Big Allis—has had to be closed down, just at the time an overload can be expected, and on the heels of the closing of their new Indian Point nuclear plant.

The big first-page headline in the *Times:* Con Ed receiving power *from TVA.* When I think how the conservatives in New York pounced on TVA for years, now to have power from that system (by transfer, of course, to intermediate systems) keeping New York City together—is really amusing.

JULY 26, 1970
MARTHA'S VINEYARD

We had a lively dinner last night at Jerry and Laya Wiesner's home in Chilmark.

Jerry Wiesner's "vacations" are like mine here, going back and forth and working hard. All the MIT administrative people have had a rough year.

He still has that characteristic quizzical, low-key expression and tone of voice that I remember so well when he was in the middle of vast public questions, in the White House as Scientific Advisor to President Kennedy. It was the same impression I sensed when he returned from Russia after attending an international conference of scientists. He had had hopes and was persuaded the Soviet *scientific* community was beginning to see that the armament race was taking away from Russian science the funds that they needed and wanted for scientific purposes.

But last night Jerry's outlook was a different one. No sense of hope that his noble efforts toward peace were getting anywhere. (*I* thought they were "noble," though he would have spurned that term.)

What about the current crop of students at MIT? His brief answer: The engineering students haven't changed much. But in physics and biology they say that "physics isn't enough."

This startled me. For so long the physicists were the one group of scientific and technical people—students and Ph.D.s—who found that their pursuit of knowledge *itself* satisfied their purpose in life, indeed *was* a purpose. They would speak—as Oppenheimer so often did—of the "beauty" or the "elegance" of a problem in physics. Nothing else mattered much; they could exclude the rest of the world by absorption in the exciting, expanding world of physics. Jerry said—or implied strongly— that this is no longer true.

Yesterday a free-lance writer, Donald Stroetzel, asked my views on many subjects that are part of my "participating life." My philosophy was what the interrogator wanted. So I rambled on, from one question to another. The underlying theme of his questioning, of course, was my experience as a developer, and the story of D&R as the medium through which I expressed and transformed my "philosophy" into things done, or attempted.

"You say," said Stroetzel, "that the heart of your distinctive way of going at development is instilling confidence in people that they can handle the opportunities for development in their country—or in an urban area in this country. How do you do this? Give me examples."

The examples I gave were actually part of what we *do;* they are not, as I thought of them at the time, part of a process of "instilling confidence"; they are part of getting a job done that people wanted done and which I was responsible for their getting done.

When one reaches out to pick up a pencil or sets out to walk he doesn't think, consciously, about the use of his fingers or thumb, or how he puts one foot after another. The object is to pick something up, or to move from here to there. So it is with "instilling confidence"—it is the objective, not the "method," that counts.

Which raises the question, of course, of whether one can transmit to others concepts such as those of "instilling confidence" as a method, a technique for development. The result is what I was after, and I sensed, rather than thought, that the result could be achieved if people one was working with believed they could do it.

Looking back, over the last physically unhappy six months since this "pinched nerve" nuisance became an acute thing, I realize I am better now.

I'm going to try sailing *Lili-put* this afternoon. But this is only because our neighbor—and a real mariner—Jack Daggett has said he would go with me. Bending the mainsail, with that sore neck and shoulder, or fighting a pulling tiller in a stiff breeze—I'm not sure how that would go. Certainly I can't pull my dinghy up the slope of the shore, alone, as I have done now these many years. Gets me pretty low thinking about this kind of limitation. Not necessarily a permanent disability but it pursues me. But "better"? Of course.

JULY 28, 1970
MARTHA'S VINEYARD

Few people were ever as close to Eleanor Roosevelt as Joe Lash. I knew, vaguely, that he had been selected, quite appropriately, by the Roosevelt family to have exclusive access to her papers at Hyde Park, for the preparation of what is called a "definitive" biography.

For two solid years he plowed through her massive papers; now, he told me on the phone, the writing is nearly done. Could he talk to me about my own recollections?

This morning he came up on our fog-shrouded hill; an intensely interesting couple hours.

He was particularly interested in my opinion—buttressed wherever possible by specific episodes—of Mrs. Roosevelt's "influence" on F.D.R., the strength and the sensitive conscience that Mrs. Roosevelt provided to the President. Joe's book will spell out the decisive role she did play, and it will be a great contribution.

Lash found my journal entries about Mrs. Roosevelt "important." He singled out her comment at the dinner at J. J. Singh's home, defending F.D.R.'s Yalta agreement, of which she was critical at the time. "Would the American people go to war for Estonia?" was the substance of F.D.R.'s defense of Yalta.

Mrs. Roosevelt wanted very much to be asked to accompany the President to Yalta. Partly his health. But mostly, she had become fearful of the presence around him of too many "conservatives." She had lost faith in Hopkins—the only thing he was interested in was winning the war; what came after was not of first importance.

JULY 30, 1970
MARTHA'S VINEYARD

An almost classic combination of things that *could* go wrong with power supply in New York City: a several-day spell of hot, humid weather, a failure of two generators of the Con Ed system. So New York is going through more of the agonies of the City Gargantua—only short of the total failure that threw the whole of the Northeast into the trauma of a blackout only a few years ago.

AUGUST 6, 1970
NEW YORK

Last night to the Shakespeare Festival, as guest of the Tobeys, including their daughter, Nancy. *Richard III,* in the open-air theatre in Central Park. Blood and thunder and murder, but wholesale. The conniving by the big Boss, Richard, and the "taking them for a ride" by his gang seemed more contemporary than I would like to think: the Anglo-Saxon Mafia.

AUGUST 9, 1970
MARTHA'S VINEYARD

Yesterday morning, under the most beautiful old linden trees, Joe Flom and I met with Professor Eli Ginzberg of Columbia, indubitably the country's leading authority on manpower. Ginzberg spoke with verve and that youthful smile of his about the billions upon billions the U.S. is spending on manpower training, doing it chaotically and with great waste. The waste comes about chiefly because "the American way is to pour in a great gob of money *before* we have spent a much, much lesser sum figuring out what the hell manpower training is all about."

The property the Ginzbergs have occupied on the North Road each summer for seventeen years is surrounded by walls seven feet high formed by enormous boulders. These are the highest walls, and the biggest boulders, to be part of a "fence" ever seen on the Vineyard. They were the work of the fabulous Vineyard family of Tiltons. Huge men, proud of their strength, great fishermen. They enjoyed showing how strong they were by moving boulders and building walls higher and tougher than anyone else's. Pry the boulders up by main force, get them onto a wooden "sled" and then a team of oxen would drag them to where the Tiltons wanted them.

AUGUST II, 1970
MARTHA'S VINEYARD

Helen asked me this noon: "So many of your contemporaries (even younger) ask you how you feel about retiring. You are now past the usual age, yet the very thought is repugnant to you; wouldn't it be worthwhile setting that down in your journal notes?"

It is. And I do.

AUGUST 13, 1970
MARTHA'S VINEYARD

My morning before-breakfast walk-run (now known as "jogging") is one of the best things about this far from usual Vineyard summer. I have gradually extended the "course"; it is now a full hour, and half is uphill. When I get back I am more than glowing.

AUGUST 14, 1970
MARTHA'S VINEYARD

Roger Baldwin at age eighty-six is as full of physical vigor as ever. But he isn't nearly so sure about most of the things he has spent much of his life about. He is disappointed in the United Nations, for example. "We are back on the old track of power, not reason." When I said, again, that internationalization may be more likely to issue from economic forces, such as multinational business, than from the neat structure of international political organization, he looked at me with those crinkly wise eyes and seemed to half agree—but only half.

He has the longest personal history as a revolutionary and reformer of any man alive—and honored more in his lifetime than any social rebel I can remember. So I asked him, who had been the leader in civil rights activities and radical labor unionism, "Roger, what do you say to the present young, to the generation of the present? What do you advise them to attach themselves to, in the way of causes?"

"David," he said in the saddest way, almost a contradiction in this gutsy, hearty man of the bellowing voice: "I don't know what to say to them. Surely no longer Labor as a cause. Surely not international organizations. If they turn to politics, they will be bound to be disappointed if they think that electing some different faces will achieve very much. Look at the Gene McCarthy thing. High spirits. But he was a dud, and is a dud. And they will be electing other disappointments. I just don't know what to tell them.

"Maybe this environmental thing will provide a cause. But I doubt its durability, for a whole generation."

Our daughter Nancy is at "Topside," with her sons, Allen and Daniel. Daniel is a charming, handsome boy, quiet and reserved. That he is sparing of words and bounce is in direct contrast to his brother Allen.

Allen has become a big, broad-shouldered young man, and a stream of words keeps pouring out of him.

Inside the agriculture building at the fair, I was greeted by Pare and Elizabeth Lorentz. I said to Nancy: "Pare Lorentz is the greatest artist with film, ever." Said daughter Nancy: "You don't need to say that to me, who saw *The Plow That Broke the Plains* six times."

AUGUST 16, 1970
MARTHA'S VINEYARD

A jolly, extraordinary evening at Alfred and Fefa Wilson's last evening, at their Lambert's Cove home. Among the guests were Brenda Forbes, an actress and personal and professional protégée of Katharine Cornell, and Brenda's mother, Mrs. Wall.

The mother is as remarkable in her way as Roger Baldwin, in his. She is eighty-eight years old, yet yesterday went out fishing and caught three bluefish. Still without doubt a beautiful woman; what a beauty she must have been as a younger woman.

She told of seeing Greta Garbo at Antigua last winter. When this old lady told of Garbo, *she* became Garbo, the deep voice that stirred the world, the profile that no one who has seen some of her films can ever forget. Mrs. Wall had been in every film Garbo ever made, so she could approach her at Antigua, whereas no one else could.

Then she told of Marlene Dietrich descending a winding staircase in a Hollywood house, swirling a loose long gown; when this old lady told of this descent, her hands and arms reaching up and fluttering down, you could *see* Dietrich. That scene was as real to us as if Dietrich herself was there.

Laughing and relishing all this spectacle around the dining-room table, some of us tried to prod the Grande Dame Wall about Garbo, she who knew her professionally and personally so long. Why, I asked, was it that Garbo, in her coolie hat against the Antiguan sun of last winter, was still so overwhelmingly beautiful? The old actress, her cheeks coloring, eyes sparkling, leaned way across the table and said directly to me: "Because Garbo always has a lover, that is why she is always so beautiful. Sometimes a man, sometimes not, but always a lover. That is what every woman needs," she concluded, nodding her head. What an extraordinary phenomenon is a first-rate professional actor.

For me the dramatic star was a gifted amateur. This was Josefa Wilson, whom everyone calls Fefa. Blazing blue eyes set in a corona of grey hair, inexhaustible energy and a presence and genius of mimicry, a pure histrionic instinct, and gestures of arms flung open; all told, a great personality.

AUGUST 18, 1970
NEW YORK

Donald Meads, Chairman of IBEC, said: "Clearly IBEC wants to acquire D&R, but with a firm intention 'to preserve D&R's integrity as an entity.' " This intention is supported by their own self-interest, about the only sure way to guarantee "intentions" in the business world.

A mixture of D&R and International Basic Economy Corporation will produce a different D&R and, as Meads believes, a freshened IBEC, freshened by the ideas we can provide.

AUGUST 24, 1970
MARTHA'S VINEYARD

Helen and I were discussing the perennial subject: "the young people." Particularly acute at this moment because our grandchildren have used "Yonside" as a kind of rendezvous-pad in a way that destroyed the "peace and quiet" that I want—and right now, desperately need.

Halfway defending the young generation, I said: "Well, we must admit that as a generation they are idealists."

That set Helen off.

"I think we have been sold a bill of goods on that idealism thing. The over-emphasis given by the news media to the goings on of what is only a minority of young people in the U.S.

"You say that they share what they have, that that is a form of idealism. It is true that those who have food, a place to sleep, share it with their friends. They also share in other ways, in rock throwing at police, in disrupting college classes, in breaking windows. They say college doesn't give them anything.

"They say they are not in sympathy with the way of life of their parents, their ambitions, or the way they make their money. They have thrown over all this to lead a 'free life.'

"But this free life is possible only as long as the checks come in from their fathers, from the profits of a business that these young idealists disapprove of.

"They look at things the way I would expect kids of a much younger age to do. But these are not children. Many we know are twenty-five, and older. I would say this was a case of delayed adolescence. The fact that some of them take jobs for a while when they need a little money doesn't seem to me to be much of a mitigating factor.

"The real point to me is the aimlessness of their lives. Most of them seem to be just drifting, without any real objective. They are entirely self-centered. They expect everything to be done for them. They feel no obligation to work to reform the abuses they profess to see about them. It is more fun to demonstrate, just to be against. They make no attempt to implement their 'ideals.'

"This does not conform to my definition of idealism. Your phrase, 'dreamers with shovels,' does. These young people may have 'dreams' but they do not take up any 'shovels.'

"I have lived forty-seven years with an idealist. I have known other idealists who have made their ideals a working part of their lives as you have done. It was hard work, many times discouraging, but overall rewarding in the accomplishments achieved.

"When you were a young lawyer in Chicago, with a growing practice that gave you recognition and the certainty of financial success, you were not happy. You felt that the public utility regulations of that time did not give needed protection to people-at-large. So you did not hesitate to become a member of the newly formed Public Service Commission of Wisconsin, with an uncertain future. And at considerable financial loss to yourself."

AUGUST 31, 1970
MARTHA'S VINEYARD

The crisis of inadequacy of electric power for New York City simply identifies the Grand Issue of the coming decades in America: further growth, and what it will cost to that environment about which so much is being said, so little understood, so little done.

Scotty Reston's column yesterday in the *Times* sums it up by referring to the "deeper environmental questions which few politicians have ventured to raise . . . in the meantime the discussions on the environmental crisis are getting wider and deeper . . . and is likely to influence almost every aspect of our national politics."

SEPTEMBER 4, 1970
MARTHA'S VINEYARD

As of this morning, married forty-seven years. And not one year off for good behavior, to borrow John Lord O'Brian's comment at his fiftieth wedding anniversary.

SEPTEMBER 14, 1970
NEW YORK

How can an adequacy of electric power over the next ten to twenty years for the northeast region be achieved with a minimum deterioration of the conditions of living?

There is one thing that emerges from my experience in public life: that action on grave public issues, whether a war or diplomacy or conservation, will not result from government action unless there is first built a foundation of public understanding.

People will believe there is a way out based upon a selective array of specific things that I believe can be done, not merely technically, but in terms of public understanding and support. We need a series of relatively small but manageable attacks on pieces of the problem, one by one.

At lunch with McGeorge Bundy I made the point that it was the region, not the state or the individual utility corporation, that must be considered. Instead of a Federal grid or regulations, the power should be shunted back and forth by the management of a big holding company, owned by the various private utilities and public authorities. The holding company was a good managerial instrument; it was the use of it for financial mischief that brought it into disrepute.

"A kind of Federal Reserve banking system for power," said Bundy. This is an analogy I want to pursue, for it has a verbal appeal and perhaps a substantive one. To have an electric-power structure that would do for electric power what the Federal Reserve system has done for the banking system. Quite a lot.

SEPTEMBER 27, 1970
PRINCETON

The cursed neck and shoulder that kept me from gardening this spring has just up and cured itself.

As the fellow says: "Long's you got your health."

OCTOBER 8, 1970
NEW YORK

In my twenty-minute talk this noon to the gathering of the IBEC "family" I said, "I feel comfortable here" because IBEC's charter and purposes and those of D&R have much in common. D&R, like IBEC, is a private company, not a tax-exempt "foundation"; it is directed to the central theme of our time: development. I referred to statements about IBEC's "philosophy" as enunciated when it was founded by Rodman's father, Governor Nelson Rockefeller, and expounded more than once by Rodman.

OCTOBER 26, 1970
NEW YORK

Have just returned from a big gala "reception" at the UN tendered by the Princess Ashraf of Iran to celebrate the Shah's birthday; which happens to be her birthday as well, since they are twins. Have there ever been any other royal twins?

Where all those people came from—part of what I call the UN Leisure Class: the people who make a career of moving from one diplomatic sinecure to another, from one elegant elaborate meal to another. I met Doug Knight, and as we carried our big platesful of goodies to a table, in a mob of a thousand, I said: "You are too young, in fact, so am I, to remember clearly the free lunch that used to pack the saloons with freeloaders; but this is the affluent 20th century equivalent of the saloon free lunch."

In the lobby people of all shapes, colors, slants of eyes, pouring out, as 6 o'clock came along, to be diluted into the massive sea of mid–New York, aglitter with the lights of the most spectacular rich city of the world. I thought: Just what in the hell are these scriveners, from all over the world, doing that will help the poor and the starving and the homeless? They looked far too satisfied with their great luck in having a government job in New York City to make me feel that they really cared about anything in their own countries—except those jobs. Unfair? Not terribly.

NOVEMBER 7, 1970
FLORENCE

Outside our window flows the historic Arno; off to the left the Ponte Vecchio. And on the Arno float the green goo and the abandoned rubber tires, discarded cigarette boxes, and other effluvium that characterize the modern version of beauty. What an unromantic sight.

But the lovely grey monuments of Florence of the 14th century mount against the sky.

NOVEMBER 8, 1970
FLORENCE

At noon went with David to collect [his daughter] Margy, at her public elementary school. A couple dozen Italian papas and mammas and grandmas, standing around waiting until the little hopefuls came out. The littlest ones with big eyes looking anxiously for their mammas, the bigger ones, the girls giggling together, the boys pushing and scuffling with each other. Margy was very modish, in long white pants and a lovely cape. Becoming quite a good-looking girl.

NOVEMBER 9, 1970
ON THE EARLY MORNING RAPIDO FOR ROME

The Italian countryside—how rich and colorful, and satisfied with itself. Everything in its place, the fields and the farmhouses just so. On the hilltops great manors and an occasional village or town. In Florence the people look so well fed; free-spenders. Not like the Italy of fifteen or twenty years ago.

NOVEMBER 10, 1970
TEHRAN

A walk through the after-dark crowded business district of this exploding city—exploding with people's appetite for luxuries that even the richest caliphs of another time could not have had. Store after store along streets—where the pavement is broken and unrepaired—displaying the most expensive and elaborate TV sets; big radios stacked up one on top of another to the ceiling. Big refrigerators, gold ornaments, the latest in ladies' knee-high boots, brassieres floating in a display in the windows. Still a few women slink by with the edge of their body-enveloping dark chadours clenched in their teeth. A bakery for cakes and cookies that would not be out of place in the Fifties on the fancy East Side of New York. Most impressive of all to me, the transformation of the butcher shops where great carcasses so recently open to the flies are now in refrigerated cases.

All this is in contrast to what I saw only a few years ago when we first came to Tehran.

I find myself uneasy with this display of conspicuous consumption, not alone because of economic misgivings. My uneasiness is the same that I feel about the conspicuous spending fever in the U.S.

What happens to the *values* of people during such a binge?

NOVEMBER 11, 1970
TEHRAN

In a country where "national planning" has had such a vocal vogue, as in Iran, I fear most that the new crop of planners under Khoda-dad Farmanfarmaian may again be delirious about grandiose planning but lack the capacity or understanding of how to carry out those plans.

Can industrial and commercial, even financial, progress as spectacular as in Iran reflect the true state of a country's health, when its agricultural gap is so wide and so static and the life of its villagers so meager?

Khuzistan, yes, that is a heartening story. But it is so small a bite in the whole picture.

Will I be able to get my dismay on this point over to anyone of consequence in this exuberant, cocky country (and I have worked as hard as anyone I know to make them cocky, from being so afraid and lacking in confidence when we began)?

On a personal note: why should I overexert myself, emotionally, about the future of Iran and of Khuzistan? I ask this question not only now, in the dark of the night, but at other times as well. Do I make a mistake to continue this bearing down so hard, when the big job I set out to do has been done, that job being to help bring momentum into this once static and (as the wise guys described it) "fragile" country?

Why not let Nature take its course, so far as my special and extraordinary efforts are concerned?

It isn't my nature to do so. But shouldn't my nature be rational once in a while?

NOVEMBER 13, 1970
TEHRAN

A delightful visit with a young Iranian, he in his last year in an Iranian preparatory school, Alborz School. I asked him whether young Iranians were writing poetry, in the tradition of a country that has had such great poets. What about art? His answers—negative—were so serious, so articulate, so earnest. Iranian education today has been strongly affected, he said, by Europe, particularly French culture. Not good, he thought; lacked the direct, simple, fierce strength of the older days, as reflected in the poetry of Hafiz.

He wants to become an architect. Is going to Washington State for training next year. "Will you come back to Iran?" I asked. "I will come back," he said, as if he had given it much thought.

"Why is it that so many Iranian students stay overseas?" I asked.

"Because the educated Iranian, particularly a doctor or architect, does not yet have the social standing and recognition in Iran that he can have in the States. But that will change."

NOVEMBER 14, 1970
TEHRAN

Of the many audiences I have had with the Shah, in some ways this one in the great many-mirrored chamber of the Palace this morning was the most memorable.

We had just shaken hands when a white telephone on a small table at my right buzzed. He answered, motioning to me to take a seat on a sofa next to his chair.

His Majesty put down the receiver, sank back into his chair, looked out in space for a few seconds, then in a very low, soft voice said to me: "We have reached agreement with the oil consortium." He went on to explain, in detail, how the agreement improved Iran's oil revenues, much needed to maintain the pace of the development program.

From this it was logical for him to talk about Khuzistan. Such feeling he has for that program, and such generosity in speaking of my part in what has been accomplished, against such an initial torrent of skepticism and opposition, within Iran, and among the geniuses of the World Bank staff.

I began by reasserting pride and confidence in what had been done to give reality to his concept of modernized agriculture, including the establishment at Safiabad of a center for research and trial. But budget restrictions had eroded that undertaking within the past two years. If we have the tools of a reasonable budget that center could become a great institution, comparable in its way to the Pahlavi Dam.

The Shah was way ahead of me. How well he understands fundamentals. "It will be done. That will be attended to. It will be ordered." And then, leaning forward in a sudden movement quite unlike his usual composure, his eyes behind those dark glasses flashing (no less), and gesturing at me (something he rarely does), he said: "And not only Safiabad, but we shall have many such centers, one in each of the various and differing parts of the country—a dozen perhaps."

On one subject the King was most explicit, and took a line far stronger than I have ever heard him take, namely—Iran must provide its own defense.

"A country like Iran cannot depend upon any other country, and particularly on a superpower, to defend it. There is no other course open. Look at what has happened in Vietnam." This was said in a deceptively quiet voice and in what was almost a soliloquy. The continued expansion of the Iranian Air Force and the Navy is the most important fact about the future of development, for it is a frightful drain on foreign exchange resources that could otherwise go for development.

Where will it end? Does he believe that Iran can have both a much greater military establishment *and* development at the pace he has set? Apparently he does.

A man definitely on top of his job, and in command of himself and his life: this was the impression that today I had of the Shah.

It was not always thus; I recall audiences no more remote in time than 1962 when he was quite evidently a troubled and unsure man.

As we concluded our talk, I said: "It is always inspiring to visit with you." I meant it. For this one man knows his great job; from the broad vision of its future, to its defense policies, to the fundamentals of its agricultural development, to the details of oil pricing.

Such winning modesty; "humility" is the word. Part of this is the softness of his voice. One might expect it to be more harsh and peremptory (actually, with his entourage I have observed that he can be just that). Imagine a King who is out in his country several days a week, dedicating this project and that plant, undoubtedly the most mobile monarch of all time, and yet one who can say: "Even I don't know all there is to know about this country, so vast is it, so different are its many parts." Then a pause and a reflective comment: "Perhaps that is why it is properly called an empire."

NOVEMBER 18, 1970
ANDIMESHK

Tomorrow we rise at six to start a long day at the Safiabad trial farm and to see the work going on on the larger-scale corporation farms. Having helped bring these large farms into reality, I find myself again with misgivings—what will happen to the small farmer, the village people Helen and I visited now so many years ago?

I warned those who came to the reception for me here that we should not neglect the work Leo Anderson and Bob Harkens and others began in direct teaching assistance to the peasant farmer. The village teacher, my favorite, dark-eyed little Tabib, was particularly warmed by this. He agreed that the American term "extension" didn't apply to village-style peasant farming.

NOVEMBER 22, 1970
EN ROUTE TO LONDON

What visual episode of this expedition was the most moving?

Beyond a doubt: sitting beside the pilot in the nose of the helicopter last Tuesday, floating, so slowly did it seem, over the gorge of the Dez and the tiny-appearing dam below, and then, miracle of miracles, returning to the plain, the greenest of green for miles and miles, half the arc of one's vision. How well I remember that emptiness of desert not long ago, and there it was now, the greening of Khuzistan. Surely this was for me the happiest sight of all.

How much of the surface of the earth is utterly barren and desolate —and desolate the lives of human beings who try to make a living on such land. Since our plane left Tehran an hour ago heading west all we saw were the harsh, dead, brown mountains, the razorback or dinosaur ridges made more antihuman and remote by the shadows of the early morning sun.

We are constantly told: there are too many people. That I don't doubt. But not because the world is fully occupied by any living thing. Those inhospitable brown convulsions below, where neither man nor beast, (nor probably) even insects, care to exist, could with skills of management and technology be made as green as Khuzistan now is becoming.

The once-desert now green was the most exciting view of this trip. But what about people of whom I saw so many on this exploration; which ones or groups made on me the greatest impression?

The answer again is easy. Not the big shots, the Ministers, the very wealthy ones at Ebtehaj's great party for me. It was the group of Iranian agricultural "experts" gathered in the assembly room at the Safiabad research and trial farm center, and those same young men when they showed us around to see their work, observe their radiant enthusiasm about the sheep, the heifers, exclaim with them over the succulent young cabbages and dark, crisp carrots, or tasty sesame seed being harvested. I recalled that when Leo Anderson and I first walked over some of this ancient land it resembled concrete more than soil, and there was a doubt whether even the strongest tractor could pull a plow through the subsoil.

What stirred me most was these young men, their glowing faces as we moved from one field to another, their eager talk about the difficulties overcome, the yields, their anxiety lest in the Tehran bureaucracy the program fail to be protected, defended, continued, expanded so that other thousands of hectares of the Khuzistan could be made to bear as these we were visiting.

These are not men dealing in abstractions or pursuing science in an enclosed lab. They were excited about the application of their slowly acquired knowledge about this empire we are rescuing from century upon century of sterility.

Action I wanted to be D&R's distinctive characteristic. This trip certainly showed me that it is not just a matter of "planning," or our desiring to get things done. We do somehow make things happen.

NOVEMBER 23, 1970
FLYING TO NEW YORK

When I went to see Prime Minister Hoveyda, in Tehran, he was standing out in the hallway and saw me entering way down the corridor. "Come in," he said. "I have been waiting for you; they have torn up this whole building and I knew you would get lost." (It was ten minutes before our appointment.)

A more informal Prime Minister it would be hard to imagine. He began to talk at once, and talked continuously and brilliantly for thirty minutes. Reminded me of the early TVA days. When you came in to see F.D.R. about something specific that he didn't want to decide right then, he would talk and talk and you would leave no wiser than when you came.

As to the issue of large-scale versus small peasant farming, Hoveyda said: "It isn't a matter of *all* large farms or *all* small peasant holdings. Each region is different, and we need both."

Which I thought made good sense.

DECEMBER 2, 1970
NEW YORK

Tonight a handsome lady said to me: "I sat in the Congressional Joint Atomic Energy Committee room [in 1947] when you were baited by Senator McKellar into making your now famous 'This I Do Believe' statement of faith." This was Mrs. David Morse, wife of the retiring head of the International Labour Organisation at a dinner tendered to David for his work for human rights, an award being made by Roger Baldwin.

David, responding to Roger, made a corking good speech. The work of the UN agencies trying to build a "social and economic underpinning" to political action, he said, was on the right track—but how long a road it was to be. What a *forceful* speaker he is, for his personality seems so gentle and almost noncommittal, in private conversation. I saw, in the ten minutes he spoke, why he was able for twenty-two years to build up that organization and hold it together.

DECEMBER 6, 1970
PRINCETON

Drove into New York yesterday (Saturday) and back, with Bob Goheen, to attend a meeting of Doug Knight's council advising on Princess Ashraf's university, Jondi Shapur.

After two grueling years of student "unrest" Goheen has come through as a man of great perspective.

The reward for this triumph of good judgment and a cool head is, of course, more trouble. This time it is the worrisome state of finances. Princeton of all places is running a huge operating deficit. But compared with many other colleges, Princeton is in clover.

That there is a genuine financial crisis among the universities and colleges of the land was set out in detail and magnitude in a report by Clark Kerr, chairman of the Carnegie Foundation's Commission on Higher Education, and a member of the Jondi Shapur Council.

Yesterday Kerr said there was no cost advantage in a university larger than 5000 to 10,000 students; a university of 40,000 is definitely not justified by reasons of "economy of scale."

"He has gone through hell," said Bob. "To think that a man with Clark's lifelong record in the area of civil rights and human rights should be attacked viciously by a group of students at Berkeley, as a reactionary!

"It stung Clark and other university people who knew his record probably more than anything else that has happened in the whole campus disturbance picture."

Princess Ashraf was most cordial.

I said Reza is very much engaged in the preparation for the celebration of the 2500th "birthday" of Iran.

"Ah, yes," she said, "the celebration will be quite remarkable. Tents will be set up for the Heads of State on the plain at Persepolis, one tent for each King or Head of State. As in the ancient days."

Kings arriving by jets, instead of on camels, but still sleeping in tents.

DECEMBER 8, 1970
NEW YORK

The Amazon River.

My God, to a river man such as I am, what a stirring in the innards at that word, that name, that picture of a river and a basin, a valley bigger than big.

At last our chance, *my* chance, to have something important to do with the future of that colossus of rivers, that behemoth of valley basins.

It is still just a chance, perhaps a meager one, but not to be dismissed.

These are the emotions, the thoughts, that went scurrying across my mind as I listened intently to Walter Rocha, a Brazilian engineer. It is with his firm of four hundred professional engineers in São Paulo that we have joined, to seek to "qualify" for a preliminary regional planning effort for Amazonia.

DECEMBER 10, 1970
NEW YORK

A strike of all taxicabs! As if "conditions of living" in this exciting, beautiful madhouse weren't already difficult enough.

The fact is, however, that without the added traffic of taxis, New York has become almost livable.

DECEMBER 17, 1970
PRINCETON

A long and revealing letter from Professor Thuc about the status of postwar economic development. The letter is a classic. A few sentences are worth quoting:

> The Vietnamese Government is actually pushing forward various development projects recommended by our joint report—among them: the fertilizer plant, the cement factory, the refinery, the irrigation project in Phan Rang, etc. Priority is given to agricultural development. . . .
>
> We expect to become self-sufficient in rice, by the end of next year, thanks to the cultivation of about 500,000 ha. in high-yielding varieties.
>
> The sad fact is that in spite of various promises no positive step has been made by our American friends, in order to help us implement those projects.
>
> In such an atmosphere, more and more Vietnamese become skeptical about the possibility of carrying on the various recommendations made by the Lilienthal-Thuc Report. . . .

DECEMBER 29, 1970
NEW YORK

88 Battle was filled with Christmas cheer, old-style, complete with grandchildren trimming the tree, the old and beloved routine of sneaking off to wrap presents and write jingles (or try to), a full table and full tummies (diets farthest from my mind). Nancy and Sylvain arrived, on schedule, Wednesday late afternoon, with the two huge grandsons. From then on life was quite different: Ping-Pong battles, much TV looking at football, gags and fun, and a very happy Helen and Dave.

Daniel interested me greatly. Seeming as tall as I am, at fourteen, but with a soft, child's voice, a reserved manner, a twinkle in his eye. About sports he sparkled. On TV we watched Brazil defeat Italy in an international soccer match (I thought how this would sadden another grandson, off in Florence). Daniel explained the action and the rules with gusto, in such contrast to his restrained and nearly silent manner generally. But it was when we began watching hockey that his talent for explaining was dramatic. The rules of hockey I never did understand. He took out a piece of paper—a brown paper bag, actually—and drew the rink on it: "The blue line is . . ." In no time he had told me how to watch hockey—a very fast game indeed. Devoted as he is to the game and full of knowledge about the technique and the leading players, he has never seen a real live hockey game.

Later last evening, when things got slow, I asked him if he could teach me to play poker. His eyes brightened: "You don't know how to play poker?" Whereupon he did as orderly a job of explanation as I have ever heard. An enchanting youth.

DECEMBER 31, 1970
PRINCETON

Tough as 1970 has been in many ways, I leave the year and enter a new one with as high a level of confidence and of strength as at any year's end I can clearly remember. Confidence and strength also describe my inward life as well.

I have before me the cover of a new recording, Mozart and Schubert symphonies conducted by Pablo Casals. The note writer comments: "How does Casals approach a composition he is about to conduct? With the enthusiasm of a youngster and the reverence that comes only with age."

I am not, as was Casals at this time, ninety-two years old; but I cherish that description: "the enthusiasm of a youngster, the reverence that comes only with age."

IV

1971

~~∙⊰◊⊱∙~~

Vacation in Antigua—Acquisition of D&R by International Basic Economy Corporation—Trip to Iran—Trip to Colombia—Trip to Puerto Rico—Trip to Iran and the 2500th anniversary of founding of Iran—Vacation in Antigua

JANUARY 5, 1971
ANTIGUA, BRITISH WEST INDIES

This promises to be the kind of "break" I most enjoy, not too long to be boring and arouse my latent restlessness; yet long enough for a complete change, sunshine, swimming and solitude.

JANUARY 7, 1971
ANTIGUA

Glutton as I am for anything that sails on salt water, this time I am having a full diet indeed.

This morning Helen and I boated over to the inner harbor, the Nelson Dockyard. What a feast of yachts, surely fifty, some huge seventy-footers, some a scant eighteen feet, that had been sailed from all over the world. All the hubbub that goes on where sailing vessels are being fitted, scraped, painted, worked over.

In the 18th century a score of the largest British men of war, ships of seventy-eight guns among them, so I read, filled this harbor during the hurricane season of July through September. Three thousand seamen lived on these ships, and the sewage must have been awful, as was the "putrefaction," as the records speak of it, and the resulting disease and death.

To listen to some of my excited contemporaries, one would suppose that "pollution" began with U.S.A., 1970.

I sometimes think that the most arrogant form of ignorance is ignorance of history, an utter lack of any basis for judging the present because of a disdain for anything that is not NOW—as they say.

JANUARY 14, 1971
NEW YORK

Helen and I to a jam-packed and exuberant reception and dinner at the Pierre, honoring Cass Canfield and his remarkable wife Jane for their leadership in Planned Parenthood.

Without some of the very people there last night, the public opinion and legislative progress would surely not have happened. From the spirited beginnings by that embattled and lonely public health nurse, Margaret Sanger, to the kudos paid last night to John Rockefeller 3d, Cass and Jane, and two politicians of a new school, Senators [Birch] Bayh and Joseph Tydings—the progress toward population control has been truly dramatic.

JANUARY 16, 1971
PRINCETON

Thursday at 11:15 A.M. in the board room of IBEC, Donald Meads, Rod Rockefeller, and I went through the ritual known as a "closing," exchanging documents; had photographs taken, thanked the assembled staff people. The several months' ordeal of my child's "adoption" by new parents was done.

Perhaps we can impart to those in IBEC who are looking for new, invigorating ideas—and Rodman Rockefeller is certainly doing just that —some specific as well as conceptual sources of strength.

JANUARY 23, 1971
PRINCETON

I prowled around a huge A&P store at the shopping center here in Princeton. The excitement, however, was the same I get when I follow my habit in a foreign country of heading for "the native market," because I have learned through the years that it is there that one sees people in their ordinary pursuits (not "showing off" for tourists) and where one learns how, and by what means, they live and make their living.

I was completely unprepared for what I saw in this A&P. An area fully a quarter block, chock full of a variety and quality of food and household articles. What seemed like *acres* of canned goods, a hundred yards of meat, in plastic sleeves, some neatly sliced for different uses. All manner of fresh vegetables. I said something about "out of season" to Helen. "No such thing as out of season these days," she said, offhand.

I felt I was really a tourist in my own hometown.

JANUARY 26, 1971
NEW YORK

The whole idea of development of the underdeveloped countries is in a decline; it lives largely today as an *echo* of what we all thought two or three years ago was "the right thing to do." It requires a new infusion of ideas; but mostly a new motivation. The advocates of foreign aid appropriations can no longer scare people with the Cold War, a line of argument I disavowed in my Newton Baker Memorial Speech in the early sixties, but it has taken quite a while for that thesis to catch up with the facts, apparently.

The country is finally beginning to "catch up" with the Atomic Energy Commission and the Joint Congressional Committee on Atomic Energy. A critical article in *Newsweek* about my special target—the failure to dispose of radioactive waste. I was just ahead of my time, with the Stafford Little Lecture series at Princeton [in 1963].*

One point I made in that time of long ago was that the AEC was both the promoter of atomic energy plants and the judge of their safety and reliability. Though I am not credited with the point in the current discussions, it appears almost everywhere. The prickliness to criticism of the present members of the AEC and the Joint Committee has now become a major part of the public doubts about the Commission.

JANUARY 31, 1971
PRINCETON

The luncheon conversation with Bob McNamara at the World Bank on Wednesday covered a wide range. Some quite specific.

As we sat down to luncheon, I said how well I could understand what he is going through: the cruel kind of comments being written about him

*Published that same year, in expanded form, under the title *Change, Hope, and the Bomb,* Princeton University Press.

lately, for in my time I had had something comparable, and that I knew it hurt, "no matter what you say publicly—that you are 'used to it'—I know it hurts."

"Of course it hurts, hurts badly," he said. "Marge is terribly torn up about it, particularly that article in *Harper's* by David Halberstam. She will be glad of what you have said to me."

I told him I was interested in talking about development generally. "With the steady decline today of support and understanding of international development, there is the greatest need for new ideas. And not just peripheral notions of how much more in money the developed countries should contribute—the Pearson Report preoccupation. We need to think through afresh, get new concepts in this whole vast area of human concern, which is world-wide economic development."

McNamara gave me a quick look. "What kind of new ideas? What is an example?"

I said we need to re-examine what is meant by so fundamental a development concept as cost.

Most of the development ideas we have been dealing with are based on determining the cost and then balancing cost against measurement of the benefit—the tired phrase is "cost-benefit ratio."

What makes urgent our thinking through a new concept of cost is the sudden emphasis on environment. I reminded McNamara that great doubts have arisen about development itself—"is development, after all, a 'good thing,' as has always been assumed?" Or is it the very thing that has brought on this crisis of a deteriorating and perhaps fatal impairment of our physical environment?

Development that does not comprehend nor weigh all true costs, or measure benefits (or lack of them) in terms of the ill effect on the total environment—this prevailing thinking about development needs a complete overhauling. But the "experts" in the banks, such as the World Bank, or the foreign aid staffs, rarely think of the cost of the development as including what it costs to sustain the environment that development changes.

McNamara listened to me for only a few moments with that head-to-one-side expressionless posture so characteristic of him when he is taking something in, or is withholding an opinion.

But that expression changed almost immediately. He lighted up, and began a brilliant discourse on how we do need to consider cost in the new light of the damage to the environment. Oddly enough, his first illustration came out of industry. He began with the automobile (he came into the public service from the presidency of the Ford Motor Co.).

"The automobile is the most destructive development ever; what it has done to our cities, to the air, to safety for people." The automobile and associated industries, he said, fought any effort to ameliorate the consequences of the automobile. And it is the cost of doing just that which was the theme of my own comments about the need for new ideas in the development field.

I found myself speaking with considerable enthusiasm about a broad-gauge view of development to include counteracting (true, at a high price) the adverse effects on development of that part of our standard of living often called these days "ecological damage."

"On this subject, indeed about development generally viewed in this broad perspective, I feel passionately."

"That reminds me," McNamara said, "about a speech on the critical need of the less developed nations that I made in Copenhagen. After the meeting a Frenchman came up to me and said, 'You are really emotional about this, aren't you?' I said I was, and should be. And I agree: you should feel deeply about these things."

Holding a sheaf of typed pages before him, and grinning broadly, he said: "I have just received, just yesterday, a staff report about Khuzistan. There are a couple sentences I want to read you because they made me feel quite good." He read: "The project's consultants, Development and Resources Corporation, are very satisfactory." And later on: "During the late fifties and early sixties the consultants contributed a great deal in stimulating and organizing an Iranian institution to carry on the work and provide training—a real example of institution building."

I was glad to report that the violence of the debate had subsided between those who, like Minister Rouhani, thought strongly that the *one* solution was large-scale agribusiness, and those like the Bank's consultant, who emotionally and intellectually argued furiously for small landownership. I never thought that this was an either/or, black or white issue. Under some circumstances large-scale agriculture is the best way, in others the small owner.

McNamara, very thoughtful and quite sober, looked out of the window. "We were wrong." He meant, I inferred, that the dogmatic and ideological and emotional opposition to agribusiness was "wrong." How rarely does one find a powerful public official who will say, so simply, to one who has taken a different view, as I had: "We were wrong."

Just in from my third outdoor run-walk of the day, a cold, sunny, good-to-be-alive kind of day. I run for physical reasons. It makes me feel good. It gives me a shallow but genuine increment of confidence, to know that I can run, that my heart can thump, thump and return to its normal (and quite slow) rhythm so readily.

FEBRUARY 2, 1971
NEW YORK

What the President of the Ford Foundation, Mac Bundy, proposed to me was as astounding and unexpected as it was flattering and enticing. Nothing less than to give my whole time for the next several years to an effort to "shape and reshape the country's mind on the whole set of environment issues."

I was shaken by the prospect it held out, from so distinguished a source, to put everything I have into so pervasive a set of questions, affecting almost everything in American life.

Of course, that is out, for I am morally committed to D&R by the IBEC transaction.

Bundy made a revealing comment: "Ralph Nader is a remarkable man in every way; and he has shown what an impact one man can have, against such odds. But what he has done, is doing, is to veto, to stop things. The missing link in all of this is what I think you could provide, and it would be positive. Not stopping things but doing things. There is quite a difference, quite."

I like to think he thought I had the savvy (my phrase) about how to get ideas accepted and acted upon in the public sphere. The environment issue is only peripherally technical and, therefore, while subject to useful technical "analysis," the chore is to get people willing to do certain things, many of which involve choices, emotional ones frequently, and usually hard choices.

FEBRUARY 3, 1971
NEW YORK

Rodman Rockefeller has an attractive boylike quality, quite appealing, and even his "business" earnestness seems like a game which he is enjoying. With as much money and family prestige as he has, it must take something of an effort, or good training, to speak feelingly and show pride in IBEC's poultry innovations.

I commented favorably on his handshaking of all our D&R employees. He grinned. "My father used to make the local committees, giving a banquet for him, furious because he would walk in and first of all shake hands with all the waiters. The political touch, you know."

There is no fable or story plot so familiar: the man who seeks or covets the return of his youth.

A more likely story is this: the man who seeks not his youth, but his prime. To have and to hold safe. *That* would be worth bartering one's soul to have. To have always those years of one's prime, when one has learned what life is all about.

FEBRUARY 7, 1971
PRINCETON

I remarked to a new Princeton neighbor, Emmet Hughes, that I was greatly surprised that Nixon was surrounded in the White House by so many awkward novices, completely without experience of government. Yet the man who has the greatest experience with the legislative and executive responsibilities of the Federal Government within my memory is Richard Nixon.

Hughes knows Nixon in more than a journalistic way since he was part of the Eisenhower entourage while Nixon was Vice President.

"It is a matter of his chemistry. Nixon never has been able to attract good people. They just don't respond to his particular personality."

FEBRUARY 11, 1971
NEW YORK

Helen and I had a delightful day today, doing the things that make New York City a jewel among all the cities in the world, just as most of the time it can be ugly, noisy, and repulsive.

We had a leisurely luncheon at Helen's favorite restaurant, the St. Regis (spending enough to keep a family of four for a week in Appalachia). Then a walk in the sunlight and sharp air, and on to the Metropolitan Museum.

Engrossed in a special exhibition, the ancient objects being from Iran, in the Elamite, Sassanian, and Achaemenian periods.

Then on to *Midsummer Night's Dream* at the Billy Rose Theatre. An extraordinarily lively, amusing, and novel setting, with actors and actresses as good as acrobats as they were as players. At a theatre I do so enjoy sneaking a look at Helen when she is laughing, a quiet delight spreading over her face. My laughter is noisy, I fear.

A good day. To borrow a phrase from "another" diarist, "and so to bed."

FEBRUARY 13, 1971
PRINCETON

Four quite young people, three men and a girl, in a double seat on a train coming back from New York yesterday late afternoon. The distinctive clothes we *used* to associate with far-out hippies now are common enough among a whole generation: always jeans, of course. Deep in talk among themselves. As I walked past them, the girl, holding the earnest attention of the men in the seat opposite, said: "The *abstract* question is *what* is success?"

FEBRUARY 19, 1971
NEW YORK

Adolf Berle dead at seventy-six.

I visited him and Beatrice Berle in the winter of 1932 when, as a member of the Wisconsin Public Service Commission, I enlisted him to come to Wisconsin—as he did—to draft a "blue sky" law for the state. "Blue sky" regulation is what we now call the role of the Federal Securities and Exchange Commission. Much of the Federal regulation of securities began in Wisconsin during those pre-F.D.R. days, as did social security, unemployment insurance—the lot.

FEBRUARY 22, 1971
NEW YORK

The memorial service for Adolf Berle, in St. Paul's Chapel at Columbia this afternoon—I have just returned—was almost as unusual as the man himself. "Let us now praise famous men" from Ecclesiastes. Then up rose his son Peter, a broad-shouldered, tall, exceptionally handsome young man, who read passages from Job.

Adolf's death may not mean, literally, the end of the era of the New Deal; but it underlines how far away and long ago is that ebullient, brash period when we, the young, knew all the answers. It was to Columbia University that F.D.R. turned for his Brain Trust; Columbia was the sanctum sanctorum of the early New Deal.

MARCH 3, 1971
NEW YORK

D&R's future and the future of the work does *not* depend upon orderliness and seven-hour management committee meetings but upon the liveliness of mind that can look ahead to what the future of development holds rather than look into the rearview mirror to see where we have been.

"You are not a yesterday person," so I was told today. "You are a tomorrow person."

MARCH 21, 1971
PRINCETON

James Hester, head of the country's largest private urban university, New York University, interests me greatly. He had just come from two "confrontations" with two handfuls of "SDS-ers." he said.

Speaking of the most recent "student confrontation" (his words), half in jest, I would say, he said:

"One of them said to me: 'Did you ever work with your hands?' I said: 'Of course, I did; I carried papers, I mowed lawns for money, I had to wait on tables and do other things to support myself in Princeton.'

" 'Ya, ya; a self-made man, part of the Establishment,' the student jeered."

You can't win.

MARCH 22, 1971
NEW YORK

His dark eyes very much alive, his voice strong and positive, Gerry Levin stopped me as we were leaving Busto's after lunch this noon and said quite simply: "I have decided to accept the challenge of Iran."† I was overjoyed and relieved, sensing that this could be one of those affirmative steps that are part of my luck.

Now we shall have in Iran a very intelligent keen young man, resolved to make the D&R-IBEC merger really merge, where it counts—at an operation point—i.e., Iran.

APRIL 4, 1971
PRINCETON

I pulled out all the stops yesterday to make Helen's seventy-fifth birthday something special. And it was.

To have seen Helen working in the garden yesterday, the notion that this was her seventy-fifth birthday seemed ridiculous. I feel more than grateful that this woman who has shared so much of my life is so well physically, and abundantly healthy in spirit.

APRIL 8, 1971
FLYING FROM PARIS TO ATHENS EN ROUTE TO IRAN

My mental attitude ("emotional stance" is perhaps a better way to put it) seems always to need shoring up each time I set out on a new phase

†When Levin took charge of D&R operations in Iran, Andrea Pampanini, formerly of IBEC, succeeded him as Executive Vice President.

of an existing undertaking in Iran, now a demonstrated success.

And a shoring-up I gave myself. "You should not go out there to plead or present an elaborate case or detailed contract for the soil conservation or agricultural programs. Remember you have promised results in the past, without having given them the details of just how you would produce. And you did produce. You are there proposing to do something for them that you know darn well you can do.

"And you must not let technical people cover everything with *their* detailed story. What the Iranians want is your ability to get results by your experience and your special intensity. You need not persuade them after what you have been able to get done, where before there was nothing but frustration."

APRIL 10, 1971
TEHRAN

I was shown into a quite small room, decorated like the living room of a modest apartment. At the end of the room, a rotund little man sat hunched over, as if half submerged, behind a desk; he looked out over the top of half glasses and made me think at once of Dickens' Mr. Pickwick, rather than one who has for eight years been the Prime Minister of an "Empire" in Asia. In his buttonhole a dark, gunmetal-colored orchid. This is part of the Hoveyda tradition.

Hoveyda was in full agreement to my central point that a "watershed" protection program should be seen as a long-term soil conservation program with implications for increased agricultural production and a higher national priority for agriculture generally.

I was satisfied. Though, of course, rhetoric does not commit a government to a program, even when expressed by its Prime Minister.

I tried my best to bring into the discussion the need for a reorganization of the agricultural activities of the entire Government. He squelched this. "I prefer to let these Ministries fight it out. The strong man prevails, the weak one doesn't. Let them get hot between them; and they do."

APRIL 11, 1971
TEHRAN

A quiet, serene palace, Niavaran Palace. No fanfare. Only a very few guards, a few young officers in the blue uniform of the Court, and the usual stately older grey-haired men who bow you in. And yet only a couple days before, the General who had ordered the execution of "terrorists" had been gunned down.

In how much danger is the life of the Shah? No obvious efforts to protect him closely. Last night he went to a public concert and ballet. An easy target, one would suppose, if he were the object of widespread hostility—which I doubt.

Before the Shah and I had begun talking, I handed him a copy of the new *Journals,* Volume V, entitled *The Harvest Years,* dedicated to him. The handwritten inscription he read carefully.

He asked what years are covered by the volume. I told him 1959–63, and said, "Those were difficult years for you and for Iran. It was a time when most Americans were expressing grave doubts, and our Government in Washington was uncertain about Iran and Your Majesty. I'm glad I never had such doubts, for the development of Khuzistan was in the TVA tradition, which we called 'by and for the people.' *Now* it is easy to have 'confidence' in Iran, but *then* was when you needed it—except that you yourself never had doubts."

As I left the King, he asked me to prepare a "piece of paper" listing the topics we had discussed and the views he held about them "so I can pass this along to the people in the Government so they will know my answers; otherwise they will not give you definite answers until they have asked me, and this piece of paper will save time. Send it to me through the Court."

When people talk about visiting Persia—few travelers have, until recently—I say to them, "You must see Ispahan, the most beautiful city in the world." I always add, "Tehran is just another bustling, noisy Western city."

Well, bustling and very noisy and traffic-choked it is. But "just another Western city" it is not.

Last evening, for example, I walked for an hour along the main business street. The stores have become conventional and the contents gaudy. Most of the people are indeed in Western clothes. But the distinctive flavor of this Asian crossroads is everywhere. Sour-looking, lost-appearing tribesmen, decked in turbans, baggy pants, and decorated sashes. Groups of blind beggars shuffling along, beating a rhythm on a drum, asking "alms." In a side street a happy-looking man holding between the fingers of his left hand the webbed feet of three ducks whose necks were turned up, and nestled on his right arm, two grey geese. Not exactly "just another Western city."

APRIL 19, 1971
TEHRAN

Yesterday I saw Khodadad Farmanfarmaian, Chief Planner of Persia's Destiny.

We discussed substantive issues, among them our watershed protection. Far more is involved, I said, than setting up some brush heaps or little check dams around the rim of the Pahlavi reservoir, to prevent silting of the lake. The whole land of Iran is suffering from soil erosion. To do something about that means changes in the way people live on the land, the way they make their living. It may require their having to move off the land they and their herds are destroying. For this, in the case of the millions of nomad herdsmen, they have not been prepared.

Justice Bill Douglas, for example, says, "But the nomads are so picturesque." They are picturesque but they are destroying Iran's land. They, and others who are misusing the land in order to stay alive, are destroying Iran's agricultural future.

The Plan Organization has in the past had studies made—piles of them—and Khodadad pointed to a bookshelf loaded with documents and bound books. He doesn't want us to duplicate what has already been done.

This nettled me. "About that file of reports, has anything ever happened as a result, or have they been merely paper studies?" He admitted the answer was doubtful.

APRIL 21, 1971
ROME

David Jr. and grandson David 3d, seen together amidst the short Italians, look like a pair of giraffes moving among the lesser animals in East Africa. Yesterday at about three in the afternoon they pushed through the portals of the Hotel Eden. What a sight for an excessively proud father and grandfather.

The whole two days in Rome were in every way a delight.

MAY 4, 1971
NEW YORK

Met Charles Evers, black Mayor of Fayette, Mississippi, who has announced that he is a candidate for Governor—of Mississippi, of all places!

A big burly fellow in a shimmering green silk suit, a rumbling voice, the manner of a completely self-possessed man. I knew northern Mississippi well—in the thirties—when black people weren't even permitted to come to a white friend's funeral, as I witnessed on a memorable occasion in the little town of Iuka. Yet here is a black man soliciting financial support in New York City to run for Governor of Mississippi. Who says things haven't changed—and for the better?

MAY 6, 1971
NEW YORK

The amount of talking about the deterioration of the environment, the amount of legislation, rhetoric, editorials, and notably citizen group activity on the subject, is monumental.

Changing the environment, including the cultural and economic setting of people's lives, to say nothing of the physical setting, is, of course, what D&R has been doing; and what I have been doing for most of my working life, as in the Tennessee Valley. The terminology—i.e., environment, ecology, etc.—is relatively new but the function is certainly what we have been doing for a long time.

The worst "pollutant" is not dumping sewage into streams or sulfur dioxide into the air. The worst pollutant we must face is a lack of confidence in America's ability to meet this test of protecting and strengthening the environment. My chief concern is a defeatist mood, a negative mood.

Most major businesses now are either resigned to or persuaded that they must take considerable responsibility and spend a good deal of money to minimize the adverse impact their operations have on the environment. But they want to know from government what is to be expected of them so they can plan accordingly. In another five years, even more changes in the direction of greater social responsibility of corporate management will take place.

MAY 11, 1971
NEW YORK

The World Bank staff has been a "project by project" staff. It is easier that way. It is simpler to present facts about the "economic feasibility" of a particular project and so it has been the doctrine that has dominated the Bank almost from the beginning.

Because we of D&R have been what the Bank staff considers stiff-necked in standing up to them with our conclusions, this has not made us friends there. "Consultants" are generally supposed to agree with the Bank staff, even though their loyalty actually should be to the borrower nation the consultants represent.

McNamara is portrayed in the critical press as Mr. Computer, or a man who has a computer as a heart or brain instead of living tissue. Talking with him, I pointed to my forehead and said there has to be some thinking before a computer has any use. He responded by saying, "Yes, man has gotten along pretty well for five thousand years using his brain and a pencil and paper; a computer might make things a little more orderly *after* the thinking has been done, not before."

MAY 22, 1971
PRINCETON

A comment from our son, from Florence, on Volume V of the *Journals:*

"It's the life of a man—and the quality and vigor of the life in those years that have created the book. . . . The substance was so fully there, that the celebration of life rang wholly true."

MAY 23, 1971
PRINCETON

A vivid exchange with Dean Acheson's daughter, Mary Bundy. I spoke of the delight I had in reading the notes her father wrote to her, in the middle of his severe trials as Secretary of State, and the country's tribulations; these notes intersperse the more serious text of his new book *Present at the Creation.*

"When Father was writing the book they couldn't find much in the way of notes for certain episodes. Then the bright idea: 'Look up those notes I sent you while you were ill at Saranac.' Up to the attic I went, and there they were. They gave a picture of Father as a warm, sympathetic human being instead of the remote and sardonic man so many people thought him.

"We are really good adult friends. It is a joy to have such a friend."

JUNE 9, 1971
PRINCETON

What an enjoyable day was last Sunday, at 88 Battle: the long-planned and often-deferred visit by Barney and Beatrice Tobey.

Barney is one of the leading cartoonists of our time; his easily recognized *New Yorker* magazine style has developed over the years while the present young cartoonists are given to squiggly lines and poor draftsmanship. What is more remarkable to me is that so serious, almost introspective a man can turn out gags—the lines of text under the cartoons—that are so humorous and topical.

Barney wanted to comment on the fifth volume of the *Journals,* which he is reading. The word he ascribed to it was "inspiring."

"You still have such faith in people, faith that things can be done that most people would say weren't possible, or even worth trying. So young people particularly need to read what you have said and particularly what you have done. *That* is what I mean by 'inspiring.' "

JUNE 14, 1971
NEW YORK

There is nothing more unsettling to this "diarist" than going into an allegedly first-class restaurant, *alone*.

"Alone?" The maître d' asks, with a look that makes the visage of Boris Karloff seem kindly. Into the rearmost part of the restaurant this nobleman whisks you; if there were a table in the men's room, that is where he would put you, rather than have a lone man use up a two-person table.

JUNE 20, 1971
PRINCETON

Last Sunday the *New York Times* began printing what is described as the first of a series of installments drawn, by their own staff, from a lengthy study of how we got involved in the war in Vietnam. The "study" was prepared at the direction of McNamara while Defense Secretary; it contained what was described as the full text of various position papers or National Security Council summaries of action taken or discussions had within the Council. All of the source material from which the study was made, within the Pentagon, had been classified Top Secret.

As Chairman of AEC I opposed the indiscriminate or too general use of the Secret stamp. I found myself greatly troubled by this practice, because it had the effect of downgrading information that should be kept secret, by lumping it with material that was kept under a Secret stamp for no strong reason.

The *Times* got this material from unknown persons; if those persons were paid to steal government documents, or if the "source" turns out to be a hysterical former public employee, the *Times* will have to answer for its methods, and justify them.

But as of now, my AEC experience, and my passionate declarations about the public right to know even about the atomic energy program, impel me strongly to approve the result—an all-out review of the absurd lengths to which the Secret stamp, wielded by subordinate employees of the Government, can inhibit that criticism of government action that keeps the circulatory system of government healthy.

JUNE 23, 1971
NEW YORK

The long visit at Princeton last Monday with Henry Raymont of the *Times* produced a two-column story this morning.

The *Times* account is the strongest statement I've made—or anyone else, I think—on the environment issue, since my testimony before the Congressional Joint Committee on Atomic Energy [in 1963]. Then, before an antagonistic Committee, I opposed an atomic power plant in New York City on grounds of public hazard. (And it wasn't built.)

Raymont in today's story recorded my prediction that the environment issue—I quote from the *Times* account—"will become a new political force that recalls the Populism of the 1890s . . . the organization of Citizens' Committees . . . concerned with the environment . . . should not be discounted. This is not a fad. This is a grass-roots movement. What it has done is to repudiate, with very serious consequences, the Government bodies as the source of protection in this field. . . ."

Maybe this will be the only way we'll ever get it recognized that people simply no longer believe what they're told.

JUNE 29, 1971
NEW YORK

Interviewed for a half-hour on the NBC network's *Today* TV program this morning, as "guest" of the accomplished Hugh Downs.

The issue of government secrecy took up much of his questioning and my responses, since the Supreme Court is right now considering the legality of newspaper publication of the "top secret" Pentagon Papers.

"Do you think," Downs asked, "there was unnecessary secrecy in the Atomic Energy Commission when you were its first Chairman?"

I said I thought fighting against oversecrecy was one of my greatest problems as Chairman, between 1947 and 1950. There was, I said, a kind of phobia developed that because much of AEC's work was necessarily secret, "everything was secret—and that is nonsense."

"I think one of the gravest mistakes in our whole national life was the unwillingness of the Government, which resulted from a misuse of secrecy, to permit public discussion of whether we should make an H-bomb, a hydrogen bomb. This was about 1950. At the time I was gagged (because of official secrecy). I thought it would be in the public interest to discuss this. I think if it had been publicly discussed, perhaps we'd have taken at the time a new look at the atomic arms race before it got completely out of hand."

Downs asked: "If your opposition to the development of the hydrogen bomb had resulted in our not developing it, what would the dangers have been then of other powers developing it and putting us behind?"

I acknowledged that those dangers certainly existed. However, we were told at the time by the zealots for a crash program for an H-bomb that if we developed the H-bomb, this would *assure* our security. Nothing is further from the truth, as we all now know to our sorrow. We had very little to lose by discussing with the Russians whether this was not the time for *both* nations to put a stop to the atomic arms race.

The chance that they would agree was perhaps one in a hundred, maybe one in a thousand, but it was worth taking two or three months of exploration to find out.

JULY 4, 1971
MARTHA'S VINEYARD

A second day in a row of sharp, shining air, a clear view from our hilltop north to the soft blue of the Sound, the tawny cliffs of the Elizabeth Islands, and to the south the broad Atlantic so close I feel possessive: an ocean all for us. Nudging the windows that hedge in this table in my study, pink wild roses, cosily decorating the boulder resembling a Thurber dog that we have absurdly named Mr. Mitty.

JULY 5, 1971
MARTHA'S VINEYARD

Visited last evening at his Vineyard home with Jerry Wiesner, president-elect of the Massachusetts Institute of Technology, perhaps the most appropriate head of a modern institution of learning in my memory. A technical man (electrical engineering, electronics, etc.) but with the broadest kind of cultural interests *plus* (the essential plus these days) experience as an activist in government and politics.

Jerry had the look of a man who has not only ridden out a storm but is satisfied that the storm produced some good results. Now the students are back at the work of studying. I detected no bitterness. Some of the scenes at MIT of a year ago were ugly.

A well-balanced, cool, thoughtful man.

Is calm at MIT a reflection of a change of mood in the country generally? Just as university students everywhere *anticipated* a general mood —an ugly one to some, violent, "irresponsible," noisy, not logical, but definitely *there*—so the subsiding of the rhetoric of campus revolt, and some of the visible manifestations of insurrection among students probably reflect the coming of a similar subsiding among most other dissident groups.

A revolution, in the realistic, classic sense, is a flame. It either bursts suddenly into action, or it dies out. It cannot sustain itself on the embers of discontent.

JULY 7, 1971
MARTHA'S VINEYARD

The mailman, a dark-haired, youngish man, brought his jeep to the door, meaning that he had a registered package. Sticking his head out of the window he caught sight of me, bedaubed with white paint, dripping with sweat.

"I heard you on television the other day. Enjoyed it. It is about the first time I heard an intellectual who said something I could understand. Made sense."

I thanked him; said I appreciated his comment but wasn't so sure about the word "intellectual."

"It's no crime being an intellectual, if he talks so I can understand him. You did."

JULY 11, 1971
MARTHA'S VINEYARD

An unbelievable, hysterical "to-do" is going on over the so-called Pentagon Papers. So out of scale have these Pentagon essays become that most people forget that they were not written by deciders but by anonymous "analysts."

They have been the occasion for some of the most splenetic, gloomy prose about the downfall of America we have heard from the word-people in a long time.

The U.S. is *not* like that, not at all.

JULY 14, 1971
MARTHA'S VINEYARD

Ged and Ellen Bentley are here from Princeton for what, happily, has become an annual visit with us at "Topside."

Being with Ged Bentley, whether we sail or not, is always a delight and a stimulus. Scholar as he is, and has been his life long, about a remote period of English literary life—the times of Shakespeare—he is extraordinarily sensitive to contemporary life, and particularly to changes he observes among younger people. Since young people provide a forward clue to the movement of thinking and motion of all of us, I always listen with care and respect to what he says about the young.

To me the young are the videttes, the outposts that sound the alarm about what is coming.

Ged's observation of the young settles on two chief characteristics: they are highly moral, and they are mystical.

To the more casual and less perceptive, the casual sex-ing that goes on among the young, the whole quasi-hippie bit, seems at first glance remote from anything "mystical."

But Ged has the advantage of having been brought up in a Methodist parsonage in southern Indiana, both his father and mother being professionally involved in what today would be considered an almost fundamentalist religious tradition. He insists that his mother believed in her dreams. "She had visions; no other way to describe it." Rural Methodism of that time was not only mystical, in that sense, but highly moral. Many kids today believe in the unseen. They have a strong impulse to share with each other, and to disavow comforts and good middle-class clothes. They have a disdain for ambition, for "getting ahead." And, therefore, they fit into a tradition of morality of an earlier time.

But the kids, Ged went on, would be the last to recognize this, or agree.

"The only thing in which they are different from that tradition of the mystical and the highly moral is their attitude and practice about sex relations. That is new and different."

JULY 17, 1971
MARTHA'S VINEYARD

At Cedar Tree Neck, I prowled all over that beloved moor. I looked out over an oak woodland. My eyes rested with joy on the dark, dark blue of the fresh water pond, a gem against the tawny dunes and dark forest. What a good, satisfying sensation. Henry Hough and I provided some of the initiative and funds that will keep all that forever as it was this afternoon, when it might so readily have become a "development."

JULY 28, 1971
NEW YORK

New York City can be dirty, noisy, overcrowded, rude, unlivable. . . .

But it can be the most beautiful, happy, entrancing, captivating place in the whole world.

That was tonight. Beatrice, Barney, and his brother, Bill Tobey, took me to see what was billed as *Two Gentlemen of Verona* in the Delacorte open-air theatre in Central Park. What a lark! The play was an uproar from beginning to end. A lithe, vital, nubile, black projectile of a girl—Jonelle Allen—stole the show, but the whole performance showed imagination and the joy of life.

The most fun, and the most New York flavor, was the audience, a great cross-section of young people. The cast was "jumping" but so, almost literally, was the audience, me included.

No set at all. A rock band banging away. The sky was clear and steady; planes with their blue and red lights occasionally drifting over, like Christmas trees lit up. Away off there came the quarter moon, with three young Americans in a capsule zooming on their way to roam about on it.

When New York is as good as tonight, it is terrific.

JULY 29, 1971
NEW YORK

One of the unassuming giants among university presidents has been John Dickey of Dartmouth, recently retired. An impressively tall man of lumbering gait, intense, inquiring eyes, a gift of economical speech. His work at Dartmouth was outstanding but few people know as well as I of his competence at his several tasks in the State Department. He is now concentrating on a study of Canadian-U.S. relations.

Perhaps the most important relationship of all is that of the U.S. with Canada. What an extraordinarily neglected field this has been.

The tension and even bitterness among Canadians toward the U.S. has reached a high point, said Dickey. But why?

Dickey will produce some light in a neglected corner of U.S. policy and practice. Here is a case where private American business organizations—i.e., nongovernmental—are at least as significant in producing the antagonism and frustration Canadians feel as anything our government can do.

JULY 30, 1971
PENN STATION, NEW YORK

Astros on the Moon—big headline in the *Daily News.*

But here at Madison Square Garden and the surrounding terrain, the oddest lot of adolescents, in their uniforms of disordered clothes. Pouring in from all directions toward the Garden. "There will be 20,000 of them listening to rock music here tonight," explained the taximan.

This outpouring of youngsters is here to yell their joy over ear-splitting rock music, all competing to show they are each dressed differently from their friends, or different as a phalanx, from their "elders."

Will we have a contemporary and realistic history of the special phenomenon of crowds of this particular period?

9:45 P.M.

On the Metroliner to Washington (as jerky as a fractious mule, speed or no speed).

Luncheon meeting this noon of the directors of the Twentieth Century Fund. The subject: "Energy." What an abstraction that wonderfully sturdy word "energy" has turned into—unhappily.

I said only one thing that made sense, to me.

"My AEC successor, the late Gordon Dean, thought the AEC's problem was to get the confidence of the Congress, which meant the Joint Congressional Atomic Energy Committee, which meant actually two members: Congressmen Holifield and Hosmer.

"The AEC may have the confidence of the Joint Committee—that can be purchased by agreeing with them.

"But they do not, obviously, have the confidence of the public. They are simply not trusted.

"Regaining the confidence of the 'concerned citizens and housewives' is the AEC's problem, *not* being cozy with the source of funds."

AUGUST I, I97I
WASHINGTON, D.C.

This afternoon I am to attend a ceremony marking the twenty-fifth anniversary of the enactment of the Atomic Energy Act. I look forward to this with a vague distaste. The speeches will be about the past by people who are looking back to the days when whatever the AEC, and particularly the Joint Congressional Atomic Energy Committee, said *had* to be believed. No longer is this true. I am proud that I have contributed to the skepticism that sooner or later will require the AEC and the Joint Committee to face up to the ultimate fact and not just pat each other on the back.

Watched the TV shots of the men on the moon. The ghostly figures of the astronauts were like Rip van Winkle with his pack on his back among the weird shapes of his twenty-year-long dreams.

The casual, businesslike way these brave men up there drill holes, bounce about in their weightless state! What men can do dealing with inanimate objects—almost nothing seems impossible. But dealing with each other, with living people—there we are as awkward and unsure as ever we were.

8 P.M.

IN UNION STATION, WASHINGTON

At the AEC anniversary ceremony, the chilliness toward me from Senator Pastore and Chet Holifield was as anticipated. But the wow of a welcome I had from what must have been a thousand people of the lesser categories of the AEC was unmistakable, warm, more than friendly. More than one staff member—identifying themselves—came up to me afterward to say how they shared my publicly expressed concern for the "naiveté" the AEC and the Joint Committee show toward the great hazards that have not been faced, much less resolved.

I learned a new way of stating what is one basis of my continued criticism of atomic energy: the "magnitudes" of the radioactive material that will be pouring into and out of these new reactors. These vast amounts of this poisonous material change the very nature of the problem, as so often magnitudes do.

AUGUST 10, 1971

MARTHA'S VINEYARD

From the Iranian Ambassador in Washington, Dr. A. Aslan Afshar, dated August 2nd, a formal invitation to Helen and me "to attend" and "to participate in the festivities" celebrating the 2500th anniversary of the founding of the Persian Empire.

A heartening, warm letter yesterday from Herman Wells, chancellor of Indiana University. A long one too, from so laconic a man.

Herman's background as a business school teacher and administrator, and as the product of an Indiana farm, gives no clue to the cultural wonders he has performed in a state, and region, where cultural interests were dormant, indeed I thought were nonexistent. I refer particularly to art and music, and even "exotic" foreign languages (Russian, Arabic, Chinese).

He has performed what is a miracle of educational and political leadership. To transform a university from a less than average state university into a locus of intellectual and artistic ferment and achievement, which he has done, is something no other university president has to his credit within my memory. To bring the people of a state along (and the chronically skeptical legislature) not only in agreement but pride and approval of educational pioneering: here is a feat that matches any in the political field. The Kennedys did fuel a spiritual fire on the national scene, particularly among a new generation. But back home in Massachusetts and notoriously in Boston, politics was not only as dismal as before, corrupt, thugish but, if anything, got worse as the Kennedy family stirred the nation outside their own bailiwick.

Herman stirred Indiana at all levels, and this is the real test of what can only be called leadership at its highest and best.

AUGUST II, 1971
MARTHA'S VINEYARD

For years I have been expressing the idea that our policy of building a great American wall around Communist China was an error of the greatest dimension. So the dramatic change that came with the Kissinger visit to China and the oncoming Nixon visit I thought was an important step toward realism, a hopeful, affirmative move.

But in the journalistic euphoria—such as a Seymour Topping series in the *Times*—I hear echoes of the acclaim for Communist Russia of thirty or so years ago. This is the future, that euphoria said. As a consequence a whole generation of young idealistic Americans had their minds confused about Communism—and later were profoundly disillusioned.

Why can't we have some balanced reports about China now?

Why don't we look into the difficult problems and obstacles the Chinese face: their primitive agricultural production, their floods, their unused resources of manpower, the consequences to them of repeating the earlier insensate drive of the Russians toward industrialization at all costs in an agricultural country?

This would show our concern and sympathy without presenting their brand of Communism as the kind of heaven that an earlier cadre of journalists and shallow idealists pictured Soviet Russia. The price for that uncritical embracing of the Soviets we are still paying.

It is an old story: something we want so very much to believe we insist on believing. For a time.

AUGUST 15, 1971
MARTHA'S VINEYARD

Our Bromberger grandsons, Allen and Daniel, allergic normally to letter writing, are literally flooding us with excited postcards from France, where the family is apparently missing nothing. Little essays on each card (particularly by the reserved Daniel) explaining the card. Mont St. Michel: the tide comes in "twelve miles," underlined twice. Napoleon's tomb; the chateaux of the Loire—a little excited message about each to their grandparents.

Who says travel isn't an awakening process?

AUGUST 16, 1971
MARTHA'S VINEYARD

Last night Richard Nixon, President of the U.S., announced action so drastic and forceful, no one who thought he knew what a wavering man Nixon has always been would have believed he could possibly take it.

I listened to the wage-price-freeze statement. Ah well, thought I, this is Nixon again; the freezes last only ninety days, which will do nothing. But then the 10% tax on imports; actually that meets the issue of Japanese flooding of the American market. Going off the gold standard, accepting the fact that the dollar was not worth more than 75¢ so long as we were importing $2 billion more in the second quarter of this year than we exported.

When we get into as great trouble as the economy is in, even a Nixon can take hold.

Thought I: Well, I am tomorrow going to spend several hours with the Oracle of What Is Wrong with the American Economy, Eliot Janeway. *Then* I'll learn whether this is good news, and what it means.

We did have lunch with the Janeways. I didn't learn much about the meaning of the Nixon measure except this important conclusion: *something* had to be done; this is the right direction. Said Eliot, "This action goes to the root of most of our troubles."

As we arrived at the house overlooking the Vineyard Haven harbor where they were staying, we could hear the Oracle's carrying voice booming away. This was *his* day and all the clients of his justly famous economic service and all the newspapers would want to get his views of the Nixon action. Which apparently they did until 2 A.M. last night, and all through our afternoon visit. Germany calling. London calling. Italian newspaper calling. And so on.

All of this furor Eliot took with great composure. His dress hardly fit the picture of the American John Stuart Mill: a pair of very baggy and worn pink shorts, a scanty horizontally striped sport T-shirt, all topped by his great leonine head and heavy tortoise glasses. Quite a picture. If ever I saw a man pleased—and rightly pleased—to be the center of questions from the whole world—or so it seemed—this was Eliot Janeway this afternoon.

It was the public recognition at last of the danger of Japanese commercial overaggressiveness and business ruthlessness that pleased me most. Now it is in the open. And this is just the beginning, the earliest beginning.

AUGUST 22, 1971
MARTHA'S VINEYARD

Just to be with "B. Tobey" for a day or two is to see how the world looks to a real pro of a cartoonist.

Fascinating to watch his face and manner while he is ostensibly just ambling along the streets and mixing with the crowds of people in Edgartown: making mental notes of people, oddities, situations that evoke those amusing or wry comments on life which are his stock in trade with his pen. His mind and imagination are constantly on the whirr.

It was an enjoyable time, this visit of Beatrice and Barney.

Last evening after dinner a whole evening of *general* conversation. An intellectual Ping-Pong game between myself and my cousin Peter Szanton, head of the RAND operation in New York, and now one of the country's leading "analysts," this strange (to me) new profession. Peter has an extraordinarily thoughtful strong face; he is tall and erect and youthful in appearance, and by no means a sobersides, though his profession of systems analysis is one generally inhabited by some of the most self-conscious and intellectually and emotionally arrogant men to be found anywhere.

SEPTEMBER 2, 1971
NEW YORK

A sad, utterly sad note from Colombia: Manuel Carvajal died suddenly last night, in Philadelphia.

What an exemplary man he was. From the very first day I saw him on the dock at Buenaventura on our first trip to Colombia in 1954, I was filled with pride that such a man existed. Enthusiastic, understanding, a public spirited businessman and public servant. As I said to Rod Rockefeller, who thoughtfully called to console me on the loss of a friend, Manuel—a rich man—was a kind of Latin American Nelson Rockefeller, who understood the responsibilities of wealth. "If Latin America had only a hundred Carvajals," I said, "the entire continent would be a different place and its future a bright one."

SEPTEMBER 4, 1971
PRINCETON

Forty-eight years ago almost exactly I, a skinny fellow of twenty-three, stood in the "parlor" of Helen's home, 605 East Jefferson Street in

Crawfordsville, Indiana, and said to President Grose and the assembled family: "Yes, I do; I will cherish this young woman for the rest of my life."‡ Of course I had no real idea what that meant. How can a *kid* (as I think today of a man of that age and inexperience) possibly comprehend what life together holds for the long future about which he is asked to make (and eagerly does make) such profound promises?

We, Helen and I, did keep those little-understood promises: we have cherished each other in sickness, in health, in good weather and in ill. Not perfectly, of course, but with a sense of the importance of continuity not too highly regarded these days.

Yesterday, watched the Italian mamas buy fruit and fish in the open stalls that line lower Ninth Avenue, en route to the Lincoln Tunnel. The boxes and cartons on the street showed that the vegetables and fruit had been raised in California, doubtless under the most modern of techniques, shipped in refrigeration, etc. But the mamas were the same as always: pinching the tomatoes, hefting the fish and tossing them back until they found one that they liked; all the modern methods of production and shipping hadn't affected in the least the broad-hipped Italian dames, the customers who were the reason for all that slick technology of food production in California.

SEPTEMBER 5, 1971
PRINCETON

Being the cook for so simple a meal as a robust breakfast—as I have been this morning—is like being the fevered drummer in a combo, certainly more frenetic than it would be to Helen. I wanted it all to come out together, so I could sit down and eat cantaloupe, grapefruit, scrambled eggs with bacon, toast and jelly, and a series of cups of coffee which must be very hot, for me.

It is very quiet in this big house, and I like it. Good for reflection.

That dratted sprain in my instep, or ankle, kicked up today. I tried to take the weight off the foot by hobbling around on two canes.

All of which made me uncertain about my ability to make my forthcoming trip to Colombia. But Colombia and the Cauca Valley (CVC) mean a great deal to me: the CVC was the beginning of the career in overseas development to which I am now so heavily committed. More important still: those men in Colombia are my *friends.* It will be a time of mourning for Manuel. I should be there.

‡Bishop George R. Grose, president of DePauw University, performed the marriage ceremony.

I think about Eleanor Roosevelt and Franklin, suddenly stricken, paralyzed. Not just a measly, bum, painful ankle, but his whole body and his whole life at stake. She wouldn't let him begin the withdrawal that is the onset of invalidism and self-pity.

SEPTEMBER 7, 1971
TAKING OFF BY AIR FOR COLOMBIA

In the long watches of last night, at the Roosevelt Hotel, the pain (and swelling) in my ankle and instep gave me little sleep.

"What a stupid thing, to start out on this kind of expedition. Why not be sensible, cancel the expedition, go back to Princeton, and wait till the damn thing is well enough?"

Then the rest of the dialog between me and myself in that little hotel room, in a long night punctuated by much pain. "You have made a commitment. Your own respect for yourself would be badly damaged if you would be all that 'sensible.' "

I have written all this introspective tripe for a special reason. One day years and years from now someone (who? I don't know) will read these notes; they will see how contrary to fact is the notion that D.E.L. always had things going for him. And mostly this is true. But not without some of the silliest doubts a man ever had.

Some of my partisan friends insist that I can see ahead, see what is coming, or should come. "Your trouble," says Helen—and others—"is that you are ahead of the times, so you don't get credit for your prescience because by the time your predictions come true your foresight is so far in the past as to be forgotten."

Overstated?

But there is not a little evidence that I have called the turn. This morning's reading of the papers and news magazines provides some case material.

Item: as I left the White House in May of 1969 (when I handed President Nixon our Joint Development Report on Vietnam postwar) I said to TV reporters I thought Japan should carry at least one-third of the cost of Vietnamese economic development since it was she who would benefit most, and would push everyone else out of Southeast Asia. Very little attention was paid to this, or to a similar though less precise statement at the end of my article in *Foreign Affairs* of about the same time.

Today, only seven or eight months later, this Cassandra-like cry: "Beware Japan," is hardly shocking. It is, above all, the basis of much of the Nixon import surcharge which could change the whole picture of our relations with Japan. In my lecture in Tokyo for *Asahi Shimbun,* the largest Japanese newspaper, I was euphoric about what I called the Pacific Basin. I predicated that glowing future upon a liberal trade policy by *both* Japan and the U.S. But that liberal trade policy was liberal only on our side; Japan shoved her excellent products into the great lush American market, but prevented American products from entering the Japanese market. I didn't believe, from my conversations in Tokyo with Japanese businessmen and economic public officials that Japan would be so stupid. But she was. And the "economic collision course" I predicted to Ambassador Alexis Johnson is a *reality* today, as real and present a danger, in the economic field, as it was twenty-five years or so ago in the military (cum economic) period that culminated in the "day of infamy" of December 7, 1941, the attack on Pearl Harbor.

Another instance of looking ahead: on the editorial page of the *New York Times* this morning (and a long story in the *Wall Street Journal*), there is comment on the effect of an AEC order of the other day, finally taking cognizance of the full range and the impact of atomic power plants on the total environment, and of some of the hazards of such plants. That the order was forced on the AEC by a scolding court decision involving a plant near Baltimore doesn't change the implications, which are to cause a review of atomic power plant approvals in more than ninety locations throughout the country.

The *Times* editorial blandly says that the euphoria about atomic power plants is being replaced, witness the AEC order, by a recognition of their dangers and limitations. Well, when I faced a very angry Joint Congressional Atomic Energy Committee, called on the "carpet" by the Committee to recant my Stafford Little Lectures' skepticism about the peaceful atom, the *Times* news columns hardly noted my appearance. It is all recorded in Volume V of these *Journals* of almost ten years ago, but the *Times* writers of today don't find it necessary to refer to my warning uttered that long ago.

SEPTEMBER 10, 1971
CALI, COLOMBIA

There are satisfactions in this world greater than those I have experienced in the last couple days here in the Cauca Valley. But they are few, and less tangible.

I look out upon the green mountains that close in this city, hear the rush of the water of the Cauca River, a river that has become synonymous, in this valley, with my name and ideas and works. I am received by scores of people I have known for many years who greet me with such a light in their eyes and the strong, double *abrazos* reserved for true friends among these people of the Valley. I see the splendid new medical school and hospital, and the brand-new university almost completed, the housing settlements on the edge of the city for thousands of poor people, replacing the noisome shacks I saw in the same place in 1954, see an extensive industrial development of medium-sized plants (steel fabrication, concrete, pulp, etc.) and a four-lane highway circling the city. And then they say to me, "It was the impetus of your Plan Lilienthal for CVC that brought much of this about." How could any one mortal not feel that it is not in vain that he has sweated and groaned and stood up under grave frustrations and difficulties?

9 P.M.

A good day. A "full house" for my speech to the Pan American Management Conference, though early in the morning.

I got a lot of questions, submitted in written form. Two of my impromptu responses I thought showed just the right kind of candor, even bluntness, and certainly no evasion on my part. Parts of the audience applauded some of my answers—which has rarely ever happened to me before. Especially my impromptu phrase—the growth of U.S. "cultural humility."

Rodman Rockefeller made a big hit by speaking in Spanish in his opening pleasantries, with very much the touch of the experienced speaker. His speech, however, which he read, word for word, hardly looking up, was a sober and "constructive" statement, quite defensive of American contribution, and because it was so serious and factual was naturally somewhat on the dull side, judging by the fact that there were no questions submitted to him.

Rodman was generous in thanking me for arranging that he attend and participate. He enjoyed not only the audience but much more the opportunity to meet all kinds of people. This he does *extraordinarily* well, friendly, interested, absorbed. I would say he is much more at home "out among them," as this week, than plowing through administrative and management matters in an office. Me, too.

SEPTEMBER II, 1971
LEAVING CALI FOR BOGOTÁ

Colombia is an airborne country—and no wonder, considering how the mountains divide it, and this despite the fact that in the years since we first came here some impressive highways have been built.

Rodman and I are traveling together. I'm inspired by the delight he shows in being in Latin America, the knowledge he has of the continent, his interest in promoting education and health. Right now he's talking, in his highly charged Spanish, with Mario Lazerna about education.

His father, Nelson, helped found the Universidad de Los Andes, and Laserna is the first rector of that small but influential university, from which I hold an honorary degree.

At age sixteen Rodman spent several months in a Rockefeller Foundation experiment station in Honduras; later he spent summers on his father's ranch in Venezuela.

BOGOTÁ AIRPORT

Rodman has an exuberance and sureness about his opinions that reminds me of his father when I spent an evening with him at the time he was Latin American Coordinator. The subject—I was then AEC Chairman—was the application of atomic energy to the problems of Brazil. It was the propaganda value for the U.S. of an announcement about this possibility for the development of atomic energy in Brazil that seemed to Nelson the important thing. When I said I didn't think peaceful atomic energy was at a point where such a sanguine statement could or should be made, Nelson disagreed, argued hard and positively.

And Rodman, the son, is equally positive. He said: "Freedom is one of the most dangerous things imaginable. Only 25% of any population are able to handle freedom. Because they are not able to deal with the freedom they now have, many of our young people are in such confusion.

"My father has had the liberals' doctrine of 'participatory democracy' clear up to here [motioning to his neck]. Destructive. It is a variant of the kind of freedom that so few people can handle."

12 NOON

For two and a half hours we have been sitting in this plane in Bogotá, waiting to take off for New York. "A technical problem; there will be a ten-minute delay," is the message, and when an experienced traveler hears *that* he knows that he is in for it.

3 P.M.

Now back on another Avianca aircraft, the one in trouble having been led away, shamefaced, the entrails of one of its motors exposed to the daylight by the inquiring mechanics, who finally gave up and sent it to the humiliation of a machine shop.

Rodman's conversational abilities and energy are formidable, intensely interesting, and wide-ranging.

Somehow the name of Herman Kahn came up—goodness knows we had plenty of time to have almost everyone's name come up.

Said Rodman: "Herman Kahn's Hudson Institute is the most amazing place in the world. Those fellows sit around a table and brainstorm for hours on end; completely undisciplined, disorganized talk, and no conclusion, of course. I think it is a shocking and fruitless way of going at things. They have an engineer among them who is unbelievable. They think that low dams are what the underdeveloped countries need, rather than high dams, and that led to Kahn's proposal for damming up the Amazon River and putting a large part of Brazil under water—which aroused the Brazilians so that I don't think Herman will show up in that country again.

"But my father is crazy about Herman. My father likes to have a man around who tosses out what may pass for ideas, and the wilder the better, because he feels he can sort out something from this outpouring that he can put to some practical-action use. That's the same way Father used to use Adolf Berle. Berle would expound this stuff, that to me didn't make any particular sense, disorganized, frenetic, all over the place. One time when Adolf was talking that way, I started to disagree and argue. My father banged his fist down on the table and stopped me. 'It's our business to listen, not to argue.' "

4 P.M.
IN FLIGHT

We finally did take off; we are now about halfway to New York but only after we passengers were again "evacuated," and were herded, after this delay of eight hours, into the *same* plane that brought us from Cali and that had been disemboweled for some internal malaise.

The long delays—hours and hours—enabled me to listen to a remarkable story of what it's like to be the scion of a world-famous family, certainly the most notable family, everything considered, that America has ever produced. To wit—the Rockefellers.

SEPTEMBER 14, 1971
NEW YORK

A letter from the Ambassador of Iran to the U.S. stating that we are to be the "personal guests of His Majesty" at the celebration of the 2500th anniversary of the founding of Iran, and telling us when we are to take off from Tehran for Shiraz, with accommodations provided.

SEPTEMBER 19, 1971
PRINCETON

My commitment to action is my role in life. It is my strong impulse to "go up to a problem instead of waiting for it to come to me" that marks me off. It is my nature to accept responsibility eagerly, it is my conviction (inchoate and rarely expressed) that it is through me that some consequential things get done and important ideas become reality.

It is the present vogue, particularly among the young, among black people, and militants and rebels generally, to put the blame for everything—including acts of violence they have committed against others—on "society" in general, blame everyone except one's self.

This is a form of anarchy far more devastating and ruinous to all of us than the classic anarchism of Emma Goldman and Alexander Berkman of the early part of the century. That was a political doctrine. It was often called "philosophical anarchism," and earned that dignity, for it had some philosophy behind it, a philosophy of freedom from restraints that became an unreal fantasy.

But the anarchy of blaming society so as to avoid any individual responsibility has no such philosophical, rational basis whatever.

A long, animated lunch, Helen and I, at the kitchen table, the viands, last evening's chicken, cold; plenty of wine, and best of all, spirited conversation. Really good conversation "after all these years of marriage" is the best kind. And why not? If we had much to talk about—as we did—when I was "seeing Helen home" from the library as a student, why shouldn't there be much to "converse about" now, with so much knowledge of each other and of how we see the world, present, future, as well as past?

SEPTEMBER 22, 1971
SAN JUAN, PUERTO RICO

This long-planned trip to Puerto Rico has a specific business purpose: to expand D&R's work assignments on this island, and obtain a new contract or engagement. The agencies with which we already have contracts for technical and management assistance welcome the idea. They see that the Government needs *something:* they are full of the *language* of planning, but action and clear lines of how to get from plans to results are lacking.

What interests me here is a fascinating problem in human personality and the *how* of the presentation of an idea. That idea is regionalism, or regional development.

It isn't an easy task of explanation and persuasion. "Planning" with a capital P has been an accepted slogan in Puerto Rico for decades since Governor Rex Tugwell's days. But the realities just aren't known. The essence of regional development is action. When one calls for action the "overeducated" drag out all the finespun reasons why action is "premature," or why there should be *another* commission to study something, or they are tender-minded or scared about fights over "jurisdiction" between two agencies, or noisy personalities. Anything but getting going.

This was roughly the impasse that existed when we began TVA, though few people now realize this. The fledgling TVA of 1933 to 1936 faced the Washington-based Federal agencies steeped in their concern for their "jurisdiction," and the lower-case local politicos, plus the academics and intellectuals who never want to move but only to philosophize.

Regional integrated development is not just a concept to be "explained" and expounded; it is a method of action.

6:30 P.M.

One of the greatest "difficulties," as several conferences with agency heads here in San Juan has disclosed, is that those responsible for parts of the problem of economic development not only don't agree on the facts, particularly about availability of water for industry and agriculture, but don't seem to have that rapport and close touch with each other that is necessary if conflicts or competition for different uses of resources (particularly water) are to be resolved or harmonized.

For example, the dashing Madison Avenue-type Puerto Rican young man (35), Casiano, promoting industry quite successfully, admitted that unless industry can be guaranteed a water supply, prospects for further industry will "grind to a halt." This is for locations on the South Coast where heavy (or as he put it, "dirty") industry is located.

On the other hand, the head of the Aqueduct and Sewer Authority, the water supplier for the island, Wilfredo Vivoni, is dejected because he says there won't be water unless a tunnel project (Toa Vaca) to bring water from the North Coast is activated. It is now stopped dead because of the highly theoretical criticism by one of those Harvard-MIT abstract-reasoning "consultants."

The Secretary of Agriculture says he is under orders to expand sugar agriculture on the South Coast; sugar is a greedy user of water. It is clear there won't be enough for both sugar and urban and industrial uses.

So nothing happens. The pieces simply have to be put together. That is what practical "integrated development" is about.

Can I make this point with Governor Ferre at our scheduled meeting? But how, in the abstract, can you explain to a rich businessman, now Governor, a subject so remote from his experience?

SEPTEMBER 25, 1971
PRINCETON

What was to have been the crucial high point (even *the* point) of my Puerto Rico trip was to be this conference with Governor Ferre. This we had on Wednesday at eleven, for about an hour. It turned out to be amusing, not to say downright funny. A comic "routine" that had to be seen to be believed.

Luis Ferre is as great a contrast to the great Governor Luis Muñoz-Marin as any writer of fiction could invent. His background, his physical appearance and posture, his methods of functioning.

A highly successful businessman, with inherited wealth buttressed by taking business advantage of the needs of an island that has been busting its seams with growth. Growth that has been stimulated by large infusions of the adrenaline of industrial and commercial investments from "the States," and those in turn given a great boost by the total exemption from Federal income taxes and large infusions of money and technical assistance from the Washington Federal Government.

We sat at the huge table in what they actually call "the throne room," very high-ceilinged, but not as dark as when I was last there with Muñoz. In bounced an athletic, trim, middle-aged man, below average height, a broad somewhat synthetic Rotarian-style smile. (Muñoz had come into a room like a bear, ambling, his white suit much wrinkled, in planter style.) Ferre wore dark, formal clothes, a white handkerchief poised in his breast pocket.

He knew about TVA; in fact, he said, smiling brightly and in the most friendly way, "I know about the systems method; you see, I am a member of the MIT Corporation. In fact, I use the most scientific systems methods. In the next room I will show you how I keep *instantly* informed, so I don't have to wait for the facts until some agency reports them; I have all that information by computer right at my desk in the Cabinet room next door."

He moved quickly as he led us into the Cabinet room. By his own chair was a white object, hooded; under the hood was a television-type screen, and below it many keys, with letters and numbers, much like a typewriter. With help from a young assistant ("I don't yet know just how to use this"), he punched keys, and on the TV screen came a line of type and numbers. "Cement production for August." "Number of telephone complaints" about this and that. "Number of letters of complaint" about power interruptions.

Turning, he grinned and said: "You see I can keep up with what is being done and what people think without waiting for reports weeks and weeks later."

He settled back, with satisfaction, and said, "This instrument gives me a new modern way for decision-making."

Of course, I definitely don't think "decision-making" is made easier by more information than anyone could possibly make use of. Certainly increasing the amount of information and "facts" by this gimmick, if anything, makes it more difficult for the head of so complex and human an enterprise—such a living organism—as Puerto Rico to come to decisions.

The mystique of the computer that can *talk* to you, and therefore can answer your questions, and can think, has been carried to its reductio ad absurdum in that little room in a 16th century Spanish colonial fortress.

SEPTEMBER 30, 1971
NEXT STOP PARIS, BY AIR FRANCE

How well I remember our trip to England—it must have been in the early sixties. I was to be honored at a ceremony at Oxford. It rained like billy hell. I cancelled out, stayed at the hotel in a cowardly way nursing nothing more serious than a fiery throat. "Nothing daunted," Helen put on her rain clothes, joined an American Express tour which made a stop at Oxford. She stood in the rain, a nameless American tour lady, and watched the gowned procession go by, of which I would have been a principal part. She laughed about this last evening at dinner; I still don't find it funny.

OCTOBER 1, 1971
PARIS

I recall so vividly what Eleanor Roosevelt said about pushing Franklin, after his polio attack had paralyzed him: she would not let him think of himself as an invalid. And that great woman said something of the same kind when she was asked, late in life, how she could possibly keep going at such a pace, never really giving up or letting go. Aches and pains, she said (I paraphrase), are part of getting older. But once you give in to them you start "down the road to becoming an invalid."

In far lesser circumstances, that phrase of hers has recurred to me more than once, as I fought off the pain in my foot for every step I walked in Colombia (where I had to get about with a clumsy cane) and in Puerto Rico last week, going down stairs that nearly blinded me with pain. But once I give up to pain something bad will have happened to my spirit.

OCTOBER 3, 1971
PARIS

Chartres Cathedral! What a majestic way to speak the glory of man. A worshipful feeling within me, looking up to these magnificent circles of color on a perfect October day. That dark ancient cathedral and those unbelievably beautiful windows are a testament to the faith in God of men centuries ago, otherwise how could they have built so great a structure, a hymn of belief and a poem of severe beauty?

We were driven to Chartres and back through back country roads lined with trees already turning yellow, huge fields of corn that would have done Iowa or Illinois proud for size, being cut and harvested by big puffing machines.

It was late Saturday afternoon when we returned, through St. Cloud. Thousands of families walking, playing, just enjoying the wooded and the broad green places that make Paris a more livable place than any other great city I know. The beginning of a sunny weekend, and they were all out. Cars, cars, cars.

OCTOBER 9, 1971
PARIS

Last Thursday we drove through the Loire Valley. It was sightseeing of the conventional kind. But the weather was so beautiful, the woods so green and beginning-gold, that in spite of my sales resistance to sightseeing, it was thoroughly enjoyable.

OCTOBER 12, 1971
TEHRAN

Last night Helen and I had an experience of a lifetime filled with experiences. At ten or so, we drove through the streets of Tehran, and saw the most magnificent display of illumination that the mind of man could conceive. "Spectacular" is a mild word. Street after street arched by a million lights.

We were awed. Said Helen, "It is like Illumination Night at Oak Bluffs on the Vineyard, but this is Illumination Night magnified ten-thousandfold." Several millionfold, she could have said. Color, grace, buildings dripping with lights, forming figures, symbols.

OCTOBER 14, 1971
HOTEL DARIUS, PERSEPOLIS

This hotel is brand-new, barely completed, like most everything in this amazing country where things are either very, very old, or just born, or being born.

How beautifully organized and smoothly executed, this sixty-nation gathering of big shots and those who are just full of themselves, all of whom have an invitation to this celebration of the founding of the Persian Empire.

Early this morning a note of sadness and nostalgia: a headline, *Dean Acheson Dead at 78.*

What a remarkable man and what an extraordinary part he played in the history of the world. With his delightful quality of wryness, he couldn't be called a cynic, not a full-blown one. There must have been in him an infrastructure of hope to sustain him through the trials and exhausting and often hopeless struggles of his public service. Happy for him, thought I, that he apparently died suddenly with no long humiliating immobility of body and mind.

Being me, I couldn't help thinking of my own inevitable chapter marked "finis."

The group assembled in this hotel is as fantastic as the occasion. Just now, looking out of the window into the hollow square, in the dying light of a desert sunset, I see a group of a dozen men from the sheikdoms, drifting about. Where will they find a place to say their evening prayers, I wonder, in this oh so antiseptic place?

What a stroke of pure imagination to tie this celebration into this ancient spot, Persepolis, into the remote past, into the glory of Cyrus and the continuity of the Persian Empire. At a time when the concept of royalty is everywhere definitely on the wane, someone of genius saw that the love of pageantry was anything but on the wane, and has made the most of it.

3 A.M.

Just back from the festivities after the formal dinner—Sound and Light, an electric display—telling the story of Persepolis in the setting of that grand ruin. It was a sight and an experience that lived up to every possible expectation—the beauty of the setting, the excitement of men and women of so many countries and so many exotic costumes. This is surely an experience to be placed alongside the most memorable of my life.

The Shah was most kindly and particularly gracious as we were presented to him. ("You are still working with us, I hope. You must. We are very serious." This is what he said as we shook hands.) Most of the people were the conventional diplomatic professionals one sees in any capital in the world.

This afternoon, beneath the towering walls of Persepolis in the brilliant sunlight, as great a spectacular as ever I—or anyone else—has seen in modern times. For more than an hour, in close marching formation or on beautifully schooled horses, squad after squad, the history of ancient Persia as a military power streamed by. History, but more alive than the present they seemed, in bright dress and shining weapons and armor. An absolutely flawless major ballet, this ancient edifice towering over it all; from the walls men dressed as Achaemenian warriors, shields held at the ready and leaning on spears, with the mountains as a further background.

The arrangements are perfectly carried out; one more evidence of how well these Iranians can do certain things that call for discipline, careful planning, and the use of money without stint. It all seemed not contrived, but real.

OCTOBER 15, 1971
PERSEPOLIS

After all this display of wealth and lavish hospitality, a great and gnawing doubt in my mind tonight, as Helen and I prepared to go to still another sumptuous dinner, described as a "private dinner given by the Shahanshah and the Shahbanou for the distinguished guests."

The doubt is this: how will the people in the villages, and the rising middle class, beginning to feel their oats, take to all this expensive display? Will they share the pride and confidence in their country that the military figures and the civil service obviously have? How much more important it is to have an affirmative answer to *that kind of doubt* than to impress the essentially inconsequential diplomatic professional corps who like ourselves are enjoying all this richness.

Some of the doubt came to the surface, and some was partly dispelled, by the way in which the lengthy ancient military display came to a conclusion. There were companies of present-day troops and women in uniform. I surely expected the "Pahlavi period," as the program described it, to be followed and the parade concluded as it would be in Moscow or Peking—by the rumble of great tanks and overhead the roar of Phantom jet fighters of the Air Force.

Not at all. The end of this display of military glory was a colorful squadron carrying on pennants the flags of all nations—the Universal Training Corps, a UN-style Peace Corps, which was the Shah's and Princess Ashraf's idea and sponsored by them. And after that in most unmilitary fashion, young people, marching it's true, but without weapons—the Literacy Corps, the Health Corps, etc. And finally, not in step at all, but simply walking along, "civilians" from all tribes, including some girls in colorful tribal costume. A sign that I am not completely wrong in my hope that this Shah has ideas about priorities that are not solely or perhaps even chiefly military, as are those held by most of the other nations of the world today.

So this was a good hopeful touch and I was proud to see it.

OCTOBER 16, 1971
FLYING OVER THE MOUNTAINS FROM SHIRAZ TO TEHRAN

Last night a spirited and convivial buffet dinner in the "main tent" (as the circus master of ceremonies used to say, and in this case quite accurately). Quite a contrast to the utter formality and strict protocol of Thursday night's Grand Banquet (the banquet of the century, the headline writers here programmed it). But not just a homey little potluck affair either—probably three hundred or four hundred people.

The Shah came in with the President of Russia, with the Titos, Papa and Mama, both broad-beamed and oh so Slavic. And Prince Philip, slender and tall, a balding young man, with his buck-toothed but appealing daughter, Princess Anne. And other "Heads of State." The Shah seated those at his table himself, with the same personal supervision that used to amuse me about Lyndon Johnson at after-dinner White House entertainment.

The Shah seemed absolutely tireless. What a day it has been—several days it has been for him. With the Empress (who smiled in a determined way, though she must have been practically exhausted), he greeted the guests and took his time exchanging words with them as they left. It was by this time after midnight, and yet he seemed as composed and as interested in each guest as if this were the first hour of the evening.

OCTOBER 17, 1971
TEHRAN

Never have I been in a hotel quite like this one. Big, elaborate, brand-new edifice, loaded with servants, from bellboys to reception clerks—and practically empty. Not only empty now, but likely to remain so until the guards are pulled off. For the hotel is sealed off to guests other than the "personal guests of His Imperial Majesty"—and we are a very limited few. And one can't use money in this place, not even for a postage stamp.

A letter from Bernardine Fritz told the sad news of the protracted and painful dissolution into death of a woman who once meant a great deal to me—Jarmila Marton. Still a relatively young person.

I first knew her—it must have been 1941 or '42, in Beverly Hills. Unbelievably violet eyes, the high cheekbones and molded features of a pure Czech—but most of all a strong, domineering personality, yet one who would do anything for those who were in trouble. Reminded me of Eleanor Roosevelt in her reachings out to help every social cripple who came along, with a mixture of generosity and determination and steel.

Images of all kinds of the epic celebration still filter through my imagination and immediate memory. The little side-pictures were the most amusing. As one example: the Cardinal representing the Vatican, in the grandstand with us yesterday in the blazing sun, at the military pageant. A girl usher handed him a tiny rolled umbrella. He opened it, graciously. And there he stood, with a little umbrella splotched with the most violent colors, he with his black "dress" and a wine-colored band around his comfortable and ample middle, and wine-colored sox.

Lunch today with Ahmad Ahmadi, now deputy to Agriculture Minister Rouhani, and Hassan Shahmirzadi, now head of the Fars Paper Co. at Haft Tapeh.

They both reported, with a sparkle in their eyes, my appearance on TV; the Shah whisking others in the reception line past him, and stopping me, calling me back, having a conversation of sorts with me.

As Helen predicted, this made a big impression on my Iranian working friends, however unimportant it surely must have seemed to others, ourselves included.

OCTOBER 19, 1971
TEHRAN

The longer I go through the rigors and trials—and successes—of what is coldly called "administration" or "the executive function," I find the satisfying and meaningful part of my life are the people, the personalities one encounters. And my ability to draw them out, to quicken their spirit, to make them outreach themselves.

Yesterday morning Mansur Rouhani, Minister of Agriculture, was discussing his national agricultural policy recommendation—a remarkable statement it is too. One of the objectives, said he, is to stop the outflow of poor rural people to Tehran, which is overwhelming the city. But the villages must be consolidated and made more attractive, and how to do this was the body of his recommended policies.

"Why shouldn't the peasants flock to Tehran? Look at me. My father was a poor peasant in a small village. The other young people in the village say: here is a son of our village who came to Tehran and now he is a Minister. If he can do it by going to Tehran, so can we." A touching example of what we in America would say showed his real democratic sense, *not* being ashamed of his "humble" beginnings but also speaking of them as an example of an important policy point.

OCTOBER 25, 1971
10 P.M.
TEHRAN

A *happy* King: that is what I thought as he greeted me at his splendid Niavaran Palace office late this afternoon.

His brown plaid suit, colored shirt, and gaily colored necktie were quite a contrast in dress to the succession of servitors through which I passed, all in their long-tailed coats and gold buttons.

Looking reflective behind dark glasses, he talked about the celebration for a few minutes, quietly, without the indignation he showed in the course of yesterday's meeting with the international press.

Much of the criticism and adverse comment about the lavishness on display came from foreigners. This, the Shah said, is because they cannot understand what the monarchy means to Iranians. "They look at the results we have achieved in changing the country and strengthening it, at the feeling the people have for the monarchy, and they say, 'How can Iran do these things through the monarchy; why isn't the monarchy like that of England, a showpiece, a ceremonial showpiece?' They think there must be something hidden to explain how this works in Iran. So they attack this mystery in all sorts of misstatements, some of them malicious; but at the bottom is ignorance about Iran and her history."

It was my view that no part of His Majesty's program for the future could be as important as bringing agricultural production and the life of rural people more in tune with the great advances in the industrial and urban sectors of Iran's recent history. "They are out of phase," I said.

"Yes, that is true. But it is understandable. First we had to increase production in industry and that has happened. Now we are in a position to do much the same for agricultural and rural conditions which are way below our standards, as I know so well and have said so many times.

"I am determined that Khuzistan move ahead rapidly and completely," he said. "I want to go down there and fly a helicopter or a plane myself to every part of the region; spend two days at it. I told our people that at the present rate it would be one hundred years before all the land is developed in that one project. I wouldn't be alive to see it, at this rate. But the *country* can't afford such a leisurely pace."

He then went on to say that Iran had determined it needed to be part of the marketing of its oil "downstream, even to including the gas pump. But it is filled with difficulties, we have found so far."

"I have yet to have known a responsible leader such as you," I said, "who could so readily move from the fine print of operating detail to issues of the broadest world-wide consequence."

"We Iranians must be able to protect ourselves—and we can—without having to call upon the U.S. or any other superpower—the story of Vietnam shows that you of the U.S. can't protect a small nation, actually; and if the 'big thing' happens [meaning a world war with atomic weapons], well, there is nothing that can protect *anyone* if that happens."

Toward the end of the audience a stony-faced minion came through a far distant door with tea. His Majesty's tea was in the same narrow little glass that appears toward the beginning of almost every conference. For some reason a full cup with saucer (gold-emblazoned, of course) was handed to me. This little detail is not the only one that caught my eye. In the room where I had waited to be called there was a gold telephone on an exquisite table next to the desk. Elegance, elegance. Yet underneath, a box of Kleenex.

OCTOBER 28, 1971
AIR IRAN TO ROME

The Prime Minister has established the tradition of always wearing a tiny orchid in his buttonhole (I remember my visits with Nehru, the tiny rose always pinned to his severe black up-to-the-neck jacket).

Looking down at a folder on his desk on which lay my letter, he put his hands on the letter, smiled broadly again, and then used a word that surprised me. "Prima facie," he said, "the answer is affirmative."

Hoveyda is a *jolly* man. He laughs easily, loves to tell anecdotes, and tells them very well.

I referred to his request that I prepare some suggested paragraphs for his New York speech. "A ghost writer for a Prime Minister"—he liked the phrase, as he does others that show he is quite familiar with American slang, particularly political slang.

OCTOBER 31, 1971
FLORENCE

Two days of such satisfaction and pride as surely come to few men. Our son is indeed a man of stout heart, wide interest and curiosity, warmth and infinite consideration, and sensitivity for others. I said so to Helen as we returned to our quarters from an evening of spirited talk. "We are the parents of a great man."

And *his* son will surely be another extraordinary person—indeed, he already has an understanding plus charisma that are quite overwhelming.

So we are really happy tonight, as we prepare to return to Rome tomorrow and then on to other happy events.

NOVEMBER 1, 1971
FLORENCE

Last evening David, Peggy, Helen, and I talked, around the supper table, for hours. While the chitchat about the children, or reminiscences about the time we lived in Norris, Tennessee, etc., were pleasant and fun, David talked about his interests in the field of general ideas, about his craft as a writer, and its practitioners, to his "elderly" parents. This was deeply satisfying.

NOVEMBER 5, 1971
NEW YORK

Political and diplomatic and international institutions—how much do they contribute to the fundamental of a "world order"? On this I am definitely prejudiced, have developed a strongly bilious view. The flamboyance of Willkie's (and Joe Barnes') *One World,* the inspired rhetoric of a Norman Cousins, and the abstract world-government legal structures devised by such noble but unrealistic minds as Grenville Clark— or Joe Clark—how much have they contributed?

But the underlying forces of so-called private transactions in the world of trade, of energy supply, of negotiation over goods and commodities and terms of exchange—these seem to me the unspectacular levers that really count these days—as perhaps they always have. These may pull the world apart, become the brew that poisons, and lead to war, *or,* as I believe, *can* help knit the world together.

NOVEMBER 9, 1971
NEW YORK

In the Roosevelt coffee shop this morning with a TV mobile spotlight glaring at me in that crowded, noisy room. For at a table right next to me, the center of worldwide attention, six Chinese, in their blue-grey uniforms (high at the neck, identical in style), part of the advance troupe of the newly admitted Chinese delegation to the UN.

The Chinese kept their composure, in all the TV commotion. They ate, in dignity, their identical meals (one fried egg and bacon each; one at least ordered *coffee,* not tea). Their spokesman signed the single check in flowing calligraphy.

6 P.M.

The homely little drama of this morning's breakfast scene took up much of the 6 o'clock TV news I have just seen. Big close-ups of the two waitresses, including the blonde one that served me *my* scrambled eggs this morning. They will hardly be fit for their serving duties tomorrow, after this burst of TV exposure.

The lobby of this hotel—the Roosevelt—full of people and buzzing with vitality, is like the stage set for a very contrived play. Those burly men, their shirts open at the neck, booming laughs: the United Mine Workers' Executive Committee meeting here, and congregating in the lobby. Or the parade of airline crews, some in the uniform of senior officers of BOAC or Lufthansa, or the blonde tight-pants brigade of stewardesses speaking German like mad, or gargling Scandinavian speech. And up on the 14th floor are those solemn, ultra-serious Chinese disciples of Chairman Mao.

The subject of the Committee for Economic Development deliberations this morning: improving the environment. (What else *could* be the subject of a conference these days?) A fragile little professor of economics at Princeton delivered himself of a paper on disposal of "solid mixed waste" (garbage to you). Then a solemn popeyed man from some "Center" for environment something or other (the proliferation of Centers is a prime characteristic of these days of grants, grants, grants) who described almost with love in his even-toned voice the various methods of incineration of this delicious brew that the housewife spews from her kitchen. All manner of burning, resulting in "residual recovery" and other pretentious verbal jargon, disguising the simple fact: garbage or used bottles "compacted" and "dissolved and disintegrated."

Another member of this circle, a big husky fellow who should have been watching a pro football team, interrupted. "Noise—that's a major source of pollution of the environment."

I stood as much of this as I could. After an hour I said that the discussion of solid waste disposal and of noise reminded me of the story about Cal Coolidge. He had attended church; was asked what the preacher's sermon was about. Said Cal, "It was about sin." "And what did the preacher say about sin?" "Said he was against it."

Everybody is against solid waste, garbage, and noise. But there are serious conflicts, serious differences of opinion about some of the sources of impairment of the environment, serious difficulties and great costs in improving the environment to get what we want—electric energy. Why not talk about a conflict to be resolved and not just agree that we are against the sin of pollution?

NOVEMBER II, 1971
NEW YORK

Listening to economists has hardly been my favorite form of entertainment, or source of enlightenment. But it was otherwise this morning, at a cozy little seminar, gathered to hear Milton Friedman, Henry C. Wallich of Yale, and the redoubtable Paul Samuelson of MIT. It was attended by three hundred earnest seekers for light, of all kinds, among them those looking for a tip about how to beat the stock market. Sponsored and "chaired" by Oz Elliott, the enterprising publisher of *Newsweek* magazine.

I was seated at a table with the four performers. A more amusing quartet I have rarely met. Economics may be dismal, but Friedman and Samuelson, plus Elliott, turned out to be anything but dismal.

Friedman, a diminutive man with a broad, shining bald head above the brightest and most amused eyes: "I was in Iran a year ago; exciting place. I wasn't there five minutes until I understood the country. Talked to the man in charge of planning. They are trained to the old meaningless orthodoxy, charged with having it repeated in a country where it has no place whatever."

Ozzy was brilliant in introducing the "panel." About Samuelson: "He wrote a textbook on economics, and appropriated a title that put off any competitor. Just called it *Economics.* It is the standard for all colleges, selling into the millions for years. Thereby in his person he disproves the old scornful adage about economists: If you are so smart, why aren't you rich?"

These are brilliant, quick-spoken men, indeed. Wallich thinks things are coming along well. Said such a startling thing (on first impression): that inflation has become deflationary, because the expectations of inflation produce deflation. This rather floored the others.

The stock market was given short shrift. Says Samuelson, "If, as Shakespeare says, history is a tale told by an idiot, then the stock market is a tale told by 30 million idiots."

Both Samuelson and Elliott have just returned from Japan. The Japanese believe the dollar is overvalued. According to Ozzy, when John Connally said the Japanese demanded that our dollar be devalued, the Japanese Finance Minister is reported to have said: "Up your yen." (This bit of topical vulgarism won't be understood in 1990 when this journal entry will—or will not—be printed. But it was funny this morning.)

That handsome statesman George Ball (now a partner at Lehman) arose to ask a question: why didn't the economists discuss the international effect of Nixon's New Policy of August 15, which Ball referred to as "Texas economics"—with undisguised disdain, as well might the true internationalist he is. Ball said the idea that it is up to the world—particularly Japan—to make up for the $13 billion gap in the U.S. balance of trade is pure nonsense. Said Samuelson: "We are swinging our weight around [a reference to Connally's appearance these days on the Japanese scene] without the weight to do anything about it."

NOVEMBER 15, 1971
NEW YORK

This afternoon and through dinner at a meeting of Doug Knight's Overseas Advisory Council about the Iranian university, Jondi Shapur.

Clark Kerr, no longer the harassed and thin-faced man I saw at UCLA, when he was the head of the California universities system and in the midst of his major troubles with a revolution of students. He looked ten years younger.

At dinner I got Reza Ansari to talk about his six or seven days in Communist China, last April. His visit, accompanying Princess Ashraf, was about the first such "official" visit by foreigners.

The picture he drew was in such contrast to the near euphoria about their trips to Red China of Scotty Reston and Seymour Topping of the *Times.*

Reza "documented" his views with "instances." "We visited several hospitals, at the request of the Princess. In Canton and in Peking. They must have been the best they had or we wouldn't have been taken to see them. They were terrible. No good equipment, actually filthy. The universities we visited were just getting over being closed completely, as they had been for a period. The Princess asked to see some of the beautiful temples. All destroyed, except one at a resort place. Destroyed all those beautiful things that remind them of the past that they hate. In the stores—we visited several in Shanghai and Peking—there was almost nothing on the shelves—about four items and little choice of kinds of cloth or other things.

"I would certainly not want to be a Chinese today."

Most of the advances they have made are the good product of an older and earlier generation, he said. Jim Killian agreed; they have many brilliant and able scholars and scientific people but they are not allowed to contribute, except perhaps in certain cases of "programmatic" work —meaning, I suppose, atomic weapons development.

As I left Clark Kerr said: "I have followed your work with great admiration. I think you probably know more about what is going on in the real world these days than anyone."

I wish I did. But I certainly don't. If he had said "as much as anyone else" I would think he had something. For I am less tangled in the details that fascinate so many observers. And I can discount as only of passing interest many events and much rhetoric that earlier in my experience I would have taken to have some basic importance.

As he ruminated sadly, in a very quiet, withdrawn, elder statesman way, Jim Killian's sole comment on Reza's account of what he had seen really happening in China was this: "It is the terrible regimentation of millions of people that is the worst of all."

NOVEMBER 17, 1971
NEW YORK

A long visit this morning with Rodman Rockefeller.

"I made an extensive statement recently about the social responsibility of private business," he said. "The *New York Times* printed a piece way back in the paper; and the headline was 'Rockefeller's *Son* Said. . . .' I want to build IBEC as *my own* achievement, and to do that I must show a profit, a substantial profit. David, you have made a name for yourself, and made a fortune by your own efforts. That achievement is yours. But I haven't, yet. That's why I won't think about anything else until IBEC is a solid, profitable success—my success."

I said, "Profit in the old sense is no longer the sole test of business achievement, as it is no longer the sole test of any other kind of achievement. It is what you produce or cause to be produced that furthers the welfare of the whole people that is the hallmark, the measuring stick. Profit, yes, but not in the old-fashioned sense of what shows on the 'bottom line' alone."

Feel tired, somehow, for the first time for a long time. When I mentioned this to Helen over the phone just now, she laughed heartily. Said I: "And what are you laughing about?"

"Of course, you are tired; do you realize how you have been going, since the first of September? Not only travel—Puerto Rico, Colombia,

Iran, Europe—but new, exciting things you are creating and pressing hard for? You are entitled—to be tired."

What a happy, easy visit we had with our son. Arrived yesterday from Italy; drove out with me last evening. What added to the satisfaction was the loving way he spoke of his sister Nancy. "Such a sweet and considerate girl . . . she seems still a girl, so slender she is. But I was so moved by the way she and Sylvain took over a most difficult situation when Pam [his daughter] was injured in an automobile accident."

David and Nancy haven't had much in common, so each of them admitted, for years. Being thrown together because of Pam's auto accident has changed this completely, as if they have discovered new friends. What a warm feeling this brings to their mother and father.

NOVEMBER 21, 1971
PRINCETON

The urge to write and publish is certainly strong in me.

What would be the cost of giving myself over to writing, full time, by giving up D&R (as someday I surely will do)?

I am now engaged in mind-taxing, stimulating, and often frustrating work, dealing with consequential issues. If I were to leave the arena of that kind of work would the stimulus and drive be gone, with the work? Is it an illusion that my work stands in the way of my having stimulating ideas worth writing about? Or is the exact reverse true: that it is the fact that I am heavily committed to that work that provides the spur without which I would have little consequential to say or write about?

I can't be both a full-time writer and a full-time executive. But is that the choice?

Surely I can't say that I "don't write." In fact, I write a very great deal —in my journal notebooks, of course. And letters that sometimes attain the stature of minor state papers.

Eventually these writings are published; my views are not arrows shot into the air to be completely lost. My journals are published. Some of the thoughts and ideas in those journals of 1959–1963, and earlier, have foretold events. My disdain for bomb shelters, at the time a hot issue, certainly did foretell what an oddball idea this widely embraced campaign really was; my concern about the hazards and the unproven reliability at the time of the peaceful atom, expressed in the Stafford Little Lectures and in Volume V of the *Journals,* certainly foretold the current skepticism about the atom, and influenced the result.

The Soviet-American Strategic Arms Talks (SALT), now entering their third year, have just resumed in Vienna. In my Stafford Little Lectures at Princeton back in 1963 I said that "the very process of seeking to negotiate disarmament treaties" at that time "does not give proper weight to the dangers to peace and to ultimate disarmament" of those very negotiations.

This morning a *Times* editorial—almost ten years after my Stafford Little Lectures statement—says: "So far, instead of curbing the nuclear missile race, the talks seem to have stimulated it. Both sides have pressed ahead with strategic missile deployment over the past two years. From the start the proposals of both sides have envisaged larger forces than they had when the talks began. And the military of both countries have pushed their missile deployment ahead as if to beat some expected cut-off date."

The concluding paragraph of the editorial contains this sentence: "Political facts have more to do with the American-made obstacles to a first-stage SALT agreement than the nation's strategic needs." (I think the same could probably be said about the Soviets.)

DECEMBER 1, 1971
UNION STATION, WASHINGTON

"What a beautiful day; this is why I like living in Washington—more sunshine here than any big city I know," Bob McNamara said. "I am very subject, psychologically, to weather, to climate. When it is overcast as it is in so many places—Germany in the fall and winter, for example—that gets me. In Bonn you can hardly breathe. This brilliant sunshine is for me."

He was just back from Asia. "I'm convinced that the Chinese are going to inherit the earth. Wherever I went, Singapore, Hong Kong, Malaysia, it is the Chinese who do things. The Indians talk about doing things, but they prefer to split hairs and treat everyone in an arrogant way—difficult people. The Japanese are do-ers too, but the Chinese are the best."

I said I wanted to talk about the results of our actual D&R experience in overcoming rural poverty through an agro-industrial complex at the sugar cane and refinery enterprise at Haft Tapeh, in Iranian Khuzistan.

"I agree," I said, "with the proposition of your address to the governors of the World Bank that rural poverty is the greatest cause of misery and of potential and actual political instability, that rural unemployment is the major cause of the crowding into the cities, that the 'urban problem' is just another face of the rural problem.

"But how to do something about it? Look for some manageable case or place or set of circumstances where a beginning can be made. I think Khuzistan may be that place.

"The Haft Tapeh complex in Khuzistan has shown the reality, not just the rhetoric, of what can be done with an industrial center to which there is naturally added a 'new town' with the amenities and income that go with employment in an industrial setting based on agricultural production—sugar cane into sugar into paper—and from there on.

"I believe we should and can find a way of replicating that example.

"This is largely Minister Rouhani's concept, and I discussed it with the Shah at length. I think he agrees. What the more abstract and abstruse 'planners' in the Plan Organization think about it, I don't know. But it is a revolutionary concept for Iran. Iran is a country where we have a combination of circumstances that made such an idea possible to try out in a specific way. Would the Bank encourage this concept, be prepared to finance it, in part? Could the Bank make a 'program loan' for this kind of undertaking, not connected with a particular project?"

On this question I got a vague response. I feared McNamara was still a captive of the World Bank bureaucracy's "project" fixation.

DECEMBER 4, 1971
PRINCETON

Word just received that, with our Brazilian engineering associate, Serete, we have been awarded a contract for studies of the vast Amazon River Basin. I found this news quite exciting.

Spent a couple hours on the next volume of the *Journals,* conferring with Helen. How can I possibly sandwich in the editing of this next volume with all the other things that are consuming me these days? But somehow I must.

The greatest satisfaction I derive from my work is seeing a man unfold, his hidden, almost frozen talents thawed out, his self-assurance, his striking power, unleashed. It's a great experience to see; it is the almost complete compensation for my work and worry, more than the tangible "business" results.

Walt Seymour is the latest and in some ways the most surprising illustration. He is simply going great guns. Best of all, he is enjoying as tough a series of jobs as he has ever had, in a great career.

The other day Walt came into my office, the tenth time in a couple hours; a big grin. "This is *fun,* this job is fun. I have no business being paid for doing something that is such fun." To hear this from an associate: that's the payoff for me.

DECEMBER 6, 1971
NEW YORK

I went to Lazard Frères at 44 Wall Street this noon and had almost an hour with André Meyer and with his brilliant young partner Felix Rohatyn. I was very full of beans, enjoyed yelling "hi" to one and all and generally shaking up the discreet merchant-banker 19th century tone of the place. I was overwhelmed by pleasant nostalgia when André took me into the little cubbyhole which was my office when I was working there back in the fifties.

The meeting was in such contrast to the times when I stood in awe of this man because of his genius for acquisition; I had thoroughly enjoyed that experience, so strange for me—a public servant. I think he did, too. As I left he said I looked young and strong. "But don't you get very tired on these long trips?" I said that I didn't particularly; that what really tired me was being bored. To which he replied, in a sad tone indicating that he was always bored—which I doubt. Not willing to leave it there, I said, "My work is so exciting that I rarely know what being bored is." Which is an approximation of the truth.

Felix Rohatyn and I had a vigorous little talk. Told him how delighted I was to see how he spoke out about the way the New York Stock Exchange was mishandled, and the grave danger to the whole country if its mishandling produced a panic. I said I remembered him as a financial genius but with a strong sense of public purpose. He peered at me and said, "Did you think that later I had sold out?" "No," I said, "perhaps just forgotten your public convictions."

We both remembered Nate Greene of Lazard. He could work in Wall Street, be a close advisor of André's, work on deals and so on, but he never lost his personal identity with his own convictions. Nor did his courage ever weaken about expressing just what he thought. There aren't very many men which nothing can shake or buy or flatter into something complaisant or acquiescent. "I see now that you haven't lost that quality either," I said.

André was more nearly himself this time, as I remember him, fondly and gratefully, over many years in the past. He is a genuine legend. And so damn human, with all the crankiness and pettiness that so often go with being a human being.

Even in the grey-blue of this overcast day, the Verrazano Bridge, over which we are passing as I write these notes, is an inspiring edifice— much more than a roadway between two bodies of land, it is a work of art. Who says that modern objects are not beautiful, in the classic meaning of "beauty," simply because they are contemporary and are useful?

Dinner tonight with Dana Atchley.

"What you have," said Dana Atchley, "is eagerness. And anyone who is built that way—not just enthusiasm, which can be intellectual—will never be bored. Being bored is the worst disease of all. It's the source of what people call being 'tired.' Restless, *that* you are, but it's the eagerness that keeps you going."

One of the many foreign-dignitary patients he had at Harkness Pavilion [of Columbia Presbyterian Hospital] was Madame Chiang Kai-shek. She took the whole twelfth floor, and when she left, with her entourage, all paid for by the U.S., everyone in the whole hospital hated her for her arrogance and ugly nature.

"One day," said Dana, "Mrs. Roosevelt was due to visit the Madame, who was to stay at the White House as the President's guest when she left Harkness. I sat in the waiting room where I was to meet Mrs. Roosevelt. I waited and waited. Finally she came bursting in, out of breath, apologizing profusely. 'I'm so sorry I am late, Doctor, but I took the wrong *subway.*'"

DECEMBER 8, 1971
NEW YORK

The journalistic formula that the Shah is an "absolute monarch" is a poor joke, when one reflects on how his "absolute decrees," as in the case of these research centers, are simply ignored by one and all. The administrative frailties in Iran are almost beyond belief.

The latest instances are over the agricultural research centers outlined in our proposal to the Ministry of Agriculture way back last June, and as specifically directed by the Shah, in writing. D&R has yet to have a contract.

DECEMBER 11, 1971
PRINCETON

Bruce Bliven's (he's now 82) Christmas greetings are invariably gay and witty.

"Rosie [his wife] is blessed with eternal youth. I myself don't feel like an old man. I feel like a young man who has something the matter with him."

DECEMBER 12, 1971
PRINCETON

General Sarnoff died this morning, so the radio—his child and creation—has just told the world.

Add up the pluses and minuses of the political consequences of that "little black box" (as radio was called at first) as it emerged from an oddity to the single most important social invention of the century, and a vote on the question "Is it good or bad?" would be a close one.

I am to be an honorary pallbearer at the General's funeral Wednesday morning. *That* will be a production and no mistake. The General doted on publicity as much as anyone I have ever known, including Baruch. I'm sure he would have expected to have the most linage and air-wave space squeezed out of his last appearance. These broadcasting people will not disappoint the old boy. He probably would say: Don't stint the publicity; after all, you only die once.

DECEMBER 15, 1971
NEW YORK

The first hour or so of the IBEC board meeting yesterday was a bore. Rodman Rockefeller, President of this big company, talked about the "fantastic" tabulation that displayed all the numbers about IBEC. Nothing said about the goal of the company.

Then everything changed. A vigorous young man, Leo Denlea, spoke about Brazil. Not about "numbers" or poultry or seeds or housing or other fragmented items, but Brazil as a vast country, as a region calling for development.

And to top it off in came two men to talk about IBEC rural black housing in South Carolina and Virginia.

Whereupon the whole sleepy overstuffed board—myself as stuffed and sleepy as anyone—came awake.

Dick Dilworth presided; alert, handsome, with the best manners of anyone I know (and don't let anyone tell you manners aren't a mark of a man's insides). His face shone with pride at the story of these two hundred black families being housed.

This sounded like the spirit of the IBEC of Nelson Rockefeller's day, years ago.

DECEMBER 17, 1971
FLYING TO ANTIGUA,
BRITISH WEST INDIES

Immediately behind me in this plane are Helen and Nancy, chatting merrily, for they do enjoy each other so. These two, so dissimilar in appearance and background, are strikingly alike in many ways.

I had never before been to the ultra-fashionable Temple Emanu-El, where, appropriately enough, the once Lower East Side David Sarnoff was eulogized. The Temple made one think of Solomon's temple—Solomon in all his glory was not arrayed as this—great pillars reaching to the sky, gold everywhere, hardly the austerity of Chartres Cathedral. As in most such funeral gatherings in New York City, this contemporary Babylon of business success, what we witnessed was actually a corporate funeral.

DECEMBER 31, 1971
PRINCETON

The practice of a reflective end-of-the-year journal entry is as old as my keeping of a journal. And that covers a span of more than fifty years.

But somehow as this year ends, I don't feel like a backward look. Not because it was a year I would rather forget because it was uninteresting, or disappointing or tragic. But the very reverse: this has been such a good year, such a beginning of still another satisfying and riskful new chapter that my interest is in looking ahead rather than savoring the immediate past. The look ahead fills me with anticipation and impatience to be in the midst of that immediate future.

As to that part of my life I call my "work," it was clearly one of the very best I have known. And my personal life—that set of emotions, controls, and non-controls within me—it was a great year. Never in recent years have I found greater relish in living.

V

1972

~~◄╫►~~

Trip to Brazil—Vacation at Caneel Bay—Trips to Brazil
and study of regional development of the São Francisco
Valley—Trip to Iran—Address to American International Club of Geneva on growth and the environment—
Vacation in Antigua

JANUARY 9, 1972
PRINCETON

Last Wednesday Helen and I were the guests of Iphigene Sulzberger,
at her New York home.

A little wisp of a lady, now eighty (she proudly tells us). Now and then
the fire of her father, one of the founders of great journalism in this
country, shows in her eyes, when she is indignant. Keenly she still misses
her husband, Arthur, his personality, his sense of humor. A dynastic
feeling that is more personal than organizational, though the *Times* is
as personal an institution as we have.

A long talk, after dinner, with Harrison Salisbury. He has made a
great success of the "Op-Ed" page. Harrison is first and foremost a reporter. For him not to have been selected to visit China this summer,
when Reston and Topping made such a journalistic coup by their trip
and report, is something I regret. Nothing in Harrison's demeanor suggested that he felt left out, when he had earned the chance. But it must
have been a disappointment.

Harrison knows the Russians as well as any journalist, by dint of
years of travel among them, even to the writing of a stirring account of

[255]

the defense of Leningrad and, as I recall, the writing of a work of fiction about Russia.

I asked him how he would compare Russia and the Chinese, the People's Republic brand, of course.

He said they are very different, though each is Communist. The difference, if time proves him right, has a great bearing on the state of the world.

The Chinese are prepared to turn their backs on the rest of the world; they have no strong compulsion to expand their influence; they *have* the world. Their culture, their ideas, their history are what is important to them.

This is in contrast to the defensive and insecure and, therefore, aggressive Russians.

An interesting view by one who knows the Russians, and I assume is guessing, as all of us must, about the Chinese.

JANUARY 14, 1972
AT KENNEDY AIRPORT WAITING
FOR THE FLIGHT TO RIO

Not starting this long trip under quite the best conditions. The orthopedist stuck a yard-long needle into my ankle, and I've walked quite a lot. The cursed thing hurts.

JANUARY 15, 1972
COPACABANA PALACE HOTEL,
RIO DE JANEIRO, BRAZIL

The view out my window of the vast crescent bay and the beach has so often been described in superlatives. But unbelievable is the reality, this Sunday noon: there must be 300,000 or 400,000 people swarming on the shore, with a background of surf, of tall luxury buildings and the peaks of the hills that ring the bay.

A big program (which Rodman Rockefeller is reviewing in detail) has been laid out. It should be a memorable experience indeed.

Two big fellows in greenish suits patrol the hall outside Rod's door; they met us and will be with him day and night, probably going into the surf with him. Reminds me vaguely of my AEC days of "bodyguards."

7 P.M.

Could there be a more magnificent view of the city than that I saw from the top of the hills surrounding Rio this afternoon? With a backdrop of the ocean and the great sweeping bay, the almost too dramatic sudden upthrust of the green granite cones, and spread out below a great city of tall buildings. Is this the greatest view of a city? Probably not, probably it is second to the panorama of New York City from the harbor or from the Empire State Building. The climb to reach this eminence is through a dark green forest, within a few miles of this modern city—that is unique so far as my experience goes.

On the steep slopes a reminder that all is not luxury and big deals. The squatter houses, the "shanties."

Being Sunday, and this the summer season—it was quite warm but there was a breeze from the sea—the road to the hilltops was filled with family excursions—a gay sight too.

JANUARY 17, 1972
RIO

Transforming "Brazil" from a great space on the map or a mental picture of a turbulent, disordered country into something real, within my personal ken—that is what this expedition is doing—and this is only the second day. To add to my store of places seen and new ideas explored is one of the delights of my kind of life.

With Rodman leading off, we met with the Minister of Planning, João Paulo Dos Reis Velloso, for an hour this afternoon. A startlingly youthful man. I heard an impressive presentation of how Brazil is going about the job of the development of a country of such size and sweep.

What I find most dramatic and epochal is not only the "numbers"— that is, the unbelievably great size of the unpopulated Amazon Basin (almost two thirds the area of the continental U.S.), or the 30 million almost destitute people in the northeast—but the variety, the diversity. For side by side with this vast empty space traversed by one of the greatest of mankind's rivers are great and sophisticated cities such as the one in which I write, and the metropolis of São Paulo, and the new city of Brasília.

The Brazilians are using the modern devices of government—various sophisticated forms of financial subsidies—to direct and stimulate activity. They understand the difference between those areas that can be made to move only by government activity directly (roads, direct government services, etc.) and those that can be left to individuals or entrepreneurs with the underpinning of credit, subsidies, financing, research risks—all the tools of a non-ideological state.

I *was* impressed.

The puzzle is how a country torn and bleeding with violent expressions of political differences, and held together by military arms—which is certainly the case though their presence isn't much to be seen—can muster intelligence and competence in non-military arts—that is a murky field for speculation. Can it last?

But it doesn't sound like Argentina, certainly not like Colombia in the years I have observed that contradictory country.

Certainly the economic and physical resources are impressive beyond words. Have these people learned how to adapt democracy by the limits they place upon its traditional Anglo-Saxon or European exercise, or have they invented something that can be made to work in South America and only there—or more precisely, made to work in the unique kind of society to be found in Brazil?

Among the IBEC group I found Rodman increasingly impressive and effective, and certainly friendly.

The most delightful man in the entourage is new to me: Berent Friele. A Norwegian by birth, sent to America by his family to learn the commercial side of the coffee trade, he came to Brazil where he lived many years, knows everyone, young and old, has learned the ins and outs of a strange political climate. A most relaxed and cultivated man, not too strong physically now, but a good companion.

I found Rodman referring more and more to "my father" in his presentation to the Minister, and in his conversations. No wonder, really: this week is the 25th anniversary of the founding of IBEC by Nelson Rockefeller, in Brazil. But leaning on his father's name is in such contrast to the insistence of so many men on avoiding that very dependence on their father's reputation and accomplishments that I was struck by it. Our son David, for instance, went to the other extreme. I found Rodman's pride in what his father had started more understandable and sympathetic than the reverse attitude.

JANUARY 18, 1972
BRASÍLIA

His Excellency Emilio Garrastazu Medici, President of this amazing empire, is the very picture of a strong self-assured man. And it is an empire, being several countries, not one, several in difference and several in sheer size.

A big man, physically, not austere but warm in personal manner, though his pictures show him to be cold and colorless.

The city of Brasília, seen for the first time from the air as I saw it coming in this morning, simply has no contact with humankind. A set of rectangles set on end. It was almost like a model in small scale at an

architectural show. Built all at the same time, there is none of the variation of taste—good, bad, and dull—that marks most cities that have simply grown.

Our first visit was to the Minister of Foreign Relations, Mario Gibson
Alves Barboza. Fluent in American speech and without mannerisms
other than those of a cultivated university professor or intelligent businessman. A diplomat, he has served in Washington and in the United
Nations.

He gave us a big luncheon, magnificent in food and service, in a
building that is open to the air in an imaginative way; within this very
"modern" setting there were many very old things of beauty from early
colonial days. The only other building I have seen that combines this
modern feeling with a sense of bringing the out-of-doors inside is the
Palace in Saigon, strangely enough.

The Minister is a great TVA enthusiast. He made me feel at home by
saying, in a quiet voice: "You are well known in this country; far better
known than you realize; perhaps as well known and regarded as any
living American."

The Minister of Interior, Jose Costa Cavalcanti, a General, did not
resemble the picture of a Latin American military man at all. His "jurisdiction" is very broad. It includes control at the center of the agencies
known as SUDAM (with which we now have a contract) or SUDENE; in
other words, the development of Amazonia and the adjacent region of the
northeast.

We had an hour yesterday with the Minister of Agriculture of Brazil,
with the elegant name of Luiz Fernando Cirne Lima. He has a college
crew cut, sharp eyes, a strong square head that turns and pivots with
intensity.

Said I: "Looking at this land around Brasília I would say that its poor
vegetation is due to lack of phosphate."

If I had exploded a firecracker under his chair, the reaction of the
Minister could not have been more vigorous. He whirled on me, as if to
say, "Where did you come from?" and said in a strong voice: "Phosphate
is the number one problem of this whole country's agriculture."

He had hardly said this—music to the ears of a fanatic on the subject,
as I have been for many years—when Tony Secundino of our party, head
of IBEC's Agroceres, sat bolt upright. His short fighter's neck came out
of his coat like a cork out of a bottle, his grey curly hair stood right up,
his left eye—is it glass?—stared wildly like Long John Silver's. "Right;
right. It is the number one problem of this country. And how did you
know?"

Then the Minister's face broke into as much of a smile as so intense a technocrat's could: "Oh; you are the Lilienthal of TVA. Of course, you know all about phosphate."

And we were off. I had found two more converts, or addicts. I shall write them both about the latest developments coming out of the Muscle Shoals National Fertilizer Development Center, and mark the chapter in *TVA: Democracy on the March* that tells how we got farmers to make the best use of triple-super years ago.

Later, Rodman said: "When the Minister and Tony joined in the cry 'phosphate,' Dave, you should have seen your face. It lighted up, and your hands gestured—you were excited."

I was, and am, for it could mean as much to these lands as it did to the deprived, one-crop cotton lands of Alabama and Mississippi in the thirties.

Further, on a TVA theme, warmly received by the Brazilians and by Rodman, I spoke of the "mystique" of a river, how it can be a unifying force in development. "It isn't just happenstance," said I, "that there is hardly a city anywhere or a civilization that isn't closely related to water, to a river. New York, St. Louis, Minneapolis, Chicago—or Alexandria, London, even Susa on the Karun, and Lisbon. And in Brazil, Recife, Belém—and Manaus and Altamira on the Amazon system will show the same thing as time goes on. Altamira can become a second Decatur, Alabama." No one in our group would understand that, but by the time I get through sending them the facts and pictures about what happened in this one-time depressed and dispirited city, they sure will know.

JANUARY 20, 1972
BELÉM

I am writing these notes on a bench in the almost deserted plaza in the heart of Belém, the capital of the huge state of Pará; five minutes away, one of the gaping mouths of the Amazon, almost exactly on the Equator.

The waters of the vast river, surely more than a mile across, come thousands of miles across the breadth of Brazil from the mountains of Peru and Colombia. It is to help design a TVA (as they say here) for the awesome river basins of the Amazon that I am in this north Brazilian city.

Unlike Rio, so metropolitan, or the shining newness, rather dull, self-conscious uniformity of Brasília, this is a city with more than a touch of its Portuguese colonial beginning. Many of the houses have decoration fussy and nonfunctional, but with a specially pleasant appearance, being colored in pinks and blues. The streets of the business section are lined with huge mango trees, luxuriant and glistening with a green that is heavy and unrelieved, a passion-filled kind of vegetation, as are the clusters of jungle through which we passed on a visit, on the outskirts, to an agricultural research station.

The strangest contrasts: 20th century skyscrapers of the most modern design, apartment houses equally tall and contemporary. The roar is that of a city of more than 700,000 people.

JANUARY 21, 1972
BELÉM

How surprised I am to find myself saying: Belém is an interesting place; indeed it is one of the most interesting of cities.

We began the day—early again—with a ceremonial visit to the Palace of the Governor. It was the Palace that was impressive; the Governor was a smiling, square-built, dark-complexioned, unpretentious man. He told us, sitting primly in a circle in the grandeur of his audience room, of his recent visit to TVA; of the noble sweep of the Amazon—for this city is the capital of Amazonia.

The building was like an illustrated chapter in the 350-year history of the Portuguese domination of this rich land. The marble staircases, the intricate pattern of the floors, the portraits of many a hard-visaged former ruler of this state of Pará, with its command of a river so vast and flowing with hardly a ripple through a dark and largely undiscovered and unpopulated empire of forests.

And what we heard in our meeting at SUDAM following the call on the Governor told us that the minerals lying in that jungle may be one of the greatest treasure-houses to be found anywhere in the world today: iron, manganese, copper, probably coal, cobalt, gold in quantities. Two minerals not yet found in quantity: petroleum and uranium.

Pleasant to watch the river boats, fishing craft with one huge brown lateen sail, dugouts, steam boats.

Rodman seems to get younger and even more boyish as I see him in this out-of-the-President's-office setting. His *relish* for new things and people is really a delight.

The trip is getting newspaper publicity, naturally enough, in the provincial press; the number of pictures of Rodman coming down the ramp of an airplane from city to city and columns of interviews which he gives with enjoyment, almost gaily.

One of these casual interviews produced the day's sensation. It seems Rodman was quoted as praising the way Brazil has gone about its economic development, emphasizing the "private sector," and this was construed in Caracas as a slur on Venezuela, where, of course, the Rockefeller interests have vast investments in oil and land, reaching back many years. Much to-do, over not much. "Venezuela can get hysterical, more than any other Latin country," said Rodman.

What makes this episode more significant is a proposition Nixon is said to have laid down in his State of the Union message. I gather it condemned expropriation but then went on to declare that the U.S. would vote against loans by the World Bank to countries that would confiscate American property. This was taken to be against Chile chiefly, but probably Venezuela bridled, too.

Today we spent a couple hours at a tropical museum—the Museum of the Amazon Wilderness, it might well be called.

A violent burst of tropical rain gave it a special flavor. For the first time I saw the weird, ominous creature, the giant iguana, perched on a tree, glaring. A pair of shrieking, six-foot sea otters, the greatest swimmers ever. A tapir. A pair of jaguars. To top it all, out of the murky water of a large concrete-lined tank came the head of an anaconda, a snake with a head so huge as to be unbelievable. He (or she!) inched its way up the side of the concrete wall toward the top of an island, the muscles contracting against the rough surface and slowly, slowly twisting the creature so it followed that smug and ugly head, writhing, until the entire snake was there to see: eighteen feet of muscle. No banker calling a demand loan could give more of an impression of steady, irresistible *squeeze.*

10 P.M.

Just back from a dinner offered to the "Rockefeller mission" by the smiling Governor and his Generals (an attractive group of young technocrats and military men). Rod was on the phone (between bites) five times —three to New York.

It seems that there is a tempest brought on by the newspaper version of Rod's remarks concerning Venezuela and Brazil. The Rockefeller representative in Caracas asked Governor Rockefeller to issue a statement saying that Rod was misquoted or misrepresented; that the Rockefellers really love Venezuela. The Governor's letter went directly to the President of Venezuela.

Said Rod: "Well, I'm sorry the letter was sent, but that is that." He seems to take the whole thing in a steady way, surprised that his freewheeling remarks were taken so seriously.

One other remark about his father amused me. "You know, my father is a hypochondriac. When he travels he has a kit of pills, all kinds of pills. A wonder they don't arrest him for pushing drugs."

I am no one to talk when it comes to pills, the number and variety I take a day, on Doctor's orders. It is the sign of a good, red-blooded American these days that there is a pill for everything.

JANUARY 22, 1972
BELÉM

Exhausted, but happy and solemn. This has been such a day as rarely comes to any man, even one who has seen as much of the realities of this world as I have.

A vastness of forest and of great waters. The largest area I have ever seen in such detail and duration completely unpopulated, almost literally without human beings, to the horizon hour after hour of flying across the basin with the theatrical name: Amazon.

JANUARY 23, 1972
FLYING BY BRAZILIAN AIR FORCE PLANE TO RECIFE FROM BELÉM

By Air Force plane to Altamira, a small river town (a future Decatur, Alabama, I describe it to myself), and then to a work camp via a fleet of Cessnas belonging to the company building a major sector of the Trans-Amazon highway.

I was surprised to find how moved I was by what I saw: a red gash through the forest, with huge scrapers and loaders roaring through the strip, steep cuts—some of them surely forty feet deep—the sides the color of fresh bleeding wounds. Along the strip the wreckage of noble trees, hacked down by axes—i.e., men, not machines—to make way for the gargantuan earth-moving equipment, piloted by a diminutive man made smaller by the monumental size and shaking sound of these bruisers.

The crews who fell the trees ahead of the scrapers and earth movers are set down at intervals in the forest. Their tools are air-dropped to them, with supplies. The contractor says they do better work if they have to cut their way back to base than if they are set up to move on from an already cleared section. An odd but probably effective bit of work motivation.

I had a strong impulse to walk in the forest, not just along the road. I found that I completely forgot my five months' lack of trust in my left foot, clambered over the edge of the road, and began walking up the slope through the forest. I know I overdramatize, but it was not just a walk along a road, not just a moving among the trees and heavy leaf litter. I was walking where no man had ever walked before, in the middle of the vast Amazonian forest, a jungle that covers half the area of Brazil. "This is the way it was at the time of creation"—I found myself mentally repeating the phrase. This was indeed "the forest primeval."

And the *rivers.* Such expanse of water, one tributary after another as we flew the course. Only once did I notice fast-flowing water—the exciting white water of rapids, of falling water, the kind of water on which much of my career and reputation rests. But mostly the Amazon rivers (the plural is intentional and descriptive) are a leisurely, meandering watery maze running over what appears from the air to be the kind of flat land of the Platte as Lewis and Clark first saw it in what is now Nebraska.

Actually the forest is not flat, but undulating, sometimes sharply. I saw this as I looked down the course of the newly gouged-out road, with its deep cuts and depressions.

What will the pounding of the heavy rains—the average is 80 inches a year—do to the roadway, and to the cuts, some of which already show ugly stabs of erosion? Tony Secundino, one of the party who knows Brazilian soils (and many other things equally basic, as I learned anew almost every hour), insisted that the soil is such a heavy clay that the cuts will not erode badly, and that vegetation or slabs to protect the cuts will not be necessary. I hope he is right; I would like to come back and see for myself. If he is not right the cost of maintaining the highway could be enormous. But the roadbed itself is compacted to a solidness quite different from that of the red roads of East Tennessee, for example.

Unlike the "business" journeys where I am responsible, which are unremittedly serious and tense to the point of solemnity, this group knows the pleasure of mixing serious observation and talk with fun. Yesterday afternoon was one of the pleasantest I have known in a long time. And so well organized. Of course, it was the contractor who made the arrangements, and in my TVA or AEC days I was so stiffnecked that I would have frowned on the idea of a contractor providing such innocent pleasures as a boat ride on a Conrad-type battered river boat, or an elaborate al fresco lunch with drinks.

A heaped plate of food, eaten on the deck of the little boat; alongside a smaller boat which was the "kitchen." And what is that piece of meat? Alligator. (Tasty too; the next time I am very hungry I can start chewing on my briefcase.) Wild duck. Wild boar.

As I got off the little Cessna at a work camp, a flush of nostalgia; how many such camps I have visited, the boss coming to see how things are going and, in my earlier days, pretending I could spot "good housekeeping" or the reverse, or good or poor morale, etc. (After a decade of this visiting new camps in the early stages of dam building, I really did develop a kind of lay observational technique.)

The young Brazilian in charge of this sector of the road brought his family to see us off; a slender girl, described as one of Brazil's champion tennis players, with five of the most beautiful children I have seen, the youngest about two, the rest of them just barely beyond the ten months' minimum spacing of Nature at its most fecund. No tennis out there in the forest.

10 P.M.
RECIFE

I was prepared to see signs of distress on every hand. Far from it. This city of more than a million people is as prosperous-looking as any I have seen in a long time. True, the country areas are dried up and there are many farm people on their uppers. How can it be that the city, the capital of a region of 30 million people, should be so obviously well off, the commercial sections of the city so beaming?

Some miles away we were taken to a perfectly delightful old Portuguese city, Olinda. I did so want Helen to see it. The church of a convent is what such a place of worship should be—gleaming white and gold, not the dour grey and dark of the Italian churches which I simply find unappetizing.

It was to Recife, a Dutch city in the 15th or perhaps 16th century, that the Sephardic Jews fled who were expelled from Spain. Then the Portuguese defeated the Dutch, and the Jews were given the option, so I was told, either to return to Holland or to New Amsterdam. They went to New York and there established the first Jewish synagogue in America, still to be seen in the Greenwich Village area—about 12th Street, as I recall.

JANUARY 24, 1972
RECIFE, IN THE STATE OF PERNAMBUCO

Pernambuco—I like that word.

I have had my breakfast out on the veranda of this hotel. A furious 70-mile-an-hour race of wildly driven cars already zooming by at seven, people ambling out to the beach which lies just beyond the racetrack of a street. My room is, I think, the smallest I have ever lived in with the exception of the cells at the YMCA in Chicago, a couple of centuries ago.

I haven't referred to the heat in the course of these fragmented notes. This morning it is the chief and central subject, even at this early hour. After all, we are very near the Equator. It is not as sticky a heat, at that, as Bangkok or Saigon, or, for that matter, in late June or mid-August, New York City, Princeton, or Washington. But a special blaze of the sun.

A visit with the "group Rockefeller" to the offices of SUDENE this morning, and then I leave my friends—it has been as friendly and harmonious a group of men as one could possibly wish for—and head for Rio, then home.

1:30 P.M., AT THE RECIFE AIRPORT

Any airport on a Sunday can be pretty full of chitter-chatter, but an airport crowd with a high Latin American density is the highest in decibels and excitement. The whole family, and their cousins and their aunts, make a festival of the departure or the arrival of one member of the clan.

FLYING TO RIO, 5:30 P.M.

This flight, tourist, was like being at a big family picnic. The place was jumping the whole way because of the young children. Talk about "permissive"—these young ones had the run of the place. One little square-built boy yelled the whole way, in the furious, completely unrestrained way David Jr. used to do when, by God, he didn't want to be restrained, or frustrated and he wanted the world to know it.

IN FLIGHT, FROM RIO TO NEW YORK

Of one aspect of Brazilian life and its fast-blooming economy we heard more than any other: the phrase, and the reality, of "fiscal incentives."

Anyone in the country will be forgiven half his income tax if he invests that sum in an industry that is described as furthering the development of Amazonia or the northeast. So we saw a half-dozen brand-new factories or enterprises—tile, textile, cattle raising, etc.—owned by a private concern but a major part of the investment coming from these "fiscal incentives."

It has certainly stimulated the rich people to invest in needed industry or agribusiness enterprises—no doubt at all. It is in fact the center pillar of the New Brazil. The investment of such a fiscal giveaway, as it would be called by many a liberal in the U.S., need not be in a particular industry; those who turn their tax obligations into invested assets can put the funds into a development bank—there are several and they are large —or can join with others. No need to search out a profitable enterprise for such a tax shelter investment.

The plan seemed to me to have advantages over tax exemptions— though these also exist under the present Brazilian effort to move ahead. Italy could have used such a plan instead of the fuzzy program for the Mezzogiorno but there is this hitch in applying it to Italy: the big Italian earners simply do not pay taxes, certainly don't pay full taxes.

But a doubt has just crossed my mind. Only the Brazilians who have large incomes can benefit substantially, or at all, from this fiscal incentive scheme.

So the new industries and modern agribusiness and cattle raising that are coming along will be owned by the same people who dominate the Brazilian scene now. This is no way to "restructure" the distribution of income. And without that, is there any way the 30 million very poor rural people of the northeast will ever really get out of the slough of poverty? Isn't it a scheme that gives the already rich an opportunity to insure their continued domination of industry and of capital-required areas?

JANUARY 25, 1972
STILL FLYING TO NEW YORK

It was a memorable experience "discovering" Brazil. What a blessing to be the kind of person who can think back on so strenuous a past week and see it as a new beginning. Welcoming it for its newness, its opportunity for adventure and stamina, as I welcome the sight of that dawn outside the plane.

JANUARY 29, 1972
PRINCETON

"If, sir, you were deprived of all printed matter, as a punishment, excepting only one book, what book would it be? The Bible? Shakespeare?"

My answer: the New York telephone book.

JANUARY 30, 1972
PRINCETON

I'm beginning to take walks again! Short, but definitely pleasure-type walks. The exultation of once again walking (after more than *five months* of hobbling, painfully too, most of the time) gives life a different cast. The pain isn't completely gone. But like the Nixon term about the Vietnam war—it is "winding down."

Helen reminds me of the many anecdotes that, in my serious days of journal writing, I didn't consider justified "recording."

For example, said she, "You didn't write out the comment of the deranged lady who kept phoning you (and me) in the middle of the night, while you were AEC Chairman, about how the atom was causing her such distress." She told Helen in justification for disturbing us at our home at 2 A.M. that her husband was in "an insane asylum." And then, in a comforting tone: "You know, ma'am, heredity runs in his family."

FEBRUARY 7, 1972
NEW YORK

A visit, in my study, yesterday morning with Richardson Dilworth, who lives in Princeton and is one of that elite corps of advisors to the Rockefeller Family.

Recently, Dilworth, "reluctantly and only temporarily" accepted the Chairmanship of IBEC.

I had suggested I would like to talk to Richardson very informally, in Princeton. Most of our visit was about the Brazil trip.

Dilworth said that Rodman had returned not only sanguine but "enthusiastic" about the prospects in Brazil, and of the opportunity it gave for D&R to contribute to IBEC its ideas of regional development in the focus of Brazil. So he listened closely to this part of my "report."

When I said that I thought IBEC had become "fragmented, was carrying on many largely unrelated enterprises," he agreed. It was because D&R and my TVA experience looked toward integration, toward the interrelation of functions that I thought, and Rodman had thought at the very outset of negotiations, that D&R could provide a useful managerial input for IBEC.

He made clear to me that he, and others of "The Family" group are watching Rodman's efforts with a combination of skepticism, concern, and hope.

FEBRUARY 15, 1972
NEW YORK

Sat beneath the big eagle in the *New York Times* publisher's dining room this noon, and fielded questions for over an hour from that very bright group who direct the destiny of the most powerful newspaper in the world. Do they realize, that group of something less than geniuses, what power they have? They seem so lacking in arrogance, personally, so eager to ask questions and weigh the responses I made, that the arrogance of power—the power that corrupts, so we have so often been told —seemed the last word one would use to describe them, as individuals. But the words they use in those editorials—that's another matter. Their printed words so often seem lacking in any sense of humility, and what is arrogance but a total lack of humility or perspective about one's limitations?

"Punch" Sulzberger has become a stocky, sturdy, tested man, a square, set jaw, a lived-in face. That he has a sensitivity about public matters I would doubt. His questions were mostly about matters close to home, the New York power picture, for example, which finally begins to worry him.

Nothing I said on this subject gave them much comfort. I said that there was no short-term solution, and that there would be bad times for New York. I stressed that only public understanding, based on an objective analysis widely discussed and comprehended, could permit the kind of decisions that would have to be made.

FEBRUARY 16, 1972
NEW YORK

I think I am at my managerial best when I draw out the views of those I work with. That I make up my mind entirely on my own quite frequently is apparent, for I do respect my instincts and hunches. But when I have a problem affecting this, or other organizations for which I have been responsible, my method is consultation. (This extends to somewhat lesser as well as major matters; for example, the many times I get Miss Baron's judgment about what to do or not to do on matters that seem to fall within the range of the quality of judgment I have found she has.)

D&R should produce its own leadership, and it has.

I followed this principle in TVA. I made Gordon Clapp personnel director from a junior post dealing with education; then promoted him, then a very young age, to be General Manager, then after looking outside for a new Chairman when I left, had Truman name him Chairman. Much the same story about Red Wagner, the present Chairman.

TVA has *produced* TVA-style people. There is always the danger that an organization will become ingrown by this incestuous process. But the alternative is not a good one, in most cases.

FEBRUARY 19, 1972
CLEARWATER, FLORIDA

A weekend visit in Florida with Ted and Nell. Technology might be as destructive of human values as the abstract intellectuals say it is; but without the jet plane, spending a couple days in Florida with my beloved brother just wouldn't be thinkable. A plus for the berated "technology."

A picture of the "social history" of contemporary America can be drawn by seeing what has happened to Florida, the older-people capital of middle America. Middle class and middle geographically.

Ted took us to St. Petersburg, where retirement for the middle class had its origins. Florida's changes are startling since the days when we used to come there, to Captiva, for a winter convalescence from flu—which was the usual thing for me for years during the winter. A continuous stream of "developments"—many of them like Ted and Nell's of "mobile homes," thousands of them spread over a far-from-enchanting landscape.

In St. Petersburg we went into a vast retail conglomerate, Webb's City, where prices are the lowest, and *everything* is to be purchased. We saw the faces of a new kind of poor. It is not the poverty of the cities, but of the "elderly" middle class. Heart-rending, much of it. Every nickel counts; the faces are sad, the mouths drawn down, and particularly today for it is cold and very windy in this "sunshine capital."

In a restaurant where we had an excellent lunch, an old lady with the inevitable blue hair. We overheard her say to her equally venerable, equally blue-haired companion: "As long as I don't think about how little time I have left I get along pretty good."

FEBRUARY 23, 1972
NEW YORK

At luncheon today: "You really should plan to go to China, and soon." Thus spake Seymour Topping, beyond question one of the best informed journalists about China and Southeast Asia.

"The Embassy at Ottawa is flooded with applications, but I'll help, and I think the reasons why you would be helpful to the Chinese with their development problems will be apparent to them."

Strange, I've never had the slightest interest in visiting Russia. Absurd, but true. But China is a different matter.

FEBRUARY 28, 1972
NEW YORK

Have just "seen" the President come down the steps from *Air Force One* at Andrews Air Base, Washington, with the cheers of a big crowd. Truly a great event, his trip to China. How well it illustrates how the office of the President can be used to establish foreign policy without the need for any Congressional authorization or concurrence whatever.

MARCH 4, 1972
PRINCETON

A stimulating and encouraging two hours or so last Thursday with Louis Cowan's graduate seminar of journalism and business-school students at Columbia. Most of the session consisted of my responses to their questions.

Some of the questions were very broad, but thoughtful: What do you consider the principal obstacle to progress and development in under-developed countries, such as Malaysia (where the questioner came from)? I took a quick aim: Lack of confidence that they have it in them to produce the kind of changes they want (I used the Persia case as an illustration).

Another question: You say that the U.S. is closer than you can remember to being willing to accept "planning." But can the national government cope with technology and planning? (I had remarked that public confidence in government and in business was at an unusually low level.)

I said I thought the rise of local environment-protection organizations meant a diffusion and decentralization of concern and of political power upon which planning, beginning locally, could be and was being built. For example, almost all the recent rash of anti-pollution legislation and regulation was the result, not of a national effort or of professional political opinion and conviction, but of these local amateur citizen groups.

Certainly the anti-pollution legislation and regulation are a major example of national planning, though rarely referred to in that way.

MARCH 8, 1972
NEW YORK

To a concert of the Bach Aria Group at Lincoln Center, guest of the Tobeys. Never believed I could stand a whole evening of Bach, but these cantatas, and arias from his cantatas, I enjoyed enormously. The oboist, Robert Bloom, and the flutist, Samuel Baron, I appreciated mostly.

Temper and indignation have their place in management. It is my way of showing intensity of feeling, and of letting others who would rather elide than decide know that I want answers, not soothing syrup.

But mostly I get syrup.

MARCH II, 1972
PRINCETON

Just been reading through portions of a remarkable study of the history of Chinese science and technology: *Science and Civilization in China,* by Joseph Needham, Volume IV. The several hundred pages dealing with civil and hydraulic engineering—including land use—were a revelation.

What the ancient Chinese did with their great rivers, the rambunctious Yangtze and the ugly Yellow, is a great epic, and largely unknown to me. Will I have a chance to see these rivers, hear the plans of the new Communist Chinese for their future? I hope so.

What I read into this account of Needham's explains why I have what might appear to be two contradictory views about the work of D&R, and before that, of TVA. On the one hand I am not that impressed with the engineering side, the techniques, the calculations, the design and construction side. Much of it doesn't seem to me as creative as many other outlets for my own interests or talents.

But what does fascinate me and drive me is the conviction, long and deeply felt, that watercourses and the way they are dealt with profoundly shape the social organization of men, and therefore the destiny of individuals. No one can read, even hastily as I did this morning, what Needham says about the history of the ancient Chinese people's dealing with watercourses (including canals) and the land dependent upon the water, without seeing that the institutions of China, and such abstractions as centralization and the warlord system, were the result of the topography and hydrology of that vast area.

This is the part of my work that keeps me fired up, not the design and building of the structures and the agricultural technology that goes with it.

Long ago I noted that our English words "riparian rights" can be translated as "rival rights," and from that to fighting and the exercise of power is not far off. The fight for water is a basic force in shaping people's politics, government, social organization.

It is this that makes our work significant, to me. Technically trained men would not be so likely to see this as I do, who have only such technical knowledge as I have "picked up" by contact with our work and our technical people.

MARCH 12, 1972
PRINCETON

A new kind of small dinner party, eight plus us, here last evening, with a slight touch of elegance. Which means that we asked that it be black tie. So what with two tins of caviar, stored in our refrigerator for such an occasion, and a good company well put together, it was almost gala.

Two guests were as close to being familiar with contemporary China as one finds, after twenty years of no visas to Americans into China. One was Walton Butterworth. He was with General Marshall on his abortive effort to straighten up Chiang Kai-shek in the late forties. The other Bill

Nancy Lilienthal Bromberger.

Son-in-law Sylvain Bromberger.

David Lilienthal, Jr., and David Lilienthal, Sr., at Topside, 1979.

David Lilienthal, Jr.'s children (Florence, Italy, 1970): (lower) David Lilienthal III, Michael Lilienthal; (upper) Margaret Lilienthal, Pamela Lilienthal.

Nancy Bromberger's children: (left) Allen, (right) Daniel.

David Lilienthal and Beatrice Tobey.

Richard Freeman, Helen Lilienthal, David Freeman, David Lilienthal in Knoxville, 1979 (*Photograph by Robert Kollar, TVA Employee Communications, Knoxville, Tennessee*).

Mildred Baron.

David Morse.

(left to right) Reza Ansari, Leo Anderson, the Shah of Iran, in Khuzistan, Iran.

John W. Macy, Jr., President of D & R.

Rodman C. Rockefeller *(Photograph by C. Sangiamo).*

Gerald Eades Bentley.

Gerald M. Levin.
(Photograph by Al Freni).

Ambassador Ellsworth
Bunker, 1970 *(Wide World
Photos)*.

Brazilian Minister João Leitão de Abreu.

Sol Linowitz, Assistant Secretary of State for Latin America.

(Seated left to right) General Manager Leon Ring, David Freeman, Helen Lilienthal, and Richard Freeman. (At podium) David Lilienthal.

David Freeman, David Lilienthal, Richard Freeman, Knoxville, Tennessee, 1979
(*Photograph by Robert Kollar, TVA Employee Communications, Knoxville, Tennessee*).

Helen Lilienthal, Barrett Shelton, David Lilienthal at Decatur, Alabama Airport, 1979
(*Photograph by Robert Kollar, TVA Employee Communications, Knoxville, Tennessee*).

Cass Canfield, Sr., David Lilienthal's editor at Harper & Row.

Lockwood, born and with his childhood in China, now one of the few recognized experts on the Far East and particularly Japan.

What did they think of the Nixon foray into China? Both were cautious. Of course, it was long past due to be in communication with present-day China. But the summitry method and the Nixon-Chou TV extravaganza one could see worried them.

I have been saying that I don't see how Nixon can win the election, my theory being that so many people are uneasy and grumbling that "it is time for a change" and "throw the rascals out." If you are the incumbent when things aren't going well the advantage becomes a great handicap.

Mary Davis, a clear-headed, forceful gal, wife of my law-school classmate Wendell, took issue with this. "Things aren't that bad," she said. "Who is there among the Democrats that people, and particularly young people, feel would make things better? McGovern, weak, 'puffy.'" (What Beatrice would call a marshmallow.)

A very great deal in what she said.

The other day I read an article in the *Radcliffe Quarterly* by the historian Barbara Tuchman. Her comment about the oral history, tape-recorder source of biography or history was that it culled mountains of trivia. What a serious-minded, humorless woman she must be, to think that only what happens—events—constitute history or biography. If she had ever participated in events of consequence—surely writing about other people's deeds is not participating—she wouldn't be quite so eloquently contemptuous of the memoirs or journals of participants. Her point that participants cannot be objective is so obvious as to be tiresome.

But the context of the times in which people live and events occur is as important as the events; and contemporary records of that context (what is sometimes portentously called "social history") is part of the record which can either be reconstructed by a historian—from what?—or set down in the contemporary records of individuals, called diaries, or in newspaper accounts, etc.

Just written a longhand letter to Jeanette Mirsky thanking her for the loan of the massive fourth volume of that giant tour de force *Science and Civilization in China*. "I found . . . what the ancient (and contemporary) Chinese knew and *did* with their watercourses great reading."

MARCH 14, 1972
NEW YORK

This noon a luncheon meeting with some of the trustees (including some new ones) of the Fund for Multinational Management Education. Heard encouraging evidence that the idea has some strength and is producing some results in the training of management talent in several Latin countries. I found this reassuring, as I had become quite skeptical, had resigned as Chairman a couple times. But today I was rather proud that I had helped to get the enterprise under way, some several years ago, and that I had contributed a fair amount of money to get it started.

MARCH 15, 1972
NEW YORK

Saw a rerun of one of the great performances of all time, Charlie Chaplin in *Modern Times.* That music-hall turn of his, in the night club, is the funniest and most perfect bit of fooling I have ever seen, and the humor and sadness and faith and courage of the ordinary man. Comes in handy, that last, in the light of the overwhelmingly favorable response to George Wallace's blatherskite appeal in the Florida primary.

This will dignify Wallace with every repressive group in the country, including the Republican Party management, somewhat shaken by the scandal about the furtive settlement of the ITT antitrust case.

Hard times ahead, my boy. Hol' on.

MARCH 19, 1972
PRINCETON

The report of the future of the world by the Club of Rome (so-called) has just about commanded more newspaper coverage than any event since the outbreak of World War II. And no wonder: the report said that a big computer at MIT laid it down that the world would "collapse" in a hundred years, or less.

What "made" the story were three things: (1) it was gloomy and catastrophic and so appealing to the newspaper sense of what is news; (2) the word came out of that modern Delphic oracle, a computer; and (3) it had the imprimatur of MIT, which is to the technical world, at least, the Holy of Holies.

The whole thing seemed outrageous to me, if only because Aurelio Peccei was the originator, so it was said, of the Club of Rome. Peccei was our erstwhile "partner" for a while [in Argentina, in 1960] until Gordon Clapp and I cancelled our contracts because of differences over business ethics.

On a walk in the bright, snappy sunshine of Princeton, I heard the story of how the Club of Rome came about, and particularly how this global death-warrant was devised, from a member of the Executive Committee and a chief technical man in the Club of Rome.

Johnny Wheeler, the world's greatest living theoretical physicist, by my judgment, phoned early this morning. He had as a guest a scientist from Geneva; Johnny thought it might be interesting for me, as it would for his guest, to take a walk together, and hear what his guest had to say about the state of Europe. To which I agreed heartily, delighting in Johnny's company and in the good sense of his remarkable mind.

The guest was Hugo Thiemann, Directeur Général of the Battelle Center in Geneva. His business card says he is "Ing. Dipl. E.P.F., Dr. Es Sc. Tech., Dr. Es Sc. H.C." No dummy, if degrees can assure that a man is educated.

What did I think of the report of the Club of Rome? Said I: If it is the purpose of those associated with that group of scientists to persuade the people of the world that dire things are in the early offing unless action of a drastic kind is taken, they went at it, in my opinion, in the worst conceivable way. First, the report was put out quite obviously to scare the hell out of people, which is no way to have a lasting, persuasive effect on the public mind.

Second, and more serious, by citing computer results as the basis for their conclusion about how long it will be until there is a world "collapse," they will run into the general skepticism of the ordinary citizen about the computer. He runs into the nonsense and errors of the computer almost every day—his bills are misstated, the damn things break down, they generally have produced a sense of disbelief about ordinary, simple everyday affairs; so, however firm the scientists' conclusions may be—which I certainly doubt like hell—to point to the computer and say that this highly fallible machine was the source of this tale was a serious tactical error.

This brought from Thiemann the damndest story I have heard for many a day of human beings who are supposed to be geniuses and technically beyond question or doubt—but ordinary mortals.

More substantive even than this tale of human frailty and "propaganda" and "fanaticism" was the role of the men at MIT who formulated a particular set of assumptions, a formula for the programming of a computer.

The history, the origins of the Club of Rome went like this: Peccei brought together a small group to contemplate and consider the "problématique"—i.e., impending disaster. The world was prodigal of its resources, was grossly multiplying its population, and by industrialization was polluting and, indeed, *consuming* the vital elements of the atmosphere. A group should be brought together to state the "problématique" (I repeat that term because he did, looking at me sternly each time he used the word). If the situation were adequately described, then perhaps "something would be done about it" (I loved that phrase, because *doing* something is far removed from what that particular group would be qualified to have a hand in).

Peccei got a grant for this purpose from Fiat and Volkswagen, than which, I thought to myself, no greater users-up of space, peace, quiet, and pure air could hardly be imagined.

At their meeting in Rome it was decided that one of their number, a Professor Forester of MIT, should formulate a "model," a simulation that would take into account population, resources, food supply, etc. From these factors, Forester said, he would prepare a number of models, which after review could be fed into the big computer at MIT.

On the plane back to the U.S., Forester, on a couple pieces of paper, did design a model. He later said that he had the model even before the meeting, and in its uncriticized state he and a young protégé and student, whose name has been in all the stories but escapes me at the moment, ran the thing out.

Then, without checking with, or being authorized by, the Executive Committee or the members of the Club of Rome, Forester, "a fanatic, a driving businessman"—his words which Thiemann repeated, to my amusement, several times in the course of our visit—proceeded to publish the results, and his young assistant made many speeches and public appearances using these results. Forester had a book he wanted to get published before the Club or anyone else could get a start on him.

And so on.

My comment in the Stafford Little Lectures that scientists are very human was certainly verified by this story. The humor of describing an MIT professor as a "driving businessman type" made it difficult for me to keep from laughing, indeed I did laugh, and I thought Wheeler enjoyed the joke but Thiemann, still resentful of the way the MIT profs ran away with the "big story," didn't think it was funny a bit.

Of course the "model" determined what the computer would say about the short-lived future of the world. And the model has been criticized by other model makers. But in the meantime the columns of guff that the press have been publishing has been monumental.

These people go at the problem of making the world realize that it must "do something" to be saved. Properly executed, such studies have a great value in defining the problem, or parts of it, though this will all be in the broadest of terms. But *I* should write about what can be done, and what *has* been done, to enable man to cope.

Lunch with the Australian Ambassador to West Germany, who said many interesting things about Australia. Not the least, that Australia has become the channel of interchange of ideas within the international community with Japan. I could see he anticipates Australia will assume much the same role, in the Pacific at least, with the People's Republic of China, though at present they do not have diplomatic relations.

The archenemy Japan is now the bastion upon which Australia depends—that is what, between the lines, I take to be what he sees. Already, in economic matters, they are partners—iron ore, etc.

I referred to my friend, the former Minister of Development, Court. "A great man," he said, very simply. The Labour Government victory has meant that Court, of course, is no longer in the Government. But his description of him as a great—i.e., a very unusual—man pleased me very much.

MARCH 23, 1972
NEW YORK

I never feel comfortable in the company of professional economists. Or in a discussion *by* economists. It is the one profession that has been constantly wrong, wrong, wrong, and yet is never fazed about coming up with new pretensions. The chief pretension right now is what to do about inflation.

Ken Galbraith is one of the high priests of this theology, but the most human of the lot. Sat next to him this evening at a long table in the beautiful library room of the Century.

Ken has changed considerably in appearance, as his fame and ubiquitousness has increased. One can see that he takes his place in history very literally. He may be right about that. An unbeatable combination: self-admiration which he has turned into a virtue; a brutal skill of cutting derogation of others which he has developed into a form of art; an extraordinary gift for words; a manner that says, as plainly as his exceptional height, that he has no doubts about his pre-eminence; the self-assurance that comes from being a Harvard professor and yet one of the most highly paid authors—put these together and you can see why he considers his place in history is made.

I certainly have no cause for complaint about his manner toward me. On the contrary. But instinctively I react against self-advertisers and those who chop down people with sarcasm.

One should be wary about one's emotions of antagonism toward highly successful men: is this just a form of envy, or competitiveness? Perhaps.

My only comment during the several hours of the session was to declare against professionalized economics and economists. Obsolete, said I.

MARCH 28, 1972
CANEEL BAY PLANTATION,
ST. JOHN, U.S. VIRGIN ISLANDS

Only one table was left by the time Helen and I reached the terrace looking out on the unbelievably azure-green beauty of this bay. We wriggled into the table; the legs of my chair got somewhat tangled with the chair of a lady on my right, she sitting with two little boys, and across from her a stocky man whose face and figure faded into the shadows. The lady, with a very attractive, lively, friendly face, moved her chair, asked me if I had room, and Helen and I ordered our drinks.

The lady, after a bit, leaned over the edge of her chair and said: "I overheard you saying something about New York. Did you come from New York?" Yes we did, just this morning and it was cold there. The conversation grew—the man in the shadow being talked to by an older lady, and our neighbor lady was gently supervising the two quite young boys, who were prattling about what they had been doing that day.

I said we actually lived in Princeton—it is unusual for me to talk so readily to "strangers," but by this time the lady had turned her chair and was part of our table. And do I know Richardson Dilworth? Yes, he is Chairman of a company my company is associated with. Then she said something about sugar cane, which had been grown on St. John years ago; I said my company had started sugar cane in southern Persia after a long, long lapse. What is the company?

By this time I thought the anonymity was going to be embarrassing if continued, so I said I would like to introduce myself: I'm David Lilienthal.

What a piece of Lilienthal luck, to find ourselves at her initiative in a pleasant conversation with Happy Rockefeller. Said the Governor: Yes, Roddy is a great admirer of yours. Was very enthusiastic about the trip to Brazil he took with you. I said there was a report that he (the Governor) might be speaking to an IBEC management meeting on the 13th. Yes, he said, I have agreed to do that. We will see you there. "I am much impressed with Rodman; in fact, at times I feel almost as if he were my son; the generation gap is about right," I said. "That's a very fine thing for you to say," said the Governor.

"These boys [referring to the very young boys, by this time on their way elsewhere] are Roddy's half brothers." I didn't realize until later how that remark of mine about feeling almost in a father relation to Rodman might sound to a much younger wife.

Both Helen and I were much taken with Happy. (It is difficult to use any other name for her, so strongly has that quite appropriate nickname been planted, by the great public furor over her divorce and Nelson's, and their marriage.)

She has an open countenance, easy and friendly; a particularly pleasing voice (rare in women, I find), obviously no "side." Said she, in explaining to him why we were talking away so, without "introductions": "You two [referring to her mother sitting next to the Governor] had me out of this conversation so I just butted into the Lilienthals'."

MARCH 31, 1972
ST. JOHN, V.I.

Stroking hard for the pleasure of swimming I pulled up on the sand before our cottage, and dripping and puffing I found myself waving and saying "hi" to a man in tomato-red shorts with a woman with her wet hair stringing over her shoulders. Hardly a dignified way to greet the three-term Governor of New York State and his First Lady (second lady, literally).

"You know Joe Swidler;* I recall that he worked with you."

I replied that Joe's first job after graduating from law school was in my law office in Chicago. Governor Rockefeller looked down, very thoughtful, as if he were composing a "statement." "Joe has done a great job for us. A man of great integrity. Difficult job, particularly siting [of power plants, he meant, of course], what with the environmentalists." A nuisance, is what his tone implied.

The workings of my memory, or non-memory, are fascinating to me. When I can't remember a name, offhand, it bothers me. Most other people will say: "Well, the name escapes me; I'll think of it later." Or, just let it go. But remembering people's names has for so long for me been almost a professional necessity, and my pride in having this ability so great, that when I can't remember a name, from yesterday or forty years ago, I can't let it go at that. I don't like to confess it to myself but there is some element of fear in the almost frantic feeling I get that I must at once drag that name out of that mess of wires known as the memory part of the brain. Strange business, this digging into one's memory.

APRIL 8, 1972
PRINCETON

Returning from over a week of absence from my work I pawed through memos and files, and said to myself: There is nothing that hap-

*Appointed chairman, New York State Public Service Commission, in 1970; he had been chairman of the Federal Power Commission, and was TVA general counsel in the 1930s.

pened, or did not happen, that would have been changed by your being here. Which is a mark of great improvement in the ability of the organization to carry on without me.

A pleasant thought. But not quite true, however.

What I provide is a strong conviction against D&R settling into the comfort of a traditional engineering and agricultural technical organization. The tendency to do just that is increased as the pressure of "meeting the payroll" recedes.

It is by no means enough that D&R is doing better along conventional lines; the question must be faced every week, indeed almost every day: the question is not what kind of an organization it is, but what kind it should become.

If D&R is half content, it is half dead. When it becomes fully content (not likely while I am around, certainly), then it has no real reason for existence. It will then be like many other organizations in the development field. Our constant goal should be different and distinctive.

With lapses from grace, it's true, this is what we have been and still are.

APRIL 10, 1972
PRINCETON

The word-people and the policy analysts cop out of decisions and responsibility for them by presenting the alternatives and showing how unsatisfactory both or all are.

This is a luxury (or a form of dishonesty) not open to politicians and managers.

This is just where the environmentalists leave us, about power supply. They are getting closer and closer to realizing that by merely defining the damage to the environment that ensues from increasing power supply they are simply describing one of these cop-out "dilemmas."

It is the absolutist position that bothers me most about the energy problem. Or any form of the many environmental issues.

What is most needed are cases and illustrations of how, by putting absolutist positions aside, we can live by protecting the environment without cutting off our lives or denying people what they want and what they can, reasonably, expect and have.

The monthly meeting of the Century last Thursday put me at table between Bill Paley of CBS and John Oakes of the *Times*.

A greater contrast in strong and influential men would be hard to find even if one were looking for such.

Paley is a big genial fellow who gives the impression of being able to live with all kinds of viewpoints. His strong friendship and support of Ed Murrow when Ed was at his most "controversial" illustrates one side of this likeable man, in a prickly kind of business, the use of public airwaves for private profit—and he has been one of the most successful of profit makers. On the other side, he is highly regarded by very conservative people, of which there is an oversupply in the circles, social and business, he inhabits.

John is a quite different man, except in this, that the influence of his words on the *Times* editorial page is comparable to Bill's electronic word-production. John has strong convictions on a few topics, notably now "the environment," so strong that they intrude into the discussion of almost any subject whatever. But his personal manner is just as genial, smiling, almost conciliatory as Paley's, perhaps more so. But underneath this is an absolutist, by my standards.

The man who "put together" our table at the dinner was an interesting and unusual fellow: Arthur Tourtellot. At first one is put off by his appearance, that of a don or professor. Pince-nez kind of glasses, but with heavy shell rims, hair pulled over the top of his bald head, noticeably short in stature; a deep deliberate voice embellished with elaborate phraseology. But a fascinating conversationalist, one of the few I know.

He and John, sitting side by side, said they thought the books I had written that would last were the *Journals.* I demurred, thought the TVA book stated propositions that today were as valid as in 1943. No. In a hundred years the *Journals* will continue to be a prime source of reference by public figures and scholars to identify what kind of a world it was in the period the *Journals* cover—so they said, staring hard at me as if I would be the last to know how important they were.

I refrained from saying—give me credit—that if they were so important, how come the *Times* Sunday book section hadn't reviewed Volume V?

APRIL 12, 1972
NEW YORK

Just back from a tiny motion-picture house off 68th Street, where I saw one of the most realistic and honest of films, *Tomorrow.* It is based on a story by Faulkner, laid, as I could see at once, in the piney woods of northern Mississippi. (At the end there was an acknowledgment to the community of Tupelo for their cooperation, so it *was* in that area I knew so well, years and years ago.)

How could the well-cared-for city people possibly understand, or comprehend the truth of the portrayal of these scrub-country poor? It set me to saying to myself: The rural poor *everywhere* should be your chief concern.

APRIL 15, 1972
PRINCETON

The first day of really heavy gardening. I had a grand time—and my muscles creak tonight.

Just flowers? No vegetables? All that work, and nothing to show for it. This represents a good many people's notion of the gardening I do.

APRIL 17, 1972
NEW YORK

An impromptu lunch today with a friend of many years' standing, Quincy Howe. He became one of the country's best-known radio news commentators. A crackling, staccato Boston voice, which he still has, and a deep knowledge of history. He is a delight to be with. (Imagine any of our present-day TV commentators knowing the philosophical difference between Metternich and Mao Tse-tung! *Quaere*—does the European-centered and -educated Kissinger know the difference? It could make a lot of practical difference these agonizing days of the resumption of the Indochina war.)

Howe knows the broad spectrum of history, but not a thing about what D.E.L. has been doing with himself. Assumed I am "taking it easy." To tell him that I am running a business, I knew, would convey practically nothing. I said I wanted to write a book, but didn't quite see yet how to manage it along with my work. He said, "You are in an ideal situation then, for absolutely no one can write a book and do nothing else. Either he dawdles between spells of writing, or he does it along with some other work, which is what you can do. Better not to try to do nothing but write. Except your *Journals,* of course." He did know about their existence, though obviously not their contents.

APRIL 19, 1972
NEW YORK

All day, beginning at 8:30, in perhaps the best example of group thinking I have been party to since I guided the five men who produced the *Report on the International Control of Atomic Energy.* The group today, the "senior staff" of D&R: Seymour, Frederiksen, Pampanini and Silveira. There was an assist from Levin, especially invited.

This is a group of exceptionally intelligent and seasoned men, who know what they are talking about, and who can differ with each other, as at times they did, with a sense of common interest and basic agreement as to objectives and methods. This process is the product of valid on-the-ground experience and tested judgments stretching back over some years in D&R (and in my case particularly, beyond that, in TVA and AEC).

A sense of achievement, as we "adjourned." Most important to me, they (and I) were (to use the sedate Walton Seymour's term) "having fun" in their work.

And no wonder. The subjects we were dealing with were of great interest to grown men who sensed that one needs purposeful and stimulating work.

I was very active in the discussions, injecting the idea at every turn that we must keep ahead of the needs of less developed countries, and not be content with supplying the, by now, traditional needs—agriculture, power, etc. E.g., export know-how, or in the case of land use or environment, how to use the technique of the earliest TVA days to overcome local government subdivision and private land ownership, obstacles to sensibly planned use of land. That device was the *ownership* of land by government agencies, such as the margin of the road to Norris, the Freeway (free of ugly billboards), or acquiring by TVA of a "protective strip" above the level of water in the reservoirs, and planning that for the kind of private development which after-the-fact regulation or zoning could never do—has never been able to do.

APRIL 22, 1972
PRINCETON

Suddenly it is spring.

The miracle of miracles, beside which the ghostly television prowling of the men on the moon seems almost ho-hum.

I wonder if I would feel this sense of rebirth if I could no longer be an active part of it, breaking open the soil I have tended and "improved," preparing a bucket of manure and bone meal to put into the holes, and plopping in some new plant, packing it down with my hands—all the rest of the ritual so well known and each time so happy.

MAY 2, 1972
NEW YORK

I spent some time studying a long paper drafted in the D&R office in Sacramento about the New Rural Towns concept for Iran. I liked the paper, but thought it missed an important element, that "new towns" in the rural areas should be part of the basic objective of improving rural life, not seen as something separate. My concern was that without that perspective the whole subject would become a playground for the physical planner, who thrives on just such a disembodied proposal.

Moreover, I felt that the proposal as drafted, excellent though it was in many ways, did not sufficiently emphasize that those who plan such towns should be men able by experience and temperament to carry out such plans, "implement" them, as they now say.

MAY 5, 1972
PLAZA HOTEL, NEW YORK

The whole future of America and the peace of the world is resting on a razor's edge of crisis on the battlefields of the Northern Province of South Vietnam, to read the pundits and hear the squish-voiced TV commentators from the battlefield.

While this is purportedly going on eight thousand miles away, the tubby European Henry Kissinger, the architect of the U.S. policy, stands before an audience of us fat cats in the Baroque Room of the Plaza, and talks as if he were before a Harvard seminar on the painful issues of the day. It is simply a small piece of a global jigsaw that he, Kissinger, is evolving for a doctoral thesis or for a book, dismissing what is going on in that "remote and not too significant part of Southeast Asia" (so he says).

Kissinger's words and his demeanor as he spoke, extemporaneously and without either a manuscript or notes, to the Asia Society tonight, was a tour de force of serenity, of the detached egghead (to use the phrase of the Stevenson days).

He impressed me and Helen greatly. For his composure, his ability to seem to respond to a question from the audience (or to say, "I would not put the question in that way"), to exhibit qualities of humor and wit I didn't believe so harassed and overworked a man could display. His guttural accent is quite noticeable but not distracting. His ability to kid himself, his European detachment and almost resignation are so different from the messianic tone of most American political discourse.

He said that he had written his graduate thesis on the subject of the balance of power and Metternich (this was in response to a question that tried to line him up with the "balance of power" theorists).

Most of the people in that crowded room (perhaps three hundred) were strongly opposed to the policy of Nixon and Kissinger. Kissinger said the differences have become so "liturgical" as to defy rational exchange of views.

Yet the respect for the man and his coolness and super-rationality was so great that he was greeted with a standing ovation and a strong wave of applause as he concluded.

MAY 6, 1972
PLAZA HOTEL, NEW YORK

I was so lost in admiration for Kissinger's handling of himself last night (one platform "artiste" admiring another's skill and aplomb in fielding questions) that it was only this morning I realized how we had been conned. It came on me, as I walked in Central Park before breakfast, that this "professor," the most influential non-political personality in the world, had concealed the fact that what the Nixon-Kissinger policies add up to is 19th century isolationism.

Let the inconsequential nations do what they choose to do without the U.S. messing around with them. Let Japan become strong enough to take our customers for goods. Let China do what it wishes. The only countries that matter are the Soviet Union and the U.S. because they have the only consequential military power.

Because he said what he did in the objective, non-polemic, sanitized words ["world order," etc.] of the Council on Foreign Relations or Harvard International Center, it didn't sound like withdrawal from the world. But this morning I see that is truly what it is.

No wonder the former avid internationalists—"World Order," "One World," "World Constitution"—such as Fulbright, are so nonplussed and frustrated. They see what their world-order business has gotten us into, in S.E. Asia.

They won't blame themselves for not seeing what it means if you really try to "enforce the peace through the United Nations, etc." Enforcing the peace, or "peacekeeping forces" (same thing), means shooting or bombing people who don't see it your way.

So they take the only escape hatch they can see, to withdraw and let one nation take on any other it thinks it can subdue by force of arms. Hitler knew what it meant for his world ambitions when he heard people sing hosannas: "Blessed is the peacemaker." The isolationists invite the tough guys to take over, and to find "friends" who will supply them with the arms to do that.

But to hear Kissinger last night on his broad philosophical theme of the Nixon Doctrine, this withdrawal is a part of a great historical pattern for building "world order."

I wonder how many other people saw what this skillful performance added up to. I didn't at the time. I knew that he was ducking the critical questions of the *hour*. Literally of that hour, considering that the North

Vietnamese appear to have accomplished in a military way what they didn't effectively in 1968, at the time of the so-called Tet offensive.

Helen and I had an enjoyable visit with David Rockefeller and his wife. There is something boyish and, therefore, disarming about him, despite his reputation as a bold, successful financial man. She, with her hair very short, and an eager, most friendly manner, is a delight.

Had a little talk with John D. Rockefeller 3d, whom I haven't seen except at a distance for quite a while. John put on that very rueful look, twisting himself in the way he has, and then said: "Nixon's statement today didn't help much"—a gargantuan understatement.

What a rebuff the President has given John 3d's commission's recent report on population, a commission the President himself had picked. Not only against abortion, talking loftily about it, but saying that couples could decide for themselves about contraceptives, as if anyone had suggested that people be forced to avoid conception. The President's statement, as I read it this morning at breakfast here, sounded right out of the Nixon of Whittier, California, with an admixture of Billy Graham. As if overpopulation is not our most—or almost our most—grievous social problem, the excesses of population growth being one of the chief centers of many other ills.

MAY 8, 1972
PRINCETON

Tonight the President told the country and the world what he proposes to do about the war in Vietnam, now that there appears to be a serious attempt to grind out a victory on the battlefield for the Communists, and a sore degradation for this country.

The Nixon rhetoric of "negotiation not confrontation" lies in shreds. The very measures—mining the North Vietnam harbor of Haiphong to prevent the entry of Soviet ships, together with the increased bombing —this was the President's "confrontation" with Hanoi, but also with the Soviet Union. Unlike most of the ultimatums in the classic pattern—i.e., through notes and diplomatic messages—this was directly, face to face, the head of a great nation at war directing his words to the heads of another great nation.

How can the Congress withhold its support of the President, who has himself cornered? How can Russia ease itself out of what is surely a less important issue than the building of trade with the U.S.?

Dr. Kissinger must have known exactly what was coming when he spoke to us last Friday night. Some of the phrases the President used were ones that Dr. Kissinger used.

When I sat in on the Johnson-Ky council of war at Guam in 1967, the Air Force Generals described various targets. Some of these were the bombing of the docks and mining of the harbor at Haiphong. President Johnson asked questions—the obvious ones: How will this be taken by the Russians and Chinese? He did not approve those targets and did not give them serious consideration, so far as one could tell. Now, years later, this is what we are doing.

Those who blamed us for not blasting the hell out of everyone and "getting it over with" years ago will have much to say on their side.

The American people have been calling for an "end to the war"; the candidates keep saying it. Everyone assumes that this is what the American people want at any cost. Now will they grow angry not at Nixon but at the Communists?

Last fall, in a review of Joseph Lash's book, *Eleanor and Franklin,* I wrote that those who have said with considerable contempt that the Cold War is an obsolete scare-phrase will find that the Cold War is far from over. It is no longer so cold, but certainly the period of détente is over *again.*

MAY 12, 1972
PRINCETON

Red Wagner, the present Chairman of TVA, and I are to appear on the *Today* TV show next Thursday morning. The occasion is the 39th birthday of TVA.

Red will try to tell the TVA story as a record of accomplishment. I may have a chance to say something of the TVA-type development overseas, in other words, D&R.

"How old were you when you joined TVA?" I asked Red.

"I was 22. And you were only 33 when you became a director. It was a young man's organization. Today when we find a man of 38, or in his early 40s, we think we are lucky. It's not easy to find young men for jobs as you did in the early days."

MAY 13, 1972
PRINCETON

A notable achievement yesterday: I managed to do nothing the live-long day. Whenever the impulse to do something hit me, whether down here in the study or in the garden, I somehow curbed it.

Decided I must be more "tired" than I have any reason to be. So I'll try to stretch the "do as little as possible" hiatus a couple days more.

I can manage to lie motionless in the sun (we have had summer weather suddenly) like a lizard. But the damned mind and imagination keep churning out pictures and ideas and recollections and "arguments." The range of these ruminations is absurd. Perhaps it is because hard physical activity turns this off that I throw myself so often into almost exhausting physical effort. Helen's remark: "You have always been like this, even before we were married when you were a student. You seem to believe that physical fatigue is a way to relax; being tired physically is being tired in every way." Of course, she is right, and Atchley confirms this, as a physician. But I can't get it through my noggin.

MAY 15, 1972
PRINCETON

The Brazil trip is "on." So Walt [Seymour] and I leave June 6th, for a two-week stint.

This morning's after-breakfast subject was a rare one. Helen asked me whether I think about being old; went on, at my urging, to say how she feels about age, the calendar that is mounting for us.

This was ticked off in her mind by yesterday's *New York Times* review of a book by Simone de Beauvoir on being old: a sad book, apparently. She did refer to those great figures who have continued to create and produce far into old age, and to the importance of financial security (or poverty) on how one takes the onslaughts of old age. But mostly it was a book describing the despair that old age brings most people.

Helen's response was so like her. "I don't feel I have to keep up with the many things I used to do—because of the children, or because of your official position. Yes, I agree that the word 'retired' applies to me, and I don't resent it: on the contrary. But despair? Not at all.

"But then you haven't reached that stage because you are so active and involved in your work, piling new commitments to the future on top of what you have."

The period of feeling tired that I have been going through has led me to think more about age than I ordinarily would, or should. The fact that the "succession" to the direction of D&R is in my mind from time to time, and even more frequently in the heads of my younger staff friends, brings the question of a change in my life style to the fore, but not yet because of what the calendar tells me about my age. But again: "despair"? No.

And when I heard the outline of the ambitious program for Brazil, in a phone conversation with Walt Seymour, I felt exhilarated; many have been the times when the prospect of such a schedule would make me fearful—can I make it? This was true twenty-five years ago, when "old age" was certainly not the cause of this trepidation.

6:15 P.M.

A few minutes before five, a call from the office: the radio reports that George Wallace was shot while campaigning in Maryland. The latest word sounds as if his wounds are so serious that he will not be a candidate when the Democratic convention opens in July. But he will be a part of the American political scene, whatever happens as a result of this shooting. No one can any longer discount the reception his harangues have received throughout the country, his appeal to the people who need someone *to blame* for inflation, unemployment, busing, the lot.

MAY 16, 1972
NEW YORK

The oncoming expedition to Brazil looks more exciting as an experience, and more promising for D&R as an enterprise, every day. This noon I lunched with a remarkable gentleman, Berent Friele, who knows more about Brazil than any dozen Americans. I have asked him to accompany us, and I think he probably will.

With a good group of "experts" now working for us in Brazil, with a good Brazilian engineering firm as associates, with the effects of our earlier trip still visible, this may be the best prepared effort ever to build a stronger and more effective D&R, in a country that is as juicy and self-confident as it is big.

MAY 18, 1972
HEADING FOR PRINCETON

This is the first time I have taken the train home (or to New York) for seven or eight months. Quite an event. I have been driven by car partly because it was the "convenient" way; partly because the damned foot did hurt. So this time it did not hurt—and this is another milestone.

The *Today* show, early this morning, was a good, solid—though not spectacular—exposure of D.E.L., as well as D&R. Getting up at 6:30, and responding before twenty-odd-million people (so they say) found me relaxed and self-assured—so I was told—and I know it without being told.

Though it was to celebrate the fourth decade of TVA, the delightful and thoughtful Barbara Walters threw the first question to me (to Red Wagner, on the show, it should have been, I suppose) and said some pleasant things: i.e., "your name is well known in Iran," and took other opportunities to say that D&R is furthering the TVA concept in several places outside the Valley.

I thought Red's handling of the criticism of TVA was admirable:

strip-mining, etc. Red's strength of stability and articulateness does not include fire or warmth, I fear. The latter I still have; how much clarity is another matter.

As we left, the ten minutes over without a blooper, Barbara Walters, in the corridor, spoke to me with considerable feeling about how much she liked Persia when she was there for the "celebration"; how impressed she was (she is no fool nor is she easily taken in) with the Shah and Empress, whom she interviewed for the NBC network; how much she would like to go back to see more of the country; how aghast she was at the poverty. ("It probably no longer impresses you, who have seen so much of it elsewhere, but it did hit me hard.")

Though I didn't get to talk even for a few moments about what I saw for the future of the Valley, I did get in some comments about Iran and even what "my company, D&R" is beginning to do in Brazil.

Miss Walters is no slick, plastic, synthetic TV talk-show type—as is McGee. She is what we now call a "concerned" person.

As we left the "Today Studio" she stopped me. With an incredulous look she said, facing me: "I knew you were a kind of legend; I know how far back your work goes. So I expected a kind of trembly, doddering old man about 90. But you are so young."

MAY 20, 1972
PRINCETON

The magnificence of the unfolding, these latter days, of the great mounds of rhododendrons that form the background of our beloved herbaceous border. The Spectabile, completely covered with the delicacy of a rare kind of shining pink.

The first iris are opening: I know each one of them, the tall whites that open first here at the porch, the purples still rolled tight but soon to unfurl.

It is a great garden this year.

MAY 22, 1972
PRINCETON

Richard Nixon, the Foe of Atheistic Communism, is in Moscow— "live," as they say about TV that will be showing him in his every move. The harbor of Haiphong is mined. Here is our Hero cozily nesting with the very men who supply the arms that keep the Vietnam war going on, and on, and on.

The President will probably be able to announce another "week that makes history" with some sort of agreement about tapering off anti-ballistic missiles and a trade agreement. But the war will go on.

MAY 25, 1972
PRINCETON

A new D&R brochure has been on the agenda for longer than I care to recall. At last, a suitable proof, from a New York design outfit, after I had rejected with some distaste something concocted by some printer in Sacramento.

Could I write something brief for the flyleaf?

D&R was founded on two basic principles: that the development of resources must be governed by the unity of nature—and that the people who depend on those resources must participate actively in their development and must control them for their benefit. We believe that D&R's considerable and tangible accomplishments for its clients have been due to the way D&R has employed the methods of modern private business management to carry out these two basic precepts. D&R's credo is that of Francis Bacon: "In order to master Nature we must first obey her."

A cry of distress from one of our engineers. "But what does that mean, 'unity of nature'? No one will understand it. I don't. Can't you revise it so even a clunk like me can get what you mean?"

I sheathed my verbal claws, but what I thought was: I took that phrase and concept from the TVA book [*TVA: Democracy on the March*], where I used it thirty years ago. That book was read, in many languages, by more than a million people; that book, built on that phrase and concept, brought most of the important business D&R has had, starting with Colombia and Iran, and now Brazil.

However, thought I, I will revise it so it will have some meaning to those who didn't go through the TVA experience, and aren't acquainted with the concept that is at the base of their jobs in D&R. There is nothing in the text of the brochure (except a phrase or two I stuck in about "integrated regional development") that gives any real idea of the distinctive set of ideas and methods upon which D&R was founded and made its mark in the world!

So I meekly revised the flyleaf statement, and I hope all the little engineers may understand a bit better what it is they do. But I doubt it: for the compartmentalizing of work along technical lines is what they understand; and without the concept that binds it together we are the same as a lot of other piecemeal development enterprises.

Might as well face it: I have a job of education to do among most of our own people, to say nothing of the prospective clients.

Here is the way the revision reads:

D&R was founded on two basic principles: First, that development be not piecemeal but guided by the interrelation and unity of all resources, natural and human. D&R's development credo is that of Francis Bacon: "In order to master Nature [for man's benefit] we must first obey her."

Second, that the people who depend on Nature's resources must participate actively in their development, and control them for their own benefit. We believe that D&R's distinctive and tangible accomplishments
for its clients and for the strengthening of their environment have been
due to the way D&R employs the methods of modern private business
management to carry out these two basic precepts.

Actually, I think this restatement will be better.

But the "unity of nature" has a great meaning, just those few words.
It is for that reason that when I was a stripling in TVA, I insisted on
titling our first region-wide report: *The* Unified *Development of the
Tennessee Valley.* And for the same reason used that great word "unity"
in the first "plan" for the Khuzistan, *The Unified Development of the
Khuzistan Region.*

Putting together the pieces of a schedule for a business trip overseas
involving a number of people in a number of places can be as complex
and time-consuming as doing the work that occasions the trip itself.

But the Brazil trip has more subtleties than usual. Finally, I had to
decide that the absolute top priority, in importance and in timing, was
a meeting requested by Leitão de Abreu, "head of the Civilian Household." So I asked Friele, now my pal and a delightful, understanding
man, to make that clear in Brazil, build on that, and himself phone the
Minister to fix a date. Then make all the other pieces try to fit that. Until
we meet De Abreu (who has something very specific involving D&R and
me to discuss) we won't have guidance about where the bureaucratic
conflicts between Ministers are, where the private-enterprise ice is thin.

But this is a pretty good example of one phase of development work
overseas that bewilders and sometimes sinks newcomers to the field—
and old hands too, for that matter.

MAY 27, 1972
PRINCETON

Today is "the day"—our annual garden party, a big bash indeed. The
crucial question always is: will it be a cold, rainy day, no day to "show
off" the really quite beautiful garden Helen and I have produced?

So the banner news this morning is: a perfect late spring day; a clear,
sparkling sky, a flamboyantly eager sun casting all kinds of fascinating
patterns among the rhododendron, and bringing out the colors of the
flowering plants. Even the Oriental poppies (green jaws closed so tight
yesterday) opened scarlet this morning, and the first of the slothful single
peony opened—it has been a late season for peonies. The iris are flying
full tilt; the name "flag" sometimes given them is so appropriate. The end
of anxiety—a fair and perfect day.

And to top it all off last night a golden full moon showing between the leafing out of the tall locust trees to the east—and this will be a great setting for those who stay for a buffet supper.

MAY 29, 1972
PRINCETON

Helen and I sat facing each other in the sunshine that brought out the early morning glory of our garden's array of colors.

What was even happier than seeing this splendor we have fashioned with not a little thought and considerable sore muscles was the thirty minutes of talk.

I wanted to sound out my ideas, against her critical faculty, about what this summer might yield in the way of headway in editing Volume VI of the *Journals,* and what I might say if I accepted the invitation to speak to the American Club in Geneva in the fall.

Would a look at what we *had* done in Persia seem to be the nostalgia of an old geezer, a backward look, a self-justification of the kind that is so tiresome? No, says Helen, in her quietest way; what has been done, the results contrasting with what you started with—this, said she, "is a blueprint for the future."

What a title! I reminded her that "blueprint for survival" was the title the British scientists gave for their Doomsday warning that the world was on its last legs; "strategy for survival" the title of the Club of Rome Gloomy Gus computer exercise. So a statement that all over the world there are instances of people working to develop and manage and so organize themselves that the future could be not one of mere survival but of hope and, well, development.

Later, here in the study, while she was tying up the *Journal* manuscript we're taking to the Vineyard, I said, rather too soberly: "That talk in the middle of the garden this morning was collaboration at its best."

She said, "Besides, it was fun."

That surely is the test. Nothing I write, or that she helps me get said, will be all that historic or world-shaking; I know that perfectly well. But that the doing is fun is the real test of whether it is worth doing, spending part of our life and energy on a difficult task, but one that is "fun."

JUNE 2, 1972
PRINCETON

Last evening I found myself spontaneously clapping my hands, not for Richard Nixon, but for a President of the United States with the manhood to give voice to ideas in which I so deeply believe.

The occasion, of course, was dramatic and novel beyond stating.

Alighting from a helicopter at the foot of the steps of the House side of the Capitol, under the eye of twenty-five million people (at least), proceeding to the House chamber for a remarkable "report to the Congress" on his "summit" talks in Moscow.

He expressly disclaimed any "spirit of Moscow" atmospherics which made the Spirit of Camp David and the preceding "spirit of . . ." exercises so meaningless. Nor did he assert that his trip unwound the arms race or brought peace, which it definitely did *not*. Instead he used essentially the language I wrote into the original International Control of Atomic Energy report: a place to begin, a foundation on which to build.

He called on the Congress to *act* on this initiative, as part of its oft-asserted but rarely exercised co-responsibility with the Executive.

What made this extraordinarily well delivered address so particularly impressive was that it represented such an 180-degree reversal of an earlier Nixon's cheap and bitter chauvinism: the Red-baiter, the cynic, the pushy boy from Whittier, California, the detestable below-the-belt fighter.

Lunch and a visit today with one of the most interesting and unusual men of the Princeton faculty, Jim Billington. His knowledge of Russian history and their Cosmos (to play with Justice Holmes' phrase), his affection for the people, have impressed me no end.

What he wanted to talk to me about is a "study" David Rockefeller has encouraged (and supported) him in doing on this subject: how can American business structure itself so that trade with the Soviet Union can be facilitated? Would I be interested in joining a group—half Russians—to meet this fall to discuss this very matter? I told him of my strong allergy to "conferences" if the number of participants is large and the underpinning and purpose haven't been worked out beforehand with care and understanding.

Billington is a dissident, and like not a few American academics, pretty restless, thinking seriously of leaving academic life for a different career.

JUNE 5, 1972
SACRAMENTO

Twenty-four million acres of desert! This afternoon, with my D&R associates, I spent a couple hours at the offices of the Bureau of Land Management, discussing D&R's recommendation to the Bureau of how to plan and carry out plans to preserve this huge area from destruction. Destruction from hundreds of thousands of wild-riding motorcyclists and thousands of crunching dune buggies, creatures with broad tires that tear up the landscape for the satisfaction of their cruising owners, week-end escapees from the smog of Los Angeles.

The California Director of BLM is Russell Penny, a sturdy, enthusiastic dynamo of a man of about fifty, not by any means the stereotype of the Department of Interior bureaucrat. Nor is his job the stereotype of anything the world has seen in this period of passionate concern about the environment. The Bureau is the proprietor and trustee of many millions of acres of land belonging to the people of the nation, some of it desert (which to many people is no longer considered "wasteland" but something to study and enjoy and protect), but also forests and mountain country.

Penny spoke with great respect for the "D&R approach" embodied in a report prepared for the Bureau perhaps a year ago. Now we hope this will be followed up by other work for the Bureau.

The combination of affluence, leisure, mobility ("everyone these days is on wheels") has made the planning for and management of the public lands of the West almost as much of a crisis problem as the concentration and degradation of the cities has produced.

These are men in the Bureau of Land Management whose work has received very little attention over the years except when there is controversy about granting a lumber company the right to cut timber, for example. They have been essentially passive caretakers. I predict that *that* role is a thing of the past.

They must learn to manage as proprietors under conditions of great public scrutiny and public interest. Otherwise the Secretary of the Interior, Rogers Morton, would never have come across this desert to "dedicate" some areas for recreation, and talked freely and with emphasis about the "archaic" system of land use of the U.S. public domain, and the importance of "planning."

Penny spoke of TVA many times during the afternoon, referred to passages in *Democracy on the March* which he thought pointed the way to involving local community participation in the planning and execution process. The seeds of ideas planted so long ago in such different circumstances in that Valley have long life and vitality, to be considered relevant to the life cycle and public use of a vast desert.

JUNE 7, 1972
FLYING FROM LOS ANGELES TO NEW YORK

Greeting me at her doorway, with that glowing smile, Bernardine [Fritz] soon brushed back the years since we were the young rebels of a complex family. Five minutes after we began talking, eagerly and with the enthusiasm of our youth, Bernardine seemed the same special person that she was for so many people all over the world—Gary,

Chicago in the days when it was a center of intellectual and artistic ferment, New York in the twenties and early thirties, Paris and the expatriate literary community of which she was so much a part, China and her great Shanghai salon that attracted some of the most extraordinary literary people of the world. And here she and I were, in our seventies, but bubbling over with the intense feelings of those earlier days.

She talked to me about her almost frantic disposition to libraries of a mountain of letters from Russell Davenport ("such tender, heartbreakingly beautiful letters, hundreds of them"), from Tennessee Williams—and a dozen other people to whom she meant so much, most of them now long dead.

Bernardine has something less than a clear idea of what I do, except that she is proud of it. That I keep on going, more than full tilt, doesn't seem to surprise her. Her look of affectionate approval at my enthusiasm about my life of work reminded me of the way she would encourage my ambitions when I was a teenage, untried kid, and she a "grown up" nineteen-year-old news reporter—one of the first "feature" gals of those days.

This was a morning when I felt dispirited about going on with D&R. This doesn't happen too often, and I recognize the feeling as being one of the least admirable of traits—being half sorry for myself.

Then I look at the record of D&R's achievements of the past twelve months, and the exciting and varied prospects immediately ahead, and I am half ashamed of the gnawing of my doubts. For it is negative doubts that wear men out, and make them bitter. (The worst possible fate for anyone!)

As I reviewed the story with the Sacramento staff yesterday, D&R has made great progress in Iran, and is becoming involved in crucial ways in the whole span of agricultural development throughout the country. These add up to some of the most important substantive issues of the next five-to-ten-year period of the Persian development.

Another kind of encouragement. D&R somehow attracts new problems that literally seem insoluble but to which a guy like myself can't resist applying some innovative talents and considerable hard experience.

JUNE 12, 1972
NEW YORK

Lunch at the Century. As I sat down next to bearded (and worn) Augie Heckscher, he gave me a great big grin, said to the men across the table: "Imagine that; we are just this moment talking about you, in connection with Welfare Island."

It was clear that no one is happy about the way Welfare Island is developing, sticking low-income housing into the equation, and thus changing the whole basic concept that D&R worked out when I was on the Committee headed by Benno Schmidt.

"I was saying that at the first meeting of the Committee you had said: What should be done with Welfare Island? Maybe the best thing to do would be to do nothing—not during this generation. And it now looks as if that was about the wisest thing that has been said. We are about to ruin it forever."

JUNE 17, 1972
PRINCETON

A strong urge to hear David's voice, so I called yesterday, and in a moment, his voice as big as life and even clearer.

I asked about the proofs of his new novel; expects them any day, with publication in October. The title? *Walking Davis.* Said I: "You stick to your talent for brief titles." "Yes; if I were Tolstoi, the book would have been titled *War And.*"

JUNE 21, 1972
SÃO PAULO

Lucas Nogueira Garçez is the very picture of a forceful, driving man, a big solid, bulky figure, grey close-cropped hair, a broad brow topping a square bull-like head. He was Governor of the State of São Paulo not long ago, is now head of the State of São Paulo's power company, head of a group of industrial concerns in this dominant state.

So with the mild-mannered Milder (Presidente of Serete) sitting on the edge of his seat as in the presence of some elemental force, for that is the impression Garçez gives, we spent perhaps a half-hour in Garçez' office this morning.

Garçez' abiding interest is in his role as a teacher of hydraulic engineering in the university, and like many Latin executives he prefers to be called "Professor." He spoke, mostly in Portuguese, about TVA as if it were the eighth wonder of the world—the leader in demonstrating how engineering could serve people and shape their destinies. It was just as well that I could not understand most of what he said, as the flow of words, pounded out with his heavy voice, was filled with "Mr. Lilienthal."

He expressed himself as pleased that "with all your other work all over the world you should come to Brazil with your company to help guide us in developing the north."

The approval and support of this tower of a man, with his leadership intact in this country, will be as important to D&R's future as anything that could come from some of those who sit in the Cabinet.

The understanding of the deeper meaning of TVA, and of his respect for the way TVA put things together, overcoming the separatism of technical and bureaucratic barriers, was what impressed me—and this is always what I despair of having understood in the U.S. Indeed the lesson begins to wear off after a while even in Persia.

Milder said some impressive things to me this morning that raise in my sights the high priority of the Amazon job, and the related northeast. Milder is from the south, from São Paulo. He said that two things make the Amazon undertaking a crucial event at this time in Brazilian super-development. One is that many of the leaders of the south feel as he does: that the north (Amazon basin and the northeast) must be developed; otherwise there is fear that the political stability that has marked very recent Brazilian history may be disrupted. "It is not solely, or even primarily" an economic question; it is the social and political importance of making progress in the north that gives the north, including the Amazon, the highest priority in the whole country.

The other face of the challenge of the Amazon, in the national picture, is as a measure of Brazilian determination about maintaining the confidence and momentum of recent years, in contrast to the disastrous period of upheaval and chaos.

JUNE 23, 1972
BRASÍLIA

Back from dinner and an evening at the home of Minister Leitão de Abreu, a whimsical, quiet, understanding kind of man. As his guest he had the Minister of Interior Jose Costa Cavalcanti, in charge of all regional development throughout the country.

Cavalcanti was head of the Brazilian delegation to the just-adjourned Stockholm international conference on environment. He said one thing I found both amusing and revealing about the Chinese.

The Chinese were quite lost. Although they were very bright and their English in private conversation was even better than the simultaneous translator's, for of course they spoke to the conference in Chinese, they had no notion of how an assembly acts. If a resolution was up for debate and adoption or rejection, they would offer their views in the form of a completely new resolution on a completely *different* subject. The chairman finally stated that the new resolution would have to be treated as an amendment to the resolution before the assembly. This the Chinese couldn't understand, thought it was an effort to put them down. Most of their resolutions were about "imperialism" or the war in Vietnam, and not about pollution or whatever the environmental issue was that was being discussed by the assembly.

This amused the Minister, but was also a commentary on how genuinely these highly intelligent, educated people have been isolated from what is commonplace in most countries.

Minister Cavalcanti told of a conversation with a highly educated Chinese member of their delegation. He was curious about how lost they seemed to be about the procedures of an assembly. "But you are a people of great wisdom," said the Minister. The response: "Yes, we Chinese have wisdom but no experience." To which I added—some of us have experience but no wisdom.

I had hardly been greeted by Minister Abreu as we came into his house (a house filled with books and a comfortable used library), than he called me aside and said: "The President wishes to see you tomorrow at 3:45." Berent, an expert in the ways of Brazilian hierarchy, considers this very significant; that it was at the President's request and at the suggestion of the head of the Civil Household. So we have a "business discussion" with the Minister of Interior and a succeeding visit with the President set for tomorrow.

JUNE 24, 1972
BRASÍLIA

Saturday we had a lengthy and specific meeting with Minister Cavalcanti, and a principal aide, Walter Ferri. The result: an invitation to make a proposal for D&R's services to the Ministry. The Minister made it plain that our services are wanted, needed, and for what purposes. The Minister said: you know the subject of regional development and administration better than we, so please, you make the proposal.

The resemblance to the Tennessee Valley was made much of both by the Minister and Ferri. They spent a good deal of time asking questions about how we did things in the TVA, with nods of agreement that this is what would move the São Francisco Valley development along.

The difficulties are obvious. But this is much further than I could have reasonably expected us to get: (1) explicit statement that our work should continue in the Amazon beyond the report due in October when the contract expires and (2) inclusion of the São Francisco, which would open the door to general advisory services on other regional developments.

JUNE 26, 1972
BRASÍLIA

The most absurdly unbelievable things happen to me.

The outwardly dour President of the Republic of Brazil spoke with the greatest of warmth and intensity: "I want you to work directly for me and to report to me in the development of this country; I want you to move the development of the São Francisco Valley ahead rapidly. I want your support."

So the word will go out that D&R is to have a hand in reshaping and reactivating work that began in the Valley of the São Francisco River seventy-five years ago—indeed, 150 years ago.

JUNE 29, 1972
RIO DE JANEIRO

Yesterday was crowded with meetings and with interesting people. Beginning early we met in Brasília with the two young men at the top of the Ministry of Interior, then in a breathless hurry, the appointments and meetings virtually overlapping, on to the Minister of Mines and Energy, on to the Minister of Foreign Affairs in his beautiful palace, then a hurried lunch and a plane to Rio, meeting people on the plane, thanks to Friele, on to a 7 o'clock (and rather upsetting) meeting with the Minister of Planning and finally the world-famous little guy, Delfim Netto, who is Minister of Finance. In two cities.

What a region it is—the São Francisco Valley—and what a river. I had no real appreciation of its magnitude or potentialities until we heard the full story this morning in the offices of SUVALE, the aborted regional agency. In land area the size of Washington, Oregon, and California combined! Much, much larger than the area of the Tennessee Valley. And the river's volume of water at its minimum far greater than the Tennessee's average flow. The hydro already installed, and the potential planned is larger by far than the five rivers of the Khuzistan will be when fully developed.

JULY 4, 1972
EN ROUTE TO MARTHA'S VINEYARD

An entire DC-3 all to myself. And I worried in Rio about whether Miss Baron could manage to get me a reservation on the 4th!

A busy, productive morning at my desk—sans air, for the air-conditioning was off and one can't open the windows. But I left a jam-full "out box" and cleared desk. With one exception: a yard-long telex giving me the exact titles and addresses of the many men in Brazil we met and to whom I should write various versions of "letters of appreciation." Three of these I did write: one to the President; a covering note to my favorite Brazilian (as, apparently, I am one of his favorite foreigners), Leitão de Abreu; and a longhand note to Berent, my friend and mentor. He deserves much of the credit for what we were able to accomplish, and not just opening doors, as the phrase has it.

JULY 7, 1972
MARTHA'S VINEYARD

It was more than setting sail into a fresh breeze this afternoon; it was conquering the most subtle of enemies, apprehension about my physical fitness, after almost a year of pain and shaky lack of confidence in that left foot, after the injury of last August.

A resounding moral victory over fears, the establishment of confidence in yet another sphere, and one that is a reflection of the vanity of a man about his physical abilities.

So I begin my seventy-fourth year tomorrow, full of bounce. Which is as it should be. But frequently isn't.

JULY 9, 1972
MARTHA'S VINEYARD

If I manage to do some good reflective thinking and sound writing this summer, it will be sitting where I am now, in my study looking out on greenery, the busyness of towhees, and the craglike composure of Mr. Mitty—the huge boulder that resembles a Thurber dog. At my elbow a colored telephone, and in back of me a typewriter. Soon there will arrive a brand-new filing cabinet. All the physical ingredients of a "creative" writing summer.

Most favorable augury, however: I have an overwhelming sense of good health and good spirits.

Sailed again yesterday, this time using the jib in a fresh breeze, but not going out of the outer harbor. Spread across the distant Sound like the fluttering flags of a ship dressed for a gala were scores of sailing vessels. It was a day for sailing; the sky so blue, the breeze steady and happy. A "race" by big schooners and gaff-rigged traditional New England craft almost made me believe, as I crisscrossed the water in my small boat, that this was a hundred years ago or so, when Vineyard Haven's harbor was filled with hundreds of big deep-lagged ships.

My blue work shirt sticking to my back with sweat, I have just come from one of the outlandish kinds of activity that seems to please my restless nature—with a long-handled pruner, clearing away the growth along the big rock wall that bounds this place on the east. It is a mystery why I take such satisfaction in standing back and admiring the grey boulders of that wall, exposed by my snipping from the quite handsome greenery. But I fairly lick my chops, walking back through the meadow and viewing my handiwork.

Helen and I sat on our long white bench on the open porch deck, in the early morning sunlight, happy as ducks on a pond. *She* because for almost the first time "you seem to be having a great time at the very beginning of a vacation up here, when so often in the past you are so tired, or troubled somehow, that you aren't enjoying yourself—and therefore neither am I." *I* because her description is accurate: I am well, happy, composed, rid of the sticky burrs of discontent or worry about my work, or the state of my physical health.

JULY II, 1972
NEW YORK

A day of concentrated intellectual and tactical wrestling with ideas, indeed a whole chain of problems.

What was it about? A critical review and revision of the draft proposal or work program we are submitting to the President and Minister of Interior of Brazil for a D&R role in getting the hundred-year-old São Francisco Valley development really rolling, the pace they so much want but haven't been able to attain on their own.

I did this review together with Walt Seymour and Andrea Pampanini —close reasoning and intense argufying with respected and astute associates—and even more important perhaps, warm friends.

We sorted out the future of the vast undertaking we are exposing ourselves to in Brazil with a precision and instinct about what we could do to justify our presence that I found even more impressive on paper than in the conceptual stage of our discussions in Brasília and Rio.

When men like each other and respect their several talents as much as Walt, Andrea, and I do, even so long-focused a day as this leaves one tired—yes, but a different kind of tired than even a short day filled with frustrations and, God forbid, boredom.

JULY 12, 1972
NEW YORK

The "proposal" then went to be typed, and packed up to be carried to Brasília and its destiny—and ours.

I was enormously pleased that my central idea becomes the theme: a unified development program for the São Francisco. We had dealt only in the general area of "advisory and consultative" services. This unified development program document will force us to bring together all the technical fleece and threads, into a fabric.

A good document, a good set of ideas.

JULY 14, 1972
WOODS HOLE, WAITING FOR THE FERRY TO THE VINEYARD

Is there anything more nondescript and ostentatiously informal than a summer crowd?

I used to resent getting on a plane and expecting to land on the Vineyard, and then being told that we would be landing at Hyannis, requiring a swift car drive to catch the ferry.

The drive through Falmouth, with its magnificent trees, was a pleasure. And now the ferry has just fog-horned its way in, huffing and puffing to get into the slip. The ferry *is* the best way to get to the Vineyard, even with such deep fog as today.

JULY 18, 1972
MARTHA'S VINEYARD

A spell of exceptionally humid weather, with fog rolling in during the night, and no breeze. In New York it must make Manhattan seem like Bangkok.

Gerald and Ellen Bentley left this morning, after nearly a four-day visit. It was a happy visit. Ged and I had two spirited sails, and there was much jolly conversation and laughter.

I continue to find Ged as interesting and companionable a friend as ever I have known. Partly because he takes things as they come. Partly because his field of knowledge is remote from my own, so I am constantly learning new things from him. Partly because he is a conversationalist par excellence, ranging from a superior talent in the telling of anecdotes to the kind of perception that a lifetime of literary scholarship can give, and which my habit of living with action does not.

Ellen's temperament is as opposite to Ged's as Helen's is to mine, but, to continue a very inexact parallel, she does complement Ged's easygoing ways with the disciplined, realistic viewpoint that years in business have given her. To which is added another interesting component: her knowledge of Denmark and Danish folkways, for which, by the way, she has something less than complete admiration—indeed can be very critical.

Nancy, Sylvain, and the beefy young grandsons will arrive this noon for a few days' visit. I rarely see Allen and Daniel, and haven't visited with Sylvain for nearly two years. And though I shall enjoy an opportunity to talk to Nancy particularly, it is a pity that I see so little of those two boys, who in no time at all will have left the nest and be adults, setting their own course.

JULY 20, 1972
MARTHA'S VINEYARD

Over the years of the earlier journals, the grandsons, Allen and Daniel, have been recurrent characters, as round-eyed babies, as hyperactive toddlers, etc. But on this visit they are, or seem, no longer children but emerging almost grown-ups. When they first came through the door day before yesterday I was flabbergasted: huge, brawny, though Daniel is only fifteen and Allen just past seventeen, they are the size of grown men.

Neither of the boys has sailed. We crammed our hulks into the little dinghy, rowed out to *Lili-put,* and the sail was the kind of getting-acquainted excursion I enjoyed beyond words. I brought the boat out of the crowded harbor—there was only a light breeze—then handed the main sheet and tiller to Allen, saying, "You take her." He gulped. "The only way to learn to sail is to sail," said I. And an hour or so later each of them was sailing *Lili-put,* and doing it quite well. It breezed up; as the main sheet pulled, their eyes would gleam: "So this is what sailing is about."

What impressed me most about a happy afternoon was the relation between the brothers, whose record for fighting and bickering is about like most brothers', including Ted and myself when we were in our teens: horrible. When I would say: "Allen, how about letting Daniel be the skipper for a while," he would turn it over without even a grumble. Later Daniel would ask Allen if he didn't want the tiller—a kind of voluntary sharing which showed that their manners, under even that kind of test, are as good as they seem when "in company."

Very proud of them, and pleased for this chance to know my "flesh and blood," sans parents.

JULY 22, 1972
MARTHA'S VINEYARD

A long talk with Helen, seeking her counsel—as I do constantly—but this time in a formal and organized way. The subject: my plans for this summer.

The outcome of an hour or so analyzing the question: get a prolonged period of doing nothing under pressure.

This probably means no sustained effort to write a book or complete the editing of the journals, both of which I had planned to do this summer.

The reasoning: I have had a strenuous—and productive—year; even more to the point, I will have an even more intense winter. For such a period, I should be rested and physically and nervously refreshed.

What about the speech I have agreed to make in Geneva on October 13th?

Her recommendation, to which I agreed: keep that date, plan to write the speech, but not under a tense deadline schedule, picking it up and putting it down during the next few weeks. The reasons for accepting the invitation—and encouraging Georges-Henri Martin to get the invitation for me—still stand: the speech can command a good press, as a speech before the American business community and the foreign diplomatic staffs in Geneva, with the friendly assistance that Martin and the *Geneva Tribune* can give it.

What about fitting the Geneva engagement into a trip to Iran? Is there a possibility that the Amazon report, due October 17th, will require my presence in Brazil, and thus conflict with the October 13th date?

We just don't know enough about how these will mesh at this time.

I was praising Nancy about how fine the boys were; how proud she should be, and Sylvain, with the "products." Nancy, obviously pleased but equally obviously not wanting to show it, looked to the ceiling and said: "Well, maybe all those diapers [at this a shudder] were worthwhile after all."

Sylvain's response was, as one would expect from so serious a man, solemn. "Luck; just luck." I demurred. "No, a good home life, intelligent parents, good inheritance," said I.

Looking very lugubrious, Sylvain shook his head. "We have friends with teenage, even pre-teenage children. Home life very much like ours; good intelligent parents, good inheritance, as you say. But the *number* of tragedies. Hard drugs. Dropping out of school. And the worst of all, disappearing, just leaving home and wandering. Their parents not knowing where their fourteen- or fifteen-year-olds are for months at a time. Terrible anxiety; cruel and exhausting.

"There was a time when a kid would get fed up with his home and parents and run away, as the phrase was. After the first night on the road, or even by the time he got to the edge of town, he would come running back. But these kids don't do that because they are joined by others doing the same thing. They have the support that the lone wanderer of another time didn't have. They are in groups, and this keeps them going, and going deeper and deeper into trouble."

"Don't tell me this is common," said I, knowing better, remembering the stories I have heard from friends.

"Yes, it is common," said Sylvain, ending the conversation.

JULY 25, 1972
MARTHA'S VINEYARD

Some measure of the interest in China these days: by 8 o'clock the big noble "whaling church" in Edgartown was filled last night (with a crowd of people in the streets "turned away") to hear Scotty and Sally Reston talk about their visit to China of a year ago. The talk was livened by beautiful slides Sally had taken, and by Scotty's salty comments.

JULY 26, 1972
MARTHA'S VINEYARD

This island has been boiling this spring and summer with an issue that has been neglected and allowed to get almost out of hand. The rate of building of new houses on small tracts, mostly by "off-island developers," is a threat to the island's chief assets of beauty, a source of pollution, etc. And the patchwork of limited planning activities fails to cope with the problem.

Senator Kennedy introduced a comprehensive bill that proposed a trust, to be administered by the Secretary of the Interior, with an Island Commission.

The howls of indignation that arose! "We don't want Washington to tell us how to run our island," etc. But the introduction of the bill, and the careful attention to the details of how such a measure would operate on the part of the Senator's staff—particularly a young man, name of Gifford—have produced a demonstration of how a people can be forced to tackle one of the most intricate problems of planning for land use I know anything about.

Last night Helen and I plodded up the creaky steep stairs of the Agricultural Hall in West Tisbury (actually the meeting room of the

"Grange," once important in this island, now almost an anachronism). The place was packed, people sitting on the floor. The precise purpose of the meeting was to give the people of the island and particularly this part of it, a chance to express their views about various provisions of the bill.

I was much impressed by the quality of the discussion. Technically, it would have done credit to a convention of professional planners. But it was better than that, because of the intimate knowledge of the areas being discussed. The ability of laymen who are involved, because of their own property or because of concerns of a broader character, to absorb and analyze and decide about technical matters was something to ponder, and be reassured about.

JULY 28, 1972
MARTHA'S VINEYARD

Early last night a moon, full to bursting, sailed slowly over the dark outline of the trees, as I watched from our deck. Utter stillness, not a sign of human habitation, and the birds all gone to sleep. Yesterday afternoon a spirited sail that nearly pulled my wrist loose, holding the main sheet against a sturdy blow from the southwest.

There is so much to feel happy about: a life-long record of doing useful things under great difficulties, and without a serious blemish or loss of temper or unworthy conduct.

For years and years people have assumed that I have an emotional curve that is a straight line across the chart. Perhaps it is because under pressure, particularly "in public," I keep my voice low and my feelings under control. How often young people particularly who have read my journal descriptions of periods of doubt and of discouragement will say: that is what happened to me, but I never thought it happened to you. But it does.

JULY 29, 1972
MARTHA'S VINEYARD

The Presidential campaign has begun, and it is hardly August. And on what kind of issue? The emotional "health" of the Democratic candidate, not for President, but Vice President. The charge from the head of the United Nations, Waldheim, that the U.S. Air Force has breached the dikes on the Red River in North Vietnam.

The American people have much to suffer through before this particular campaign, begun so prematurely and on such strange issues, is finally decided in November.

Six hours of sailing yesterday afternoon with Tom Mendenhall, president of Smith College, who lives down the hill. Born and brought up far from salt water, he is, I do believe, as passionate a sea-sailor as ever I have known or sailed with. Has just bought a new sloop, built to his specifications; a beauty it is, too. With a steady southwesterly breeze and lively water, we went through tricky Robinson's Hole into Buzzards Bay, and came back to the mooring off the Daggett place as the sun was setting —an almost ideal sail.

To all the agonies and worries of *any* university head these troubled days in education, he has added the special problem of a newly aroused and highly sensitive generation of young women, aggressive about being women—"don't tread on me, I am a woman." This has brought on confrontations and the occupation of university buildings at Smith. As if this weren't enough, there are a hundred and fifty black girl students, with the double hang-ups of being girls *and* black.

He didn't complain about all this, not at all. Just recited some of the episodes.

"One of the black graduates is the daughter of Percy Sutton, President of one of the boroughs of New York City. She was prominent in a militant demonstration. Her father wrote that he was sorry his daughter had given me this embarrassment, but I am proud of her, just the same. Only by this sort of action can changes be made."

I'm beginning to be troubled that I have done so little work of the kind I had planned for this summer. Perhaps while I am dawdling up here, and only occasionally thinking directly about the development theme for Geneva, I'm really sorting the ideas out in my nonconscious.

JULY 31, 1972
MARTHA'S VINEYARD

The last notes in the entry for the 29th appear to be true: way in the back of my head I have been thinking, or speculating about what it is I have to say in the Geneva speech.

Last night I scrawled in characteristic large letters all over a sheet of paper: GROWTH UNLIMITED.

This morning I made an extemporaneous "speech" to Helen—somewhat dazed by my sudden vehemence—that growth, and expansion— development, in short—do *not* mean destructive acts against the environment and our survival, as it is now so popular to say, but just the reverse. The *wrong* kind of development should be compared with the right kind. The right kind strengthens human life, gives the means for voluntary balancing of population in numbers, and a distribution of people rather than their concentration.

This would be a "statement," a credo, a prelude, in perhaps two pages, a provocative introduction. To be followed by cases, by illustrations of growth that support my contention: Persia, Brazil, TVA.

PLANNING FOR THE 21ST CENTURY.

That planning must be based upon an understanding of the dynamics of human nature. And human nature demands change and growth. To deny growth and expansion *and development* to the millions of people of the earth who have only begun to develop would be the most serious of all threats to peace, an almost sure guarantee of war.

Went to a cocktail party given by Joe and Trudi Lash for Evan Thomas, Joe's editor at the Norton publishing firm, and for the president of the firm, a big strapping reserved kind of man, George Brockway. Norton is riding the wave of prestigious success, and much of the credit they give to Evan. Joe's second volume, *Eleanor: The Years Alone,* is just published. His first, *Eleanor and Franklin,* won about every possible award: National Book Award, Pulitzer Prize, Book-of-the-Month, etc.

It couldn't happen to three better people: Joe and Trudi and Evan. At Harper, Evan was the editor of the book Helen suggested while I was AEC Chairman, in which she wove with artistry excerpts from my speeches into a coherent volume: *This I Do Believe.* So the reunion with Evan was a pleasant occasion.

Helen and I were leaving and on the porch when a short, solid-looking woman with tousled blonde hair came charging out of the door. Lillian Hellman gave me a smile and a vigorous handshake: "I didn't intend for you to leave without speaking to me." She looked me over deliberately and carefully. "I must say," she said, "you are exactly the same; haven't changed a bit."

AUGUST 3, 1972
MARTHA'S VINEYARD

A trip to Edgartown. To the library to collect an armful of books, mostly mysteries, to sandwich in with such heavy-goers as Tuchman's *Stilwell* and Lash's new volume on Mrs. Roosevelt.* Some shopping: I love to go into a well-stocked hardware store to buy turpentine, say, for a painting job, and then buy oddments right and left, which I did. Sat on a curbstone watching the hairy, self-conscious male young-uns and the hip-waggling gals, and occasional tourists with cameras growing out of

*Barbara W. Tuchman, *Stilwell and the American Experience in China.* New York: Macmillan, 1971; Joseph P. Lash, *Eleanor: The Years Alone.* New York: Norton, 1972.

their chests. A dinner looking out on the harbor, and then home to the hill.

A more isolated "private" place it would be difficult to find, the way we live; this was borne in on us last night as we sat reading in what is almost a tree house, the wind rustling, inky dark, the quiet so quiet one can almost hear it.

AUGUST 15, 1972
MARTHA'S VINEYARD

A cable from Minister Cavalcanti received yesterday formally accepts our proposal, subject to contract terms. Friele reports that he will see our friend Leitão de Abreu next week to arrange for a signing ceremony toward the end of September, perhaps earlier, for which I will be present, also perhaps the President and a decoration, and perhaps a designation of me as "Advisor to the President on Regional Development" for the whole country. I put this idea into Berent's mind; if it works out it should give us a nation-wide, perhaps world-wide, standing. It also makes it that much more important that we get together a group of D&R people of the highest caliber, omitting the acceptance of mediocrity that I find too much of, particularly in D&R's Sacramento office.

AUGUST 16, 1972
MARTHA'S VINEYARD

From eleven yesterday, when he arrived, until he took a plane to Rio, via New York, I spent with Hal Frederiksen. We covered almost the whole range of D&R's work and problems. In particular, Iran and Brazil.

I spent much of the time on the pricing policy of D&R. I repeated my strong preference for a fixed price for the complete job in Brazil—which is what I thought we had proposed, only to find that the proposal was the conventional cost-plus style, with all the delays and red tape of such an arrangement.

I must have made it pretty strong. In any case, I talked to Boyd in São Paulo, learned that *he* thought the Brazilians would even prefer a fixed lump-sum contract. So Hal's instructions from me are to see that is done. This time it had *better* be settled, as I thought this had been when the matter was first discussed with me before the complete proposal went off to Brazil.

I ought to be able to write a draft of that Geneva speech. Get it started. Sit down and write and stay writing until you have a draft.

Joe Lash is working on a biography of Roger Baldwin. Trudi said:

"Roger doesn't know himself; his picture of himself is not quite what Joseph is finding out—natural enough. It is the job of his biographer to find out just what kind of a person he really is."

I said I was determined to write a book, beginning this summer, but running a company at the same time didn't make it all that easy. The writing itself will be difficult.

"Oh," said she, "but you write so easily; I have read your *Journals* and it comes so simply and easily."

"But journal writing isn't writing," I said. Somehow the lack of necessity of having an organized structure or sequence—the sequence determined by events or feelings at the time—accounts for the impression of ease. This is what David has said about what he calls my journal style.

Now, why can't I do the same with the Geneva statement, or the development book?

This morning I am going to sit here and put on paper what I said on the subject of economic growth and development, in a loud and most emphatic voice to Helen a half-hour ago on the sundeck.

AUGUST 17, 1972
MARTHA'S VINEYARD

I am so torn. About what? I think it is because I am drawn by a desire, almost a compulsion, to express in words the total of my life's experience and convictions, and, against this pull, the equally strong desire, necessity even, to express myself through direct experience with people, people who need what I think I have learned, and can practice.

Putting into words what I believe, what I think, this pitted against doing; words against experience. I am what I *do,* or I am what I *say?*

On the way back from a swim up popped the structure for the Geneva speech. How strange are the workings of the mind, to be going on thinking or imagining back there in the recesses of the head, when the body is just fooling around on nothing except enjoyment and laziness.

AUGUST 18, 1972
MARTHA'S VINEYARD

At dinner last night, Amyas Ames said, "New York City is today half black; it will before long be the principal black city of the world. Whatever we do to promote an opportunity for black people to express themselves, give them an outlet that can only be called artistic—theatre of their own right in their local areas—helps make New York livable. Is it livable? Who knows; but we can in this way try to make it so."

I found this encouraging and innovative. But it occurred to me that this is pretty much a current revival of the now old-fashioned settlement-house spirit of Jane Addams in Chicago and Henry Street in East Side New York, though the black constituency is different from the Jewish and Italian immigrants that were the center of those earlier social-worker efforts.

He said one thing that bothered me: that the root of what is troubling people and making them feel without purpose and function is "mechanization."

That people thrown out of lowly jobs should regard the "machine" as their enemy, or that socially minded people bewail the loss of the craft spirit, because of the machine, that I understand.

But *defining* "mechanization" as the enemy, by a sophisticated and very well-intentioned man—this bothers me. It fits into the theme I'm trying to structure and expound: that the right kind of development and growth holds out the best, perhaps the only, hope for billions of people throughout the world.

AUGUST 24, 1972
MARTHA'S VINEYARD

Bleary-eyed and dog-tired, I have just completed the initial rough draft, twelve typed pages, of the Geneva speech. Whew!

It is more than the rough draft of a speech. It is an effort to clear my mind about where I stand on growth and the environment, about the hottest of the great current issues.

The long-term impact of the TVA book continues to impress on me that however I decry the "word people," writing a book can be a way of producing action; it can be almost a form of action itself.

AUGUST 30, 1972
MARTHA'S VINEYARD

A call from Friele from São Paulo: the date of the taking off is now September 16th, and the expedition will combine the Amazon and the Planning Committee with Serete, with the ceremony of signing the new contract for São Francisco.

A good session with Helen about the "preparation for the printer" for Volume VI. She has done a very workmanlike job of analyzing the entries, so I can run my eye down the listing and see what was covered, by time and by subject, and her general judgment about what needs to be done by way of editing: cutting, untangling, etc.

I hate to yield to the idea that I have already too much on my plate to contemplate the long job of getting out another volume during the coming twelve to eighteen months. I think as of now that she could do the editing on her own, subject to a series of questions to be put to me.

AUGUST 31, 1972
MARTHA'S VINEYARD

Einstein's time-space—i.e., relativity—explanation of the universe was, so it seems to me, an attempt to apply determinism to physical phenomena. This had to be abandoned, so I understand, by reasoning and experiment. Hence the quantum or wave effect, incalculable and absolutely unpredictable.

I like this admission of unpredictability.

Marx thought human affairs could be predicted: economic determinism foretold, for example, the collapse of capitalism. Which it has done no such thing. Then, because of that intellectual miscalculation of economists—Marx was the father of modern economists, so I think—many economists have tried to convert their bankrupt and obsolete profession by transforming economics into mathematics, and we have this nonsense of econometrics. Again, a form of deterministic thinking.

The root of much of my skepticism, not too emotional a term, about economists and economics is that I believe in a random, unpredictable world of men.

SEPTEMBER I, 1972
MARTHA'S VINEYARD

A bit of irony this: Pampanini reports by phone that the Philadelphia division of the U.S. Army Corps of Engineers requested D&R's help on two essentially local flood-control needs, one on the Schuylkill River, the other on some little stream in Jersey. No competition, just picked us out and said would we do a planning job for them? Contract signed at once, yesterday.

Pampanini says the young official (a civilian, of course) he talked with seemed intelligent and enterprising. When Pampanini told him this was no way to go about flood control, according to D&R principles (and TVA's), he agreed, but said there were no funds for anything but local works within a particular Congressman's district. The disastrous Scranton–Wilkes Barre floods of this spring haven't changed the century-old local pork barrel method, apparently.

Helen and I spent much of the morning going over her suggestions for revisions of the rough draft of the Geneva Statement. I gladly accepted almost all of them.

Since I completed the first draft I have added a couple concluding pages, the substance of which is to make explicit and public what I have been wanting to say for some time: that the conservatives are now ready, willing, and eager for planning.

SEPTEMBER 11, 1972
NEW YORK

The assistant bell captain at the hotel is a grinning slender man. I have often listened to his stories, particularly about his son, in the Air Force.

"Yes," he said, "we did go out to Seattle for his wedding; then we stayed on for two weeks, going all the way through Oregon. Had a wonderful time. I made $2400 on the races here, and that's what the trip cost, so it didn't set me back any. Went first class, too."

I pondered this story all the way downtown. A *very* contemporary tale it is.

SEPTEMBER 16, 1972
PRINCETON

I am walking again!

Best news in a year. What it means to me to be able to walk without pain, pain that I had for almost a full year! For me not to be able to walk as I pleased and when I pleased, was to lose part of my humanity, as if a part of me had been shriveled and departed.

10 P.M.
ABOARD VARIG, FOR RIO

Berent Friele handed me a volume, a present to me: *Brazilian Poetry.* Again the doors open wide of understanding of a country and a people and a history and a culture completely unknown to me, and to most North Americans.

How exciting it is to see life on a wider spectrum, and that is what education and experience—and living, for that matter—are all about.

So I'll be working on rivers and irrigation and how better to organize the conflicting agencies competing with each other in the São Francisco. But what I shall be really doing, to my greatest satisfaction, will be learning about a way of life, a history, and even poetry, as in the case of this beautiful little book about poetry.

SEPTEMBER 18, 1972
BRASÍLIA

(In a "guest house" out in the middle of nowhere in this strange city.)

Today, at five, the end of the trail that began in late June: all the questions about a major commitment between Brazil and D&R resolved.

The end of a trail but more truly the beginning. Beginning of as tough an assignment as any since the beginning of Khuzistan so many years ago. And with expectations higher than the sharp blue cloudless sky of this central plain.

"Never has there been a contract worked out so quickly and so smoothly. Usually it takes months and months."

Thus spake the Minister of Interior, as sturdy and square-built a man as one ever saw, and his two younger brilliant aides, Henrique Cavalcanti and Walter Ferri, shook their heads almost in disbelief.

What "did it" was largely that Minister Leitão de Abreu had persuaded the President that this was a great idea; and the President's approval of the contract before there was a contract really put it through.

On our side, we have performed well. The proposal drafted in Sacramento was a model of clarity and understanding; it was in their hands almost as soon as the mails could reach them. It was acted upon without delay.

SEPTEMBER 19, 1972
BRASÍLIA

This almost empty guest house is somewhere on the outskirts of what will one day look like the Brazilian version of Beverly Hills: new stylish one-story attractively designed houses, tile roofs, pastel shades, distinctive. Here and there a raw, very dry woebegone landscape—I like green.

Very early the workmen arrive, diminutive dark fellows, working away at the foundations and the structure of new houses. These I assume will be largely for government employees of many countries. Down the street—I have just come back from a pre-breakfast walk—a sign tells us that this sad-looking lot will be the home of the Romanian delegation. However little good it may be for the not overly prosperous peasant of Romania to have a rotund and well-fed Party member living in Brasília, having to build a residence for their Ambassador provides plenty of profit for Brazilian contractors and for these hapless-looking men from the poor country around this sumptuous capital.

I put my huge black signature on the contract document with the cameras flashing and TV clicking. A little speech by me: "The São Francisco, in the poetic Brazilian phrase, is *rio integra,* the river of integration, linking the north and the rest of the country." The Minister made a long and impassioned speech in which D&R and Mr. L. figured prominently.

The stage of Brazilian development that began with the Serete Amazonia undertaking, and was carried forward in late June with the São Francisco, went into another stage, with euphoric statements on all sides.

SEPTEMBER 20, 1972
3 A.M.
BRASÍLIA

A night when I should by rights be sleeping the sleep of the resolution of uncertainties, I am battling one or more mosquitoes! Tried to ignore them, took a sleeping pill. Still that ominous little whine in the ear, and the procession of welts on my hands and forehead.

Quite an anticlimax. Isn't life full of just such descents from the solemn, even pompous ceremonials? Here I am *licked,* by the hum of a mosquito!

Finally I gave up trying to sleep, even with a sheet over my head, took my little flashlight and padded my way into the living room. A big bird flew up, circled to avoid the beam of the flashlight. I thought it looked like an owl, the usual posture. Flew up into a dark corner. Or had the loss of sleep and the battle of the humming of the mosquito unbalanced my mind, in the middle of the night?

II A.M.

It *was* an owl; how reassuring. There he sat, with his tufted ears and wide staring eyes in the bright light of day.

The Minister of Interior took us to the Palace, including Berent, who was evidently not on the official callers' list. We sat with the Minister while we waited for the jumbo-size buzzer that barked out: the President is ready for the next visitor.

Cavalcanti reminisced about his early years as a young First Lieutenant at a primitive outpost on the Río Negro, at the headwaters of the Amazon on the border of Brazil. His "command" was a platoon, and probably a pretty ragged lot at that.

The President came to greet me, a strong handshake, grabbing my arm, to which I, without thinking, responded by grasping his, in a pale version of the Brazilian *abraço.*

A commanding presence, this President. Huge head, large nose, very blue eyes, heavy eyebrows. And most surprising, a quizzical smile directed toward me. I said something that inclined me to rap the table hard. When he asked why I felt strongly about Brazil—that part of my Geneva speech had been read to him by Leitão—I spouted in a strong voice. As we left, he used the word—with approval—"enthusiasm" (the Portuguese word is not dissimilar).

Later, when we saw Minister Leitão de Abreu, his eyes twinkling, and clasping my hand warmly, he said, "You have a friend in the Palace," meaning himself, but also the President.

SEPTEMBER 23, 1972
SÃO PAULO

My bags are packed and I am ready for the next leg of this journey. I have just talked to Helen in Princeton; the *real* occasion for my calling her so far away is one of those absurdities that show that I am a long way from being the smart fellow I am usually pictured to be. I took a heavy blue overcoat instead of my light cashmere. I have imposed on her good nature once more to bring my fall coat to London.

SEPTEMBER 27, 1972
LONDON

My rendezvous with Helen came off with beautiful timing: she arrived at II P.M., from Kennedy; I from Lisbon at 6:30, both on schedule and happy to see each other. Tuesday and Wednesday were filled with the pleasure of seeing the West End of London again—much of it on foot.

Have just had a phone talk with Sir Dennis Hamilton, editor in chief of the *London Times* newspapers. He had read my Geneva Address and said some good things about it; said the *Times* would report on it; would I send other "pronouncements" on the subject? Particularly interested in what I had said about Persia.

Tuesday morning I phoned the office of Lord Thomson, the owner of the *Times* papers. I asked for his secretary; then a flat Canadian voice said, "Hi, David, glad to know you are in London. Read your speech; thought it made good sense; passed it on to our *Times* editorial people; they will probably want to see you; certainly I do."

SEPTEMBER 30, 1972
FLYING TO TEHRAN

There was much unadulterated sight-seeing in London, not excluding the old standbys of the British Museum, an elegant 2:30 P.M. roast-beef gorge at Simpson's, beef and kidney pie at a Dickensian bar near the Savoy, two plays, and the delight of "just walking," endlessly, through the most interesting and varied street scenes in the world—to my way of thinking.

The highpoint of sights was a forty-five-minute visit with Lord Thomson of Fleet at his office.

The eagerness about everything, of a boy to whom everything is new, the carriage of a human bulldozer, his shoulders hunched forward, the big jowls on either side of very round eyes that peer through glasses as thick as the bottom of a bottle, that voice: staccato, strong and more than positive. Not quite the overwhelming volume of Roger Baldwin's, but the same impelling and compelling effect. You would never think of him as a man approaching eighty. Even less so when he tells you, in short, machine-gun bursts of words, that Monday he takes off for a ten-day visit to China, with eight "of my boys" from the *Times* papers, a journey that will include Thailand ("we own a paper in Bangkok") and Bombay ("we own a printing company there"), and Tehran ("we may do some business there soon").

"If I were twenty years younger, I would head for Asia, that's the future, believe me. No, I am not Canadian. They gave me a title so I took out British citizenship."

He said he thinks a lot of Americans. "I *bloody* well ought to; I own more than fifty American papers, including one I bought from Bill Fulbright in Arkansas."

OCTOBER 6, 1972
TEHRAN

The Shah's personal warmth has never been higher. Such a relationship should grow in depth—but so often it becomes merely nostalgic or formal, with an eye on the clock and with nothing much to say.

As I waited in an elegant white, gold, and red anteroom, I heard the pounding of a helicopter overhead. An officer dripping in gold braid, a heavy gold ceremonial sword clattering at his side, came rushing through the hallway, brushing past an elderly gent armed with a long-handled mop who had been dusting the dustless floors. The Shah was returning from the ceremony of opening Parliament. Five minutes or so later I was ushered in; as usual with me, the audience was solo.

Seated in chairs that faced each other, we had been talking together perhaps ten minutes when the gold-plated handle of the double door rattled and clattered. The Shah must have guessed what was up; he took off his dark glasses, looked in the direction of the door, and in a moment it came open and a beautiful dark-eyed little girl of perhaps three came dashing full tilt across the huge room like a young gazelle. I rose to greet a Princess. The Shah, still seated of course, said, "This is the youngest," and to the child in English, "Say hello to Mr. Lilienthal." The little girl, looking at her father, stuck out a fist and the introduction was over.

Whereupon she tore to the other big door and began working at that handle, got it open. Outside two attendants, looking a bit abashed, grabbed her, and we resumed our audience.

I remarked that the Crown Prince had become quite a big boy. A beam of paternal pride lit up his face. "Yes, and he is a nice boy, too. Has such an interest in technical things. He takes machinery and electrical things apart and puts them together with great pleasure and skill."

At the beginning of our talk I thanked His Majesty for being willing to see me. He smiled in an almost shy way and said, "This is Friday, and ordinarily I do not have audience on this day. But what else would I do with the day that I would enjoy more?"

I had nothing in the way of serious problems or obstacles to report. The agricultural research centers program he had directed us to help prepare I said was now ready for submission to the Ministry of Agriculture. I thought it a good, solid program.

The Shah settled back into his chair, looked very solemn and thoughtful. He told me that in the next Five-Year Plan—which will be twice as large as all the previous four programs put together—a chief emphasis would be on agriculture.

Then for the first time I can recall he picked out a Minister for mention: "Rouhani is a strong man; he understands agriculture, and the kind of technically advanced agriculture that we need." I agreed, and added that his deputy for research was a very able and capable man.

The Shah spoke of the benefits to Iran of our long association with his country. "You bring your long and successful experience to us, so we can take advantage of what is known elsewhere; and you protect us from making the same mistakes that have held up development in other countries. I hope this cooperation will continue in other areas of our development in this country. We need your judgment and experience. We know that you believe in Iran and we believe in you."

I said that there is bound to be criticism of "foreign consultants"— as there has been. Some Iranians naturally feel they don't really need outside advice. But in the many years we have been in Iran we have been treated with the greatest consideration and brotherliness, with only a few exceptions.

He responded that, of course, there might be some resentment against "a certain kind of contractor, a certain kind of consultant. We appreciate the kind that you and your company represent."

The Shah spent a good deal of time discussing oil and gas. "You Americans will have to *import* each year $25 billion of oil in the coming years. Not all of it will come from Iran, but it must come from outside the U.S.

"We are going to enter the American market through an arrangement with Gulf, and perhaps also Ashland, perhaps later with Cities Service. That means that in many thousands of filling stations we will have a participation in the sale of our oil. That is what I have been driving for.

"But the crazy Arabs. They are demanding terms that can't stand up to the pressure of time. They want to get money for their oil by making impossible demands which won't last. And what will they do? They will have vast amounts of money in their bank accounts, but they don't know what to do with it. I hope they will see that it is to their interest to invest the money from their oil in the oil business, as we plan to do. I want them to come forward with this idea, which I have been pressing for years, come up with it as *their* idea."

The Shah asked: "What is going on in Brazil? I read an address of yours that spoke of your work in Brazil. You sounded optimistic, as I recall."

So I described the dimensions of the Amazon, and of the São Francisco.

As he talked about Brazil, the fact that he had indeed read my Geneva Speech became evident. So that speech has had an effect on the thinking of two Heads of State before it was ever delivered. Even if I never make it, it will have been worth the effort of this summer.

The Shah said he had visited Brazil some years ago when things were very bad in that country—disastrous inflation, for example. "How did they ever get into that fix?" I explained how well they were overcoming inflation by an ingenious device of sliding devaluation, and how the military protected the Ministers and their technical work from cheap and emotional attacks and from the legislature that have caused so much interference with the economic progress of the country.

"Yes, that is the kind of thing we get from our legislative body; I agree. But"—and this said *sternly*—"the military must stay out of civil affairs, completely. Completely."

Did he say more than what must be obvious? Or is there before him constantly a problem of keeping the military from taking over more and more and destroying the development that is going on so well?

"You have been in Iran over a period during which great changes have taken place so you know them better than most people. I can remember visiting Dezful with my father. Everyone in that city was afflicted with trachoma. Imagine. That impression never has left me, never for a moment."

And the dark shadows in his eyes—for at this point he had taken off his dark glasses—confirmed the depth of that memory of a young man confronted probably for the first time with great human misery.

I had several times shifted in my chair thinking he must want the audience to come to a close. But he didn't give any signal and we went on. Then he said: "It has been good to see you again. We want you to continue to work with us." As we reached the door, he turned to me and looking at me hard said: "Come to see me anytime that you are here or want to see me. If you find any obstacles in your work, you come to me at once. We can't afford to waste any time. Bring those problems directly to me if you are hampered in your work. Remember that."

OCTOBER 7, 1972
MESHED

Am I the fellow who told prospective visitors to Iran that modernization has about taken over, that they are just too late to see the Persia we saw sixteen years ago, the Persia of tradition, of Omar, the Thousand and One Nights, etc.? "That is about gone," said I, sadly.

Well! I am simply goggle-eyed by what we were permitted to see this morning at the Shrine of Imam Reza here in the Medina of the Shi'ite branch of the Moslem world.

Because we were the guests of the Minister of Agriculture and have become a trusted name in this country—I can't think of any other reason —we infidels were allowed to walk through the vast enclosure of the Shrine, so thick and solid with worshippers we could hardly pick our way through.

Of course, Frederiksen and I had removed our shoes; Helen and Rita Frederiksen were two blackbirds in heavy silk chadours, warned that only their nose and eyes could show, and as little of those as possible.

Nothing I have ever seen anywhere in our travels hit me so hard. Could *this* be the One World our orators prate about? How can these prostrated people, the hysterically weeping women, the gaunt-faced old men, the forms scattered far and wide through these series of enclosures, with the gleaming blue domes and golden spires, be *part* of the same world of "spectacular progress" the Shah declaimed about yesterday in his speech from the throne just a half-hour before we sat down in the calm of the Palace to discuss the most sophisticated problems of the world?

The people we saw at their worship were from all over Iran and the entire Moslem world, including Pakistan, Afghanistan, and even Saudi Arabia and the medieval Persian Gulf states such as Bahrain. So it was a mixture of the devout, many of whom had traveled many miles, with their foodstuffs, etc., to spend a week or two camping out in this mecca.

Goggle-eyed I was and still am!

The Governor General, our host here, is the "Master of the Shrine" (ex officio, I suppose). He gave a "special dispensation" and so not only we men but also our women (a low order of being among Moslems) entered the Court, and the Shrine as well.

OCTOBER 8, 1972
MESHED

I could hardly sleep last night—though this is a very comfortable guest house—for thinking of the scene of those several hundreds of people swarming over the marble floors of the Shrine. Was this actually some movie, on location, those extraordinary costumes covering thousands of "extras," with their white turbans, dark eyes, tattered clothes?

I had real pangs of conscience picking my way through the clusters of people so intent on worship, sidestepping a man all in white, his body flung forward head-down on the floor in prayer; a woman nursing her baby. Particularly when our mentor from the Ministry, Mr. Motamedi, urged me to look through the openings in a high gilded-iron fence so I could see the Tomb itself, a highly emotional scene like a mountain revivalist meeting (I thought). On the loops of the grating were hundreds of tiny padlocks, each with a strip of cloth. Placed there by worshippers, like the candles in a Roman Catholic church.

What troubled me was that our "guide" was pushing aside sorrowing women, clinging to the grating through which we could glimpse the Shrine, at a distance. No women, and few men, were ever permitted to get closer than this to the center of the Shrine. That was a bit too much for me. I didn't want to invade such a private, personal ceremony, even *with* "special dispensation."

We visited the Museum of the Shrine with a slender, most intelligent and well-informed young man. Wall hangings (more than rugs), quite ancient many of them. Nothing I have seen at the Met approaches them for beauty. Some made of countless tiny jewels woven together, others with gold and silver thread. The most beautiful was a sepia-toned jewel-encrusted rug portraying the four seasons—a miracle of imagination and skill.

OCTOBER 9, 1972
TEHRAN

We were gathered around the familiar table in Minister Rouhani's office. Big, burly Bert Cutler, face impassive, reciting the "troubled times" he and his D&R group had experienced in one of the basins where there was serious overgrazing from too many sheep and goats; what he proposed should be done.

Said the Minister: "There is only one short-term solution—evacua-

tion of the people and animals that are more than the land can bear."
"Yes," agreed Cutler, "but they must have someplace to go, some other
way of making a living, and that is what the plan we are developing can
provide, *if* we are given time."

A conversation in Farsi followed. Minister Rouhani said, "The troops
are already on their way to that valley; the people will be moved and their
animals."

Bert's impassive face looked very troubled. "It will be difficult to
work with the people under those circumstances, and perhaps dangerous
for our D&R group. But we will do the best we can."

How could we, Americans, argue about the use of force in a country
not our own?

I said to the men afterward: look at the way our settlers "solved" the
problem of the Red Indians, who were also nomads, when the settlers
wanted the land—we shot them, or herded them into "reservations" far
from their hunting lands.

The whole picture is not that bad, for in those mountain valleys, says
Bert, it is a good life people can have without "modern" implements. And
this is what many of them want, actually.

OCTOBER II, 1972
TEHRAN AIRPORT READY TO TAKE OFF FOR GENEVA

At 3 o'clock this morning, shivering and shaking with a series of
chills, despite a sweater and two heavy blankets, I was really too
weak—and disgusted with myself—to do anything but lie there and
shiver.

This is not the first time I have left Tehran in the embrace of a stupid
cold. I had to jog my sense of humor during the night when I thought of
what a mess it would be if I couldn't make that address on growth after
spending weeks on it this summer and having it built up by two Heads
of State.

OCTOBER 12, 1972
RICHEMOND HOTEL, GENEVA

A troubled-looking Georges-Henri Martin showed me what it means
to be a friend: he met me at the airport. "Troubled" because I had cabled
yesterday morning that a "sudden acute respiratory trouble" made it
necessary for me to ask him to cancel a dinner in my honor set for
tonight, sponsored by the Institute for Education in International Management located here.

I had all I could do to get on the plane yesterday morning; but by the time we arrived I was without any obvious fever. I was mighty grateful that Georges-Henri had set up an appointment for me with a physician.

He prescribed a whole series of drugs to relieve the symptoms—including a glass of hot "grog"—a toddy.

What was "planned" as a day of rest to offset this flu turned out to be hours of trying to cut the speech down to thirty minutes. Helen manned the guns to help, and disregarded my irritation, for I felt rotten and the last-minute cutting was nerve-wracking. But it was something I had to work out myself. Whether that will in fact cut down a 1½ hour speech into thirty minutes, only tomorrow noon will determine. And it *is* a good clear statement of what I believe.

OCTOBER 13, 1972
GENEVA

Well!

I made it to the finish line; the speech was to a big and unusually intent audience of the American International Club (most of whom I rather guessed were from a dozen countries in addition to "America").

To my great surprise, the fire and belligerence and positiveness came through. Perhaps I overdid my being so positive. But I wanted people to know where I stand. What is the point of shilly-shallying?

OCTOBER 14, 1972
GENEVA

A deep overcast and haze, and the damp chill in the air that one comes to expect in Europe through all the months of winter. Yesterday was full of sunshine for me. I had pulled myself together and made one of the very best forensic efforts in years. Even my voice, so croaky for days, behaved through the entire hour (a question period and a reception).

OCTOBER 15, 1972
VEVEY, SWITZERLAND

Have just come from a walk in the town of Vevey of a Sunday afternoon. Very much the highlight: a circus. Helen and I joined the throngs of papas and mamas and their goggle-eyed offspring, gawking at the animals in the zoo. And a very impressive menagerie it was. We expected the mangy, sorry-looking half-dozen tigers and a bored elephant of the country European circuses we have seen. Not at all. Six of the biggest, proudest polar bears I have ever seen—imagine!—several well-upholstered two-hump dromedaries, swaying from foot to foot, contemptuous and sneering, a giraffe that looked sixteen feet high, and craning over, almost nipped off my hat. I have never been so close to so many exceptional animals, for there were practically no barriers between them and the queues that passed.

The "creatures" most interesting were the local country people and their children. They were diminutive but delightful.

OCTOBER 16, 1972
VEVEY

We are now heading home. In a week I'll be back, either in Princeton or at my desk. Between now and then we have many miles to cover, by rail through the Alps and then into northern Italy, and a reunion with David and his family, a prospect I find exciting and happy.

OCTOBER 17, 1972
EN ROUTE VEVEY TO FLORENCE

The number of times I have flown over the highest of the snow-covered Alps, giving them only a casual look.

This train ride has been one long excitement. Not just the "panorama magnifique"—as one of our Swiss compartment companions said—but the richness of the valleys. The vineyards are being harvested, and how golden and rich they are. But the most impressive of all is the sheer stubbornness that led the Swiss to build massive stone walls right up to the top, bring soil to fill back of the terrace walls, and plant vines everywhere.

OCTOBER 22, 1972
FLYING TO NEW YORK

The last wing, I suppose one should say, of our long journey. It has seemed long. Too long.

The visit with David and his family was one of the best we have ever had. When we arrived Peggy was ill, but she recovered quickly, and David and the children were never more interesting and loving.

David 3d is only an inch shorter than his 6'5" father! The face of a poet, the grin of a small boy. He looks forward to the coming year with great anticipation, a little apprehension. For this coming summer he returns to his native country for the first time since he was twelve (now seventeen plus) to enter college. It will be a great year for him, and a difficult one for his parents.

OCTOBER 28, 1972
PRINCETON

THE WAR IS OVER.

Now, of course, that isn't what the headlines said yesterday, but that is certainly what they imply.†

The "morning after" is not quite so exuberant. The details to be settled could still upset the settlement.

NOVEMBER 4, 1972
PRINCETON

Last Sunday he played tennis; on Monday morning, my classmate and friend, Wendell Davis, set off for his law office. Last night he died after a heart attack that very evening.

I take these deaths of others pretty hard. Not made any easier by the discussions about who is to succeed me in D&R, or as I prefer to put it, while we discuss how to establish continuity in the work I have had under way not without some success these seventeen years.

NOVEMBER 6, 1972
AT PENN STATION WAITING FOR THE 4 O'CLOCK TO PRINCETON

I go home—something I rarely do in mid-week—to prevent the vote for Nixon being completely unanimous. As the polls predict, it will nearly be.

NOVEMBER 8, 1972
NEW YORK

There are a good many lessons that will be drawn from yesterday's election. "Nixon by an avalanche." One is that you can't beat a resourceful incumbent with a cluck. Truman won against great odds because he was not only the incumbent but a tough, straightforward, earthy man.

The best evidence that it was the weakness of the "head of the ticket" is that the Democratic Party is stronger today than it was the day before the election.

I thought McGovern's views on foreign policy and action about as wrong as could be, and would have been uneasy on that score had he been elected.

†At the Vietnam negotiations in Paris, Kissinger had said "peace is at hand."

NOVEMBER 9, 1972
NEW YORK

It is almost impossible at whatever cost to get a really good meal in New York. Going to the Century, in the evening, where, it is true, the food is more than passably good, is like dining in a retirement home. No thanks. So I went to the Press Box, where the maître, Bruno, knows me. And what a dinner I had.

Now to bed, to read the last few pages of Dickens' *Great Expectations* (which I have been reading for four months!).

NOVEMBER 15, 1972
NEW YORK

I enjoyed today. Even a session at New York Hospital, having iodine poured into me (it is opaque to X-ray) to see how my plumbing is actually behaving. The "help" there I had a good time joshing, and my distinguished urologist, Dr. Victor Marshall, looked at the X-ray films and said: nothing wrong there.

I won't deny that two weeks ago I began to be fearful that something *was* wrong. But I really am a healthy character, and strong beyond my deserts considering how I make things just as hard for myself as possible.

NOVEMBER 19, 1972
PRINCETON

A visit at Bill Dix's yesterday afternoon. A long and absorbing talk with the new dean of the school of engineering, Robert G. Jahn. Engineering students who come to Princeton have much of the prevalent student desire that what they study should have "relevance" to present-day social needs. Many of today's young people are searching for something special to them and their future world—even as some of us did, though much less was made of the notion that we were, consciously, "searching."

The sharp lines of the classical definitions of engineering (civil, electrical, mechanical) are blurred by the needs of the community, and of the work of the world. I asked, "How do you as an educator make students realize this, how do you revise the curriculum to accommodate the fact that those classical definitions no longer satisfy what the new engineers must meet?"

It was a vague kind of question; I really had in mind that in TVA and in D&R, development of resources, of urban society, and of agriculture, requires engineers to have a broader spectrum of interests and training than prevailed when a man could say that he was a civil engineer, or a mechanical engineer, and that was that.

His answer was surprisingly specific. The school picks out current *issues* that call for engineering training, and focuses on them. The *application* of engineering training brings down the walls of the classical definitions and divisions of engineering. Environmental protection, urban problems, transportation, providing for energy needs, even the newer needs of the medical profession.

"Physicians have become the victims of new engineering technology" was one of the provocative things he said. He used a term new to me: "bio-engineering." The use of the computer by the medical profession, the improving of sophisticated mechanical aids for the physically disabled—as he talked I understood that engineering and other simple almost unrelated physical activities are on the way out. What should take its place is engineering as part of a complex and *unified* set of skills and judgment. This has been my goal for technical people in TVA and more latterly in D&R.

Bill Dix said an interesting thing about D.E.L. "You are an anti-historian. Your interest is not in the past but in the future. The future of Brazil, right now, is what occupies you; and before that, other futures, a year or so from now, other futures."

The contradiction here, if there is one, is that I have also been in the process of publishing my impressions and reports of the past, in what may prove to be one of the most extended of American journals. This isn't inconsistent with being an "anti-historian" since the journals are written at the time and refer to that present, or, as in the case of Brazil and Iran, the future of those countries.

Barbara Tuchman, it is claimed, is a "historian"—i.e., a scholar. (But not by me. I maintain she is no more nor less than a newspaper reporter out to substantiate her prejudices.) In a sentence in chapter 11 of her *Stilwell*—which off and on I have been reading for some time—she says: "History is not what is true but what the public *believes* is true." (That is almost exactly what she tosses off at the end of a paragraph.)

Almost to a man and woman, those who have "reported" on Vietnam set out to dishonor the U.S., its leaders, and the Vietnamese people. They have already written more horror books about the American part in the war than have been written about the Civil War, or probably World War II. Much of this, probably most of this, I find cheap sensationalism, and without a shred of fairness or objectivity. But if Tuchman's Law is valid, then these newspaper reporters (not scholars by any measure) have set

out to make the public believe that what they write is true. And, therefore, it is true!

NOVEMBER 24, 1972
PRINCETON

I thought I had seen every kind of beaten, bitter, disillusioned crier
of Doomsday. But no. I reached the peak last Tuesday afternoon (that
would be the 21st of November, 1972, not 1872, it should be recorded). In
a big office on Sixth Avenue I listened for an hour to Daniel K. Ludwig
("one of the richest men in America, in the world" as he was described
to me) passionately, solemnly declaring his own life an utter failure (though he didn't quite realize it was that) while he said, inter
alia:
    "This country is bankrupt. It's too late to turn it around. Ever since
Franklin Roosevelt we have told people they don't need to work, the rest
of us will take care of them; ever since then this country was on the way
to its doom. We don't even have an army that has the guts to take over,
as they did in Brazil, which is what saved Brazil. And the last election
just confirmed it—too late now."
    Ludwig is the owner of three million acres of land in the Amazon
Basin. Some of it contains iron ore and bauxite, in the Jari River area,
some of it he is devoting to a wood products business (a Malaysian kind
of quick-growing tree), some to rice, some to cattle. So he is an important
figure.
    I had explained that my company had been engaged by Brazil to do
development work, and since he has been so active I wanted to get acquainted, get such views about Brazil as he wanted to give me.
    "Rice? Yes, I played around with rice. My damned experts, they *lied*
to me."
    I broke in to say that sometimes experts overestimated, were given
to wishful thinking.
    "*All* experts will lie to you. Always do."
    So that settled both rice and experts.
    I spoke of forest products. Suddenly he warmed up. "There I have got
a winner," he said with relish. "Let me show you something. I just do this
for the fun of it, but sometimes we do get a winner."
    He opened the drawer of a table and brought out pieces of wood—a
cross-section, eight inches or so wide, of a tree, and a large shell of wood
veneer.
    "These come from a tree seven and a half years old." And he went
on with enthusiasm.

But soon he was in the most bitter mood I have ever heard. "No one is willing to work."

Ludwig is a self-made man. His sole education was in elementary schools. Went to work in a shipyard, proud that he developed a method of building ships by welding instead of riveting, etc., has made a real contribution, I think, to ocean transport, including the sea train. Why then is he so full of hatred?

Ironic. Out of the window of the new Burlington Building you can see the row of glittering new glass and steel skyscrapers along what was so recently a pretty dingy Sixth Avenue. New York City, bustling, vigorous, the very center of the business and the communications world, the financial center par excellence. "Rotten—the whole country is rotten, nothing can put it together again."

So . . . one goes to the zoo to see strange and hideous animals, with long horns or, like some monkey, with a purple bottom, and I find even the most aesthetically repulsive animal interesting to observe. So it is with the Ludwigs of this world.

DECEMBER 5, 1972
NEW YORK

Music in Princeton at last, after all the missed opportunities because I'm in New York most of the week. In Jadwin Gym heard a resounding Mahler Fifth Symphony, by the Chicago Symphony Orchestra.

The last movement begins in a delicate, reverent whisper, builds up to a crashing affirmation. I felt as if I had written the music. I came away, after that tumultuous closing, saying to myself (almost aloud): By God, no problem can lick me; nothing is quite impossible for me. Bend to the storm, for the moment, yield a foot or so when the going is tough—but never, never lose courage or fighting spirit or a sense of movement. That's it. Keep moving.

DECEMBER 9, 1972
PRINCETON

I do live the life of a human chameleon, and yesterday was a special example. In the morning I wore many hats, until noon; in the afternoon at Princeton lived in the groves (dripping wet it was) of Princeton academia—my first meeting of the Advisory Council to the Department of Near Eastern Studies.

I thought I knew what "Near East" means. But they define it at Princeton, for the purpose of research, thesis writing by seniors, and graduate and Ph.D. work, to include not only the "Middle East" but practically the whole of the world of Islam, in North Africa (Egypt, Tunisia, Algeria, etc., etc.).

One bright-eyed historian, wanting to be a pioneer, has invented psychohistory. He has been in analysis in the hands of a psychoanalyst, Freud-style, so he can qualify as a psychoanalyst himself. To what end? So he can psychoanalyze Ataturk, about whom he is writing a psychobiography.

Of course, it is the great creative Turk's mother that explains everything. I found all this amusing rather than repulsive. One can't reject this hooey out of hand and completely. Of course, there is basic sense in the notion that to know about a great leader's inner life helps—or is relevant to—an understanding of the events in the outer world in which he participated or which he led or obstructed.

As a responsible executive and manager, I know that we judge people and their potentials by a hunch ("experienced judgment") about their personality and background. But to make a cult of this, to become a psychoanalyst yourself to do this kind of appraisal would be ludicrous in the world of affairs.

Still, anyone in the academic life who is reaching out for something new is better than the geezers who just continue to use and repeat the lecture notes they made twenty years ago.

The men around the table included three men on the Advisory Council I found very worthwhile. One is a studious-looking young man, a Vice President of the Federal Reserve in New York, Richard Debs, with the kind of Lebanese parentage that marks Ralph Nader as an exceptional man. Debs is a Ph.D. and a graduate of a law school. Terribly worried by my remark that the "energy crisis" in the U.S. means that the U.S. balance of trade and payments will be out of kilter to the tune of perhaps twenty to thirty billion dollars in ten years, because we must buy so much oil and gas from the Middle East.

The critical importance of the Middle East to the West, and particularly to the U.S., is a consequence of our utility companies' refusing to make realistic projections of demand for power over the years, something we of TVA and D&R have been trying to persuade people about for years. The banking and international monetary people in the State Department and the Federal Reserve think this money crisis (for that is the real consequence of the energy shortage) came on "suddenly, in the last eighteen months." Nonsense.

Another of the outside non-academic people is, by name, Holden, son of the former president of Vassar; the third, a Mr. Rea of the rich Philadelphia family. Both clear-headed men.

Rea said: I learned this noon that every single one of the graduate students intended to become teachers, intended to follow the academic life with their training in Near Eastern studies. This is the result of a deliberate policy instituted by Goheen fifteen years ago. But why? Why, with all the need for people trained in knowledge of the increasingly important Middle East, should teaching be the only vocation to which they expect to devote themselves?

One of the most philosophical answers was given by two of the professors. "It is an easy life. Paid for twelve months' work, actually only teach eight, all kinds of fringe benefits, pensions, etc., and none of the pressure of the competitive life." An honest if, to me, disturbing answer.

At the dinner meeting I spoke with some passion about how important it is that those who have an understanding of the Middle East's culture, history, an interest in its archeological remains, should be available for work in that region on behalf of American or other Western business. Said I: "When we are looking for a water resource engineer or a watershed protection technical man (as near Khorramabad) it is a great advantage if he has some background of knowledge and interest in the Near East and its way of life." This I assumed is one of the important things that a graduate of Princeton concentrating in the Near East would have.

This precipitated some discussion from the outside people, but the academic people, it was clear, regarded this as a "primitive view"—that job opportunities should not be a measure of what you get out of and put into an academic period of study.

Ah me. We people of the mundane world that lies outside the uncontaminated groves untouched by "utility."

DECEMBER 10, 1972
PRINCETON

Last Wednesday I sat in McNamara's reception room, looking at probably the saddest examples of portraits in Washington: the glum faces of all the preceding Presidents of the World Bank. The pixy face of Gene Meyer; next to him, Gene Black, looking far less like a statesman without the black Homburg he still wears as a badge of the international great-one; George Woods, bland and washed out, the portrait looking like the product of an "artist" in the window of a five-and-ten, a colored tintype, whereas George had a glint in his eye; and finally, a picture of Jack McCloy, the perennial stand-in Repubo-Democrat of the Stimson-Acheson Period of dual citizenship, one foot in each Party and getting the best of both.

I was interrupted in my reverie of these masterpieces of portraiture, and the fading eminence of these men (and myself), when a bright-eyed little lady with bobbed grey hair appeared around the corner.

"I am Miss Moore, Mr. McNamara's secretary, and I want to shake your hand" (which she and I did, solemnly, suiting the action to the word, as they say). "I wanted to shake the hand of a man who stood up and told the Senate of the United States right to its face what you *did* carry in your head." The reference was to my so-called reply to Senator McKellar of so many years ago. So I thanked her, she excused herself with no more comment but with a happy smile, and I resumed my musing about the Great Men on the wall of the reception room.

McNamara came pounding out, coatless as is his custom, a great big cordial welcoming smile and handshake.

I had wanted to converse about Brazil and about Iran, but he was full of the places where people are very poor, and where the current drought threatens starvation in the next several months: Bangladesh, even Indonesia.

When I saw that neither Brazil nor Iran was on his mind, but Vietnam might be, I asked him about Harrison Salisbury's strong invitation to me of the other day to write an Op-Ed article or two about a postwar reconstruction program. Should I get into that subject again? Wasn't our report a futile exercise?

He replied: Not at all; it has been influential. I should certainly write such a piece.

I said I thought the only thing I could say would be to stress the moral issue that will confront America when the "hostilities" are over.

He said, of course, that should be what I should say. He had to speak to the Ford Foundation board next week, and wanted to stress that issue himself. I referred to my [1960] Newton Baker Lecture about "foreign aid": its purpose should be to express American idealism; not what we got out of it, but the kind of country we really are.

I have never seen him more full of fire.

"I am going to the Middle East in a couple weeks. We in the Bank have shown the Arabs that we want to work with them, something really new for the Bank. They are going to have enormous sums of foreign exchange selling the oil and gas we need to keep our country going, and Europe too. Why don't they invest their surplus in helping the developing world, such as Sudan or Indonesia? How?" (Here is the "official" gimmick, I thought.) "By buying World Bank bonds and thus helping spread development into countries that need financial help."

I commented on the huge amounts of "cash" the oil companies of the Persian Gulf would have in five years, ten years, more than they could possibly use for their own internal development even if they wanted to or had the capability. And the effect this will have in continuing the drastic unbalance in our own and the world's monetary systems.

"You have been thinking about this. Can you give me your ideas about this?"

I said, "Let's put that over until some other time."

I rose. "You don't know, Bob, how good it is to be dealing with a man in this Bank who is almost by instinct affirmative. Not constantly negative. I have suffered from that negative attitude here for years."

He roared. "Jesus, can you imagine how frustrating it is, that caution, that negative look at life. Sometimes it almost drives me nuts."

One dramatic episode: in trying to explain my initial reluctance to write the articles for the *Times* about Vietnam, I said I had taken responsibility for that job, from President Johnson, only when it was put up to me as a kind of duty. And I had to pay for it.

"Would you believe it? Just taking on a clearly nonmilitary job producing a postwar development report estranged my son; not only my son but my granddaughter."

Bob slumped way back in his chair at the lunch table, one shoulder way down. The brilliant, lively eyes so evident when talking with gusto about the Sudan, or our duty to the starving people of the world, gave way to an almost opaque clouded eye. His face seemed to shrink in size. I was shaken by this transformation.

"I could tell you stories even worse about myself, many of them."

Suddenly he sat erect again. "David, do you know where Easter Island is?" I said I thought it was somewhere in the Pacific. "Yes, two thousand miles from California. Well, Marge is going out to that dismal little island soon. To see our son."

He didn't need to fill in that picture. I inferred that their son had left the country, isolated himself, because of his father's part in the war.

A man who has suffered, and continues to suffer, the javelins of the wise-guy journalists. The latest and most personal is in David Halberstam's *The Best and the Brightest,* though the chapter picking him out is I guess the same as the malicious article in *Harper's* of months ago.

DECEMBER 12, 1972
NEW YORK

Rockefeller Center was never more resplendent: a score of ever so white angels blowing triumph through brass trumpets held high toward heaven. Watched this last night on a long walk, but more entranced by the look on the faces of the young children watching those lights, and the giant tree, and all the other tasteful (not gaudy really) signs of Christmas celebration. Chinese mannikins in Saks' window, for example. It didn't occur to me, as too often it does, that this is part of a commercial sell-the-goods operation.

DECEMBER 17, 1972
PRINCETON

I was much concerned about where in the world I would find time to keep my promise to Salisbury to write the postwar Vietnam articles for early January publication. The end of the war doesn't seem all that near, judging by Kissinger's press conference yesterday and the assurances North Vietnam has received of full support from both China and the Soviets.

All the hurrah from the intellectuals that the Cold War is over, about which report I have been so scornful, seems a bit laughable today. But things do change; or as the all-wise columnists say: "But *that* remains to be seen."

I have little use for what Truman called "the professional liberals."

DECEMBER 23, 1972
ANTIGUA

What a shriekingly amusing time we—Helen, Nancy, and I—have had this summery afternoon. Can there be anything more amusing than to be witness—at a safe distance—to the embarrassment of others, particularly when they happen to be the big and powerful?

In the roadstead of this little harbor a yacht—only slightly smaller and less grand and opulent than the *Queen Elizabeth II.* Literally. The owner was aboard the plane on which we ourselves arrived, complete with seven teenage, long-haired girls—his daughters and their friends, we were told. His name, Levitt, the builder of Levittown and many times a millionaire.

We rather resented the presence of this huge liner, chiefly because at night it was lighted up so brightly as to spoil wholly the effect of the full moon on the white sand.

This morning every sign that *La Belle* was preparing to leave. Her crew of more than a dozen busying themselves in all directions. One of the two anchors came rattling up. But the second couldn't make it. All afternoon they tried this trick and that but the anchor chain remained steady; no anchor came up. Men swarmed around the bow, peering over, shouting orders; others were in little boats doing this and that, even swimming about the chain as it stubbornly refused to move.

Finally the chain began to move, link by link; the men at the mechanism high above in the bow became very busy. The points of the anchor showed above the water, the great chain clanged against the steel hull. A hollow iron clatter-bang. Then, as one man, the four crew members on the bow and the two on the bridge yelled, barked, shouted, *but* not in nautical language. The shouted command: *"Whoa."*

I thought: "Whoa" indeed; what would Admiral Lord Nelson think if a crew of his men-of-war yelled at an anchor as if it were a horse, when his fleet once crossed this bay?

DECEMBER 26, 1972
ANTIGUA

The night before Christmas a gaggle of teenagers, Antigua-style, appeared, as is the custom here, to sing carols for the mostly English guests. While the leader was sorting them out and humming do-re-mi, the skinny little black girls in the front row went into vigorous go-go movements, not of the kind favored, I would say, in the little country church from which they came, torsos twisting, little bottoms waggling— the works. Then the leader's hand came down, and they sang out: *"Sigh lent night, 'oly night . . ."* etc.

The first return to reality came last night. The Xerox of a letter about postwar reconstruction in Indochina: a most cordial and unguarded letter from Marshall Green, Assistant Secretary for East Asia and Pacific Affairs. It helps to quiet any doubts I had about the timing of my renewed expression of interest in the subject of reconstruction—to Secretary Rogers, to Harrison Salisbury, and to McNamara.

I shall follow this up, perhaps by a visit.

But between the time when I told Salisbury and McNamara I would write a basic statement about the moral basis of a strong reconstruction effort, and the present, Kissinger's famous "peace is at hand" statement gave way to renewed warfare.

Not having seen a newspaper or heard a radio for nearly a week, I don't know what the recent developments are. In a week we shall be getting ready to return. I may then find Vietnam is high on my list of "priorities."

The D.E.L. physical activity department has been going at high gear. Four rather vigorous swims from our front porch, as it were; an hour and a half walk, with Nancy, to the top of the hill and then on to a site overlooking the wide sweep of the froth-girt sea, and a prowl through what is left of the barracks of the 18th century British troops who held this strategic area for the Crown.

A comfort to know that whereas last Christmas, out here, walking was painful because of that ankle tendon injury, this year I hardly notice it.

Have done a lot of reading, in my usual manner—i.e., reading three or four different books, and different kinds of book, simultaneously.

DECEMBER 27, 1972
ANTIGUA

Once more "Nancy has gone." It was a joy having her here with us for a week, soaking up rest and sun. A person who enjoys life quietly, softly I might say, soft as her voice and gentle as her manner.

But the passivity is only on the surface. The intense, almost fierce, passion for the truth, the insistence on literal honesty—her own word to describe this trait which goes back to her childhood. With it a strong sense of justice—"it isn't fair." I can still hear her say this with such intensity as a child. She was shy as a child among adults, but a very popular girl among her contemporaries. I note a touch of bitterness at times in her comments about public issues, and we stayed away from such—after all this is her holiday as well as ours.

The warmth and humorous glint in her quite beautiful eyes so often sends a pang through me: I see my mother's eyes. Indeed, physically, as Helen and I have remarked, she is like my mother: the oval face, the wide-apart eyes. But not my mother's temperament, which was fiery, often belligerent, and usually full of fun—not humor, but fun. Mina did have a sense of fun, particularly noticeable because my father simply had none, though always equable and good-natured to a fault, like Ted.

The guest population is at its height, this being the period between Christmas and New Year's. Until yesterday it was like being in a more or less upper-class or professional English club.

Then today there descended on us eight young Italians. The four girls are very tall, very long legs, very thin, and no breasts (though they did wear a wisp of something where their breasts would be if they had any). In swimming they are like sticks, so thin and strung out.

But this afternoon they appeared in sport clothes; what *class,* the way they wear their clothes and carry themselves.

DECEMBER 28, 1972
ANTIGUA

A most sagacious friend said: "Don't decide important directions when you are pressed and tired. Wait until you have had your vacation. You'll come back with a perspective you probably don't have in the center of pressure and a certain fatigue."

Such advice is not so obviously right as it might seem. Reminiscent of some of Justice Brandeis' comments. For example: never make an important decision (on a public matter, he meant) unless one is in "concert pitch." Physically, he meant, but emotionally as well, I should think. Another aphorism attributed to him: the outside of a horse is good for the inside of a man.

"Concert pitch" and "perspective that comes after a change of scene and a rest" are not easy states of being for a man with management responsibility. But this doesn't make the counsel less wise and true.

Now what are the "products" of this vaunted "perspective" earned by a week's rest as of this morning on this Caribbean shore?

It can be applied to quite particular, specific problems.

The world isn't going to stop, or break into little pieces by what you do or don't do about the things that absorb your attention and cause you to lie awake at night.

This is a view difficult for me because temperamentally it is against the grain of an intense and egocentric person. More especially it is contrary to long years of the nature of my working life. My strength in getting things accomplished has been this very intensity, this non-thinking (i.e., non-conscious) premise of my life—that what I set out to do or am doing *is* very important.

It certainly was decisive in shaping TVA, not to say saving it from an early death, by failure or decay. Currently, my strong feeling about the neglect of the Persian peasant has kept that issue a strong one, despite the fact that most of the Shah's government entourage are rich men's sons who couldn't really care less. To this broad statement, Minister Rouhani is a notable exception, he the son of a villager.

Perspective should extend beyond the "allocation of your energies" in a working sense. It should take in the manifold and fascinating non-work opportunities for personal enjoyment, satisfaction, and self-expression. You are not—be fair about it—one of these one-track business types who without their work are without compelling interests, curiosities, and personal relationships that make for a civilized individual. By no means.

You don't have—as in youth we think we have—an unlimited amount of time, in years, in which to spend your energies, satisfy your interests, and enjoy the sensibilities that are yours.

The two days before we left—i.e., December 18th and 19th—I spent most of the time on Brazil, more specifically the commitment that during February I must present D&R's report and recommendations on how to reorganize the development of the São Francisco region.

In our tiny little library at the office, a map of the São Francisco region spread out before me, I thought I saw, confirmed, my earlier hunch: the "drainage basin" of the São Francisco River is not A Region.

True, our contract wrote the drainage basin concept into the engage-ment. I did get in, in the contract revision, a phrase something like that in the TVA Act—the drainage basin plus the contiguous area affected by the development of the drainage basin.

To make it really productive requires the addition, in some fashion, of the coastal area between the course of the river and the sea. I had my eye on the State of Bahia, or in any case, the capital city, the beautiful and historic Salvador, with its deep-water port and its significance in the life of that part of Brazil—and her history, for that matter.

DECEMBER 29, 1972
ANTIGUA

Those intellectuals who consider themselves qualified to be *the* crit-ics and analysts of American (or Western) standards have one thing in common. They denounce or deplore the destruction or deterioration of the culture of other peoples by their adoption of American standards and values. This is a major theme of the professional American journalists and writers of books about the war in Vietnam. This feeds the character-istic American love of self-guilt, and is accepted pretty widely as gospel.

Their picture is that of a pure and simple people and society slugged into acceptance of values alien to them, the raucous coarse impure stan-dards of American life, and particularly those subsidized or pushed on these noble simple people ("villagers" is the favored phrase) by the cal-lous Americans.

This well-accepted notion is largely bunk. The reason it is bunk is that the people who study and write about it are so remote from the kind of life most Americans generally want for themselves.

I record instances that lead me to reject the conventional picture.

Clothes fully as much as the books that are read, the music listened to, the public issues believed in, reflect an important part of a "culture." I doubt not it has always been so.

When it is "the thing" in New York or Paris for women to wear dresses that are above the knees, or even halfway to the thigh (or long hair, to the middle of the back, among the young, another part of the same phenomenon), then a month or two later that is the kind of dress one sees on the streets of Tehran or Tokyo—or in Antigua.

This manifestation of what people want (which is the basis of their "culture") further demonstrates that the process of accepting American or Western modes is a purely voluntary, certainly a non-coercive, process.

I could make the same point about the kind of "popular" music people want to hear, particularly the younger generations around the world. No one compels the young Vietnamese or Japanese or Swiss to listen to rock and roll or buy by the millions the records of these alleged musicians.

The most serious fault of the sociology intellectuals is that they assume the role of judges of "good values." Having no use for contemporary American values—i.e., what people want—they assume it is a mark of outside coercion or of inner decay and degradation that those "false values" are accepted or adopted by the people in other countries. Particularly the simpler societies and less developed countries.

Have just heard from a neighbor here that President Truman died day before yesterday.

Grateful that the doctors were not able to keep this doughty fighting figure alive when he was no longer aware of being alive—a cruel and inhuman misuse of medical knowledge.

What a man he was, this man under whom I served with such pride, and who honored me by standing by me in my "troubles" without condescension toward me or self-pity for what he was "doing for me."

I expressed my sentiments about President Truman the other day in a letter to Margaret about her biography of her father.

Here is a quote from it:

> Of all the years I spent in the service of my country, the most satisfying—and therefore the happiest, despite the turmoil, and at times the malice of powerful enemies—were those under the guidance and protection of the President, your father. Greatly as I believed in him and honored his straightforwardness as my boss, I never fully realized what a superb human being he was to work for and with until, during the past two days, I read your memorable book. What a *genuine* man he emerges in these loving pages.

DECEMBER 30, 1972
ANTIGUA

I cast my eyes on those of my "possessions" brought along on this lazy expedition. Inanimate objects, all.

Yet how much each of them evokes the most startlingly clear, vivid, warm recollections and living associations: people, events, lows and great highs.

That inanimate "objects" have such an ability to be alive through imagination has hit me strongly on this sunny island afternoon. When I acquire something inanimate, with the thing newly possessed I also possess and can hold the occurrence, the event, the person linked to that thing and to that act of acquisition and possession.

DECEMBER 31, 1972
ANTIGUA

The sun is down beyond the bay and the dark green hill to the west; the afterglow is all that remains of the last of the daylight of 1972. A good year, all in all, it has been for me. For mankind? It is far too early to judge —a century too early perhaps. How lucky I am to be alive and part of this amazing year of 1972—and the decade for that matter.

What a wonderful way to see the end of a memorable year—and, therefore, the beginning of a new one—to spend a few hours with a great poet, the greatest singer of the wonders of this country, of the joy of being an American, since Walt Whitman.

We had a long leisurely luncheon visit with Archibald MacLeish at the Macy home, part of the Mill Reef Club estates. With him were the lovely, devoted Ada, his love of a lifetime, and Milton Eisenhower.

Archie does not seem to change in appearance or certainly in vigor of voice and imagination and manner, though, as he has pointed out, he has recently had his 80th birthday.

He wanted to talk about the state of the world, and to some extent we did. "Are you frightened by Nixon, and this 'anger' which he explains as the basis for all-out bombing of Hanoi?" Archie put the question to Eisenhower.

Like his great brother, Milton Eisenhower isn't given to very direct answers. But he did say he was puzzled, perhaps frightened. He settled down to a mood of recollection. "You know, I came to know Nixon very well. I accompanied him on long trips, while he was Vice President—to Russia, to Latin America. If he were seated right there"—pointing to an easy chair on the ocean-view terrace where we were having a truly imaginative MacLeish rum drink—"you would not find a more pleasant person. Interested in you, in what you are saying, charming, a good man to be with."

All of which led Helen and me to think that this was the Eisenhower way of saying: No, I'm really not all that frightened. He has his ways. And he may "pull it off"—an expression that came out during Milton's comments.

Speaking very slowly, solemnly (he does not have the lightest manner under any circumstances, I thought), Milton Eisenhower said: "I am quietly organizing a very high-level committee to see to it that Agnew isn't the candidate in 1978, to promote the candidacy of Chuck Percy. A highly personable man, excellent speaker, attractive family . . . an ideal candidate."

Later Helen commented, *sotto voce*, that it might not be irrelevant

that Percy, in addition to his charm and his views, would have the Rockefeller money, his daughter having married Jay Rockefeller.

But mostly we spoke of how good it is to have been permitted to be
alive in the most exciting period perhaps of all history.

MacLeish is a delightful, thoughtful, sensitive man, who knows what
it is about, and best of all, can say so in the most important language of
all, poetry.

VI

1973

~~◦~~

Trips to Brazil and proposal for organization of regional development of the São Francisco Valley—Visit with Shah of Iran in Washington—Trip to Brazil—Trip to Romania and Iran—Vacation in Antigua

JANUARY 2, 1973
ANTIGUA

Now we come close to the end of these days of swimming, three to four times each day. An end to vast quantities of sun, which has browned or reddened me almost beyond recognition. And the casual hours without cares.

I confess I'm more than ready to pick up the skein of the active life, with all of its risks and worries.

JANUARY 7, 1973
PRINCETON

The reality of life and living is so full of meaning, is such a dare to do, to overcome, to create. Then how explain the attraction of illusion, of unreality, and why disguise the nonsense of illusion by calling it "bright dreams"?

When you set up an illusion as your passionate goal, you are inviting disillusion. This axiom should be self-explanatory. But instead of that explanation, so many people choose to explain this as desertion of ideals, "death of dreams and vision," or personal rottenness.

To move the world toward something better than we have we must first understand the world. The world-law people, such as Cord Meyer, Jr., or Norman Cousins, never did understand it.

JANUARY 10, 1973
NEW YORK

We are having the kind of weather I like best: very cold, very dry air. Took two long walks daily in Princeton in the wind last weekend, and all I lacked for utter physical satisfaction was my dear departed horse, friend Mac. How he would snort and blow steam from his nostrils, and buck-jump as I rode him in Norris on such days as these.

JANUARY 12, 1973
PRINCETON

The most stimulating part of today was spent on the periphery of Princeton University, with my latest enthusiasm, Dean Robert Jahn.

I repeated to Jahn how impressed I had been by his definition of the modern outlook of the engineer's role in society, which he has embodied in several papers, extraordinarily articulate and persuasive. He hastened to say, in his reserved way, that what he had said on this score wasn't the prevailing view in the profession; indeed, he was by no means sure that it represented the view of his fellow faculty members of the engineering school. Of this I have no doubt. Such ideas move slowly.

JANUARY 20, 1973
PRINCETON

A visit from Mehdi Samii, who told me, "I am leaving public service by the end of this month and His Majesty has asked me to organize a political party.

"His Majesty, I am completely convinced, is uneasy about the one-party system which has grown up. He senses that to assure the continued strength of Iran, to force it to face the questions which great success, too-great success, in the economic field has brought, and will continue to bring, there must be discussion, free debate over the direction of the country, its policies. To accomplish this a two-party system is necessary, essential. Not an 'opposition' party in form only, but a genuine one."

But is the Shah aware of what it would mean to begin to relinquish the complete authority now in his hands, making every single one of the decisions? Is he really prepared for a constitutional role as sovereign rather than ruler? Is he able to adjust to this change?

"The Shah knows," said Mehdi, "that I have had—and expressed to him—strong reservations and concern for my country and for him in the present course, that no issues are resolved until he has decided them. How bad it is that discussion and debate are so limited, that there is so little opportunity for the airing and weighing of differences on policy.

"I realized the risks to me personally. It might be construed as opposition to the Shah, just the beginning or announcement of such a party. It could get out of hand and become the center of dissent and protest of a kind that could only cause trouble rather than be constructive on issues.

"I thought it over carefully. I told His Majesty I would do it. I would first bring together a small group, not more than thirty or forty men. They will be mostly—unfortunately this is true—Anglo-Saxon-educated, English and American. Then we will increase the group to perhaps seventy."

Does the Shah sense a rising tide of dissatisfaction and discontent among the poor; does he feel that the leadership by the Prime Minister has been too compliant, tended to cover over basic problems?

Or was this the wise and far-sighted act of the kind that led him to announce and to enforce the sixteen points of the White Revolution, against which he must have been warned by many, including perhaps the ghost of his hard-bitten, ruthless father, whose methods did so much to set Iran on the road into the modern world?

JANUARY 22, 1973
NEW YORK

At noon appeared at the office the Consul General of Brazil in New York, carrying with him a beautiful decoration, a big blue and white cross, making me, as he said, entitled hereafter to be addressed as "Comendador" of the Order of Rio Branco. Berent, who was with him, brought word that I was to propose just the kind of Brazil-TVA I thought was desirable, and not worry too much whether other agencies of the Government would fight it. The President will settle that part. Well, we shall see.

JANUARY 23, 1973
NEW YORK

Lyndon Johnson dead. The very whirlwind of energy and believer in pressure has ended where all human beings end. And by some ironic twist he died just as an agreement to end hostilities (I didn't say the end of war) seems again close to a fact.

Now the judgments about Johnson, so bitter and mostly unfair, will be mellowed, in the good American tradition, by his death.

Odd how we behave, vengeful toward a man until he can no longer feel the bitterness and vindictiveness, then all schmaltz and sentiment when he is no longer around to hear it.

How tawdry and shoddy are those word-people of the press who vilified Nixon for not telling just exactly what was going on in the negotiations. This is my first, and unhappily rather negative and vengeful reaction to the glad tidings just announced by the President on TV.*

What I say should be about the moral issue that now confronts this country, the *opportunity* to once more demonstrate the compassion, the concern for those in need, turning our backs on those who speak only words of ugly criticism.

A time to be affirmative, positive, hopeful, to look ahead.

JANUARY 25, 1973
NEW YORK

There is more to life for me than my work: I need to remind myself of this more than most people for the simple reason that my "work" is itself a way of life. I thought of this last night as, with the two beautiful Tobeys as our hosts at supper and at Alice Tully Hall, we drank in the delicacy, the grace, and the glory of an evening of Bach arias. I thought Helen enjoyed it very particularly, and that alone makes me happy.

After the concert we came back to the hotel in time to hear Charles Collingwood's *Perspective on Vietnam.* This included excerpts from Kissinger's press conference of yesterday morning, and parts of what I said when Charles interviewed me recently. (Though he did "use" much of that filming, he had to leave out some bits that I thought were good, because deeply felt.)

Much of the comment by Sevareid was on what I had said about America's moral responsibility to herself, to her own standards of compassion. Sevareid particularly endorsed my impromptu conclusion that rebuilding Vietnam would not be too difficult a task.

JANUARY 27, 1973
PRINCETON

Spent most of yesterday and today thinking about and writing my convictions about American policy toward the reconstruction of Southeast Asia. The piece is 90% done, with that wonderful Helen stepping right in to type the rough, after making some good suggestions as I read it aloud to her this noon, over our sherry.

*The cease-fire in Vietnam.

Many of the ideas—indeed, the central one—is what I said, quite impromptu, in the Collingwood interview on TV. But I added one thought I hope will attract some agreement, or controversy—anyway, attention.

It is a warning that we must not let this postwar period be one of recriminations and vilification of those people with whom we have gravely disagreed about the war.

JANUARY 29, 1973
NEW YORK

It is a pleasure and a delight to watch a skilled editor sharpen up—by striking sentences or paragraphs and thereby increasing the force—what is written. This I witnessed once again sitting with Harrison Salisbury for only thirty minutes while he read and suggested specific ways to cut and, therefore, concentrate the impact of the Op-Ed piece I put together over the weekend.

He will use it soon. For the Vietnam issue is, as Harrison said, "front and center" these days.

I was stubborn about the final paragraphs. And no wonder. For the *Times* itself has contributed to the "mutual recrimination." The analogy to Reconstruction days after the Civil War he thought wasn't justified; I did.

Salisbury asked, "Do you really believe that if the fever of emotion subsides this hatred and revenge will not also subside?" I didn't think so.

So the piece may appeal to others as well.

JANUARY 30, 1973
ABOUT TO TAKE OFF FOR RIO

Within D&R as it now is, I feel better than for some time. Partly because I clarified my own role as the one who will decide whatever is to be decided—no more of this experiment with a "consultative system," or a troika of men with such widely different backgrounds and experience as Seymour, Pampanini, and myself.

FEBRUARY 2, 1973
FLYING TO ARACÁJU IN THE STATE OF SERGIPE,
NOT FAR FROM THE MOUTH OF THE SÃO FRANCISCO RIVER

Now we begin seven days of traversing the full length of the river we are supposed to convert to a kind of miraculous Paradise. The height of these expectations is going to be a serious handicap, but also these hopes and expectations give an importance to the work that should help get up the steam of action; the rhetoric is already at full throttle.

On Wednesday, postwar development of Vietnam became first-page news, with a statement from the President and the dispatch of Kissinger to Hanoi.

This morning's Rio papers spread that story—a Marshall Plan for Southeast Asia—all over the first page.

No one has asked me about participating, directly or through D&R, should all this flurry become more than chatter. But at least I have once more planted my flag on terrain where I am most comfortable and best known: the ethical principle I believe must underlie reconstruction, or the relief of poverty, or whatever.

How should the development of the São Francisco be carried on; or more precisely, what kind of agency should be created that can "integrate" the many and disparate parts of development? *Or,* should we leave things as they are; say that the way things are presently organized— "sectorally" as the economist says—is doing just dandy and should not be disturbed by any nonsense about the need to have the sector pieces put together into a unified or integrated way?

Of course, proposing a change that would diminish or affect the way things are will always arouse objection, as I know so well looking back on the various fights with the Washington departments in the early TVA days.

Why should this Government reach out for me, one who stands for a different way of developing a region than the "sectoral" one, if they didn't consider that with the present method the full potential of that vast region isn't being reached?

I committed one of my not infrequent outbursts yesterday, at the conference table in the Ministry of Interior where we were meeting.

The river, said I, is being most successfully developed for one resource and one only: vast amounts of cheap hydroelectricity. That power is being almost entirely exported to other parts of the country, outside the Valley. That is being well done.

Isn't this a kind of internal colonial exploitation? And isn't it settling for far less than the Valley is capable of producing?

Frederiksen slipped me a copy of the approved budget for the São Francisco undertaking. I was supposed to grunt OK. But it was far from OK. I want the number of "part-time specialists" cut down by one third or a half. These characters come in for a couple weeks or a month, cost

Brazil a huge amount, file a report that they could, for the most part, write without leaving their desks. I'm fed up with this phony business.

The resident staff are paid very substantial salaries, probably more than, with their record and competence, they would be getting in private employment in the U.S.

Add up all this and allowances and benefits, and they are receiving more than I get for holding down two jobs, President and Chairman, and producing almost all the business that keeps the company going.

It is Brazil—and the other countries we serve—that foots the bill for such cushy employment contracts.

And exemption from most U.S. income taxes to encourage people to work in a hardship post, such as Rio, for God's sake!

This goes on with all American contracts everywhere, I'm told, which doesn't make it any less questionable to me. And probably the U.S. Government agencies do much the same.

PENEDO

A flight in a splendid Varig plane to Aracáju, then into an automobile and a fast ride, northeast, for hours and hours; a stop at the fascinating primitive town of Propriá, where I saw the only "navigation" on one of the greatest of South American rivers. Sailboats without keels carrying rice and charcoal to the shore, where it is unloaded on men's backs into tiny two-wheeled donkey carts. I hope we make something important out of moving things on this great river. We did on the Tennessee and it wasn't much less primitive. Sand and gravel with wheezy old tugs and barges.

This time we saw people and cattle. The country is very rolling, much of it green with acacia bushes. Even now, at the end of the dry season, a great many puny cattle. Brazil, I was told, ranks fourth among the cattle-raising countries of the world.

So cattle are important even though almost nothing whatever has yet been done to improve forage or improve the breeds, or provide supplementary feeding. I was told in the early TVA days: you can't raise cattle in that Valley—too hot. Now it is one of the greatest prize beef cattle regions in the U.S.

That didn't "just happen" because of any speeches we made. We worked at it. And if they will work at it here, with some guidance and perhaps encouragement and inspiration from us, this and other "impossible" things can be made to happen.

Frontier is the feeling this great expanse of almost unoccupied country gives one.

FEBRUARY 3, 1973
PENEDO

A terribly hot, wearing day, first, in the Cessna to Propriá, then following the great river to Paulo Afonso Dam. It was worth it; for one thing, the Paulo Afonso cataracts seen from the air, flying low in the cramped Cessna, from Penedo, then on the ground, seeing the dam and the unbelievably violent spilling water—like a dozen Niagara Falls it seemed to me. There was something wild, untamed, about the way the water that did not go through the turbines came charging, savagely, from a dozen spillways.

I couldn't sleep properly—or improperly, as it turned out, naturally —because of the heat. So I set out about six to look for a market. And found a remarkable one at the foot of the hill. Even at six it was crowded with country people displaying their mangoes, cut meat (unrefrigerated, of course), great sacks of corn, some of it milled fine, sacks of manioca. The people paid not the slightest attention to the tall guy, obviously a foreigner, in his butter-yellow short-sleeved shirt. Along the quay, perhaps five hundred people waiting for the ferry or for small canoes to carry their chickens, bedsteads, reed mats, fish traps, etc., across to the other shore.

FEBRUARY 4, 1973
PETROLINA

What really concerned me was whether, with the kind of staff we have, D&R could come up to the needs, to say nothing of the expectations, of those who brought us here.

The "judgment" that is involved is an important one. It deals with nothing less than the kind of "findings" and "recommendations" we can make, a week from tomorrow, to the question: how should Brazil so organize the development work in this vast and notorious Valley so as to bring out its greatest possibilities?

Yesterday I saw a great engineering spectacle, the beginning of the harnessing of the São Francisco River at the point where the river falls several hundred feet into a deep and rugged canyon. The organization that planned this, and that has other plans and works under way to increase the electrical output of Paulo Afonso several times, must be a substantial and able institution. Would the country, and the asset of this remarkable river, be better off by putting the power development inside some other agency, with the delays and second-guessing this might involve?

Integration and unification of development can be achieved without central control. That is the chief lesson of TVA, during its forty years of development. One region can be successfully developed even though in all other parts of the country the same resources are developed on a national basis.

FEBRUARY 5, 1973
BOM JESUS DE LAPA

Today had a great deal of the kind of interest that means the most to me.

So often I complain that on such trips to see what can be done I say: but you didn't take me to the *back* country. That complaint would not fit this trip, and particularly this day. People not picturesque, but poor. Land that was poor but inviting development. A valley as green as the Tennessee Valley with the blue haze of the rim of mountains that encircle the broad valleys there.

FEBRUARY 6, 1973
TRES MARIAS DAM

What does it add up to? What can we do—what can *I* do, since it is to me that they look for a stirring idea to tie it all together?

Can this river do for this great inland empire of Brazil what we of TVA made the Tennessee River do for the industrial and municipal development it touched?

And yet.

This river, they say, doesn't go anywhere. It has no real outlet to the sea. We flew over the mouth, over a huge sand bar reaching out into the ocean. The river has dams that block the use for shipping, except with fantastically expensive locks. Since power is the dominant use, irrigation will have difficulty getting a good share of water, to say nothing of the problem of maintaining a deeper channel for (presently non-existent) navigation.

Highways and ordinary country roads are badly needed—this is obvious.

I don't find that my chief technical staff, smart as they are in their particular expertise (or at least the jargon that goes with irrigation, agriculture, power), have a broad enough understanding of resource development; they also lack the capacity to express themselves in words that persuade and move.

Can I turn over this offspring of mine to such less than outstanding leadership when I move on?

FEBRUARY 8, 1973
BRASÍLIA

Leitão de Abreu was all set to have me see the President. This was farther along than I thought we were.

I made a special point about the fellow who cannot bring his produce to market because there are no roads, or is a couple hundred miles from a veterinarian to treat his ailing cattle.

It is people like this that the present uncoordinated form of organization and administration is quite inadequate for. Leitão took this in, obviously much impressed when I said I thought this would be of the greatest concern to the President.

Even the well-heeled private investor wants to reduce the risk to him by having the Government provide an important part of the cost through canals and roads. Which is right and necessary. Otherwise nothing will come of it.

But the poor and often quite ignorant *small* guy is a private enterpriser too; you must reduce the risk for him too, by providing a modest road and access, and bringing the rural credit facilities close enough to him so he can make use of them. Sometimes he must travel several hundred miles to make his credit application. The same for veterinary service.

So, whether they are big or small like the struggling farmer way back in those little squares of clearing we saw so often on this trip, they must have the Government reduce their risk, in many ways. Then they too can make headway.

FEBRUARY 13, 1973
BRASÍLIA

My "oral presentation" of our present views about "institutional changes" for the Valley of the São Francisco turned out to be quite successful, judging by the acceptance by Minister Cavalcanti of our major points. I made a point not to go into details.

The virtue of this kind of informal presentation of ideas is that an experienced guy can observe how his "story" is going, not press where, by facial expression of the listener, he can see that the point is understood, and go on to something else. Reading a written presentation means that you plow through things that need no elaboration. And it does not flatter a listener that you bear down on a point that he already understands, bear down on it because it is in that confounded written statement.

The central point of my discourse was that there needs to be an *overall* comprehensive direction to the Valley's development. This will be the theme of the written report, still in draft form.

This will step on a good many toes, chiefly the powerful and well-run public power companies who have had almost complete control of the principal asset of the Valley, the energy in its waters. To put any limitation on this long-established regime will take much persuasion, or the force of Presidential edict, or, more likely, some kind of compromise, a balance which we should be experienced enough to devise. Or try to.

But the court of *first* resort, the Minister of Interior, Costa Cavalcanti, got the point, expressed agreement. To my surprise the present head of the Valley agency, Colonel Wilson Santa Cruz, was in agreement with our thesis, seemed pleased that in us he had an ally, though our recommendation called for a phasing out of SUVALE.

The written report will be ready before I leave on Thursday.

The language problem is always with me in discussing ideas that are not readily explained even by one sophisticated English-speaking person to another, much less when I make my points to a man whose English is good enough for ordinary purposes but where the nuances of organizational matters are hard to transmit.

The hours I spent on the speech for Geneva—though the speech was entirely ignored in the U.S. press—have helped greatly to carry over to the Brazilians, and I hope Iranians, what my oral discourse in English can't do. The Geneva Speech was translated on the initiative of Rubens Vaz da Costa and published in an attractive paperback, read widely, and appeared in full in five different leading Brazilian newspapers. Part of that speech was given over to the unified approach. So it isn't as if most of these people—including the President—who have little or no English, haven't had some considerable exposure, in their own language, to these fundamental ideas.

Part of my responsibility as a man of experience and of a certain reputation is helping those I work with to feel their importance; to do this they must be "included in," as the Goldwyn phrase, turned around, would have it. This was why I wangled it so that Frederiksen went with me for an hour with Leitão de Abreu, and then by just avoiding all attention to "permission" or protocol, I simply took him with me to see President Medici a half-hour ago. Frederiksen says he needs to learn about many things, and never a truer word was spoken. The inside workings of the high levels of government and of business are a total blank to him. Out of this I hope he will develop a kind of confidence that will show in his manner.

Them as shall be nameless cannot say that today I fell again into my nascent defect: diffidence. When the General Adjutant opened the great door to the President's office, I charged across the almost fifty yards with a swinging stride, shoulders back, big grin. After an enthusiastic *abraço,* a big dimpled smile of welcome, he said to the Chief of Protocol, "He looks younger than last year."

FEBRUARY 14, 1973
BRASÍLIA

My son is a writer, a professional, but I only write journals as the impressions come to me.

To be a writer I would have to meet my emotions face to face, not casually and at random, as in the occasional journal entries in which I say, or try to say, how I feel. I would have to tear the words out of myself painfully and with precision, not just dash them off. I put words together, and occasionally a phrase or even a sentence has the touch of a writer's instincts and even skill. But when I disclaim, quite honestly, that I cannot be called a writer, I speak the truth. And this despite all the words I write and all the pages of those words that have been put into books.

FEBRUARY 15, 1973
GALEÃO AIRPORT, RIO

Dr. Rubens Vaz da Costa, head of the National Housing Bank, said he agreed with our recommendations about an overall agency for the São Francisco Valley.

I got the impression that the word may have gone out that the President is prepared to do something about the improved organization of development in the Valley and is only waiting until he can point to this "distinguished expert" and his opinion to justify it.

FEBRUARY 27, 1973
NEW YORK

Trying hard to analyze the energy issue, as it unfolds. It strikes me as a good example, offhand, of the need for a unified approach, my special theme for so many years. A big enterprise, not a bunch of isolated non-related pickings at the phase of the problem that is at the top of the heap.

A strange, a foreboding encounter, my luncheon meeting with Walter Levy this noon. He is recognized as "one of the world's leading oil economists." Only rarely does one see a considerable intellect—and he is certainly that, in his field—who has become a crusader; a Cassandra with a Viennese accent. His profound conviction is that a terrible confrontation, a kind of war, impends between those nations—the oil-producing nations, chiefly Iran and Saudi Arabia—who have the Western world by the very throat, and the Western nations who must have that oil in order to live but are, as he puts it, being coerced and dictated to, not negotiated with. The issue is one of naked power.

Walter's prescription of what to do about this is candid and frightening: the Western world, including Japan, must join together to resist. The result at present is completely "unacceptable." Does this mean war? "War" is the term the producing nations use, says Walter.

I listened attentively. Said I wondered if he realized the political aspects of such a position? Yes, he did. He was making a campaign of it. At Amsterdam in late March he will talk to the European Common Market countries urging resistance on a common front.

MARCH 1, 1973
WASHINGTON

However much the diplomat Jahangir Amuzegar is in appearance, certainly in two hours of talk at lunch he demonstrated again a trait of the well-educated and privileged Iranians of his generation. I spoke of concern lest there be a "confrontation"—a "ganging up" as he put it—of the Western oil companies and their governments to maintain some balance with the producing countries, something that Walter Levy had elaborated upon. This could cause havoc, I said, for everyone.

Yes, said Amuzegar, it is possible but quite unlikely because "the majors"—the big American and British oil companies—have reached agreement and are not likely to take or join in any such step.

Amuzegar seemed composed and unconcerned. "The majors are very close to the Nixon Administration," said he. Then I said there was a new factor, the threat to the stability of the international monetary system and the U.S. balance of trade of these huge cash payments chiefly to Saudi Arabia and Iran.

He agreed, this would add a new dimension. But there would be ample room for "accommodation."

AT UNION STATION, WAITING (IMPATIENTLY)
FOR A TRAIN HOME

Even in the midst of World War II there wasn't anything like the outward display of "security" I observed around the White House this noon. Neat, smoothfaced young officers in dazzling blue uniforms, with sidearms sticking out all over them. Then it occurred to me that Golda Meir, Prime Minister of Israel, is having a meeting with Nixon this noon.

Of all the statements about our dependence upon the Middle East for our very life, none impressed and depressed me more than an impatient comment by Bob McNamara. I had commented that in addition to everything else in this complex issue, there was the fierce antagonism of the Arab states to Israel, with the U.S. tied to Israel's survival by many commitments, including arms and culture.

McNamara said he had just returned from visiting Kuwait and Saudi Arabia, hoping he could persuade them to purchase World Bank bonds (Kuwait did buy seventy-five million). I said this was fine, but those countries, if they invested in the World Bank, would expect a big quid pro quo.

Suddenly he burst out, this slender man with the rimless eyeglasses, sitting there coatless as is his custom.

"I spent twenty-five minutes listening to King Faisal pouring hatred and scorn of the most venomous kind on Israel," he said. "If we are dependent upon the Saudis for our fuel—and more than half will come from them—we will find we must pay for it in more than dollars."

A grim statement, while the White House prepared at that very moment just down the street to receive the little, wizened Milwaukee school teacher who is the Prime Minister of Israel.

MARCH 4, 1973
PRINCETON

Said Jahangir Amuzegar, by phone, "I have thought further about what you said to me at lunch the other day. You may be right about the possibility of a confrontation by the Western oil-consuming countries, a joining together to hold down the terms of the oil-producing countries, such as Iran.

"I want to be guided by your counsel that Iran should present its case to the American and Western countries. You recommended this more than two years ago. I didn't believe it should be taken seriously and neither did my Government.

"But on thinking it over, I think you may be right.

"We would like to have your advice at every step," he continued. "You see, we Iranians have come to trust you more than any other foreigner. And no wonder; you have never misled us."

MARCH II, 1973
PRINCETON

Tonight a deep, all-enveloping fog. Serene. It smooths out all the sharp reality, replacing it with the even greater reality of a dream world. The arms of the big apple tree beside our front door seem to float. The intricate maze of the branches of the tall locusts weave softly in the fog, like the fronds of seaweed or coral, in a deep grotto of the ocean, seen as one dives into the down-under.

This afternoon Helen and I went to the Art Museum to see the much-publicized Norton Simon art collection. A Bellini portrait I thought great, strong and real. But for most of the rest, I wonder why all the fuss.

Bidding up the price of art objects by these merger experts and grocery-chain characters has done the world of art no good. You don't judge the value of a work of art, or music, by what some accidentally rich man is willing to bid for it against the bid of an equally undiscerning and almost equally rich guy, both of them making their bids and their judgment after getting the advice of . . . their tax-evasion lawyers.

MARCH I2, 1973
PRINCETON

The only "news" that is really important is the account Dr. Haynes recited to me this afternoon, after one of his characteristically thorough examinations: you are in splendid health. *Every* basic factor.

Dr. Gottlieb, head of the Princeton Forrestal Lab—the center of fusion research—is a great big man with an enormous and handsome head, long partly grey locks, strong face, and penetrating eyes. I listened to his explanation of what they have been doing with the $35 million invested in capital and how much more in operations in that strange place and felt: The man has management sense as well as being a scientist par excellence.

I was most impressed with the fact that he doesn't regard his laboratory and fusion prospects as the only things that count; it is part of the broad picture of American need for fuel: that the continued dependence upon the Middle East, or even on the oil companies, should make everyone realize at long last that this is not an issue that will simply go away.

The gadgetry at this laboratory is fantastic. Even the measuring devices are complex beyond anything in the Manhattan Project or its successors. The great heavy ribbons of beautiful copper for the containering magnets, the manufacturing competence of that university labora-tory—more like a 21st century factory than a part of a university.

Quite an experience.

MARCH 19, 1973
NEW YORK

Said Polly Bunting:† "I like the idea of a dinner at one on Sunday. It has quite a tradition behind it—the time when the minister was invited for a chicken dinner with the family. When I was an intern at Johns Hopkins it was the time when we all got together, and if there were personal grievances or irritations, we got them out—at Sunday dinner—at one."

This was at our 88 Battle Road dining-room table, festooned with that fabulous lace tablecloth, a gift from Bernardine, the ironing of which was one of Margaret Morton's delights.

Polly is a delight. She is now an assistant to Princeton's new presi-dent, with, I gather, rather vague responsibilities thus far. "Yes, it is different than when I was at Radcliffe. But a switch I find is a good thing. And it couldn't be better than to be at Princeton at this particular time."

"President" Bowen seemed more like the name he preferred: Bill. He seems like "Bill," but he wears the toga of one of the most distinguished of American universities and has made a notable beginning. How young he seemed, down the table at Helen's right hand, at ease, talking with such vigor and without the caution and circumspection that so often is the case with men who head a faculty, the most cantankerous of all bodies of men to administer, much less manage.

Bowen has exactly what is often referred to but rarely exists: an open countenance. And such good sense. What he said about the row going on in the Institute for Advanced Study right across the way was so wise, so mature and understanding. He questioned as I do the basic concept of the Institute, that there is a virtue in men being completely free of any responsibilities—to teach a class, to advise students, to meet a deadline. Of course, they become inward to a degree, and being inward, become "arrogant"—his word (one I would endorse).

MARCH 20, 1973
NEW YORK

A visit with Berent Friele this morning brought news that I found surprising—and satisfying. Ludwig is in "deep trouble" in Brazil—Lud-wig, who showed me that he thinks I am just a soft-headed idealist,

†Former president of Radcliffe College.

Ludwig the 19th century exploiter, the super-tough big shot in the Amazon, with three million acres of land, a fiefdom along the Jari River. How did this happen?

President Medici, the four-star General, visited Ludwig's operations on the Jari, and was shocked and dismayed at the treatment of the working force, the terrible living conditions, the miserable wages, the rising discontent among the working people.

Said Berent: By contrast he visited Antunes' operations in magnesium and iron, and found good living conditions, schools, health services.

On his visit to Antunes at Amapá, the President hardly listened to the recitation about magnesium; he spent his time looking into living and working conditions.

Berent pointed to the Portuguese translation of my Geneva Speech, with its emphasis on human beings. That was why the President and Leitão de Abreu liked that speech so much.

Whenever an American enterprise produces a bad impression overseas, it affects all foreigners adversely. But it is one more confirmation of a sound principle, for me at least: to say my say, express my convictions, and try to demonstrate by my actions that I mean exactly what I say.

MARCH 24, 1973
PRINCETON

Mary Davis had us to an impromptu cocktail affair last evening for Ken Keating, a Harvard Law School classmate of Wendell's and mine, former Senator from New York.

He is a personal friend and political associate of Nelson Rockefeller. Nelson will probably again run for the Republican nomination for President, so Ken opined (probably a guess, but an informed one). "When you get that political bug in your system, nothing can cure it." Yes, said George Gallup, at my elbow: "Political ambition is a terminal disease." Which I didn't think was bad.

MARCH 25, 1973
PRINCETON

I have become so accustomed to the idea of having had several careers that it came as something of a surprise last evening—dinner at the Bentleys—that there are some people I respect who consider that side of my life something remarkable. More than remarkable, worthy of emulating.

So I was struck that Bob Goheen should remark on this, because he has done that very thing. When he took the presidency of Princeton, he said it should be for fifteen years only. Now, having resigned after a most fertile and productive tenure, he is in the midst of another and in most ways very different career: head of a Council of Foundations. And at a difficult time for foundations, for Congress has put them under a severe set of regulations.

MARCH 28, 1973
NEW YORK

From my western windows I am looking out on one of the choicest views in all of New York, perhaps of anywhere: the setting sun, orange and gold, lighting up a low bank of clouds on the farther side of the Hudson. But this is the last time I shall see this particular view: next week D&R will be moved to the Time & Life Building (to an office I haven't yet seen), and one more episode in my working career will have come to a close, a new one opened.

In the past I have been unhappy and restless about *any* move, whether to a new office or a new job or a new home. This time I am not fussing about it at all. Steadily the concept of reducing the size and importance of the central office of D&R has taken hold, the concept of having most of the staff where the work is going on. This move is in a way symbolic of that change.

APRIL 1, 1973
PRINCETON

A vigorous walk in a half-rain, half-mist. How the garden must love it. And I do too.

The circle of trees of the flowering crab—on the Common—has turned green. I stopped to touch and almost fondle the stubby early leaves. Along each of the branches a string of droplets. No necklace of pearls could be more beautiful, for these are fresh and alive, against the dark of the twigs. I brought out a box of grass seed; dusting it on open patches of the lawn, watching the grey wisps of seed float and scatter and lie on the open ground—what a good feeling to be planting in a rain.

APRIL 3, 1973
PRINCETON

Happy Birthday to Helen—and a beautiful early spring day it is to express joy on such a day.

We go to New York for a fancy luncheon at the St. Regis, to the Tobeys for a drink and supper (and if I know Beatrice, a birthday cake and candles, for she is a great celebrator of events) and to the theatre.

APRIL 4, 1973
NEW YORK

Yesterday in California, Nixon and Thieu issued a joint communiqué with a strong statement on U.S. support for a major reconstruction effort. Will this signal our return? Seems doubtful, since the Nixon Administration is very Party conscious and I am a Democrat.

APRIL 5, 1973
NEW YORK

Planning—other than physical planning—is a *political* process. Therefore, the extremes of close intellectual analysis, the setting out of the illusive overcertainties of numbers and precise categories, are not relevant to the kind of planning we are undertaking to do for the lives of the people of the São Francisco Valley.

A political process: what does this mean? It means making goals and methods plain to people whose lives will be affected, persuading them by making things clear to them, not just clear to the technicians but to the people.

How many times I have said and written something of this kind. And yet I found this afternoon that I had to explode to our little group working on the São Francisco. I have been through this process of "upsetting" technical, overeducated people for so long, so long.

But I shouldn't be discouraged. For Walter Rocha came all the way from São Paulo to talk to me for four hours, an outgrowth of a similar oral chastening I gave him last Christmastime and again in Rio in February. *"Now,"* said he, over a long luncheon discussion, "now I understand what you mean." As a consequence he has resigned from his engineering firm, Serete, persuaded an investment bank to support a new company he has formed to pursue "how to make things happen through ideas"—his quote of me. So while it is often uphill work, these ideas do "take," some of the time.

I am trying to overcome and counterbalance the narrow but efficient kind of technical education these men get. Said I: "Read poetry; poetry may be more important in understanding what makes things happen in this world than logarithms."

APRIL 13, 1973
PRINCETON

I should never forget (and those who observe me should not forget): things don't *always* work out for me, lucky as I am. Don't work out in my work or my health or spirit.

What I would like to believe—do believe—is that "with a little help from my friends" (in the words of the old Beatles song) I become balanced and sensible again.

In scanning portions of Adolf Berle's diary or journal, I see that even he had times that were not consistent with his best side. I was glad that Beatrice Berle, who edited his journals, didn't cut out all of these less than worthy passages. A man who has the good luck to take a leading role in public affairs or private undertakings should be permitted to growl, or feel sorry for himself, or even be hateful at times, or vain, or jealous— these are human qualities that link him to his fellows.

APRIL 21, 1973
PRINCETON

Spring in all its glory, the glory of growing things. For me this means digging into the stubborn clay and making it fit for the roots of my new roses, patrolling the whole circle of the perennial border to speak to every old plant-friend and encourage the new. Watching Helen sitting by the side of the border moving her beloved forget-me-nots, which cast a blue haze over much of the border, finding an open space for the ones that are crowded, digging out the weeds. When I came on her whacking away I was about to say how hard she was working, but before I could go into that routine, she smiled up at me and said: "I am having such a good time."

APRIL 25, 1973
AT THE NASHVILLE, TENNESSEE, AIRPORT

The whole range and the variety of contemporary life: it is all there in the Tennessee Valley; so I have always thought. What we witnessed since Helen and I arrived in this Valley Sunday night confirms that feeling with an impact from which I am still reeling.

Here was an undertaking grown vast and full of meaning, which I had the good luck and toughness to start so many years ago.

The warmth toward me of old friends or people who worked with me and reminded me of what I had said to them, long ago and well remembered; the excitement of seeing young men take over and carry on, with the same vitality, creativeness, and intensity that the organization showed when I was around.

The theme of TVA remains much the same; the application of that underlying theme (or themes) changed as conditions changed, as new ideas came along. What a heartwarming experience this has been.

APRIL 27, 1973
DRIVING TO TRENTON

What greatly concerns the American media these days is one of the strangest twists in the troubled skein of contemporary American life. Even stranger than the wild preoccupation with the price of steak of a week or so ago (not the components of the price for meat, nor the causes of that cost, nor inflationary spiral as a peril—but that one commodity).

Today, and for the past few days, it is what is now known simply as Watergate. An apartment hotel in Washington where I stayed now and then in that city I find so repulsive. But Watergate today is the code word for the most self-righteous outcries about the ethics, not to say the criminal conduct, of the men around a President just the other day elected by the largest popular vote in the history of the Republic!

These White House staffers now cringing before the storm of innuendo of wrong-doing and stupidity are the very same who ten days or so ago—give or take a few weeks—were on the cover of the news magazines as the stern, strong, powerful, dedicated new breed Nixon had brought out of private business life to "manage" the country. Their every personal characteristic and habit of life was mulled over by the journalists and the second-guessers among the columnists.

Today their name is "mud," a sticky slimy excrescence.

How many times I have seen something of this sort. I used to say that having a public man's picture on the cover of *Life* was the "kiss of death." Although it didn't happen to me after the *Time* cover story about me, for example, it did happen to many. It accounts for my leaning way back, trying to keep a low profile, because the reward for a good public job is not the blatant snow job of a lyric magazine piece but the satisfaction of a job well done.

APRIL 29, 1973
AT KENNEDY AIRPORT, WAITING TO BOARD VARIG FOR RIO

It says something about TVA that Red Wagner has been reappointed for a nine-year term as TVA Chairman—by a Republican President.

(It tells something about changes in the value of the dollar in the intervening years since the early thirties that my government salary as

Chairman was $10,000 a year, Red's is $40,000 today.)

Wagner is a very competent man, of this there can be no doubt. Indeed, in an extemporaneous speech in Decatur I said he was the "most competent Chairman TVA has ever had." What I meant—though I didn't expand on the statement—was that he had a good generalist's command of the basic facts about one of the broadest-ranging enterprises this country has seen, next only to what I faced when I took over (or was "took over" by) the AEC in '46. The largest power system in the country, a pioneer in nuclear technology and in the techniques of environmental protection; a chemical engineering program of the broadest scope and magnitude; a big dam-building program with the labor relations problems that go with it; a financial burden that is huge, borrowing hundreds of millions of dollars in the private capital market and therefore having to take responsibility for interest costs and the timing of offerings. A novel program of education, and of outdoor recreation.

To grasp this, to be able to explain it to Congressional Committees, to deal with the natural grumbling of more than 150 municipalities when their rates are raised, as they must be with rising costs, to be responsible for reclamation of the devastation caused by strip mining, a lively and usually acrimonious issue throughout the country—all this and more adds up to a monumental burden.

He carries all this with surprising good humor and composure. In private—and in his recent conversations with me he grew steadily more open with me—he does resent much of the criticism that is coming his way. In public he shows himself a confident man doing his job. But the extremes of the environmentalists, quite simply, "get his goat." In his internal burning about criticism, he reminds me of Gordon Clapp, who kept his temper in public but was deeply hurt or violently angry at times.

Red spoke of many instances of the nonsense of those who long for the simple life, and are articulate about it, but are as foolish and unrealistic as people can get. For example, a letter from a college student who wrote of the "inherent richness of rural poverty," which the TVA rural program was destroying.

So absorbed have I been the last few days since we returned from the trip to the Valley that I have not yet written about that visit.

In the perspective of a few days on the scores of happy episodes, what stands out?

Item: The new Decatur elementary school meant so much to me, because in a specific way it showed that the leadership of Decatur (chiefly my dear friend Barrett Shelton) was not solely concerned with new industries and added income—a result they have achieved in an extraordinary way, as a trip along the waterfront industrial area makes so vivid. The education of children is what the new income is used for, black and white together, and the way that is taken for granted pleased me enormously.

Another outstanding impression is in a lighter vein: In the vast new concrete fortress of the Browns Ferry atomic energy plant in North Alabama—out on the bare reaches of what was once a cotton field—the young man who will carry the awful responsibility of its operations showed us the great control room, the eyes of the many dials peering at the human intruders. At the center of the great bow of control devices, what looked like the board of some game. Each of the buttons numbered, corresponding to the nuclear uranium assembly way down below in the bowels of the impatient monster.

I knew that if anything goes wrong there must be some way quickly to change the rods of uranium and stop the "reaction." Above the checkerboard a row of four brilliant red buttons, and on each the single word SCRAM.

I liked this further evidence of the inventiveness of the American half-slang language, which produced Jeep, for example. But SCRAM. These are referred to quite seriously and with no grins by the operators.

Of a different kind: How impressed we both were by the emphasis on and preoccupation with education in the Land Between the Lakes wilderness project, the almost 200,000 acres in the long peninsula between the vastness of Kentucky Lake and the neighboring and contiguous Barkley Lake.

Thousands of young people from several states come to this beautiful place to camp and hike, yes, but accompanied by their teachers to learn about the natural wonders of an almost untouched region.

VARIG—8:30 AIRBORNE; NEXT STOP RIO

Red's difficult public posture, as he carries on this great task, throws a curious ironic light on the change in TVA since my day as an original Director and its most influential pathfinder and protector—which is essentially the job of the Chairman. I used to say that it was my job to be the fighting buffer, protecting the working staff from the onslaughts of Congress, the press, and the utilities, so they could get the work done—and this was notably true in my AEC Chairmanship.

The differences between Red's problems, between those he must fight off so the work can go on, and mine, are striking.

The utilities together with the Washington centralized bureaucracy were my most obvious and flamboyant foes. I represented the vanguard of Socialism or worse, the promoter and operator of public ownership.

Now Jim Watson, TVA's Manager of Power, has been made head of the Electric Power Research Institute, a combination of the utilities and

TVA to find new sources of power—nuclear, coal. The organization, long talked about ineffectually, was actually brought to pass by TVA leadership. That fight is over.

Similarly with the fertilizer industry. How they beat at TVA—and me. Now they are in bed with TVA. More than that, they depend, openly and not out of the side of their mouth, upon the national chemical research program at the Shoals—it has become a fertilizer industry darling.

In my time we had staunch Congressional fighters for TVA—Norris [of Nebraska], of course, but also men from the Valley: Hill, Kefauver, Sparkman, Barkley. Now Red tells me there is hardly a voice raised in support of unpopular things TVA must do—surface mining of coal, raising rates, etc.

I gave Red no advice. But I managed to say what he didn't need to be told, that where he thinks he is right, he must just put his head down and go plowing ahead, support or no support. And I think he will.

At over six hundred miles an hour I am being propelled toward a tough job: facing a group of Brazilian governmental vested interests and explaining why, in the interest of their country, they should happily agree to have their jurisdictional toes tramped on. How to present our proposal for a São Francisco corporation that will be persuasive—quite a task. But I'll try it.

MAY 1, 1973
RIO DE JANEIRO

In theory, after a long flight (over nine hours) one should not try to do any work for a full day. Yesterday morning and afternoon I went right at it, reviewing drafts of all we should give the Ministry of Interior's Council, examining our recommendations about reorganizing the structure for the development of the São Francisco.

MAY 2, 1973
RETURNING TO RIO FROM BRASÍLIA

A memorable day. The first and major part of the São Francisco responsibility presented to the (previously doubting) Comissão of the Ministry of Interior with great success, confirmed later by the Minister, Cavalcanti, and his deputy.

More than that, Leitão de Abreu, in a morning meeting, approved the basic idea of a unified agency for the whole Valley.

As a next step I urged the Minister to get a small group from the affected Ministries to work, at once, on a draft of a statute. A timetable was set up—proposed legislation to be ready for Congress by July 1st, the new agency to be in being by January 1st.

MAY 3, 1973
RIO

After a period of almost exultation over the excitement of turning a country's development policies almost 180° into a new course, seeing people completely different from those I would see in the retired quiet of Princeton, or stirring up a staff with a combination of ideas, zoom, and laughter as I did today, I realize that this kind of life is, as the kids now say, "my thing."

MAY 12, 1973
PRINCETON

Hard work in the garden and even harder work at the typewriter. Filling in some of the bare spaces with some of the most graceful columbine I have ever seen. Writing an informal synopsis, in the form of a letter to a *New York Times* man, of my idea of how to go about making up the inadequacy of fuel and power supply. So I sit here with my sweaty blue shirt and wet corduroy knees, muddy hands, joining together two of the kinds of work I most enjoy—ideas and making the spring garden a thing of delight.

MAY 13, 1973
PRINCETON

Helen listened to my letter to the *New York Times* describing the article on energy. She has an uncanny way of getting to the heart of things. How quickly she can spot one of my vague or non sequitur passages, and indicate how to correct it.

Frustrated as all get-out she has been since before I returned ten days ago. The reason: in gardening she did something to a sacroiliac joint, and has been in bed much of the time. Not in pain (she says) but playing it safe, which means no gardening and seeing me out there working away when she can't. I know the feeling.

MAY 17, 1973
NEW YORK

Ever since Dr. Haynes put me on a low-cholesterol diet I have been eating food not fit for a working man. At the pace I work and move about, it just isn't the right way to live.

MAY 19, 1973
PRINCETON

With the customary cooperation of Mother Nature, the annual garden party was really a great success. After a tumultuous couple days of high winds, raw weather, very cold, the day was beautiful, and the garden aglow. As interesting a group of people as ever we have had as guests, and a good mix: not just university and not just business associates. A social triumph for Helen and a gardening one for me.

MAY 22, 1973
NEW YORK

Now everything in the press and on TV is on one note: Watergate. Ugly as the story is, without a doubt, the newspapers and TV are blowing it up as if nothing of the kind had ever happened before.

And such self-righteousness: the editorials, the columnists, the pipsqueak journalists. Those who are behaving most rationally are the politicians.

The lesson of the Senator Joe McCarthy period hasn't been learned, quite obviously, except by members of the Senate.

MAY 29, 1973
NEW YORK

Every now and then it comes over me that I am doing the kind of work I am best fitted for, but that I may be in the wrong organization to do it. There is an aura of the tenure-protected servant, conventional-style; the snobbery about money matters for the Corporation; a preoccupation with salary, benefits, allowances for the individual—these and similar characteristics of a staid bureaucratic type make me wonder if I should not openly recognize that I should turn in my suit and go elsewhere.

Why can't an outfit that is capable of doing such great things for the public interest—as D&R has definitely done—also be carried on with something other than this above-the-battle atmosphere about finance, about arithmetic?

Just in passing I remarked to Pampanini that I noted that we are in good shape for cash, having just reduced our loan at the bank to $50,000 out of a credit of $250,000.

He said we really didn't "need" cash. But it isn't a matter of needing the cash; cash, money, has an *earning power,* particularly these days, and we should be getting it.

At one time as I recall D&R had retained earnings in excess of one million, which of course we invested and on which we earned a return. The fact that we don't need the cash—what the devil has that got to do with it?

I must be in the wrong kind of organization.

MAY 30, 1973
NEW YORK

A very long session today with Katsuhiko Takahashi, a puzzling person: Japanese in appearance but quite American in manner and style of thinking.

He confirmed my feeling that the conventional development pattern of service, with its emphasis on "consultation," is a sick business, whether being carried on by the World Bank with its multiple and repetitious Missions, or by the regular consulting organizations such as Arthur D. Little, which is advising Japan's Foreign Ministry on how to invest in the U.S.—as if they would know anything except the merest platitudes on that subject.

He said that the Japanese were no longer satisfied with fine, beautifully bound volumes of reports ("stacked this high and gathering dust") and wanted to combine feasibility studies, etc., with business and investment judgment and sources of funds—much the theme of the long memo I wrote last August, on the Vineyard, about the shortcomings of our agricultural program.

The reason Henry Wallace thought about hybrid corn—which revolutionized corn growing and, therefore, the great corn-hog industry—was that Henry was the kind of fellow who walked between the rows of corn, and thought: Why not shorter stalks and more ears? It is walking between the rows, in the fields, using the term literally but chiefly symbolically, that gives brilliant scientists and clever inventive men ideas for research and investigation that they wouldn't get in a lab.

Japan has problems, despite or perhaps because of its spectacular success and growth. American multinational companies have comparable problems in the process of grabbing off so much business throughout the world.

Success has a high price tag on it, as both Japanese and American multinational enterprises are learning.

JUNE 1, 1973
NEW YORK

A long and quite explicit letter from Walter Rocha in São Paulo yesterday—special delivery, plastered front and back with dozens of stamps—laid out a proposal in writing that startlingly reaffirmed an idea on the philosphy of development I wrote a memo about long ago, before the creation of D&R, but which I never was able to get André Meyer to move on—due to my tepid approach to him perhaps.

Or it may be, as Rodman wisely said the other day: Sometimes an important idea has to wait for the time when it is recognized and can be effective.

I do feel—even before breakfast—that this idea's time has come.

JUNE 3, 1973
PRINCETON

Watergate and its opposite number, the Pentagon Papers' theft, are products of the secrecy phobia as an essential ingredient of "national security" that goes back to a considerable extent to the Secret Atom period. For the excrescences of that period, through which I had to live, a casual look at Volume II of the *Journals* provides many examples. Nixon rose from deserved obscurity through the secrecy route—Alger Hiss et al. No reason to believe he has changed one whit. It worked before; he thinks it will work again. Let's hope not. But in destroying Nixon, don't destroy the country in the process, please.

JUNE 4, 1973
PRINCETON

Rocha has made it clear that what he wants is what I can contribute on the business judgment side, and by using my knowledge and acquaintance of American business and financial institutions and people. He tried to be polite when I reminded him that I am the founder of D&R and its chief officer, and he must take D&R, too.

He pointed out that there is nothing in D&R's engineering and agricultural expertise that qualifies it for the purposes of developing new business opportunities in Brazil in the way he and his bankers have in mind, or to put it less abstractly, "You do not have in the organization anyone else who can contribute."

Samii has made the same point about the long-discussed Iranian private-sector economic consulting organization, and similarly, though to a less explicit extent, so did the Japanese intermediary we saw the other day.

The long-term point is this: if it is not D&R but D.E.L. who will make the Brazil thing go—if it does—with considerable time and energy input from me virtually alone among the present D&R organization, and similarly the Iran idea, then since I must shift out of D&R someday—whether in a year or three years—why not set up a different kind of organization now, and act only as a consultant to D&R as occasion requires?

The *National Geographic* for this month has a long and richly prestigious article on the Tennessee Valley—"the peaceful Valley." Can this great achievement, so graphic and beautiful, possibly be what only forty years ago was, as Forrest Allen said, "something in Dave Lilienthal's briefcase"—as it almost literally was.

JUNE 6, 1973
NEW YORK

At dinner at the Tobeys, Barney said a most affecting thing, particularly from one who tends to be on the gloomy side.

He was quoting with great approval a fellow cartoonist he saw at the *New Yorker* cartoonists' weekly lunch, after they submitted their drawings and gags for the judgment of the art director.

"We artists are a lucky people. We see things other people don't; shapes and designs that to most people don't exist, we see. And if what we have done today, professionally, doesn't satisfy us and we are downcast about it, we know that tomorrow what we are striving to create in a drawing or painting may with a single stroke of the pen or brush come alive.

"Now, most people repeat tomorrow what they did today. Not artists. So we are lucky."

JUNE 10, 1973
PRINCETON

The mythology of disarmament. With the Russians descending on Washington to continue the SALT negotiations, this could be a time to recognize that preoccupation with weapons is not the road to peace, but a source of futility, frustration, emptiness, and worse: an intensification of the arms race.

I have just reread my Stafford Little Lectures on the subject—made in 1963, on the eve of the Geneva arms negotiations. With the substitution of Nixon, Washington, and SALT for Eisenhower and Geneva, it stands up. And particularly taken in connection with the equally startling prediction about the Chinese and the true road to peace, developing a sense of community through specific measures such as are now increasingly part of our relations with the Soviets and Chinese.

I said years ago that energy and fuel needs have been dealt with in a piecemeal and, therefore, ineffective way.

Now this is the subject of almost hysterical declarations on all sides. This is what I have been preaching during these years, including the basic proposition that our experience has shown that the "experts" in the academic and non-action world and among officialdom have been chronically underestimating the increasing need for electric energy and fuel.

My concern about the world having a better understanding of these problems makes me fidgety to begin major writing to include this set of ideas.

But why disturb the equanimity that I have earned? Why can't I be content to settle back to do my daily work, in itself a big undertaking?

JUNE 11, 1973
NEW YORK

I need to comprehend that D&R is the vehicle for carrying out the ideas, the drives, the purposes of my life. It is not just a business, to be given up if now and then I am bored or harried. It is the way I express what I have learned, what I believe, the faiths and dreams I have had during a long and very busy life.

It is a personal platform from which to affect minds and events; as its head it gives me a status that an emeritus, an elder statesman, does not have; as a man of action I command respect for ideas because I am part of an enterprise that has accomplishments to its credit and an ongoing action program.

JUNE 24, 1973
PRINCETON

Allen Bromberger arrived yesterday; he will drive Helen, and our summer things, to the Vineyard tomorrow.

Now eighteen, about to leave home and enter college. A serious, solid, and thoughtful man, transformed in so few years from the spindly, tense child. He can converse with so excellent a choice of words about impersonal things—e.g., the content of a broad orientation-style course he wants to take.

When I commented to Nancy about how *interesting* we found Allen, what an adult he was, she said: "That's the sad part of it. When finally they become interesting as individuals, they leave home."

JUNE 25, 1973
NEW YORK

The Presidency of the United States of America: what a resounding power for good, what a glorious symbol of this great people. This is what one felt watching the beefy, back-slapping Brezhnev, head of all the Russians, agree to close and peaceful relations with Russia's rival and enemy.

And there was Richard Nixon, who brought this event off.

Then the sad aftermath: a thin-faced, troubled, half-bald, bright lawyer, John Dean, testifying before the TV, for all the world to see, that the President has grossly lied and fouled the great name of his country. How can you compare the drama of these contrasting events—the Soviet détente and the crass venality of Watergate!

JUNE 28, 1973
FLYING TO THE VINEYARD

There it is, off the port wing: *The* Island. Oh, blessed isle. But that rhapsody was an English poet's about England. This is not England. But it is as near to my sense of roots as any spot on this earth, since I learned that my sentimental posture about the Middle West was just that: a posturing. Of all the places where I would want my ashes to be scattered—if that means anything—it would be in the little cemetery in West Tisbury. Odd?

JULY 4, 1973
MARTHA'S VINEYARD

First thing this morning, padded out to the deck, barefooted and in pajamas, holding the rolled flag, like a Torah, and then into the socket and there she flies in the stiff breeze. One of the most beautiful sights in all the world, the flag of the United States of America. Too bad I don't live so I can float it every day, and not just on special days, such as this.

What a country it is and how supremely fortunate we are to live in such a country. With such strong feelings I looked at a *Today* TV show, two people being interviewed about their organization against war, any war. Suddenly I became absolutely furious.

Not one word about the U.S. being number one in the most important of all measures—freedom. What the hell good is literacy and health care without freedom for people?

When I see David Rockefeller or Armand Hammer of Occidental Petroleum, or Nixon, throwing their arms around the Russian and Chinese leaders, and the writers returning from those countries emoting about them, without one word about what has happened to freedom of the individual in Russia and China! Then I look at that flag straightened out in the breeze on our deck under the sky, and groan.

JULY 5, 1973
MARTHA'S VINEYARD

Why is it that the course of events everywhere, but particularly in the U.S., is being determined more and more by the word-people? These wordsmiths include prominently the academics, the intellectuals, the newspaper writers and columnists, and now the TV commentators.

I see the sad decline in prestige of those who are prime movers, who can stand the gaff of competition, of contest, of fights, of assertiveness. When this is combined with conviction, even vision, or intensity of purpose, it can induce action in others.

These are almost the opposite of the traits of those intellectuals and writers who only plant such doubts, specters of introspection, that they call *ideas.*

These latter are without any incentive in themselves to act, but they can make the prime movers feel so unsure and hesitant they no longer produce events rather than theories and models.

The "stop growth" concept swept the country, the world, last summer with its satellite doubt or negative concept: ecology *über alles.* The devastating effect on the prime movers upon which everything really depends, continues.

One Daniel Bell has just published a book that is an illustration. Bell predicts that those who have "knowledge" (including scientific and technical) will drive the society of the early future. The prime movers with responsibility for decisions and power will be as nothing.

The mood of defensiveness will be increased. When will the prime movers wake up to find that this kind of passive nonsense comes from those in enclaves of the universities or editorial rooms who must protect themselves from the rigors of the real world? That world is a harsh, competitive, bruising arena where only the super-adrenalines can perform their vital and life-giving function—which is action.

Another misbegotten product of this substitution of words for reality is the current fad (or is it more than a fad that will pass?) for labor-intensive production.

Unemployment (hardly a new phenomenon) is a continual and shocking curse in underdeveloped countries particularly, despite the figures that show greatly increased productivity (rising GNP). The same passive types called for non-capital-using methods of producing food or relatively simple objects (hand tools, housing, etc.), which is another way of saying quite simply: the use of maximum human labor—the backs and hands of human beings—rather than more efficient use of machines.

I have seen labor-intensive methods, and with few exceptions they are reactionary, oppressive, anti-humane, and self-defeating.

I saw labor-intensive raising of cotton in the South: a nightmare for the black men, women, and children chopping and picking in the fields. Their lives were barren, their freedom restricted by the low productivity which put them in the hands of the landowners and storekeepers.

I saw labor-intensive coal mining in 1933, at Coal Creek, Tennessee, and the miserable life this created for those miners and their pathetic families, the high cost of that coal disguised by disgraceful payments for that "labor-intensive" way of producing coal. (I haven't any recollection of hearing from those writers of books and articles about TVA's strip mining in Appalachia, speaking out against the horrors of labor-intensive coal mining.)

I have seen dams being built in India by labor-intensive methods, whole villages of women and children carrying aggregate and cement in head baskets, as low a form of life for those people as imaginable.

These are among the "triumphs" of the word-people whose phrases now condemn relieving men of the brutality of labor-intensive methods on the ground that to do so will "solve" the admittedly serious problem of unemployment.

Isn't this the Luddites burning farm machinery all over again, to "protect" the jobs of farm workers? Isn't this what Senator Norris used to describe to me of the fight of the Ohio farmers when the first wheat binders came to the farming country where he was brought up—and which he contrasted with the progress that mechanization and electricity brings?

All this ties into the extremism and shortsightedness of the professional environmentalists.

JULY 8, 1973
MARTHA'S VINEYARD

Surely a birthday—the 74th—permits a bit of retrospection, as well as the more normal looking ahead. It has been a good year.

The deepest satisfactions and joys have been in what is usually, discreetly, called "my *personal* life."

So, I have survived, no mean achievement. And I say: bring on the 75th birthday a year hence.

JULY 15, 1973
MARTHA'S VINEYARD

An evening at Leona Baumgartner's, with her husband Alex Langmuir and their other guest, Jean Gottmann, now head of the department of geography at Oxford.

At Oxford they get six months off every year. "What do you do during the rest of the year?" I asked, ruminating about how I won't even give myself two solid weeks—or days. "I go to conferences," he said quite simply.

The subject everywhere seems to be one note: Watergate. The consternation and indignation about this stinking White House is more than justified. But carrying it too far, again indulging in doom talk, may lead to sympathy for Nixon, and from sympathy to support of a sort.

With only the gentle warning of distant grumbles of thunder, suddenly this hilltop's trees were lashed with a ferocity of a gale, then rain driven against this redoubt with the force of a giant fire hose. The rain drove right through the outer skin of the house into pools. And I, who had just returned to bed to try to catch up on the sleep I didn't get last night, was thoroughly awake as leader of a sop-up brigade.

Later I heard that what we had was a localized tornado. I had no reason to doubt it as I walked down the road beyond the mailbox: big branches snapped off and strewn along the sides of the road.

This has been the most aqueous spring and summer in anyone's recollection.

JULY 22, 1973
MARTHA'S VINEYARD

Rodman Rockefeller got off the plane from New York yesterday early forenoon for a vacation kind of weekend with us, and was greeted by fog and a continuation of rain, rain, rain. But however disappointed he must have been—as I was for our plans for a sail, the beach, etc.—his good manners never faltered, though the lousy weather continued the whole day and into the night. And this morning the fog holds out.

Mostly he, Helen, and I talked of personal matters. The new house he is building at Tarrytown on a bluff overlooking the Hudson River. "Windows that are each nine feet wide and twelve feet high, with thermopane glass an inch thick." Or their summer house in Vermont, which can take care of fifteen guests at a time.

In contrast with the Helen and Dave "camp" on this hill, this sounds like bragging. But there wasn't a single note of that kind. Whatever he thinks of the way we live—with Helen, who is *not* forty-one, making and serving dinner for seven last evening, and cleaning up afterward—there was nothing but good manners and cordiality.

At dinner Kenneth Keating, soon to head for Israel as Ambassador, at a critical time indeed; Mary Davis, looking pale, I thought, and troubled; Beatrice Gould, attractive and more interesting than I can remember her; and Bruce Gould, the very picture of a retired sage.‡

I was glad of a chance to talk about Iran with Ken. I didn't get the impression that his month-long briefing at the State Department has made him as fully aware as I am, or the facts warrant, of the new and added tension in the already cruelly tense confrontation between the Arab countries and Israel, caused by the dependence of the West, and particularly the U.S., on the Persian Gulf oil.

A day together in the rain and fog and eternal green of the Vineyard, talking about everything under the non-sun, and a day in misty sun and a sail in *Lili-put* in quiet water and gentle breeze, and an opportunity to swim in the cold and very salty Lambert's Cove beach, today gave Rodman Rockefeller and Dave Lilienthal a far better foundation for an understanding of the business and development problems of D&R than any number of "meetings" in an office setting: stiff, formal, impersonal, with both of us on guard and "negotiating."

A very companionable man.

JULY 26, 1973
EN ROUTE TO WASHINGTON

Friends, and even acquaintances, ask: "Do you include everything in your journals, or do you pre-edit, excluding matters of embarrassment to others? How do you have the 'courage' to expose just how you feel?"

"Cutting" after the writing is an absolute necessity: there is just too much material to publish. Helen and I between us must have cut half of the 1964 entries, as either banal, too personal, too lengthy, or too complicated to be understood.

The one thing I don't want to happen with the journals (not necessarily the portions considered worth publishing but the complete story as filed with my papers) is this: that I portray myself to myself as (1) never

‡The Goulds were the editors of the *Ladies' Home Journal* for many years.

making a mistake; (2) always succeeding; and (3) never having ignoble or petty reactions to events.

JULY 27, 1973
WASHINGTON

From the time when I was the Peck's Very Bad Boy of the atomic energy scenario, critic number one of the AEC's attitude toward safety, to the almost literally open-arms reception I got yesterday noon from the new Chairman, Dr. Dixy Lee Ray, is about as wide a spread as one can project.

"Your coming to see me at just this time is divinely inspired, if it is not blasphemous to say so," she said. The new legislative proposal that would change the administrative structure for energy is now the subject of hearings before the Government Operations Committees in both Houses. Essentially it places the overall responsibility for energy in a new agency.

She recognizes that the technical people of AEC are really oriented toward atomic energy, of course, whereas a far broader scope, to include coal conversion, would be the subject of the new agency's function—including what is now done (or *not* done, in my view) by the Department of Interior's Coal Research Bureau.

I commented that the thesis of my writings (e.g., the Stafford Little Lectures) had been the lack of a concept that covered far more than the one way of meeting our energy needs (i.e., the atom).

I mentioned my skepticism about what the simon-pure analysts could do to get us along toward an energy program. I recalled that a Navy strategy analyst had been made the head of staff for a small group in the Office of Technology.

Oh yes, she knew all about this man. "We set up extensive briefing sessions for him; this was after he had been on the job a full six months. Now you know you must be able to get a good grasp of a new subject quickly or you are no good in this field. I myself am a biologist, but I learned, and learned quickly." (I nodded my head, recalling how in three weeks I had had to learn most of the fundamentals, and certainly all the terms, of atomic energy.) "After a long briefing by Commissioner [Clarence] Larson, the Navy analyst looked up and asked: 'What is enriched uranium?' And when Larson later talked about how much electric energy, at what cost per unit, would be required to produce the stuff, the analyst asked, 'Tell me; what is a mill?' " At which Dr. Ray glanced at me with those shrewd blue eyes and actually looked sad.

I have just this minute come from Blair House and one of the most satisfying and explicit meetings with the Shah in all my years "in his service."

(The street floor of Blair House is quite a different place than it was when last I went through the doors; that was one rainy dismal night, duly recorded in the *Journals,* Volume II. The subject: the bomb, of course. President Truman, Dean Acheson, Eisenhower, I believe: should we continue technical cooperation with the United Kingdom?)

After a minimum of pleasantries, with unaccustomed vigor—hands gesturing—the Shah said, "I told the American press, and the Senate Foreign Relations Committee: Iran is not an archaic country; we are not a Middle East country. We are definitely not Arab. In ten years, as more of our people have become literate, we will be like France"—this was said leaning way forward in his chair, fixing me with his eyes—"and perhaps better than France.

"We are arming ourselves because we have the same needs for defense that other countries have, perhaps more so. It exasperates me"—an understatement, judging from his expression—"to have the newspapermen ask me: 'What country do you fear?' I respond by saying, 'Do you ask other countries, Britain or France, when they have a military program, what country they fear? No, you don't.' "

Looking at me in that personally friendly way that has become his style with me these past years, he said, "You have seen the transformation over the years, the many years that you have worked on our behalf. In this country you are listened to and trusted. You will be listened to when you say, as you have said many times: this is not an archaic country."

This was my cue to talk about how important it is *now* that American public opinion understand Iran, the new Iran, and its evolution. I said, "Now, at last, it is recognized how much we of America depend upon Iran. I can recall how the American Government had no confidence in Iran or your regime. Even so great a liberal and humanitarian as the late Ed Murrow, with his *Fragile Regime* documentary. . . ."

He looked down, bemused. He could remember, as I did, how the U.S. Embassy—i.e., the State Department—forced deflation that brought the country almost to the point of collapse.

To my comment about the American people needing to know about Iran now more than ever, now that we are more than ever dependent upon each other, he responded, with considerable force. "I have told the press what kind of country Iran is. Our goals. Our resources. I made it plain to them."

I said he came to America only once in a while, saw the American opinion-formers only now and then. What I have learned about affecting public opinion—such as "selling" TVA to the country—is that the evolving picture and the facts need to be provided on a continuous basis. Some mechanism needs to be set up, in America, to keep people informed.

He got the point—in part. "There is no one better able to perform what you have described than yourself. With you it has been a matter of your personal experience, the things you have seen. You know my goals as no other American knows them."

To be the center of propaganda for Iran—which is the way it should be construed, necessarily—that may be a poor posture for me and perhaps not an acceptable one for Iran.

JULY 28, 1973
MARTHA'S VINEYARD

Jahangir Amuzegar, when I saw him in his office in Chevy Chase, told me that in the last couple of weeks the Russians have achieved their historic goal: direct access to the Persian Gulf and the Indian Ocean. I exclaimed: "How is that?" Through the coup in Afghanistan, and the pincer on Pakistan. I thought: No wonder the Shah feels the increased need for a strong Air Force and a strengthened Navy. But I have seen nothing of this in the press accounts of the deposing of the King of Afghanistan. How come?

The Shah, his right fist clenched, aroused, eyes flashing even behind dark glasses, sitting in the Early American parlor at Blair House, had said, "We know that wherever there is a sign of weakness, the Russians will exploit it for their purposes."

What a dramatic confirmation of my steady song of derision and disbelief about the theme of the super-wise Harvard intellectual types, the Schlesinger-Galbraith axis, and the *New York Times* editorialists: "The Cold War is over and gone; it never really existed."

AUGUST 2, 1973
NEW YORK

Up at six, on a grisly rainy day, to do a few minutes' stint on the CBS morning news program, with Richard Hottelet doing the questioning.

I suggested as the news peg the State visit of the Prime Minister of Japan, and the joint communiqué (by the Prime Minister and Nixon) that Japan would contribute to the reconstruction of Indochina. Dick said that Kissinger told him yesterday that the PM had volunteered a figure of $50 million for Vietnam "aid" in the first year, four times that much thereafter. This I took to be a "good sign" of the Japanese judgment that South Vietnam is politically viable.

I issued a warning that if American carpetbaggers started making big costly contracts that would exploit the people of Vietnam, I would "explode." But they will try, and where there is a big profit to be made in an underdeveloped country the American contractors and business types will gather like the vultures that most of them are. About the people for whose protection and benefit (presumably) this terrible war was fought they couldn't care less. So carpetbaggers—my phrase—isn't too far off as a description.

AUGUST 3, 1973
MARINE TERMINAL AIRPORT, NEW YORK CITY

There are certainly more unpleasant and more frustrating situations than to try to return to Martha's Vineyard when it is enveloped in dense fog. Offhand, I can't think of many of them.

Whether we will fly, where we will fly to if we do (Hyannis, or wherever), is still wrapped in vague pronouncements by the Lords of the Desk here.

So I wait. And wait. And wait. Dripping, for it is 100% humidity; noisy; uncomfortable—these seats are not all that responsive to the human rear or back. But I am a friend to all mankind, the afterglow of a thoroughly good fourteen hours. I demonstrated this when, going to the office at 7:30, I shared my inner peace and, by contrast, my joy in living, with two rather harried-looking "colleagues." And that this revved them up I didn't need them to tell me.

FOUR HOURS LATER

Not yet on the Vineyard, but this seems the last (or "terminal") lap.

If you aren't prepared to take such days "in your stride" (as Gordon Clapp used to say), you should not "reside" on an island subject to fogs.

If you aren't prepared—and eager—for whatever may come in the exciting, worthwhile work upon which you are engaged, and ready to take on the problems and the risks when they occur, not when it is "convenient" for you, then get out of the hot kitchen, to paraphrase Harry Truman.

It takes a lot of living to feel deeply, to understand, to communicate and give to others, to draw upon what others have to give you.

AUGUST 7, 1973
NEW YORK

When Davey left for Italy, he was a long-legged boy of eleven. He phoned me today, having arrived a few hours before on the Italian liner

Michelangelo; he is eighteen, and never during those years has he seen his own country, not once.

Immediately, he wanted to get to the Vineyard, with two friends. Miss Baron pulled off one of her wizardries, and in a few moments had three places on a plane leaving for the Vineyard in a matter of a couple hours. Helen will certainly have her ordinarily completely nonplussed hands quite full—for in addition to the Brombergers, now "in residence" at "Yonside" with Daniel and his friends, here are three more boys.

They know they are welcome, and that Helen will manage somehow; which I suppose she will.

AUGUST 10, 1973
MARTHA'S VINEYARD

Davey remembers the smallest details of our wanderings in Princeton years ago—when he stood under the blown-over willow tree on the Institute Circle where I took his picture, where we stopped to reach across the fence to feed apples to the Oppenheimer horse, and so on.

He and his cousin Daniel are getting along like a house afire; laughing, joking, and the grins bring out the dimple in Daniel's round face, the light in his eyes. Can these two be related by blood at all? One can't see any marks of that. But both a source of such pride to their grandparents.

AUGUST 11, 1973
MARTHA'S VINEYARD

David and Daniel and I had our first sail yesterday: a blustery, very gusty southwester. I thought they enjoyed it, particularly when, with Daniel at the tiller and main sheet, a blow hit us that heeled us way over. Daniel yelled: "Hey, now what do I do; we're going over." Which we weren't of course, but it did add spice.

David's two Florence friends who accompanied him are most well mannered and as bright as all get out. And so handsome. I feared that, with Nancy and Sylvain, this would be too much for Helen, who feeds them dinner. Not at all. Buying huge sacks of groceries and washing stacks of dishes (we are now beginning the paper plate period!), she takes with her accustomed aplomb.

AUGUST 12, 1973
MARTHA'S VINEYARD

It was nine years ago this month—while we were on the Vineyard, in fact—that there came news that Nate Greene had suffered a stroke.

It is not that I miss Nathan and grieve for him more on an anniversary of his death; hardly a week goes by that I am not reminded, by one event or another, of how much I depended upon his comprehending friendship; quiet, self-effacing, wry at times and never stuffy, always loyal to what he believed I stood for, or should stand for.

Those two "elderly parties," laughing and chatting together; what are they doing walking around the West Tisbury burying ground? Choosing a burial plot is what.

Soon Helen and I will own somewhat more island real estate (about 15 feet by 20, I would guess). The superintendent of the cemetery looked out on the extensive array of ancient headstones, some even the graves of pre-Revolutionary times. The names are fascinating, particularly the first names of women.

"Those over there"—he pointed to the old part—"there's nothing there but bones, and most of them haven't any relatives on this island, never are visited. We have to keep those graves up just the same." Nothing romantic about it to him.

We have decided that we have deeper roots on this island than anywhere else, so we might as well have our ashes deposited here as anywhere.

AUGUST 25, 1973
MARTHA'S VINEYARD

Have just walked mostly through underbrush along the stone walls that mark the borders of this place. From the downside saw the clump of "grandfather" beech—once a mere 6 feet in height, now towering 60 feet.

The observation deck on our house is now built; a great success. To climb its stairs and come out upon that view is to breathe a new life. We now have one of the greatest views on this island, north toward the Elizabeths, and then to the south, the Great Ponds and the sand and surf of the ocean.

AUGUST 27, 1973
MARTHA'S VINEYARD

"Roger, you are about to go on a canoe trip in Missouri? You keep going great guns. How do you manage to retain your vigor and fire, your optimism?" (Roger Baldwin is eighty-nine.)

"David, I asked Pablo Casals this question—he must be in his middle nineties." Roger leaned over as if he were about to give me a piece of classified information or some delicious but scandalous gossip. "Pablo said: 'It's *enthusiasm,* that's the secret.'

"And David, that's what you have."

Well, most of the time.

"Do you still write those amazing journals—every day—still?"

I admitted I did, though not necessarily every day.

"Don't see how you do it. You are so in tune with the people you meet. You must like people or you wouldn't describe them so carefully, so sensitively. That takes a lot of energy, to be in tune with people that way. You aren't like a violin or a harp, you are a whole orchestra. Keep on writing them that way; the events are interesting, much of them, but it is what you record of your impressions of people that makes your journals, far as I know, unique among diaries."

I take this advice quite seriously, because I am spending a fair amount of time cutting the 1965 entries. As with the 1964 ones, I do cut about half, for I wrote reams and reams. The cutting is mostly so I can reach the Vietnam entries within this volume: Volume VI. But with that kind of advice from Roger and other respected people I hold my hand about cutting episodes and personal reactions that have little or nothing to do with "events" or with "development."

We have been up to our eyebrows with guests at "Yonside." Allen Bromberger, back from the wars of his bus trip across the country, complete with an Abraham Lincoln under-the-chin beard, walked in the other evening, followed by five huge young men, friends from Newtonville. No advance word, of course. As I looked at this troop (in their teenage uniform—i.e., deliberately ragged T-shirts and purposely ripped blue jeans), I was more than taken aback. Even Helen looked a bit nonplussed.

But they pretty well take care of themselves at "Yonside"; the refuse and cartons, etc., become mountainlike. "Oh, we'll clean this all up when we leave, Grandmother," said Daniel. And they will; in the meantime it looks like the East Village. But they do have a good time. Being out from under any semblance of parental or any other discipline or authority is a tonic.

At first I was furious to see these galumpuses of young men that the grandchildren bring with them, with no request for permission, no "forward planning"—just walking in. I got over this chiefly because Helen took it so well, partly to cool down my indignation.

"We want the children to feel that 'Yonside' is theirs; we would be unhappy if, as last year, they made no use of it. So it is just a matter of better planning."

So be it.

Another chapter closes: have just made a gift of *Lili-put* (and little *Put,* the dinghy) to the Girl Scouts at Plymouth Bay. It has become very expensive for what little use I can make of it, sailing single, and it is a pity to see her lie there all season hardly used, and during the winter piling up great expense.

I feel somewhat as I did about making a gift of Mac, my horse, years ago.

I hope the youngsters—the Girl Scouts—who learn to sail in her will appreciate her responsiveness to wind, her spaciousness, that they will enjoy her half as much as I have, these several years.

Such are the goodbyes that hurt; but not as much as goodbye to people you love and cherish.

AUGUST 31, 1973
MARTHA'S VINEYARD

Because the Vineyard—meaning Indian Hill, and our houses on this hill—have come to be such a part of Helen's and my life, we like to say: "The grandsons feel they have their roots here more than in any other place." But it is true.

No doubt about it, as this summer is demonstrating. The way they embrace this place, feel at home here, love the swimming and the free-dom. The way they feel they can bring their friends to share it with them shows that we are not wrong in that saying: "This is where their roots are."

David 3d returned from his Western trip so alive and full of himself. He has wanted to return to this country for years; there is no let-down and no need to adjust, judging from his wide-eyed account of his trip, or the warmth of his manner.

SEPTEMBER 3, 1973
MARTHA'S VINEYARD

A big gathering of old friends, and some new. We had kept "secret" the fact of our 50th wedding anniversary, but the lively bash of perhaps thirty-five people turned out with felicitations of considerable warmth— and, I thought, surprise. It isn't true, as so often said, that divorce is now so common that changing partners two or more times is the rule. Still, you have to have outlived many of your contemporaries to be eligible for a golden wedding, and have managed through all kinds of weather, the most difficult (and rewarding) of human relations.

What set this occasion off for me was the presence of three as handsome and lively young men as ever I have seen: Allen and his bright-eyed brother Daniel, and the startlingly distinctive David 3d. All of them tall, husky, and raring to go.

SEPTEMBER 5, 1973
MARTHA'S VINEYARD

Told Scotty and Sally Reston how much Helen and I appreciated their good wishes on our wedding anniversary, delivered by their son Tom. I was pleased, I said, to see Tom because, so he told me, development of people who have had the short end of the stick has been a chief concern of his as a student at Harvard.

Said Scotty: Two years ago Tom was sure that the only answer to the problem of giving the very poor a better chance was violence. "Happily he no longer feels quite that way about it. You have found a way—the work you have done in Iran and now Brazil—that he wants to hear about."

SEPTEMBER 7, 1973
MARTHA'S VINEYARD

A memorable hour and a half with Scotty Reston, with Sally, in their little green house back of the *Gazette*'s establishment, in Edgartown.

By common consent Scotty is the most influential journalist in America today. After listening to him late yesterday afternoon I thought, Scotty is one of the few genuine statesmen, a private man with a sensitivity to the state of the Republic.

"Distinguished," even as I saw him yesterday: an old blue tunic, flowing (loosely indeed) in a wide circle around his now impressive front; his grey hair long and flowing over his expansive forehead; his eyes peering over half-glasses, at me and then at the yellow foolscap tablet on which he was writing some "of your thoughts."

After some personal pleasantries he said: "You wanted to talk to me of your ideas about energy."

I put it something like this: Those who have been responsible for seeing to it that this country has an adequate supply of energy—electricity and gas and petroleum—have failed us. What is their current "answer"? Spend vastly more money on "research and development," or in exploring for oil, or arranging for oil from the Middle East. The figures go up each time anyone talks about it.

But my theme is that it doesn't make sense to turn over even greater resources to the very ones who have failed us—despite plenty of signs of their inadequacy over recent years. We need new brains, a new team, a new approach.

We should build not on the discredited ones but on those new people in AEC, among the junior officers of the oil companies, among the coal companies.

I mentioned my failure to get my basic ideas published in the *Times:* the *Magazine* article of several years ago, the more recent one. It was my fault, I recognized, because I don't have the special skill for that kind of presentation. But I thought I would have another go at the Op-Ed page.

"Of course, I would be for that, in a way," he said. "It might get people's attention, as the farmer said explaining why he clouted the stubborn mule over the head with a four-by-four, 'That's to get his attention.' I agree with you that finding new faces within the Administration who could do something about the President's position would be more effective."

The most impressive thing Scotty said was about the proper attitude toward the President, generally. "The talk about impeachment, of course, is and always has been silly. He will be President for another three and a half years. We must do whatever we can, all of us, to encourage those courses he must consider which we believe will keep the country from falling apart. More than that, that will get us moving again after this sad and destructive period."

After which Scotty talked at some length about his opinion of Kissinger, about the way in which Kissinger had been willing to come to the Restons' home to talk with Bill Fulbright particularly. "When he first came into our living room, with a grin he said, 'Is it safe to talk here?' The bugging of pals that has been going on was what was at the bottom of this jest, but apparently Kissinger has been bugged, too."

SEPTEMBER II, 1973
PRINCETON

Be glad to erase and forget the past few days. The muscle pains and aches turned out to be fever. A rough time it was. The worst part, really, is the preoccupation with one's health, with the bottles of antibiotics to be taken (and the dopey feeling they produce), instead of thinking about the beauties of the world around one—and the past few days were magnificent, with great distance over deep blue water.

But I got on the plane this morning and am glad to be back in this comfortable and beautiful house. I'm all for the house on the Vineyard so long as it is the outdoors that is the center; but being dopey, inside the house, it is better to be dopey here.

SEPTEMBER 15, 1973
PRINCETON

The worst thing about an illness—the very worst—is that one's outlook narrows, draws in, from the wonderful vista of an exciting world, down to the particulars of that one body, yours: "how much temperature," or what back ache. What a letdown—from the whole world to one's petty symptoms.

Where a few days before—when I took my sturdy health for granted —everything was interesting, sometimes troublesome or puzzling or disappointing or challenging, down to a preoccupation with self. Ugh.

I think I'm over that particular focus that held me for several days last week. What has been hanging over me has been the question: can I manage the long flight to Brazil, first to Rio then after the ordeal of customs inspection—two tiresome hours—on to Brasília?

SEPTEMBER 20, 1973
APPROACHING RIO

For all the *pre-angst,* the overnight trip went even better than usual.

What made the trip particularly pleasant was a book: Joyce's *A Portrait of the Artist as a Young Man.* What a delight to read prose that is poetry, and poetry that needs no embellishment or tricks of rhetoric to hold one spellbound. One reads the *words,* not just splashing through a paragraph at a time as I do with so much of what I read.

SEPTEMBER 22, 1973
BRASÍLIA

It is more than ever evident that this one man, Minister Leitão de Abreu, with his baldish elliptical-shaped head and perpetual grin, is the main element in such position as we have in this fantastic country. More satisfying even than that, he has become a good friend, in a personal sense—and is there really any other basis for calling a man a friend and having him show that he likes and trusts you as a person?

Hal Frederiksen and I, yesterday morning, spent almost an hour with Leitão in his funny little office with the now familiar round table, adjoining the Inner Sanctum of the Presidency.

I told him our story: We had been asked by the Ministry of Interior (on instructions from the President, we doubt not) to make recommendations on "institutional" changes in the way natural resources activities of the national government should be organized, for planning and administration. Such recommendations were to be made long before the completion of our analysis of the Valley's substantive "potentials."

We objected: the kind of organization for development should be designed *after,* not before, we had developed a picture of what there was to develop. But Henrique Cavalcanti had insisted; the Government was entirely dissatisfied and disappointed with the way things had been going for many years in the Valley's development; wanted to present the Congress with legislation for a new agency (referred to in those early discussions as "A Corporation"). The deadline would be July 1 for introduction of the legislation, after consultation with the Ministries involved. *So,* illogical as it was, we proceeded to make recommendations, and later to "clarify" them, when opposition developed to the nature of the recommendations.

Then, at a meeting a few days ago of a specially constituted Council representing various Ministries, Henrique said, "D&R has contributed nothing of significance" or usefulness.

On being pressed on this, with considerable spirit and even temper on my part (this was day before yesterday afternoon), he said he didn't mean to imply lack of confidence in D&R's capability, but the various Ministries could not accept or agree on any of the institutional changes we had recommended. He himself did not see any need whatever for a Valley-wide agency or improved cohesion in the work going on in the Valley.

I said to Leitão this reaction was not a surprise: *no* bureaucracy in my experience had ever been open-minded about any change in its prerogatives or jurisdiction; no changes of authority could be expected, if they depended upon getting the agreement of the affected bureaucracy.

We believe that the lack of maximum progress in the development of the Valley was due in very large, perhaps major, part to the organizational confusion, overlapping, conflicts between Ministries.

The Minister said I should tell the President this story.

Which I did; with the help of a fine gentleman who acted as interpreter. It was at this point that the President, frowning as he tried to understand my English (which he does quite well), came up with the sentence which was translated as "I will remove the differences."

My explosion of indignation yesterday and the audience, whatever else it produced, certainly ended the lack of opportunity to discuss our ideas and get the Ministry's reactions. Morris McClung and Hal spent, literally, *hours* with Henrique yesterday. We got a picture of what he thought our report should be, and it is a sad picture, for it shows the baleful and dehumanized influence of the mathematical economists and logicians. But we can adapt ourselves to that kind of nonsense. (Though I'll be damned if I care to sign a report that obscures the reality of valley development and increase of human opportunity with a lot of this garbage that has become a stock in trade of mathematical economists, in which equations become more important than the driving force behind development, an understanding of what it takes to move people and get things done.)

Leitão's dinner for us last evening was at his place in the country. A kind of Brazilian Camp David; in fact, the Minister wore a sport jacket with "Camp David" and the U.S. seal on the pocket, a memento of his three-day visit to the U.S. with President Medici.

Built of fieldstone and native hardwood. The distinctive thing was the waterfall built almost right into the simple house. The waterfall came from a big spring, dashing against rocks put into place, producing a pleasant "rumble of water" (Leitão's phrase).

The meal itself was served not outside by the barbecue pit, but at table, quite decorously. But the great slabs of barbecued beef, pork, were brought to the table on long skewers, and sliced at the table; delicious.

The Minister is the very picture of a relaxed man (though with much on his mind). But his slender little wife showed the effect of living with a man so much under the gun of major and general responsibilities—apparently the President doesn't make a move or a decision without Leitão being in the middle of it. (Evidenced by the presence in the forenoon of the world famous Minister of Finance, Delfim Netto, a rotund goggle-spectacled wavy-haired young man. And by "rotund" I mean he stretches out in all directions. A lively face. He remembered he had met me in his office in Rio more than a year ago.)

Had a good talk with Dias Leite. All his mind is directed to "March 15th"—a date, but also a signal—i.e., when he will again be a private citizen, the new President being in office. I said it was good that the new President, General Geisel, would be a man who understood the fuel and energy picture so well, as head of the national petroleum corporation, Petrobras.

"Why yes, he understands it very well indeed. And I have informed him several times of matters we have discussed together. So there will be continuity with what you have been doing. Definitely."

It was the first time I had heard any expression about "continuity" between Medici and the succeeding Presidency. I take this somewhat with a grain of salt, but the general predictions are that the new President will carry forward the policy of the Medici regime, and since they have been so successful and to the satisfaction of the people, generally, this makes sense. As if sense is always the criterion in public affairs!

The high point of the Brazil visit came with Rubens Vaz da Costa, in his great office atop—27th floor—the National Housing Bank.

Rarely have I been more impressed with a public servant. The manner of a professor, superficially, but as he discussed particular economic problems, the hard-nosed experienced administrator showed through. I was so heartened by this man and his understanding of what I am about that this morning I wrote one of my most purple-passage letters to him.

I expect—so do others—that Rubens will be part of the incoming Geisel Administration.

SEPTEMBER 24, 1973
AT RIO AIRPORT

Feel pretty rotten (took my temperature, some fever again, muscle ache like mad).

BUT,

1. I *didn't* cop out; if I had I would feel much worse and the "worse" feeling would continue; and

2. I am heading in the right direction: home.

A telex in: The Iran National Water Plan contract formally signed— a big four-year pioneering job. Does pioneering never end? Of course it doesn't, not even after all those eighteen years.

SEPTEMBER 29, 1973
PRINCETON

Once more the McNamara–World Bank annual meeting (this time at Nairobi). Once more the theme: "more help for the poor countries." For "help" substitute "non-interest loans." What they mean is "help" in subsistence agriculture.

Like most crusades initiated by well-motivated people, this one is strong on rhetoric (with most of which one cannot possibly disagree) and weak on how to get things done that will really help.

Why are some countries "poor"? This isn't a question that good motives will resolve.

McNamara now has surrounded himself with fancy mathematical economists as he surrounded himself with "analysts" in the Defense Department; the bitter fruit of that reliance is too well known: the bloody Vietnam debacle.

Some countries, like some people, are poor and nothing can be done to change that. You can't "educate" a population into prosperity or even decent conditions of life if they simply do not have the basic natural conditions, of soil, of water, of climate. You can mitigate but you can't make a basically poor country over, and if you put much effort into it, you squander resources better applied to countries that do have resources.

How long some things take to mature!

On Gordon Clapp's and my first trip to Khuzistan our car came around a curve in the highway and there we saw a picture that we never could forget: the great pylons of fire, flared (i.e., wasted) gas from operating wells, energy that had been wasted by the tens of millions of BTU since the British first found oil, more than fifty years. Which set us to thinking about transporting that gas to the U.S.

Now in so many years (eighteen, about) it is finally to be "collected" and manufactured into a form that can be brought to the U.S. to meet our increasingly serious shortages.

Yesterday an announcement that the Iran Gas Co. has signed a 22-year $2 billion deal for the "collection" of flared gas in current fields in Khuzistan, to be transformed into forms of hydrocarbons that can become feed stock for synthetic natural gas (SNG) to be processed in Iran and transported to the East Coast of the U.S. by Transcontinental Transmission Co.

OCTOBER 9, 1973
NEW YORK

On the radio, the voice of the Russian Ambassador at a meeting of the UN Security Council expressing condolence to the families of those civilians, including Russian citizens, killed in the bombing of Damascus by Israel a few hours ago.

Fanatical demonstrations by the Russians in the UN are a well-remembered staple. But Malik said things about that terrible incident that caused me to think: the world is closer to World War III than at any time, not excluding the Vietnam war.

Arriving at 1 Beekman Place tonight for dinner at the John Rockefellers and then on to an opening of Ispahan art at Asia House made both of us nostalgic. Hand in hand, we walked up to 23 Beekman Place, Katharine Cornell's house, where we lived when we first came to New York almost twenty years ago.

I sat at Blanchette's left hand, the Iranian Ambassador on her right. Such an intense, interested woman she is, and how she turned to talk to me with youthful enthusiasm when I mentioned our liking so very much her daughter's book about her African experience in the Peace Corps;

told me all about her divorce, her three boys, how she is working on the staff of *Newsweek* to get training for what she most wants, to be a good writer. A characteristic Rockefeller story about the book; the publisher insisted on titling it in a way that showed the author was a Rockefeller; the girl would have no part of it, insisted on her married name.

One of the warmest spots of the evening was a talk with Rodman's mother, Mary Rockefeller, who said: "Oh you work with Roddie—he certainly needs you; he is growing up, don't you think?" I said he was a young man reaching out for new ideas.

I was called on, at Asia House, to make a talk, with a warm introduction from Phillips Talbot. I said that what binds countries together in mutual understanding is not so much their economics, but the work of artists, that the exhibition we saw—and how supremely beautiful it was in all the richness of its 17th century love of beauty—reminded us once again that the only thing that truly endures is the work of the artist.

Later in the evening I was carried back to the earliest days in Iran, when a young man spoke words so familiar at such gatherings: Do you remember me? Ahmad Tehrani! Our young Khuzistan Development Service lawyer when we first came to Iran. "I was so proud of KDS and what we were doing. Now I am Ambassador to South Africa, and I tell them in Natal, you should go to Khuzistan to see how to develop your part of the country."

OCTOBER II, 1973
WRITTEN PARTLY AT THE OFFICE,
COMPLETED IN PRINCETON

Phone conversation with Jahangir Amuzegar.

"The strongest impression—and greatest concern—I brought away from the World Bank and International Monetary Fund meeting in Nairobi is this: a conflict between the oil producing countries [OPEC] and the ninety-seven developing countries. They are no longer on our side; they ask: What will you, the oil countries, do for *us*?

"I am really worried that we of OPEC will lose not only the support of the industrialized countries, such as the U.S., and their understanding of the rightness of our position as oil producers but equally serious, the support of the ninety-seven or more developing countries whose progress is tied in part to oil prices and supply or whose 'promise' for development may turn on oil."

Amuzegar's voice—the only way I had of judging his demeanor and degree of concern—showed a quality I had never heard before; the pace of speech was slower than usual, the words almost solemn.

OCTOBER 14, 1973
PRINCETON

I do believe I'm becoming almost human. Last weekend I sat for a whole afternoon before a TV set watching a ballgame between the Mets and the Cincinnati Reds. And again part of yesterday; tonight picked up the finale of the second World Series game, from the middle of the 11th to the end, and such an exciting bing-bang of a rouser it was. (Would have missed this but I called Mildred Baron to inquire about her cold; when I asked about the Mets, and she said they were in the 11th, that ended the phone conversation pronto.)

I am doing much reading—almost at the rate of a book a night. My eyes are red, particularly since I often read a couple hours between two and four A.M.

I have revived interest in my record player, which on the Vineyard I play constantly. The complete Bach flute sonatas are an utter delight. I balanced them by the blare and inspiring whine of Scottish bagpipes.

OCTOBER 18, 1973
DRIVING HOME FROM NEW YORK

A long talk with Rodman in my office. It is plain that he sees me as a softie who can be gotten around by pleasant talk and by stalling, stalling.

But Rodman did make one remark about the kind of man I am. "There's no English word for it, but the Spanish have one—it means a person who is not willing to let well enough alone; wants to change everything. 'Restless' isn't quite it."

He is a frank and explicit worshiper of power, and power over people. So that he would like to use me is understandable, particularly since I am indeed a schmo and "good guy."

OCTOBER 22, 1973
PRINCETON

Ishmael Jackson was here to wash and install the storm windows. In the driveway, a white auto van, aluminum ladders on top; an assistant in tow.

Ishmael several years ago, when first he put up our storm windows, was a by-the-hour employee of some firm. Today he heads the Nassau Cleaning Company, owns a fine van, has a list of clients.

If these shallow smart-aleck intellectuals at MIT or the Club of Rome were capable of digging into the facts—or recognizing the relevant facts

—and of understanding fully the evolution of Ishmael from an hourly worker to an entrepreneur, then such idiocies as the "limitation of growth" or the zero-growth doctrines would be seen for what they are— dehumanizing and without reality judged by the way people strengthen themselves.

Alas, that amount of human understanding isn't what our intellectuals and most of our students have facilities for comprehending.

OCTOBER 24, 1973
NEW YORK

The time when "everything happened": that was last weekend. Nixon "defies" the courts over those absurd "tapes," fires Archibald Cox to keep him from uncovering the mess; has the only Mr. Clean around the White House, Elliot Richardson, resign; is assaulted by a wave of public anger and cries of "impeach" the s.o.b. (so the overdramatic, congenitally livid TV journalists describe it); capitulates and says he will turn over those tapes (which I would guess will ultimately turn out to be inconclusive if not innocuous); and then Metternich Kissinger and Peter the Great Kosygin announce that they have insisted on a cessation of fighting between the Arabs and Israelis—which at the latest report last night neither has any present intention of doing.

Helen came in yesterday so we could go to dinner at Rodman and Barbara Rockefeller's apartment. The architect I. M. Pei and his wife dropped by before dinner. He looks like a fellow caught between vast acclaim and real trouble: his famous John Hancock Building in Boston became an eyesore before it was occupied, many of the windows being boarded up because they just plain popped out—and a building in Houston, I hear, having comparable problems.

OCTOBER 31, 1973
PARIS, EN ROUTE TO BUCHAREST

My first close look at an East European crowd; at least I assume that is what they are: the large clutch of people waiting for the plane to Belgrade and Bucharest. Waiting is the word, too, an hour's delay "because of technical problems." The air was filled with what I took to be Slavic, perhaps some Hungarian sounds, far from melodious.

Our ticket said "first class." No such thing on this route, and a good thing too, for anyone interested in what the people who travel look like and behave.

From 30,000 feet it should not mean much; but somehow to cross Germany, Munich, Austria (Salzburg), Zagreb in Yugoslavia—all for the first time, seemed quite special and exciting. It is common knowledge that it doesn't take much to arouse my enthusiasm and excitement.

NOVEMBER 2, 1973
BUCHAREST, ROMANIA

If coming to Romania, en route to Iran, was to "get some rest," it has hardly been a success: from the time we were greeted at the plane until the delightful family-style dinner party last night, it has been an active time. But since one purpose was to add another country and region to the parts of the world we have seen, and perhaps even to see if at some future time D&R couldn't have a role here, it has been far better than I could have imagined.

What has chiefly interested me is my first opportunity in many years to meet the kind of young men who run a Communist country.

The Vice President of the National Council of Science and Technology, Professor Mihai Draganescu, is a bulky, extremely serious, driving sort of man, a great square head and shoulders to match. An electronics man, but with a passion for general philosophical ideas about how such a country and such a state of technology as the one they are reaching for can be fitted into the kind of "one-world economy" that he sees is coming; much "money" (his term) is the power that pulls it all together.

In this questioning mood about non-scientific concepts, Draganescu is a familiar figure among scientists, but though more articulate and sobersides, among businessmen as well.

We did our share of sightseeing too: the Gold Treasures of splendor and antiquity. The outdoor Museum of Village Life.

NOVEMBER 3, 1973
BUCHAREST

A visit with the president of the Academy of Agricultural Research. All very formal. Whether D&R can provide some help to Romania— which I did discuss—I don't know. But the blue-plate-special propaganda spiel the stolid, satisfied-looking Professor Serban Tideka gave me indicated that *he* thought Romania needed nothing. The usual "in" line, though he was courteous and gracious in the extreme. Proud that Romania beat everyone else who competed to supply sunflower seeds for Iran. "And they gave us 10,000 hectares of land for development in the north"—this was Dan Vamanu's translation and means that Romania does have a large-scale agricultural project approved for Iran.

We drove all day, after this meeting, across the whole of the country in a northwesterly direction, across the Texas-like flat-flat plains of the Danube Basin (a kind of Communist food factory—state-owned agriculture) and then into the hills and finally to the great dam of the Arges, adjoining Hungary. A dam that resembled the Pahlavi—a double arch, 165 meters high—with the white snow-covered Carpathian Mountains as a backdrop.

I was exhausted, slept twelve hours; feeling pretty rotten, slept again today.

NOVEMBER 4, 1973
ATHENS

In a few hours Helen and I will be going to the Archeological Museum here in Athens to see something that she has thirsted to see ever since last summer. When I said that for our wedding anniversary I had found at Tiffany's a beautiful emerald ring, pear-shaped and devastating, she said: "What would I do with a very costly emerald ring, or any other such jewelry? But if you want to get me something for an anniversary present that would mean a great deal to me, take me to Athens on this next trip to see the great new things at the Archeological Museum" —and so we shall go, to see the murals from Santorin.

And did.

In company with swarms, tidal waves, of English "public" school youngsters. (The ages? I would guess between twelve and fifteen.)

Learned that they had been packed off in a big cruise ship for a two-week travel to Spain, and to the fascinating excavations going on at the island of Santorin. What a menagerie that cruise ship must be; but British children somehow seem more self-controlled than the queues one sees being marched into the Metropolitan in New York.

NOVEMBER 6, 1973
TEHRAN

Yesterday morning there was a call from the Secretary to the Minister of Court: an audience has been arranged for you with His Majesty tomorrow at 11:30 at Niavaran Palace.

Very pleasing that the Shah had taken the initiative. It will come at the very beginning of my stay, so I can plan what should follow.

The word is that the Arab oil producers have announced a 25% reduction in oil production. The battle is on, apparently. Prices will go up drastically, as there will be competition for the 75% of production that remains. How this will affect Iran, one of the OPEC countries, it not joining in the Arab "pressure" group, I may learn this morning.

A pall of deep haze and smog hangs over Tehran, obscuring, obliterating, the ring of mountains which used to be so brilliant and dramatic on such a sunny day as this. Iran, like the rest of the world, I guess, will have to pay a price for "progress." But it need not be that way.

Just back from an hour's audience. It was in every way a successful one, covering the broadest ground and His Majesty's reflections at this historic time, but also being quite specific.

His Majesty met me in the great hall of mirrors. I remarked on the "beautiful weather." His response was characteristic: "But the country needs rain."

He seemed more somber and subdued than usual; the lines of fatigue were plainly drawn.

I spoke of the idea that came to me, quite spontaneously, that there should be a long-range and comprehensive plan for the Kerman region, as a region. Unless this was started at once, "vested interests" would be established that would be wasteful and full of duplication.

"Kerman is a blank; nothing has been done there and everything can be done: ports, mines, cities, a center for power production. But it needs to be planned—that is the way we went at the Khuzistan and the results show it."

Khuzistan and what was done there—and is continuing—was mentioned often by His Majesty and with satisfaction, to both of us!

His unease about Russian objectives in the Persian region he was very frank about. "They have never changed their objectives; they want to control the world for Communism. That has never changed."

This statement was in such contrast to the détente with the Soviets that has been going on with such rhetorical flourishes for years now.

I criticized the American alarm about dependence on oil from the Middle East; it has led to a basic policy that is negative and corrosive: "We must no longer be dependent upon oil from the Middle East." Instead, we should, in America, be developing energy resources in a positive way for affirmative reasons.

He replied, "The Arabs are frightened peoples. They are frightened by the modern world, and so they strike out with oil as their weapon. We shall not join them in blackmail to change American foreign policy or any other form of blackmail."

I reminded the King that I had a deep-seated concern, expressed here in Iran, lest Iran depend too heavily upon Japan.

"The Japanese are in a vulnerable position on their fuel supplies—this is so well known—and Europe is even more so," the Shah said.

NOVEMBER 10, 1973
TEHRAN

Mehdi Samii, to my great satisfaction, looked healthy and spirited. Mehdi's comment that best characterized the man was about his new post, head of the Agricultural Development Fund, actually a bank to strengthen and encourage agriculture.

"It is so new, and there is so much for me to learn. I am stretching my mind on new things. And they are important. The future of agriculture, I believe, is with the medium-sized independent farmers who run their own farms. The very large agribusiness operations in Khuzistan haven't yet produced much. The very small peasant farms are for subsistence, and with only five or ten hectares will never be much more than that, will not contribute to the food needs of the urban centers. The in-between farmers could make all the difference.

"But they hold back in investing in their farms because there is no assurance that they won't be nationalized in some further land-reform program. And our Fund and private banks hesitate about lending them money and they hesitate about borrowing. So I am trying to get assurance about titles. Get those concerns out of the way and these family farmers could make all the difference."

The Shah, so a newspaper story reported, forbade all top officials of the Government to own stocks in private companies, and required them to dispose of shares they owned. Mehdi said this wasn't likely to be very effective; it was a roundabout rather than a direct way of fighting corruption and favoritism because it would be so easy to evade by transferring shares to others.

"It has never been a policy—as it is with you—that public officials could not have an interest in private companies that might be affected by their public actions. But whether this is an effective means of stemming corruption, it shows that the Shah is aware of the problem, which is worse now than it has ever been, much worse."

I said that in all the years we had been working in Iran neither D&R nor its personnel had ever been approached nor had we ever engaged in anything that remotely resembled buying contracts—and so forth. So I was surprised by the implications of the report of the Shah's actions.

"No, you have not had the problem. Your reputation along these lines was and is well known, and no one would try that with you. But it is a problem." When he said this Mehdi looked very sad.

NOVEMBER 12, 1973
TEHRAN

The recognition that it was our concept for Khuzistan almost eighteen years ago that "triggered" the whole sweep toward development in the country is told to me time and again. The continued expansion of the sugar complex, the growth of a huge nation-wide power system, the belated recognition of the place of agricultural research (using the term in the broadest sense). Not the least, the recognition that D&R represents a kind of integrity and honesty that is not present everywhere among the "contractors" or the public servants or the private businessmen—of these things the praise is unanimous.

The difficulties we went through in the early days are completely forgotten: skepticism and vitriolic criticism, the doubting Thomases, the strangling agonies of bureaucratic red tape, the breaking through of new ways.

In short, now that development is a key theme in this remarkable and wonderful country, what we did as pioneers seems "easy."

NOVEMBER 15, 1973
ANDIMESHK VILLAGE

We escaped the constant threat of death and destruction on the drive along the truck route from Ahwaz. Giant trucks that hold to each other's tails in close formation, like lumbering, roaring elephants. Passing the cavalcade in a car is a test of one's good luck.

The landscape a dreary one, but enlivened now by recent plantings of some kind of desert juniper, and the great tongues of flame from new oil discoveries, sometimes six such flares together, while huge self-contained drilling rigs prove that the Ahwaz area is one sea of the most critical fluid in the world today: unimaginable quantities of oil. One well is almost on the grounds of the new and splendid Ahwaz Hotel—imagine a modern hotel in Ahwaz fifteen or even ten years ago.

In a strange way, I found comfort in the fact that the main street of Ahwaz is much the same as it was when first we came here almost exactly eighteen years ago. Now many of the former open stalls are enclosed with plate-glass windows and some have air conditioners. But the people in this busy, lively city have not changed all that much in appearance, in their garb, their manner. This may become one of the centers of power for the modern world, but seeing the street scenes you would not mistake this city for some equally affluent city in central Indiana, or Bucharest, for that matter.

We headed for Haft Tapeh. Not to see the sugar cane that flourishes, despite the early predictions of failure when we vouched for it, nor the plant making paper out of the cane's stalks, a plant being expanded with private capital. Instead, to see a small, beautiful, tasteful museum beyond the village that had been erected for the sugar-refinery workers. The museum was built by the site of an excavation of an ancient civilization—Elamite (i.e., 2250 B.C.), predating Susa, and contained the treasures found in the dig.

The stop there was especially for Helen, who ate it up, to my delight. (I myself find this intense absorption in solemnly digging into the tiniest fragment of rubble, of broken pots, not quite worth all that effort and scholarly preoccupation.) Helen will give me a lecture about it with the slightest encouragement.

Stood up for five consecutive hours, greeting the now large contingent of D&R people, and others. Particularly did I enjoy reminiscing with Ata-ollah Akhlaqi, a politician and member of the Majlis [Parliament], whose knowledge of Dezful (he was once the Mayor of this, the "oldest town in the world") and whose anecdotes of the early days of KDS are delightful.

NOVEMBER 18, 1973
TEHRAN

Much troubled in my mind by more talk about corruption in the granting of contracts hereabouts.

"In this country," Ebtehaj told me, "people believe men are dishonest because so many of them are, in small things and large. The reason you have never been approached for anything improper is because everyone in the world knows that you are a completely honest, incorruptible man. I have that same reputation. I will work with you, but not in any way that would profit me financially."

NOVEMBER 22, 1973
IN FLIGHT TO ROME

Thanksgiving dinner is about to be served to Helen and to me—the sole passengers in the first-class section of Iranair—but it won't be turkey, surely.

Helen and I enjoyed each other so much on this trip. I made a conscious effort to think of places and things that I knew fit her special interests—such as the stop in Athens, the new museum in Tehran, the Haft Tapeh dig. We had a fairly active social life with Iranian friends. But more than this, our hotel accommodations—a quite attractive living room joined by our separate bedrooms—made for a homelike atmosphere ordinarily so difficult in a hotel; we even developed a routine about breakfast, and it is surely known that the secret of a good marriage is a pleasant and relaxed routine. I told Helen, "I have my home with me."

Hard as I worked—I really did, and long hours and intense situations too—having her with me made it much more natural for me to grab a ten-minute lie-down, even a snooze, between meetings.

And I was so very proud of her with company, her wit, her good looks, and particularly her animation, livening up social gatherings that with me alone would have been serious, almost solemn.

But best of all, I could talk out problems that bothered me, and get those incisive insights, usually delivered with very few words, that have helped me over a good many of the rough spots since the early days of D&R; some of which, as it happens, occurred in Italy (on our way to and from Iran) and in the same Rome hotel toward which we are going, very rapidly now, for the plane is nearly at Rome airport.

NOVEMBER 23, 1973
HOTEL HASSLER, ROME

How green is the Italian landscape as one drops down to Rome, after the bare bones of Iran.

When we registered here at the Hassler, after our flight from that other world, the receptionist pulled out a card to check our guest status. Notations of every stop we have made here. The first one was in early *1956.*

It was here that Gordon and I drafted the original contract to be submitted to Ebtehaj, as I recall; it was here that later John Blandford§ and I debated how we should organize ourselves.

Nostalgia pursues one, sparked by a look at that much-thumbed card at the registration desk of the Hassler.

NOVEMBER 25, 1973
FLORENCE

A happy, jolly reunion with the Florentine Lilienthals. Last night a big turkey and much laughter. Peggy was at the top of her vivacious form. Margaret, only twelve, is physically very much a woman, in every other way still a girl, handsome, giggly, loving, no longer a show-off brat.

§D&R's first chief representative in Iran. He was TVA General Manager in the 1930s, later Assistant Director of the Bureau of the Budget.

David, stooping as he walks so as not to touch the ceiling—or the sky. Quite a picture, he walking through the streets of Florence, his mother alongside, way down there about the level of his shoulder.

One of the few times he had a good word to say for his native land: Watergate shows that the American people are no pushovers, react sharply to the kind of corruption that is accepted as "what goes on" in Italy and many other countries.

I asked him why he preferred to live in Italy—with its political confusion, noisiness, lack of public ethics, etc. But, said he, Florence isn't just another Italian city: "It is an international city, in every sense. Here we can meet people from all over the world; it is a center that makes me feel at home, as a writer."

NOVEMBER 27, 1973
ROME

Said David, "When I am with you folks I am not conscious of your age; both of you step out vigorously, and you don't *think* like old people."

I resisted Helen on our taking the extra trip and time to come to Florence. Why not suggest David come to Rome for a day? But Helen persisted, in her understated way (which always "works" with me). How right she was, and how deprived I would have been if we hadn't made the trip and had that memorable visit. And we would have missed the delightful hours we spent with Margy.

AT THE AIRPORT, ROME

For the first time I became aware of the celebrated beauty of Florence as a city. Austere, but still indubitably a beauty to make me catch my breath, literally, as one vista after another opened up. This time we could actually see the center of the city. For here automobiles, the blessing of the century and its curse, had been banned.

FLYING THE ATLANTIC

In retrospect: You are returning from the longest and most intensive exposure to today's Persia in many a year.

You were among the very few who sixteen years ago had faith in that country and in its King and in the destiny of that land. How now, prophet —for you did prophesy its renewed greatness. Almost alone you were. The bitter skeptics within the country; the homegrown intellectuals and professional Persian doom-sayers alike, to say nothing of the Communists; the high-toned "experts" (*vide* Ed Mason) of the State Department gave it no chance.

What then do you feel?

A warm feeling of home; that's first. Not a "home" of tranquillity and orderliness. But more to my style, a place of vitality, a nervous restlessness. A confidence that in Iran is no hysterical hatred, such as the Arab nations show. Steadiness. Looking at their own growth. Taking changes as if they were foreordained.

But on the fearsome side, suddenly I was almost overwhelmed with the acknowledgment, oddly for the first time, that my second country also has corruption. I would like to believe that what exists in Maryland (*vide* Spiro Agnew) and Indonesia or Nigeria does not exist in Persia. But I was assured by such a calm man as Mehdi that it does. This troubled me. Partly because I feared that D&R was not at all times being considered on its merits for work in which I believe (e.g., the Karkheh Basin development).

What a great feeling. To be looked on as their friend and benefactor, because of my work, by so many of the leadership of distinction, and by the hired drivers of cars (one of whom embraced me with gusto and loud cries as I entered the Ministry of Water and Power).

Helen and I had our elegant dinner (at 37,000 feet) sitting at a formally set table in the upper deck of this monstrous big aircraft.

Shades of that single-motored Bellanca, TVA's first airplane, piloted by Tom Kesterson, the first plane in which I flew. The wings were canvas-covered! The landing field at Knoxville a tiny island in the river. No meals at a table, none at all!

NOVEMBER 28, 1973
NEW YORK

Said David (I paraphrase, of course), "Your work is your life. You have recited some of the unpleasant sides of that work. That is the price you pay for the good satisfying hours and days, the sense of accomplishing the things for which you founded D&R and which are part of the purpose of your whole life. Don't look at those harassing episodes separately from the whole story—and it is a unique story as your life has been unique."

DECEMBER 1, 1973
PRINCETON

I should just loaf over some of the many books I keep adding to the already overflowing cornucopia of books in this blessed house, books that already line the walls of this refuge, my study, where I am writing these notes; line one side of the graceful living room (in which, appropriately, we do not "live"); line one wall of my bedroom, line both sides of the wood-burning hearth in the upstairs sitting room; line a wall in the sun room, and scatter through the guest bedroom—and wherever there is space for a book.

The outpouring of books—almost every one of which at some time or another one or both of us have read—is a further mark of the oddness of my life's pattern—a craving man, unhappy unless he is *doing* something (often the action is with little or no real significance) and yet a bookish fellow fascinated by words, enjoying the writing of millions of words, chosen often with the greatest care, words weighed to see whether they do express precisely what I feel, or on a lesser level, what I see or am part of.

A contradictory kind of cuss indeed.

Running my mind back over the weeks we were out of the country, and especially in Persia, it is the mental picture of particular individuals that stands out, rather than abstract issues about "development policies" or "political forces," though I was certainly in a setting alive with just such questions.

First of all, of course, the figure of the Shah, thinner and more strained than when I first met him. But I have written about His Majesty at the time of the audience.

Ebtehaj, lounging (imagine Ebtehaj lounging!) in his office at the top of a new private bank, his fires banked, surrounded by literally scores of glossy photographs from his past. (Where are the pictures that predict his future, this man who saw the future so clearly when he sat in the seat of power?) His warm reaching out to me: "Don't lose faith in Persia, David," said so earnestly and half tragically.

His disciple and my oldest—in duration of friendship—most respected and beloved friend in Persia, Mehdi Samii. So thin, almost gaunt he seemed.

When a man is as patently genuine as he (I didn't say "sincere," a far lesser word), it gives you a sense of confidence that the environment and the genes that produced one such man have certainly produced or can produce others of the same kind. It doesn't take a large number of such men to give a country and a community a healthy tone.

Against this optimistic appraisal, I cannot forget or overlook that there are a great number of Persians who are or will be "spoiled rotten" by the easy money, the flood of prosperity, the boom-town spirit.

Haven't I been the lucky one, to have seen and been part of so many transformations of the life of people—the Tennessee Valley, Persia, Brazil. I should include in this roster of "experiences" what happened to the American people during a profound depression.

DECEMBER 2, 1973
PRINCETON

Lining with concrete the great west canal of the Dez irrigation project, which I watched during our Khuzistan trip, was intensely interesting. A huge machine pours cement, smooths it in place, and then a big vibrator spreads it into a plate. A sophisticated piece of modern machinery.

From where I watched this operation, across the canal I could see villagers—children included, of course—threshing rice, whacking the stacks of gathered rice with flails, the same method that has been used since time immemorial.

What do the village people think of this machinery which digs a great ditch, then lines it with concrete slabs? The D&R engineers of whom I asked the question said the village people just take it all for granted; makes no impact on their thinking. I wonder.

DECEMBER 9, 1973
PRINCETON

Thoreau said: "I left the woods for as good a reason as I went there. Perhaps it seemed to me that I had several more lives to live and could not spare any more time for that one." And then he continues: "It is remarkable how easily and insensibly we fall into a particular route, and make a beaten track for ourselves."

From that man of another time and temperament comes this summary of what eats at me (though I overdramatize it without a doubt). Have I made a beaten track for myself without considering whether I can "spare any more time" for that beaten track?

Beatrice says if *your* beaten path is one you have sought all your life, and is satisfying measured by your lifetime values, then just because it is a beaten path doesn't signify that it is wrong to stay on it.

Fatigue is something I somehow refuse to recognize as one of the important facts of life. But it is good to remind myself that an obviously sturdy and healthy man can have episodes, and that the "cure" is a bit of good sense about rest.

So, tomorrow I am not going into the office; this afternoon will watch TV football and play records.

A phone call from Louis Cowan. At his home he had a group of people: Mac Bundy, Kay Graham, Arthur Schlesinger, and the like. He said: "Inevitably, the subject became 'energy.' I said there is one man in this country who has predicted just what is happening and why, and that is David Lilienthal. Whereupon Mac Bundy started right off: 'Louis, you are absolutely right. Years ago he was right about this.' And went on to expand on this theme."

Said Louis: "On such a grey, rainy Sunday, thought this might make you feel good, to know that people like Bundy say these things about your foresight."

DECEMBER 13, 1973
NEW YORK

I am not a loner. I live by exchange of ideas and the stimulus of discussion and disagreement with my intellectual equals. This is what made the days and years working with Gordon so satisfying, in TVA and D&R.

The only way, Helen seems to think—and I half agree—that I can find some other use for my energies and experience is to quit D&R outright. "Then you can think what other things you could do that would be satisfying, but you can't do that *while* you are still enmeshed in D&R." ("But be damned sure," says Helen, "that Miss Baron goes with you, whatever it is," and how right she is.)

It is always sad to leave anything that means much to you, particularly if you have literally created it. But everything comes to an end, everything. And I may be ready for still another career!

DECEMBER 17, 1973
PRINCETON

The "energy crisis" dominates the verbalizing of the intellectuals and the press and the TV, much as Watergate did.

"Stop using so much energy," which they call "conservation."

To the extent that this means being less wasteful, it is hardly a great discovery.

But a column by Tony Lewis in the *Times* this morning, quoting Carroll Wilson,◖ carries the true story of what is behind it all: it is the negative defeatist retreat of the "limits of growth" phobia, in its latest form.

◖AEC General Manager, 1947-51.

Last night David 3d phoned us. He is transferring to George Washington University in Washington, D.C.

He is visiting with Sylvain and Nancy, and will go to Florence tomorrow. He had "transferred" but not without finishing his first semester at Oberlin. The small-town atmosphere of that middle-Ohio town was not to his liking. He had "problems" with other students—and why not, considering that he has been out of this country for seven important years. Washington, he says, will be more to his liking. He wants to study "constitutional law" and government!

In other words, he is in the process of trying to "find himself."

DECEMBER 20, 1973
FLYING TO ANTIGUA

An "ideal," "programmed time" for a Caribbean fortnight, a good *affirmative* time for such a break, such a refreshing of spirits and ideas and energy.

(With all the crap about lack of gasoline, this plane is two-thirds empty! The feeling grows on me that the wildly publicized "energy crisis" is mostly a way of getting increased gas prices—21% increase announced today—and electric rates—increase of 23% applied for, which will undoubtedly be granted.)

The kids in the next aisle in this "economy" trip have voices such as Dante, with his most torture-inventing skill, never could imagine. The screaming voices of little girls who are not too well "brought up" (I use the phrase to expose my snobbish side) are a curse in a cubicle like this plane.

DECEMBER 24, 1973
ANTIGUA

On this tropical oasis it is hard to believe there is a world of troubles out there. Dozens of smiling black servants fetching and carrying; the biggest thing to complain about is that our cottage phone is out of order (imagine *that* as a source of bellyaching, I who come here to escape a phone).

Three swims today; sun and breezes; books to read, including the delights of [Merle] Miller's oral biography of that salty, earthy "old sonofabitch Harry Truman," to use his favorite phrase. And the nagging trouble in my gut almost gone for the first time in six weeks.

DECEMBER 28, 1973
ANTIGUA

A youngish couple, obviously English, had one distinction: they had a whole bottle of Mumm's champagne during the al fresco lunches, and champagne and another bottle of wine at dinner. The son of the Mumm company, thought I. (Up here champagne is $22 a bottle—but this is BWI dollars, i.e., $11 U.S.—as I learned when I procured two for a small dinner of friends here.)

This noon the man joined our out-of-doors after-luncheon group, and I began to notice that he had an extraordinarily sharp and critical mind. He tore into the British—how stupid they had been in not recognizing the pride of the people in the colonies, such as Antigua had been—whereas the French gave the residents of Martinique and Guadeloupe a vote as French citizens, poured money in rather than draining it out.

Hearing this quite passionate and on the whole knowledgeable talk about development, I perked up; I have been almost ominously silent at these informal gatherings, since one can pick up some pretty tiresome people who hang on like limpets.

I learned he was William Davis (editor of *Punch*). He turned toward me, and soon we engaged in a most intense conversation—mostly him speaking, but me egging him on.

But it was when I began on economists that I realized I had found that rare bird, an economist who shares my profound skepticism of most of the tribe. He had been financial editor of the *Manchester Guardian*. I wondered how that background qualifies him to be editor of a most prestigious humor magazine, its humor being a quality many non-Britishers would say hardly exists. (It is a particularly acute British quality, I think.)

He recognizes that this is a puzzle to many people—*Punch* and economics. But it doesn't faze this intense young man with piercing blue eyes and the manner of a crusader. "Humor is a weapon," he said, among other things.

Anyone who holds in derision all this precious nonsense of the latter-day economist is ipso facto a treasured addition to that legion of people who are my teachers.

DECEMBER 30, 1973
ANTIGUA

Dinner tonight on the star-lighted terrace with a celebrated German archeologist of Greek antiquity, Dieter Ohly, and his almost equally distinguished archeologist wife.

Tall, awkward, middle-aged, bald, a wisp of hair over a broad-beamed head. Director of the Munich (Bavaria) Archeological Museum. That museum owns two of the great Etruscan vases, the third recently acquired by the Metropolitan in New York for a million dollars. Tried to restrain themselves about the shenanigans by which a notorious Italian dealer in antiques managed to get that great vase out of Italy (illegally, of course) and sold to the Met.

He will be in residence at the Institute in Princeton until spring. Told a story about an Italian historian, on the Institute faculty until, unable to stand America, he returned home. When he came to America, he brought his dog, and knowing that an Italian dog could not exist on American food, he brought with him "a calf"—i.e., the frozen carcass of a small cow. The Germans thought it so funny and so did we. This historian also upset the regime at the Institute restaurant because he had to have his spaghetti twice a day.

Mrs. Ohly is a most alert and handsome young woman, full of smiles. But when she spoke of the "decline of the German university," there was no smiling, no laughter. A cloud, sudden as the tropical showers that in a moment erase the bright sunshine. "Bremen is already Communistic. Even in the University of Munich and other universities in Bavaria, the most conservative of German states, not only do the students have a vote on new faculty members and other university matters but even the women who clean up the floors.

"The outlook for West Germany is not as pictured in the American press. It is dismal; the universities, in fact the whole country, are going down and down. And not because of unemployment or lack of prosperity. It is something deeper."

VII

1974

∽◯◠

Trip to Brazil and presentation of report on São Francisco Valley—Discussion of cooperation with Swedish firm of Gränges—Vacation in Antigua—Trip to Sweden and Iran—Visits with Thomas Hart Benton—Trip to Brazil—Trip to Vienna and Iran—Beginning of Public Service Management assistance to Government of Iran—Vacation in Antigua

JANUARY 3, 1974
ANTIGUA

Coming into the Cabinet Room at the White House, I had found General Eisenhower and Admiral Leahy deep in conversation—Ike always earnestly throwing himself into whatever he said, which is why, I suppose, he was taken to be a wise and thoughtful man on any subject.* We were there to discuss whether the bomb test planned for Eniwetok should go ahead with public disclosure. But what Ike was saying to the President's chief aide was: "It's those damned little hors d'oeuvres they give you at these Washington cocktail parties—that's what does it."

It wasn't too long after this "significant" discussion in the Cabinet Room (with the President [Truman] appearing shortly afterward) that Ike was hospitalized with some kind of bowel disorder.

This inn has not only physical attractions—the half-moon bay beneath hillsides rising and green—but the denizens are more interesting

*This refers to a 1947 meeting (see *Journals,* Vol. II, *The Atomic Energy Years,* pp. 212–13).

and congenial for our style than we have found anywhere else in our wanderings in the Caribbean. Most of the guests are English, as is the owner Peter Deeth, and his attractive son Paul.

And not only one "class" of British. For example, a round-headed, square-shouldered man of perhaps forty, with a belly like a balloon, which he carried as a mark of his success in life. He spent the whole of one afternoon here at the dock trying to learn to water ski. Surrounded by his laughing children and other guests, he would put on the skis, be pulled up by the tow line of a motor boat, and immediately plunge forward on his face. Then he would repeat the operation, again and again. All with complete good humor, and complete lack of success. I admired this version of John Bull stubbornness.

The English have a social pecking order that is more pronounced than we Americans, it seemed to me. Peter Johnson, a huge robust-speaking man, lives in a big house on Long Island at Oyster Bay. Was, or is, in some business concerned with recording devices (originally Dictaphone), very conscious in the pleasantest way of his record in the Royal Navy. Other guests are classified downward from this pinnacle. The nearest to the "top" I assumed was the editor of *Punch*. I assumed that the Becks (the widow and her grown son) would rate high in the English social pecking order since they are obviously very well-to-do and the top family of the Channel island of Guernsey (close friends of ours, here) with a three-generation tomato-under-glass industry. Helen inferred they may be established in Guernsey, but not quite up to the Johnson— i.e., British—social scale.

All of these people have manners that I find most appealing. Hearty laughter, but none of the high cackling laughter that a couple drinks at the bar seem to produce with some of my American compatriots.

JANUARY 4, 1974
FLYING TO NEW YORK

Aboard this plane we saw the first newspaper for two weeks. Greeting us, on the first page of the *Times,* the slightly condescending and benign picture of Herr Doktor Kissinger, *der Mensch Wunderbar,* lecturing the class from his exalted podium at San Clemente, saying the same things he said two weeks ago: the oil-consuming nations must join together, otherwise there will be a major depression, world-wide. This is substantially what Walter Levy, speaking for the private oil companies, said last summer. Frightening the oil producers with a major depression for the industrial countries, the consumers, isn't too likely to produce much of anything.

Herr Professor says we must recognize that this is an interdependent world. At the same time the Nixon Administration says the U.S. must become "self-sufficient" in fuel. Try to match those two!

JANUARY 5, 1974
PRINCETON

Yesterday afternoon, palm trees, the beneficence of the sunshine, the lapping of the seas on the shore; and last night the brilliance of snow over the moonlit landscape. This morning, the eastern dawn lit up what must have been trees and shrubs but was actually, as anyone could see, a fantasy of silvery ice.

JANUARY 10, 1974
NEW YORK

The monthly dinner at the Century was far better attended than I would have supposed, considering how unpleasant the weather has been. Met Fred Friendly, still booming. "I remember the last time I saw you was at Robert's house [Oppenheimer] when he was dying." Then he turned to Max Frankel, now Sunday editor of the *Times,* a boyish beaming fellow, the brightest-boy-in-the-room type. "I said to CBS that they have a film of how Iran looked fifteen years ago, the one Ed [Murrow] did with you; they should do another showing the change—the before and after Lilienthal. This fellow built the new Iran, built it, mind you, with his bare hands."

I didn't think Frankel seemed too impressed. I wouldn't have been, with such hyperbole. So many of "those present" worried about the Shah "raising oil prices by four times, overnight."

A real undercurrent of concern from friendly people: "What about the Shah? Has he moved too fast and too far?"

I say: "He knows what he is doing; and why should he continue to subsidize the Japanese with oil at cheap prices?"

But it is a warning. I wish Amuzegar were back; I would like to urge him to be more specific about what Iran is prepared to do for the less-fortunate developing countries—the point I made with no success whatever with Minister Ansary.

JANUARY 15, 1974
NEW YORK

John Dickey is a towering figure with a powerful voice, a voice that an outdoor tent-show evangelist would envy (if there are any speakers left who don't mouth a microphone). Adding to his height and girth, he

414]   *The Journals of David E. Lilienthal*

had a fur cap perched squarely on top of his vast dome of a head.

He was so warm and cordial. Now he is in New York working on American-Canadian relations for the Council on Foreign Relations.

I mentioned the Passamaquoddy tidal power project—that friends in Maine had been asking me if the change in the energy picture might not make Passamaquoddy closer to an economically possible undertaking. Said John: This would take approval and, more to the point, much money "from Ottawa." That seems out of the question, if the U.S. benefits from the project.

"Three years ago when I began this study of political and economic relations between the U.S. and Canada, I found relations were quite bad. The force of the 'new nationalism' in Canada has made this worse. I must admit that in the past three years those relations have deteriorated.

"The western provinces are perhaps the most violent against the U.S. When Seattle wanted to change the height of a Columbia River dam to increase power output, British Columbia simply tore the place apart, though they too would benefit from it."

John attributed this particular form of animosity toward the U.S. to that "stupid" proposal to treat waterpower on a North American basis. Proposing to take water from Canada to supply the U.S. was like sticking the Canadians with a sharp prod—a bit of nonsense even to propose.

JANUARY 17, 1974
NEW YORK

I have learned to say "No," as a reflex, to all invitations to "public dinners in the Waldorf Ballroom." It takes special untalent to compete successfully for the title of the phoniest, more tiresome, most meaningless routine in this glossy city of phony-ism. But the Waldorf public dinners win hands down, particularly when it is a "testimonial" to some temporary somebody who will be a nobody tomorrow.

Last night's "Tribute to David Morse," attended by an overflow crowd, was the shining exception. The subject was one of the warmest and most worthy, most practical men of high accomplishment for human causes. And the sponsor was Dr. Howard Rusk's World Rehabilitation Organization, which has been providing medical and physical therapeutic help and training for thousands now for a good many years.

At the conclusion, Rusk read the citation David (and the International Labour Organisation) received at the time of the award of the Nobel Peace Prize—"a universal man." I was seated next to the Morses at his table, and I wondered how he could manage to control his emotions well enough to respond with the remarks that were expected of him. But he did, in words that bore the mark of true eloquence, which is not to be found in the words alone but in the character and works of the man himself. I was terribly moved.

One man spoke to me whom I didn't recognize at all: he had been a young lawyer with Electric Bond and Share when Chairman Groesbeck and I were negotiating over the sale of their Knoxville utility. (This would be 1934 or 1935.)

This reminded me—and I retold the story with gusto—of Groesbeck's long, long, long phone calls to me from New York. At the conclusion of one of these calls—he was an interminable talker—Helen said, shocked: "Dave, was that a long-distance call? Why I can remember when we only sent a telegram if someone had died and for a long-distance phone call —well, it had to be a dire emergency and then it was mighty short." She was right; that's the way we were brought up.

This was a labor audience, largely the garment workers with their various specialist unions (the detail of labor specialization is astounding to me).

By David's arrangement I sat at our table next to the Ambassador to the U.S. from Romania, Corneliu Bogdan. A most attractive dark-haired man, quite young, knowedgeable about TVA and particularly about D&R (David Morse's briefing, of course), wants us to come to Romania to see what kind of help we can be, particularly in the field of joint ventures with American firms.

JANUARY 22, 1974
NEW YORK

A walk through a Marboro bookstore on 57th Street is enough to discourage one from giving up very much to write. Stacks of "remaindered" books, some of them quite excellent ones, or by people I know (e.g., Senator Paul Douglas). A dollar apiece.

A walk through the Princeton University Bookstore last Saturday overwhelmed me with the same feeling. Among current novels alone, scores of them, most of which I have never heard of, most of which probably will not be heard of by anyone a year hence.

I do have a life. Do I want (or *need,* for my "fulfillment") to exchange living for writing?

Lewis Strauss ended his long battle with cancer yesterday; Thursday I go to his funeral here, which will be one of those public-relations-style funerals at Temple Emanu-El.

My first comment was hardly a worthy one. I said to the driver: "Well, I have *oversurvived* a good many of my adversaries."

Glad I wrote him a friendly and quite sincere personal letter some months ago when I heard that he was very ill.

The obituary in the *Times* was long and wandering, and its interpretation of the meaning of Lewis quite cheap—quoting those who found he made a serious issue out of every difference with associates (true enough). Of course his part in the action to go ahead with the hydrogen bomb was made much of, and that is correct and part of his contribution to . . . I am not sure to what, considering that the arms race has been accelerated and security is no greater since that act.

JANUARY 23, 1974
NEW YORK

One of those eleven-hour days, hardly leaving my office and desk from 7:30 until 6:30. But so far as I can tell, none the worse for such an absurd, intense bang-bang of a set-to with a variety of concerns, all of them interesting. To me, at least.

The morning was largely given over to a seminar in the realities of management, as applied to this small but very fully occupied group of as diverse personalities, scattered locations (geographical, that is), and varying talents as I have encountered since I turned in my suit, with sighs of relief, as Chairman of AEC. In a real sense I have come to feel that "great" as were the issues and the consequences of my work on the AEC, D&R's progress is equally important. What this much smaller enterprise has done, and the high stakes of public import for which it is responsible in that vital place called Iran, stands out as a kind of peak of significance.

There are very definite limits to accommodation when the issues have been made clear. My reservation about myself is whether I have made my views and judgments clear, or even whether I have expressed them at all. One of the virtues of spending so many hours in the seminar sessions is that I find I am making my own convictions more clear.

The buzzer: "Chairman Ray of AEC is on the line; wants to talk to you urgently." So I took it.

The Chairman wants you to attend the Lewis Strauss funeral tomorrow representing the Commission; would you be willing to do so?

I was flabbergasted. Questions of good taste aside, the irony of my representing the Commission at a funeral, and a big public funeral, of a man who, as everyone there will know, made things damn difficult for me and the four of us on the first Commission, to say nothing of the ugly treatment he dealt out to Carroll Wilson.

Well, new people, new ways. So I'll be there. The Chairman said she would "notify" whoever—the funeral management perhaps?—that I am there in their place. Should I be put in a separate section of pews with a placard: official mourners from the Atomic Energy Commission?

JANUARY 24, 1974
NEW YORK

Other than a funeral, there is only one other circumstance of life (which shall be nameless) which makes me feel more thoroughly alive. No disrespect to the solemn rites over Lewis Strauss which I attended at the ornate Temple to Financial Success located at 65th and Fifth Avenue. Instead of feeling depressed or even very thoughtful, or introspective ("Are YOU next?" etc.) I walked from 65th down the Avenue, observing the bright eyes and very much alive young people with great delight, for what I was thinking (perhaps "feeling" is the better word) was: what a wonderful thing to be wholly alive in body and spirit.

That is banal, that comment, but no more so than the manner of a big funeral in that cavern of opulence. The eulogy by a rabbi was certainly a masterpiece, not of understatement. As I listened to the recitation of Lewis' "credentials" entitling L.L.S. to entry into the Valhalla of Conservative Adoration as pronounced by Robert Taft and H. Hoover, "How great are the virtues of understatement."

I feel like instructing Helen not to permit anyone to put on such an extravagant orgy of praise. But then Helen wouldn't permit it; indeed, would quietly walk out of the proceedings.

Lewis did so many good things in his lifetime that it wasn't necessary or becoming to make him out a demi-saint or a Jewish George Washington.

JANUARY 29, 1974
NEW YORK

David Morse and I make a good team.† His background of devoted public service in the U.S. and internationally and his backing of a good versatile law firm (in New York, Washington, Paris, and Beirut) matches my public service history, with the D&R technical staff (strengthened and broadened) to correspond to his firm's ability to put transactions together.

I mustn't underestimate how much added time it will take to get this new relationship going. But since I have made up my mind that D&R has

†Later in the year Morse became a Director and Vice Chairman of D&R.

much yet to deliver, and much yet to create, the time and effort will be well worth it.

On an impulse, phoned Nancy. I asked about the local (largely volunteer) newspaper she helps to run in Newtonville.

"It's doing all right; makes some of the local politicians think twice now before opening their big yaps. But it doesn't make any money. We do well to break even but we do that. Besides, it is fun."

I thought about that for a bit, quite overwhelmed with pride for my daughter.

Said I: "If you can do something useful and have fun too, *and* break even, I'd say that's pretty much the definition of a good life. That's about what I have done most of my life, what I am doing now: doing something I think is useful to others, having fun, and breaking even."

JANUARY 30, 1974
NEW YORK

Phoned the dentist for an appointment; talked to the hearty Mrs. Hart, his technician. Said she: "Katharine Cornell asked me to send you love and kisses; she is in the chair right now."

New York oddments:

On the plaza before the Time & Life Building, "our home," a long line of bicycles, most of them heavily chained, some of them having their front wheels taken off and chained. Brings back childhood recollections of the courthouse square in Valparaiso [Indiana], with the iron hitching rack with farmers' teams tied to the rail, while the Porter County farmers did their Saturday shopping for the week.

JANUARY 31, 1974
NEW YORK

A visit today from Robert De Giacomo, a longtime friend of my son and his family. "Oh yes, David 3d is doing very well, I think. Yes, he sees a good deal of our daughter Jane, but they are both working hard at school." (This last remark due to my grandfatherly frown indicating that I wondered if David was at George Washington to be educated or to pursue Jane.)

I recounted this, by phone, to Helen, with some mild sarcasm about how hard David was working at his studies. Said Helen: "As I recall, there was another pair of young people at college, in Cambridge, who studied together." That took care of me. She went on to "refresh my memory" about what we did more than fifty years ago. Touché, touché, old boy.

FEBRUARY 3, 1974
PRINCETON

Last night's reading finished off two famous old boys and got them buried. The Duke of Wellington and Alexander Graham Bell. Great detail about how from their seventies on they disintegrated, physically, and lost their spirit. Preoccupied with what Wellington called "the other side of the hill," etc.

Yesterday I did two hours of the briskest kind of walking, bundled up, for it was deliciously cold. Today jumped furiously on my stationary bicycle; did shadow-boxing on the back porch (too sleety slick for outdoor walking today).

Yesterday in Helen's and my after-breakfast think session, I decided to take action on the D&R history, calling Tom [Mead] to come out to discuss it, decided (just like that) to set aside $100,000 of our money, to be matched, I hope, by some foundation grant, and developed the idea of a big publicity spread announcing the expansion of D&R into new areas.

FEBRUARY 4, 1974
NEW YORK

A clue to the times: driving in to New York this morning, early, blocks and blocks of automobiles lined up, waiting their turn to get a few gallons of gasoline. This was repeated everywhere on our route and down Nassau Street.

Moreover, "energy" has become by all odds the most important single topic of discussion. All my past efforts to arouse interest in the subject of how badly we were handling energy, how little it was understood, particularly by the smart-aleck "analysts"—none of what I had to say made any impression. But now it binds, a bit, and becomes something to worry about, and *perhaps, maybe,* to do something effective about.

FEBRUARY 7, 1974
ON THE TRAIN HEADING FOR PRINCETON

My first trip by train to Princeton (or anyplace else, for that matter) for months and months. I don't particularly like making the trip to and fro by car but it does save my energy, which is about the only commodity I have that needs conserving. Certainly perking ideas I have in plentiful supply these days.

Spent the morning at the hotel, mostly on the phone and poring over newspapers that are filled with items that fit the strategy matrix I have been trying to develop for a couple years.

The broader aspects appeal to me. There is a world-wide shortage of the kind of fertilizer needed in Asia. Without such a supply, now so traumatically short, the widely touted "green revolution" and new seeds fall on their face, and in the fall carry not only a sad burden of hunger to millions but deflated expectations. These have been publicized so widely by Jim Grant and Chester Brown (his book, *Seeds of Change*).

D&R would approach such a subject from a generalized "resource base" point of view. But I want to see it tackled from the special angle of a businessman's calculations, which must be specific and (if I can be pardoned for an unpardonable term) project-oriented, a business point of departure.

I provide what I call, without apology, an idealistic perspective: The hungry people.

It is to put these two together: the businessman's craftsmanship ("crafty"?—not necessarily) and ability to deal with concrete and specific situations, and the perspective upon which D&R was founded and that I represent—*that* is what I want the immediate future of D&R, the new D&R, to spell out. Not really new. This was the original concept back in 1955.

FEBRUARY 8, 1974
PRINCETON

A heavy, a dense snow. Like a solid curtain, drawn down by some magic, unseen mechanism. Beautiful, restful. A sight to quiet that chronic restlessness that keeps me from doing just nothing, as I should after so much excitement of mind and such a whirligig of motion as marked the recent weeks of my work, and the heady, near delirium of the new ideas that keep bouncing around in my head, a fermentation of ideas and projects that become well formed so often out of a deep sleep.

FEBRUARY 19, 1974
NEW YORK

Thinking I needed some recreation after such a trying day, I trotted over to a movie house showing a burlesque on Western movies, *Blazing Saddles.*

I had to stand in line in a cold rain, for the privilege of buying a ticket, then a further stand in line clutching my little red ticket before we could be admitted. (I hope it will not be so complicated when the Angel Gabriel, if indeed it is he, asks for my ticket, later on.)

As we were all standing and shivering, and me feeling like an utter fool, a man in a long flowing velvet cape moved near us, and I looked up to see an arm reach out from the cape shaking a hand full of coins. All he said was: "Retarded." Said I: "Standing out here in the rain like this, I sure am retarded."

P.S. The movie was at about the level of the old male-only, two-bit burlesque-vaudeville, in which there are no double entendres—they spell out the gags in about the style of a college hazing. I left in the middle.

FEBRUARY 21, 1974
NEW YORK

Yesterday David Morse swept into D&R with a burst of enthusiasm, energy, and initiative that did my heart good. From the time we sat down to lunch at the Century until we parted on Fifth Avenue at 5:30, the doldrums and stagnation I had feared were setting in were gone.

He brought back a story from the Ivory Coast and Senegal that was more than talk. And the leisureliness that (Frederiksen definitely excepted) characterizes D&R staff (or so it seems to me) was replaced for one whole afternoon by the briskness that makes life invigorating, and fatiguing too, I expect.

David is personal counsel to Senghor, President of Senegal. I had looked on this connection as something less than monumental from a development point of view. Then he unfolded a Dakar newspaper which showed pictures of Prime Minister Hoveyda signing an agreement for a refinery, with David's picture representing Senegal. This joining of Iran and Senegal (at the "highest levels") was no mere coincidence for the future of D&R. Made me repeat Josephus Daniels' amusing counsel to me, as a young man: "Never follow an unlucky man."

The involved and unplanned circumstances that led to David Morse becoming a partner of mine at this particular time is more evidence that I am lucky and that I don't too often "follow an unlucky man."

FEBRUARY 22, 1974
PRINCETON

This very morning's *Times* reports on page one the offer of the Shah to pledge a very large sum (the figure one billion is used, but it amounts to more than that) for loans to alleviate the effect on the "poorer countries" of the higher oil prices. This announcement confirms how close I came to predicting these things in the talk on Iran I gave at Asia House earlier this month. It also makes me slightly annoyed that I didn't at least attempt to get my remarks published, and so get "credit" (what good is credit, except for one's vanity?) for our special knowledge and our identification with Iran.

FEBRUARY 23, 1974
PRINCETON

The Arab countries' cut-back on production is what caught the public eye the most, but it is the price increase and the consequent huge revenues that have brought the importance of Iran to the fore.

The image of Iran has changed, by the evidence of the number and kind of business types who want to see me these days. The reason: they are trying to find out, through a meeting with me, how to go about working themselves into the money harvest in Iran.

In my Asia House text, I refer to the position of the "raw-material regions," and the leadership Iran has provided or fortified vis-à-vis the industrialized countries. I say that the industrial countries will have to adjust themselves to the posture of the raw-materials countries.

Part of that adjustment must come from a new set of ethics for those Americans and others who procure raw materials absolutely essential to the West's very survival.

The bribing and corruption that has become standard practice among almost all those dealing with these countries will produce, in them, an international Watergate. In D&R we have been inflexible and will continue to be on this practice of kickbacks in one form or another, so common, so accepted.

Says X, a brilliant head of a trading group: "David, you are not living in the world as it is. We have to do this paying off or we won't be able to do business."

I predict that this policy is not only ethically wrong but will account for the further decline of American business reputation throughout the world.

FEBRUARY 24, 1974
PRINCETON

There are times—this morning is one of them—when I have a sense of having failed.

In what way?

I know that I have done a workmanlike job. D&R, and I, are again doing important things. My ideas about many areas are being adopted— whether it is coal and its place as a source of energy, or the unified development concept I designed and made work in TVA, or my strongly expressed concerns about safety and the hazards of atomic power, or the place of Iran on the world stage.

But I have failed to keep my name known and recognized. I no longer write articles or give interviews. "Whatever happened to David Lilienthal?" is a fair question.

Now and then—this morning was one of those times—I become restless and frustrated by my poor personal "public relations."

Two TV shows about Iran this day (not one, but two!). On the whole very fair, not the old picky kind. The long one on NBC was most impressive, in that it included not only the military build-up (the Iran Navy and Air Force story) but also included pictures of village schools and the Literacy Corps. That kind of social program Charlotte Curtis of the *Times* missed completely in covering the 2500th anniversary celebration a couple years ago, treating it in her absurd way as if it were a kind of social gathering for royalty. The meaning of that celebration escaped her, though it was there for her and others to see.

What Iran is doing is news now. It is what she is doing (and what I am doing) that counts, not the newspaper stories.

MARCH 1, 1974
PRINCETON

Yesterday, Tom Mead accepted responsibility for undertaking the D&R history. I have lined up the structure of a way to use our $100,000 to begin the operation, and as incentive (or "bait") for a university-cum-foundation partner.

At a time when I seem to have my plate full and I sleep only on weekends (eleven hours here in Princeton last night!), I have taken on a big, new, and fascinating merry-go-round.

MARCH 2, 1974
PRINCETON

When I am giving my money away I manage to get things moving rapidly and with a certain panache. Have just come from a half-hour with Bob Goheen at the little house in which he and Peggy now live (after the uncomfortable grandeur of Prospect House).

I told him of the D&R history project; I had taken Tom's draft of a proposal, which he read (and later asked if he could keep). "I find this exciting—and characteristically generous too."

He will move on this, interesting Princeton in the idea, and probably be helpful with some foundation ("It should be a natural for Ford"), but the decisive thing is how it can be made to fit into the structure and interests of a university. He will explore this at once with Morroe Berger, head of the Near East studies department.

I think about it a good deal, in spite of all the other exciting and controversial things that I am in the midst of.

MARCH 7, 1974
IN FLIGHT APPROACHING RIO DE JANEIRO

This will be another of those very brief forays into Brazil. Here it is Thursday morning; less than a week hence—i.e., Tuesday morning—I am to be back in New York and Princeton.

How we will get along with the presentation of our unified development report I have no idea; it stands to reason that the bureaucrats to whom it will be submitted next Monday will continue to be skeptical. On the 15th is the changing of the guard (the inauguration of the new President).

But I am not going to strain; the problem of doing something really fundamental about this Valley has been with the Brazilians for decades and decades; in the meantime the land in most of the area has become poorer and so the people have become no better off, probably the reverse. But there will be chinks of hope—the minerals; the improvement, slow but sure, in cattle raising; the general improvement throughout the rest of the country.

Besides, the small staff working on this study hasn't had the full kind of information really needed.

MARCH 8, 1974
RIO

The pressure under which our valiant, small staff group is working to get out the São Francisco report is something that doesn't appear in the report itself, nor in the memos in the files. One has to see it, as I have here since yesterday morning when I got off the plane and went right to work.

It will be a big document because unless a report is big and fat, it isn't worth the money. Will they study the whole? I doubt it.

It is a good job considering that the Valley is as large as the Iberian Peninsula, and diverse—really three regions, not one.

The vitality and happiness of the people in the crowded downtown streets where I went to buy Helen a birthday present. The mixture of brand-new office buildings and here and there the baroque and much-decorated buildings of a quieter time, with the restless flow of people, mostly some shade of brown, is truly enchanting. Though this is summer, there is a lovely breeze today and I could stay here most happily a long time.

MARCH 9, 1974
RIO (AT THE AIRPORT)

"You lucky man; traveling to those far places. And your work—'development.' Fascinating, I'm sure."

But how damned uncomfortable it is to get from one place to another. This is the "mobile age" but what that means is being jammed, packed, and standing, standing, standing, waiting and waiting.

It's worth it. Definitely. But in all the abstractions and the wide, wide world of generalizations about "the impact of technology," etc., there won't be found much about the just plain discomforts of getting around, of surviving in the close-packed urban centers, just the "swift magic" of jet travel.

"Swift." Ugh. In the air, yes, swift. On the ground, it's one wait after another.

To bed at one. Up at six. It is now almost nine, and this plane isn't yet ready to take off. Fighting to get tickets checked, standing for a full hour in a whirling crowd—of happy, good-natured people, I must add, for South Americans on a weekend particularly enjoy crowds and noise. Then pushed into a bus, and now in this really elegant plane.

BRASÍLIA

A very tired public servant, after five exacting years guiding Brazil successfully through a resurgence and a good record—this was Leitão de Abreu at his country "cabin" for a family dinner. What a warm friend and believer in me he is indeed.

The only "outside" guest was Henrique Cavalcanti. How fortunate that was, for we heard that he has been named again to his post as second man in the Ministry of Interior, responsible for the São Francisco Valley and our work and recommendations. He told Frederiksen that the new Minister, who takes office next Friday, has already decided that there is to be a Valley agency, and that he and the new Minister of Agriculture are going to work together to promote the region's food production potentials. Frederiksen told me tonight that at the last meeting of the Council to the Ministry, he had said that perhaps Brazil should consider whether food might not be more important ten years hence than energy, which now is pre-empting the river's water irrevocably, and putting a stop to any increase of irrigated agriculture in the basin.

MARCH 10, 1974
BRASÍLIA

Said the soft-spoken Chief of the Civil Cabinet: "Mrs. Nixon arrives on Thursday to attend the inauguration on Friday. She presents a difficult protocol problem."

At this point I must have looked puzzled. "Protocol?"—the wife of the President of the U.S.? Mrs. Roosevelt presented many problems on her many travels as F.D.R.'s eyes and ears, but protocol, never.

"You see, Mrs. Nixon is not an official, so . . . She must be appointed to some commission so she will have an official standing."

I found this amusing.

Finally the point of TVA is being understood by our own D&R Western contingent: that the *river* provides the unifying element.

The failure of the original São Francisco Valley Commission—frequently pointed out in our earlier discussions—was not due to inconsistency between the TVA concept and Brazilian conditions, but a failure to recognize how its central theme is necessary for overall development here.

The unifying element is *water*. The allocation of most of the river's water to power has prevented any real planning and coordination for agriculture, industry, etc.

Hal Frederiksen has done a brilliant job, though tardy in seeing that point, in building the whole framework for "realizing the Valley's potential" around the allocation of water use as the central theme of planning, the means of control, the handle by which the unified plan can be realized, implemented.

I wonder once more: Why should I wish on myself a big added load? Absurd on the face of it, except for the fact that taking on new risky things seems to be part of my nature, as long ago as the beginnings of TVA (Phil LaFollette thought it was "a poor risk for your career" and I was then thirty-two). I am now no longer thirty-two—or even seventy-two!

MARCH 11, 1974
GALEÃO AIRPORT, RIO

The "report" (all forty pounds of it!) on what we think Brazil should do about the São Francisco we carried up the stairs, grunting a bit melodramatically, and plunked on the Minister's desk at the appointed hour: 9:30. Only the Minister and Dr. Henrique Cavalcanti present for Brazil; for D&R there were Morris McClung, Hal Frederiksen, and myself. I nodded to Hal, who made a twenty-minute statement that I thought was workmanlike, solid, and sensitive to the issues and the obvious restlessness of the audience. Definitely a very exceptional man, Harald. The rehearsals with me over the past couple days, when we were together most of the time, he had taken very much to heart.

This was a strange episode. A year and a half ago the Minister and I had stood in the very same room, signing a contract in the presence of dignitaries. The study, our findings, and the recommendations were, ostensibly, directed to him. But Friday of this week he goes out of office, becomes a private citizen after many years of public service. The new Minister, who can make all that work amount to something in the world of fact and action, wasn't there, naturally, though Henrique, designated to continue as Secretary General, was. What Henrique and Leitão de Abreu said in a low key Saturday night was confirmed by the almost casual attention given to Hal's extraordinarily good presentation—i.e., that the new Minister "has decided" that a Valley agency will be confirmed according to our recommendation.

Flew from Brasília to Rio, fighting our way through this airport, one of the very worst in the wide world; now here I am again: we overfly Brasília on our way to Kennedy. Nothing about the air travel in Brazil is calculated to make life easier for an already tired guy.

MARCH 12, 1974
FLYING TO KENNEDY

This plane (poor Pan Am) is one quarter full, and only half a dozen in first class.

I bought Helen a birthday present (a pair of amethyst earrings), nothing prodigious but a remembrance of her upcoming (April 3) seventy-eighth birthday. I declined the proffer of a "wholesale" figure on the receipt for Customs. I know that the other way is the "custom for Customs" but I'd rather pay the full amount.

I can't help being amused. Is such "virtue," a moral revival in America, the consequence of Watergate? My guess is that the natural self-righteousness of the American people alternates with "putting it over," and that perhaps we are on a holier-than-thou bust at the moment.

The McClungs gave me dinner last evening and a chance to rest before taking this trip. They have two lovely little girls.

Judy and Francis Borcalli—McClung's irrigation righthand man— came in for a visit. These two, with an infant, had lived in a village in Afghanistan where D&R did such a good irrigation project, some years ago.

MARCH 14, 1974
NEW YORK

"The Shah is a—you have an excellent American word, a Congressional word—whip. No matter how much the country is doing, he whips us to do more, always more. He knows that sometimes what he demands is impossible, but it keeps the pressure on. Whip."

Jahangir Amuzegar got off these enthusiastic comments while we were on the 40th floor of the Time & Life Building, paying a visit to Ghaffari, who, as Jahangir said, is "Mr. Energy" in New York: representing the National Iranian Oil Company and the gas and petroleum as well.

For a time Jahangir had trouble getting any attention from the press or the magazines. He called on me to help, which I did (an Op-Ed piece through my discussions with Harrison Salisbury, a full-length article through intervention with Bill Bundy of *Foreign Affairs.*)

But *now.* Wow. He makes a statement or a speech to the Security Analysts Society, for example, covered by "all the wire services, and the *Wall Street Journal."* He is carried away by the attention paid to him. And no wonder.

MARCH 18, 1974
NEW YORK

It takes me a while to get used to seeing so casual, informal, and youthful appearing a man as Bill Bowen presiding in the "President's Room" of Nassau Hall [Princeton]. A tweed jacket with leather patched elbows, a mop of hair over a pale face (he has just come back from a bad case of flu, he said).

With us was one of my very favorite of men on the Princeton faculty, Morroe Berger, probably the best informed man on Egypt anywhere in these United States. Also John Lewis, dean of the Woodrow Wilson School. And Pampanini, who drove out from New York in a spiffy orange rented car to pick me up at 9:30.

Both Berger and Lewis were very affirmative about the D&R materials project, as described by Tom Mead in an expanded memo. Lewis had reservations, but was affirmative on the whole. The reservations were of the kind one would expect from a scholastic administrator, concerned about how this, to them, unknown "Thomas Mead" would fit into the faculty structure.

MARCH 19, 1974
NEW YORK

At 12:30 today, through the door of the handsome Platt Room on the fourth floor of the Century, came Erland Waldenstrom, a very tall, spare, long-faced, solemn man of about sixty, in tow of David Morse. By 3 o'clock he, as chairman of the great Swedish firm of Gränges, and I for D&R, had agreed on the first stage of a "joint venture" in Iran, perhaps elsewhere as well.

This may be—at this moment of exuberance I believe it firmly—the first of a series of joint ventures with private firms, the kind I have been maintaining are what the *future* of development should hold, rather than continuing only the "foreign aid" or "international public lending" phase of development, a phase I believe has seen its day. For D&R at any rate.

MARCH 21, 1974
NEW YORK

"Confined" to bed here in the hotel by some damned bug that last night and this morning fevered me quite some. I have just had "clearance" from Dr. Hoskins to be on our way to Antigua beginning tonight. Probably mostly fatigue. I really "put out" like mad Tuesday.

The upshot: I have just signed a memorandum of understanding unique, I think, in development history, certainly a first in the story of D&R.

David Morse has made all (OK, 75%) of the difference for D&R in the past several weeks particularly. The Gränges are *his* clients; it turns out they thought he had done them a great service in getting me to consider and then to commit myself to the furthering of their world-wide ambitions and diversification in development.

That sounds stuffy and indeed conceited; but that is the way they put it to him. Like the Brazil contract, the engagement was conditioned, explicitly, as well as induced, by what I could contribute personally (and by my "leadership"—a strange word considering how my colleagues periodically crawl over me).

MARCH 24, 1974
ANTIGUA

About the relation of the state of men's minds to their bodies, many thousands of words have been written and much nonsense spoken. Some has been by medical men (e.g., my dear friend Atchley, father of somatic medicine) and by self-styled experts in the human psyche.

In my career and personal life I am a living example of this inter-weaving of physical illness and mental and spiritual state.

But I never knew until my current reading of Flexner's classic life of none other than the oh so solid, unemotional George Washington that

Washington so unexpectedly confirms this bond between body and spirit.

And the story's application to my own half-dead years of "retirement" immediately after I left the AEC is startling.

Washington, victor over the British, back to his beloved (but I suspect, boring) Mt. Vernon acres—and boring wife. Would the colonies which he freed from "British tyranny" tear themselves apart or would they adopt a framework for a united nation? The prospect looked dark. He was torn between doubts and his desire (so he said, repeatedly) to follow the path of a quite private life.

His health during this period of indecision and unhappiness was "failing." Rheumatism so he could not raise his arm, could hardly turn over in bed for the pain in his legs, etc.

Then this passage from Flexner (*George Washington and the New Nation,* p. 160). Washington felt a haunting sense that "I am passing rapidly into the *vale of years* where the genial warmth of youth that shines its votary with a generous enthusiasm becomes extinct and where the cheerlessness of the prospect often infects the animal." He speaks sadly of "the increasing infirmities of nature and the growing love of retirement." But why seek consolations in retirement? He was only fifty-six years old and comfortably rode twenty miles almost every morning.

Then the punch line, looking back on my withdrawal symptoms when I too was "only fifty-six": "Why not"—(the words of Flexner)— "wash away the specter of old age in floods of purposeful activity?"

I have been less successful on this holiday by the sea in cutting off all thought of my work for a spell than when we were here before. Full of ideas of where we go from here with the concept and record of D&R to build on!

MARCH 28, 1974
ANTIGUA

Henry Fonda, the actor, is playing the role of Clarence Darrow on Broadway, so I noticed before we left. Which led me to comment to Helen this morning over our beachside breakfast how I regret that I was not writing a journal during the years when I knew Darrow (and his eccentric wife, Ruby) in the earliest years of our life in Chicago in the twenties.

This is not the only episode that would make interesting reading as part of a contemporary record spanning so many years and so many turns and twists of American life, public and private.

During many months I saw a good deal of him, and her. They were an extraordinary couple, and Clarence's misanthropy might be attributed to Ruby's bewildering, unpredictable conduct and character (so it seemed to me as a man in his twenties).

What does the compilation of my papers given to the Princeton Library include that refers to Darrow? I wrote an article for *The Nation* about a famous Detroit race-riot case in which Darrow was counsel for the Negro defendants. I assume that article is in the files. What about my correspondence with Freda Kirchwey, then editor of *The Nation,* about that article? The article itself gives my impression of Darrow as a lawyer in that case as seen by his young junior counsel—i.e., D.E.L. (The judge who sat on the case later became a Justice of the U.S. Supreme Court, Judge Frank Murphy.)

At one time in the twenties I committed myself (on my initiative) to the writing of a biography of Darrow. He provided me with the transcript of some of his closing statements to the jury in famous labor cases, and I culled accounts of many of his cases, and other more personal material, including his many "lectures" on philosophical subjects.

I gave up the biography project, because, as I recall, his pessimism and negative outlook on life as stated in his writings depressed the hell out of me, being so contrary to my own temperament then—and now, when I am considerably older than Darrow was.

What could have happened to the documents? Did I profligately throw them away?

If I were of a mind—or disposition—to write an autobiography, a form of looking backward, as Bruce Bliven and Cass Canfield have often urged me to, then today's recollection of yesterday would be the focus of my writing and recall.

Why do I find the idea of a conventional autobiography of so little interest?

It is precisely because it would require that I keep thinking about the past, and embellishing it, no doubt, as most autobiography is embellished or colored by an old man's memory—or a young man's, too, for a good many autobiographies have been written by men in their middle years, and some of them absolutely first-rate—e.g., Graham Greene's or even Benjamin Franklin's.

The fact is I am far more interested in (not to say excited by) what will happen (or can be made to happen) next week in New York, or in succeeding future weeks in Stockholm and Tehran, than in what happened in Chicago in the twenties or in my boyhood in Indiana.

How does this "brave renunciation" of the past fit with my publication of journals of things past, and my current unhappiness that Volume VI, though the manuscript has long been written, is still not ready for the printer and won't be until I can squeeze out the time to do the final editing?

MARCH 29, 1974
ANTIGUA

Another talk with Helen (post-breakfast, of course; when else?) about planning "my writings."

She took a firm, affirmative position, as opposed to her more usual inquiring, exploratory stance.

"You write your journal entries rather easily, in contrast to the hard going when you are writing or trying to write a 'set piece.' You write your journals about events or reflections that grow out of the day's activity or what those activities set in motion in your head.

"Isn't there a way to capture that informal style and outlook as part of that book we have been talking about for so long?"

This morning, I thought I got a glimmer (only a glimmer, true) of how this could be done.

The theme of the book is the thread that runs through the contemporary world: development. Development and growth are the chief concerns of our time.

My whole viewpoint about my experience in development is that the spring from which it all flows is not "economics" or "sociology" or "political science" but people, separate individuals. This conviction is particularly borne out by the first part of the manuscript of the journals written in Peru in 1965—a series of portraits of people—not officials particularly, but the people who spurred that effort toward development and those who "squnched" it.

So why not begin the book with a portrait gallery? F.D.R. and his dreams for the Tigris and Euphrates as he flew over that region (now, years later, *my* region, you might say) or Harry Truman greeting me with similar concerns about the Missouri, or Ebtehaj, or Nehru, a string of people, interesting people, some famous, some only local but full of personality.

What ties them all together, these strong people? The very tie or theme that characterizes the whole of modern life—i.e., the promise, the tantalizing promise of development.

APRIL 6, 1974
WASHINGTON

I don't recall when I have laughed so heartily as at the Gridiron dinner tonight. Laughter of any kind, hearty or not, in this city at this time is the rarest commodity.

This room facing Lafayette Park overlooks the White House, and there is a full moon tonight. What has gone on in the past year and a half in that symbol of American respect for its democracy is hardly a laughing matter.

The skits were extraordinarily clever, and without malice. What a huge crowd it has become, that affair. Of course, I met so many men, a good section of the notables of yesteryear and not a few who still hold sway.

APRIL 8, 1974
PRINCETON

On the way home, Fletcher Knebel, now a successful novelist (who lives in Princeton), asked me if, seeing the Washington scene at its most garish, I felt a hankering to be back in that life. I could honestly say, and "without mental reservation," that I had no vestige of such hankering.

Said I: The Washington press corps makes me uneasy, creepy, even more than in the years when working with them and knowing them was part of my *working* life. Lord Acton's overquoted axiom, "power tends to corrupt," explains my revulsion about these interesting, brilliant, but corrupted journalists. It is not only those who have the power who are thus corrupted; power corrupts those with whom the powerful deal, who, as in the case of the Washington press, must, or do, cultivate, flatter, cozy up to those who have power.

It was a wide-ranging hour and a half I spent with Robert McNamara and his patient little wife Marge at their home on Tracy Place [in Washington], and while he drove me back to the Hay Adams Hotel in his tiny Pinto we continued to talk most intensely.

For twelve years they have lived in a quite spacious house in a residential area not far from the center of the city. Beyond the big windows of the living room, a small quite formal garden, on each side two large dogwood trees. How they love that spot, for they referred to the comfort they get seeing the green, and "soon those pink dogwoods—how they light up the whole place." Somehow I hadn't believed that the tense McNamara (and never more tense than that Saturday noon) had so much feeling about flowers and green. He spoke with quiet feeling: "We have a conservationist in this house; our daughter is entering the Yale School of Forestry and Environment."

Their son, who suffered so about his father's part in the Vietnam war and I gather made his father suffer—as my children did me—works in a community agricultural project in the West somewhere, and will be going to Davis to become an agriculturist of sorts.

Bob himself is chuck full and overflowing with a preoccupation about "agricultural productivity," but it takes the form of concentrating on the "productivity" of the very poor. This has filled his speeches and public statements, to the point where I began to wonder if he has much grasp of how poor people fit into the overall development process, for certainly the very poor (the sub-Sahara starving millions) almost exclude consideration of less clinical cases of need, and indeed seem to me to obscure the methods by which people who have a better chance can get their heads above water.

So on the drive back to the Hay Adams I said I didn't think enough attention was paid to the question: *Why* are these people very poor? Is it because the natural resources, the land and water, that should sustain them simply aren't there? Does it make sense to expend scarce resources of funds, seeds, fertilizer, and particularly human energies to get these miserable people over one starvation crisis when we know their basic resources won't sustain them for long and the whole process of rescue has to be repeated in a couple years? Should we not question whether they should continue to live where there is little prospect that the foundations of their life will support them continuously?

At this line, Bob's jaw muscles tightened; the network of fine wrinkles seemed to deepen in his taut face (I had never seen him look so tired as on this visit).

He said of course he recognized that the world has only so much in the way of resources or skills, so it did not make sense to expend them, pour them into a hopeless situation. Some people living in such a region, perhaps, should be moved to a more hopeful place. Malians (he shook his head, a bad memory crossed his face)—shouldn't they move on to the Ivory Coast, for example?

"I emphasize the very poor, and the spectre of starvation in Africa and perhaps India, to stir the conscience of people. I do recognize that we can't waste limited resources just to keep a hopeless situation going. But I still feel that unless we look hard at such areas, we can't know whether we might not be overlooking some one element that could change the picture."

He told a story of a visit to some very poor agricultural cooperative. The man he put in charge said the people simply won't work. That simple. Just won't work more than four hours a day. Can't get productivity up on four hours. Then the manager changed the nutritional pattern, which did improve the picture substantially, but not enough. Try some other move, said Bob.

I was somewhat shocked intellectually by this social-worker preoccupation, as I would call it, on the part of someone who stands for the whole spectrum of development, though at the same time full of admiration for the humanitarianism of this allegedly "computer minded" man (as his Vietnam enemies described him).

A former senior member of the World Bank development technical staff said to me: "Tell Mr. McNamara how you feel; give it to him straight. He doesn't listen to his staff; perhaps he will listen to you." I give him full marks for patience—he did listen and, better still, he responded.

Because of his reference to the Ivory Coast I said Minister Diawara has asked us to pick up our development work there where we left it off, after eleven years of first-rate planning work, this time to implement what we had laid out, now that they have the money to carry things forward (cocoa and coffee prices have made them almost rich). Bob said he was delighted to hear this. After we have put forward some proposals, particularly respecting agriculture, we should informally get word to him about them.

I also told him about the latest important news about D&R: the "partnership" with Gränges; told him what a remarkable man I thought Waldenstrom is, and why I thought Gränges could supply some of the missing managerial "how to do it" that Iran and other countries needed.

Bob said, "I would like to meet Waldenstrom, when he comes to Washington or I go to New York." The fact that this big Swedish firm would join up with a small, consulting, idea outfit such as D&R seemed to fascinate him. It does me too, for that matter.

APRIL 20, 1974
PRINCETON

Jim Emmert dead. From the first time I saw him, a shambling Hoosier living penuriously (by his choice) in a hall room in Cambridge where we were in the Law School, until we visited together when he was Chief Justice of the Supreme Court of Indiana, he never changed. A rough-hewn man, a natural man.

And sad news about another big figure in my life: Bill Voorduin, a really great "big dam" engineer, seriously ill, according to his daughter, with whom I talked by phone yesterday.

APRIL 24, 1974
NEW YORK

Lunch yesterday with Joe Flom.

Despite the evidences of personal prosperity, he is full of gloom: "The country is coming apart at the seams," pretty much the same mood and even the terminology one hears all around.

Not from me. One can't preach "change," as I have for so very long, and expect things to remain the same, not only personal "morals" (meaning, usually, sexual behavior) but also conformity with legal restraints about what is mine and what is yours.

Joe joins the ranks of those who have "made good" according to the

ambitions and standards of twenty-five years ago when he got out of law
school: fighting for an education and getting it, starting at the bottom in
law practice, and allowing: "I have all the money I'll ever need—but *so
what?*" He put to me this last question, rather an exclamation, with that
sidelong look of his.

He couldn't quite disguise his fascination with the kind of interesting
(though absurdly ill paid) work that I do.

APRIL 28, 1974
PRINCETON

A very brief story in the *Times* this morning that almost all of the
present Iranian Cabinet members have been either replaced or the present members given different portfolios. Will this include Vahidi (our
power proposal would be a dead letter, for practical purposes, if we had
to deal with still another Minister)? Tomorrow I should know more.

Could I have imagined years ago that a change in the Iranian Cabinet could be so important to my work and, therefore, to me?

The warmth of my personal life, the mounting evidences of a healthy
life, and not only physical; the expanding interests in people and persons,
the beginning of what could be a major "collection" of contemporary
drawings, mostly *New Yorker* cartoons. I now own eight of these and plan
to have several times that number before I'm through. My first collection
of anything since I "collected" cigar bands and stamps as a youth!

It was a happy week, a glowing week. Is there a less well worn term
than "fulfilling" to describe what goes on in the heart of a man who has
had a life as varied as mine? On the verge of my 75th birthday, *not* to be
plodding along, not to be losing my enthusiasms but adding excitement
to daily life—that's the way it is this spring.

I leave it to others to despair about America. I am as dismayed by the
smell in the Nixon Administration as anyone, though not quite as self-
righteous as some of the former F.D.R. and H.S.T. graduates (some of
whom were not as pure as they would like to have us believe).

What heartens me is a wholly personal view of the life around me,
and in which I participate. So I sleep badly, so the tremors of rampant
inflation and their effect on my income give me something to think about,
negatively, still I am so fascinated and delighted at the changes that I see
I can't let the more cosmic events, as portrayed by the word-people of the
press, oppress me too much.

Mr. Tom Moore, who now and then drives me to or from Princeton,
said: "No, I couldn't make that Puerto Rico trip, to play golf"—he plays
in the high sixties—"but instead we will be going to Spain. We go some-

place like that every year." A taximan, indeed. "Where else, than America?" as they say.

The faces, the demeanor, the way people dress that I see on the streets of New York; this is the greatest cavalcade imaginable. By the time I have seen a dozen interesting figures on the street, I'm grinning like everything.

An hour-and-a-half visit, in the garden, with Professor Morroe Berger.

Told him I wanted to bring him up to date on the gift to Princeton of the D&R files, and of my gift to Princeton, both of these to be without the condition originally discussed with President Bowen, Berger, John Lewis, and the latter with Princeton's counsel, Tom Wright. While the papers will not be signed and the first portion of my gift not made until this coming week, the terms are settled. The materials would be available to scholars, for teaching, research, and professional use. Morroe has no doubts about the use of the material throughout the university, and not just in the Near East department or the Woodrow Wilson School; sociologists and engineers among others would be involved, he was sure.

Princeton has not in the past given much attention to Iran, in its teaching and scholarly activities. Instead, the emphasis has been on Lebanon, and, more recently, strong concentration on Arabic language, and history in North Africa (Morocco, etc.).

Now Princeton wants to give most of its teaching, research, and development attention to Iran. Goheen, when president, explained this to the Shah a year or so before he left the presidency. Out of this came the Pahlavi Fund grant of a half-million, "and we want and expect this amount to be greatly increased from the oil companies, among others, and also additional grants from the Shah."

Princeton believes that the Shah is interested in strengthening "intellectual and scholarly ties" to the U.S. From Iran's point of view, this is good policy, to avoid the impression that it is only because of the U.S. as a source of military equipment that the Shah is concerned about this country. The Princeton connection fits and furthers this concept.

Then, said Berger, there is the long-standing connection and association of Iran and D&R, which has a special place in recent Iranian history, plus the standing and reputation of D.E.L. Add to this the gift and transfer of the D&R papers, and the bond becomes stronger.

Princeton is increasing its faculty commitment to contemporary Iranian public policy, while continuing its credentials in the area of culture, history, etc., and has added a Professor Clinton to the faculty for that purpose.

"It's very appropriate, this gift of the papers, with the purpose of providing a base for study of D&R's development contribution to Iran. Iran is the only country in the world, so far as we know, that has adopted a distinctive policy for development, and that is the unified development theme of D&R, as in Khuzistan."

APRIL 30, 1974
NEW YORK

At the Century for lunch. McGeorge Bundy, President of the Ford Foundation, said: "Your name came up today; complimentary, it was . . . Yes, the enthusiastic word was from President Bowen of Princeton."

Hope this means what I *think* it means, that Bowen, like Goheen et al., is already seeing the potential significance of this undertaking, and laying the groundwork for supplementary foundation support. Certainly Princeton's prospects for substantial sums from Persia depend upon some new, fresh ingredient, and the "source materials on the development process" may be it.

MAY 2, 1974
PRINCETON

Yesterday morning at the office, Andrea handed me a telex from McClung in Rio: the new Minister of Interior notifies us that our contract is terminated. And this at a time when only the day before it was announced that the new President, Geisel, presented a draft of a new corporation, COVALE, that embodies the essential and controversial proposition we advanced and stood firmly for (against the skeptics)—i.e., a Valley-wide agency.

MAY 3, 1974
PRINCETON

Did I say "Brazilian bumps," yesterday? Having our recommendation publicly adopted, and then, presto: You're fired. Andrea has just talked to Morris McClung in Rio. The new Minister called McClung in, said our work had been very useful, was going to be used in the creation of a new corporation, as we had recommended; the report was going to be very useful. But it will take a couple or three months to get the new agency set up and functioning, and during that time there would not be anything consequential for D&R to do. Hence, to save that money, he rescinded our contract.

And paid us for the most recent invoices, almost upon presentation —which relieves any cash problem.

The significant thing, of course, is that instead of our being repudiated and professionally humiliated, the Minister went out of his way to commend our work. Which may well mean that when the COVALE, our recommended TVA agency, comes into being, we may be engaged again.

Something upsetting, however, is going on in Iran, with the wholesale changes in the Cabinet membership. It will be an unruly kind of time to be there, but that is exactly the time I should be there, and that I most enjoy. I not only make speeches about change, I really relish it, though at times, of course, I grouse and fuss.

The "documents" are ready to sign that commit Princeton and D&R to a joint inquiry into what I call "the development process."

Four of us, Tom Mead, Morroe Berger, and [Princeton Librarian] Bill Dix, all excited and full of ideas, met for lunch at Prospect this noon.

The deed of trust I thought could become a historical document. It borrows heavily from Tom's and my memo about what this is all about, what could come from all this future analysis of the maze of D&R paper detritus and the memorabilia of nineteen years of work, the successful, the frustrating, the good ideas and the boring engineering-style English (is anything uglier and more awkward than the alleged prose of men trained only in engineering?).

I walked through the east campus with Berger, past the glowing giant tulips of the Prospect garden, the dazzling display of row upon row of dogwood in supreme flowering, past the sober hirsute students occupied with their own thoughts, looking neither to right nor left—and I thought: What a privileged man you are, Dave. To be welcomed and, indeed, respected by the academic community as one with ideas worthy of the study that is called "scholarship" and also an activist, a do-er, even a businessman, and a prosperous one, able to give $100,000 to a university for a study program growing out of his work as a do-er.

Can anyone have it better than that?

MAY 4, 1974
PRINCETON

Abolhassan Ebtehaj came to my office Wednesday morning, for a long (one-and-a-half-hour) talk. He has lost none of the fire and passion which made him the hero among most of the young Persian intellectuals of the early days of our work in Iran. Though he is again simply a banker, as he was when the Shah put him in charge of the first Plan Organization more than twenty years ago, it is still public issues that concern him.

Chiefly that our plan for the development of the Khuzistan should receive so little support and little sense of urgency.

He showered contempt on the policy recently announced that Iran should become a leader in producing electricity from the atom—this while five million kilowatts of hydropower from the Khuzistan go unutilized.

But most of his words, intense and unsparing, were reserved for his disagreement with the Shah's policies and the picture of himself the Shah has presented to the world in recent interviews.

If there was any strain of the dictator in the Shah or the secret police were as horrible as is sometimes charged, surely Ebtehaj wouldn't be allowed to talk this way in Iran and outside.

MAY 7, 1974
IN THE SAS AIRPORT LOUNGE WAITING TO TAKE OFF FOR STOCKHOLM

Of the many takings off for Iran of the past almost twenty years, this may well be one of the most notable.

The first almost complete reorganization of the Cabinet. "Shake-up" is the newspaper term. But actually this isn't as significant as it first appears, for the Ministers and Ministries most consequential for our work—agriculture and power—are unchanged, though probably increased in importance. The big change is the designation of the clever and ambitious Hushang Ansary to the new Ministry of Economic Affairs *and* Finance. A kind of super-Minister.

The chance of advancing the "new dimension" of D&R I have for these years been pressing for, but this time with the presence of a distinguished Swedish industrial firm, Gränges.

The effect of the decline of our standing and function in the São Francisco Valley—i.e., the termination of the balance of our contract (another six months)—is modified by a telex stating that the Deputy Minister of Interior, Henrique Cavalcanti, wants us to remain for some further work. Could this be negotiated into something more substantial? In any case, it is clear we are not in a Brazilian doghouse, as the first curt message from the new Minister seemed to indicate.

It will be a comfort to leave behind "the Nixon Tapes" and "the Transcripts." Or will we? It was sickening enough to read in the *Times* some samples of this extraordinary display of crude cynicism and depravity. But to have to hear it again and again is almost too much.

Will it stir the American conscience and indignation? Or have so many people been brainwashed by this most diligent artful crew, become so bored, so concerned with their own more useful thoughts, that once again evil men will prevail?

The best thing that has been said about the indecent exposure—or the exposure of major indecency—came the day the transcripts were published last week. Eric Sevareid on CBS burst through the bounds of desiccated comment on TV to speak from his heart and soul—and it was a great picture of the outraged conscience of a true and (one hopes) not an old-fashioned—i.e., out-of-date—American.

The Walton Butterworths put on their annual May wine and strawberry bash—a huge party—just down the street from us. We knew only a few of the guests—looked like the country club and Wall Street group. (I didn't notice a single individual from the Princeton faculty, although Emmet Hughes and his blooming young bride probably count—he now teaches at Rutgers.)

When I saw George Gallup, it came over me that this relaxed, smiling, Middle West–looking man, broad-shouldered, youthful-appearing really, is not a man but an institution, and, unlike many such personalized institutions, has also become himself an adjective—e.g., a Gallup poll.

How much this man has affected the political and social life, the thinking and decisions of the American people! Whether for good or quite the contrary, I couldn't say. I think on the whole it has been a bad thing, because we Americans appear to have taken it so seriously.

MAY 8, 1974
FLYING ACROSS NORWAY AND SWEDEN FROM BERGEN

Mountains, white in the mist, and for part of the way the deep dark inlets—I suppose these are "fjords." But it is a desolate scene.

Bergen: How do the people sustain themselves? From the air, great grey flat granite. Can it maintain any living thing? Apparently, for there are clusters of houses. And even on a tiny island completely cut off from the land, a village of sorts.

Iran has its great central desert. That desert is tawny, and very tiring to the eyes and spirit—mine, at least. This desert is white, and deeply broken. But desert it is.

MAY 9, 1974
STOCKHOLM

To be valued for those qualities, personal and professional, on which one himself sets the highest value, that is what creates a good partner-

ship and in time that very rare and precious relationship, a good friendship.

At a small dinner last evening here in the restrained elegance of the
Operkeller, Erland Waldenstrom quoted Bergson, characterizing my
years of journal writing: "To think like a man of action, and to act like
a man of philosophy."

MAY 10, 1974
STOCKHOLM

On a bright early spring day, sparkling air, lakes everywhere, roads
all to ourselves (how rare this has become), spruce and birch covering
the rolling hills: beautiful and serene it all was.

And then by contrast, the power of man and his machines: down into
the great iron-ore mine (one of the oldest such anywhere), over 500 meters down, with the digging being done by remote control, a man watching a bank of three small TV screens punching buttons that loaded and
moved the cars way down in the earth.

Dinner with a truly remarkable man, the long, thin, thoughtful but
warm Erland Waldenstrom, and his extraordinary wife, full of enthusiasm and interests. They all seem excited at the beginning of the Iran
adventure. And frankly, so am I.

David Morse and I, by dint of a flood of telex messages, have laid out
a program that will kill ordinary people, for seven days. How overwhelmed I thought John Silveira would be by all the requests to meet
everyone and see everything.

MAY 11, 1974
AT THE STOCKHOLM AIRPORT

The Swedes may not fully realize it but their profusion of female
blondeness has affected the American "culture." Except that here being
a "blonde" is common statistically, whereas in the polyglot American
female population to be a blonde (whom gentlemen still apparently "prefer"—not me, definitely) requires oceans of Clairol.

This is Saturday so there is a good deal of family travel complete with
little, very little, girls, blonde and cute as all get out.

The cuteness diminishes as a function of age, I notice.

EN ROUTE TO FRANKFURT VIA HAMBURG

Stockholm to my eyes is a very appealing city in appearance. I say
this with not a little surprise, as the mental picture I had was that of a

stuffy, stolid place. Not at all, physically. In the center of the city is a small lake ringed by public buildings of good if less than imaginative proportions—the Palace, the Parliament, and so on. Against the skyline, the spires of cathedrals—one slender spire actually lacy. And to top off the delight of a city so close and intimate, a three-masted schooner and a line of smaller working vessels, their bowsprits extending out along the wharf, right in the middle of a metropolitan city with the bustle of cars.

The sunshine has been like sparkling autumn rather than spring as I know it, except for the gleaming fresh green of new leaves. And a sky of a metallic blue.

Parks and water—rarely have I seen more of both in the heart of a city. Erland Waldenstrom's home was once a hunting lodge for Kings of Sweden, in a forest, but close to the heart of the city. Low ceilings, sprawling rooms—in other words, a country place. Neither Erland nor his intense and handsome wife are given to elegance (though he dresses as a French industrialist might, double-breasted, careful, she however in country tweeds).

David Morse and I have spent a good many sessions of talk about the purpose of this trip so far as our Gränges associates are concerned.

What can come out of our introduction to Iran of this first-rate Swedish industrial firm is certainly anything but clear. Minerals—their mining and processing, metal production and fabrication (particularly steel, copper, and aluminum)—would seem to be a long-term possibility.

With his obvious imaginative outlook, will Waldenstrom find interesting things that Iran greatly needs but which go far afield from minerals? I am banking on this, though why I have this feeling depends almost entirely on a hunch. The hunch is that he would not be setting out on this trip to Iran, and entering into a wide-ranging contract with D&R, if he were not in his mind thinking beyond mining.

Perhaps mining as a place to begin. They are presently negotiating with owners of lead and zinc deposits, relatively minor ones. If they proceed with this, it may give them a place to begin to develop broader interests.

A comment to us yesterday by Sven Ersman, the chief executive: "May I be candid? Sometimes Erland will take the initiative in directions which his executives do not have the capability to pursue." In other words, keep the damper on the boss' enthusiasm. How many times such a comment must have been made about D.E.L. by his more down-to-earth "executives."

MAY 12, 1974
TEHRAN

Began this morning at six and was on the run all day with my little Swedish adopted family. It went very well indeed, and our partners are all smiles. Even the Swedish Ambassador was impressed, though I made no bones about my desire to keep him on the edge of things, if not out of our activities. I want this to be economic and technical, not Foreign Office stuff, though probably I won't succeed. As usual, I stayed away from the American Embassy.

MAY 13, 1974
TEHRAN

For the first time I can now remember I find myself too tired to do the kind of journal writing I want to do, where much is going on for us, as it is these days in Tehran.

"Presenting" this delegation of Gränges to top officials, as we have been doing almost continuously, turns out to be mighty strenuous.

I would like to write a description of our Sunday morning meeting with the most relaxed Prime Minister I have ever met—Hoveyda—his feet stretched out from a half-reclining position onto an ottoman—and so on.

But I am too bushed.

MAY 14, 1974
TEHRAN

How well I remember Rouhani saying, some years ago: "But you must remember we are a poor country."

Now, suddenly, what seems to worry the Ministers we see (but not the bouncy Prime Minister) is "How can we use the annual sixteen billion dollars of revenue, when last year it was only two billion"?

Ironic, that.

MAY 15, 1974
TEHRAN

A jolly party of a part of the innumerable Farmanfarmaian clan. But I couldn't bring myself to get into the spirit of the affair. It wasn't that I was tired. I just couldn't sufficiently forget that these people are living high on the labor of very poor people crushed by the fierce patriarch who fathered the twenty Farmanfarmaian sons and twelve daughters.

One of the "sisters" of the Farmanfarmaian tribe gave me the big social-worker frown of the very rich person: "Why is it, Mr. Lilienthal, that in this country we don't have enough food? It is so difficult to get good meat that I have about given up having parties."

Why indeed? I tried, above the hubbub, to say that so much attention had been given to building industry and making some people rich that those who raised the food weren't educated in how to do it. I yelled something about how complex farming really is compared to building a dam or mining iron ore.

But if food is hard to come by for the rich, or nearly rich, imagine what it is like, and will be, for those who aren't.

Of course, what Iran will do is use its swollen sudden wealth to import frozen meat from Australia. But for such a gathering as last night, frozen meat isn't good enough.

Before dinner, David Morse and I stopped for drinks and a chat with Khodadad and Joanna Farmanfarmaian at his home, perched like a house of magic on a man-made cliff looking out on the mountains in one direction, the twinkling city on the other. What a gem of a home; but I felt it was the home of an unhappy man, a man who will never be content until he is back in a major role in the government.‡

When I saw how utterly beaten and haggard is the little Napoleon, Hushang Ansary, now the top Minister of all, I wondered just what it is about high public office that makes a man living a comfortable, luxurious life, as Khodadad Farmanfarmaian does, now simply die because he is not in the center of power. He at least, unlike many men less candid, said plainly: "I want power; I reach for power. Nothing less will satisfy me."

MAY 18, 1974
TEHRAN

Back from two fully packed days in Khuzistan. The presence of our Swedish associates or clients or tourists—I'm still not sure, nor are they, what the accurate term is—stimulated the kind of overall expedition that I haven't taken for a long time.

To them, as to most casual visitors, looking up at the vast curved tower of the Pahlavi Dam was an experience that widened their eyes and produced gasps. Particularly because the "lake" is full of the greenest of water, and the spillway was a mini-Niagara.

To me the greatest satisfaction was flying high, in our small chartered plane, over the irrigated areas. The green checkerboard with

‡He was appointed governor of Iran's Central Bank in 1968.

strongly accented borders to each of the huge segments represented achievement, in spite of the bureaucratic lethargy of the present Khuzistan Water and Power Authority and the anomalous position we of D&R are in, having a broad generally recognized responsibility for results, but with no longer any real *authority.*

D&R's hopes and expanding role are only ripples in the perspective of the troubles that continue to infect this part of the world. Poor Nobel Peace Laureate Kissinger trying to disengage the Syrians and Israelis in the Golan Heights while terrorists massacre school children and Israeli jet bombers kill hundreds in Lebanon in reprisal.

Helen's reading to me from the vengeful pages of the Old Testament, while we were in Antigua, comes back with a certain horror across the ages: violence, mass murder, more than an eye for an eye, brought up to date with explosives and area bombing and slaughter of innocent people.

Reading some scholarly accounts of Khuzistan's history, seeing the Elamite artifacts at Haft Tapeh, the remnants of Susa, and the Tomb of Daniel, as we did Friday, make me realize how lucky I have been to represent a modern and humane as well as an effective roadway to something better than slaughter as a means of having one's way.

My lust for a look at ports (second only to public markets and bazaars) was nearly satisfied in our expedition yesterday. After flying low over the refinery of Abadan, by car and on foot we gaped at the port of Bandar Shahpur and, later in the afternoon, the port of Khorramshahr. Such a profusion, higgledy-piggledy, of almost every kind of objects, off-loaded from huge cargo ships in the blazing sun. Tractors, brand-new and shiny, from Romania, orange-colored mini-bulldozers from Japan, truck tires as big as the side of a barn, stacks of grey aluminum ingots.

I miss not having Helen with me, though it wouldn't have been her kind of trip, with me going from one place to another. But it does get lonesome and I do feel tired.

MAY 19, 1974
TEHRAN

An amusing and colorful letter from Helen today, describing a bar mitzvah which she attended.

"Each of the two boys involved read a too-long paper written for the occasion. One boy read a rather impassioned paper on Israel, the other read one on Golda Meir.

"Also each of the boys read a portion of the lesson for the day, which I thought was an unfortunate choice for the present occasion, since it was from Leviticus, and dealt with the punishment that should be meted out for various misdemeanors, which was usually to take the culprit out and stone him to death. This didn't really jibe with the paper telling how peaceful and high-minded the Israelites had always been, and are, nor with the later remarks by the Rabbi to the same effect. It did go along with my Antigua Bible reading however."

Spiro Agnew is in Iran, just another anonymous, unrecognized addition to the hordes of salesmen seeking orders, contracts, making "contacts." John Silveira's son Johnny tracked Spiro down, got him to agree to speak to his school next trip on the subject of "the responsibilities of the Vice Presidency."

No dyed-in-the-wool bureaucrat ever admits he was wrong. But when one such brags about the success of a project he opposed at length and without reservation, that's an occasion for scorn or indignation.

The chief high-staff opponent of the Dez project almost fifteen years ago was the head Loan Vice President of the World Bank, S. Aldewereld, a beak-nosed, guttural-voiced Dutchman. Tonight he was guest of honor at a small dinner given by my now friend Minister Rouhani. And such encomiums by Aldewereld on the great success of the Dez Project!

As John Silveira said: "Why didn't someone tell me he was the guy who said there was no need for the power from the dam, and that a few diesel pumps would take care of irrigation? I would have said: 'Why don't you World Bank fellows *admit* you were wrong?' "

MAY 21, 1974
TEHRAN

Homesick for Home and Garden. This is the time when the iris begin to hoist their orchid-tinted sails, and the first roses unfurl.

Here roses flourish with wanton abandon, with no tiresome, expensive attention, pruning, special treatment of the soil, and spraying and dusting. Along the new autobahn circling the city an unbroken array, *miles* of gorgeous roses—what we call hybrids—growing in the gravel thrown up by the road construction.

Hossein, D&R's driver, knowing of my admiration for roses, brought in a huge armful from his own garden. "Hundreds," he says, wondering what the fuss is about. What I envy most is not their profusion of color, but the healthy foliage. Apparently black spot and fungus are not known here.

On the dot of four, the very tall saturnine attendant decked in the world's longest swallowtail coat, having beckoned to me, knocked once on the handle of the double door, waited a few seconds, and ushered me into a room blazing with mirrors. The man halfway across this space came toward me with hand outstretched and a smiling word of welcome. I couldn't help thinking: Here is, at the moment certainly, the most influential man in the world; upon his judgment and his hold on the loyalty of 32 million people the immediate future of all peoples depends to a degree not true since F.D.R. The voices of all the other of the world's great captains and kings are muted and uncertain compared to that of this soft-spoken figure.

I said there were reports I wanted to make. One was Khuzistan.

His Majesty seemed interested that I had been in Khuzistan. "When? That is when I was there as well." He didn't comment, looked as if he expected me to express an opinion.

"I found that our basic confidence in the land, the water, the climate, has been more than justified. But, Your Majesty, I am an impatient man. Things aren't going as rapidly as I would wish or as they can.

"I have in mind particularly the time it has taken to get water to all the land, or the fact that our unified plan for fourteen dams, seven million kilowatts of power and much irrigated land, except for the Dez area, is still not a reality.

"Part of the trouble is that in the recent past there were budgetary constraints—lack of enough money. But that's certainly no longer true. The slowness in getting all the canals completed and lined (there are still 30% to be completed), to bring water to the land of the large farming corporations is administrative—how to overcome a shortage of cement, or higher costs to the Iranian contractors, who slow up when they find that they are being pinched by inflation."

The Shah's face became very somber; he looked down, studying the floor. "I place the greatest importance on improving efficiency in the Government. I have given Amouzegar full support. It can be done but it is very difficult. We have become accustomed to slackness over the years and this must cease or our whole program will be endangered.

"We did it in the military; that is being efficiently run. But in the military you can give orders and the orders must be obeyed. In the civil government . . . well, it is a far different and more difficult thing."

I didn't notice any particular interest from His Majesty in talking about Khuzistan. When I said I had visited the ports, that led him to say that there would be a railroad connecting Khuzistan ports with a new port at Bandar Abbas "for thirty million tons—that's the kind of thinking we have in this country."

The Shah said Iran would have 20 million kilowatts of atomic energy; he had a couple days before seen Dr. Dixy Lee Ray, the AEC Chairman, who extended U.S. "cooperation."

I couldn't resist a sour and not creditable remark: These days you can't really count on anything that the present U.S. Administration says or promises. The Shah drew himself up. "Well, we also have the French."

But my comment about the disgracefulness of the Nixon Administration led him to turn on me, with the kind of intensity I have rarely seen, as he said: "What has *happened* to your country?"

I said to His Majesty that this was a sign of a general let-down in standards and values, not confined to the current Washington scene. It was like a sickness, an infection that was now coming to a "crisis." I heard myself predicting that what the world was witnessing of cynicism and corruption in the highest places did not represent the whole of American society. I thought it was particularly encouraging to see how much civic spirit there was, not in Washington, but where it counted most, in the communities, with the concern and the action about impairment of the environment.

Then the Shah said some remarkable things about the effect of prosperity—referring to the sudden "affluence" of Iran.

"I know that with all this new wealth we are earning for ourselves there is the danger of permissiveness." (He used that phrase several times during this almost soliloquy.) "The signs of it are beginning. I know that. But it will not be that way here, not for the next fifteen years, not while I am here."

I was struck by this spirit of self-examination, of questioning, of awareness of the price of prosperity and the limits of a ruler's power, not associated with the picture of an "absolute ruler," the term so often used by the journalists.

Now, the part of the audience I enjoyed most, talk about the D&R papers and Princeton. Apparently so did His Majesty.

I felt encouraged to introduce the subject since it was clear he wasn't asking me to leave, for here came tea, served by an elaborately dressed, very British serving man, bowing low over the gold cups, his jacket glittering with gold buttons.

"You are *giving* D&R's years of records to Princeton?"

He leaned over, took off his glasses, raised his eyebrows in the way I have learned means he is more than politely interested. This encouraged me to haul out of my inner jacket pocket the brown brochure of the Shiraz Conference on development, with IRAN prominently displayed together with the insignia of Princeton. He looked it over appreciatively. Then I went into my thesis—and one that Bob Goheen had approved, indeed had rehearsed with me: that the Shah has previously shown his desire to establish and to strengthen ties between the intellectual, commercial, and academic life of America and Iran, witness the Pahlavi Foundation at Princeton. The jointly sponsored Shiraz Conference (jointly between Princeton and the leading Iranian universities plus the Plan Organization) added to the vitality of those ties, examples and demonstrations of the Shah's interest in both the cultural heritage of Iran and non-material bonds to America.

I handed His Majesty a copy of the "Deed of Gift" of the D&R Papers, remarking that I thought it was a historical document worth his reading. He accepted this, too.

As the audience ended—it lasted almost an hour—he walked me to the door, saying, "I must get a note of the name of that Swedish company with the strange name." "Gränges," said I in my best Swedish accent, and took the folded deed of gift from him, stopped, and pulling out my pen, wrote "Gränges" as well as "Waldenstrom" on the back of it.

So ended another, and in some ways one very special, of a long line of meetings with Mohammed Reza Shah Pahlavi.

MAY 25, 1974
PRINCETON

The trip to Khuzistan and the ports removed any doubt there might have been that we were "just another consulting outfit" who writes reports rather than *does* things.

That I have not worn out my welcome is reassuring. Particularly with the King. But even more with Persian friends—Samii, Amouzegar, Reza Ansari, Shahmirzadi, Ebtehaj, and then the whole crop of New Iranians, young enough to say they "heard of you when I was just out of college."

The prospects for new, interesting, and important work in Iran continue bright. Frederiksen's idea for a farm-management training service, on which he and I worked hard before he left on his latest trip to Iran, has been very well received. Likely we will have a contract for this new idea, one that grows out of our TVA experience. His proposal for a service to provide logistical planning, as well as financial, for the expansion of the national power system seemed to hit Vahidi very well, when John Silveira and I saw him on the last day of my trip.

All in all, it was one of the best visits to Iran in recent years.

MAY 27, 1974
PRINCETON

On the cover of the *New York Times Sunday Magazine* an overpowering portrait of a stern Shah, in full military regalia. In the magazine an article by some English journalist. A slick personality article, as unperceptive of the quality of leadership of the present-day Shah as it is superficial and ignorant of what is going on in the country I so recently saw, and whose history and path I have had not a little effect upon these eighteen and a half years past.

What is going on in Iran is a transformation—physical, mental, economic—on an epic scale. Very little of this is reflected in this kind of journalism, nor in the interviews the Shah gives to almost any journalist who asks for time.

Which stirs in me a desire to have my say, to write and speak about a phenomenon of change without parallel in modern times.

If I am to write about Iran, this is surely the time to do so. But if I did, wouldn't it also suffer from the disease of journalism, which is to speak of today, to the current issues, the things that interest people today, which are usually best expressed in clichés?

The last couple days taught me what I didn't recognize when first I arrived—how tired I was. Aching muscles that hadn't been used for almost three weeks, except for getting out of automobiles (or climbing the steps to the D&R office). But I have been resting, and am ready for the fray beginning tomorrow.

JUNE 2, 1974
PRINCETON

Helen's spring garden party (and mine) yesterday was the largest and the most enthusiastic of the series of such bashes, which have become a minor institution hereabouts. After an early morning rain and afternoon "threatening weather"—this holding of everyone's breath about the weather adds something to the excitement (not too strong a word).

What impressed me most—and others too, I guess—was the mixture of different kinds of people and different interests.

For example: [Ambassador] Ken Keating, fresh from a plane from Tel Aviv, his presence all the more dramatic because he and Mary Davis are to be married. The beaming Nobel Laureate Eugene Wigner; Glenway Wescott, who has just finished his memoir. "The best thing I have ever written," said he to Beatrice Tobey, looking, so she reported, very boyish. Bob Meyner looking more than ever like a retired Notre Dame football coach, with his Helen, showing with dark places under her eyes the wear and tear of a fighting primary campaign—she again seeks the nomination for Congress. A covey of young people, new to these parties, including the very tall and handsome junior Archie Alexanders, coming on in New Jersey public life. Dottsie Greenbaum, as cocky and self-assured as ever, overcoming the kind of physical difficulties that would immobilize a lesser soul. The bouncy ex-Mayor of Princeton Ray Male (and the even more bouncy Mrs. Male), full of ideas for an article I "simply must write" about the relation between action and integrity. Harry Smyth, whose Smyth Report really introduced the non-atomic world to the atom years ago, now full of ideas sparked by the Indian underground explosion of a bomb—which has rather shocked the world. (This morning I pressured him to write a solid piece bringing the subject of international control of the atom out of the closet where it has been resting, covered with the clichés of the Kennedy-Humphrey-disarmament talk nonsense.) Not by any means the least, my niece, Elise Lilienthal Copeland, very self-possessed and extremely pretty, with her serious and strong-looking husband.

I did enjoy seeing so many people I like and who respect me. But the telling thing is that somehow we are able, year after year, to get together at a single party such a diverse group.

JUNE 8, 1974
PRINCETON

The other day I read a feature in *Newsweek* (called "My Turn," a kind of guest editorial). The writer spoke of the impossible kind of life wives of public officials have.

But it did remind me of an episode in the recent visit to Iran.

Minister Rouhani, a powerhouse who operates way beyond *any* rated capability, had invited a dozen of us to dine with him at the Royal Country Club. There we sat for an hour and a half, including his wife, but no Minister.

Finally he turned up, ebullient and without apology. "I love to talk," he said. Said his wife to Pat Silveira: "He stays at his office till all hours; often it will be twelve midnight before we sit down to dinner set for eight."

Went to the Century monthly dinner Thursday night. Joined Jack McCloy.

We hadn't really visited for a long time. I couldn't see that he had changed one bit, the same burly shoulders, steady eye that bores right into whoever he is talking with, a youthful almost boyish grin, particularly if the joke is partly on him. I don't know anyone who has been *in* more things of a public or quasi-public nature, though except for being the "Governor" of Occupied Germany, only rarely did he give up his personal status as perhaps the most sought-after lawyer. And he practiced law, not "influence" or "connections" or "glamour," à la Clark Clifford.

(I sometimes forget that Jack was a member of Acheson's State Department Committee on Atomic Energy in 1946, out of which came the Acheson-Lilienthal Report.)§

We were joined by another man out of my past, Nobel Prize physicist Rabi (Robby to everyone).

Rabi is full of smiles these days; always had an engaging manner. Only when I said I was trying to prod Harry Smyth into writing an article for *Foreign Affairs* (without Harry's cooperation, so far) did a shadow come over his face. "I am beginning to think that the Indian explosion of a bomb may bring us into the most dangerous period of all."

Last week I sat with Ozzy Elliott, publisher and "boss man"—his phrase—of *Newsweek*. A gaily-colored bow tie approached, extending way out on both sides like a sloop—sailing wing and wing—the phrase when the jib and main stretch out on both sides.

Out of the bow tie a voice, strained. It was Arthur Schlesinger and he was in full cry. Shook hands with me absently; he was in hot pursuit of Ozzy.

In a lecture-platform voice he said, with not a little emotion: *"Newsweek* has quoted me as having written that I think Kissinger is a great national asset. That is not the full quote and without the qualification. What I said in a long article in the *Wall Street Journal* was that he was a national asset *but* his method of conducting State was distorting, etc. . . ."

Ozzy put on his most indulgent, placating expression. "Arthur, I am sorry what we quoted wasn't the full meaning you had in mind; so we can expect a Letter to the Editor; be glad to print it."

Mollified, Arthur grinned: "Well, I know you don't personally write the whole magazine," and disappeared down the stairway.

Ozzy sized me up, as I began to sip my first J&B. Head cocked, the critical, skeptical professional, editing a mass-media magazine, who has everyone and his uncle trying to find an angle that will produce favorable mention in so widely read and influential a place as *Newsweek.* That impressive super-acquiline nose and bald dome making him, in this cautious mood, look like a predatory eagle.

For almost an hour it wasn't a luncheon conversation at all, but a good journalist probing, one question following another. (This was in contrast to the second hour and a half, which was relaxed and fun.)

Of course I had intended the luncheon to be a means of interesting him (and *Newsweek*) in the "meaning of the Iranian transformation" (rather than the trivial though entertaining accounts of Iran appearing so often lately).

§The basis of the United States proposal to the UN for international atomic energy control.

The first question set the tone: friendly but damn professional; like a press conference, not hostile but so the interviewee would know who was boss, and no fool he.

"What would happen if the Shah were hit by a truck?" meaning, suddenly died, of course.

So, quite soberly, I said there were two sides to the answer. One the formal one: I explained the constitutional provision, sponsored after his present marriage, providing for a Regency Council headed by the Queen. There is a Cabinet, made up for the most part of able, seasoned men; the Prime Minister, who is also leader of the "official" political party, has been in office for ten consecutive years, something that doesn't happen in an unstable country.

That's the formal side. The other side is psychological, emotional. The Shah's sudden death, particularly if it was by assassination—after all this has twice or three times been attempted—would cause great shock, mourning, and loss of strong leadership and a great human symbol. But the result would not be a military take-over, in my opinion.

His next questions were less grave. The Shah's age (fifty-four last October); what can they possibly do with so much oil revenue; what has D&R's work done for food, for industry? What will D&R's next tasks be? "A national water plan; that's practically drawing a picture of the future of the country, isn't it?"

At the end of an hour and three drinks for each of us ("Oh, come on, Dave, have another with me; after all this is Friday afternoon"), Ozzy stopped the Iran questions (all of them good, for he is an intelligent man and a real journalist—too few are).

He said: "How does our country look to you now? After all, you have seen a good deal, experienced some hard knocks in the public field, been a successful businessman, and now working overseas. Have you greatly changed your ideas about the country, and in what ways?"

I said I did not join with those who were despairing. "I am still an optimist, more so now than for a long time, though I know all about the sour side."

Ozzy said *Newsweek* had a page given over to outside views, called "My Turn." What about writing a page—1500 words—for that? Not about Iran, etc., but a very personal piece. "Think about a piece for us, and we'll talk about it next week."

JUNE II, 1974
NEW YORK

At noon today the sun was bright and gay. The wide plazas at the corner of 49th and Sixth Avenue, before the Exxon and McGraw-Hill towers, were a carnival, a scene one might have found in an open square in Marrakesh. Here was a crowd of young people and, within the circle, a voice explaining the demonstration of yoga, going on: "Notice that you don't strain; you roll into the next position . . . ," etc. At another part of the dual plaza a black bongo band, in costume. And so on—this was New York City, the metropolis to end all metropolises, reverting to the primitive village at noontime. I enjoyed it thoroughly.

A telex from Frederiksen from Brazil. If I understood what he said, we are not "out" of the São Francisco job, certainly for the time being, and *he* thinks we will be retained after the new corporation for the Valley is set up by law.

Our great friend, the gentle, literate Leitão de Abreu, has been named to the Supreme Court, so we will have a friend in Brasília though not in the Cabinet, as before.

Dr. Hoskins gave me a pretty thorough going-over; says there is no physical reason why I can't indulge in whatever summer activities I want.

Went to Barbara Nicholls' gallery; bought several more cartoons, including a terribly funny one by Charles Addams, who I met at the opening. I am getting quite taken with the idea of a sufficient number of contemporary satirical drawings that make a collection of interest not only as a modern art form but as a way of describing what it is in present-day American life that seems funny or outrageous or even shoddy.

I brought a big sack full of roses from our garden. A few I have here in this cubby of a hotel room. One, a pure orange, has slowly been opening from the bud it was when I cut it. It is comforting and pleasurable to just sit and look at it.

JUNE 15, 1974
PRINCETON

Ozzy Elliott sits on top of a powerful magazine; in his office, shirt sleeves rolled up, where I visited with him Wednesday noon.

He meant just what he said at the Century the other day: he does want me to write a "My Turn" page, a personal statement about how I see the country. Perhaps tomorrow morning I can set out some brief, understandable examples of my theme.

The theme is a simple one, one I have written about—and lived. That an affirmative, positive outlook, a confident go at things, will produce economic and social results; a defeatist, negative, fearful mood—such as now holds the country in its grasp—will defeat us.

My guess is that Elliott's interest in having the piece—if he continues to be interested when he sees it next week—is because I have a record of doing things rather than just writing about doing them.

A group of the "highest tycoons" came in to see him last week, he said. They were discouraged; why do we get blamed for everything? What are we doing wrong? Why are the people so "disturbed"? They were plenty worried, he said.

Perhaps an obvious piece, however vague, will be welcomed.

When we had finished talking about the article, I said I expected to be given some editorial help by one of his "boys." "I'll do it, myself," he said, "in my clubfooted way." And then he took me to visit the news and production department, and I met Kosner, the bright-eyed, eager-looking managing editor, and a blond chap I took to be the head of the news department.

Then he pointed to a glass-enclosed room lined with what looked somewhat like electric typewriters. On spindles long yellowish limp coils, flat, vaguely like something you might see in a sausage works. "Those perforated coils actually set the type," said Ozzy, "set it in Tokyo as well as two places in the U.S. where *Newsweek* is actually printed." What about the printers? "They stand by the machines, under our contract, but do nothing."

JUNE 18, 1974
NEW YORK

At exactly six the phone rang here, and that big deep voice: "Dad, this is . . ." and of course I broke in: "David, you are here."

With that warmth that is especially his, he wanted me to come out to the Joel Raphaelsons, where the three Florentine Lilienthals are staying the night. Against my better judgment but according to my real desires, I did go, adding to Marikay Raphaelson's domestic problems.

A few hours before I had a copy of David's new book, *Mr. Nicholas,* and when he phoned was almost halfway through it. Enjoyed it—and surely it is timely, what with wiretapping and surveillance still being the big news of the year; the invasion of privacy is what the novel is all about.

JUNE 23, 1974
PRINCETON

Our garden continues to be full of color and form. This is surprising for it is a spring garden. A solid mass of purple clematis against the east cedar fence, contrasting with the climbing roses. A profusion of golden day lilies is beginning. The "form" is supplied by astilbe, cocky plumes, white, pink, cream. And the delight of the spring garden, the columbine, still full of color and luscious foliage.

But best of all about this early summer (or late spring) garden is not the flowers but the trees. We are so lucky: the east rim of the garden is bordered by our neighbor's great trees, very tall, not less than sixty feet, slender and luxuriant. One of the delights of the outdoors, particularly this season, for me, has been watching the wind.

I learned the pleasure of *seeing* the wind while on the Vineyard. But in this garden the trees, through which the wind riffles or blows, are seen against the sky, very close at hand. I have sat by the hour, almost, admiring the greys of the very tips of these slender trees (some locusts) while the breeze, when it is still, or the gale, when it storms, plays through the tops, like the wind that moves the top gallants of a full-rigged sailing schooner or ship.

An hour or so ago they took off in the car for the Vineyard: that huge grandson Daniel, with a delicious grin that would stop anything, took over the wheel of the Olds, and alongside, his indomitable grandmother. In a downpour of rain. Packing an already full car in a torrent of rain is not her idea of a way to take one's leave. So I am alone, or as I prefer to think of it: on my own; or better still, enjoying the rare blessing these days of privacy, however temporary.

Last week was a full one, but not a harassing kind of fullness.

A letter from Elliott: the "My Turn" article I produced last weekend (meaning, actually, in almost three pretty full days) Oz called "nice"— what a word for a serious article. In any case, nice or splendid, great, stimulating, timely—he said *Newsweek* would publish it after some cutting, but it would not appear for some weeks; the pipeline is full of other "My Turn" pieces.

Another big story about Felix Rohatyn of Lazard in the Sunday edition of the *Times*. Has developed the reputation of a financial wizard.

When I first visited with Felix he and his wife were on a plane, with us, returning from Europe. He was full of talk about broad social and political issues, found my work interesting and my background of public experience much to his liking.

What did success with a big, big S do to Felix? Made him very rich and very well known in the financial and political world, certainly. But in the fine print today's story told something of the "price"—as I interpret

it. It was stated that he and his wife are "separated," she living with the
three children.

JUNE 26, 1974
NEW YORK

Kosner, the managing editor of *Newsweek,* phoned. The "My Turn"
piece he likes very much, is sending a photographer over for a picture,
and may print it, after I have cut a couple hundred words to make it fit
the space. He said it might be the issue of July 8th, which would be a good
birthday present.

JULY 4, 1974
MARTHA'S VINEYARD

It has been a week since I left the role of the guy responsible for an
enterprise that once more is feeling its oats, for the role of *patriarch* of
a clan, the phrase Ged Bentley used, in a birthday note received yesterday.

A patriarch I would define as an old man surrounded by his progeny
and their progeny, at his ancestral seat. With the arrival yesterday afternoon of a dazzlingly beautiful blonde baby of eight months, Jerusha, the
child of Pamela and her Irish husband, Michael Black, another generation is added. It is indeed a gathering: there is grizzled, bearded David,
curly blond-headed Davey, a solemn Allen (Nancy and Sylvain's elder)
looking with his black beard and steel glasses like a character out of a
Chekhov play. Twelve-year-old, smiling Margaret, with infinitely good
manners. Tomorrow or Saturday, Daniel will be arriving, a solid seven-
teen-year-old with twinkling eyes, and his parents, Nancy and Sylvain.

For one day (the 8th) I will be expected, I suppose, to live up to the
soubriquet: patriarch, who has outlived so many of his contemporaries,
and greet this small circle of splendid children.

It didn't last long, my gesture of renunciation, of late last summer,
giving up sailing by gifting my beloved little sloop to the Girl Scouts as
too much for me, and for those who disapproved of my single-handing
Lili-put across the Sound. For yesterday, with Jack Daggett's help, I
picked up a Dyer Dhow, a new 9-foot sailing dinghy, and hoisted its red
sail before noon today, sailing it off the Daggett beach, first with Jack,
then a second sail with Gregg, his solemn and brilliant twelve-year-old.
I am awkward with the little catboat, but gradually will more or less get
over that. Instead of spending hours going into the harbor in crowded
Vineyard Haven, now I have a boat on the shore five minutes' drive from
"Topside."

And to make it still a different kind of summer, I have that Hill Top cabin, leased for July. The little cabin sits on the most favored spot on this island, I do believe, perhaps the most beautiful anywhere. "A Three Hundred Degree Look"—that might be a good title for that spot. The Sound near and in the distance and in the foreground, the two delightful freshwater ponds.

If this is the fate of a patriarch at his three-quarter-century mark, all that should bother me is whether I deserve such good luck.

JULY 8, 1974
MARTHA'S VINEYARD

It wasn't the biggest Family Reunion in the world by a long shot, but it certainly set a record for this one. A combination of three birthdays: Davey's 19th and Sylvain's 50th on the 7th, and my 75th today, and a gathering of generations, climaxed by that utterly enchanting eight-month-old Jerusha.

Each family gathers its own "traditions." One of ours is measuring the height of each of the children and grandchildren on the inside of the coat-closet door in the living room, marking the rise with the date of the measurement and the inches. Jerusha standing on her tiny toes (with some assistance, naturally) was almost exactly the height of Daniel at the same age—he is now over six feet.

I had a handful of birthday cards, but only one phone call—so far. This a cheery one from Beatrice. She kidded me about heading the dynasty gathered around; but I was glad as could be to hear her voice. She never fails me, whatever the occasion.

JULY 9, 1974
MARTHA'S VINEYARD

A phone call from Rodman. He and David Morse were lunching together; wished to send their birthday greetings.

I well know that I have, more than once, become enthusiastic about some man or turn of events only to find weeks or months later that my enthusiasm was overdone, in some cases grossly overdone.

But this time I have the proof of a couple years of trial: "getting acquainted" with what David can do, with his temperament (judicious, unlike my own) and with his ability; and of course, what he has done to help me formulate my ideas of new dimensions for D&R.

In the shade cast by our new Tower, Helen and Margaret have been engaged in deep and animated conversation. "Girl talk," perhaps, or family gossip. That twelve-year-old doesn't yet know, I suspect, how much those talks with her grandmother, in many ways the most remarkable and stable personality I have ever known or am likely to know, will mean to her in later years.

It is one thing to be in charge of an event with people who will "do what they are told," so a schedule or deadline is possible; but a family gathering of more than a dozen loved ones ranging from 75 years to 7½ months, is a real test of skill and planning. And she did it.

JULY 12, 1974
MARTHA'S VINEYARD

I am learning quite a bit about today's young people. The lesson comes from observing Davey, Allen, and Daniel, all approximately the same stage of teenage-hood.

This generation apparently simply must have cars. They dress in the most ragged of clothes, are prepared to live on hot dogs, don't spend their money on booze, really. But a car they must have.

Under the "education trust" we established for each of the grandchildren (six—i.e., including David's and Nancy's children), Allen (a student at the University of Massachusetts) talked the trustee into providing him funds for a sports car as part of his education and maintenance. A couple weeks ago someone ran into him at an intersection, completely demolished the little car, and banged him up. The other day he appeared here in a second-hand van, which he will use in carrying out the contracts he has for painting houses in Newton. The car-truck wasn't in too good shape; he worked hard to refurbish it. That motor vehicle is important in a way that my L. C. Smith typewriter was when I went to college—a machine I used to pay part of my expenses, as secretary to an officer of the Tri Delt sorority.

Davey has been sulking lately; the reason: the trustee had the temerity to ask his parents *their* opinion about his buying a car. "It is none of their business."

I rented a car so Daniel would have mobility out here without taking our car when Helen might need it—I try not to set foot in a car, having all the taxi rides I can stomach. The attraction of spending time with us here at "Topside" would be about nil if Daniel didn't have full availability of a car.

JULY 16, 1974
MARTHA'S VINEYARD

Why I don't "unravel" this summer (though there have been other summers when this was true, come to think about it) puzzles and annoys me. But I will stay on for most of the month.

Daniel and I have set up a horseshoe-pitching "court"—quite professional it is, and the other day the Daggetts and I moved my little 9-footer to the large pond, and sailed it a bit. But I guess I do miss the precious sails in *Lili-put*. When a strong north breeze comes along, as it did the other day (with the accompanying clear sparkling air when the wind sets in from that direction) I become nostalgic for those spirited single-hand sails straight across to Falmouth and the mainland.

JULY 17, 1974
MARTHA'S VINEYARD

From this quiet hilltop, looking over the blue of the Sound and the ocean, the telephone carries messages from me to so many places: Senegal and the Senegal River, the Ivory Coast, Iran, Venezuela. It is a heady feeling, countering the dejection I feel when I am "resting."

JULY 19, 1974
MARTHA'S VINEYARD

The night darkness can be ever so dark from this lookout spot. And then suddenly the black was riven with great flames of lightning, over the Sound and then seaward. Magnificent, we standing there in the glass-circled room, watching with honest awe one of Nature's greatest displays, a summer lightning storm. Followed, at this hour, with a strong westerly wind that tosses and whips the treetops on this hill, more with exuberance than with anger. A different kind of delight than that I get watching the spring breezes move the very tall locusts that rim our garden in Princeton.

One quite young oak just outside the window of my "study" seems to fight back. The older now quite huge trees cannot tell the youngster to relax and take it as it comes; the young don't take to that kind of advice.

And neither do I, come to think about it.

Of the young males I have seen a good deal this summer. Daniel particularly. He who has the reputation of being laconic has opened up, as I felt sure he would if the elders would wait till we got on an activity that interests him, or showed an interest in what he has been doing. I began asking him about the jobs he has had. His description of the life of a busboy in a restaurant and as a clerk and stock boy in a small local drugstore opened the gates of communication with his grandfather.

Late yesterday he was beginning the painting of the porch railings (after the most intensive scraping and sanding of old paint I have ever seen—he is thorough and believes in doing a job his way). I was interested in the whole painting sequence and for fifteen minutes, painting away the while, I learned about primers, lead and latex paints, the effect of moisture, sun, and so on.

Suddenly he caught himself: "Lecture over." A delightful boy emerging into manhood. Proud that somewhere he not only has our daughter's genes but, presumably, some of mine.

His cousin Davey, returned here from his wanderings, is a different style entirely. Full of himself. When he tells a story of what happened to him the other day on the streets of Edgartown, the curls that cap his head shake with his gestures, his great long arms swing, he keeps his eyes on his audience for effects.

Whatever their future throughout the years, right now they are *great* to be with.

Tom Benton is not only the portrayer of Americana par excellence; he is a piece of Americana himself, every inch of his banty rooster sixty-odd inches. His visit the other day to "Topside," with Rita, was memorable.

Tom is eighty-five. He never quits painting. He has now set out on a new mural for the Country Music Building in Nashville. His lesson to me is: "Keep going." That's what his presence on "Topside" said to me.

There is nothing about Tom's appearance, manners, conversation, that remotely suggest a "painter," and a distinguished one too. His hair is bedraggled, he explodes into a cackle when he talks—and he talks a lot, mostly in exclamation marks liberally laced with his Middle West repetitive style of profanity.

As he came into our big room, Daniel, in his tattered teen costume, was about to leave; this tall grandson and diminutive Tom shook hands. "What are you doing?" asked Tom, looking up to Daniel. "Working, eh? Good. Go right out there and go to work. Good for you."

Daniel grinned that dimpled grin of his. Said later: "I like him."

What a picture, I thought: this link between Daniel Bromberger, seventeen, about to try his wings, and Tom Benton, eighty-five, rowdy, lusty, narrator, with his brush and imagination, of the America of the trans–Mississippi River West.

Rita looks more like Earth Mother each time we see her. She said Tom had seen my optimistic piece in *Newsweek,* called Roger Baldwin, and said, "Let's all go out and see Dave and Helen."

When you are with Tom Benton there is not much time for anything resembling serious discussion of the kind Roger likes, and excels in. Tom's high-pitched cackle takes over. So Roger sat in a corner, saying to me separately, "I'll be back; there are many things I want to talk over with you."

Last January Roger was ninety! He has just come back from a river canoe trip. "Everything about me, physically, is just as it was. All the parts work. The only competition I have is with the calendar."

A telex from McClung in Rio. The São Francisco corporation we recommended is now law. The legislation signed by the President. This is mighty satisfying news. For virtually all the wiseacres said Brazil would not change its functional piece-by-piece department-by-department way of going at the São Francisco development. But the law just passed, so I am informed, does in fact adopt in essence our recommendation for unified development and an agency that represents that principle.

JULY 20, 1974
HILL TOP CABIN, DAGGETT SHORE

I need being by myself, as some people need being surrounded by people; otherwise they say they are "lonely." With too much of other people after a while I draw into my shell.

This morning I had a lively time with young Gregg Daggett, bringing my new birthday telescope up here, and having him use it to pick out the great views on such a sharp "northy" day: even Gay Head, and Woods Hole.

With the telescope at 60 magnification, he and I watched the brigantine or clipper-schooner *Shenandoah* hoist sail across the Sound and take off like a shot, on a broad reach with this spanking north wind to send her flying.

But when that was over, it was so good to be once more alone, tracking along the boulder-strewn shore, then in the lee provided by the Cedar Tree Neck cliff, and up to the top of the cliff.

I am a lucky fellow.

Next week to New York. I have been a stranded islander for more than three weeks, and that is about the limit at one stretch.

JULY 26, 1974
HILL TOP CABIN, DAGGETT'S

I walked through the Sanctuary woods (swishing a branch at the damned biting black flies) to be by myself in this oasis of blue water and solitude.

(I should ask some of my dedicated super-ecology friends—most of whom live, by their choice, in elegant New York apartments—how they decide which forms of "wild life" are threatened species to be protected and which are damned nuisances or carriers of disease that in turn "threaten" other species, including the human. What about black flies or mosquitoes?)

I spent Tuesday forenoon and all day Wednesday in the office, and between the pressure I put on myself and the incredible din of mid-Manhattan, I produced as much fatigue in that short venture into New York as a normal person would use up in ten days.

One other tempting effort to add to my responsibilities, to celebrate entry into my 76th year. I have revived my interest in doing something definite, professionally and in a business way, about Western coal.

Yesterday I phoned the Sacramento office requesting them to give thought to a project for evaluating water availability and resources in the Western coal area. A study by the National Academy of Sciences (just published) seems to throw doubt on the availability of water for mine-mouth coal plants; this should be something D&R Sacramento should know a good deal about, or could find out.

JULY 27, 1974
MARTHA'S VINEYARD

Said Helen: "It's a good thing you have decided to be cremated, otherwise I can just see you sitting up in your casket and saying: 'Just a minute; I've got an idea.'"

This was apropos a long discourse from me, while we sat in our big room here, of how I happened to propose that we help Iran's Government become more "effective"—a proposal to which Amouzegar responded with such warmth. "I am hooked," said I, referring to the letter of response to this invitation from Amouzegar. "Of course, I could later say that the terms and arrangements aren't satisfactory, but on a matter of such consequence, if they really want me, I can't very well pull out."

Then I went on to describe the latest rebirth of my coal ideas of so long ago—the letter from American Electric Power and from Red Wagner.

Hence the comment about getting me into ashes lest I interrupt the funeral with a "new idea" from the casket.

Vanity comes in a variety of shapes. Such as the inordinate satisfaction I got this morning that I could *still* (that's the key word about my form of male vanity)—could still split logs with my ten-pound sledge and a steel wedge.

It is only fair to recall that for three years I have had an unreliable ankle tendon, and that for months my thigh muscles gave me fits. So hauling that big oak log out from the underbrush where I salted it away to season, heaving it to the saw horse, sawing off lengths, swinging the axe and sledge, and cheering as the tough old oak split! This swinging of the big sledge has much reassurance in it.

The scratchy sounds come from the activities on this house of Daniel, clad in his very professional-looking white overalls. The rubbing off of old paint and applying new will go on as long as he is here. I can't help recalling those painter grandsons when they were round-eyed little boys, around this place.

John Silveira went to the "social sciences and development" conference at Shiraz, in my place. He made one comment about it in a recent letter that sums up in simple words something of what I have tried to say, critically, about the limitations of those who deal in abstractions. Said John: no matter how hard they try, the social scientists always seem to be on the outside looking in.

John used the term "comprehensive development"—an improvement on the unified development phrase, I rather think.

JULY 29, 1974
MARTHA'S VINEYARD

Henry Hough gave a dinner party at the ancestral place, "Fishhook," last evening, in memory of his late father, George Hough, Sr., the redoubtable "Pat." That house, and that colorful old boy, his father, are very much a part of Helen's and my life as summer Vineyarders (half of our married life, at that—27 years).

On a dark misty night, it was to "Fishhook" that Betty Hough took us when we made our first visit to Martha's Vineyard, back in 1947. I was Chairman of AEC; terribly tired and drawn.

There were many times when we would wander along the road to see Pat at "Fishhook" from the nearby "Allen House" where we stayed for two summers. We also made regular pilgrimages to see Pat after he sold us the "Topside" property and we built this house.

So it was a happy nostalgic evening, for Henry had invited Tom and Rita Benton and Roger Baldwin, also long-time friends of Pat's; they used to visit him, and drink his whiskey, and Tom and Pat would trade lies by the hour—both good story tellers.

At table, Tom tried to draw me out about what I am doing in Iran. I was laconic, and not "putting out." Tom was in high gear, not without some help from several stiff bourbons. He has been made much of lately, partly because of his famous mural work, and partly because of his good stories about his fellow Missourian Harry Truman, for whom he did the murals at the Truman Library.

The praise for Tom was coming fast. Tom nodded toward me: "Ya, all I do is paint. Dave there, he *does* things."

JULY 30, 1974
MARTHA'S VINEYARD

Is retribution finally overtaking Richard Nixon? The TV is now full of the hearings and speeches of the Judiciary Committee—and its damning votes.

Wrong-doers and cynics ("idealism is for punks, not realists") can prolong the process of exposing and of catching up and punishing Nixon, armed as he is with the almost unlimited power and access of a President, of a President who wants to swing his club. But that story is surely nearing its climax, with a trial of the President likely, if not certain.

A year ago at this time the story was the highlight on TV; it has taken all that time to close the noose—so it would appear with the votes on impeachment of last night.

But it will drag on and on. Better that way, I suppose, than to throw the rascal out, a rascal who was re-elected so recently by an overwhelming vote.

"I am shy, and have difficulty overcoming my reserve." I was surprised to hear this candor from so famous and successful a man as bewhiskered Joe Lash, probably the most accomplished biographer of recent years: *Eleanor and Franklin* and *The Years Alone*.

Joe called on me here for an hour or so yesterday afternoon. He is preparing to edit the diaries of Felix Frankfurter. In reading material at the Library of Congress for his new book on the relations between Churchill and Roosevelt, he came on the Frankfurter diaries. They go back to 1911, when he was a legal assistant to Henry Stimson (one of Felix's greatest heroes) through the years of his law professorship and as Justice.

I learned more about Frankfurter than I could possibly impart; true, I did have a very active correspondence with him over the years, and asked his advice—or received it without asking—more than once.

Time was when his severest critics were of the conservative persuasion—because of his part in the Sacco and Vanzetti case, his relation to F.D.R. as Governor and particularly as President.

But his service as Justice produced another kind of criticism and from the liberal corps. This centered on the Justice's severe and, I thought, almost doctrinaire concept of judicial restraint in passing on legislation challenged on constitutional grounds. I had thought he carried this intellectual position too far.

Apparently those who one would suppose most admired Felix have pretty well abandoned him on this major issue. I could just see how some of them felt partly envy, because he was the first law-school teacher, the first academic for that matter, who not only wanted to enjoy great practical influence on public policy and events but achieved it to a marked degree.

But the dissent among liberals went farther than that: they really profoundly disagreed. In the introduction to the diaries apparently Joe will give considerable attention to this.

The other area that was a surprise is what Joe reported about the extent of Felix's political activism, while a Justice, amounting not to the role of counselor (à la Brandeis, and before him, Chief Justice Taft) but to that of advocacy.

Lash is a hardworking, conscientious, and diligent researcher, with a point of view and considerable personal humility of the best kind. But there is an almost lyric, poetic quality in his writing, which I think accounts for the great success of his books about Eleanor Roosevelt.

AUGUST 6, 1974
NEW YORK

The President of the U.S. admits, at long last, that he has been trying to mislead the country and even his own lawyers. This is too much for even the hard-shell characters we saw on TV last week during the House Judiciary Committee hearings. The stock market booms in the hope that the President will resign, anything else than what is on everyone's mind, the impeachment of the Chief Executive.

AUGUST 9, 1974
MARTHA'S VINEYARD

Watching and listening to Nixon last night you could believe that he was being honored—honoring himself—for some great achievement "in the national interest." I could hardly believe (trying the while to keep from rushing to the bathroom for a good throw-up) that that foxfaced creature realized he had dishonored the great office he bore; rather than turning to a nation-wide audience to celebrate some victory of unselfishness, by resigning before he was ignominiously tossed out.

"I am not a quitter," said he, quitting. And the reason: not that he had himself caused his downfall, but that he had been advised he would not have the "political" strength in Congress to remain. *Why* they all turned against him—about that not a word nor a hint.

We are well rid of him.

Had it not been that a Mr. Mediocrity by the name of Harry Truman had suddenly succeeded a giant of a President, to most everyone's dismay, and then proved to be one of the greatest of all, I would have thought as I saw Gerald Ford that we are in for the most bland sub-mediocre period of non-leadership since Warren Harding. But appearances are often deceiving. Harding looked like a President, so they said, and what a mess. Truman looked like what he was, bless him, and what a strong, wise leader he turned out to be.

AUGUST 15, 1974
MARTHA'S VINEYARD

Davey left yesterday on his return to Italy. What most impresses me is that he is one of those particularly articulate, talented ones who are *searching,* for just what they don't know.

Yesterday morning Daniel and Davey took me to the South Beach, my first visit this year. How invigorating and life-giving are the cool waves; to become part of the green water and swim hard against that primeval force of an incoming wave, and then walk the sandy shore.

AUGUST 18, 1974
NEW YORK

Roll all the fiestas, carnivals, county fairs, and outdoor vaudeville and one-ring circuses together and you still wouldn't have a fair idea of what I saw in Central Park this afternoon. A whole city having a mass picnic, a great and gay and happy throng.

I would never have had the wit to plan to see this spectacle, and be part of it. "This is our backyard," Barney and Beatrice said as we entered the park at 72nd Street and Central Park West. What a yard.

Apparently this only occurs on Sunday afternoon, and this is a beautiful summer day, following yesterday afternoon's wild and tumultuous storm.

This morning I had pretty well decided that I simply could not add the responsibility for inviting the Shah to a meeting in New York "in his honor," under the aegis of the Iran Council of The Asia Society.

It is a mark of the influence David Morse has on me—or in any case of the good sense of his recommendations—that he made me see that in a completely different light. Now I am persuaded by him that I should take that responsibility "as a great personal honor," Morse says, but he, David, will see to it that the logistics will be cared for by him and people he will bring together.

The clincher in the brief talk we had was this: if anyone else, the Johnny-come-latelies about Iran, heads this occasion it will be a blow against you, and D&R. Says David: "You are the person people think of when they think of Iran, and you have earned that position through long years of effort in their behalf. Now to have someone else take that role would not only be the loss of a great opportunity for serving Iran in the U.S. but would be interpreted as passing you by, as evidence of a decline of your position when the contrary happens to be the case."

AUGUST 20, 1974
SACRAMENTO

I have the distinction, said I to myself, of being the first one to tell Nelson Rockefeller's son Rodman the news—that his father had been named Vice President—and the first to congratulate him as he sat at our table having breakfast.

Now, that is surely news enough for one day.

But actually, the day was full of news, all good, after hours of discussions, and more important still, of decisions.

Rodman was the star. No longer the negative, cautious, guarded, scared man, he not only agreed and committed himself to seeing that D&R gets the long-needed infusion of added capital, not only listened carefully through hours of exposition and argument about the conflicts, programs, and the prospects, but came up with some questions that showed insight, and new ideas and initiatives.

AUGUST 23, 1974
LOS ANGELES

My taste for nostalgia, family reminiscences, and backward looking has definite limitations. I had almost a full day of it yesterday, with Bernardine, and later when we were joined by her brilliant, spirited sister Alyne, and her husband Max—Ernest Hemingway beard, but anything but a tough-guy manner.

I expected Bernardine to be almost an invalid, but except that she has a great hoarseness, and doesn't move much, physically she seemed about as well as any old lady of over eighty. It was spirit that distinguished her. That has become almost extinguished.

A half-day of "do you remember" or looking (and laughing) at family pictures will take care of me for the rest of my life.

AUGUST 24, 1974
LAKE TAHOE, CALIFORNIA

One of the greatest of America's natural beauties: the forest, the ring of mountains, and most moving of all, in this setting, a huge lake of purple water so clear that the boulders a hundred feet below the surface are visible.

Almost as much a treat was the two-hour drive from Sacramento through pine forests.

I hear so much of how "spoiled" is such a place as this, built up, commercialized, but what I see is how much of the area is still in state forests. The Frederiksens took me in their motorboat through this unbelievable water to Emerald Bay, past the green of Sugar Pine peninsula.

There is another side. From this cabin, the roar of automobiles along the highway; the houses are close together; at night the distant lights of the gambling casinos—why in hell come to such a magnificent place to pull the arm of a gambling machine?

SEPTEMBER 3, 1974
MARTHA'S VINEYARD

Mike Lilienthal (looking like a dramatic-type bearded movie actor, and handsome in a particularly virile way); Anne Shattuck, slender, fragile-looking, but as strong and resilient as a Damascus blade.

"Annie" is well organized and businesslike and practical. She says, "I know we have got to make our living out of what we know about pottery and selling it."

They want to set up a pottery in New England. Of course, I knew that their "call" wasn't entirely social, not by any means. They need capital, and where else to get it but from Grandfather Lilienthal? The question is: what are the figures of capital needed?

Anne impressed me enormously with her knowledge of the costs, the "cash movement" (meaning the cash requirements from month to month). I loaned them somewhat more than they asked; their needs will be greater than they estimate—it's always that way.

I welcomed the chance to encourage two talented young people in setting up their own business of producing beautiful things (Mike is a genuine artist and no mistake) and earning their living in the way that fits their training and their desires.

It is a tough time to start a new business, now when so many established businesses are faltering, and gloom is thick as the clouds outside on this rainy early fall day.

SEPTEMBER 4, 1974
MARTHA'S VINEYARD

Tonight Henry Fonda presented on TV his version of Clarence Darrow's courtroom appearances that made such a smash hit on Broadway last season, a performance I didn't get to see because it was completely sold out for weeks.

Toward the close of the hour-long program Fonda, as Darrow, told the story of the trial for murder of Dr. Sweet and the ten other black people in Detroit in the early twenties. As Fonda spoke to an imaginary jury, I was taken back to my own days in that courtroom, as a young lawyer Darrow brought to Detroit to assist him—though precious little I contributed. He tried the case as a trial of the white man's treatment of the black, through the ages.

The article I wrote at the time for *The Nation* about that trial is in my "papers" somewhere. But the memory of that experience, never erased, tonight became vivid and present as I sat in our big room here on this hilltop while outside the storms of the last several days were subsiding. Once again we could see ever so plainly the waters of the Sound and the string of lights that mark Herman Melville's great whaling city of New Bedford.

Our 51st wedding anniversary; "observed quietly." Alone, for almost the first time this summer.

SEPTEMBER 5, 1974
MARTHA'S VINEYARD

A great treat tonight, a visit with Thomas Hart Benton, and his wife, and our favorite, Rita. Without her, Tom would have probably never amounted to anything; probably become an East Greenwich Village wino, in spite of his great talent and stamina.

Rita made us a huge batch of spaghetti, of which I devoured more than my share. Good conversation with Tom before a fire in their home that lies practically on the lip of the waters of Menemsha Pond.

What moved me most was listening to Rita, at table, tell me about "Jack" Pollock, the splatter genius.

"He came to us when he was only a boy, seventeen, a student of Tom's at the Art Students League. The boy never had a mind. Never did have a brain. But a great sense of color. He was a favorite of a Long Island lady, who kept him. One day she came to his place; he was out of his mind with anger, threw paint in all directions in a big tantrum. She saw it; said it was wonderful. 'If you do more like that, I'll buy them all for $300 apiece.'

"Jack stayed with us, shared what little we had. He painted like Tom, his teacher, before he discovered this splatter painting. It had design and movement and color, though I don't wonder you can't see much in it. But those paintings we stored in our attic at home in Kansas City—I wouldn't sell them. Gave one to the Modern Museum, got a $60,000 tax credit for it. But he never had a brain."

Seeing Tom walk out to where the bourbon was—only his third drink —he looked like some comic character, with his toes turned way out as he walked, à la Charlie Chaplin; from the rear, the wide, blue, very droopy drawers and hair in disarray, Walt Disney's picture of one of the Seven Dwarfs.

He took us out to his studio, where he is finishing a small mural painting for the Country Music Building. The way Tom *constructs* such a painting. A very rough sketch, then a series of drawings, and the components of such a drawing—the individual figures. Before the whole goes on the wall, the spaces are worked out with the precision of the design of a delicate machine.

As Tom hunched over beside the fireplace, I got him to talking about one of his favorite men and subjects: his fellow-Missourian Harry Truman, in retirement at Independence.

"Back in '62 I let some of his pals persuade me to do a portrait of the old boy. What they wanted, of course, was a painting that looked exactly like the official photographs which were no more Harry Truman than those awful juiceless official biographies.

"He gave me half a dozen sittings, and I did a number of sketches. Had him looking straight at me, like the photographers do. What the hell was the matter? Then I said: 'Mr. President, will you take off those glasses?' He said, 'I haven't been without glasses since I was a little boy.' But he took them off. They were very strong, you'll remember, Dave, and made his eyes look very large. But because of the glasses I couldn't find his eye *sockets;* when he took them off I could put his eyes in those sockets after he put the glasses back on. Well, finally I gave it up, and he let me off; was awfully decent about it.

"Years later, after he had his stroke and looked like a very old man, I tried again, but this time I had him reading, not looking straight at me with those glasses. Here is the result; not bad, but Margaret didn't like it at all. Naturally."

SEPTEMBER 7, 1974
MARTHA'S VINEYARD

On the hollow drum of our roof the musketry of heavy, unremitting, wind-driven rain, all night and increasing in fury, or earnestness, into the morning. Pulled myself into the pants and jacket and goofy hood of my daffodil-yellow foul-weather gear; went out into the storm. Ostensible reason: to inspect the other house, bring in armloads of oak for the fireplace (it's cool and raw). The real reason: I am a cornball, a Walter Mitty type, determined to make himself as dramatic as possible. Always.

SEPTEMBER 14, 1974
PRINCETON

Phoned David in Florence this morning. They still don't know what kind of ailment Peggy has. It has been weeks and weeks since she was bitten by some insect. David sounded low.

As I checked out at the hotel early yesterday morning, exchanged greetings, as usual, with one of the cheery bellmen. "All set for next month," he said with a particularly broad smile. "Our retirement home almost built in Sun Valley in Idaho."
"Retiring?" I said.
"Yep; thirty-two years of dragging these bags around."
What a country and what a time—I never get over marveling. He must have some kind of pension, and savings, to build a home in Sun Valley, and all these years a bellhop. His son, I know, was graduated from college, is an officer in the Air Force. And my bellman retiring, at age sixty-five.
Such a case is by no means unique. But why doesn't one of those gloom-dispensing journalists report on such cases, and right in the middle of a stock-market panic, which is what we have today.

SEPTEMBER 18, 1974
NEW YORK

Came Miss Baron, in the midst of much other turmoil: a message from a Finnish journalist, representing a Vienna newspaper, who a couple of years ago had written with enthusiasm about our Khuzistan work. Could I see him? No, of course not—look how my office was crowded with people. Strong advice from M.B.: see him; he knows Dr. Gremliza, one of your favorites. So from refusing to see him, I ended by taking him for a humble lunch downstairs, and was delighted.
"Bread upon the waters," said M.B. For this eager, blue-eyed Finn will make things more interesting in Vienna when we arrive there, and may be the fellow to write an article about D&R.

SEPTEMBER 19, 1974
NEW YORK

Saw a late afternoon showing of a new Ingmar Bergman movie: *Scenes from a Marriage.* A tour de force of its kind. Almost entirely in very close-up of the two man-woman characters, and words, words, words. Introspective to a painful degree.

There is an appeal these days in the dramatization of futility. Which is what this picture is, with all of its polished camera work and well-defined personal tensions, and lack of tension. Didn't bother me.

I am less puzzled—and no longer at all frustrated—by a major theme of the picture. Namely, that sex isn't the whole of man-woman relations, or life itself for that matter. And "sex" is the word; not "love," but sexual intercourse.

What puzzles me far more, about myself, is something quite different. (And how self-centered one can become living alone in a big city as I do much of the time.)

It is my continued strong interest in the profession that produces words—usually referred to as the literary life. When I am not able to sleep in the early morning, I read a biography. The passages about the business of being a writer of fiction fascinate me, so I underline or mark the passages.

Aren't these strange texts for a fellow who spends his days as I do, in a professional way, ironing out a new organization of a lively and unusual business?

Does all this interest in the lives and ways of novelists, as recorded in their biographies, show that this is what I would most like to have been able to succeed in doing, rather than what I am, what I have become? Is all this journal writing in the middle of the night a clue to my deeper ambition, one that I recognize is beyond me in any distinguished way?

SEPTEMBER 21, 1974
PRINCETON

Mary Keating called to invite me (and Helen—who was still on the Vineyard) to lunch, from which I have just come. Ken Keating, the Ambassador to Israel, proved to be exceedingly interesting—I was the only guest.

I asked him about the spirit of the Israelis, and on this he was eloquent and emphatic. "It made me feel somewhat ashamed about our draft evaders and deserters to see how the young people rallied to the colors when the Arab War broke out. (Of course, the cases are so different; their country was under attack.) But the inflation rate is ruinous—over

35% and still going up. Some people are leaving the country. At one meeting saw a big sign, 'I Want to Go Back to Russia' and then some reference to the high cost of living, etc., in Israel."

I asked for his appraisal of President Ford. It was most impressive. "I served with him in the House for ten years; he is a midnight lamp burner; works hard; knows his subject. Is particularly strong in foreign affairs." (Which surprised me, as the press rarely remarks on this.)

About Kissinger, now that Nixon isn't there, Ken wasn't too sure. "It was Nixon who made Kissinger. He talked to Nixon as President two or three times a day. Once when he called from the Embassy he told the President he couldn't make any progress with the Syrians and would have to give up. The President said: you stay right there until you get an agreement. Nixon had a good sense of strategy; I am not sure how Kissinger will get along without the benefit of what Nixon had that Ford may not have."

SEPTEMBER 24, 1974
ABOARD A DOMESTIC FLIGHT TO BRASÍLIA FROM RIO

Travel is an obsession in Brazil within the country. So here I am squeezed between two large gents, headed for Brasília.

It seems not inconceivable that the Minister of Interior will say: "We do not need D&R for the next phase of the São Francisco, though it was you who laid the groundwork in your big fat report."

I can identify very little support or understanding in Brazil at this point. Leitão de Abreu is now on the Supreme Court: what can he do?

In the meantime, "back in Iran" the prospect never was brighter. Long letter from Mehdi, enthusiastic about our farm management project and genuinely warm and understanding. We go to a formal dinner next Tuesday night at the Iranian Embassy where we will see Hushang Ansary and doubtless others.

Besides, we are "related by marriage" with a country and a ruler that are making world history. At the UN the President of the U.S. and Secretary of State are pounding away: oil prices must come down or the world faces a profound economic collapse.

So what goes on in Iran is no longer a regional or provincial matter. Sunday the geniuses who prepare major *New York Times* editorials gave the whole editorial page to a demand that (somehow) the world force the oil producers—usually referred to as the "Arabs," almost forgetting for the moment that Iran is not Arab, and that Venezuela, Nigeria, Algeria, are involved—to lower prices.

Just how this kind of fierce talk is going to drop oil prices isn't yet disclosed. Stop-using-electricity "conservation" seems to be ended. But only a small fraction of American energy comes from imported fuel oil. And the price of alternate energy sources—coal for example—goes up almost as much: TVA reports paying $30 for poor coal (Anderson County) and the demand now is for $50, up from $9 (only a couple years ago, $4+).

The big headlines of the Brazilian papers scream: Ford Says Petroleum Prices Threaten a World War. Of course, I can't believe our Boy Scout Master, non-elected President said any such thing. Surely he is saying that a world-wide depression is threatened unless oil prices are reduced, or something of that kind. But probably all over Latin America this same headline or its equivalent.

Our first appointment was to see the new Minister of the Interior, name of Reis (I'm told the R isn't pronounced).

The tall, bespectacled Minister, in quite good English, proceeded to praise what we have done for their country by this study. I countered by saying that the report wasn't prepared because we wanted to "write a book but to get *action.* Brazil is a country of action," etc. "What can we do, now that that part of our work is done to help produce action along the line of the recommendations?"

The Minister said our first recommendation had been that an "enterprise" be created—meaning the Valley-wide agency provided by legislation soon after the new President took office. The next phase will also require "your technical people and you. When we receive the Portuguese translation of the report—you say it will be ready and printed in about ten days?—then we will study it and analyze it and be ready for other projects and things the report recommends."

What could be more fair?

The Minister said the President was soon to announce a big program for the northeast, and the São Francisco is partly in that region. Also for the Amazon. Apparently the new Minister hadn't heard of our work on the Amazon. This represents a neglect on our part, I must say. Perhaps he didn't know that we had been associated with Serete—we deliberately played that relationship down.

SEPTEMBER 25, 1974
BRASÍLIA

We read stories in the *New York Times* about "The Generals" who "run" this country under a military dictatorship. The picture is of burly, harsh-voiced characters pushing people off the sidewalks, as I recall had been written in the early days of our visits to Iran.

Yesterday afternoon we spent an hour with General Golbery, the Chief of the Civil Cabinet. A mild-looking little man, in his late sixties, I would guess, heavy glasses, a soft voice, and a warm smile. None of the Generals we have come to know, except former President Medici, could be distinguished from, say, high-school teachers, even the broad-shouldered Cavalcanti.

Golbery told us that our work had been a great help to Brazil. Couldn't have been more affirmative. Besides, he had read and understood the summary and statement of programs (two of the four volumes of the big monster of a report).

He has arranged for us to see the Minister of Planning, Velloso, today; we guess that the President is relying on these two as far as the São Francisco is concerned.

A period during which the "head of the President's household," smiling and speaking excellent English, told me I had done something important for his country, that they had confidence in what we recommend, that there had to be one organization instead of many for the Valley, and, with a small bow from a sitting position, that my name is so well known throughout the world, so many important works accomplished, etc., that the President expected us to carry on into "the second phase" of action.

As Adlai Stevenson said, and as I like to remind myself, such praise, like pipe smoke, is pleasant enough so long as one doesn't swallow it. But will there be a contract, and when? That will be the test, not the extravagant praise and how obviously impressed they are.

Leitão de Abreu came out of the elegant courtroom of the Supreme Tribunal Federal, looking much fresher and less harassed than when I used to see him in the office next to the President. He had missed me at the reception last night—I should have planned better about going to the American Embassy. But after an hour's dashing about with a lost taximan, we gave it up. I hate to hurt the feelings of a man I like as much as De Abreu and who has made our work here successful—so far.

AT RIO AIRPORT, 10 P.M.

Since 5 o'clock I have been going through a kind of din, cattle-car jamming, from one place to another, by every means of conveyance, and then locked in a hermetically sealed metal lozenge with several hundred other people—the ride from Brasília to Rio, what a drain it is, although the lithe young girl attendants do a job of feeding that would make a professional gymnast envious.

I must begin to ration myself. Not be so willing to take such trips just because of my loyalty to the work and the people, ours and those of the

countries we try to serve. "If only you had a greater sense of moderation."
Yeah. But then you wouldn't be you.

SEPTEMBER 30, 1974
PRINCETON

Confirmation from Minister Diawara that the Ivory Coast does indeed want us to go ahead with their projects.

OCTOBER 2, 1974
NEW YORK

Back at work. Up at 5:30, David Morse and I having breakfast in his
and Mildred's jewel of a little house in Georgetown, filled with the beautiful things—pictures, art objects—that I associate with a wealthy background. A portrait of Lincoln, for example, painted just before his death,
owned by Mildred's grandfather, Oscar Straus. Exquisite things, all in
such good taste.

The huge dinner at the Iranian Embassy last night, the guests mostly
the "Foreign Service" bureaucracy that inhabits the Washington scene,
year in and year out. The professional Foreign Service characters who
make a life of attending such "glittering" functions I find quite uninteresting.

But the setting is rather overpowering: the mirrored halls are saved
from being cheap show-off by hangings and vases of such beauty that
they take your breath away—but those are of a long time ago, centuries
in fact.

My chief impression about the Washington trip was the avalanche
of gloom. I would have expected it here in New York, or, what with
constantly rising food prices, at the supermarket checkout line. But these
European Chaos-Is-Upon-Us boys chill the bones. Of course, the Finance
Ministers gathered in the meetings are producing a panic of major proportions in order to prove that their personal and official fears are justified. That is the nature of a panic—the prognostications of the fearful
produce the very results they predict and fear.

Next: Chaos.

I don't take too much stock in Total Disaster, provided the U.S. holds
fast. And it can.

OCTOBER 12, 1974
PRINCETON

A couple hours this morning with Tom Mead.

Is my notion that the D&R Papers could provide a treasure of material on the nature and dynamics of the development process a good one?

Listening to Tom's frustration as he is wading through masses of papers (mostly trivial and grubby details), it came to me that it is not the papers but the whole story of development that we should search for, that scholars and students would find interesting and stimulating. The papers and the process are not synonymous.

My affirmative suggestions were that Tom deal with specific cases—agriculture, health, the power system, and then identify the consequences of these beginnings. He will prepare a memo for me, I hope, to clarify what this is all about.

OCTOBER 17, 1974
AMSTERDAM AIRPORT

I wandered about the Amsterdam airport grinning like—well, like a happy man, pleased with himself. Reason: an interview with me by Phyllis Meras, in the *Vineyard Gazette* for October 11. I had definitely given up any hope that the interview—that was back in late August—would appear, because I didn't think what I said to her could make such sense to her. But it turned out, despite the delay, to be just what I hoped it would be. The themes: (1) food; (2) development is a job that only the people of the country being developed can do. An old conviction of mine, of course, and basic to the D&R philosophy (though not to most of the current third generation of D&R staff, I fear).

OCTOBER 19, 1974
VIENNA

Among the beautiful people of Vienna vastly enjoying an opera in perhaps the most beautiful and elegant opera house in the world, La Scala not excepted. Having after-opera supper at the Sacher. And so on —a couple days of pleasure in a city that is bulging with prosperous-looking people.

As I watched the opera tonight—a Tchaikovsky, *Eugene Onegin*—and looked at the throngs of lucky Austrians (they have no "defense"—i.e., military millstone—around their necks), I thought of my father as a boy, at age eleven, carrying pipe in a plumbing equipment shop. And his great-grandson, Helen's and my extremely handsome grandson Daniel, traveling with us now on a trip of exploration such as would never have happened to me, so opulent, expensive, and intellectually exciting.

The tickets to the opera—they are very difficult to get—from the Finnish journalist who came to our office some weeks ago, and with whom (his lovely wife included) we had dinner after the opera. They live on a hill in the environs of Vienna from which on a clear day they can see sixty kilometers, and occasionally the spires of Pressburg, not too far from the village where my mother spent her early youth.

What contrasts on this trip.

IN FLIGHT, VIENNA TO TEHRAN VIA IRANAIR

Sacher torte mit schlag, etc. (cum calories galore) and the charm and obvious prosperity of Vienna—that's over, and a happy interlude it was. Now I'm back on the job, and more suddenly than I could have anticipated.

For as we settled ourselves in the plane, a youngish man across the aisle called my name and introduced himself: Cyrus Ansary, my tablemate at the Embassy in Washington, brother of Hushang.

Daniel has been both a joy and a puzzle. He keeps a completely immobile face most of the time; then on comes that one-sided warm smile, and one melts. Is he enjoying this experience? Helen, who knows him better than I because of this summer, says he is—and he says so. He reminds me so much of his mother at that age, reserved with adults, but anything but, among her own generation.

OCTOBER 20, 1974
TEHRAN

This afternoon David Morse asked Daniel some questions about the school busing war going on in Boston. What followed was a genuine tour de force. As David said, when Daniel left to dress for dinner: If only we had a tape of that; his analysis of the Boston school situation, the balance and thoughtfulness and eloquent statement. And this is the very quiet Daniel. "He is a deep well," said David Morse. Indeed.

OCTOBER 21, 1974
ANDIMESHK, KHUZISTAN

Once more a look at what we have wrought, or made possible to be wrought; this time a long, very dusty journey through an almost 15,000 hectare land project by a group of private investors under the management of our D&R alumni now in the "private sector."

Much of the time this morning (we got up at four, departed from the hotel at 4:30) we saw the beginnings of large-scale agriculture—land leveling (or to use a better term, land shaping) to a degree of high precision. Even to the point of what they choose to call a "laser beam" that adjusts a big earth-moving machine "electronically" to cut into the powdery soil to the exact depth to provide that billiard-table flatness that good irrigation practice requires.

"The answer to the problem of drainage, to avoid what is called water-logging, is a perfect surface, so there is no standing water." This is what Leo Anderson preached years ago. These huge machines, with the laser impulses, set the depth of cut precisely without the drivers having anything to do with it; the tractor operators do nothing but operate the big machines as they would any earth mover.

OCTOBER 22, 1974
ANDIMESHK

D&R brought into being—indeed, created—this huge enterprise, made it possible. Now the Khuzistan Water and Power Authority, a creature I insisted years ago take over the operating and policy responsibility, has done just that—but in a definitely bureaucratic spirit, bureaucratic as I defined it years ago in my TVA book. (I.e., chiefly concerned with the bureaucracy itself, and the individual promotion and well-being of the bureaucrats.)

KWPA, an Iranian-staffed and -run outfit, has built a beautiful modern office building instead of that Victorian-style defunct hotel in Ahwaz where it, and we, started; it has built a fancy clubhouse, where we dined last night; and it has cut itself off pretty much from the lives of the poor peasants, and become, in turn, the outsiders, the foreigners in their own country, to the aggressive corporate farm managers of the huge agribusiness enterprises, one of which (the Shell Oil Company's 15,000 hectare operation) I visited at sundown yesterday.

During a troubled night I looked back on D&R's beginnings with the rosy-tinted vision of all nostalgia and backward looking. I compared—in flashes—the days when Leo Anderson ran this regional development, he with his explosive, profane, driving manner, knowing just what should be done and when, which was instantly. And it was done, even though money was often scarce. A picture of Iranian helpers sitting around a table in a steaming little aluminum trailer, they the students, our D&R people the teachers and the drivers.

The D&R people themselves, in this night-long troubled non-sleep, all seemed giants (Gordon, Voorduin, Anderson, et al.) and in contrast the present D&R men, second-raters, refugees from the California water department I usually refer to as the Sacramento enclave.

Some of this sour outlook stems from being denied use of our usual commodious quarters in Andimeshk because, of all indignities, it was being occupied at Tehran's direction by the German Ambassador!

It is now no longer dark of night, as I write; it is the crisp coolth of a desert morning. Things look different. I fought to have the responsibility and decision-making transferred from us to an Iranian "institution," KWPA, and to Iranians. The transfer is complete. So D&R has become largely an advisor whose advice is rarely given forcefully, and even more rarely followed.

The unified comprehensive concept has been pretty well destroyed by centralized control from the Ministry of Water and Power—as we predicted when this bureaucratic change was made several years ago.

I was so keen to have private farming corporations move into the carrying out of the development of these lands, and that too has happened, in a big way, bigger than I could have dreamed possible. That too reduces the need for a strong D&R, minimizes the kind of challenge that kept such men as Leo Anderson fighting and creating.

Of course, looking back from this day ten, fifteen years later makes those earlier people and those earlier activities seem much better than they were. But can there be any doubt that where functions diminish and phase out (even though that was exactly what I wanted, as a matter of principle), vitality diminishes and the quality of people changes?

When I crawled out of an uncomfortable bed at 4:30 this morning, I had made up my so-called mind: you've had it; get out while you are ahead. And ahead we are—such kudos, such new opportunities, such ideas about Iran.

But the fanciful idea of turning in my suit is balked by several things: First, the horrible picture of getting up each morning at 88 Battle Road with nothing to do but invent a reason for being—the slow death of "retirement." (Not a real picture—I would find other things to do than putter—and besides New York has come to mean so much to me, so very much.)

And second, I learned from the months I spent "resigning" from TVA that, as Mal Sharpe advised me: "You will know when to leave TVA; something more challenging will come along, though you don't know nor can you imagine now what that will be."

OCTOBER 24, 1974
KERMANSHAH

A beautiful—indeed, spectacular—city with a backdrop of brown crags against the bluest of skies. This is the beginning of the long-planned trip to the Karkheh River Basin, to be continued tomorrow by charter plane and car.

Such prosperous-looking people, babies fat-faced and healthy, miles and miles of small shops chock full of goods of all kinds. Here and there a store with fancy sports cars displayed on the floor of the store!

But the old bazaar, a series of mud-brick arches, is very Middle East and 15th century. The "traffic" problem as we strolled along, agog, ranged (as it did when we visited the Ispahan bazaar) from a very white donkey who brushed me aside to the biggest, most elaborate Japanese motorcycle, and astride it a very proud and arrogant young man who appreciated our admiration of his mechanical pride and joy.

But this is very fatiguing. Both David Morse and I admitted tonight to being tired; having to climb four flights to our room (the elevator, naturally, wasn't working) was the last touch. But Helen seems as full of vitality, anecdotes, and good humor as ever. Indomitable.

Yesterday we went from Andimeshk to the Dez Bazaar, largely for Daniel's benefit, and Helen's. To see this tall, wide-eyed grandson buying a Lur felt hat, and David Morse's relish at the sight, he having fallen completely under Daniel's reserved charm.

And a visit to the Kermanshah Bazaar where Daniel insisted on buying a kilo of Iranian tea; he came off triumphantly with the tea in a brown paper bag—how this went with the Customs in New York we often wondered.

OCTOBER 25, 1974
TEHRAN

The flight in an Aero Commander over the Karkheh River Basin was a delight, a revelation about its possibilities, possibilities for a quite different kind of food production than the vast flat plains of the Dez River —i.e., the Khuzistan.

After our charter plane arrived at Hamadan this noon, Daniel looked very sad, didn't want to go on our visit (to what was a particularly uninteresting city, after all), was obviously feverish, achy. Now what? Anxious moments before we found a place at the airport where he could lie down. When we came back from our tour of the city, he was much improved.

I put him in the co-pilot's seat on the return flight to Tehran, thinking there was less air motion up there. The young Iranian pilot let him fly the plane for a full half-hour, and told him about all the instruments, the radio, navigation techniques, etc. Daniel perked up at once, clung to the wheel till his knuckles became white, and afterward explained to us with vivacity what he had learned—probably the shortest and most effective instruction in flying in the history of aviation. He ate it up, his fever forgotten.

The trip to Hamadan (the site of the ancient Ecbatana) was a let-down. Tried to get into the Tomb of Queen Esther. The taxi driver, puzzled: Esther who? Finally, in the outer crypt, saw over a kind of altar, near a window, a candle demurely perched on the altar. Examined the gaily-colored altar cloth to find the letters on it read: POPEYE in English!

OCTOBER 27, 1974
TEHRAN

It was last spring at an audience that I spoke to the Shah about the responsibility he had placed on the new Minister of the Interior, Jamshid Amouzegar, to strengthen the country's civil service and make for greater management effectiveness. On an impulse, shortly after my return, I wrote a long letter to Amouzegar saying I thought D&R might be able to contribute, out of my experience with the Iranian establishment, and David Morse's work in management training in the ILO.

This noon I learned how affirmatively and enthusiastically Amouzegar received this suggestion—it wasn't much more than that though I have in the meantime given it considerable thought.

He said: "As soon as I got your letter saying that you and Mr. Morse and D&R might help us I showed the letter to His Majesty. He was as pleased and enthusiastic as I. He directed me to enter into whatever terms you thought were right, so we could have the benefit of your help as soon as possible. On whatever terms—money is not a problem; you should have the greatest degree of flexibility."

I had suggested in a letter that perhaps the Ministry of Energy—still called Water and Power—was a place to begin. He responded affirmatively.

The Minister proceeded to describe the problem on which he needs "help": essentially the salary scales within the civil service, particularly the relation of one set of services and professionals to others. He gave illustrations.

"This situation is our most urgent and most pressing problem. It may well require a revision of our employment laws. Unless it is remedied soon, it may wreck the Iranian civil service."

Then, leaning toward us, and with intensity, Amouzegar put it all very simply: "We are the patient; you are the doctor. As the doctor, you must tell us what we should do, for the short term *and* the long term. If what we are doing, the direction we are going you find is the right one, that is one thing. But if we should change directions, that you must tell us. You are the doctor."

This phrase—"you are the doctor, we are the patient—tell us what we must do"—so impressed David Morse that he has kept repeating it each time he has described the public sector assignment to others. And he adds, "What a personal tribute to you, David."

The Minister expressed himself as delighted that D&R had the services of David Morse, and about the almost unlimited confidence the Shah had in me. So we would start this not just as another survey, or just another "consulting contract," but in direct communication at the top of the Government.

All of this is sobering, exciting, and will take careful thought. I would like this to be a modern and contemporary new aspect of D&R services. This is an area where ideas count, and imagination. Not just an opportunity for the sort of "job classification" and "salary classification" that TVA did so many years ago. I should make clear that this job should fit into the mosaic of D&R's past history and goals, and results. I want to assure D&R's continuity, by the continuity of the concept, the standards, the honesty of this undertaking. The impulse to pull down the pillars, to sulk, or to explode is very strong.

OCTOBER 29, 1974
TEHRAN

A visit with Mr. Ebtehaj, back at his bank after surgery for ulcers. With the old fire, he told us more stories about his seven and a half months "in jail" in 1961, and of the efforts of his enemies to get evidence that in paying "Lilienthal and Clapp" large sums there was corruption, or in any event, that he had not secured all the necessary official approvals and therefore was breaking the law.†

Later a brief visit with the finest friend I have in this country: Mehdi Samii, in his office as Managing Director of the Agricultural Development Bank.

Said he: "When I left you, at David Morse's house in Washington recently, I walked to M Street to get a taxi. Finally saw one, signalled to it; it went on, then stopped and backed up. The driver leaned out and said: 'Aren't you Mehdi Samii?' Yes. 'I was one of your guards when you were Governor of the Central Bank. I came to America, six years ago, and now I own a fleet of taxis.' "

An elegant luncheon with Reza Ansari, for some time now with Princess Ashraf Pahlavi's (the Shah's twin sister) organization for "Social, Economic, and Cultural Affairs." The guests included two other

†This unusual episode is recounted in the *Journals*, Vol. V, *The Harvest Years*.

alumni of the original Khuzistan program: Ahmad Ahmadi and Shah-mirzadi.

Reza reminisced about Khuzistan as it was before we began that program, and added one more story, one that he said showed in an earthy way the impact on people's lives and even their family, domestic stability.

Before D&R it was so hot that for four months the women of families that could afford it would take the children and come north to Tehran or elsewhere, leaving the men. A long time to be away from their women. Said Reza: "There was this stream of families heading north, and another stream heading south to Khuzistan, of prostitutes. After a while this led to divorce and broken homes. Then came electricity, fans, air conditioners, refrigerators—and the wives stayed and there were no more divorces."

Add one more for electricity and "development."

OCTOBER 30, 1974
TEHRAN

TRAFFIC. I will never complain about New York's congested traffic now that I have seen and been engulfed in such traffic as I have never seen before. Unbelievable.

Even the hardened Tehranis find this almost too much to bear. Said Mehdi Samii this noon: "This traffic is driving me crazy. Can't count on when you will arrive at a place where you have an appointment."

NOVEMBER 4, 1974
ROME

After our session with Minister Amouzegar at noon on Sunday, October 27, David Morse sat down in the conversation-filled D&R office and began drafting, in longhand, a "Memorandum of Understanding" covering that meeting. I read it carefully, thought it was an admirable summary of what had been said. Then, four days later, I again met with the Minister, though this time unfortunately without David, who had left for Paris and New York on the previous day.

I explained David's absence, said we had discussed the Minister's proposal carefully; that the subject was of such importance and so much a part of my own experience in government that I had agreed to accept the responsibility, fully aware, I thought, of the risks to me, in my standing, since our recommendations would necessarily be controversial and stir conflict between government agencies and within the private sector as well.

The simplest way was to hand him the draft memorandum of under-standing.

He read it slowly, carefully, quite pokerface. "This paper clearly states the substance of our discussion. I am prepared to sign it now, including the figure you have written in of $400,000 for the first six months' work. But I should mention this to the Minister of Plan.

"To make sure, I will get the approval of the Prime Minister on Saturday; he is head of the Budget Committee of the Council. Phone me Saturday noon after your audience with His Majesty—I will be here—and you can report on your audience and I can tell you the result of my mentioning this to the Prime Minister."

I said that my audience would probably be cut short, because I noticed that Secretary of State Kissinger, complete with his usual array of publicity, would be in Iran on that day. If the Secretary's visit is with the expectation of forcing down Iran's oil price, I said, I thought he was wasting his time and would be better occupied to do some sightseeing. Amouzegar found this amusing.

For my audience with the Shah I had walked quite alone, on the crunchy gravel, from the gate to the great marble steps and thence, still alone and unattended, to the vast corridor, where brilliant attendants in azure tailcoat uniforms gestured this direction and that until I reached a "waiting room" by this time quite familiar to me, with its red velvet and ugly early 20th century furniture. There I sat, for perhaps ten minutes.

My audience had been fixed for 11:30. At exactly 11:30 a smiling young man came to fetch me.

The door to the Shah's office was opened; inside a servitor bowed to the waist, I walked in, and as usual, His Imperial Majesty approached me from the center of this vast room, smiling broadly, looking tanned and very fit. After an unusually long handshake and an exchange of greet-ings, he moved toward a settee, while I, walking behind him, said in my heartiest informal tone: "My wife and I wish Your Majesty happy birth-day." (His birthday had been last week, with the usual nation-wide cele-brations.) "And," I continued (as I settled into the settee and he close by in his chair at my left), "it is a happy birthday for Iran, and in fact for the whole world, for you have become a center of stability and certainty for the whole world, at a time when leadership everywhere is unsure, unstable. And I include my own country.

"Think how it would be if you were not here, at this time, not only for Iran but for all of us today."

He took this comment as an expression of personal pleasantry or apple polishing, though he raised his eyebrows and looked very thought-ful; then said, with that quite amused kind of smile that doesn't show up

in the familiar photographs of His Majesty shaking hands with the visiting dignitaries who crowd into Iran these latter days: "You know—few
other people do—you can think of the country as it was when you first
came to work with us in the winter of 1956."

Said I: "It was your unfailing support and your prodding that made
it possible to begin the Khuzistan program, and carry it through. If it had
not been for you, nothing would have happened, we could not have done
what we did in Khuzistan."

He nodded and said, *sotto voce:* "Otherwise it would today still be a
wasteland."

I said I had gone to Khuzistan the first days after we reached Iran,
and then to Kermanshah, and flew in an Aero Commander over the
upper Karkheh River Basin.

I reached for the copy of *The Unified Development of the Khuzistan
Region* which I had brought along, a fat green-covered volume, this copy
with Gordon's and my signatures dated May 1959.

And this began my discussion of the Karkheh project I so much want
to go ahead. I opened the map of the region. He took off his glasses and
studied the map, frowning. This basin, from Kermanshah southward to
the Gulf, was part of D&R's original plan for Khuzistan. But nothing has
been done in the Karkheh Valley. I pointed to the dam sites and the
mountain valleys with their agricultural potential.

"And you say this is now going to be developed?"

I said D&R had been asked by Minister Vahidi to submit a proposal,
and I had said I would take responsibility to see that the 36-month preliminary work would go forward if it were treated as was the Khuzistan
region, as a single comprehensive job, not broken up into separate bits,
as is the prevalent custom, unfortunately.

His finger traced over the parts of the Karkheh Basin, as I referred
to the effect of dams in the upper basin mountains on preventing devastating floods in the south. "And here, toward the south, live some very
poor people, very poor, which this development could help." He r'ared
back: "Yes, poor; and very close to the Iraq border." The political point,
of course, had been made without my mentioning it. But he will not need
to be reminded again.

I made only scant reference to the Karun Valley, to the west of the
Karkheh and north of the Dez. But I particularly pointed out that the only
dam so far built in the upper Karun was what we in the Unified Plan had
called Karun #2 but had not built, now the Reza Shah Kabir Dam, about
to be "topped out."

Although I had been told, twice, by Amouzegar that the Shah was
much disturbed and "furious" when he learned recently that the dam's
foundations were leaking badly, that there would be perhaps two years'

delay in delivering a million kw of power from the dam while extensive repairs and grouting were made at great expense, the Shah made no reference to it, so I didn't. Perhaps this was wrong on my part.

I had been prepared, fully, to express my opinion: that this represented carelessness, or lack of care and faulty, bad engineering, not to be *fully* informed about the foundation of a dam on limestone (like Kentucky Dam of TVA). Amouzegar had urged me, when David Morse was with me, to speak out. "The Shah greatly values your judgment. His own advisors have told him that the catastrophe could not have been avoided, that everything had been done according to the best 'international' standards."

The Shah came back to the map of the upper Karkheh. "This work could prevent soil erosion and the silting of the reservoirs." This has long been a source of worry to him, to the point of his insisting that the silt in Pahlavi reservoir be dredged out, at great expense.

I referred briefly to Minister Amouzegar's new Ministry, that some people had thought that the man who had successfully confronted the oil companies and led the way in OPEC had been demoted, but I knew from the audience, last spring, that he had been made Minister for strengthening the public administration because His Majesty considered this of supreme importance. As of course I did.

I handed the Shah the memorandum of understanding, which I said had been prepared by "my colleague" David Morse, describing his background and talents. He read it through, slowly (he is actually a rapid reader). I had taken the precaution of writing into the blank space about the fee a number I knew would be adequate but represented the value of the service—i.e., $400,000—a substantial sum for a six-month preliminary work.

"The topmost priority for Iran is what we are asking you to apply your experience and judgment to: improving the public administration, putting an end to red tape and delay."

The Shah, his voice low, intense, his face clouded in concentration, is the man described in a cover story in this week's *Time* magazine as The Emperor of Oil.

I find this quite remarkable, giving this such importance, this grim intention to reset the whole mechanism of government, on the civil administrative side. This is a picture of a sovereign of an underdeveloped country, fiercely moving to absorb its great wealth, cash flowing in like a spring flood.

My ofttimes expressed personal concern, and professional concern, for D&R, that I am just "repeating myself," and D&R is doing the same thing (a concern that the facts do not support), is dispelled by this sudden new assignment.

He made no comment after he had read the memorandum of understanding. I said Amouzegar had told me that after the audience I should check further with him, but that the paper correctly reported the substance of the meeting he, David, and I had had, that Amouzegar would check with the Prime Minister and the Minister of Plan and let me know definitely today (i.e., Saturday).

"Amouzegar will continue to represent us in OPEC, of course. But his work on the public services is 'of the very first importance.' It was one of the points of the White Revolution. Amouzegar is a tough man."

I said: We will try to come up with more than a conventional study of public administration, and it will not be simply a copy of American or British methods. We must take into account as best we are able the way Iranians look at things.

I got to my feet; the Shah said that if I would wait for a brief time, Amouzegar would be the next for an audience, with the Council of Ministers.

Amouzegar came bustling in, dressed in a pale blue suit. Apologizing for the delay, he said he had talked to the Prime Minister about the agreement, also with Majidi, the Managing Director of Plan Organization, and to His Majesty. The Prime Minister said it was all right "but we thought we should have a brief statement as part of the memorandum of what we can expect to get for the $400,000. This is to protect both of us from questions in Parliament and perhaps the press, you know."

(I thought to myself that this was encouraging, to have evidence of this kind that the approval of the Shah does not mean that Parliament and the press are not able to ask questions and criticize, as is so often assumed by such hotshot journalists as have been interpreting the Iranian scene of late.)

Also, "I would like to have the agreement be between yourself and the Civil and Administrative Services of the Iranian Government, and I would sign the paper on behalf of those agencies, rather than as a person. It is too personal as it now reads, on our side. It is quite all right to have it personal on yours."

Of course, I said this was quite in order; we submitted a draft only, and would make the additions he suggested. Perhaps after three months, there could be a report of what had already been done.

From the "crudities" of the bathroom at the Hotel Daryoush in Kermanshah to the luxury of lying full length in a steaming bath this morning at the Hassler: if not quite the extreme extremities of travel amenities, those two come close to it.

We had barely arrived yesterday early afternoon before I was on the phone to Florence, heard that resonant voice of our son. He would come to Rome to see us, and then Helen would go on with him to Florence while I headed back.

Rome at sunset on a pleasant Sunday was sheer delight. For years I have differed with Helen about Rome: it seemed a good place to stop over but not to visit. But not so last evening.

The whole western sky was rosy, the clouds purple and orange and red as the sun receded, gently, slowly, delicately serene, not with the indecent haste of a tropical sunset of Brazil, or the "let's get it over with" of sundown on the desert of Khuzistan or Arizona.

As we leaned against the stone parapet overlooking the now to us so familiar Spanish Steps it was dramatic with the drama of the stage scenery of ornate Italian opera. The whole of the heart of Rome was the foreground, the sun touching all those famous domes and spires, softening to nothing the noisy raucous sounds of the millions of Fiats, etc. that have made Rome at times an abomination.

NOVEMBER 5, 1974
ROME

The visit here with David was the happiest chapter of the whole trip. Not even the audience with the Shah of last Saturday gave me greater joy; nor the increased awareness of how better to run our operations in Iran.

David arrived Sunday afternoon. That evening he and I took a walk. He was in a mood to talk about himself. I found that despite the toughness of being a "professional writer" and the agonies of the two months while Peggy was so mysteriously ill, he is ready for what comes, "a happy and a lucky man," his phrase. Lucky because he is doing just what he most wants to do—write; happy because he has a family to care for, and love, and be proud of.

While we were looking out over the hypnotic panorama of Rome, on a quiet night of moon and stars, he began to talk about the brief visit with Beatrice and Barney Tobey last summer.

"They opened up to me—and it was so moving. Suddenly, Beatrice made a comment about my work. From anyone else than Beatrice I would have thought: Who asked you? But what she said was so quick, such a flash of insight, that I have thought about it time and again ever since. It has affected my outlook, the new direction that I had been reaching for on my own."

I leaned over the parapet at the head of the Spanish Steps, looked out over the scene that Keats had found so warming; kept silent for a long time. Then I said that it was extraordinary that this little woman, my cousin and closest friend, should be brave enough to break through the barrier that encases most creative people—such as he is—to offer a word to which he had so completely responded. But a similar experience has been mine with this remarkable and pert woman, with whom he and I share (in different degrees) a common bloodstream.

In quite another area I had found that Beatrice's judgment was one to lean upon, where earthy, peasant-style, uncomplicated advice was needed. One thing that had so impressed David about the intuitive reaction of Beatrice to his writing was that "she really doesn't know much of my problems as a writer, and yet here comes this lightning glimpse."

And so with me, I said to him. She really doesn't know the full story about those problems of mine on which I have sought her opinion. Instead of stirring me up when I am in a fighting mood, for example, she sets out a balanced viewpoint.

NOVEMBER 9, 1974
PRINCETON

Arrived "home" (is 88 Battle home without Helen, visiting in Florence with David?) bushed but no longer introspective, and after a steak dinner prepared by Margaret Morton, to bed and a good sleep.

Today I gathered together all my paraphernalia: spades, forks, richly crumbly compost from my treasured heap beside the garage, bone meal, grit, and dug holes worthy of the rather special King Alfreds in the west border. To my dismay, found the clay inert and heavy, no place to put a good bulb. Dug way deep, and instead of Elamite artifacts, as per Haft Tapeh, nothing but chips of rock and bits of broken china and glass. Our predecessors made a dump of what should have been a border. It gave me great satisfaction to tear it all out and replace it with honest earth, wherein at this moment nestle some of Holland's best products.

General Alfonzo Ravard is a notable figure in his Venezuela, but relaxed in a deep chair in Rodman's office he is a pudgy little man, very round-eyed and professorial.

Said I: "General, D&R simply isn't interested in taking on the kind of nation-wide overall planning study the Minister's letter describes. I know and you know what will come of all that: exactly nothing but reports, to add to other such reports.

"General, you didn't change the face of your country—as you most certainly did over many years in the Guyana region—by such vague philosophical stuff. Let's move, let's start, let's get going with the bulldozers, and with that kind of job we'll join in."

Rodman felt let down. "But isn't it necessary to have a broad picture of the country as a whole before starting development? Didn't you have such a broad analysis before you began in Khuzistan?"

(I should write Rodman about this, for he has been bitten early in life with the "national planning" and systems analysis bug, which his father now describes in his most recent grandiose "Committee on Critical Choices." Rubbish and fit only for the academic palate.)

In the sourest moments of the morning (about 1 A.M., indeed) I had imagined I would open the meeting about possible D&R participation with Ravard in Venezuela, by stating, in a flat and belligerent voice, that it must be understood that D&R is a fully autonomous and independent outfit, though its shares are owned by IBEC. Instead of such a self-conscious stance, which would have been offensive, though accurate, I positioned my chair directly opposite the General and "took charge," as indeed was expected of me. (David Morse, more given to the diplomatic tone, said immediately afterward: "You were belligerent today.")

I focused on what we want—that is, some form of participation with General Ravard, whether a joint venture, a joint company, or whatever. He must have in mind a number of his fellow Venezuelans, men with whom he has worked during the years, who could form a small unit, which we of D&R would match; set up an office in Venezuela, present a joint budget, and get going.

Actually, this was the kind of thing Rodman himself had in mind, even suggesting the amount we could expend while we tried to get the kind of work that would support the joint effort and be satisfying and satisfactory. Gradually it was evident that this did appeal to Ravard, but he wanted to impress us with the fact (which I don't doubt) that he had many other business opportunities and therefore would be limited in the time he could give to this venture.

Since I was in this mood of putting things out on the table, I went into the problem of Ravard's relation to the process of nationalizing the foreign oil companies as an appointed "observer" for the Government. If he joined in a venture with D&R would this be criticized and made much of? D&R is a "separate" company, it is owned by IBEC, which is owned by the Rockefeller family, and the Rockefellers in the public mind and probably in fact are large owners of Creole and other Venezuelan oil companies that are going to be nationalized.

My point was the one I had made to Rodman, with David Morse present, on the preceding day. It was that being in a close venture with General Ravard, who has influence in the dispute between the acquiring government and Creole and the other oil companies, involving many millions of dollars of Rockefeller investments, "could cause your father embarrassment" in the confirmation hearings where he has plenty to bother him as it is, and even more so when he becomes a public official, the second man in the Executive Branch, the Vice President.

When I had said this, Rodman said, "It is thoughtful of you that you should have that in mind." I said I had had many years' exposure to the kind of sordid and unworthy inferences that confront men in public life. I had had my share, so I was sensitive to the possibility and indeed knew that the time to think about such matters is *before,* not in the midst of criticism, however "shameful" on the part of those who use such inferences.

"Yes," said Rod, "and you survived."

Rodman closed the meeting with Ravard this way: "You are the most independent man in Venezuela without a doubt. And here is our counterpart, the most independent man in our country," gesturing toward me. (If he truly means that and will apply it by maintaining the arm's-length relations I believe are essential between D&R and its "owner," it will have been a good afternoon.)

NOVEMBER II, 1974
PRINCETON

As I opened my *New York Times* this morning I saw, on page eighteen, a full-page paid advertisement about the Shah's press conference of the morning of November 2 (probably just before my audience that same day).

The subject: oil prices. There reproduced was the full text of the questions put by the correspondents and the Shah's answers.

Even more interesting was a comment about the way "the American press misconstrued due to accidental or deliberate distortion" what the Shah had said in response to questions at what must have been one of his biggest press conferences.

The occasion for such a large number of "American correspondents," of course, was Kissinger's entourage of fifteen newspapermen, who are part of his "sweetheart" contingent wherever he goes.

The Shah's comments, vigorous and sharp and anything but conciliatory, answer one question much in my mind: is American and world opinion of any importance to Iran? It is evident that His Majesty feels strongly about this.

He is trying to turn around the very bad press built against him (a rotten piece in *Harper's* magazine is the latest).

That *Harper's* article by Frances Tree really got my goat. (It was written, as was her Vietnam piece of irresponsible sensationalism, "disguised" under her married name of Fitzgerald.)

In the entire piece it is impossible to find a single word about the constructive things Iran and the Shah have been doing all these years. And the misstatements of fact are shocking.

Had me steaming all morning.

Had such a pleasant interlude this noon. Lunched at Prospect House with Bill Dix, a gentleman and one who has made the professionalism and sensitivity of a Great Librarian an exciting thing indeed.

With Andrea Pampanini, Bill took us through his creation, the Firestone Library, floor after subterranean floor. The happiest part for me was not the rare books (though who can sniff at the Gutenberg Bible?) but the young people, the students, in their cubicles and lockable "carrels" (a new word to me). Alive and full of purpose.

Long, long ago in the midst of that scorching fight with the World Bank over a loan for the Dez Dam, Ebtehaj said: "And furthermore, one of these days Iran will be lending money *to* the World Bank." It seemed bravado at the time. But here it is. See the World Bank press release:

> The Imperial Government of Iran and the World Bank have signed an agreement for a loan to the World Bank of $150,000,000. The loan will have a maturity of 12 years and the interest rate will be 8% per annum.
>
> This is the second loan made by the Imperial Government of Iran to the World Bank. This borrowing will bring the total amount borrowed by the World Bank from Iran to $350,000,000.

NOVEMBER 12, 1974
NEW YORK

Whenever have I seen so many cops? Walking across 50th Street past the Waldorf, the place was blue with them. Why? The arrival at the Waldorf of the leader of the Palestine Liberation Organization, who will have his say at the UN this week. With memories of the [Olympic Games] massacre at Munich in 1972, and terrorism rampant, it would be a good deal to expect the Jewish population here—or their militant members—not to "protest," and it is up to the police force to hold things in some sort of order. With TV cameras, there is every reason to expect a lot of pushing and shoving. I hope nothing more.

NOVEMBER 13, 1974
NEW YORK

Breakfast at Harmon's coffee shop. There was David Tobey looking like the very picture of doom. His bosses at Philipp Brothers, he said, "think that the world is collapsing." (*Their* world, of plunder and rapacity toward the underdog nations, just may be collapsing, at that.) Said David: "I think so, too."

I whacked him as he left, saying: "Shame on you, a young fellow like you, with your prospects and all, talking like that. Of course it's not collapsing."

The waitress said: "It *is* collapsing. How can I survive with prices going up and the landlord . . . ?" And across the way, a quiet, grey-haired lady wearing a hat—why did I find *that* so significant?—eating her breakfast, broke in, in a soft voice: "It is collapsing, and I know it. You'll get no votes for the future here."

Then I opened the *Times* and saw the picture of two of the leading professional economic masochists, Galbraith and Barbara Ward, glorying in predictions of chaos. The reporter even said Barbara's tone was "ebullient."

NOVEMBER 16, 1974
PRINCETON

Russell Lynes has a beaming, somehow Oriental smile. Wise and warm. I had more than an hour as his luncheon companion at the Century Thursday. (He is now president of the Century Association, that remarkable collection of what Whitney Seymour called "the ragtag and bobtail of the best people of New York.")

I expressed my consternation and indignation about the nasty article *Harper's* magazine published about the Shah and Iran, with the unusual twist of a derogatory editorial line on the very cover.

Said I: That article—forget the very many misstatements of fact—was written in the spirit of Goebbels, and concluded with a plain and unmistakable "invitation to assassination," which is literally true.

Russell, one of the best writers and editors in this country, is listed as a member of the board of editors of the magazine.

I was left gasping, mentally, when his only response to these strong statements about the irresponsibility of the magazine was to say, with that wide smile: "I am on the board of editors, but I rarely read the magazine; haven't read the article you mention." And that was that.

I said I continued to keep a journal, beyond (in time) the five volumes Harper & Row has published. I got the impression he had never heard of those volumes and had the vaguest notion of what I do with myself.

I wanted his advice: should I try to write a book, a distillation of my experience in development?

"Oh, I wouldn't worry about writing a book. Even those of us who make our living by writing find it very difficult and confining. If you keep your notes as you go along, someone will come along and write that book about your ideas and what you have done." A big grin: "I'd forget about a book."

Have spent much time, each morning, thinking how we should approach the "Amouzegar Project," as we call the public management job.

One precept I laid down: in staffing the enterprise, start with the dictum: "Who is the best person in the country for this particular job?"

With some "instant replay" assistance from the redoubtable Miss Baron, I thought at once of the longtime and vigorous Chairman of the U.S. Civil Service, John Macy, and in a few minutes she had him on the phone and I'm to see him next week.

NOVEMBER 17, 1974
PRINCETON

Propped up luxuriously in bed. It is an overcast grey day.

Have just read through, carefully, a report (filled with figures) that astounds me. It is the TVA's *Annual Power Report* for the fiscal year ended June 30, 1974.

By all odds the largest power system in this country—24 million kw of installed capacity, revenues of over $886 million and so on. The numbers, taken in a big dose of reading this report, are simply staggering.

And add to this the more recent tracks of your own career—TVA is now the largest atomic power producer and more, much more, is on the way.

NOVEMBER 18, 1974
NEW YORK

Pampanini handed me this morning a very workmanlike and lengthy statement on how to go about the Amouzegar Project, putting into good form the approach I have been talking to him about, and including, in good English prose, a statement that is an encouraging measure of his analytical abilities; I daresay it takes more than analysis to get this big undertaking really going, but it helps. So I'm taking him to dinner tonight to celebrate Round One.

Much hangs on how well I get John Macy "fired up" about D&R when we meet tomorrow morning.

NOVEMBER 19, 1974
NEW YORK

It is twenty-five years since I sent John Macy to give those superbrains—and superegos—at the Los Alamos [atomic energy] Lab some sense of organization. Then he was tall, slender, athletic, and with an eagle eye and a short crew cut—a distinguished man who did an impressive job under great difficulties.

Today this same man walked into my office, still very erect, slender, athletic, still with a short crew cut (though his hair is a brilliant white). What had been added in the intervening years is the result of a remarkable subsequent career: Chairman of the Civil Service Commission guiding the largest body of public servants ever, and simultaneously ("I wore two hats," he said) four years as President Johnson's personnel director.

"President Johnson said: 'Why can't I have the benefit—when I am appointing men—of your methods in the Civil Service, picking people for their merit?' And so instead of patronage and political recommendations, I proposed people for Johnson that it was up to him to appoint," said Macy.

(Now I recall that it was because of Macy that Johnson named me and D&R for the Vietnam postwar job—which I could have gladly done without, I guess.)

Will John accept? That he is intensely interested was clear. As I said —and it struck home—"this could be the capstone of your professional career, this task of redirecting Iran's entire public sector management."

He has, of course, personal problems before he can decide. Committed to his present job as chairman of the National Council of Better Business Bureaus ("what I am in this job is a mendicant, rattling a tin cup to raise funds from businessmen"), and he has a family problem, two children still in college. The customary array of personal problems for anyone when discussing an overseas post.

He would add great stature to our standing in Iran if he could be persuaded.

NOVEMBER 22, 1974
PRINCETON

My concern is that we begin the Amouzegar Project with a broad perspective, lest we find ourselves piling up "facts" and prosaic and shopworn precepts about "good public administration," whereas I see this as a far broader task.

For example: why should the Shah and Amouzegar and Vahidi be so concerned about strengthening public management in Iran? Not to meet the standards of public administration experts. What are the distinctively Iranian conditions that make this so important?

Then: do we want to make recommendations that will make Iranian public sector management be "just like us"? Definitely not; yet that was the apparent goal of the U.S. AID Vietnam Mission on public administration (there were a flock of them at work on it).

That remarkable wife of mine: a brief meeting in my study (hers too, come to think about it) this morning made this plain: she has already edited ("prepared for the printer") the MS for most of Volume VI!!

Looking at what she has done over the past months convinces me that she can turn out an edited version of the journal MS for '64, '65, '66, and '67 that will require very little change by me. She has identified the questions she thinks I should be the one to pass on, but by sampling these questions, I find that she knows the answer to her own questions as well as I do.

And why not? She has lived through these events and ideas, knows what is a sensitive subject and what is not, knows what clarity of prose means.

A long talk with Frederiksen from Caracas. No doubt that his energy and ability to take the initiative have brought us very close to a new area of work.

"Dave, the Ministers and heads of regional authorities down here have never heard of D&R, nor of IBEC. They call it 'IBK,' and don't know what it does.

"But they know all about Lilienthal and TVA.

"Most of them know David Morse and his work, and would be glad if you two could come down in early January to present the proposal."

So I have agreed to go to Venezuela in January. Hal will be here the week after Thanksgiving, so we can spend a couple days on the proposal.

Looks encouraging.

NOVEMBER 24, 1974
PRINCETON

The other day I overtook Bethuel Webster, headed as I was for lunch at the Century. He was just back from a "conducted tour" that included several days in Iran—Ispahan, Persepolis, etc. Said Beth: "You know, we didn't see anything of the work you have been doing out there and didn't meet anyone who had ever heard of it or you."

I repeated this to David Morse, later. While he was in Iran everyone he met, among the higher ranks, and visitors too, spoke of me as a "legend," knew of our work, praised it. Said David: "Beth and his companions"—which included Francis Plimpton and a former British Ambassador to Iran, Roger Stevens, who organized the "tour"—"must have talked only to bellboys at the Hilton."

Other friends have asked me, "Why is it with all the publicity about Iran there is never any mention of your work?"

This and other instances raised again the question: have you overdone your "low profile" policy? If it is a policy, and not just an acquiescence in the fact that constructive things that are done in Iran, since they
are not considered a "crisis," aren't of interest to the press.

Then I looked in my early [TVA] *Journals* when I had too much
publicity, all of it derogatory and even vicious, whereas A. E. Morgan and
Willkie, et al., were being praised to the sky by the press. Yet I survived
and so did my work, and neither of them did.

So again: isn't the anonymous role better than pressing for personal
or company publicity? Or have I carried this out-of-sight policy much too
far? And if so, should I try, really try, to do something about it?

NOVEMBER 25, 1974
NEW YORK

A cable from Amouzegar's deputy: the contract has been signed and
mailed; the money is on its way to our bank account.

Now we are truly ready to make commitments to people, to
schedules, to the design of the undertaking. John Macy, a key person on
the professional side (and our kind of man in every way), thought about
our offer over the weekend, will go with us, including five months' residence in Tehran.

My goal—getting a preliminary team into the field "during November"—will be achieved, including "the return of Walt" [Seymour]. He is
ready to leave the blessings of retirement to take a look at the Ministry
of Energy, both from the organizational viewpoint and, I hope, the substance of a power-planning study. This has been languishing lo these
many months.

Helen is all set to start, in earnest, to take full responsibility for
editing the MS of Volume VI, 1964–1969 or thereabouts. There is much in
this volume of considerable interest.

As an example: pages are devoted to the fight I made, shoulder to
shoulder with Reza Ansari, to preserve the regional and decentralization
aspect of the Khuzistan project. We lost that fight. Rouhani, Minister of
Water and Power, won; KWPA was made part of his Ministry, and the
collateral but essential services and functions of health, social welfare,
were amputated, and KWPA began its decline.

Now, according to an account in the *Tehran Journal,* instructions
are going out that all development work is to be decentralized and region-
alized!!

So it takes time to win a fight like that. TVA won it because I stood
off Ickes, Fortas, Corcoran, and the Washington agencies generally with

vigor and much support. But the central agencies won the war, in the sense that they prevented any other regional agencies of that genuine kind from being formed.

There is now a real chance in Iran to pick up where we were when I took it on the chin, along with Ansari, almost ten years ago. Particularly is there a good chance since we have now been "commissioned" to make overall recommendations on organization throughout the Government, with particular reference to water, power, and agriculture.

NOVEMBER 28, 1974
THANKSGIVING DAY
PRINCETON

The East Room, on the fourth floor of the Century Club, a round table elegantly set for lunch; four of us drinking martinis, then sitting down to lobster bisque laced with warm sherry, followed by a splendid minute steak. Around the table the team that will go to Iran very shortly to reconnoiter as significant an undertaking as any of us have shouldered, and particularly the writer of these notes, who has "assumed personal responsibility."

At exactly two minutes before 2:30—Morse has been looking at his watch for thirty minutes—the clang of a telephone. David Morse is on his feet. "That's what we have been waiting for." In a few minutes David returns, holding his arms up, his thumbs up. "The answer [from John Macy] is yes, definitely."

Only a month ago, in the office of Minister Amouzegar, the proposal was made, and, orally, accepted. Now the contract is agreed upon, the funds are on their way, and on Monday, December 2, the first group will be in Tehran. With Macy committed (so David reported) to resign his present post and head the field group on this "A Project."

It was good to see Walt Seymour back in the fold. He is his usual cautious jurisdiction-minded self, but the warmth and quiet enthusiasm as well as clear straight thinking were back, after months of the doldrums. I find that when a man announces that he is retiring, from that moment on he is not much account so far as ideas or spirit are concerned. Walt has "had it" on the retirement binge.

NOVEMBER 29, 1974
PRINCETON

A call this morning: Ed Morehouse died last night. Aside from my brother Ted, my longest friendship was with Ed. He was one of the most potent influences in my professional life. An extraordinarily well organized mind, but little imagination. In those earliest days of my public service, in Wisconsin, he supplied what left to myself I could never have provided: a knowledge of economics and a technical capacity that I wholly lacked.*

DECEMBER 4, 1974
NEW YORK

Lunch with Cass Canfield. He is pleased to learn that the MS for Volume VI will be forthcoming from Helen this spring. Talking to her today she seemed quite confident. I don't feel badly about "shoving" off the editing job on her; she does enjoy it, does a splendid job which will require only a modicum of review from me I think. And it makes her feel that she is functioning, as I feel I am in my work.

DECEMBER 7, 1974
PRINCETON

The D&R board meeting began at 9:30 and went on through a luncheon. The luncheon was tendered by Rodman, for whose hospitality I gave credit, in a little speech—but which D&R will doubtless pay for, if I know this young scion of a generous father. I think Rodman must be a throwback, genetically speaking, to his wizened great-grandfather, whose dispensing of dimes has become an American saga.

Rodman arrived late, after breakfast with his father. Acknowledging my congratulations on the end of the Vice Presidential confirmation hearings before the House Judiciary Committee, Rodman leaned over, looking as angry as so bland a man can, and said: "Do you know who was the worst inquisitor on that Committee? A Jesuit priest."

The highlights of the board meeting were our two Latin American members: General Alfonzo Ravard and Bernardo Garces.

Said Bernardo, while we were waiting to begin the meeting: "The last time Dave was in Bogotá the President was Lleras Camargo—or was it Lleras Restrepo? Anyway, Dave came to lunch at the Palace, and the whole Cabinet was there. Before we began to eat the President looked down the long table and, in Spanish, said, 'The two best friends Colombia has are David Lilienthal and Nelson Rockefeller.'"

The most favorable impression I had of General Ravard's qualities was confirmed by the six or seven hours I had with him at our dinner meeting Thursday night, the board meeting and luncheon Friday. One or two examples:

Hal Frederiksen was describing his meetings with the Minister of

* Edward W. Morehouse was chief economist of the Wisconsin Public Service Commission in those early years.

Planning in Caracas, and later with the staff of the several regional authorities on his recent trip.

The General, following Hal's words closely (with a characteristic frown when he is concentrating), interposed: "I thought it was better that Mr. Frederiksen see these people alone, without me. Not because I wasn't greatly interested in joining with D&R if contracts were made, but for a different reason. I did not want any of the government people to think that I was a kind of intermediary, because I have been in the government for all of my professional life. I wanted them to decide about D&R wholly on the merits of D&R.

"Although Mr. Lilienthal wasn't present at that time, it was his reputation and judgment that they were relying upon, not mine—and you will see in the newspaper interviews the Minister gave that he spoke of Mr. Lilienthal and only incidentally D&R."

The General's statement was so quiet and to the point of public ethics that it impressed me again that here was a man we could team up with, knowing he is our kind of person, and this even in a government not noted for particularly high standards in this respect.

The other example showed his tact and yet complete honesty. Rodman spoke with rising excitement about how important land reform had been in Venezuela; that this had to be taken into account in whatever we of D&R did in the agricultural field. He leaned over and bore down on this, speaking with his customary self-assurance. "Isn't that true about Venezuela, General?"

General Ravard turned in his chair. "I would qualify what you have said," he said with a gentle smile. And then he proceeded to destroy Rodman's thesis. "This was true, in a way, for a time, but it is no longer true . . . ," indicating briefly what had happened to change the picture. The combination of tact—of the kind *I* am rarely capable of—and yet not agreeing, even with a Rockefeller, just to be agreeable, made me feel more secure in trusting this man and wanting to work with him.

DECEMBER 8, 1974
PRINCETON

Helen tells a story about Daniel, who made such a hit with all of us, and particularly David Morse, on our Iran trip. It is a mother and son story.

Helen found a large poster of giraffes, which she had put aside for Daniel, who was much interested in these critters.

Helen offered it to Daniel last summer; he put it up at "Yonside"; as he and Helen packed up to drive back to Princeton, she said his mother, Nancy, had said that Daniel no longer was interested in giraffes. Daniel took down the poster to put it up in his room at home, then asked his grandmother: "Are there any other things you have that my mother says I don't want?" This is a variation on the annoyance I feel when I hear Helen mention what things I don't "like."

DECEMBER 9, 1974
PRINCETON

That fellow David Morse: what a man. When I suggested that we might have dinner together Tuesday night, he said he had a special engagement that he enjoyed: a dinner given for the football Hall of Fame. He was an end with Rutgers, and afterward played professional football with the Washington Redskins! And there on my desk is a big picture book of his being host to the Pope in Geneva.

DECEMBER 10, 1974
NEW YORK

After the D&R board meeting, I raced to Princeton to attend some of the sessions of the Advisory Committee to the department of Near Eastern studies.

Once again I was disappointed and frustrated. I had made the point that this department should spread its influence, through its graduates, into other fields than academia. (In fifteen years, practically every Ph.D. and almost all other "concentrators" in Near Eastern studies have been prepared for and gone into teaching.)

Except for one faculty member, no one supported me. This man agreed with my statement on this score, saying that the Princeton faculty is "too nervous about its virginity, that it may be seduced by businessmen into producing graduates who might go into other pursuits than teaching."

The Middle East has become a matter of the greatest interest and concern to the Western world, and therefore trained men and women are needed to add some understanding of that region, its history, its culture, its sensitivities, and least of all perhaps, its languages.

These senior faculty men, tenure-blessed all of them, of course, enjoy what they are doing, enjoy the life, the surroundings, like being with bright young people. So why should they endanger the institution in which producing men like themselves is their sole purpose? Or are these students attracted to teaching because they are much like their teachers in their desires and aims for a certain kind of life?

On the way home I talked with one professor, agreeing with him that it is a good deal to expect a change by people who have lived their lives as teachers in the ideal conditions of a university campus. Said he: "Yes; it is a good and happy life."

So I had better stop my evangelical efforts. The people D&R sends to these various countries, and particularly one with a long cultural history, Iran, simply must learn about that country "on the job." As indeed did such a diamond in the rough as Leo Anderson, and others who have become fascinated by being in a land with such a stirring history.

DECEMBER 11, 1974
NEW YORK

Got to the office particularly early, after a memorable breakfast of cold, sticky, gummy oatmeal at a coffee shop on 44th Street. Opened the door, saw a yard-long yellow telex on Miss Baron's desk. And the roof fell in.

My concerns expressed so often, and even at the board meeting, about the quality of our people (and the quality of ideas, for that matter) in the National Water Plan were apparently shared by the Iranians in the Ministry. Demanded that the whole staff be fired and replaced!

In the presence of David Morse, later, I talked to Hal Frederiksen. Either we should "turn in our suits" and rescind the contract or get an adequate staff. From Tehran later a cry from Silveira (who was supposed to be monitoring this program all along) calling on Hal to drop everything and go to Tehran for three weeks. References in the telex from Silveira about "hand-holding," meaning buttering the Iranians up, gave me more confirmation that we do not have a competent managerial approach to our job at that office. Too much emphasis on "getting along personally" and too little critical understanding and strength.

This is not the stuff of which good management is made.

Barney and Beatrice had supper with me at the Century tonight, and pleasant it was. They both seem in good spirits; Barney's work is going well. He had a great topical cartoon in the last issue of *The New Yorker,* a businessman striding along with his attaché case and a sole bicycle wheel under his arm. These days on the sidewalks before the great buildings in mid-Manhattan are row after row of bike racks. All the bikes are manacled to posts with big chains, and most have had a wheel removed, for "security."

This morning Bernardo Garces came to the office. He had a conversation with General Ravard after our board meeting that he thought I ought to consider in connection with our projected trip to Venezuela.

It appeared most likely, said Ravard (though it had not been made definite), that he would be asked to head the new public oil company that would be formed to operate the oil industry after the impending national-ization of oil in Venezuela. "You should be sure to get well acquainted with the other men in Ravard's consulting company, for if he became the super-minister of oil, of course he could not join with us in the kind of regional developments we hoped would come out of our journey in mid-January."

DECEMBER 12, 1974
NEW YORK

A long visit with Mehdi, at his suite at the Pierre.

David Morse was with me at a late afternoon session and heard in detail what Mehdi had to tell about the kind of people we must deal with in working out the "public sector" study and recommendations. It will put us right in the middle of a fierce fight for the Prime Ministership if and when Hoveyda resigns. Amouzegar is desperately ambitious for that post, and is a rough and ready man, according to Mehdi, though of course charming and affable with us. And on the other side the equally incredi-bly ambitious and very active Hushang Ansary.

Mehdi has the face of a man who appears somehow surprised, and delighted. Even when he is talking about things going on in his country that clearly worry him, he worries about his country and not the personal effect on him. So many men of great abilities and responsibilities show that their concern is mainly about the effect of worrisome things on them, on their career, their future. Not so with this remarkable and lovable fellow.

I repeated what I have been saying for more than three years: that Iran should tell the world, in detail and continuously, what they are doing to build their country and the life of the disadvantaged people. It is a great story. Instead they have permitted the international debate and discourse to go off, particularly quite recently, on the subject of oil prices.

The point has been reached, I said, where Iran, as one of the largest of the oil producers, is being blamed for inflation, for the threat to the stability of the international financial structure, for the threat of a vast world-wide depression.

Mehdi threw up his hands and said, "But we don't know, in Iran, what to do about it. And besides, I am afraid the Prime Minister, perhaps His Majesty, feel this way: it doesn't really matter what the American people think about us."

After a solitary dinner at La Provençal on 62nd Street, I walked down Fifth Avenue to the hotel, slowly. I couldn't share the exuberance of the holiday crowd, even the delightful picture of small children, with their parents, headed for the glitter of the lights and the magic of such show windows as Schwarz' toys, or the bejeweled, animated belly dancer figures in Saks' window, or the charming scene of a Dutch city in the KLM window—features of as noncatastrophic a scene as one could imagine.

DECEMBER 16, 1974
PRINCETON

A delightful afternoon on Friday here. We had David and Mildred Morse for lunch, and with them Dr. Edward Bloustein, the president of neighboring Rutgers. A handsome, very youthful-appearing man, with a head of tousled hair, an athletic figure, and a most open manner. His wife is equally attractive, full of enthusiasm, a hearty laugh—it was the fact that all of us *laughed* that made it a happy interlude.

David told a story of an experience he had with Khrushchev, while ILO Director General.

He visited Khrushchev officially in Moscow. He told Khrushchev that his grandparents (perhaps it was his parents) had been born in a village in Russia, that he had heard, as a child, stories of the village, the stream that ran through it, etc., much like the stories my darling mother told me about the tiny village of her childhood in the vicinity of Pressburg in Hungary.

David took a Russian plane to return to Europe. He couldn't help noticing that the plane didn't seem to be going in the right direction, was going east rather than west. They began to fly lower, then began circling. A member of the crew came to him, pointing out a village, and explained that Khrushchev had given orders to fly his guest over the village of his forebears.

"A very human man, Khrushchev," said David. We were enchanted.

DECEMBER 20, 1974
NEW YORK

How refreshing to watch a real pro in action. That's what we saw yesterday, for several hours, with John Macy beginning to find his way on an "awesome" assignment, strengthening the management capabilities and structure of a whole country in a feverish period of growth and change.

He asked such good questions, was so well organized, avoided digressions. I can see now why he was such a trusted advisor to two Presidents, Jack Kennedy and Lyndon Johnson, neither of them easy to help, because neither knew much about public management.

DECEMBER 24, 1974
CHRISTMAS EVE
ANTIGUA, W.I.

Just before a lingering sunset, all orange and gold, two sails tacking again and again into the narrow neck of the harbor.

At that distance the sails, fore and aft, seemed *flat*. And flat they proved to be. A Chinese junk, high poop, painted red, finally managing to have the wind at its stern, down one of the sails (like a slatted window shade it was) and on into the inner harbor.

A fitting overture to still another Antigua holiday, begun after a tiring journey from New York via six hours and more in the crowded airport of San Juan. Really "exhausting." Ten minutes after we finally were in our rooms, I was swimming and forgetting the vows I took in San Juan that never, never, never would I make this trip, which for years had been so easy with a non-stop from Kennedy.

DECEMBER 26, 1974
ANTIGUA

True, I haven't mastered the art of doing nothing, but I have certainly given it a hard try these latter days. The early morning swim in the magic light, the sun just emerging over the green rim of hills; lying in the sun, moving through *Death Comes for the Archbishop* at a word-by-word pace, and then it's time for a pre-luncheon swim, a long one, fighting off the drowsiness and, of course, succumbing to it for a siesta, another swim and a half-hearted game of rummy, going up the hill to dinner, some more reading—and the day's "work" is done.

The remarkable thing about such a routine is that a man who has for months been so revved up as I can stop thinking so completely.

Well, not all that completely. A splendidly illustrated article in the *National Geographic,* quite favorable, and with a spectacular color picture of our showpiece, the Pahlavi Dam, but still no acknowledgment that we had ever been there.

Then reason drove out such grumpiness: I *wanted* it to appear that the Iranians did this all by themselves, as a means of building their sagging confidence—lack of confidence, really. And the Persians themselves know about us, so what does it matter that Americans don't?

DECEMBER 27, 1974
ANTIGUA

The tips of the palm fronds glisten with the rain that came on suddenly. On this shore, looking out onto the bay and its resting yachts, the rain is a curtain, a soft grey translucent sheet. The whole familiar view is transformed from brilliant sunlight to a misty loveliness, brought to us out of the south. And the sun breaks through while it is still raining, until gradually the wind shifts back to the east and this haven is itself again.

How fortunate for me that I have met and known one who could make me aware of and sensitive to the nuances of life; not alone to the sights of nature—such as this impromptu downpour—but to almost everything about me, and to ideas, thoughts, imaginings that taken together have made a new beginning of life for me.

Yesterday afternoon Helen and I walked to the top of one of the hills that embrace this bay, called Shirley Heights. A stiff walk it is for us who don't walk uphill much.

The view must be one of the greatest in the Caribbean, perhaps anywhere. Deep blue of sea, for almost 300°, way below and off to the horizons. The walk is made particularly dramatic by the ruins of the vast military and naval establishment that held this island of Antigua and, through this bastion, controlled most of the eastern Caribbean for the British in the 17th century.

I say "ruins"; but some of the structures are far from ruins: one series of stone arches is as fine, I daresay, as anything the Romans built when they were in their greatest period of building through the territories they occupied far from Rome.

Helen's stamina continues to amaze me. Even she remarked on it, a rare thing for her, as we trekked along on an hour-and-a-half jaunt, much of it—half, of course—steep, uphill. "Not many women my age could manage this or would even try it."

DECEMBER 30, 1974
ANTIGUA

As our car entered the grounds at the Macy establishment at Mill Reef, Archie MacLeish put his head into the car to say that Kenneth was with them, was looking forward to seeing us; "I should tell you that he has terminal cancer of the bones." Kenneth, their son, a first-rate journalist and explorer of dangerous places, knew he had little time left. This gave a sad and reflective tone to our post-lunch visit.

He talked with spirit and irony of his work, for seventeen years, with the *National Geographic,* where he did some classic text-cum-photograph stories, one in the current issue, one famous one on the Hebrides, another on the Great Barrier Reef. At times the pain the poor fellow was suffering was too much. "Perhaps you had better go down with me, Mama," he said a time or so. She went to administer a shot and then she would return. Later Kenneth would rejoin us.

What a sorry turn of the cards: for those two noble souls, Archie and Ada, to have to stand helplessly by to watch their son's suffering, and before long see him die.

I asked them a question I have been putting to myself—though not morbidly, I must say: "What is the best way to live when one is 'old'—or so the calendar says—and when so much of the work one set out to do one has done?"

We four talked quietly, objectively, about how best to spend those few remaining years (few by definition because of our advanced ages) and how to think of death.

Archie MacLeish, that smile as warm as ever, leaning over to emphasize what he must have been thinking about quite a bit: "It isn't that, at eighty-two, I fear death; in fact, at times I would rather welcome it. What I cannot reconcile myself to, however, is that after one has learned so much, seen so much, come to understand so much, that one day it should entirely disappear into nothing."

Looking fondly at Ada, she so blue-eyed and pert (also eighty-two), Archie said: "There is something we four alone, sitting here, can say that we could not say almost anywhere else. We are fortunate to have lived almost the whole of our lives with one other person. It isn't just that all passion is spent, spent in a way that is so convenient"—a characteristic chuckle—"it is that we have found a way through these long years of being together to *explore* ever more deeply the full meaning of passion, of all manner of passion."

Archie and Ada's answer to my question: Keep working. Said Ada, "Archie is working as hard, perhaps harder, than he ever has."

Said Archie: "The only way I can reconcile the puzzle of death is to say: Now, today; each day."

I think I knew what he meant.

Said Archie, laughing: "I have probably the most superficial knowledge of Persia—as it was called then—of anyone."

Then he told this romantic story: "Back in the early twenties I was appointed secretary to Delano—Franklin Roosevelt's uncle, you'll remember—who was head of a League of Nations Commission to investigate the growing of poppies and to try to put an end to it, and the opium trade. So we traveled to Kermanshah and Hamadan—ancient Ecbatana, you know. They were growing poppies all right. When the Delano Commission asked them to stop it, the Persians said: 'We need exports; but we have no means of exporting, no railroads. Poppy seed can be packed on the back of donkeys or camels.'

"So the Commission said: 'Why don't you build a railroad? Where should it go?' So I had a map, and there in Kermanshah I said, 'How about this way?' and drew a line from Kermanshah south through the mountains to the Persian Gulf. We showed this to Reza Shah, the present Shah's father. He took a blue pencil and drew a line much like mine, and said: 'This is where the railroad will go.' No big studies, just the Shah's order. And it was done."

A great story; such a good story I hate to "research it." But this much is surely true, that the old Shah did order a line built, and a great achievement it is through those mountains.

DECEMBER 31, 1974
ANTIGUA

Tonight begins a new year, by the calendar. I am trying to learn to disregard the calendar, or at least take it less solemnly. But beginning a new year means closing the story of 1974.

It was a good year because it was a *happy* year, in my personal life.

Watching the sun going down—what magnificence, these tropical sunsets—I found myself counting, on my fingers, and saying to myself: Only three and a half more days. Which means that I am "vacationed out," and ready to go back.

VIII

1975

Trip to Venezuela—Visit to South Carolina—Trips to
Iran and further development of Public Service Management assistance

JANUARY 1, 1975
ANTIGUA

Helen says, "What you do is *public* service, not private business.
What you build (a dam, a reservoir, an irrigation network) is much the
same as those built by a private business, and so too are the staff you
employ and direct to do those things—much the same technical kind of
men. But what you do is different and is public service because your
purpose is different; and the way you do these things is different. It is the
way you do the things you do through D&R and not the physical results
that distinguishes you from other managers of such undertakings. The
very fact that you tackle these development matters on a regional and
decentralized basis is evidence of that different way."

JANUARY 2, 1975
ANTIGUA

As an addendum to yesterday's entry about the difference between
D&R (and TVA, too, for that matter) and other methods of achieving
development, isn't the word "spirit" as a mark of the difference better
than the somewhat hard and "managerial" term, "the way"?

Whether development is carried forward by a private firm, to get the
work done but doing so at a profit, otherwise it won't be done, or by a

[513]

public body (AID, or the Corps of Engineers, without financial profit), the spirit is what counts. And that term includes and is almost synonymous with the preoccupation with human beings as the end and purpose of what is done.

JANUARY 3, 1975
ANTIGUA

Last night, as I was about to dress for dinner, I thought once again about the moving experience we had seeing Archie and Ada and their pain-racked son, Kenneth; of how much Archie's poetry has meant to me, and to the strengthening of America's confidence in its deeper values and trusts. So I sat down and wrote him in longhand (I don't believe in waiting until a man's funeral to tell him of my admiration and love for him).

JANUARY 5, 1975
PRINCETON

St. Francis could not have taken his birds much more seriously than I do the ones I have under my wing, around the ancient apple tree outside the dining-room windows. Instead of reading the accumulated mail, the mass of Christmas cards and messages, etc., I stepped out into the gay sunshine and refilled the feeders, sprinkled the ground with seeds, and generally enjoyed myself.

To top off the homecoming, I covered parts of the perennial border with salt hay, particularly the candytuft—which does get burned by the wind from the north, and the primroses, which came through the heat of the summer and look very happy, cozy against the new growth of rhodo. A brisk walk, and I felt I was home again.

But it was a good vacation.

JANUARY 7, 1975
NEW YORK

Yesterday was a happy day. I found that in John Macy, now a full-fledged and full-time D&R partner, I had found truly a kindred spirit, not just on the level of professional and intellectual competence and excellence such as Gordon [Clapp] exemplified (and hardly anyone else to the same extent since his death). His set of values—there is no better word —is the kind I have, and most respect and greatly admire.

To others involved in the "Public Sector Project" I have to explain over and over again that this is not an exercise in "public administration" techniques. But describing as I did to John what I have learned about Iran's development objectives, he could see at once that what we look into in an organizational sense and what we later will recommend must be wedded to and made to serve those particular and distinctive Persian goals of today.

So he and I had a highly stimulating and exciting time. He is fully committed to the work, and is becoming aware of what *I* and D&R hope to be from here on out, a concept which in recent years has been more than somewhat eroded and I would myself say, tarnished, by the efforts and intention of the Sacramento leadership to make this an engineering and technical agricultural consulting company.

If that is all that it is, and I could do nothing effective to return it fully to the original concept, then why should I try so hard to insure its continuity?

Phoned the Macy home about eight to correct a date I had given him. Mrs. Macy said he had already left for the city.

Then she uttered one of the finest encomiums on D&R I have ever heard. "I am very enthusiastic about going to Iran with John. But what makes me happiest of all is how eager he is to go to the office now; for months he had little spirit for what he was doing, but this is a new lease on life for him, because it is his kind of work. That's what means the most to me."

JANUARY 11, 1975
PRINCETON

Two days in bed with that old time enemy, "The Flu." And I'm due to be up at 5:30 tomorrow morning, for an early morning flight to Caracas.

So I decided to go, and without looking backward. If you're going to lead the pack, you should lead, be out there where the younger critters can see you.

Now we have three new recruits, all of the very first quality—Morse, Macy, and now, this week, Joe Blatchford. No doubt in the world that we are entering a new chapter, and reaching for a high level of excellence.

JANUARY 13, 1975
CARACAS, VENEZUELA

The view of present-day Caracas from the wide window of this hotel room that overlooks the city, hemmed in closely by spectacular green mountains, surely must be one of the most dramatic sights in the world. *Until* you look more closely. For on the mountainside are the shacks of the very poor, mingled with the skyscrapers.

Foolish it may have been to get out of a "sickbed," with fever, and make this trip, but it was something I had to do, or so I thought. Not that my presence and participation with General Ravard, Hal Frederiksen, and the Ministers is likely to make the difference in getting an early contract (which I want, for D&R), but copping out, as virtually ordered by the doctor, would not have helped either. But I didn't go to a dinner given us by General Ravard, and as a necessary concession to that ole devil flu I stayed in bed.

During the past fifteen years I have definitely changed, as to taking risks. I now take all kinds of risks, of which taking long trips when I'm not really up to it is only one kind. This is a "personality change." Contrary to what one might expect, it was in my younger days that I was most fearful.

JANUARY 14, 1975
CARACAS

This strange country has been so bubbling with internecine fighting, low-level "politics" that permeate and poison everything, public and private, that it seems a most unlikely place for D&R to spend energy seeking a long-term development engagement, and having secured such a contract, to be willing to put up with the rough edges of a country for which the word "unstable" is an understatement.

But their need for the kind of regional development ideas we stand for, and the presence here over a long period of so outstanding a man as Ravard, encourages me to agree with Frederiksen that we should make a strong effort. (His reasons are not entirely mine, but still . . .)

I continue to be enthusiastic about Ravard. He is a hallmark in any country of good technical capability and of development ideas that parallel my own, to a remarkable degree.

What will $10 billion a year of cash do to this country of less than ten million people? To be able to observe this close at hand will be worthwhile, as an experience.

JANUARY 15, 1975
CARACAS

When I strode into the President's office, Carlos Andrés Pérez was sitting behind a desk far off, and came to greet me and my entourage with the athletic figure and self-assurance of a boxer. The office itself was decorated in pastels, instead of the dour mission-oak effect that I recall, though of course there were the usual huge paintings of the Liberator on an enormous horse.

It was all cordial; we want your "great experience," etc. Across from me sat the Minister of Plan, Rodriguez, beaming but saying not a word. An empty charade, at this point. The Minister had read our proposal, agreed with it. It is what happens *after* they agree (after they say yes) that really counts.

JANUARY 16, 1975
CARACAS

Blatchford said he, while here, had just finished rereading "your book"—which usually means *TVA: Democracy on the March.* He said those things about the book, written in 1944, that I most wanted to hear, but wouldn't have expected to have this tall, very experienced and well set up youngish man get out of it on a rereading—i.e., reading it in the light of today, and not as a historical set piece of the New Deal days.

Let me paraphrase what he said: That it is "positive," that the theme and the story it tells are "fresh and crisp," and have as much applicability to today as anything now being said, more so.

Blatchford is respected here for his work with the poor—I noticed this at the Miraflores Palace yesterday particularly. Improving living conditions in the towns and big cities will be part of our obligation under the proposed contract with D&R.

But don't we stand for a later chapter of development, less of the volunteer-social-worker approach? With more reliance upon moving this country into strengthening its food productivity, through technology and organization, rather than putting so much reliance upon improving the conditions of *campesinos* who have cut themselves adrift from the land, and have become, actually, squatters and day laborers.

As I reflect on it, there is precious little in my 1944 book about working individually with the poor people on the Tennessee hillsides, which Joe finds so "relevant" and exciting. The really important things are: better use of resources, better education, better fertilizers, better farming methods, more use of electricity.

So, greatly respecting Blatchford's past achievements and his human motivations, still I wonder if there is a satisfactory role for him in the current D&R organization and goals in this country.

Will the figure we are using for the four-year work seem too high, and how about the fee? I believe we should keep these figures higher than the overeager Frederiksen would prefer, perhaps higher than Ravard believes will be appropriate.

I made my point and will be ready to leave it at that. The point being quite simply the old one: the laborer is worthy of his hire. And the further point that unless we ask for a substantial, and to them even an unprecedentedly large fee and charge, the Venezuelans will not fully respect and make use of our judgment and recommendations.

To oversimplify: what one gets cheaply, one holds cheaply.

Yesterday noon, a rare treat, and the first kind word for a U.S. Embassy luncheon invitation in a long time, indeed since Helen and I (particularly she, the archeology buff) met and visited with Ghirshman, in Tehran, he the great French leader of the Susa explorations.

The treat: the guest at a luncheon for twenty at the spectacular Ambassador's residence was Samuel Eliot Morison, a well-worn old sailor and historian (*The Admiral of the Ocean Sea, The Northern Voyages, The Maritime History of Massachusetts,* etc.).

He totters as he moves, yet he is on a long cruise (in a Grace Line freighter) to Bahia and Buenos Aires. His response at table to Ambassador McClintock's graceful speech was delightful—a clear soft voice, brief, full of feeling. He didn't indulge in bathos as he said that he had written his last book and taken his last yachting exploration.

Just received a "formal report" from Hal and David. Hal finished "the figures" last night at 3 A.M., what it will cost Venezuela for D&R's and Ravard Associates' services over the next four years.

They took to heart my crankiness expressed so strongly last evening. The second man in charge, Benchimol, studied the figures, and accepted them for recommendation to the Minister tomorrow.

JANUARY 17, 1975
FLYING TO NEW YORK

How well I recall one of my first "successes" in negotiations while on Wall Street. Said I to André [Meyer]: "Well, I got agreement." "Tell me precisely what they said." "That's it; we are agreed in principle." "In the business world," said André, "that means 'we will think about it'—and now comes the tough bargaining."

So when Hal Frederiksen reported that the Minister had said after days of discussion of details that our proposal was fine and he agreed, I wasn't surprised this morning to have the Director General of CORDI-PLAN, Helly Tineo, finger the paper as we sat at his table: "Of course we will have to examine each sentence with care, and then the lawyers will go over it carefully, and perhaps in a few months we will know."

Hal's face dropped at least a foot; mine even more, if the truth be told.

So we will not be able to book the revenues, or hire people right bang-off.

I am afraid I bristled some, and said, "I must be candid; we have many other obligations and if at the time you make up your minds I am engaged completely elsewhere, you must remember that I can't be in two places at one time."

JANUARY 22, 1975
NEW YORK

This was a day when I could actually *feel*, in a tactile sense, the weight of experience, pressing down on a wide array of problems and issues, and producing answers, responses, clarification. Experience that is not just backward looking, nostalgia, the old soldier fingering his medals of battles long gone and by most everyone well forgotten. No, this was experience that sharpens today.

It doesn't happen to me, this kind of proof that experience enables me to say (or think), "Why, I have been here before," or *"This* is the way we should go; I know this to be true because something inside me tells me so, clearly and effortlessly." And across the table the less experienced men recognize that it is not a pile of facts but the fruits of experience that guide my responses.

All of this apropos two long sessions chiefly with John Macy. John has become a center of gravity, of force for me. It has been a long, long time since I was so close with a thoroughly first-class, broad-gauged, completely cultivated mind and personality. I'm enjoying it thoroughly. And in the exchange it is apparent that so is he.

He combines a high degree of professional attainments—the highest in the public administration field of competence—with a humane outlook, a conviction that all of this governmental "administration" technology is only worth talking about or working to improve *if* it gives people, individuals, a better, wider opportunity for their talents and prospects.

So it is not professionalism for its own sake, just as I eschew planning as an end in itself, or science, or technology. He exemplifies that humanist outlook I tried all one summer back in '66 to describe, in those tortured Fairless Lectures at Carnegie.

Humanism plus action: that is the formula for me, and today we begin to demonstrate how it can be made to have a real impact on the increasingly tense Iranian scene. Tense largely because the great goals will be ashes without a more skillful and professional touch about managing things in that country. The noble and exalted goals of the Shah and his people can't be sustained for long by rhetoric.

Nor can they be attained wholly by absolute power. Macy spoke a profound aphorism on this score today. Said he: "Absolute power"—such as it is conceived that the Shah possesses—"cannot achieve, absolutely. For without *acceptance* by the people of the goals and methods, absolute power can issue decrees and ukases and orders, but the performance depends upon understanding and acceptance, which means education."

Macy is a do-er, and his manner in my office gives me a good picture of how he operated within the White House and particularly with such a difficult but active man as Lyndon Johnson.

He has already assembled a team of six or seven pros, in various sectors of the field of public management. Think of that: on November 2 Amouzegar gives me this assignment. Macy accepts the post, clears his deck, and today has a full-fledged group of seniors ready to take off February 4.

JANUARY 25, 1975
PRINCETON

Spent nearly two hours this morning with Tom Mead, talking with him about the "D&R Papers" project at Princeton and listening to his doubts, uncertainty—and enthusiasms too. But he wants to plow ahead in better organization of the papers.

What Tom couldn't get clear is that the development after D&R moved operations to the Iranians is important even though D&R itself isn't represented in the papers after that turnover. And results—some of the results—are spectacular, the sugar project, for example.

FEBRUARY 1, 1975
PRINCETON

Last week began with a memorable afternoon of talk about the Public Administration Project. David Morse, unusually subdued, and John Macy, at his outgoing best.

I keep badgering my friends and associates with this thought: the inquiry and the purpose of their work (and mine) is not to add still another chapter to the techniques or literature of the profession of public administration. The "strengthening of public sector management" is part and parcel of the development goals of present-day Iran, and must be related to and in furtherance of those goals.

John Macy came up with a way of expressing what I so much wanted to be accepted and acted upon as the purpose and guiding principle of the public sector management assignment in this way:

Translate into management and needed human skills the specific objectives of development as set out in the new Five-Year Plan itself.

He put it more succinctly than this, but that was the burden. Nothing could be further from the conventional overprofessionalized approach to public administration than this.

I decided that I should make absolutely clear that this enterprise, being carried on so far from me, should be run by Macy, so I put that into a memorandum the following day. We'll hear some complaint about this, but in principle it is correct.

I spent long hours (one evening I left the office at 9:30) reviewing parts of the 1966 journal manuscript, cutting much more even than Helen had.

She said to me yesterday that I should not cut illustrations, cases, even though to me they may seem too detailed, for example, expositions of what we called Atlantico #3, a fascinating irrigation and agricultural project in the north or Atlantic region of Colombia.

"You are so much interested in the abstract principles of development, which you state very well, sometimes even eloquently, that you don't yet fully realize that to many people those have little meaning until concrete cases make them clear and of interest to outsiders." Of course, she is right; this is a point she has made to me again and again.

Thursday she came to New York. We went to the Tobeys for a relaxed drink and one of Beatrice's gourmet meals. (She doesn't know *how* to prepare anything but a delicious and interesting meal, Barney said.) A brief glance at Beatrice's recent paintings—strong they are. I so admire her, for many of the facets of her personality, but as much almost as any for the resolute way she continues to paint, for her own satisfaction.

FEBRUARY 2, 1975
PRINCETON

Barrett Shelton of Decatur and I have been friends and battlemates for years and years. To overhear our long phone conversation a few minutes ago, you'd suppose we see each other every other week. That's what rapport means, I guess.

The subject I called him about, of course, is my concern about the immediate future of TVA, with all the outpouring of antagonistic newspaper space of late—it looks like a well-planned campaign.

Most serious is that there will soon be a vacancy on the board, and if this is filled by a cheap county-courthouse Tennessee politico of the same stripe as young Jenkins, Red Wagner won't be able to function and TVA will be in the deepest trouble since Arthur Morgan tried to torpedo it forty years ago.

Barrett, who knows public opinion in that Valley as no one else does, assures me that the within-the-Valley criticism is dying down. "We down here are not all that provincial any more; we know what is going on elsewhere, and that electric rates are going up everywhere, that the risks of atomic energy are a nation-wide issue and not ones invented by TVA.

"The next board appointment," says Barrett, "is [Senator] Spark-man's. But John needs help, needs light. The friends of TVA should help him by suggesting names because others are pushing for candidates, one of them a vice president of the Alabama Power Co.—imagine."

I should call Sparkman. But I ought to have some names to suggest. And I simply don't, and Red tells me he doesn't either.

What a joy it is to find that not only do I have fast friends in Persia but still have them in the Tennessee Valley.

A long brisk walk on a sun-drenched day of unbelievable beauty—beauty of air, of silence, of inner peace and outward perspective.

What made my heart leap was to look under the lee of the big azalea near the house and there, bless their tiny brave hearts, the butter yellow of winter aconite, like golden nuggets.

Another post-breakfast talk with Helen about the journals. Not just the Volume VI on which both of us are now working (1966) but a restatement of what they are: not a historical record, not a memoir, not a "book about development" (though they are all of these too). My son put it best years ago: how life looks to one particular man, as he undergoes a great span of experiences, some intensely personal, some quite "technical."

I only wish he were here to help me pound out the Diarist's Note I want to write.

FEBRUARY 4, 1975
NEW YORK

The public sector management project received a big shot of adrena-line today: a letter from Minister Amouzegar (telexed from Tehran) ex-pressing considerable satisfaction with the preliminary results thus far and proposing that the program outlined in a letter of January 10 be broadened. Not only broadened, but in the most significant ways: first, that we include his own Ministry, in some ways the most sensitive and significant for intergovernmental relations within Iran, for Interior supervises the provinces, the Ostands. This is the kind of assignment that can be spelled decentralization with a capital D—which is my meat.

So it does look as if it will not be many weeks until my stated goal to John Macy will be ripe for exposition to the Minister, and reach the contract stage—i.e., treating this as a several-year project with a budget of several million dollars. So I wasn't too far off in setting May 1, or even mid-April, as the time to work out a new and extended engagement.

FEBRUARY 8, 1975
PRINCETON

Sat next to Robby Rabi at the Century dinner Thursday night. He is as full of bounce as ever, with that mischievous bright-eyed grin and chuckle that I remember so well. Part of his good spirits and cheerfulness derives from the only clear conviction he has about human affairs or any effort to improve them—viz, that nothing will come out well, no matter what. I know dour people who have that outlook, but not another exuberant and jolly one. No need to worry yourself about anything because nothing will be any good. That's not exaggeration.

Of course, he wanted to reminisce about the recently deceased AEC, now made up of two parts, the regulatory one and the research half.* "Both will be bad, of course," says Rob.

He wanted to speak some wisdom about Lewis Strauss. "Strauss was brilliant but not intelligent." Rob *enjoys* his Jewishness; recounts with that slant-eyed almost Chinese smile his own humble beginnings, but how pious and ritualized was his home. "Now with Lewis, it was a different thing. I would say Lewis was bar mitzvahed but not confirmed." Just what that means, technically, I don't know, but I got the drift.

Our table conversation hit on one subject which I enjoyed: his admiration for Helen. "And how is she? She goes on those long trips with you; imagine. I remember her when you lived in a suburb of Washington. I would like to see her again. You are busier than I; I'll call and see if you and she can't come and have an evening with us." Said I: "I like her too."

FEBRUARY 11, 1975
NEW YORK

David Morse slumped back in a brightly-colored living-room chair in Rodman's spacious drawing-room office, and for twenty minutes recited the flawless qualities of a paragon whom he interviewed in London, part of Rodman's effort (no longer a covert one, as it was for so many months) to find a new President of D&R.

After an hour's discussion it became clear that for about a year both Rodman and Bob Helander of IBEC had been trying to interest this man in the Presidency of D&R. Until David spilled the beans last October, none of this was disclosed to me.

This gave me the opportunity to decry the lack of corporate ethics in

*Research and production functions of the AEC were vested in the Department of Energy; the regulatory function was transferred to the new Nuclear Regulatory Commission.

this way of recruiting a man to succeed a top officer without his partici-pation or knowledge. The scorn I felt I kept in good control, but two little boys who had been brought to the woodshed for a paddling and some straight talk never looked more shamefaced.

This is not a "job," not a "position." The Chairmanship of D&R is as much a public responsibility as any I have ever had.

FEBRUARY 26, 1975
NEW YORK

Rodman said to me, "Don't let the Treasurer out of your control; if you do you will be the prisoner of Sacramento"—his exact words. This was when he was told that the finance and administration division would be moved to Sacramento—after I had fought it off ever since Christmas-time of 1973.

Right, but an inadequate description of the situation. No matter where the financial control resides, physically, geographically, if all the chief executive officer gets are reports, justification or rationalization, then he—i.e., D.E.L.—has no way of measuring the dynamics of perform-ance. Reports are a rearview mirror, telling you what did happen, not where you are now or where you will be six months or even six weeks hence.

A report long after the fact is useless.

This is an absence of financial planning—with a vengeance.

MARCH 15, 1975
PRINCETON

The D&R Super-Roller-Coaster—up and down—this week put on a classic, indeed, a gourmet performance.

Monday, no cash in the till, and a big payroll coming up on Friday. Instructed the Treasurer not to issue a check for my salary, the second time I've felt that uncertain in a single month.

Wednesday morning, Frederiksen appears with an elaborate state-ment, featured by the comment, "D&R is in very good financial condition, the best in many years"—this at a moment when the company was "insol-vent," by which I mean unable to meet the legitimate claims of its credi-tors—i.e., its staff salaries.

A red-hot meeting with Hal, in which I stated—without persuading him in the least—that the company was overcommitted in terms of peo-ple required to carry out our "about to be signed" contracts for services, always in the future. He lowered his head and resisted every criticism or suggestion that we cut back on expansion until we had absorbed, with competent people, what we already had under way. I decided I would defer this until we had raised the capital to get us out of the immediate cash "bind." It was a strained session.

Thursday morning, I had arranged for a meeting with Rodman on the cash funding crisis. At about nine, Hal closed my door and handed Morse and me a letter, dated the previous Monday (the 10th of March). Said he was resigning.

With Hal, went in to see Rodman, with Morse and Helander. Rodman stated strongly that he had respect for Hal as General Manager, that he had no intention of forcing (by voting his ownership shares) a new President on me or on D&R to take the place of Frederiksen. I told Hal strongly that so long as I had faith in his competence and performance, he need not concern himself with imaginings about what Rodman thought of him, that I was running D&R. But whether he stood by his written resignation or withdrew it, as David Morse urged him to, was a wholly personal matter with Hal, and I would adjust to whatever was his personal decision. We have had so many months of Hal's long spells of unease (hours and hours of it) and suspicions of IBEC's intentions against him.

On the constructive side, IBEC, without question, provided the added equity investment promised last summer, on the basis of apparent good prospects, particularly in Iran, as outlined by Hal. We were again in funds.

Yesterday before breakfast, Hal phoned to say he had decided "to stay on."

David thought the week was a good one in that it brought the issue that has been bugging Frederiksen clearly before Rockefeller.

One further benefit: it brought from Rodman Rockefeller one of the clearest statements of the theme of D&R in contrast with other development firms, and having stated that, why he had such a strong feeling that we needed as a President (replacement for me) a man of such stature that new directions along the same or a similar theme would be possible.

For a change of pace, and as confirmation of what I *say*—i.e., that there is more to life than D&R—I saturated myself in the sounds of the Bach Aria Group on Wednesday evening, preceded by a delightful family-style dinner with Beatrice and Barney, and Miriam Drabkin.

Thursday Helen came to the office to smile at the cartoon collection on my walls, to dine (with much laughter) over silly "in" jokes of ours, and to see a moving performance by Fonda of highlights in the career of Clarence Darrow; a nostalgic experience for the grey-haired lady at my left, and her no longer young lawyer companion—and once law colleague of Darrow.

Further change of pace: entered the appropriately modest-sized office, in Firestone Library, where a great man, Julian Boyd, is editing the papers of another great man, Thomas Jefferson, eighteen volumes of which have already been published, forty-two still to come.

The first sight that greets you coming into that office is an empty cardboard carton under a burdened table. In large letters it says: Creative Playthings.

Well, what Julian Boyd is doing—has for some years been doing—is certainly creative. And the passion for being systematic that character-ized Jefferson marks everything this scholar is directing.

Julian had two other guests: Joe Johnson and Dean (of the Graduate School at Princeton) Jerome Blum. We were shown the photocopies of letters written by Jefferson in a precise and tiny script. For example, the famous and romantic Head and Heart letter, which Jefferson wrote with his left hand (because of an unexplained injury to his right) to Maria Cosgrove. He had not only written this long passionate letter, but had *copied* it for posterity.

Hours and hours Helen, Mildred Baron, and I have been spending on the Volume VI *Journals* "preparation for the printer"—and this on top of other pretty heavy work.

But it turns out to have more than a retrospective or an editorial value, by far. Much of it underlines how much I have to do to explain D&R to a new generation within the organization, and to the public. Tom Mead's work at Princeton will have something of the same consequence, I believe.

MARCH 16, 1975
PRINCETON

For ever so long, Helen has been gently but persistently prodding me to do a book on "development."

I agreed (1) that I would never write the book myself, what with the more than full plate I have; (2) that the *Journals* contain in themselves everything I want to say, though, as Helen points out, those thoughts are scattered throughout the published and the still to be published volumes; (3) that Helen can do the book herself, by putting together what I have said about development through these years of journal and other writing (even going back to *TVA: Democracy on the March*); and (4) that she demonstrated in the *This I Do Believe* book that she can put together a more than satisfactory book providing the connecting tissue.

So this is a good day: to have something decided that sets her on a big task in which we can work together, but which will be essentially *her* book, and will keep her fully occupied with interesting and demanding work for at least a year or more.

MARCH 20, 1975
PRINCETON

A phone talk with Jerome Wiesner. "We—MIT—agreed with the Shah we would train a group of Iranian nuclear physicists for the big expansion—twelve atomic power plants, I believe—they are buying. I have a problem: a coalition of students at MIT is preparing a protest; partly those who don't like the Shah, some who don't like atomic energy or atomic weapons—and so on. Can I tell them that these plants are part of a well-worked-out national plan for energy to take the place of oil when it is exhausted? Is there such a plan?"

No, there isn't. We (D&R) were asked to help on a plan for electricity supply, but it doesn't exist, right now.

"Yesterday two Iranians, professors at the university, asked me what I would do if I were asked what they should do with their money—invest in the U.S. or Europe?"

Put it into Iran. Our 1957 plan for the five rivers of Khuzistan would produce about as much as the proposed nuclear reactors, and those dams would also irrigate large areas of the land. Then there is education, village amenities, etc.

MARCH 21, 1975
PRINCETON

A call from Assistant Secretary of Defense for National Security Affairs, Robert Ellsworth. Explained that military equipment for Iran "is part of my . . . well . . . jurisdiction. The U.S. has agreed to work with Iran on a nation-wide communications system, which would include nonmilitary as well as military functions. This will require *training* a great many Iranians. But they don't have the people to train. Noticing in Sunday's *Times* that D&R is studying the administrative structure of Iran, it has occurred to me that our two organizations should be in touch with each other; perhaps we can help you and we know you can help us in this problem."

I explained explicitly that our "assignment" excludes the organization of the military establishment of Iran (which Ellsworth seemed to recognize at once). Still there are many activities and responsibilities of the Pentagon in Iran that are not military, of which training for a communications system is certainly one.

I suggested he message the head of their Mission to get in touch with John Macy. I started to describe John; he broke in: "Oh, I know John Macy; and when you send a message include greetings from Bob Ellsworth."

"The head of the U.S. Military Mission's name?" An off-stage yell: "What is Rocky Brett's first name—oh, Devol." "No wonder you call him Rocky, with that first name," said I. So I telexed John and he will message through to Major General Brett. This should add a new and important dimension to Iran's understanding of how easy it is to enter into these big flashy programs (with all that oil money) and how hard to find the men able to carry them out.

I want the Iranians—who are proud and don't particularly like to be reminded of any deficiencies—to realize that they can't just buy trained people without the danger of colonialism—i.e., the importation of too many outsiders. They must take the training of Iranians seriously.

MARCH 22, 1975
PRINCETON

Four hours with Leo Anderson, as absorbing and enlightening and wide-ranging as any similar period in my recent experience.

Yes, he is more than ready, willing, and (with his long illness behind him) able to devote himself to D&R's agricultural work, even full-time if there is enough work of the kind that interests him.

There could hardly be any better news than this.

When he was told that we had signed a contract (and just a couple days ago) to take on the Karkheh Basin, that did it, for he volunteered that he thought the opportunities for that upper basin were as great as any-place in Iran, perhaps in the world. I am equally keen that that region be another high-water mark of achievement.

MARCH 23, 1975
PRINCETON

I am going through the Vietnam agonies *twice;* once in the journal entries made in November 1967, which we are reviewing and shortening (but very little; they are very graphic), and then, second, in the press and TV. For that war is starting up all over again, a war for the *ending* of which Kissinger received a Nobel *Peace* award.

I am impressed, as I read the entries made in Saigon in November 1967, with how much I admired the people, including even covert allusions of admiration for the Viet Cong and the North Vietnamese.

But the flood of human beings pouring out of the North of Vietnam, pictured so graphically in the TV and press, is a most sobering spectacle. How much of this disaster can be charged to the hatred, nothing less, of the press and TV, who refused even to report on the kind of heartening things, particularly among the younger people, that formed a substantial part of what I was involved in and wrote about?

I notice that almost the most cocksure of all in the press, the editorial and reporting pages of the *New York Times,* this morning began the first steps of a withdrawal from their extreme position. They must sense that if the ordinary people desperately abandoning everything to leave their homes before the onset of North Vietnamese armies were all that eager to be part of the North Vietnamese "solution," they wouldn't be leaving in a wild rush. And that when the American public again sees the wholesale massacres, the kind that bloodied the Tet offensive around Hue, there may be hell to pay, looking for American scapegoats. I could nominate a few, gladly.

MARCH 30, 1975
MILLS HYATT HOUSE
CHARLESTON, S.C.

Could hardly take in the grandeur and good taste of the streets lined with some of the most beautiful houses in the world—surely, in the U.S. Walked and walked and walked, trying to keep up with my almost seventy-nine-year-old spouse.

Between the fatigue I brought with me from the last three weeks of seven-days-a-week work, and that innocent little "cold" I dismissed as "nothing at all," I was utterly bushed at day's end.

But beginning with our arrival Friday, what severed me completely from the life and world I have been living in was neither the "antebellum houses" nor the slowdown that the lousy cold commanded. It was an unbelievable change in this heart of the South.

A large gathering of Negroes, all part of a family group. Three generations. Grandmother, distinguished-looking, in a pink ensemble. Her sons and daughters-in-law, in full command. A grandson, alert, cuddling a couple toddlers who were everywhere. All of this in the main dining room of this hotel—in Charleston! And nary a raised eyebrow so far as I could see among the other holidaying guests, obviously from the best middle-class families of South and North Carolina.

APRIL 3, 1975
CHARLESTON

Yesterday morning to the magnificent showplace, Middleton Gardens, some miles out of the city. Too late, just, for the full-blooming glory of the great mountains of azaleas. And the sun fitful at best. But a milky haze gave the vistas and waters that special quality of delight we call Japanese-y.

Between quite stormy, windy, showery weather and a return of that dratted virus (to which I had said farewell almost a week ago, so I thought), it hasn't been quite as good a holiday as I had hoped for.

Bill Bundy is credited with being the principal architect of American policy for Southeast Asia—i.e., Vietnam. Our national interest was at stake, he said; if Vietnam fell before the Communists, all of South Asia would fall.

This morning on the CBS morning news he said some remarkable things, proving that he and others like him who put such faith in a stop-Communism policy backed by a large American force now thought the apparent defeat of South Vietnam would not "significantly" affect the posture of America elsewhere; the other countries of Southeast Asia were solid and would not be affected. "As for our relations with Russia [which I had assumed had "won" the war], the defeat of South Vietnam [and of the U.S. in support of South Vietnam] might even be helpful as it would remove a source of friction."

That qualifies as about the most astounding picture of an apologetic kind I can remember. Say to the Czechs: Stalin's taking you over improves American relations with Russia as it removes a source of friction, that source being the struggle of the Czechs for their liberty!!

APRIL 13, 1975
PRINCETON

A four-hour session with a group of professors in the engineering and science department at Princeton University.

We discussed the significance of the D&R Papers. What value do they have, now that the great storehouse of boxes is in fairly good shape?

I brought Hal Frederiksen back here and we looked at Tom Mead's prospectus. Hal provided real ideas about those papers—and the physical and social consequences that lie behind them in Khuzistan. As stimulating as anything I have heard since I first conceived the idea of a rescue operation to save them from being put into a cavern of a library and never *used* for practical and teaching purposes.

APRIL 20, 1975
ABOUT TO LEAVE NEW YORK FOR LONDON—AND THEN ON TO IRAN

What a morning to leave our garden. At 6:30 I walked, step by step, the whole length of the curving borders, to see what had happened to *each* plant, *each* flowering bulb, since I made my tour at seven last evening. And then to give the rose border a final look, particularly the five new dormant bushes we put yesterday into enormous holes David and I dug, down to the full eighteen inches deep and eighteen wide that so rarely have I managed before.

The deep joys of the first signs of the early spring garden—some of those scarlet tulip bulbs of last fall's planting are flaming now. And the huge trumpets of the daffodils, crisp, proud of themselves, strutting their stuff.

But there were even greater delights: the presence in Helen and my home of that grizzled tall sequoia son, with his quizzical smile, eyes sparkling as he gets off a quip at his and my expense about the domination we share at the loving hands of our joint General Manager, Helen.

I feel at peace. I know I am loved and return love. Not only respect, in full measure, but something deeper by far. Why shouldn't I be at peace?

APRIL 21, 1975
IRANAIR TO TEHRAN

Been reading some of the Public Sector Management material.

The centerpiece is a long, informal, vivid piece by Frank Sherwood. Apparently I had made it emphatic that all the highly technical public administration this and that didn't much interest me. What I wanted above everything was a basic *theme* broader than highly show-off jargonese. The way to *that,* so John Macy recommended, was through a reading of my *Journals.* (I would have thought *TVA: Democracy on the March,* and *Management: A Humanist Art,* would also provide clues of my notions relevant to public management in Iran.)

I am to propose a theme, with my trademark on it; it will be a radical one, a far-reaching one, and yet one that is do-able, given Iran's past and its capacity to absorb and support revolutionary ideas and programs.

APRIL 22, 1975
TEHRAN

Have just received a great shock. A telex from Mildred Baron tells the story about the plight of Professor Thuc.

Sent a message to see if the Defense Department could put Thuc on a list for evacuation—the least we can do.

Spent most of the day with the dynamic, enthusiastic John Macy, going over the draft report, the substance of which we will present to Minister Amouzegar on Thursday.

APRIL 23, 1975
TEHRAN

My most important achievement has been getting a hotel room for Leo Anderson. The scramble for a place to sleep in this boom city is almost unbelievable. Why tours and tourists are encouraged by full-page ads by one branch of this government while "serious" travelers are unhoused (or sleeping in hotel lobbies) is one of the many oddities of Iran's "lack of program coordination."

My message about Professor Thuc produced a request to Ambassador Martin [in Saigon] to try to put Thuc and his family on the list for evacuation of those closely associated with America.

The diminutive professor and I were truly partners, trying to design a road for the future of Vietnam that would not be simply one of bombing and bloodshed and hatred. This is not simply trying to rescue a personal friend. To have his creative association with me be the cause for his execution when the Communists take over Saigon would be just too terrible an injustice to bear.

APRIL 25, 1975
TEHRAN

John Macy and I spent a memorable two hours yesterday with Amouzegar.

John made some casual comment about last night's rain and the day's fine weather. This prompted a careful and solemn explanation by Amouzegar of how essential it is, for a good grain crop in the dry farming areas, that there be *four* rains in springtime, spaced precisely fifteen days apart (this is a serious man, and chitchat about "the weather" as a conversational opener brings on this kind of serious discourse).

The Minister had only a few days before had a lengthy report from Macy about the progress of the public management work he leads. Amouzegar launched into a warm and emotional encomium about John Macy and the work of the group he leads, and how fortunate Iran was to have the "help" of such a man, who has so completely identified himself with Iran's needs, goals, and—though he didn't use the term—culture.

The confidence he showed in these words was heartening and deserved. He marked John off as different from the flood of what John calls "peddlers," the horde of briefcase proposal-carrying tycoons and salesmen now filling Iran (many of them, according to Amouzegar, forced to sleep in saunas for lack of hotel accommodations).

Later in the talks, he characterized D.E.L. and D&R as something more than "consultants" thinking only of themselves; in almost twenty years we had demonstrated that we had Iran's interests at heart. He quoted His Majesty's repeated estimate of me, a measure of confidence which John characterized as "terrifying," confronted as we are with a problem that has baffled and divided those who have confronted it, for years: how to enlist and stir and motivate the great army of the bureaucracy, and the citizens too, to put the goals of their country ahead of their innate lethargy or self-interest or just plain ignorance.

Macy spread the folder containing the summary of the preliminary findings and recommendations before Amouzegar, and began to read the preamble; this irritated me since Amouzegar had the words before him and was reading them.

So I interrupted. John Macy had assembled a group, had interviewed almost two hundred important figures in the Iranian scene, and we were presenting a diagnosis and recommendations—scores of them, actually —for the second phase, that of "implementation."

Brief as the time was—less than five months, net—we had beaten even our original ambitious schedule. This presentation today was a concrete demonstration of the underlying theme of our recommendations. By eliminating or closely modifying the constraints and multiple procedural limitations of the present Iranian public sector management system, speed and high quality could be substituted for the agonizing delays upon delays that the present system imposed, as we of D&R well know from sometimes bitter experience.

Would we prepare, at once, a "proposal" for the next phase, the stage of implementation of these recommendations?

I made a strong point to this effect: that D&R, and in this case, Macy's group, would be prepared to change their internal and determined schedule of priorities, in the implementation aspects, from week to week, depending upon the urgencies that the Minister himself encountered.

Some of our recommendations deal in long-range needs. "But," said Amouzegar, the deep lines in his noble face deepening, "I have problems I must decide by the end of the month, next week. So a proposal that looks ahead several months or several years must be given a lower importance, right now, than one with an emergency character."

Amouzegar has a gift for the graphic in discussing serious subjects. "There is a case that illustrates how I need to make quick decisions, and so do the local officials responsible to me.

"The illustration comes from the Justice Department, an official in Bandar Abbas. It was charged that a brutal murder was committed, so the Magistrate reported to me. An autopsy of the dead man was necessary for the trial. Said the official in the small community, 'We have no facilities for an autopsy, no physician qualified to perform it; the corpse must be transported to a place where such facilities and doctors exist.' It is a three-day trip by truck, and in the great heat—well, you can see that by the time the corpse gets to Tehran, there will be little to perform an autopsy on. What do I do?"

And Amouzegar added: "Whose budget can be modified to provide facilities for such future cases, in an area where a great port will be constructed? There will be more than one such case.

"I can't wait for several months or years for a change in the administrative machinery; I need quick answers, and I have no staff here, except you."

Amouzegar launched into an intense and extremely eloquent declaration of how deadly important it was that this undertaking succeed, and the dire consequences should it fail.

Not all these announcements and eloquence from the Throne, and the newspaper editorials about $20 billion of oil revenues, or the promise of a "great civilization" ten years hence, would satisfy the people. "Fourteen million people are living a nomad's life. More than half the people are illiterate. They ask why that twenty billion can't find its way into their life, they who have an annual income of less than $50."

He told an affecting story of a visit he made recently, with the Queen, to a place just outside Kermanshah. They came to a miserable hut. Those with the Queen were aghast when over their protests about the danger that she would be exposed to disease, she went into the hut. There was a very old lady with horrible skin cancer. The Queen talked with her for fully ten minutes, asked about her problems, and was greatly affected by the utter poverty. Very few, if any, of the people you see in Tehran who are making themselves very rich would have gone into that hut.

"We can't divide the twenty billion equally, of course, and much is needed for roads and factories. But surely that $50 or less could be increased, soon, to $100. Today there are so many in terrible poverty, so many illiterate and sick."

Looking me hard in the eye, he said: "How do we know that, after you have made these recommendations and after we have put them into effect, the results you predict will actually take place? What do you recommend that we do to give people faith that these changes will happen, that the results of the administrative reforms will produce results?"

I took up the question directly.

First, as to the importance of making changes, and making them soon: there must be instilled a sense of urgency throughout the Iranian system. Perhaps the Shah could do for this what he did to arouse public support for the original "White Revolution": a mass meeting of hundreds of thousands in the stadium, calling on the nation to support and insist on these administrative anti-red-tape measures; an Imperial Decree giving this the highest possible priority; a speech from the Throne to the Majlis; and so on.

Less dramatic, but worth doing: that Amouzegar take immediate action on some part—perhaps only a small sector of the problem—such as a declaration narrowing the gap between public- and private-sector compensation, and intimating that other steps to make private employment less lush and public employment more desirable, in a compensation sense, would be undertaken. Not wait until there is a comprehensive program of action, but respond to the need for urgency by doing something, a series of somethings.

As to next steps, the Minister will study our summary of recommendations, then take it up with the King. He had no doubt that whatever we thought was necessary by way of funds would present no problem. (I doubt if this can be taken literally.)

He said, "What you are doing in this work is risky for you, as well as for me; if we don't produce, it will be serious for each of us." True. More serious for him, as an Iranian official, than for us, but damaging to us just the same.

APRIL 28, 1975
TEHRAN

Lunch yesterday with Mehdi Samii. He says the industrial slowdown of Europe and the States has already cut anticipated oil revenues from twenty billion to perhaps sixteen billion—still a "sizeable income." But there are few places where there can be a cutback—he counted off on his fingers what the possibilities might be: health? no; education? no; defense? no. So the next step may be to require some of the specialized units, such as his Agricultural Development Bank, to find their own finance, outside, through private banks. This he thinks might be a "sane" move, and keep future commitments more nearly in line with reality.

I asked his advice about whether I should propose to the Minister of Energy, Vahidi, that I might be available to advise the new atomic energy program. Mehdi thinks I have an obligation to provide the benefit of my experience, etc. I am *far* from convinced.

Our proposal for the Public Sector Management program was accepted today by Amouzegar.

APRIL 29, 1975
TEHRAN

Reunion with Leo Anderson as a full-fledged and functioning D&R Director of Agriculture. What a man he is. It will be no holds barred if anyone tries to bulldoze him.

A heartening visit with the young, handsome Minister of Energy, Vahidi. He is more than ready to back (in words at least) the restoration of the Integrated Regional Concept for Khuzistan! And Mehdi Samii this noon (at an elegant small lunch with Ebtehaj) assured us that Rouhani, Minister of Water and Power, has completely changed on this subject and is more than prepared to back a recommendation for a revival of real regional development.

MAY I, 1975
AT THE TEHRAN AIRPORT, WAITING TO FLY TO AMSTERDAM

Said John Macy, at dinner last night: "The attitude of the Sacramento office in recruiting people for the work here is that they are doing some-one a great favor if they come to Iran. That's all wrong.

"When a person becomes a 'permanent' member of the D&R staff, doesn't that mean that the condition of his employment is that he is available—and clearly willing—to serve D&R wherever he is needed, with reasonable terms?"

IN FLIGHT

The Public Sector Management responsibility is a reality, with a certainty that a three-year, well-financed commitment has been made by me and John Macy.

Amouzegar, and then Mehdi and Ebtehaj, insisted that I should make myself available for counsel to the new atomic energy program. Amouze-gar thinks the Shah should have my views since I was a pioneer in this field as now Iran is.

How about preparing a memorandum which the Shah could read, but not make it in the form of a proposal but an information memoran-dum? I agreed, and may have opened a pandora's box for myself. In any case I wrote something.

At least, my conscience is clear. And it was Amouzegar and Samii's statements that I had an obligation to try to help the Iranian beginnings in this tricky field that decided me to submit the statement, inadequate as it is.

MAY 2, 1975
FLYING TO NEW YORK

I broke the trip at Amsterdam because, in a letter, Helen asked me to. "You need some rest."

It turned out to be one of the happiest of afternoons yesterday, for a gardener. For the tulips are now at their blazing incandescent height.

At Kirkenhof—a sight to behold, Tulip Heaven—I walked and walked until I was exhausted. My days of sixteen-hour effort in Tehran had caught up with me.

I who grumble at the thought of joining a "group" of tourists voluntarily got aboard a tour bus and, on a sunny windy day, saw the wide bands of tulips, fields of scarlet and yellow and pink, almost to the horizon. And bought a hundred or so to plant come next November.

MAY 4, 1975
PRINCETON

Returned to *my* garden at the peak of its early spring exuberance, on a day of luminescent sunshine! Out the window went all the persistent advice about "take it easy after that long exhausting journey—and the jet lag." So Helen and I traveled to Mazur's nursery for stacks of plants, and stiff muscles or no, we gorged ourselves with the kind of pleasure that is unique: observing the oft-repeated but always magic renewal of life in one's own garden among one's close friends, the dashing colors and form of flowers in a plot of land that one has oneself designed and tended for years.

"How well I remember the last time we were together," said Ambassador Dick Helms, in his office at the Embassy in Tehran, on the last day of my stay, Thursday. He has a strong laugh, head tilted way back.

On this sad morning the headlines were two words: Saigon Falls, and the news story that of Americans running away from the scene of their greatest testing in many years.

Helms told John Macy: "Dave and I were in the same car coming to the airport at Guam after the meeting there with President Johnson and the others [in 1967]. Somehow we were delayed and when we reached the field, *Air Force One* was already moving down the runway. Guam is a long, long way from Broadway. We yelled and waved; luckily the pilot saw us, and stopped, and the door opened while we raced up the steps."

Helms said he had heard all about the Public Sector Management project from John and others, thought there was nothing more important.

He remarked: "I suppose this is about the busiest U.S. Embassy in the world these days."

Said John: "The peddlers?"

Helms grinned. "That's what we call them ourselves. They aren't all Americans, of course, but those are the ones we get, and they come without any notion how hopeless it is to get a hotel room. Hotels completely filled. Even the saunas have rented out their hard benches."

Helms talked about corruption, as candidly and sensibly as ever I heard. "The peddlers ask me what is expected of them to get a contract by way of middlemen and other forms of bribes and payoffs. I tell them what the official answer is: 'Don't do it, it isn't necessary, and it is against Iranian policy from the Shah down.' But this is always oral.

"I say to the Iranians: if you would put that into a written statement, it would stop a lot of this, and would save me no end of problems of explaining. For after I tell one fellow trying for a contract that it is not Iranian policy to permit this, he sees a competitor who *has* paid off get a fat contract—so they don't believe me."

MAY 14, 1975
NEW YORK

My sadness is too deep to commit to words, about Vietnam, about the latest nightmare of man's inhumanity to man—the fleeing of hundreds of thousands of Vietnamese, frightened for their lives, from other Vietnamese, from the North.

Joe Slater is head of The Aspen Institute, located at Aspen in the mountains of Colorado. They have satellites scattered here and even in Germany. "Thought and action"—that slogan not only describes what they think of themselves but how self-conscious they are about how the world can be made better by people getting together and chewing things over.

Empress Farah is on the Institute's board of trustees, and she will preside at a gathering at Persepolis this fall.

As Slater prepared to leave my office, he looked sad and concerned. "There is so much cynicism and disbelief these days. Do you think this activity of ours will be greeted with cynicism, outcries about how much repression there is in Iran, how hypocritical all of this is? The Queen is getting an honorary degree at Georgetown Friday, and already the students there (and in the surrounding area) are organizing a demonstration against her."

Then he went on to give an appraisal of the Queen that gladdened my heart: how sensitive she is to the subject about which she speaks whenever she can—industrialization and culture—how can they have both?

I spoke of my own experience and my own conviction: that when you believe in something after giving it thought, don't let anything, particularly anything that is showy and cheap, stop you.

But he knows how much criticism there is in this country against Iran; not only at MIT but Stanford and elsewhere.

MAY 23, 1975
PRINCETON

Found myself reading once more "Atomic Energy for Military Purposes" by Henry D. Smyth. How it brought back that Saturday afternoon in Norris, Tennessee, in 1946, when I first knew that I was about to head that strange enterprise, the Manhattan District.

On June 7 Harry Smyth and I are once more joining forces, professionally, in a talk session here in Princeton, this time about the "Export of Nuclear Technology."

Last week was difficult, but productive. Decided to assign to John Macy the task of recommending specifics for those changes in the organization of D&R outlined in the draft statement I dictated early in the week.

On Tuesday I told Frederiksen that he was not to continue to assume that I had confidence in the way D&R is organized nor in the long-term plan of having most of the management of the enterprise in Sacramento.

It was necessary to be blunt and even bellicose with him because unless I am, I find a fortnight later that he writes that "as was agreed," etc., and goes merrily on without changing course. Too bad I have to deal with a close associate in an almost rude manner but otherwise he blandly ignores what I considered a decision and a direction.

The D&R board meeting on Wednesday was marked once more by the superior performance of our two South American Directors, General Rafael Alfonzo Ravard, and Bernardo Garces.

Ravard, his eyes lighted up with the excitement of ideas, showed how close, almost parallel, has been our experience, his and mine. And not only our recollections but achievements reflect that common experience. It is the experience not of theoretical people—though theory and philosophy are at the base of it all—but of practitioners. For that there is no substitute, I once more concluded after several hours of that board meeting.

Rodman listened to my and Macy's description of the Public Sector Management program, and then exploded a bomb that rocked everyone. Standing as he delivered his statement, he said, in effect, that he was preparing a speech in which he opposed the "transfer of American technology" to developing countries as being against the interests of the U.S.

He mentioned Iran and the Shah ("I do not know what his intentions are; I am not confident about his intentions toward us") but this superisolationist statement went much further even than half questioning our work for Iran and particularly the Public Sector Management improvement program. Should D&R help make it possible for Iran to achieve its goals?—stated by Macy as the purpose of our work—he doubted that. Didn't yet oppose it, but that was the inference.

We were flabbergasted.

Two highlights of the three days: One was an eloquent and most perceptive written statement by John Macy of my philosophy in establishing D&R, and its organizational implications. That is, that under the engineer-oriented management leadership of Frederiksen and his people, were we drifting away from the whole purpose, the distinctive purpose of D&R? He thought we were. He asked, how can this be corrected, how can D&R be brought back to its real purpose—and answered with suggestions about organizational changes. (It was to fill out that thesis that I assigned to him the job of recommending ways and means.)

The other high point, also concerned with "turning D&R around," was an evening with Leo Anderson. *He* understands what D&R was; he was part of it during its halcyon days, particularly the creation and development of KDS, our original organization in Iran back in the 1950s, the Khuzistan Development Service, and the human as well as the physical resources of that period. He pledged that he came back to D&R because he thought he could help me "turn it around." I believe he will.

MAY 26, 1975
PRINCETON

Saturday night and early Sunday morning I witnessed my first eclipse of the moon ("saw" is too tame a word for observation of this spectacle). It was a hot night; in pajamas I sat out in the garden with binoculars and watched the full moon slowly lose a slice, then as half was gone, the remainder turned orange, then blood red.

Have been giving a good deal of thought to the future organization of D&R. The notion is unworkable that most of our work should receive "technical support" from an establishment (i.e., Sacramento) 11,000 miles from the need for "support." Yet that is not only what has been going on but is what Frederiksen insists upon increasing.

MAY 28, 1975
NEW YORK

Tall, movie-star laugh, wavy-haired—in short, John Lindsay, twice Mayor of New York City, breezed into my office this morning. In his role as a lawyer freeloading for advice about Iran, he spent much time there, so he says, on behalf of some pretty tough characters who have contracts (so they say) for building recreation facilities, housing, etc.

I sounded off about the bad name American relations would get out of this building of huge enclaves—20,000 new housing units in one location—with American privileges in the middle of Iranian poverty.

He left soon after.

Spent much of the last two days getting Macy ready for his trip to Sacramento; his "mission": to lay the groundwork for the tightening up of D&R's management, and particularly the relations between Sacramento, Tehran, and the new renewed center of the company I propose to establish in New York. He will have a lively time with Hal, I prophesy. But the more I watch closely—for the first time really in quite a while—the more I blame myself for letting such unprofessional management go unchanged, or even unchallenged.

MAY 31, 1975
PRINCETON

Much is written and said about "the secret of management," or the skill of delegation.

The man who is a successful practitioner of management is he who can have many things going at the very same time. Or so it seems to me. And having them going on in the way he conceives of them and all headed for the same overall goals. This is a long way from mere "delegation."

A long phone call to John Macy preparatory to his leaving for Sacramento and a definitive discussion and program for strengthening D&R.

The essential element here in administrative terms is that I have defined what I want done, but in terms that have John fully as excited and turned on about this as I am myself.

Then at noon I spent a couple hours on a new set of ideas I have about improving the control of atomic energy, with Von Hippel, a clear-headed physicist from Princeton, and that sage of all atomic energy development, Harry Smyth.

JUNE 1, 1975
PRINCETON

I have changed a good deal since the days back in the spring of 1946 when my mind and energies were concentrating, day and night, on the atom.

But the atom hasn't changed all that much.

This became clear during the talk with Von Hippel and Harry Smyth, in preparation for the rebeginning (as it may be) of voicing my ideas about how to deal with the atom, its beneficial side, its "dangerous" side.

I summed it up yesterday by a phrase, "atomic energy is still an immature technology," despite the thirty and more years since it burst upon the world's consciousness.

For example: nothing effective has been done about waste products. Now this is more than a matter of "safety." Safety is involved, of course. This highly toxic material piles up in vast quantities in atomic reactors, as the fuel is "burned" up and the residual wastes have to be removed and stored, while fresh fuel is put into the reactor.

But in that waste, those atomic ashes, as we used to call them, are substantial amounts of plutonium which can be recovered by chemical processes, and it is the Pu that then becomes the source of bombs.

The heart of my new idea turns on this extraction of the Pu from this radioactive garbage. If that reprocessing could become the sole function of an international agency—the one now in existence—then a power reactor itself would not be a source of concern lest it be turned into bomb material. It is the reprocessing of spent material that is the "dangerous" activity. And thus far there is no known commercial plant that has succeeded in producing Pu from the spent fuel from an otherwise benign atomic reactor. General Electric built such a facility with its own money, and it failed, only a short time ago. So the field is open.

Von Hippel will moderate Harry's and my performance next week before nine people (probably eager to get off to play tennis).

He got the point of my idea; seemed to think it had technical possibility. But he went on to say that the material used in many, perhaps most, power reactors is far too low in U-235 or Pu to be useful for an explosion, for a bomb. "In other words, it is 'denatured'—the idea in the board of consultants' report of 1946."

JUNE 2, 1975
PRINCETON

After several days of heavy rain, today one of those days in early June that the English poets found stirred them. After the end, nearly, of the perennial border and rhodos, the rose garden begins to gleam, with every shade of red, of deep pink, and, yes, rose colors.

JUNE 4, 1975
NEW YORK

The hottest issue of the moment, or of a good many moments: the continued proliferation of atomic energy plants (promised though not yet delivered) to almost a dozen countries that now do not have atomic energy capacities: Syria, Egypt, and now Brazil. An excited column on this by Scotty Reston today, in his modified doomsday tone.

Against the tone of doomsday, my idea: that is, adding the recovery of plutonium to the functions of the International Atomic Energy Agency (the one at Vienna), a development function which also combines in an important way control aspects (or a control device that has a development aspect).

How can I get wider currency for this idea? If it were wholly gloomy there would be no problem: the more negative and awful an idea, the better chance it has to receive space or time from the "media."

But the heart of the idea appears to stand up to the scrutiny of such a wise scientist as Harry Smyth. I took down in shorthand his responses to my questioning, by phone, today, and it looks pretty sound and reasonably readily explained to laymen.

JUNE 5, 1975
NEW YORK

One more step, a large one, toward a substantial reorganization of D&R: told John Macy I expected him to give almost half his time to helping me establish a corporate center here in New York, "the office of the Chairman and Chief Executive Officer." After a proper time, I would expect him to help me phase out of operations until I became a Chairman of the Board to further outside interests and formulate a continuing and ever-changing picture of this distinctive enterprise.

JUNE 9, 1975
PRINCETON

Fighting my way through a draft of an article presumably for the Op-Ed page of the *Times* on the need for a new initiative for international control. This would be based on the set of ideas I have been developing about the processing of spent fuel to recover Pu.

It is hard to write when I am as tired as I really am, and there is so much else on my mind.

JUNE 15, 1975
PRINCETON

Monday I had the main features of "a new initiative" on international control in mind; by Friday morning an MS completed and off to John Oakes, at the *Times,* who accepted it in a few minutes; it will appear, apparently, early this coming week. Also proposed a second interview for the *Los Angeles Times* syndicate.

Great satisfaction out of this business of coming out of the too "low profile" period.

JUNE 17, 1975
NEW YORK

Being absorbed, as I am now, in the "nuclear fuel cycle" regurgitates those years when "the atom" was the center and focus of my worries and responsibilities—and the result is a pretty glum man at the moment. How can anyone discuss a serious subject, seriously, these days, and not cry havoc—and yet that's what I am rehearsing, day and night these latter days, since I started writing the Op-Ed article about plutonium recycling, etc.

The young man at the *Times* who is responsible for the "minor changes" Oakes requested is a good illustration of . . . something. When I asked him to identify me with the first American proposal for international control, the Acheson-Lilienthal Report, adding that I didn't think many people of his age would be very clear about it, or remember the Baruch Plan, etc., he replied:

"You're right. That's one of the problems of editing the article."

That's putting me in my place.

JUNE 20, 1975
PRINCETON

Lo and behold, the *Times* did think well of the article, for it was there, big as life, this monring. Someone else must have been "bumped," for the placing was at the top of the page with lots of white space around. And gracing it, a drawing of an insect with the title in big type: "If This Continues the Cockroach Will Inherit the Earth."

The display of the piece, and giving it a high time priority, were most impressive.

But my first reaction, and Helen's, to the title was: dammit, this is a serious, very serious article; that cute and sensational title ruins it; that will turn people off reading it.

Called Beatrice; asked for her professional opinion. "Don't you dare apologize for that title; they know what they are doing. That will attract attention when some solemn title about the dangers of the atom and so on would turn people off who would say: 'So this is more about the atom; ugh.' "

I could see that she was right, for the phone calls (e.g., Rodman Rockefeller, Mary Smyth on behalf of Harry, etc.) confirmed it.

After congratulating me, Rodman remarked on the title as provocative ("Did you write that title?"). Then he said, "Do you know, I found a cockroach at our house yesterday evening."

JUNE 21, 1975
PRINCETON

In June 1950 I wrote an article for *Collier's* magazine (which I have outlived by quite a few years, as it happens) urging that the atomic energy plants, particularly those at Oak Ridge, be sold to private industry and classified information be broadly made public to competitive industry.

Yesterday, twenty-five years later, President Calvin Herbert Ford, our non-elected by a landslide and a pardon President, made the same proposal, responding no doubt to the pressure within the Administration to keep up our enriched uranium supply for new power plants. Anything to distract public attention from the comatose state of the atomic energy industry, at this point.

JUNE 23, 1975
NEW YORK

The long-awaited mile-long telex arrived: a contract signed for the next stage of the Public Sector Management program. Macy has lived up to my expectations, and has learned a good deal in the bargain—e.g., decided not to leave Iran until the first payment of a half-million is "in the bank."

Helen off this morning, after three days of packing, with bearded Allen at the wheel. Had a reassuring talk with him last night. Determined to think up some way by which he and Daniel can get a job on the Vineyard; that is what they want most of all. And then in the fall, off to Colombia for a job on a ranch of Mario Lazerna. "I want to get more perspective, by seeing more of the world." What gusto. How proud I am of such a young man.

JUNE 24, 1975
NEW YORK

On a day of more than tropical gooey heat, I set out to sign my will at the office of Joe Flom's firm.

Flom now has an enormous law firm. Saw him for a moment, his cigar sticking out at an angle, the look of the very successful and somewhat surprised fellow who "made it big."

JUNE 28, 1975
THE PLAZA, NEW YORK

How strange that public events of these days, events that sear my very soul, so rarely are even referred to in these journals, whereas trivia —even if to me, personally, they are not by any means trivia—get long-winded introspective entries.

Yesterday, the woman whose photograph is on the bookshelf of my office—she was a slim, dark-eyed girl then, years ago, standing in the wheat field by her father's house—Indira Nehru Gandhi, brought down on her head the self-righteous cries of all the sacred cows of world journalism. In short, Prime Minister Gandhi took over the control of her vast country, and as Abraham Lincoln did when he shut off habeas corpus, the copperheads thinking he was a weak buffoon, so Indira struck down political democracy and constitutional rituals to save India—and her critics as well as conspirators in jail and the press censored and suppressed.

There has been an increase in the number of countries that will have nuclear bombs of their own.

In short, West Germany and Brazil signed a $4 billion contract for nuclear facilities including plutonium production. Our milk-toast State Department, which could have made it most difficult for Germany, said it "regretted" it.

JUNE 29, 1975
THE PLAZA, NEW YORK

With Leo Anderson and Verle Kaiser from eight until a few minutes ago, mostly listening to Leo, who was at the top of his form.

If he and John Macy can't give D&R and particularly the conceptually leaderless Sacramento group a turn-around, it just can't be done.

Leo's talk was full of gems of understanding; I thought they were gems because they spoke of my own convictions.

"In recruiting a new man," says Leo, "I don't start out talking about salary and fringes—that comes at the very end. I tell him about the job, and say: this job will give you the best *job satisfaction* you have ever had in your life."

Says Leo, "I have kicked out such AID phrases as 'counterpart' or 'advisor'; I call them our Iranian associates.

"About training: we want someone who can teach them how to solder, not the theory of heat transfer."

Oh, I enjoyed those hours. How well he has sized up how little some of these able people in Sacramento know about what D&R is all about.

JUNE 30, 1975
THE PLAZA, NEW YORK

At eight this morning I was in the office, and there was Hal Frederiksen, in from Sacramento. We completed a day of real progress, specific, and I trust, lasting. The spirit on both sides lacked entirely that edginess and even suppressed anger that has not been absent from other sessions over the past months.

Hal laid out a series of financial statements, one for each segment of the company's work, expenditures month by month.

He didn't realize, he said, that except for a pale little weekly bank-balance statement, I had not been seeing any of this, although it was sent to Pampanini, so he said. In any case, he said that for the first time he could realize why I had felt so lost and frustrated, that I needed to know where we are, and he intended to provide the data currently from here on out.

And the *spirit* was good.

JULY 2, 1975
"TOPSIDE," MARTHA'S VINEYARD

I had barely reached this hilltop when there was a call from Miss Baron, so soon after leaving the office "for a fortnight": Macy reports that the half a million is on its way, so badly needed for "elbow room" to effect the reorganization planned for months. A good way to start a holiday.

And what magnificent weather too. "Visibility unlimited" is more than a phrase to describe this pellucid air, and the familiar pale blue of the Sound, the darker blue of the ocean to the south.

So serene it is here. We are a green island within an island. And within me none of the turbulence that has been such a common experience when I have left my work to convalesce, for so often have I exhausted myself and been grossly unhappy and disturbed when the pressure let up—and not only the pressure of work, but of emotional crosscurrents. None of that yesterday afternoon, nor this morning.

JULY 4, 1975
MARTHA'S VINEYARD

A quite unexpected bonus of approval of my so recent re-entry into the atomic energy field of battle: a longhand note from Jim Conant, approval of the Op-Ed article, with an article he wrote for the *Christian Science Monitor* quoting extensively from the *Times* piece. And a postcard of agreement from another giant, Wigner.

JULY 5, 1975
MARTHA'S VINEYARD

Thirty years ago Alfred Eisenstaedt, even then the No. 1 magazine photographer for *Life,* came to Norris and spent several days taking pictures of TVA and of the Lilienthals. Today he showed up here, by prearrangement, and took dozens of shots.

Remembering the famous photo of Coolidge and the Indian war bonnet that he wore with such a naturally vinegary look, I declined to "do something"—which is what he requested. What I "do" is as little as possible, and that is what he settled for: Helen and me in the selfsame pose as one he used in Norris, showing us leaning over a balustrade.

Eisenstaedt has an enormous head and the rest of him dwindles, so at a glance he is something seen through the wrong end of a telescope.

Eisenstaedt's girl assistant (an eager young Amazon) reminded him that in a half-hour they were due to take pictures of Scotty Reston and Walter Cronkite. "They are playing tennis and will be in tennis shorts. Reston said to me that he has funny skinny legs so be sure to remember that when you take the pictures."

Sylvain and Nancy arrived in the afternoon yesterday, the first time we have seen them in a year. Our enormous pride in their remarkable sons is pretty well matched by their own, though they hide it somewhat more.

JULY 9, 1975
MARTHA'S VINEYARD

For the first time in more than two weeks since I have been here I did some considerable walking, and paid my first visit to the Daggett beach. Little Peter Daggett (but not as little as last year at this time by six inches) and I had a good reunion on the rocky shore (the tide is very low). I brought a huge lamb bone for Sparky, who was overjoyed, proceeded to bury it, and then pounced all over me, he who usually takes a week before he stops putting on his watchdog role of barking like the devil.

Keeping in touch with the office daily, at least once.

Yesterday Miss Baron with evident pleasure telephoned a cable of birthday greetings from the Minister and my friend, Amouzegar.

JULY 12, 1975
MARTHA'S VINEYARD

Twelve solid days of overcast skies since the day after I arrived, and with a liberal mixture of fog, wild winds, sudden downpours. One swim the whole time.

And yet, a happy man; no grumpiness, irritability, grousing about weather, or anything else.

Have done a measurable amount of work, literally hours of telephoning and receiving of telex messages.

A nearly two-hour phone conversation with John Macy, just arrived yesterday afternoon from Iran. Full of enthusiasm, good reports, and yet some professional warnings of shortcomings to be dealt with.

Two things stand out: the continued strength—indeed increased strength—of Jamshid Amouzegar, strength in OPEC matters, strength as a *non* political political leader, and strength in his increasing confidence in John and myself.

The second part of the report reassured me tremendously: the great impact on the work of Andrea Pampanini. I told Andrea when I asked him to "take charge" in Iran that he was to make decisions, on the spot, pull that operation together, and when necessary talk back to those Iranians delaying the work rather than humor them, be pals.

JULY 20, 1975
MARTHA'S VINEYARD

After a several-month period of vacuum about the D&R Papers, that certainly shows signs of life again. President Bowen [of Princeton] spent two hours at our office—the locale of the meeting was as significant almost as the fact that it was held.

How youthful and un-presidentlike is his mien, with that lock of hair dangling over his eye.

He will be writing a letter confirming the arrangement we think we have worked out as the next step. The most important is that Princeton will arrange to have published a statement describing the Papers and their meaning to scholars and practitioners, and giving access to them to people from outside the Princeton community. This was Sylvain's recommendation to me; happily it was the first suggestion Bowen himself put forward, without waiting to hear from us on the subject.

He was accompanied by Dean Stokes of the Woodrow Wilson School of International Relations and Public Affairs, and Dean Jahn of the School of Engineering and Applied Science. John Macy pretty well led our discussion—at my suggestion before the meeting—and David Morse attended and contributed.

A decisive mark of progress: a meeting at dinner Thursday night with Macy followed by a morning session with Frederiksen. The subject: my insisting on a Development Plan, to take the place of the scattered, item-by-item New Business proposals, the fragmented character of which has driven me nuts.

We called on Rodman Wednesday. He was so depressed, and with good reason, if reason has anything much to do with that profound state of mind that sees little hope ahead.

Depressed about the state of the country, about our "so-called foreign policy." Most of all about the obscure future of what a fortnight ago was a clear road—i.e., the sale of IBEC's 51% in a supermarket chain in Venezuela called CADA, for a great big sum.

Still, he said he is "going off for a fishing trip in Quebec and a cruise in Maine in my father's yacht."

JULY 22, 1975
MARTHA'S VINEYARD

Last night our beloved daughter Nancy took a plane for a month in Italy. All by herself. Considering that our child is now fifty years old, and the effective mother of two huge young men, one might suppose by the number of times Helen and I refer to this history-making event that she is leaving for a trip through the jungle of New Guinea.

But the picture of Nancy's first expedition into the world as non-parent-attached comes back to us: when she left for Radcliffe College from the little town of Norris. I was so impressed with that departure (though Helen was with her) that I went back to the office and wrote a journal entry which was later published in Volume I.

The "judicious editing"—Canfield's phrase—of the Volume VI MS turned out to be an injudicious attempt to rewrite the very tone of the journals. This has upset our holiday plans, and Helen has been working so hard to go through the often illegible notes of the copy editor, hardly a page being unchanged. I will write Cass a letter, complete with some hilariously funny illustrations, of why only a small part of the "editing" can be used.

AUGUST 1, 1975
MARTHA'S VINEYARD

A big party at Ralph Meyer's fabulous brand-new home overlooking Chilmark Pond and the south shore of the ocean. A kind of housewarming, I suppose, so all the Chilmark community of notables and intellectuals was there.

But it was the brief talk with Jerry Wiesner of MIT that interested me particularly.

He wanted to talk about the program for training nuclear engineers and technicians for the announced vast atomic energy program.

"I didn't ask to see the Shah. They sent for me. Would MIT train a large group of technicians? I said MIT had never trained 'technicians.' The Prime Minister said: 'I suppose you are like the Harvard people—I know MIT isn't Harvard but it is the same thing—you want a five million dollar grant.'

"That got me mad. I said we weren't asking anything; it was their idea. So I thought I had better prepare a proposal and ask for plenty. So I did.

"I saw the Shah. A touch of megalomania, I would say. Didn't think much of my warning that it would take time to train and equip a new atomic industry. Said everyone says that about everything Iran sets out to do—but we do it just the same."

I asked: "How is the program going? You have some of their students here. How is their English?"

"The truth is more than half of the forty or fifty students aren't interested in nuclear engineering at all; that is just the excuse for their being where they can get what they want, which is a good general MIT engineering training. So we splice in enough nuclear engineering to be able to say they have had some—but that's about all.

"One of the students is doing graduate work in electrical engineering. I asked him: 'Do you know Lilienthal?' 'He is our father,' this fellow said, rather awed."

Helen talked to Marge McNamara. The McNamaras have a place next to the Meyers. They have had a hard time keeping people from using their beach, as one could have predicted.

"I don't like to be a policeman, chasing these young people away. But they go right by the windows of our bathroom, and what can you do?" She looks worried most of the time in any case, but this doesn't recommend itself as a way to spend the summer.

Suddenly she said to Helen: "Bob retires in three years. I don't know what he will do then. Have to start looking for a job, I guess."

That problem doesn't seem critical. What I do wonder about is whether the antagonism to Americans may make it a problem to re-elect an American as President of the Bank to which the U.S. contributes less money than the oil producers.

This was the first day of fun I have had in this vacation period. Went to the Hill Top cabin, swam at the Daggett beach with Jack Daggett, and sailed in his Sunfish. Swimming in the Sound was just right. Isn't it about time I took time for a holiday, now that the grim business is over of *un*-editing the Harper editing of the journals?

AUGUST 17, 1975
MARTHA'S VINEYARD†

A long visit with Jerry and Laya Wiesner at their summer home. Wiesner and I had a good time reminiscing about his visit to the Valley in the thirties, with Alan Lomax, recording the songs and speech of mountain people for the Library of Congress—where, Wiesner supposed, the tapes are on file somewhere.

It seems that I helped them, or took some special notice of this project, while I was on the TVA board, but I have only a vague recollection of it. A long way from going into the mountains to record songs, and being head of the most prestigious of scientific and technical institutions.

Only the barest reference, as we were leaving for the return to "Topside," to the subject that was in both our minds, MIT's contract with Iran for the training of fifty-odd Iranians for their new atomic energy program. The student body and many of Jerry's faculty had been most vocal and critical of that contract, one that Wiesner said he had been asked to enter into by the Shah.

†The two notebooks containing the original shorthand entries for the period August 17–October 8, 1975 were lost before they could be transcribed (one was forgotten in a taxi, the other was left on the plane after a Tehran–New York flight). The entries were rewritten from memory at Princeton on December 28, 1975.

As for the theme of my Op-Ed article of June 20, Wiesner dismissed this by saying this [nuclear waste] presented no great problem; could be solidified, etc. I didn't argue with him about it. Nor refer to the passionate letter from Jim Conant agreeing with my concern.

SEPTEMBER 23, 1975
NEW YORK

Luncheon at the *Times* with Iphigene Sulzberger and a Rabbi Schindler, president of the Reform Jewish Congregations—not the correct term.

Back during the summer a letter from Mrs. Sulzberger asking for my opinion about an idea she had. She had referred to the opening verses of the Book of Ezra, which told of the role of the great Persian King, Cyrus, who freed the Jews from the bondage put upon them by the Babylonians and sent them back to rebuild the temple in Jerusalem. She was troubled, she had written me, by some of the comments of the Shah of Iran, that she interpreted as not sympathetic toward Israel. Wouldn't it be a good idea to have these passages about Cyrus in the Book of Ezra translated into ancient Persian and contemporary Farsi, illuminated in a beautiful way, and presented to the Shah as a reminder of the story of Cyrus and the ancient Judeans?

I received an amusing letter much later, from Iphigene, part of which follows:

> I am afraid, however, that I have missed the boat because the outrageous UN resolution branding Zionism as racism made me look again at the Book of Ezra, and I find that the dear old boy was racist, telling the men of Israel who had returned from captivity that they were diluting their precious blood with Babylonian wives and children and that the alien families should be returned to Babylon. This has a moral which catches up with you even if it takes two thousand and five hundred years!
>
> I fear, therefore, if I quote the first chapters of Ezra to the Shah, someone will surely point out to him the bigotry contained in the concluding chapters. Under the circumstances, the least said, the better.

OCTOBER 7, 1975
NEW YORK

I have gone over in my mind a list of public relations firms, and believe we should engage one to help in the New Direction I have set for my special role: energy. And I think Anna Rosenberg would be the best of the lot, because I think she believes in what D&R is about.

A call came in from her. Sure enough, David Morse had lost no time, and we set up a luncheon date.

OCTOBER II, 1975
TEHRAN

I proposed that John Macy become D&R President; my remaining as Chairman, Chief Executive; Frederiksen, Executive Vice President. Agreed to by Macy after several hours' discussion.

OCTOBER I5, 1975
TEHRAN

One of the longest gaps in journal writing for a long time. But not because of lack of writable events and observations. For one reason, I have used up the extra energy I usually draw upon for detailed journal writing.

But how well things are going on the D&R front! No cause for anxiety there.

Late yesterday afternoon John Macy came charging into our living room, with the best of news. He had spent almost three hours with the leading deputy of Plan Organization and a group of ten or more Deputy Ministers from many of the Ministries. Led by the Plan Organization Deputy who brought them together, and by Alimard, now Iranian head of the Public Sector Project, they supported all of our recommendations for change, particularly in the direction of decentralization, and were forming an ad hoc group to press for "implementation"—which, of course, is the key.

John was most excited and heartened about it.

Yesterday I saw five Governors—Ostandars—full of fire and understanding of the implications of what we have proposed, implications for a more democratic society.

John Macy had told me that at a recent meeting with Ambassador Helms—an old friend of L.B.J. days—Helms wanted to see me on this trip.

Helms listened to John's lecture on the progress of the Public Sector Management program, and said again he thought that without progress along the line of making things work better, Iran would face real difficulties.

Then he asked if I had informed the Shah that I was here. I said I had not requested an audience.

"It would be wrong of you, if I may say so as American Ambassador, if you did not let him know you are here, as I know he will want to talk with you. Don't do this through the Office of Protocol, but through the Minister of Court."

He went on: "The Shah has told me he wants your advice about the atomic energy program.

"A few days ago I had a visit from Dr. Enteman, the French-educated young man in charge of the atomic energy program in the office of the Prime Minister. He said that in the proposed atomic development program with India and Pakistan, Iran would expect to receive, as a matter of right and in recognition of their participation in the overall uranium enrichment expansion being managed by Bechtel, that portion of the product represented by Iran's financial contribution, rather than in proportion to Iran's *'need'* [his word]."

Apparently all this means that the French and German atomic industries will dominate the provision of the added enrichment facilities.

I countered by saying I did not want to become involved once more in atomic energy. To treat this whole subject as just one of who gets contracts for equipment, etc., overlooks the grave and even catastrophic character of atomic development when competition between countries is the key. "It must be treated as a *world* problem or we are all in great trouble."

OCTOBER 17, 1975
TEHRAN

Just outside the windows of Helen's room is a great cavern, an excavation; long steel girders support the buildings on either side. Filled with rubble. Adjoining, on the bustling street, is a half-torn-down old building.

This pleasant outlook, right in the middle of Tehran, is the home of a peasant family consisting of Papa (we haven't seen Mama yet), two sturdy-looking young boys, some chickens, and three charming sheep, one with an amusing black face.

At evening the papa drives the sheep toward someplace we can't see from the window. Occasionally he sets out green forage for them. The sheep, according to Helen, have definite personalities, the larger two gang up on the smaller black-faced clown; the boys snuggle up to them.

What the head of the "household" does for a living is hard to see, but he is most industrious in bringing trash into the cavern, and now is burning part of it in a cheery bonfire, and at other times he sorts out the trash; for pickings, we suppose.

This noisy, clattery, traffic-choked city is full of just such anomalies.

When I was lying here in the Park Hotel for ten days some years ago, sick as a dog with flu, the view from that same window was of the Russian hospital. It was part of my rare entertainment to observe the

Russian way of treating obstetrical cases, which was not exactly an example of the highest standards of medical care. Now this pastoral scene.

My time isn't taken up entirely by such observation; not quite. A lot of listening to complaints but also some of the keenest dissection of managerial problems I have heard since Gordon Clapp. The dissector, John Macy.

OCTOBER 19, 1975
TEHRAN

When I visited Abolhassan Ebtehaj the other day, he was very low. No one in the country was willing to stand up and say what they think about "conditions," and certainly about the "regime." The young men were making money, and nothing else mattered.

I had recently come from meeting with the four Deputies in the Ministry of Interior and four Governors; I told Ebtehaj that I had found it quite different than he had. I picked out Amin Alimard as an example of an intense, deeply concerned, and forthright young man, well trained, the man Amouzegar had appointed to head the SOAE (the Civil Service Commission) in his stead.

I told Ebtehaj that I thought there was a cadre, larger than either of us knew, of the same kind of alert patriotic young men that he, Ebtehaj, had gathered around him in the early days of the Plan Organization. He perked up.

"Why don't you meet Alimard?" I asked. So yesterday noon, at the Iranians' Bank, we four (Alimard, Ebtehaj, Macy, and I) lunched together.

This may have been one of the best things I have done for Iran in a long time, for it was even better than I hoped for. The best result was that it stirred up Ebtehaj into that half-frenzy of enthusiasm that is the man at his best.

Alimard was articulate, forthright, critical of his country, but not just negatively so.

OCTOBER 21, 1975
TEHRAN

Just before noon a call at the office from the office of the Minister of Court: "Your audience is for this afternoon, at 4:30; you should be at Saadebad Palace at 4:15." Like a dentist's appointment, that informal.

I had said to myself that it really didn't matter much whether I got to see the Shah on this trip. But this word—and the happy reaction among my pals, and the secretaries at the office—showed that it *was* important that I not leave Iran without this mark of standing. Far more important, this opportunity to report on progress.

I wanted to get John Macy included in the audience, and did get approval of his going to the Palace with me. Asked the friendly lady secretary: "Is Mr. John Macy accompanying you essential?" Not essential, said I, but important. So he did accompany me, briefing me in his intense way all the trip up to the hill, as he must have briefed three U.S. Presidents in their time.

Through the gate and up the long gravel walk, puffing a bit with fast walking and altitude, and gulping in the extraordinarily pure and sweet air of the foot of the mountains. Then the signal came, the attendant opened that door, and I found that the Shah had walked almost to the door, and greeted me with what is really one of the warmest of smiles, a firm handshake. I was struck by how fit he looked, in contrast to some of the recent photographs.

After being seated, I thanked him for finding time for me to meet with him and to make a report of progress since the last audience. His face lighted up: "We must meet not less than two times a year."

"It is exactly a year ago—October 28—that I sat here while Your Majesty passed on a contract for what we called the strengthening of public sector management, the need for administrative reform. Much has happened since that time." I told him with some detail about getting the "best-qualified man in the U.S., perhaps anywhere, to head up the work here in Iran" and described John Macy's work with three Presidents of the U.S. This was to be done under the hand of Amouzegar.

He knew exactly what I was talking about; said that this work of the SOAE had just been made the responsibility of Amin Alimard, "another very good man; Amouzegar has other things to do," a very cool statement indeed to describe Amouzegar's responsibilities about oil prices and OPEC.

Alimard certainly starts off with a strong endorsement from the man who appointed him, and he deserves it, John Macy and Henry Reining, his deputy, believe. Alimard was a student of public administration under Reining at the University of Southern California.

The Shah keeps abreast of almost everything he is running—and really running. Though I was somewhat nonplused by the sparkle in his eye as he asked, "And you will use computers?"

I spoke to him about the studies "in depth" we were undertaking of three Ministries—Energy, Agriculture, and Education. I said that Leo Anderson was doing the Agricultural inquiry, and reminded him of Leo as the man he walked over the sugar plantation with years ago; I identified Sam Brownell as former U.S. Commissioner of Education, and said how fortunate we were to have his help.

I didn't think the Shah was set on fire about the public sector program, not as much as he was last year when I agreed to try to push it along. But when I turned to a report on the Karkheh Basin, he really showed the strongest kind of interest.

I had brought the Unified Development Report of 1959, with its fine schematic map of the Khuzistan region. I ran my finger over the Karkheh Basin, pointing to Kermanshah, and gave him the figure I had secured yesterday—that there were a million hectares of agricultural land there.

Yesterday morning Leo Anderson had burst out with a cry of protest against our discussion about the Karkheh being mostly about dams— which it had been. I paraphrased the words Leo had used then: we should find out about the *people* in the region, what they wanted, what they needed and what they thought they needed, how they could improve their agricultural practices. To do this would require a special kind of Iranian to go into the villages and report what he found, and then shape a program around that evidence of the villagers' condition and desires.

Of course, this is an old story with me, but it does need so badly to be repeated at every opportunity, including an audience with a monarch of very great power.

I had made my point: dams alone are by no means enough. And to do the total job of education—for that is what it comes down to—requires funds, more funds than have been previously set aside.

The King leaned over the map as he had last year. I pointed to the date on the report—March 1959—only a very short time after we had first come to Iran, and remarked on how comprehensive was the Master Plan after so short a time.

I repeated what I said the year before about the proximity of the Karkheh to the border of Iraq. "The situation between the two countries is now quiet and peaceful, chiefly thanks to Your Majesty's initiative and resolve. But it may not always be so, and to have a good healthy development right across the border from Iraq might be worth more than the total of the agricultural production."

At this reference to Iraq he looked very somber indeed. He looked so, how shall I say it?—"vulnerable." Looked like a man, not a monarch.

So I said: "I look upon you as a monarch, the ruler of this country, for whom I have been working for so long a period. But I also think of you as a friend, and as a public servant, an accolade I would like to feel I have earned for myself, combining in a private company the goals of service to the public.

"For me, public service has been the greatest satisfaction of my life; fortunately I was able to make money in ordinary commercial pursuits so I could afford to do this work in Iran, which has been financially very unsatisfactory."

Not all of our talk was about solemn matters of state, or "development."

I said the American public and particularly the cult of journalists took a superficial look at Iran; even the editor of the greatest American newspaper, the *New York Times.*

"Yes," he said, "the *Times was* a great paper, ten years ago; it is no longer. This is also true of most of the Eastern U.S. press." So much for Oakes and his "The Persian Mind" Op-Ed piece.

A long look and silence. Then: "You have dedicated a large portion of your life to my country."

He was still in this mood as I began to rise, and he walked me clear across that large room to the door. Looking at the floor, he said: "If you ever find obstacles in the way of the work you are doing, bring them to me, directly. If you get stuck, let me know, directly."

"Your Majesty has said something to that effect to me before, but I preferred to try to work things out without troubling you. But I doubt if this will always be possible and I shall indeed come to you with matters I can't work out—that is, if I 'get stuck.' "

OCTOBER 22, 1975
TEHRAN

Another fourteen-hour day.

A bizarre story late today. "This is Dick Harza of Harza Engineering. Could I see you for a few minutes?"

I smelled something, so asked John Macy to stay with me and have the meeting in a public room of the hotel rather than, as usual, in our suite. First much obvious casual talk. Then he said: "I didn't know whether I would talk to you about a problem Harza has here, but I guess I might just as well."

Perhaps ten years ago, Harza had made reconnaissance studies of the Karun River in Khuzistan and located several damsites. No reference to the fact that long before Bill Voorduin had located the sites on the Karun and they were identified in our 1959 Unified Development Report. "I never saw your development report." How innocent we would have to be to believe that—but I said nothing, nothing at all, which is what unnerved him, a man obviously much worried.

He continued: "Then 'out of the blue' we had a call from Minister Rouhani of the Ministry of Water and Power, asking that we come and negotiate with him for a dam on the Karun. We got a contract and started work.

"We have run into a delay." "Delay" is what he called it. I let it lie there, until he explained that the dam was supposed to be producing power a couple years ago, that it would not be producing for another seventeen months.

The cause for the "delay" was that the foundation was seriously faulty, required a massive wall at a large cost.

He explained in greatest detail how they had investigated the foundation conditions by the best, latest methods and with the best expert consulting advice. "This is the sort of thing that happens occasionally and could not have been prevented. The Ministry agreed and so did a special inquiry by Asfia [ex-head of the Plan Organization, and himself a geologist]. This international group recommended that Harza continue to repair the damage and proceed with the other major dams on the Karun."

But that decision was reversed "by the highest authority."

"If Harza is excluded from building other dams, those dams will probably be awarded to other than American firms." At this he looked at me as if this would be equivalent to allowing vandals to desecrate Old Glory.

"So, I have come to you to ask you to speak a good word for us, knowing of your standing with the highest authority and your long experience with dams."

I explained that in 1959 we had reported on this as well as some thirteen other damsites in the region, that about ten years ago we were requested by the Managing Director of the Khuzistan project, Reza Ansari, to submit a proposal, which we did, and were told that the Shah favored granting the contract to us. That at the same time the Minister of Water and Power had been given authority to place the Khuzistan Water and Power Authority, our client, into the Ministry, and we protested this, as had the Managing Director. Whereupon Minister Rouhani "negotiated" a contract with Harza, concluding that our bid was "too high."

"You can see," I continued, "that it would be quite incorrect for me to express any opinion about the Karun Dam and the 'delay,' or whether its cause was due to careless or poor engineering, or even to read the explanation in the document proffered."

In the MS of Volume VI, now I hope actually being set into type, there was an entry reciting what happened to us ten years ago or so.‡ This sequel is some kind of a record: a big company imploring us, the unsuccessful bidder, to "put in a good word"—i.e., a professional word—absolving them of blame in what is a minor disaster for the hopes of this country.

‡See *Journals,* Vol. VI, *Creativity and Conflict,* p. 141.

OCTOBER 25, 1975
EN ROUTE TO ROME

Rouhani's arms on the long table, his hands clasped, he began at once: "Only in-te-grated regional development can solve the problems of this country. This should follow the pattern, the model, you, Mr. Lilienthal, gave Iran in Khuzistan.

"There is no other way this big country can develop; it is too complex."

I added the illustration of the Haft Tapeh workers who were so undernourished, when we began fifteen years ago, that they couldn't cut sugar cane, so D&R had to import a brawny cane cutter from Australia. He would cut more cane in an hour than the underfed peasant villagers could cut in a week; but this big bimbo, according to Leo Anderson, listening in, insisted on having two steaks by noontime.

My point, of course, was that nutrition and the health of the people of the area was an "integral" part of the successful growth of sugar. And Rouhani put in: "It must be in the same agency, all the elements. Like KWPA."

My face must have shown my incredulity, and it was reflected in Leo's as well. For it was Minister Rouhani who began the process of the decline of integrated development in the first and thus far the only place where it was actually tried.

There was still another episode in the meeting with Rouhani. A young man came in with a document for the Minister's signature. Rouhani introduced us to him: a Deputy Minister. The Minister showed us the paper written in beautifully inscribed Persian; it had four signatures; the Deputy nodded and added *his* signature.

Rouhani said: "This paper shows you how much time and energy must be wasted by regulations of the kind Iran can no longer afford. The words say that a certain company may import fifty tons of an Australian oil that is needed in Iran to rub on grapes to make them shine, in the making of raisins. That's all.

"But the regulations required that such a permit must be signed by five, no less than five, *Ministers*. We Ministers thought this was terrible so we got the regulation changed to permit such a paper to be signed by our Deputies.

"*But* the Deputy Ministers won't sign unless they have the permission of the Ministers, which is what I have just given. So not only five Deputy Ministers but also five Ministers must approve these fifty tons of oil.

"We must eliminate all these approvals on little things, and delegate to others way down the line all details."

Of course, John Macy grinned fit to kill, and started to say that this is exactly what the Public Sector Management recommendations were dealing with—then restrained himself, as I did. If the lesson is learned, that is that.

But in the morning paper (the *Journal,* I think) a long editorial about decentralization and delegation, beautifully written, making this point and making it strong. And since the editorial must surely have had the approval of the powers that be, and since the text is nothing less than a paraphrase of our Public Sector recommendations, we, and particularly John Macy, can feel that our proposals are more than just another of a long series of professorial "studies" and "reports."

The D&R precept that the test of the worth of our efforts and ideas is whether they induce and produce action may well be exemplified in this important enterprise as it has been in others concerned with physical resources of water and land and power.

It is not difficult to identify the single most significant result of this two-and-a-half-week expedition. It is the demonstration, in the most specific ways, of the complete capacity of John Macy to be the President of this company, to *run* it, as to broad issues and details. In fact, my impression was wholly confirmed that he is a superb master of details, of figures and budgeting and financial control and direction.

This means that in a very short time indeed, I can turn over to him the kind of responsibility and functions that are least to my taste and which I do least well, and thereby free myself for the leadership role that such a platform as D&R provides.

The second most significant consequence of this trip was the warm vote of confidence from the Shah.

Earlier I refrained from writing about one part of the audience because it was so personal, and so sobering. But while it is so very fresh in mind, I should write it down here.

The Shah had referred, at the outset of the discussion, to the "administrative reform" task, that he understood that I was taking "personal responsibility" for that vital task, hence the broad and most unusual terms of the contract he had approved at the Palace on October 28, 1974, and the subsequent extension for three years.

"You have made many commitments to me and to Iran and have never failed."

After we had looked at the map of the Karkheh Basin, and I had described the opportunities and what I saw as its importance to the country, he said this was a very important undertaking indeed, as he believed years ago when the Khuzistan project was begun. "It is really a part of that large plan, isn't it?"

A year ago he had approved the idea of our going ahead with it. He pushed the map aside, said he expected me personally to commit myself to see that this project is carried out in the same manner. "It is a personal commitment as in the case of the other works you have been responsible for these twenty years."

OCTOBER 27, 1975
ROME

Yesterday morning I walked in the Pincio Gardens with my son, a tall, bearded, thoughtful figure who has come to mean more and more to me as the years of his youth have edged into his middle age. The great city spread out from the battlement in the blue haze of early morning, the sky that special medallion of blue that has for so many generations attracted to Italy so many writers, poets, and particularly painters.

We walked into the huge fortress just beyond this hotel which houses the Cultural Center of France, exhibiting now, on the hundredth anniversary of his birth, a vast collection of the paintings of Corot, to look over the heads of swarms of, mostly, diminutive Italian Sunday lookers, many with their young children, a solemn, well-dressed crowd.

Corot lived a long life, and painted into his mid-eighties. I asked David how it happened—as I thought I had observed—that so many painters kept alive the spark and the drive of creativity into their old age, whereas in so many other fields creativity, and super-energy, too, wane at earlier years. In the case of abstract mathematicians and physicists, the tradition is that their greatest creativity is spent by the time they are thirty or younger still. What about writers?

What is it that ignites and renews the creative spark? For a public man, such as myself, I thought it was the tension and constant conflict in his work, against which must contend. Indeed I had, with a suggestion from Beatrice, titled the latest, on-coming volume of the *Journals* "Creativity and Conflict."

As we moved, talking quietly, from a tender painting of a peasant girl to a massive landscape—they reminded me of the American 19th century Hudson River paintings—he opined that a painter is able to draw energy from techniques which he constantly challenges. A writer—that is different, speaking for himself: working alone and not in the presence of the subject of the writing (as a painter works out technique from painting to painting, the subject first close, then moved farther away, then in a different light of a different time of day). The Monet waterlilies or the series of Reims would be examples, I suppose.

Whether all of this musing was a correct assessment doesn't matter —didn't matter—in that yesterday morning. What mattered was that I was happy, and for me to be fully happy except in the midst of some stern tussle involving my work and its consequences is rare, rare enough to record.

David brought Margaret to Rome with him, now on the edge of being a "young lady." A delightful child-woman (fourteen and a half years old). A great reader, and entranced with our hotel apartment, with its elegance (quite unnecessary for Helen's and my tastes), complete with a bathroom mural of a nude Etruscan lady preparing for her bath, accompanied by her maidens, including a gal playing a double flute.

NOON, ROME AIRPORT

Vindication sometimes comes late, usually after one is long dead. But not for D.E.L. (very much alive at this point) in my opposition to the development ("crash" or otherwise) of the H-bomb.

Here in this crummy airport lounge, not made less crummy by being called a VIP lounge, I have just read an article by as distinguished a scientist-statesman as remains active: Herbert York, in the current *Scientific American,* and it is part of a book just published, *The Advisors.* Robert Oppenheimer and his colleagues of the General Advisory Committee were right on scientific grounds; I was right in accepting their view [opposed to U.S. development of the H-bomb], rejecting that of Teller, and right in advising Truman to approach the issue on other than scientific grounds—i.e., political and statecraft.

OCTOBER 30, 1975
NEW YORK

"Getting used" to the dislocation of time in a long intercontinental air voyage: it's not all that easy, and some people just assume that it takes a week at least to readjust. I went right to the office Tuesday morning (arrived Monday afternoon by New York time), felt vigorous and cocky about the results of the three-week expedition to Iran.

But the tough part is this business of waking up at 1:30 A.M. and filling in the time until morning.

There are redeeming features. Yesterday I was on the street at dawn. One who has never seen New York in the earliest morning cannot appreciate what a great city looks like: the streets swept clear of cars and people, one can *see* the City. What a picture of strength this is, a great achievement of building, of creating—creating something both physically magnificent and in spirit beyond any human experience in any other civilization of mankind.

NOVEMBER 2, 1975
PRINCETON

My walks—those long walks uphill and down on the Vineyard or a couple times around the circle of the Institute for Advanced Study Common here—have been increasingly distressing, even painful, in recent weeks.

An X-ray film showed that I had some arthritis in both hips, which may account for the "sore thigh muscles" that have made walking often something less than a pleasure.

I relate this trouble to the only half-recognized, less than half-admitted—to myself, that is—state of being *old.* The word itself I try to avoid, even as I write it. And that is something new.

NOVEMBER 6, 1975
NEW YORK

Yesterday a two-and-a-half-hour impromptu grilling ("heckling," Anna Rosenberg, at the head of the table, called it, as a "Devil's Advocate") by five of the staff of the public relations firm of Anna M. Rosenberg Associates.

A number of times in the past I have considered the hiring of a public relations firm for D&R, and then thought better of it. I am now sure this is the time for "speaking out," to use the phrase John Macy and I have used to dub this new departure.

I was deliberately provocative in the ideas I expressed to these five sharpshooters. "Devil's Advocate" or not, I could see that these high-powered Madison Avenue types are full of nostalgia and clichés and told them so.

NOVEMBER 10, 1975
PRINCETON

The fact of my "advanced" years once in a while intrudes itself on my consciousness. This my conduct denies: my enthusiasm, my romantic notions, my planning ahead, my congenital optimism, all deny the word "old."

The joys of youth are celebrated more in retrospect, I opine, than in their occurrence. Youth is worshiped, and that is rarely more evident than today. But I can at this time more fully describe the deeper satisfactions of maturity, for these things I have: as good health as ever I have had, stamina almost without limit when it is needed by my work or pleasure, relief from the angst about money, which plagued me many of the years of getting established, and in the early New York days too.

So it is a *good* time. That it won't, can't, last forever shouldn't affect today.

NOVEMBER 15, 1975
PRINCETON

An explosion of energy, ideas, excited talk, a *do-it,* electric atmosphere: that's what happened Thursday and Friday.

I am somewhat puzzled that Macy should make all that difference.

Working with Gordon Clapp years ago, I had the satisfaction of watching a well-organized and first-rate mind at work. (I notice I just wrote "watching"—and that was often the most descriptive, the truest term.) With John Oliver there was a sense of calm but certainly no explosion of ideas. John Burnett came as close as anyone to producing the spark that set me off into a creative spin. David Morse, particularly since his illness and his steady withdrawal from the line of fire, has produced only a cordial personal warmth.

One odd thing I have noticed about my interaction with Macy. It is not only that, in his deeply earnest way, he spurs my imagination, throws back the ball of ideas I may throw into the air. It is that he is so orderly; when I launch something, new, fresh, or far from novel or worthy, I can be sure it will not be treated simply as conversation, or even hardly listened to. John writes it down in that ubiquitous black looseleaf notebook, in careful longhand, and then does something with it: a letter, a memo (he is a prodigious memo dictator, lengthy memos, good and complete and well written, if at times colorless).

The popular assumption, held by most of those who write, or are interviewed, about energy, is that the subject is simple: energy is gasoline. The "energy crisis" to them is a picture of cars lining up at filling stations unable to get all the gasoline they wanted.

Another variant is the shadow of the "Arab Embargo." And to prevent a repetition of that shutting off is the central purpose and theme of all policy issues about energy.

I must find a way of being persuasive that this is not the whole of the meaning of the energy crisis, so-called.

The fundamental nature I must somehow make clear to the American public mind.

And that fundamental understanding is far, far from being synonymous with a gasoline tank.

NOVEMBER 17, 1975
NEW YORK

An interview this morning with [John] Cunniff, the AP business editor with (so he said) 900 newspapers running his column. I disregarded the bland advice of the man from the Rosenberg firm. In short, I cut loose —about the timidity and frightened state of mind that has led to our "energy crisis"—and indicated how we should go about getting out of it: by demonstrating that this is the greatest underdeveloped country in the world.

It was good to say my say, regardless of its effects on prospective or present "clients" or D&R—just being myself.

Just before I left my office, Hal Frederiksen handed me a brief letter of resignation.

I am not really upset about Hal's resignation. This was almost inevitable; I couldn't see how Macy could do a good job of managing the company unless he had a free hand, and that would have irked Hal too much to bear. So that resignation is to the good. But I do admire Hal, like him very much, believe he has done a great deal for D&R, and for that deserves much credit, which I shall speak of tomorrow.

DECEMBER 3, 1975
NEW YORK

I took a phone call directly this noon, in the office. An excited voice: "I have just read your article in the Lima, Ohio, paper,§ and I say go right on giving them hell for being so slow." And so on, including a quote from the concluding sentence, in which I say I don't want to sound as if I were preaching. "Keep right on preaching," he said. "We're with you."

Who this was I don't know. But even though the big-city press will continue to pay no attention, here is one yelp from the grass roots. A fair trade.

DECEMBER 10, 1975
NEW YORK

Again the deep delight of hearing the Bach Aria Group at Lincoln Center. Hearing, and feeling—and in the case of the tall, dark-haired, delicious soprano—watching as well.

New York may be on the "abyss"—the word Governor Carey used

§The Cunniff interview.

yesterday—BUT where else is there so much great music to be heard, great art to be seen, so much vitality? Tonight, with the great Bach chorale still agitating me, I forget the clatter and noise and the complete immobility at noontime of mid-Manhattan.

My Cunniff AP interview certainly provided a bang of a beginning of the program of "speaking out." Eight-column headlines and big displays literally from coast to coast, in the perhaps dozen tearsheets I saw today—and probably many more to follow. I still have the ability to say provocative things, it is evident, and in this case, said things that I am betting "the country" is eager to hear. The poor tired columnists and the dull TV commentators—at least I sound alive and mad.

DECEMBER 16, 1975
PRINCETON

A session for a couple hours with two Princeton deans, Robert Jahn of Engineering and Donald Stokes of the Woodrow Wilson School. The subject: establishing a relationship with Princeton that would broaden D&R's reach for new men, drawing on the postgraduates in engineering and on whatever the Wilson School of Public and International Affairs produces. Our interest is in development, and helping inculcate the idea I have that development—not just studies—be the career of activists.

This will go well, for Princeton and for D&R, if we on our side don't commit ourselves beyond what we are capable of doing. If we hold ourselves out to provide a possible career (i.e., jobs) we should be prepared, without delay, to respond to such interest as I doubt not we will have from Princeton students and faculty too.

The fact is we aren't prepared for this, in a management sense or financially. Saying this to John alone, as I have more than once, makes little impression, so excited is he with these ideas and his new role as head of D&R. Saying the same things to these deans will, I think, implant the cautionary word with John.

Was much impressed with Dean Stokes. Not only an open and attractive man, but contrary to my early impression, quite articulate and with ideas that are in considerable contrast, in their affirmative tone and content, to John Lewis, his predecessor as dean. I think we shall hit it off well.

DECEMBER 17, 1975
NEW YORK

All day yesterday and much of the afternoon we devoted ourselves—

John Macy, Tom Mead, and I—to how best we can develop *people,* the basic resource, the ultimate source of today's much-abused term "energy." Not "people" in the broad rhetorical vague sense: but how to develop one or two young people who we find are qualified and eager to become part of the corps of developers, pioneering in a new kind of career.

We agreed to call them development interns—a term I hope will as the years go by attain as great meaning and emotional content as I feel about the concept tonight.

Strange, isn't it, that I can still get such a sense of achievement, and happiness, seeing such an idea as this take shape, a union with a great educational institution, Princeton, and a joint venture between D&R and two of the Princeton schools, the Woodrow Wilson School and the School of Engineering.

DECEMBER 21, 1975
PRINCETON

An episode Friday illustrates the way in which people try (and often succeed) in using us to "tout" their own money-making purposes. Not by engaging us—then at least the relations are open and aboveboard and can be judged by professional standards. But in slick ways.

There was a phone call from someone who identified herself simply as "Mrs. Javits" and wanted to speak to me. "He will know who I am." When I spoke to her she said, "I am doing some things for the Princess," meaning the King's sister, Ashraf. The implication was that it was something helpful to Iran; that she had been advised to see me by the Princess "who is now in Tehran."

"I may bring in a Mr. Finn."

Mr. Finn turned out to be a squat, grey-haired young man who said he was the partner of a well-known and large public relations firm, Ruder & Finn. (I wounded him by saying—I was edgy when I saw what this was all about—that I had never heard of him!)

They are going to Iran soon; expect to be employed (by whom he didn't say, but he implied it would be someone with clout in the Government) to advise Iran on its public relations problems in this country; had been told that I knew a lot about Iran and who they should see out there, etc.

I had trouble controlling my temper, and didn't entirely succeed. "You mean you are expected to 'change Iran's image' in this country?"

"No, not quite."

"What do you know about Iran?"

"Nothing, really; that's what we expected you to provide us."

No need to recite how I felt about this. It took us years and years. So in a half-hour we are expected to inform them about Iran. What Mrs. Javits said was so shockingly ignorant or askew I won't record it.

This kind of thing in one way or another presents a constant problem and a threat to D&R's good name, or the use of our time. Apparently Macy has been spending hours and hours with people, in Tehran, sent to him by David Morse. No question of a fee or a formal arrangement. What they say, of course, is, "We are associated with David Lilienthal and D&R."

The list of people who try this gambit is a long one. What can we do about it?

DECEMBER 22, 1975
NEW YORK

A shocker this morning. Our friend and "client," Jamshid Amouzegar, kidnapped, at an OPEC meeting in Vienna, schmaltzy Vienna. With him the other "oil Ministers" of OPEC. Packed into a plane by the "terrorists" (still unidentified as of this hour), flown to Algeria, then on to Libya.

"Stranger than fiction" no longer describes it.

DECEMBER 25, 1975
PRINCETON

What a good year it has been, and a year of goodness. I have discovered all over again what a fortunate man am I, living at a time when my unquenchable faith in goodness is at a premium, because the hucksters of "public opinion," the opinion shapers, as they call themselves, need to be told off.

It is so quiet here today, just Helen and me on a Christmas day, just as we really want it. Outside a whiteness, quite unmarred, snow covering everything, and particularly my beloved sleeping garden.

DECEMBER 27, 1975
PRINCETON

That one-hour "interview" with Cunniff made such a dent, was carried far and wide with blazing headlines. Why? Because I had worked out an outline?

No, it came through because I felt strongly and my words reflected feeling; the feelings were clothed in words that sprang out at Cunniff, and set him to scribbling direct quotes like mad.

I should work out, in my head, what it is I believe about the sterile vacuum of today, and the words will come.

DECEMBER 31, 1975
PRINCETON

It was a good year, with fewer of the worries and unpleasant strains, and more satisfactions at year's end than I can remember.

But the dominant feeling tonight is not one of summing up or appraising the year past, but confidence and happy anticipation of the months ahead.

It is going to be a good year.

IX

1976

~✺~

Testimony on nuclear proliferation before Senate Government Operations Committee—Vacation in Jamaica—
Low head turbines and undeveloped hydropower—Trip
to Iran—Conference of Northeast Governors on energy
and development

JANUARY 1, 1976
PRINCETON

I begin a new life each day: that I have learned long since. But clearly
a new life has begun for me, and those I love and before whom I warm
my hands and my imagination.

For me a beginning requires a dare, undertaking something beyond
my powers, beyond what I can see, but not beyond the drive I have to
accomplish something that means much to me.

And that is what I have set my heart on for the coming months: to
"speak out" about the atom.

JANUARY 3, 1976
PRINCETON

Nancy and Sylvain's sons are certainly not *vaqueros* in Colombia, as
they romantically thought or said they would be, working on a ranch
with cattle. Though they did work, and live, as farmhands. Lately they
have been the guests of the Bernardo Garces family in Cali, and apparently enjoying themselves greatly, a condition from which the presence
of two young daughters has not detracted. But they got out of their system
one kind of romance—the Colombian cowboy version.

[573]

JANUARY 9, 1976
PRINCETON

So many times, so many months, so many entries have sounded one note about D&R: financial precariousness.

Why should this seem so important? Because what I set out to do was to prove that I could be an instrument for helping people, poor and struggling people, outside government, outside foundations, and without gouging. That part of my thesis for D&R was as important as the work itself.

Last year we showed good earnings at a time when almost every other business in the country has been in a struggle. And the prospects for another good year for 1976 seem excellent.

A sad picture last night at the Century. Dana Atchley, so frail and bitter. Why he should be bitter escapes me: so many men came up to speak to him who had been his patients, who had honored him, named a building after him, given him respect. But his "machine" has worn out.

JANUARY 11, 1976
PRINCETON

What an odd feeling. Here I am wrestling with a problem without a solution: what can mankind do to save itself from utter destruction?

It is almost exactly thirty years ago (January 23, 1946, to be exact) that I sat down with four other men to face up to this problem.* The fact is that we are farther away from a satisfactory answer today, in 1976, than we were in 1946.

JANUARY 13, 1976
NEW YORK

A good day's work, after days of "thinking" once more about my old friend and antagonist (and the world's), The Atom, and what to do about it, what to do in its new guises as a widely "proliferated" object of hope but mostly, at this point, of angst.

Saturday I sketched ideas—all separate and scattered—on separate sheets. And then yesterday worked with Miss Baron at 88, as a help and a reminder that I couldn't just keep on going from one notion to another.

The product: perhaps eight pages of text, presented to a solemn "jury" this morning, as good a one as anyone ever had: Ken Fields, former

*The State Department Board of Consultants on International Control of Atomic Energy.

General Manager of AEC; John Macy; Tom Mead, intelligent but not informed about the atom—and David Morse in the very late afternoon, with the overhanging general good sense of Mildred Baron.

Then the long and wearing process of revision with four high-level kibitzers.

A good solid statement I could stand by.

"They"—that is, the jury in my office—said it was "constructive," "provocative" (I hope so), and it will have an impact on events.

JANUARY 14, 1976
NEW YORK

On December 21 last year, I wrote of a meeting I had with Mrs. Javits and Mr. David Finn of Ruder & Finn International.

Later John Macy spent some time with Finn and Mrs. Javits. He reported to me that actually the firm of Ruder & Finn, a public relations company, was trying to make a client of Iran, but he emphasized that "they do not have a client." Hardly a useful application of our time and prestige.

This would hardly be worth recording were it not for the following confirmation of my uneasiness about the whole episode, in terms of candor and the possibility of D&R being involved in what seems to me a somewhat shabby business.

Last night on the Channel 5 10 o'clock news, several minutes were given over to a rather sensational statement, namely, that Channel 5 had discovered that Mrs. Javits had since September, 1975, been registered as an agent of a foreign power, Iran, at an annual compensation of $67,500 and perhaps more; that she was on her way to Iran; that when queried about what she had done or intended to do, according to the TV reporter, it had something to do with "fine arts." Mrs. Javits also said that she was associated with the public relations firm of Ruder & Finn.

Mr. Finn, queried by the reporter, said that he did not see that there was any conflict of interest involved in the wife of a Senator who is a member of the Foreign Relations Committee being an agent for a foreign power at this salary; Mr. Finn also said he was unable to expand on what it was either Mrs. Javits or his firm will do for Iran or for OPEC.

These are people prepared to use us, our time and our prestige and the information and judgments of great value earned by more than twenty years of work; and they conduct themselves without the candor and disclosure to which we are entitled.

I take a very serious view of this whole business. At the risk of being "uncooperative and stuffy," I think we have to protect our good name and our only resource, which is our knowledge and standing.

JANUARY 17, 1976
PRINCETON

Well, that broadcast certainly did set off a flurry. With the irony that goes along with any public question, it was the employment of a Senator's wife that the press and TV made the most of.

So for forty-eight hours long spots on TV news, including a tasteless press and TV conference by Mrs. Javits.

Then this morning the Carl Byoir public relations firm says they, too, have a contract with Iran, to promote the Iran airline.

JANUARY 18, 1976
WASHINGTON

What began as a casual acceptance of an invitation to testify on nuclear proliferation before a Senate Committee promises to become quite a performance tomorrow morning. Paul Leventhal, the senior staff man of the Senate Government Operations Committee, phoned me at one o'clock Sunday, rather on the edge of excitement: "There will be a big coverage. Some members of the Committee will have some questions to ask you, and I thought you might want to know what they are beforehand." Whereupon he recited quite a number which I dutifully took down in shorthand and later transcribed. None can be answered fully. Still it is good to have them in mind.

JANUARY 19, 1976
WASHINGTON

My decision to dramatize the proliferation danger by calling for a unilateral "embargo"† certainly shook up the stance that the atomic energy establishment has been taking.

Whether my "do something, and do it now" statement may not be "historic" as the Committee staff said, it certainly will be the focus of the discussion of these issues, including the position that Kissinger may be taking in Moscow when he arrives there tomorrow.

JANUARY 20, 1976
WASHINGTON

How did it feel? To be facing again the senior circle of a Senatorial Committee, back of me the hubbub of a crowded standing room of specta-

† A moratorium on U.S. export of technology with which other countries might be able to reprocess spent nuclear-reactor fuel in order to recover bomb material—plutonium.

tors and a jammed press table, the TV lights, blinding at first and hot, the impersonal eyes of four TV cameras, the still photographers crowding before the table where I, and the two other witnesses, lined up?

This time certainly no apprehension, for I knew what I was going to say in the "prepared statement" I had thought through for more than a week, and the questions that I hoped would come would be fun to try to meet.

But the big difference came when I said—with more obvious satisfaction than was seemly: "I appear here as a *private citizen.*" Makes all the difference: I was there to say my say, bottled up for so long. But no more.

The focus of all the questioning to me and to Dr. [Hans] Bethe and Professor York, the other witnesses, was "Mr. Lilienthal's proposal for an embargo." I'm told the afternoon session of professors again was directed to dismissing my proposal. So my purpose was achieved—to stir up discussions of reality and avoid the usual "on the one hand and on the other" that surrounds most of the discussion of the atomic issue.

As Macy, Morse, and I left at the noon recess, we were met by the handsome, dapper staff leader, Leventhal. "Would you consider becoming a consultant to the Committee?" I said I would, that D&R was lucky to have a former General Manager of AEC [Kenneth Fields] as a part-time consultant and would be free for such an assignment.

I was expecting the next question. "Are you working in this field for Iran?" I interjected: "No, we have no connection with any atomic plants or companies."

Senator Percy, smiling, said: "In view of your testimony about an embargo because of the dangerous character of proliferation, have you stayed out of this field because you have a *moral* repugnance?"

"No," said I, "the reason we aren't in it is not that; no one has asked us."

Which, of course, drew something of a laugh, but I thought afterward: I hope the answer wasn't considered a frivolous one.

JANUARY 22, 1976
NEW YORK

This morning I spent an hour and a half of intensive talk with Tanner of the *Wall Street Journal*—the first *Wall Street Journal* coverage in a long, long time; Tuesday noon I had an hour with Jim Bishop, who covers energy for *Newsweek;* and then, of course, there had been, on Monday, the two and a half hours of testimony and colloquy on the proliferation issue before Senator Glenn's Committee, with a battery of four television cameras and two press tables full of correspondents, and in the afternoon, a quite stimulating hour with Elizabeth Drew, now of the *New Yorker* staff.

What really has produced all this perhaps overexposure (in contrast to the almost anonymity of the past) was the statement to John Cunniff of the Associated Press. This produced a haystack of clippings from far and wide, all over the country. In talking to Cunniff this morning on the phone—the first time I have exchanged views with him—he said that I had expressed skepticism about the impact of what I had said to him in the interview in this office; he reminded me that he had been puzzled by my skepticism and had predicted that the keynote of the interview was one that the country would respond to, was ripe for, was waiting for. Did I still have reservations about the receptivity to these ideas and particularly the themes that dealt not simply with energy in the narrow sense (e.g., electricity) but human energy and the spirit of a country restless and impatient with the timidity of leadership?

I said that ten newspaper reactions would have persuaded me, but a thousand certainly confirmed his case. Which is, of course, my case too.

But skepticism about whether the country would pay any attention to me has been removed in the sense that the newspaper coverage has been phenomenal and gratifying and so far serious. Indeed, no backlash yet. That result is a very reassuring one and personally very satisfying. So satisfying and gratifying that the physical wear and tear has not been visible. It seems to me I feel better even without sleep or decent rest than I would if I were pacing myself judiciously.

Yesterday afternoon a visit from Leventhal, a journalist by profession, who had previously been "press officer" for Senator Javits. He said he came to explore with me how much help I could provide the Committee when it began to "mark up the bill"—professional jargon for getting the bill before the Committee ready for voting in the Committee and later before the Senate. During the hearings we had promised that we would submit comments on the bill itself, from the point of view of both substance and whatever legal questions occurred to us.

But the point of Leventhal's talk with us (David Morse was with me part of the time) here in the office was the possibility of serving as a consultant or advisor to the Committee on the broad questions that go beyond the bill itself, which is essentially directed toward the organization, or reorganization, of the Federal Government's functions dealing with the export of nuclear technology.

Leventhal did not imply that he had any authority to speak on the possibility of an advisory role, but he certainly offered himself as a communication belt to the three Senators and personally (if his words were literally to be believed) would recommend such a relationship. And this is before all the witnesses before the Committee have concluded; the hearings go on at least through next week.

Leventhal expanded on this theme. Would I consider bringing together a group who could prepare a "Lilienthal report on atomic energy control," as one might say, "thirty years after"—that is, as a sequel, a contemporary sequel to our Board of Consultants Report of 1946?

Of course, I did not make a commitment on this, except to say that the matter of lack of funds adequate to cover the two or three months that such a report might require on the part of such a group would not be the decisive factor. In other words, anything as serious and as potentially helpful in the public domain should not be prevented from happening for financial reasons. I assume that the Committee itself would not have enough funds for such an undertaking, though he assured me that they do have funds for "consultants," whatever that means.

JANUARY 23, 1976
PRINCETON

The satisfaction I get out of reading just for pleasure. My multiple-book way of reading has its own delights. Variety; change of pace; diversity. The multiple-book habit goes way back, though I'm not sure that I have ever noted it in these journals.

Presently the roster includes Travis McGee (a John MacDonald creation), Ed McBain and his 87th Precinct police characters, then the sad story of the failure of the League of Nations, C. P. Snow's Trollope, Wain's delightful but semi-erudite biography of Samuel Johnson, a life of Talleyrand, begun last summer, as well as Malone's Jefferson—and so on.

I find I can pick up a book I began a day ago and left unfinished, for the time being, and one I began three months ago, and it goes on as if there was no interregnum.

Now I have just begun Jim Bishop's *FDR's Last Year.* Which reminds me of how I wept recently over the TV version of *Eleanor and Franklin,* based on Joe Lash's book (a beautifully inscribed message from Joe in our copy here, worth preserving).

JANUARY 31, 1976
PRINCETON

It turns out that it was only because I took a strong and readily understandable position that the drift to nuclear catastrophe is being seriously considered as a political issue. I believe that. Anything else would simply produce one more "study," one more analysis. I called for action, and action stimulates thought better than studies.

FEBRUARY 2, 1976
PRINCETON

As of this hour my "dramatic, even shocking" proposal of nuclear embargo doesn't seem quite so quixotic and "naive" (one of the academic-style witnesses called it!).

McGeorge Bundy had said, "But how do you expect to move the French?," meaning it can't be done. Well, last week the French and the South Koreans cancelled out their outrageously dangerous plans for a nuclear fuel cycle sale and purchase.

Further, before the same Senate Committee I appeared before only two weeks ago, a representative of the General Accounting Office gave a dismal and negative view of how effective the International Control Agency had been as to inspections and safeguards—a position that sweeps away the views of those who pictured my embargo idea as quite unnecessary—what we have can be patched up by a few bits of cosmetic tape.

FEBRUARY 5, 1976
NEW YORK

A long telephone conversation with Paul Leventhal.

We had previously discussed a misunderstanding of my testimony about an embargo—namely, that it was put forward as an inflexible position. The *New York Times* editorial and Senator Glenn's own comments seem to make clear that I am talking about an embargo as the only alternative left to us in our efforts to get genuine safeguards.

Without disclosing to whom the letter was written, I quoted the following from the second paragraph of my letter to Hans Bethe:

> The chief purpose of the proposal in my own testimony was to try to focus attention on the urgent need for an American and international consensus and policy for action on this grave issue. My proposal of a unilateral embargo or interim moratorium on export I thought might serve to sharpen what has become a diffuse discussion and clarify the need for action. Most of all I wanted to try to offset defeatism about proliferation: that "nothing can be done about it by anyone."

This surely indicates that we are talking about a means of ameliorating and fortifying efforts toward strengthening and making real the safeguard system.

Leventhal told me that Hans Bethe had written Senator Glenn with an "afterthought." Bethe's conclusion is that the best procedure would be to "patiently" discuss these matters with other nations and try to make them see that it was in their own interest to join in anti-proliferation measures.

What have we been doing, while this proliferation has mounted, except try to persuade other countries, beginning with Russia in 1947 and 1948 and going on to India for that matter, in 1974?

Someday I would like to find time to write another piece about the lack of political—i.e., human—understanding of the rarefied style of scientists, of which breed Bethe is one of the best and most lovable. Curious how he failed to recognize that he himself was strongly urging an embargo, and not a temporary one, on isotope separation facilities and breeder reactor technology.

I said I noted that last June the "supplier countries" (that would be Russia, Britain, France, West Germany, and the U.S.) were having "a very secret meeting" in London (according to the *New York Times*) to develop guidelines and principles about the conditions under which they would supply non-nuclear countries, all for the purpose of minimizing the dangers of utilization of nuclear facilities and fuel for the making of weapons.

Leventhal said that they did agree on extending the safeguards to the realm of know-how. But they did not agree on any ban on the export of fuel facilities to individual countries.

So what all this fanfare produced is an agreement that when facilities have been exported and transferred from supplier to "customer" countries on an individual country basis, the technical know-how that makes it possible to keep such facilities going should be under safeguards. Big deal.

The testimony from a Deputy Secretary of State simply says that we have all this under control and that even the passage of this reorganization bill would be contrary to the State Department's policies, which regard the export of nuclear technology and materials as part of the ways of keeping our "allies" happy with us.

FEBRUARY 10, 1976
PRINCETON

My first Princeton "teaching" exposure, as I faced the rising tier of seats and faces at the Woodrow Wilson School yesterday late afternoon.

I asked that this be announced as "a conversation with David Lilienthal on the management of development."

The opener: we have been told that "the business of America is business."

I suggest that the phrase should be: "the business of America is development."

I went on from there to talk about opportunities for a professional career.

The question part of the "conversation" led me into, improvising, some of the strongest comments I have made, in public certainly, about the low state of the business community's ethics. The papers each day tell of shoddy bribing by major multinational companies of those in foreign countries who can influence the purchase of American goods, particularly aircraft.

I took a poke at John Connor's new "profits are for people" publicity campaign, when his company, Allied Chemical, has been guilty of a crude misfeasance in the treatment of employees badly hurt by the poisons they have been handling.

Much excitement these days about the safety of atomic reactors in this country. Resignations of three G.E. engineers, followed by a spectacular resignation of Robert Pollard, a principal technical man in the regulatory branch of what was AEC. Unsafe, he said about a big plant on the Hudson serving Con Ed.

My question: how can we export reactors, and permit licensees of these U.S. designers to export, when we aren't yet sure how safe they are for the U.S.?

FEBRUARY 12, 1976
NEW YORK

Long letter from Macy, about his meeting with Amouzegar, who spent most of the time reciting the horrors of his kidnapping from Vienna. He is almost compulsively prepared to talk about it. Amouzegar makes mention of his religious belief in preordained destiny. But it took more than faith in Allah to account for his display of courage in facing and managing that situation. He is very critical of OPEC security, the official behavior of the Austrian Government, the effectiveness of international police work, and the capacity of governments involved to collaborate meaningfully in such an emergency.

He became a special target not so much for his OPEC leadership but because of the terrorists' hostility toward Iran because of its military involvement in the State of Oman.

FEBRUARY 16, 1976
PRINCETON

The D&R Papers, as an institution, are no longer just an idea of mine. The new Princeton librarian, [Dick] Boss, described the progress, and the physical result that is emerging: a several-hundred-page "catalog," a kind of index and guide to the use of this massive collection. There never has been so large a manuscript collection, said he. The catalog will be some five hundred pages long, printed, and will be sent to most of the places where there might be interest in using the story.

I jumped over lightly the fact that what Princeton has received is only a fraction of the total of the papers of D&R, which of course are increasing as we go along. Among the most notable new material are the hundreds and hundreds of pages of memos being written by the Iran Public Sector Management group.

Some of this will have great historic interest two decades from now, said Boss, and having seen how extraordinarily candid the interviews are, I thought to myself: maybe in two decades, but certainly this material must not be available for some years, for some of it would be a firecracker in the Iran setting today.

FEBRUARY 18, 1976
NEW YORK

We have had almost all manner of troubles in Khuzistan: a big flood, drought, dust storms, and day before yesterday, a tornado that flattened many of the transmission towers and put an end to power service to the Haft Tapeh area, in some places for seventy-five hours.

But there is a good, an exciting and satisfying side to the tornado. It is the word that the training for hot-line maintenance by Iranians—the symbol of our confidence in what these people could do—has paid off in a crunch. Apparently the maintenance crews went at the restoration of service—a tricky business at best—with real professional skill and patience.

Makes me proud of the tradition of D&R and KDS, to believe in the people so much that even such a way-out and dangerous skill as restoring power after a tornado is not beyond them.

FEBRUARY 21, 1976
JAMAICA, WEST INDIES

We *did* get away for a breather, after all. Slept the sleep of a child last night. No whirring in my head of ideas, or worries. Just the kind of vegetating I need after weeks of high excitement.

Reading Jim Bishop's *FDR's Last Year* (April 1944–1945).
Here is a passage that was pure F.D.R., trying to break an impasse at Yalta over whether France should be given a seat on the German

584]   *The Journals of David E. Lilienthal*

Control Commission (it is startling, considering what happened afterward):

> The President had a device . . . to introduce an innocuous but sensitive subject unrelated to the matter in hand.
> He began to speak of Iran claiming that 99% of the tribes were in bondage to 1%. It was a "very, very backward nation." If such poor nations were to institute a plan requiring five years, or even ten, and allow the 99% to purchase small pieces of property to farm them and be permitted to sell produce; if the rulers would study the American plan of the Tennessee Valley Authority which displayed in grandeur what could be done to store water and manufacture electricity for cheap rural electricity, these backward countries would in time become good customers.

FEBRUARY 26, 1976
JAMAICA

Franklin Roosevelt's death brought tears and shock in April, thirty-one years ago. To me, at my desk in Knoxville; to millions all over the world. But that was so long ago, so much has happened since, to all of us.

And yet, as I read the story again this morning in the remarkable book by Jim Bishop, once again the lump in my throat, the ache in the middle of my chest, the swelling of the eyes into tears.

He did his job as he saw it. Who are you not to do yours, to the end, wherever and whenever that "end" may come?

FEBRUARY 27, 1976
JAMAICA

Years ago when I would be exhausted and go away to recuperate, I would fight myself if I was tempted to think or to "work," when I was supposed to be banishing serious thought. Not this time.

I have been jumping up to jot down, strangely enough, in longhand, phrases that might fit into the Washington Planning Society speech, one I want very much to be another step in the "speaking out" regime I have set out for myself.

Now reading the last pages of what has been more than a book: a personal experience, *FDR's Last Year*. Truman, at eight in the morning, at the desk in the Oval Room, for the beginning of his first day, plugging away at a speech to a joint session of Congress, though there are "speech writers" who could spare him. Bishop throws this in:

"The weakness of the strong man is that he courts exhaustion."

MARCH 5, 1976
PRINCETON

Ed Thompson, editor of the sprightly magazine *Smithsonian,* wrote asking me to contribute some writing or ideas. The head of the Coal Association, Carl Bagge, invited me to be the keynote speaker at the Association's annual meeting, and spoke warmly of my position on energy expressed in a speech back in 1963.

I have been complaining to Beatrice that I was getting very little help on my "speaking out" drive from the Anna Rosenberg outfit; these and other instances show how little I need a professional public relations firm at high cost.

MARCH 9, 1976
NEW YORK

Got off my chest how I feel about corruption, the single most important issue these days. And where more appropriately than as the lead-off speaker to the Iranian Investors Conference at Asia House this morning.

A hush went over the audience of perhaps seventy-five people, half Iranians, the others middle-level New York businessmen. The papers here, and in Iran, have been full of the subject of corruption, a "shameful" story, as I said. But it wasn't the kind of realism that these largely technical "social scientist" characters were accustomed to.

What I said was simply what I replied to all those American businessmen's questions to me: Is it necessary to pay off for contracts in Iran? Is it required that one have an "agent"? I said: "I have been working, with my company, in Iran now for exactly twenty years, and *not once* was it ever so much as hinted that someone needed to be an intermediary for pay, that 'influence' was needed or to be used."

I went on to say that when such a situation had arisen—this was *not* in Iran—we simply immediately cancelled our contracts. If the price of being straight is to lose contracts or business, surely that will be worth paying, for the very foundation of private business is integrity. Integrity of contracts, integrity of dealing, and if that goes, nothing is left.

At the luncheon Ambassador Zahedi gave a splendid extemporaneous speech about relations between the two countries; moderate, sensible, well spoken.

MARCH 11, 1976
NEW YORK

Iran is creating a serious problem by not paying its bills, according to a long account in this morning's *Times*. My feeling about Iran is at a pretty low ebb, at this point, not because, as has happened so many, many times in the past, they are slow in making their payments to us, but because the evidence of bad judgment and unwillingness, for the most part, to face up to this marks most of what they do these days.

Nevertheless, when Phil Talbot phoned me asking on his behalf and John Rockefeller's of Asia House that I join in an invitation to the Queen to a public dinner in New York, I said that they could put the invitation with my name attached. If and when I put an end to my Iranian involvement, refusing to join in such an invitation isn't the way to do it.

Besides, I think the Queen represents the brightest hope for wide humanist concern in the entire establishment.

About yesterday in Washington:

Ken Fields and I met for about an hour with the Chief of the Army Corps of Engineers, Lt. Gen. Gribble. A soldierly-looking man; wearing his three stars and campaign ribbons seemed quite in place, though he is essentially an administrator of construction activities all over.

The General was candor itself. He knows how TVA introduced new concepts into river development and concern for other things than just building structures. He quite generously said that the Corps today is quite different in the range of its understanding of social responsibilities for its construction work than ten or fifteen years ago.

Looking back on the years when TVA and the Corps were by no means on friendly terms as to objectives or interests, this was quite a thing, I thought, to say to the former head of TVA, sitting there in his office.

Then to Robert Seamans, head of the Energy Research and Development Agency, in brand-new offices, in an eyesore of a building, in the worst possible taste, the kind that keep sprouting all over Washington, every fortnight.

Seamans is very tall, somewhat stooped, white hair, a youthful, quizzical face. I was puzzled that his manner gave no outward sign of the kind of concern or urgency I showed when I was in his spot, nor recognition of the current failure of the program entrusted to him, with its rhetoric of high-flown objectives, set first by Nixon and then by Ford.

It was evident that the atomic energy industry is in quite a flutter at this point. What kind of leadership they have I can't make out. But that once again they are going to try to discredit the motives of those who are crowding in on the program is evident.

The seemingly amused above-the-battle demeanor of Robert Seamans adds up to no good.

Then we marched on to the Coal building and the greatest extrovert I have met in a long time: Carl Bagge. There is a character. "Think of it; the first Chairman of AEC makes a pilgrimage to the home of the coal industry—we must record this in pictures." Which of course he did.

I managed to get him to talk about the people in the coal industry.

The picture he drew of how confused is the Washington Government picture, the indignity of Congressional hearings, and ineptitude, was a serious story, when the wind was taken out of his overeager approach.

MARCH 17, 1976
NEW YORK

Plugging away on the Washington speech, which is becoming quite a "statement." It will be the first time I have taken the offensive about the Acheson-Lilienthal Plan, ascribing the acute atomic tension now between Pakistan and India to failure to hang firmly to the basic objectives of that 1946 plan. I'll not make any friends among the scientists and their Atoms for Peace with this. I soft-pedalled this in my Senate Committee testimony; not so in the draft I now have.

My style is not only oral but conversational and hard-hitting. As David Morse said yesterday: "You have an instinct for the jugular." Wise or not, prudent or not to say these things, I'm going to say them, next Monday.

MARCH 25, 1976
NEW YORK

A firsthand report from Bernardo of the "adventures" of Daniel Bromberger in Colombia really made my day. Bernardo's obvious affection and loyalty to this remarkable wayfarer in a strange land was such that we lost the sense of embarrassment and awkwardness because the Garces family had Daniel on their hands week after week, rescuing him from his visaless existence.

Nancy and Sylvain, both looking quite perky, had dinner with Helen and me at Le Chanteclair, to thank Bernardo and his family. The tales of Daniel's journeys, his relish and zest in seeing the country non-tourist-style, were so refreshing.

MARCH 27, 1976
PRINCETON

On Monday morning (the 22nd), I spent a couple of hours with the managing editor (Simons) of the *Washington Post* and six or seven of his reporters and co-editors. They had not read my forthcoming speech to the Planners' National Conference, but said that what I considered my chief point was about the opposite of what was generally believed—i.e., that the size and complexity of changes increased the stature of the individual rather than diminished it.

My point, so central to the whole set of ideas, that this is a different country now because it is becoming more and more diffused and decentralized—that point had no "takers."

What they asked about the future of atomic energy and proliferation were banal questions.

I did have an hour with a lively fellow, O'Toole, the energy and environment specialist, they said. Tried to get him aroused by my own increasing interest in the potential hydroelectric energy in this country. He even showed some interest in one of my vagrant notions that small-scale, low-head turbines hydro installations have a considerable future.

My speech in the evening was received with acclaim, interspersed with applause or laughter at my digs, and a closing ovation.

I haven't lost the ability to hold a big audience motionless through a forty-minute speech. The ideas in the speech appealed, so the long tussle to get it out and on paper was worth it.

But at this point, it is the effect on me and on the audience that moves me; I shook hands with I guess a hundred people, exchanged greetings.

An old geezer said: "You are the youngest man in this whole conference."

This was in contrast to the complete and total disregard of the speech by the press in Washington or New York. Not a line. In short, it just didn't seem to be news.

Time was when this would have been a big disappointment. Particularly after I had spent so much time and intellectual agony drafting and redrafting and wrestling with the ideas. But, by now, I recognize that what makes news in the eyes of a newspaper editor is not a serious piece, however challenging some of the statements may be.

MARCH 29, 1976
PRINCETON

A call from John Macy, from Iran, about the signing by Alimard of a contract extending the Public Sector Management contract for another year—a confirmation of the importance of the work and of the standing of Alimard, and an assurance that $2 million will be forthcoming.

Saturday night, dinner with the Sitwells, Celia (the robust and highly talented daughter of the late Paul Sachs of Harvard) and Dick, archeologist of the Morgantina dig in Sicily, and in Greece.

The other guests were also of academic distinction, including the head of the Princeton art department and his soft-spoken and appealing wife, and Julian Boyd.

These are what in public service circles are Elder Statesmen. They seem so secure, sure of themselves, genteel until it hurts for one like myself given too often these days to some earthiness of expression, and, activist as I am, fidgety in the presence of such concentration on a narrow segment of life of another time.

I was much impressed, not to say cowed. Later it was pointed out to me that I should not feel so defensive, that Elder Statesmen and their younger brethren too, in academe, live in a narrow cubicle of life, where they know more than anyone else, but (many of them) little else do they know or understand.

MARCH 31, 1976
NEW YORK

Dis-a-pernted, to say the very least, that there was not a line in the *Times* or *Washington Post* reporting that speech to the Planners on which I had set such store. Rationalized it: there was no "news" in it by current journalistic standards, also the press release prepared by the Rosenberg characters missed the point completely.

Then a call from Helen: "Your roses have arrived from Starr ... and the *Vineyard Gazette* printed your whole speech in its last week's edition." Is this some kind of joke, they who are so sparing, parsimonious in fact, about carrying speeches and such?

Immediately, a phone call from Scotty Reston. Said he: "I'm calling to congratulate you on a very good speech."

Then this noon as John Macy and I were leaving the Century, we greeted John Oakes at the door. Said he, "Dave, that was a very good speech you made the other day in Washington." Me, still smarting just a tiny bit: But where did you read it? It wasn't reported in the *Times* or the *Post*. "I read it in the strongest competitor of the *Times*," and grinned; of course, it was the *Gazette*. Which does reach a selection of the "opinion formers" (in the winter, when they have time to read), that tribe about which I express such scorn.

Macy and I had a most productive day. Between us, I think we may have hit upon a theme for the energy program for this country about which I am so intent these days. My thought: that we develop a balanced program in which "the public interest" is the key, that being the note most needed, as we see it, in developing new sources of energy; the very considerable change the business organizations (coal, atomic energy, and hydro) have neglected in their statements and public plans. Yet it is their derelictions in this sector that have given them the most trouble in mounting and achieving new energy sources.

John came up with a term to connect this approach to the underlying basis of D&R: integrated. We added, speaking as one voice: and draw upon the technical resources of Princeton.

APRIL 3, 1976
PRINCETON

Last night celebrating Helen's birthday we had a gala dinner at Lahiere's, here in Princeton.

Trying to find a theme for the talk I'm to give to the American Philosophical Society on the 24th, in Philadelphia. I'm told that this Society, founded by Benjamin Franklin, will provide an audience of scholars in the humanities and physical sciences almost as distinguished as that which meets in Boston under the aegis of the American Academy of Arts and Sciences.

I extemporized to Helen yesterday morning, in a style of preparing ideas for a speech or article we have been following now these many years. The *time* in the history of the Republic calls for the kind of declaration I could make.

Cocktails this evening at Joe and Kitty Johnson's, with the green and pink of the surrounding trees seen through the high windows.

Guests included the Lamsons. She has just finished a biography of Roger Baldwin, based chiefly, I gather, on his papers about the American Civil Liberties Union, which are housed here at Firestone Library. The fact that we, who have known Roger as a man so well and so long, were not interviewed indicates it will not be a very personal picture of the man. Similarly, no interview with Tom Benton or Bernardine Fritz, for that matter.

APRIL 4, 1976
PRINCETON

A phone call from Florence: the resonant, sturdy voice of David, wishing his mother a happy birthday, followed by the voice of Davey (not so heavy a voice), then darling Margaret and Peggy. And later an exuberant call from Mike, very high about how well his pottery design is going, the new things they are trying—very much the successful artist-cum-businessman. And then Nancy, the quiet one, with another birthday message. At this point, the rewards for the years of anxiety, of care, and of just plain boredom—housework isn't all that enchanting, as everyone knows—are amply repaid.

A caller here this afternoon—Gail Russell—a graduate student at Princeton. Asked to see me because she is writing her Ph.D. thesis on regional development and planning in France. I recalled our visit through France back in the fifties as the guest of the then French Minister of Plan, Jean Monnet, who was at that time creating a great regional plan known as the Schuman Plan, which evolved into the Common Market.

Miss Russell has already found that planning—on its merits—has suffered in France; now they simply pick out some area that can bring in votes because it is depressed and "make contracts for a project" without respect to any plan.

I learned every bit as much in the hour and a half in our living room from this fresh-faced young woman as ever she did from me.

APRIL 7, 1976
NEW YORK

Durable. Some rare people are just that, and how admirable I find them for that quality. It is certainly the word—and the quality—to describe John Burnett, with whom yesterday I had a visit, the first in many months.

More than five years sweating it out with perhaps the biggest urban development program in this country, the New York Urban Development Corporation.

John still gives me the impression, as he did when we worked together, of a collected, compact, middleweight boxer, a big grin, explosive laugh, the once highly mobile hand gestures a bit restrained. But not visibly touched by the tough things that have happened to him, in his work and in his personal life.

I wish I could think of some effective way of having the benefit, for me and for D&R, of one of the liveliest minds I have ever known.

APRIL 9, 1976
PRINCETON

A cool spring—but still, it *is* spring; and in Princeton that means flowering trees—the tulip magnolia, the weeping cherries throwing their gossamer nets of lavender over the graceful limbs, the still flashing gold of forsythia (more abundant this spring than ever), and everywhere the saucy jonquils.

APRIL 18, 1976
PRINCETON

That great moment when I look out of my window to the east in the early morning and there is the Old Man Apple Tree, a solid mass of blossoms.

I have become so personally identified with that ancient tree: it is hollowed at the base, the trunk wrinkled in folds like an elephant's hide. But there is more than enough life in the old boy to put out graceful branches and the exuberance of blossoms and, later, fruit.

The bark is obviously full of vitality—otherwise why the exuberant branches, and then, today, the festoon of blooms, as fresh and vital as any I have ever seen.

I wouldn't say exactly that—in the contemporary jargon—I have an apple-tree fetish; but that tree does sustain me as I plan ahead for weeks of vigorous activity.

APRIL 20, 1976
NEW YORK

The substantive impression of my visit at Lazard yesterday is a clear one: weak as he may be, absent for a year from his office, André Meyer is still "in command." Not a detail can be decided without André's approval.

Said Hettinger: "André still runs this organization—and Paris, too—like a French feudal barony." I think I know what that means.

APRIL 21, 1976
NEW YORK

David Morse, at his suggestion, sat in my office reading aloud to me the final of my American Philosophical Society "discourse." Making reservations for his habitual generosity and enthusiasm, he seemed greatly pleased: "This is poetry, poetry. This is the best you have ever done. You *are* a writer."

I myself had some reservations: that the style was somewhat too elaborate. But for the kind of immediate audience, perhaps not. I did have in it, in my best "pejorative" mood, some biting things to say about the drift of economics into a "heartless" mathematics, and scorn for the "limits of growth" sloppiness and the sophomoric mentality that produced it.

APRIL 25, 1976
PRINCETON

Since yesterday noon I am dubbed "philosopher," officially. Well, not quite: I was called before the American Philosophical Society's gathering, with Franklin, Washington, and Jefferson looking on (from their portraits in the classic room of the Society's home) and formally inducted into the Society as a member. Despite my "discourse" that followed, later in the morning, I did not have my membership revoked.

In the course of his rapid-fire speech, the speaker just preceding me, the Solicitor General of the U.S., Robert Bork (mine was the one to close the Annual Meeting), made a comment to support a point he was making. It is, I think, a classic of contemporary public life, and was uttered with complete seriousness by Bork.

As an illustration of something or other, this is what he said:

"A member of Congress was expected to address the Society on an aspect of democracy in the U.S., the future (or lack of it) of Federalism. But he cancelled his participation with this explanation: 'My two speech writers could not agree on what I think on the subject.' "

That story is not only humorous, it tells a lot.

I did not think I did my best, as to delivery, and about my public-speaking ability I am hopelessly proud—after all I have been doing this since I was in high school, not to say college, and ever since. At one point my voice broke, something I can't remember happening before.

But the theme and content were extraordinarily well received. If, as such a commentator as Reston believes, the strength of Carter's appeal is to the self-esteem of the American people and to an innate spiritual quality, certainly that is what this discourse said, and the highly sophisticated audience certainly showed that they "liked" it.

APRIL 26, 1976
PRINCETON

A great sense of relief: my brother Ted got through this morning's surgery, at Jefferson Hospital in Philadelphia, with "vital signs satisfactory"—I suppose that means heart and blood pressure. We visited with him Saturday afternoon, at the hospital. Once more I realized how dear he is to me, what an utterly sweet nature, so natural, so good.

APRIL 28, 1976
NEW YORK

As the courtly and solemn Julian Boyd opened the afternoon proceedings last Saturday in the history-soaked and quite beautiful hall of the American Philosophical Society, he said, clearing his throat: "I want now to report on a meeting of the Executive Committee of your Society. We have concluded to press forward with the program for the meetings of the coming year even more strenuously than in the Society year that is now being concluded under my presidency. One conclusion we reached was that the Society would select and inaugurate younger members."

Then without a hitch, he said: "I have now a further announcement to make. The Executive Committee with the concurrence of the Society has elected to membership Mr. David E. Lilienthal, who I will now ask to step forward and to sign the historic book of membership."

That the first election of a younger member turned out to be a gent who is approaching his 77th birthday was a joke that apparently escaped everyone but Helen M. Lilienthal and D.E.L.

A pretty much sleepless night last night induced by the old demon of no cash in the till, or the advancing dark shadow of a payroll to meet without the wherewithal to meet it. How many times, O Lord, do I have to go through this?

David Morse may have saved the day and my peace of mind. He knows how tenuous our cash situation is. Said he about his talk with Sheldon Bass and Robert Helander of IBEC: "Finding the money to keep D&R in funds against the more than a million dollars which Iran owes D&R is our job; that is what we are paid for. We should not expect Dave Lilienthal to have to become involved in solving that problem unless it comes to the place where we have failed and his involvement is essential, and that should not happen."

A great happiness tonight, a very special kind of joy. Benny Goodman and an extraordinarily alive group playing great jazz to an audience of mostly outwardly staid and grey-haired Centurions and their wives. How the stern, bewhiskered portraits nearly popped off the wall of the lounge —and then as the whole place rang and burst with the excitement and rhythm of the classic jazz, even those old boys seemed to join in the verve and dash. The pianist, a huge and very black woman, made the piano shake, the cornet blasted the air, the drums reverberated—most of all was Benny the Great, with notes so pure and cadence so delightful that he transformed that often rather gloomy place into a sensual jangle of sound and motion.

Then, with the Tobeys, we went to what has become a rather famous musical of the season: *A Chorus Line.* A new idea—and a new idea for a show-business kind of musical play is mighty hard to come by.

MAY 2, 1976
PRINCETON

Helen and I gardened—with a vengeance—she putting in her beloved bright-eyed pansies, I digging swaths of astilbe to fill the gaps here and there. Now—it is 8:30 and the sun is down, ushering in the most gazelle-like thin new moon in a smoky blue sky—Helen is still at the pace she sets, but now not the trowel, but the everlasting Index for Volume VI, the last throes, we both hope.

Thursday night, April 29, at a dinner meeting of the Twentieth Century Fund. The speaker the redoubtable and somber (professionally somber, I thought) Felix Rohatyn. The subject, the woes of New York City, which has been in the intensive-care department now for months, being administered fiscal digitalis, poor-mouth-to-mouth resuscitation—a sorry story and one Felix refused to predict will save the patient from just what I'm not too clear, though it is referred to by the commercial equivalent: bankruptcy. The right term?

To my great surprise, I spoke up as soon as Felix concluded: the alleviation of New York's problems is not solely in these fiscal remedies. The problem of New York is not New York but the lack of economic development in the region upon which New York must depend. (This thesis was taken up again at the full board meeting the following day.)

MAY 4, 1976
NEW YORK

Everyone is going around in circles, saying the same damned things about the energy problem. Where is there a new idea for this vexed problem? Is it in fact a "problem"; haven't we been sucked in by our own and our so-called leaders' rhetoric, all this call for a "national energy policy"? A dud.

Late in the day expounded to David Morse an idea about a new departure in the proliferation morass: that we propose to Dr. Seamans [of the Energy Research and Development Agency] how he might solve the fierce confrontation between Iran and Pakistan about an atomic fuel-processing venture, an undertaking that would provide the *materials* for atomic bombs aplenty for Iran, Pakistan, and India, with the merciless commercialism of Germany and the French who will do anything to sell this fiendish equipment no matter what.

The idea: to propose once more as I did many months ago to the Shah that the three countries form a regional reprocessing enterprise supervised by the International Atomic Energy Agency, as near an approach to internationalization as now is reasonably attainable.

I thought my spiel impressed Morse. But would it impress Seamans, and in turn, the heads of those countries? Worth the trial, just the same.

At the Century, had a quite delightful dinner. The head of the Audubon Society and a leader in the World Wildlife Federation talked about birds and beasts; so much more relaxing than about human beings. Indeed, people whose preoccupation is with birds and animals look so much more relaxed and fresh than those who, like myself, deal with people and heartaches.

Ten minutes ago the phone rang; it was Helen. "I don't quite know how to tell you . . ." Of course, I thought: It is bad news about Ted. But no.

"Dave, Michael Lilienthal has committed suicide."

Pam, according to Helen, who talked with her, quite composed. Pam asked Nancy to call Peggy and David in Florence. Which she did—a painful task.

With Anne's help, Mike had pulled out of a period of self-doubt and at times flight from life. But with the achievements of their work and their business at a high point—why, why? No one will ever know.

MAY 10, 1976
NEW YORK

We talked to David Sunday. His voice and manner quite shattered. I grieve so for him: a great blow, about Mike. Anne told us later he had a nervous breakdown. "Mike just snapped," she said.

Both of us so full of admiration for Pam and Annie. "We have got to be strong, strong," said Anne in that thin little-girl voice. But she is not a little girl, and hasn't been: a remarkable person, and we feel as close to her as if she were our own.

Helen finished the Index to Volume VI late last night—a big and laborious job. This morning Harper's Corona Machemer, quite excited and friendly, phoned to read me the first review, from *Publishers Weekly.*

Such a good one. Confirms from a professional bookselling source Beatrice's appraisal of many months ago, that this is the best of the volumes for the general reader. The text I expect to see tomorrow, but it is a most reassuring clue of what we may expect when the book is actually in hand —which is still at least a month off.

At a meeting a couple weeks ago, Stuart Harris, the publicity chief for Harper's, got off a most discouraging negative comment: "This book doesn't have much that is exciting in it, such as there was in the other volumes." From a corner seat, the delightful smiling Corona Machemer said, in a barely audible voice: "Nothing happened in the volume: except a war."

That did it.

MAY II, 1976
NEW YORK

Sigvard Eklund, head of perhaps the most important of all United Nations agencies, was obviously sobered and "impressed" as I came into his office at the UN building this afternoon with David Morse and General Fields.

As we left he turned on the warmth and excitement he quite obviously felt, to have had in his office a person he must have thought had become a stuffy elder statesman living on the past. What I talked about, with considerable passion and particularity, was the present and the future—the increasingly alarming spread of atomic weapons; each week adds to the fears I expressed before the Senate Committee.

At the end he told me how much he had "heard" about me, but what impressed him most, so he said, was to see on Harry Smyth's bookshelves in Vienna, the *Journals of . . .* etc.

He is stocky, very European, grey-haired. When I said that on his shoulders as head of the International Atomic Energy Agency the gravest responsibility of any man in the public sector today rested, he acknowledged that statement as an evident truth. A good basis for our talk: the continuing story of one nation after another yielding to the commercial (and political) advances of the German and the French manufacturing interests.

But he sought affirmative, positive signs. One was that he did believe that Euratom (the atomic energy agency of the Common Market) would finally and shortly join the NPT (Nuclear Nonproliferation Treaty) nations. That perhaps Japan would come in. And that if any nation wants to make weapons, the simple way would not be by a commercial power reactor but by the straightforward way we did at Hanford—skip the atomic reactor phase entirely—and this they are not doing at the moment, although apparently this is the way India made its bombs, and Israel.

I did come away feeling that this guy is very much in earnest and on to his job. Perhaps in this high estimate I am influenced—and why not? —by the fact that the very point of my Senate Committee statement was the one he, although an international public servant, kept repeating— "Why is it that America has not asserted itself? Or—to use the phrase of your Senate statement—taken the initiative?"

Why indeed.

Two Rockefeller brothers at close quarters are quite enough of "The Family" for one small gathering, at the Center for Latin American Affairs.

I was quite moved that all this intimate acclaim, bringing those "prominent figures" out on a rainy night, was to pay respect to Berent Friele, an advisor to "The Family" for so many years—and what a good job he has done.

I can add only one item for future historians about Nelson, as a result of this close exposure.

He wears short sox, and without garters. All the rest of his act has been witnessed, thanks to TV and radio, many times. And it is a good and I believe a sincere performance. Forget the easy clichés about the dignity of man, the importance of people. I have the feeling he doesn't think of them as worn clichés at all.

"The happy time"—I am almost quoting verbatim—was during the days of F.D.R. And that could well be just what he meant.

In Berent's acknowledgment of the "award," he referred to me, and particularly our efforts in Brazil's São Francisco. Which is very much like him, for he did the kind of "helping hand" service for me in Brazil that he has done for Nelson Rockefeller for several decades. Berent had a sense of conviction about what we were trying to do for Brazil.

MAY 14, 1976
PRINCETON

For the very first time during this goofy "primary" campaign, a candidate discusses a real issue: the spread of atomic bomb capacities. A speech by Governor Carter covered extensively by the *Times.*

Through the whole speech and the news story, many names and contributions were referrred to but not a mention of the guy who brought this issue to the fore before the Senate Committee months ago!

MAY 15, 1976
PRINCETON

Our garden this morning is at its tremulous peak. The Spectabile rhodo is a veritable mountain of delicate pink and gold. The best of the iris, extraordinarily large, fluttering in a soft breeze. Helen's ring of blue: a border of forget-me-not is soft and luminous. This is the year of the coral bell, tall drooping green wands on which these fragile bits of coral swing, in a profusion such as I can't remember anywhere. And this morning the first open buds of the rose border.

The fact is I have been fatigued beyond the point that I should permit myself to be. But I did have the good sense to come home Wednesday noon. It is peaceful here, and beautiful.

I am one of the lucky ones among my age and generation: the luck is that I do have things to worry about, to be concerned with; that I have work to do that is not make-work but real, and that there are many who listen to me and want me to persevere. And other more personal reasons for being truly alive, not just breathing, but alive.

Elizabeth Drew did include my statement to the Senate Committee in her "Washington Journal" in the current *New Yorker* magazine. And added some quotes of a conversation we had, which reproduced the strong feeling I have on the proliferation issue. So my concern of yesterday about my role in bringing that grave issue to public notice isn't likely to be overlooked entirely.

In pursuit of Harry Smyth, I talked to—i.e., listened to—Mary Smyth. She gave me a picture of how unhappy one can be who knows he is able to function but is barred by an arbitrary age limit—at Princeton sixty-five —which apparently is why that wonderful Johnny and Janette Wheeler are leaving Princeton for the University of Texas.

Suddenly Mary paused. "How old are you? You must be almost sixty-five yourself and yet you are going right on. . . . You are almost seventy-seven? Then how do you manage that? Oh, you are in a private firm, yours. . . ."

MAY 18, 1976
NEW YORK

My idea of small waterpower has me quite excited—as if I had discovered more than a debater's gambit in the energy controversy. I may also have found that I am by way of repudiating or greatly weakening a major premise of the "industrial revolution," namely, the "economy of scale"—i.e., that the bigger the unit, the lower the cost. But if a major part of the "cost" is the adverse effect on the environment, then the economics of size may be passé in these days, and the advantage moves away from size.

Brandeis, by instinct, saw this many years ago, and I thought he didn't understand technology—which he really didn't, as of his time.

But with the preoccupation with the economic effect of great scale, and its effect in increasing the cost of making a source of energy or output competitive with living conditions, we may enter an area in which the economy of scale, so beloved of many when I wrote *Big Business: A New Era,* may no longer be a true doctrine.

My talk about low head turbines and still undeveloped hydropower may have considerable consequences for the main basis of contemporary industrial development.

MAY 19, 1976
NEW YORK

Donald Cook in a spare, ugly, pale-coffee-colored room at Lazard this afternoon was the picture of a displaced person. And his feelings, moving from running American Electric Power Co., the largest privately owned utility in the country, and at the center of controversy—which he thrives on—to sitting with a piece of yellow paper in front of him, no one to order around and no one to ask him what to do next, all of this brought back my own beginnings in what is laughingly called the investment banking business, Lazard-style. But he is a very impressive-looking man, exceedingly cordial.

I very carefully avoided reference to any but the energy kind of business opportunity that I thought D&R could come up with. In point of fact, the longer I chew it over and yell about it to my noncommercial-style colleagues, the more I can see that the hydro, and particularly the low-turbine concept, has real possibilities in it for a presentation to Lazard and others, we providing the promotion and the technical background, and they the business skills.

But I carefully avoided referring to anything in particular; after all these years of watching bankers and others gobble up my ideas and run off with them, I have become pretty gun-shy about premature disclosure. But as a shrewd man, Cook could see I did have something particular in mind and finally invited such a presentation, including such brochures as we have.

From the D&R point of view, here certainly is a place that will listen to us if we have something worth listening to of a business nature.

MAY 23, 1976
PRINCETON

Our annual garden party yesterday. After a week of cold raw weather and high angry winds, the Lilienthal weather luck about that party came through—and everyone seemed to enjoy each other (it is a kind of Princeton reunion for many of our friends). It seemed to help me to turn the corner from a period of irritability and discouragement.

MAY 28, 1976
PRINCETON

Last night I moved D&R affirmatively into the role of a business that is "available" for the promotion of waterpower, power from smaller installations, an idea that has great appeal to me. The "positioning" of D&R was the consequence of what I said on a Robert MacNeil Report program on Channel 13, presided over not by MacNeil but his very able coadjutor, Jim Lehrer.

For the first time I spoke of D&R as being in the business of analyzing and promoting an important added alternative source of energy, and one that everyone agreed had not been given much consideration, indeed almost overlooked by the Federal Government.

MAY 29, 1976
PRINCETON

I'm a bit surprised at the number of ideas that have been bubbling up in me in recent weeks, as my taking such a strong position on the infirmities of the "economics of size," begun as the way to bring down costs—which had been a staple of my thinking in TVA and is the orthodoxy of contemporary business thinking and decision.

The more I think of it, the more sense it makes—this questioning of size. The arithmetic cannot be challenged—if you can turn out a million units, the cost per unit of production is less than if from the same machine you turn out only a hundred.

But if that machine is so big that it isn't used to full capacity because of a recession, or breakdown, or if—and this was my principal point concerning big electric plants—it takes ten or fifteen years between beginning and actual production, the interest costs during the nonproductive period, and the escalation of prices, wipe out the "economy of scale" compared to a smaller plant if that smaller plant can be installed and productive in fifteen months instead of fifteen years.

MAY 31, 1976
PRINCETON

I've finally made up my mind: I will support Governor Carter. What precipitated the decision was a phone call from Bob Goheen: Carter will be holding a fund-raising meeting next Saturday night. Bob, an old-time fund raiser, knows how to do it. "If you feel like coming, bring a check for $250 or $350 for two of you."

No use putting off a personal decision any longer. How could I be "for" anyone else who has any prospect of being nominated?

JUNE 4, 1976
PRINCETON

Here I am, on a day of dazzling sunlight, sitting indoors, in the up-stairs living room. Absurd.

How come? The sequel to several days of rousing pain from an in-flamed ligament in my right foot. And under surveillance by my most loving but no-nonsense spouse, lest I wander out and start walking on that foot until it is healed.

JUNE 6, 1976
PRINCETON

At ten last evening Helen came back from the Meet Carter party (and bring your checkbook). As enthusiastic as she ever allows herself to be, but definitely impressed. And, I thought, for some very good reasons.

"Anne Martindell, the hostess for the meeting, introduced everyone individually to Mr. Carter, giving each one's name. When I was intro-duced, Carter said he was sorry you were laid up and couldn't come, he had admired you for a long time. One photographer—for the *Princeton Packet*—asked that I stand with Governor Carter, who put his arm across my shoulder while the picture was taken.

"He made a brief speech and then asked for questions, and got many. Many of them skeptical ones, which he handled," said Helen, "with good humor and a flash of the 'Jack Kennedy' touch of humor. There was something about him that reminded me of Kennedy."

Trying to formulate a sensible speech for the coal-industry meeting in Colorado on July 1. What makes the outlining of such a speech difficult is that the energy issue is so comprehensive; wherever you touch it, whether on coal or hydro or atomic energy, the issue broadens, and the strands to be woven into a unified statement are so many and so diverse.

JUNE 12, 1976
PRINCETON

High as a kite, am I. And no wonder: I have just hung up after a long phone talk with John Cunniff, who read me what he has written based upon my Robert MacNeil statement and a two-hour session with him in my tiny (but blessed) hotel room last Thursday afternoon. It will go out on the AP wires Monday for Tuesday afternoon members of the Associated Press.

The stir I am making about waterpower (I have dubbed it the "orphan" so far as the Federal Government and ERDA [Energy Research and Development Agency] are concerned) has restored whatever waning confidence I develop from time to time that I am approaching the time when I am no longer producing.

The speech for the coal industry meeting July 1 should provide a chance to say something and may create quite a bit of interest, for energy is indeed the tired old man of public issues.

In preparation for a second draft, I reread the speech I made to the American Society of Newspaper Editors back in April of 1947, almost thirty years ago!

The speech to the planning conference, in Washington, very soon to be published by *Smithsonian,* was considered full of new and fresh and challenging ideas. Similarly, I would say the discourse to the Philosophical Society, though less controversial perhaps. And now "moving water" as a source of electrical energy.

JUNE 28, 1976
MARTHA'S VINEYARD

It was Helen and not the experts (myself included) who caught a serious and vulnerable omission in the Energizing speech. (She was too preoccupied last week getting ready to go to the Vineyard to read it before I finished those two hellish days of writing it.)

What she saw was that I didn't admit that there had been abuses in the past, on environment, and didn't distinguish between the contemporary business manager and those who had (and often still do) commit these environmental abuses. I hope the correction I made this morning will be caught in some of the releases at least.

JUNE 30, 1976
AT LOGAN AIRPORT, BOSTON

In a United Airlines 747, waiting to take off for Denver–Colorado Springs.

Prescription for a comfortable air trip at the crowded holiday season: (1) get a sprained ankle, and nurse it for all it is worth; (2) get a big impressive walking stick with rubber tip; and (3) request and get wheelchairs at every stop. Talk about the Friendly Skies of United Airlines: being wheeled out by "supervisory personnel" instead of standing with the holiday crowd of vacationers, babies, prosperous "middle"-class Americans.

At noon last Thursday, John Macy, David Morse, and I lunched as Rodman Rockefeller's guests. John told Rodman the essentials of how Hal Frederiksen, with a company he has organized, is moving in on our clients and four of our present technical staff, with the prospect that at least a half-dozen more from the Sacramento group will follow. In their brochure they claimed that they had participated in the Pahlavi Dam enterprise, though none of the Frederiksen group were in D&R at any time during that undertaking.

Rodman said he would support the idea of a law suit.

I said that in my July 1 speech at Colorado Springs I was taking on the environment issue, which most people in the energy field have shied away from meeting head-on.

Then Rodman, for a straight fifteen minutes, talked about "The Cousins Rockefeller," who call themselves "The Wards."

"When I meet with them I'm the only one that isn't way overboard —vehement, belligerent even—about protecting the 'environment.' "

Macy asked about Jay (that would be John Rockefeller 4th, now running for Governor of West Virginia—a coal-mining state, incidentally).

"Well, Jay is in politics, so he plays it cool—scattering his shots."

JULY 2, 1976
COLORADO SPRINGS, COLORADO

I would say that the trip out here was a great big fat waste of energy. My speech was delivered to the remnants of the audience that survived a four-hour program. But I hadn't counted on this particular audience as the measure of the worth or reception of the things I said. So I'm not nearly all that let down.

JULY 3, 1976
COLORADO SPRINGS

My initial appraisal of my speech, that I had wasted my time, that it was a bust, turns out to be quite wrong. So many serious people have spoken to me about it, more than almost any speech. Two men said they are buying a "cassette" of the speech to take back with them—apparently it was recorded and is available in that form. Worth all the time and juices I put into planning it, and writing it (and rewriting).

Had a fascinating visit with a postwar-style German (*West* German, as he was careful to point out). Friedrich H. Esser, M. Sc. of Ruhrkehle A.G. Had a year at the School of Mines of the University of Missouri.

After he had described how all the several private German companies mining coal in the Ruhr Basin had been "put together" into a single enterprise, and cited the production totals, I could see why the Ruhr has been such a factor in the tension, to say nothing of the spilled blood, between France and Germany.

He responded to my questioning about where in the world the coal reserves and production come from. Countries with the most favorable geology for coal (i.e., for economical mining, I suppose he meant), he ranked in order: England, Australia, and the U.S. The Western coal reserves of the U.S. ranked high in favorable geology, but there is no "strategy," by which he meant what was so evident at this coal meeting: a firm policy about access to the vast reserves of the West.

What the coal people need to know is whether and on what terms coal reserves of the West could be leased for development.

The Secretary of the Interior, Thomas Kleppe, a moon-faced small-bore politico from Bismarck, North Dakota, spoke: "You and I know," he said to this audience of coal businessmen, "that there is on the President's desk, for signature into law or his veto, a leasing bill that the coal industry finds 'onerous' and opposes." (In this case, "onerous" means that the financial terms, strip-mining provisions, etc., are costly and some would say prohibitive of any extensive development of the Western coal reserves.)

"I don't know," said the Secretary, "what the President will do. I have recommended that he should veto it."

But—and here is the "catch," the picture of how major American reserve planning is decided—"I have seen the TV this morning and I see that *one* uncommitted delegate to the Republican convention who wants the bill signed is talking with a representative of Mr. Ford. Even one delegate is important right now, so I guess you can figure what the President will do about that coal-leasing bill."

The "need for certainty" about coal leasing that occupied so much ratiocination and words in memos by Walt Seymour and Tom Mead and their highly rational and intellectual discussions with Washington governmental technical people—this is what it comes down to: a delegate to a Republican convention from a state that may have little electoral weight may just decide the coal-leasing policy.

John Macy came to Colorado directly from several days in Sacramento. What was the latest in the assault of Frederiksen on D&R? Nothing good.

JULY 7, 1976
MARTHA'S VINEYARD

More than any other place on earth, this hilltop and the meadow and trees below are "home." This is where the roots are, for Helen and for me. But more so, for the grandchildren (except Margy).

This is Davey's 21st birthday. That he crossed the ocean to be here is not a casual circumstance: as he says with such fervor, even ferocity, this is one place that is "home"—his word.

JULY 8, 1976
MARTHA'S VINEYARD

So, tomorrow morning you will no longer be seventy-six. You'll be seventy-seven. I'm not too good a judge, but I can't see that I'm really much different from ten years ago. Not so far as spirit is concerned, certainly. Physically: I sense that my physical condition has not changed so far as I am aware. "Health" may be too general a term, but it does embrace more than "physical condition."

JULY 10, 1976
MARTHA'S VINEYARD

As I was emptying a jam-full mailbox at the gate, along came Henry Hough and we proceeded to have what in whaling language (appropriate up here) would be called a "gam."

"Have you reconciled yourself to Jimmy Carter?"

I said I was enthusiastic about Carter "because in his talks he pictures the same kind of small-town rural Southern background that I knew so well, in Georgia and other states, as I traveled around preaching what TVA electricity could do to change people's lives in the country. I believe in him—not a matter of reconciling myself."

Henry seemed relieved.

As we sat in the sun Helen straightened me out on something that has puzzled me. What is the point of my "speaking out" to audiences that are simply "folks," with no particular interest or "influence" in the basic issues about energy or centralization?

Said Helen, "You did this—in person at service luncheons or on courthouse steps—in the Tennessee Valley, to people who were not of the 'opinion former' group. They needed to understand your ideas, and it was from this activity of yours that you built a constituency without which TVA couldn't have succeeded. Why is this any different, essentially? Building understanding of your ideas and motivation is an important part of your life now as much almost as when you went on speaking trips in the Valley."

JULY 15, 1976
MARTHA'S VINEYARD

The mail brought my first look at Volume VI, so long in being born. A handsome book it is.

I have just had a great experience: Jimmy Carter's "acceptance speech" to the Democratic convention.
I believe the man. But mostly I have faith in the way he went about reviving the essentials of the elective ideal: carrying a story directly to people of all kinds.

JULY 20, 1976
NEW YORK

Inscribed a whole lot of these big fat Volume VI's today, ones that Macy will carry with him to Iran next week, including one to His Imperial Majesty the Shahinshah of Iran.

Landing on *Mars,* 214 million miles away. And TV pictures to prove it, what's more.

JULY 21, 1976
NEW YORK

The by-line "Ann Crittenden" in the *New York Times* business section acquired a special and combative meaning to me, after she wrote a long story about the influence of American "consultants" on the actions of foreign countries, rhapsodizing about Arthur D. Little—and not one word of mention of D&R.
Today she was no longer a by-line; Ann Crittenden was to come to the office, with Anna Rosenberg.
I went into my excited story about hydro as an approach to the "new"

sources of electricity, particularly in such an oil-starved area as New England. This caught on.

I had hardly gotten back to my desk when there was a message: "Ann Crittenden says she *must* speak to you."

Which she did. Her editor did indeed want a story for the Sunday business section, for week after next. We will meet tomorrow morning, and probably finish it off by phone from the Vineyard.

JULY 27, 1976
MARTHA'S VINEYARD

A sun-filled blowy morning here on this hilltop; the *wind* is such an intimate part of life, making sounds like those that make sailing a special human experience. Those wind-created sounds stimulate my imagination.

This time the possible theme of the speech I've committed myself to make at Lawrence University, Appleton, Wisconsin, in late September, the opening of the Gordon Clapp Lecture Series. This will be a good time for me to talk to the young people gathered at Appleton at the beginning of an academic year about their "careers."

The theme is the attraction and the importance of doing work, of pointing their lives, of developing an ability to further the public interest in whatever they do; that furthering the public interest through their efforts will be the criterion, the measure by which to judge whether a future is interesting and exciting or dull and routine, however successful by older standards.

The sad decline in public esteem of private business is largely due to disregard of the public interest as the measure of the worth of private business activity, and not just the flagrant breach of trust in the bribery and illegality uncovered in recent years and months.

JULY 28, 1976
MARTHA'S VINEYARD

John Macy off for Iran tonight via Rome. A long phone meeting with him this morning.

John was most affirmative—as is his wont, anyway—about the future of the Sacramento staff. They hunger to know more about D&R as a whole; have been kept out of this by Frederiksen's lack of interest in anything but engineering, and then only that done in Sacramento. Seems reasonably sure that the "defections" to Frederiksen have about run their course, and that replacements and new blood can be procured.

JULY 31, 1976
MARTHA'S VINEYARD

Late last night out of the dense fog a stirring on the afterdeck, the sticky door pounded open, and in walks a tall slender smiling figure: Daniel, home from the South American adventure.

Ten months away from home, on his own. Has that quiet determination of his mother. "I decided that most of the plans I had made hadn't worked out, but I made new ones, and didn't want to come back until I had got something from the time and money. So I stayed."

He has made a decision: to enter Hampshire College, a new and small college near Amherst. No question about not going to college after that wandering. So this will reassure his parents. But the underlying questioning of the young people of his generation (and Allen's and Davey's) about the value of college probably remains.

Daniel is an exceptionally perceptive fellow. Asking him what he most got out of his months of being in a part of the world he knew nothing of, he showed a clarity that I wish more young people had. "Instead of concentrating on myself, and puzzling over what I should do with my life, I found that seeing the way other people live, in places I never knew about, gave me a better idea of myself than sitting around and thinking only of myself and where I fit in. Seeing not yourself, but other people and places—that's how I begin to understand myself rather than asking myself some unanswerable questions."

AUGUST 1, 1976
MARTHA'S VINEYARD

Have been so greatly enjoying *The Thurber Album,* and laughing, not just chuckling.

His account of Jake Fisher, a very strong old boy who would argue with words and fists:

"In his seventy-seventh year Jake took to his bed for the last time. As he lay dying the preacher called on him. 'Don't you want to forgive your enemies?' he asked. Jake smiled. 'I ain't got none,' he said. 'I licked 'em all.' "*

That's a line I'll remember if that question is put to me, someday. And I could list the ones I don't need to forgive because I licked 'em: A. E. Morgan, McKellar, Hickenlooper . . . and so on.

*James Thurber, *The Thurber Album.* New York: Simon and Schuster, 1965.

AUGUST 6, 1976
MARTHA'S VINEYARD

"Making New York City habitable is more than playgrounds and even hospitals. It is public libraries. And these are closing down. Think of it, the great library on Fifth Avenue, some of the divisions open only a few days a week. Neighborhood libraries, such as the one at 67th, closed one day a week. The St. Agnes Branch at 102nd and Amsterdam now closed.

"These libraries throughout the city have been crowded. Many children found this the only place where they could do their homework, living six or seven kids in a crowded apartment.

"Libraries are a basic part of education for thousands of people, and not only the young by any means, older people, too. New York's place as a center of art depends on the department of the Fifth Avenue Library where artists and architects can find the material they need."

I am quoting my cousin Beatrice, fully aroused by what she feels is a blow at a great American tradition, the public library.

I said Helen and I were going to be dinner guests of Amyas Ames, head of Lincoln Center, and a great public servant. "If only Ames, or someone of his stature and administrative ability, would take the lead in preserving the public libraries in New York City," she said.

When Beatrice has a conviction about a number of things, she is extraordinarily articulate. About books—there she bursts into a fine flame.

AUGUST 7, 1976
MARTHA'S VINEYARD

"The New York cabbie" has become a type, but the variety of the species is actually unlimited. Last week I ran into a thirty-third-degree, widely traveled Mason.

A little man, middle-aged. Over his identification box on the right, three Masonic plaques, including that of the Shriners.

"What is your lodge?" he asked.

"A little Indiana town you wouldn't have heard of," said I, and then the memory of my father's promoting me into membership in Winamac came back to me; how I startled the natives and my dad by memorizing the ritual in two days (and forgot it all in a few months, of course).

My bright-eyed little driver told me of the lodges he had visited. The best was his own, in Bermuda, "in the Scotch jurisdiction," where they take it very seriously. "Of course I take my apron with me wherever I go. The German jurisdiction takes it the most seriously. You really have to be able to answer all the questions and know the three grips or it is no good. And in Turkey . . ."

Then it gradually dawned on me: he had been in the American military; in the Air Force, as it turned out. (Ankara is one of the biggest of American Air Force bases, or was.)

How it lights up the day to come out of one's shell and talk with people; "just a taxi driver" doesn't mean you may not be chatting with a world traveler.

AUGUST 17, 1976
MARTHA'S VINEYARD

The jabbering in the background is the TV casters trying to make something less than humiliating—to the sensible people of the country —of the Republican national convention. Such an elevation of trivialities. And Nelson Rockefeller enjoying the last glow of public attention as if it all amounted to something.

For me it was glorious: at the hilltop overlooking the Sound, the two lovely little lakes, the circle of green. For the first time since my right ankle became a basket case (how many months ago) it was a return to full use. It has been a long painful recovery. Took the Dyer Dhow for a row on the velvety surface of the Daggett Pond. It was a joy indeed.

The twisting and turning is over about a theme and title for the Lawrence University speech. Talked to Norman Clapp [Gordon Clapp's brother] and he thought the title was a good one: "The Public Servant and the Private Businessman—Today and Tomorrow."

AUGUST 19, 1976
MARTHA'S VINEYARD

Getting some great letters about Volume VI, ones that make me happy, and compensate for the rough time we had in getting the book out. The warmest, one from Dorothea Greenbaum, bless her. This afternoon an eloquent one from Jonathan Daniels. To have a contemporary of mine recognize that age is no final measure of vitality, as he does, is most pleasing.

AUGUST 20, 1976
MARTHA'S VINEYARD

The dawn from our tower: a palpable stillness that spreads over the green and blue, a stopping of all things, for a visible moment. The sun has not yet appeared, the night is gone except for a silver cookie of the newest new moon. Perhaps the Lord has decided that this is so happy a dollop of time that He will call it an Eternal Day—and begin creation all over again in some other part of the Universe.

7 A.M.

Still on the tower, my breakfast coffee in my hand: the brass of the sun through the lattice of leaves, the trees that cover Indian Hill to the east of us; and then the sunlight freed of the hill, sweeps across the cluster of pine and the whole green amphitheatre, warming everything and declaring: it is day. Another day. We say, without thinking quite: good morning; good day. Good it is, because it is new, unused, to make into something new, different from yesterday.

The Hill Top cabin: my hide-away, little used this summer.

This blessed spot. Surely the most entrancing view in the world to have as one's own, alone.

A white crane banks, turns, settles on the little pond. A brilliant goldfinch darts by; then a red-winged blackbird swoops past. Out on the Sound to the south, wings of another kind dot the blue, the tall yachts.

Last night the most chaotic swarming of local politicos, the last hours of a "convention" dominated by television. The passion for "exposure" by the characters who came to this Republican convention to be seen and heard. And heard was easy, for the empty senseless "demonstrations" for Reagan, by that time a candidate who had been voted into relative obscurity. Yet they chanted and blew their silly kid New Year's Eve horns, hoping that the eye of the TV would catch them.

The Democratic Party and Jimmy Carter will have to be very inept or lose its marbles if they don't win against such a disorganized crowd.

AUGUST 21, 1976
MARTHA'S VINEYARD

All summer Helen has been bending over sheets of paper, in the early morning, drawing her version of a reconstituted "Topside," one that will provide me with a larger bedroom, and exchanging her little bedroom into a kitchen and the tiny current kitchen into her new bedroom.

The long-range plan behind Helen's drawing looks to the time when we may need full-time in-house help for us, by then rickety octogenarians, this by my insistence, over Helen's mild dissent. A closer need is to be able to accommodate overnight people coming to see me about D&R matters. This too seems imaginative and remote.

Last week Helen engaged a neighbor, Harold Dugan, a builder. So it will, presumably, be a somewhat different house next year when we return in June.

Very pleased to receive a cable from André Meyer acknowledging receipt of the new *Journals* and protesting that my references to him were too generous, but acknowledged as a token of our "friendship." Glad he used that word and happy that he spoke of seeing me when he returns, which must mean that he has recovered to the point of thinking of coming back.

AUGUST 22, 1976
MARTHA'S VINEYARD

A mixed bag of interesting people at the Amyas Ames' summer home on Seven Gates last night. As handsome and original a drawing room as ever I have seen. Sculptured out of the sky, a vast arch of windows looking out on the Sound, giant wooden beams coming to a gentle peak. On my admiring the structure, Evelyn Ames said: "Yes, it is like a tent."

Both Helen and I were impressed with Reston's comments about Governor Carter. (He didn't call him "Jimmy.") Very intelligent, widely read, smart (which is different from being "intelligent"). And says Scotty, he will certainly be elected in November. Had high praise for Ford's acceptance speech—strong and well delivered. But the nomination of Dole as his running mate seemed a mystery. "That nomination guarantees that the Republicans will sweep Grand Rapids and Topeka."

A long talk with Francis Plimpton, who was one of the few truly distinguished U.S. Ambassadors to the United Nations. Mostly about his concern about nuclear energy, and the difficulties with the alternatives.

AUGUST 28, 1976
MARTHA'S VINEYARD

The impression I have had of Anthony Lewis of the *New York Times* has been that of a cogent and collected person, which has distinguished him from most of the commentators and columnists. This impression from what he writes was more than confirmed last evening as we talked together, briefly, and as I heard him put some sense into the random remarks of other guests about Africa, and particularly about the tensions and eruptions in South Africa and Rhodesia.

Lewis is a great admirer of Hugo Black. Had I known Black when he was a Senator, and at the time he went to the Supreme Court bench? I said I certainly had; that he was one of the early TVA's staunchest friends in the Senate.

This morning I refreshed my recollection by looking at Volume I of the *Journals.* There is a particularly interesting brief reference in a long entry of mine about a meeting with F.D.R., which foreshadows the later appearance of a liberal Democratic group in the South. Reading that entry points to the real origin of such a man as Jimmy Carter, and shows that those who think Carter's liberalism in the South is a mystery, or a phony, don't know their history.

Roger Baldwin made his annual call on us late yesterday afternoon. The warrior of so many great battles of change seemed for the first time an old man, he who has always been "beyond age." Not because of his appearance, though of course he shows the visible marks of his almost ninety years. No, the first sign of being old came when he spoke of his visit to Europe this summer. "I like Europe, because it seems so stable; things aren't changing, aren't so full of tension as in this country."

With some prodding from me, he insisted that "you and I are optimists," but he spoke with despair about the state of the world and particularly this country. When I reminded him (as if Roger Baldwin of all people needed reminding) about what progress we in this country had made (and for not a little of it he had been responsible), as in the condition of black people, he perked up. "Yes; and the status of women."

AUGUST 30, 1976
MARTHA'S VINEYARD

It is now, I believe, just two years ago this summer that I had a hunch that I could help fructify and make real one of the Shah's goals, the strengthening of public sector management. A letter from John Macy dated August 17 gave me a sense that this undertaking is really making visible, and one might hope, enduring headway where it counts most, in the minds and outlook of the youngish leaders of Iran.

This morning I heard from John: "Collaboration with Alimard confirms your favorable assessment of his capacity and backing. Receiving his full support for significant enlargement of government-wide training effort. He now describes his organization as the agents of change for government reform."

SEPTEMBER 2, 1976
MARTHA'S VINEYARD

One of the family jokes or pleasantries has been that our grandchildren have had no idea of what their grandfather does, how he earns a living. Very vague to them.

All of a sudden, it not only has come over them what I do and have done, but they are hell bent to read the *Journals,* beginning with the beginning. Davey and Daniel had quite a talk about this yesterday afternoon; quite excited they were. Allen carted off Volume I last night and, according to Davey, has fixed up a place at "Yonside" where he reads until all hours in that volume. Davey wants to have I and II to take back to Italy so he can read them this winter. He was very interested and full of questions—good ones—about the waterpower ideas I have.

What Helen and I find particularly interesting is that suddenly, so it would seem, they want to know what I have been spending my life doing, and suddenly the *Journals* are something to read as having meaning to them.

SEPTEMBER 3, 1976
MARTHA'S VINEYARD

AP and UPI stories last night about D.E.L. and D&R plus *seven* radio interviews in a single week between September 8 and 15 don't please or impress me half as much as the spurt of interest by Allen and Davey. Says Allen—quite uncertain and a bit confused about his future career —to his cousin: "I'd like to know how he did it. So I'm reading the *Journals* beginning with the first and will go straight through." (And similar comments from the other young men.)

"Grandfather, all of a sudden something you said to us ticked off this feeling that we now begin to see what it is you do."

SEPTEMBER 5, 1976
NEW YORK

Fifty-three years! We celebrated yesterday on the Vineyard with Cordon Rouge champagne, and lobster. What is remarkable is that we still very much enjoy each other's company.

SEPTEMBER 6, 1976
NEW YORK

Sunday afternoon in Central Park. A multinational, multi-ethnic spectacle, no less. I am still dazzled by what I saw: thousands of village people in the most urban setting of all. The great park of Olmsted, rimmed by tall buildings that spell superluxury, crowded with thousands of people who have poured out of their congested "apartments," out to enjoy themselves, to eat their own kind of food, to talk their non-English language (mostly Puerto Rican Spanish), to gambol and listen to guitars, watch magic, dodge bicycles.

The most lasting impression is how completely non-organized these thousands of pleasure seekers were. Each little group mingled with others with no one to discipline them or tell them how to enjoy themselves. They seemed to be there as individuals. None of your collective organized style of fun.

This was a slice of American life, of world life. Noisy—but very much alive and vital.

I felt grateful to Beatrice and Barney, who took me to see this great show, though they have seen it many times, since they live so near. But they seemed to find something new, and enjoyed pointing out this and that which I might have missed.

At 9 o'clock yesterday morning I was in the serenity of our home on the hilltop in Martha's Vineyard; at noon in this maelstrom. *Both* were American—I tried to remind myself of this.

SEPTEMBER 7, 1976
NEW YORK

John Burnett has landed on his feet, after a very rough ride on a bucking runaway steer known as the New York Urban Development Corporation.

He looks happy. Satisfaction in being taken on as executive vice president of David Rockefeller's real-estate holdings, not only Rockefeller Center but in other parts of the country. He has the makings of a strong future. He has continued and undiminished loyalty to D&R and warmth toward me.

SEPTEMBER 10, 1976
NEW YORK

A ripsnorting session on proliferation yesterday, all afternoon, with Bob Helander and Ken Fields. The meanderings in Congress the last couple weeks on this issue plus the collapse of the Administration's position have produced anything but clarification, and the cocky academics and "weak-kneed" State Department characters who declared that my embargo position was "too late," have now produced a proposal—what

ERDA administrator Seamans considers "a virtual embargo" on export of nuclear material.

With his white plume of wavy hair, more distinguished-looking than ever, Rodman came to see me yesterday.

He said, "I would like to go with you on a trip to Iran this fall, with Barbara. I have never met the Shah, and I would like IBEC to be more publicly identified with D&R."

I said: Of course; but this should be arranged by Helms, the Ambassador. That isn't what Rodman wants. I will have to explain to him, today if possible, that he will have to have very strict security protection. Terrorist opponents of the Shah's regime have murdered five Americans, unknown men, in recent weeks, in ambush on the open streets of Tehran. The Crown Prince of the Rockefeller Family would be too good a target to be overlooked, if there is as active a guerrilla organization as this would indicate. I would not particularly enjoy riding through the streets of Tehran with Rodman under these circumstances. I must tell him this, quite candidly.

Chairman Mao Tse-tung dead. They can't live forever. But what effect will one leader more or less have on the basic needs and drives of the people in the villages and cities?

SEPTEMBER 15, 1976
NEW YORK

Rodman, sober and, as always, courteous, agreed he will not go to Iran.

Mid-afternoon I sold kosher margarine and pizza with kosher cheese. In short, I was on a forty-minute radio interview at station WEVD about the [*Journals*] book and about many of the subjects in it, the commercials being for Mazola margarine (strictly *kosher*) for Italian dishes. Kosher margarine for Italian dishes ranks with our family story about getting the first Italian food in La Porte, Indiana, in the Chinese Rathskeller.

A very intelligent woman (Ruth Jacobs), the interrogator. Gave me a chance to say my say about a TVA on the Jordan, but more than that, how to try to accommodate the rights of the Arabs with those of the Israelis. I hope to get a copy of the transcript; I thought I said it well.

And a one-hour interview with a bushy-bearded scholarly-appearing man, Bill Dunlap, for a "think" article in the [New York] *News,* the

newspaper with the greatest circulation in America but the least disposition of its audience for "think" pieces, I would suppose.

Asked, late this morning, if I would substitute for a Congressman
(who had cancelled) in a Conference Board program for the following
afternoon. Definitely yes, said I. So I attended the annual meeting of the
Conference Board late this afternoon, and instead of staying off by myself
as I so often did in the past, I greeted people and they greeted and visited
with me, including Elmer Staats, Controller General of the U.S., with
whom I sat at dinner. What a solid, unflappable man, but with considerable feeling which he keeps under control.

SEPTEMBER 19, 1976
PRINCETON

From the Conference Board dinner Wednesday night, until the ad-
journment of the Conference Thursday late afternoon, I was in the midst
of the current heads of perhaps three hundred of the largest American
businesses, and another five hundred or so senior staff of those companies.

My impromptu appearance as a member of the panel was an experience of sorts. The subject of the Conference was the concern of most large
business managers and investors these days: "The future role of business
and government."

For a while it seemed that the current star would completely monop-
olize the panel discussion. A disjointed European-looking scholar, in appearance and manner, but actually the man, so I'm told, who business
people listen to with awe, today's Delphic oracle: Daniel Yankelovich.

As we were introduced, I noticed that three huge spotlights had been
turned on, shining right into our eyes on the dais of the ballroom of the
Waldorf, so we couldn't see the audience that filled to overflowing that
big room. I leaned over to Sandy Trowbridge‡ and said: "Sandy, can't you
get those goddam lights turned off?" Laughs from the audience, whispers
"the mike is on" (which it was), but the lights were turned off, amid
applause. Which set the tone of my later remarks, which were crusty and
belligerent, as I usually am in the presence of highly theoretical and
cocksure characters like Yankelovich.

No questions came to me or Sandy, the other "panelist," from the
moderator, Bill Miller, head of Textron, a dapper little country-club type.
We had to listen to a long, dull, Germanic discourse by a seer (his spe-
cialty appears to be to "survey" and analyze what people will do and

‡Alexander B. Trowbridge, Jr., business executive, and president of The Conference
Board, Inc.

think), a man whose every comment showed, as I said, complete lack of "roots" in American society.

Finally, I broke in to express my theme: the need for an ethical revolution and an ethical foundation for both the public servant (i.e., the government man) and the private businessman. Economics doesn't explain the present tense and antagonistic relation between government and business. In fact, we could well get rid of economists, so far as I am concerned. At this point, to everyone's amazement, the audience of perhaps a thousand broke out spontaneously into prolonged applause—right in the middle of a panel discussion. I've never heard this happen before.

One of the most pleasant experiences was to sit at dinner beside Sir Reay Geddes, the very picture of a cultivated British man of affairs. (Actually, head of Dunlop Holdings, a British international banking house.) A very tall, handsome man, relaxed in manner and speech, able to state opinions without being opinionated—a real skill among the British cultivated businessmen, a rare quality among our own of that same group, I fear. His speech from the dais later on was witty and subtle, with perceptive observations on American life today.

I only wish I could make my points, in extemporaneous discourse, without bristling, as I certainly did (with some justification considering how annoyed I was by the lord of the surveyitis syndrome, Yankelovich).

Last Monday I went on two radio programs (taped, of course). In all I have been through eight such in the past couple weeks. Plus two lengthy press interviews *(New York Post* and Sunday *New York News)*. The occasion, ostensibly, was about Volume VI of the *Journals*. Actually, most of the questions and my responses were about D&R, atomic energy, weapons proliferation, and so on.

After weeks of frustration, the Crittenden article for the *New York Times,* about small waterpower, actually appeared last Sunday. Truncated, but reasonably accurate. It has already produced more interest among serious people than I could have expected, and this will be manifested next week in conferences already scheduled.

The high point of the week, indeed the ultimate high point about the *Journals,* was a longhand letter from Archie MacLeish. Quite moving. Here is a part of it:

> It is a marvelous thing to see a man who has known from the start what all mankind used to know: that one doesn't find one's *self* by burrowing for it in one's own gut and testicles but by laboring to save the world, to conquer the monsters, to clean the stables. I wish you were a poet. Your Journals are and will be a famous rock quarry for builders to come (if builders do come) but what the generation needs *now* is not stone but crystal—the splinter of light which will

say: Look! Look beyond you—beyond your sick "self"! The Journals mean it: Say it!

SEPTEMBER 10, 1976
PRINCETON

A couple hours late yesterday afternoon at Joe and Kitty Johnson's, to chat with George Ball and his wife, the brilliantly alive Mary Bundy, and the pale and convalescent Bill Bundy.

George has just published a volume of his views about foreign policy. A big solid Foreign Service type he is, handsome in his white hair and big square head. Ball is now a partner of Lehman Brothers, to recoup the complete drain of his financial resources, as he explained, after so many years of public service, mostly dissenting as it turns out, in the Kennedy and Johnson period. But, he said quite candidly, "Banking is a bloody bore," as indeed it is, for a man who wants to remake the mixed-up foreign policy of our country.

Ball was the chief negotiator with Iran, on behalf of Pan Am and a banking group; the issue was the sale of a large block of Pan Am stock, at a time when it was in deep financial trouble some months ago. The discussions were with Hushang Ansary, Minister of Finance, and a very unlikeable personality.

"It was made plain to Lehman and Pan Am that the deal could not go through unless 'appropriate arrangements' were made with Ansary. We told the go-betweens that Lehman was not interested in that kind of country."

I broke in to say that in all the years we have been working in and for Iran—over twenty-one now—never were we approached with any such suggestion.

Said George: "I haven't any doubt of that; they knew they were dealing with David Lilienthal and that kind of thing would be unthinkable, with you."

Our case may have been affected by the fact that the Shah invited me to come to the country and to do this work, rather than any initiative or entreating on my part.

But I could not help feel a bit apprehensive that, however clear our own record is known to be, the assumption that corruption and "arrangements" are the order of the day in Iran might tarnish our good name.

SEPTEMBER 25, 1976
PRINCETON

The text for the Wisconsin speech, which I thought I had all wrapped up last weekend, turned out—as I read it Monday morning—to be a bore, without driving ideas.

So I started all over again. The result, a new title and a fighting speech centering on the excesses of dogmatic environmentalists. Unless I miss my guess, it will produce quite a bit of flak among the professional environmental groups, a bit of confusion as to what I mean by "moral purpose." But I think it is about what I want to say at this point.

Thursday noon lunch with the kind of unusual figure that American life is capable of producing: Charles "Chuck" Luce, a small-town boy from Wisconsin, now chairman of the board of Consolidated Edison of New York.

I wanted to talk to him particularly about the dangers I believe we are all in because of the extreme positions and great leverage the professional environmental leaders have acquired, chiefly through the use of the Federal courts. The delays and negativism that have gripped the whole field of supply of energy through the abuse of a cause I believe in, and have pioneered, in fact, are disturbing. What I have found difficult to find my way through is the problem of how to bring some judgment and sense into what began many, many years ago as a humane and progressive "movement."

The "Gordon Clapp Lecture" is my latest effort to find a theme that will be difficult for the extremists and professionals to destroy completely —or destroy my credibility, I guess is what I mean—one that at the same time will bring some sense of philosophy and basics to an issue which could be most damaging, not just to increased energy supply—which is completely stymied today—but to a public discussion, which is on too narrow and parochial a basis.

Luce cited case after case of the abuse of requirement of "environmental impact" statements, which have become a *formula* for transferring a public policy and factual issue into the straitjacket of Federal lawsuits, before judges who have no training and no mandate to try such issues.

Elmer Staats voiced the opinion of most sensible and progressive men when he referred to this the other day when I saw him. A letter from Elmer this week showed that he feels this, as a man with a long record of being progressive, enclosing a copy of a speech by the presiding Judge of the Circuit Court of Appeals in Washington gently but explicitly criticizing the use of the courts for purposes for which they are not equipped.

I warned Norman Clapp the text of my Clapp Lecture might embarrass him, as Chairman of the Public Service Commission. I said I had tried to follow up my Colorado Springs speech by a pretty stiff comment about the need for a broad base for the environmental issue, rather than the shrill and dogmatic and arrogant assumption that only the professional environmentalist could speak for the people of the country. He said that he welcomed my making that issue and far from embarrassing him, he was sure it would serve a good public purpose.

SEPTEMBER 26, 1976
PRINCETON

Yesterday in San Diego Governor Carter endorsed the nuclear materials embargo idea, my proposal of last January. The Ford Administration hasn't shown any leadership on the issue. The whole point of my position last January was that it was an American duty to take leadership in putting a stop to a drift to atomic warfare.

Just watched and listened to Rosalynn Carter on *Meet the Press*. She was terrific; if Jimmy will take the same fully alive way of expressing himself as she did there is no doubt we will elect a fully alive human being and not a TV dummy, which is what the format and the pedantic "panel" of those accursed debates made of both of them.

But it will be a close race between Carter and Ford.

SEPTEMBER 28, 1976
FLYING TO MILWAUKEE

The "proliferation" issue—a concocted word for world survival—continues to be at the very top of the news, a "top" that must compete with the relative trivia that newspapers and media give attention to. My impulse at this moment (high above my native Middle West) is to renew my demand for a complete embargo from the U.S. The reprocessing issue, of which so much has been made (by me, among others) seems secondary. "Stop the Nuclear World, we're getting off."

The great dark steel-like arc below is Lake Michigan. How many memory replays that body of water and its sandy shores evoke.

SEPTEMBER 30, 1976
APPLETON, WISCONSIN

What I set out to say, and write, way last summer, has now been delivered, in an auditorium on the campus of Lawrence University.

Was it worth all that effort, those days and even weeks of outlines? Not for this particular audience, not just as a debt paid to Gordon, without whom I probably couldn't have done the big job in Iran. But it was and is worth it to have to "speak out," to say my say, to put it down on paper and revise and revise—and think.

What impressed me most? Not the intense emotional reception given to my lecture. So intense that I broke into the text before me with some impromptu comments that brightened the rather one-note somberness of the discourse.

What impressed me most were the young students. Most of all a gal with an unformed face and soft embarrassed eyes who asked to interview me for the *Laurentian,* a college weekly. This took place almost as soon as I arrived, yesterday afternoon, from Madison. She talked to me—after a brief initial period of embarrassment—as one journal writer to another. What she said was taped, along with my heavy-footed responses, and I have made a big point of requesting a transcript of that tape. Not for what I, the "interviewed" said, but what she said. Such perception, such understanding. I felt a bond of understanding with this stranger, almost immediately.

I say "understanding"—understanding of why I write as I do, why I must put myself into what I record in these interminable notes. I have never talked to anyone who caught the point of my journal-writing impulse so fully and was so articulate about it. Because she too, at about the age I began my "diary," has begun keeping a journal.

Rolling through the countryside of Wisconsin was something good for the soul. Flying, which is of course what I invariably do, is all right for getting from one place to another. But to see the country—one of the chief pluses of this rather demanding trip—driving through the rolling hills is right, the only way.

The land I saw is a delicious morsel, warming to the senses.

The hazy golden beauty of the gentle hills from Appleton: how I drank this glory into my very insides. We went out of our way—Norman Clapp and his delightful wife, Analoyce—for my special benefit, not only so I could relish such a landscape, but so we could drive through a morain, where all was undulation crested by some of the most outrageously-colored trees in their autumnal splendor of rose, of gold, of fiery red.

The visit to Madison was packed full. Lake Mendota at the very window of my hotel room; the university now grown beyond comprehension, with more glittering bicycles row on row than there were students when I was a part of Madison forty-four years ago. Such beautiful young people, and how lucky they are, to be sure, on this lovely autumn day. Then a reunion with some old friends, and some considerably "older." I kissed Elizabeth Raushenbush Brandeis, to her surprise, kissed such fragile cheeks; changed, but really much the same reserved woman, worshipping the very mention of the name of her father "The Justice."

After the fifteen or so of us had drunk and eaten together, Norman asked me to tell my friends what I have been doing; sitting at table I talked longer than I should have, until eleven. George Gant was there, as jolly and rotund as ever, and Jeanette.

One of the major purposes of this trip, of course, was to move ahead on my most recent business crusade: hydropower and hydroturbines. This occurred in the first hours of my time in Milwaukee. And I learned almost at once that my hunch about the possibilities of an interesting and useful venture was filled with promise. In fact, the three men from Allis-Chalmers winked when they said: "You are going to hear a lot about that idea; that *New York Times* article has certainly stirred up the industry."

Further, and later, talks opened the door to other ideas, such as where the electricity customers—Rural Electrification Cooperatives, municipal, utility companies—are who need power from whatever source. That extraordinarily intelligent and politically knowledgeable Norman—quite unlike his brother Gordon in this respect—will be thinking over this concept, and I'll be hearing from him on specifics, I'm sure.

Analoyce had arranged a meeting with the board of editors of the *Milwaukee Journal,* and with a reporter, a red-haired lively young man, Hayes. I banged right into the spread of nuclear weapons, delivered with more force than I realized I could summon with a completely new group of newspapermen. My purpose was clear to me: to try to get the Carter group to put this issue high on the agenda of the next TV "debate" on October 6, as a prime issue of foreign policy (the ostensible subject of that debate).

Hayes' story on the subject in today's *Journal* was mostly drawn from my January testimony, but not entirely. Whether it will come to the attention of the Carter advisors, as I hoped if I made it strong enough to get on the wires, I may not know. But the story in the *Journal* was generous in space and certainly clear.

My stamina on this trip has been the subject of remark. The most significant thing is that I have neither made a big thing of the endurance I have shown nor actually felt fatigue. Thirty years ago I would have been "exhausted" and going through all kinds of excuses to my hosts as to why I had to rest.

OCTOBER 3, 1976
PRINCETON

To a memorial service for a great scholar and a bubbly friendly man,

Cuyler Young, at the beautiful old Nassau Presbyterian Church on the edge of the Princeton campus.

It was only a month or so ago that Cuyler, his curly hair waving in the breeze, his lively eyes excited as always, came to 88 to receive from us some boxes of plants—myosotis mostly—because his wife enjoyed them so.

What broke me up at the ceremony was the string of *little* grandchildren, the sense that life goes on, one generation shuffles out and another or several more stride on or toddle on. That, plus reading some poems of Archie MacLeish in a splendid essay by Hilton Kramer, art critic of the *Times,* has made me particularly tuned to the "old man's triumph . . . to pursue impossibility—and take it too."

OCTOBER 10, 1976
ROME

Much walking yesterday, with Helen, David, young Margaret.

David talked a good deal about the Italian version of Communism, the political movement which he describes as a grass-roots movement, concerned with local, even neighborhood, problems—a health or family planning clinic. Heading for the Pantheon, we came on a Communist Party meeting, calling for "unità." David translated the speaker's oration —about the need for a neighborhood Communist-sponsored social-services center. First time I had attended a meeting in which the hammer and sickle on a red background (with the green and white of Italy) was flying over a meeting.

OCTOBER 17, 1976
TEHRAN

Feeling very lousy, and not at all sure I can or should try to march up to the Palace, what with a temperature at the moment of 102+.

By God, I *did* it. Got up early, woozy but determined. Walked that "last mile" from the gate and the confused-looking soldiers, climbed the steps in the cold air—the Palace is more than a thousand feet above the elevation of Tehran—swept into the ornate foyer, and exactly at 10 o'clock was greeted with a friendliness and warmth as great, perhaps greater, than at any time in the past twenty-one years!

As we settled into seats, I on the by now familiar sofa, he in his accustomed chair, he mused: "How long has it been since we first met, since you began to help us—eighteen years, is it?"

"Twenty-one, Your Majesty: 1956. It doesn't seem possible. I have probably seen the improvements and changes in this country over a longer period than almost any other foreigner."

He was wearing a heavy suit—it is cold on the side of the mountain —and thrust his hands in his vest pockets, a characteristic pose, looking bemused and recalling the past.

"Then we amounted to nothing. No one had heard of Iran or paid attention to us and our needs and hopes. You were one of the very first Americans who showed you believed in us.

"What are you particularly working on now?"

This was a signal for me to launch into a description of the Public Sector Management Project. I said how remarkable, certainly unique, it was that a sovereign should so thoroughly understand how basic it is to the carrying out of his goals and those of his country that the administrative machinery be improved and strengthened, usually a subject not considered crucial enough or dramatic enough to command that much attention nor the high priority His Majesty had given it.

I reminded him that it was almost two years ago, almost exactly to the day, that he had asked me as head of D&R to take responsibility for bringing to Iran a group of the best-qualified men to advise and assist in this part of the White Revolution. That the theme of the work had been decentralization and diffusion of authority and responsibility, and that had led to giving attention to a new role of the actual managers in the Ministries, the Deputy Ministers; that since being here I had attended and participated as an observer in what had been a two-day round-table discussion group of such Deputies.

That the King was aware of what the PSM group had been involved in was evidenced by his comments. He talked of the just completed local elections for local councils and elected municipal officials. "More than 90% of the people in the localities voted in these elections."

The municipal elections were most successful, he went on, and were about what happens in their own communities, electing men who are responsible to the local people. "And now that we have begun decentralization, the local people are to be given the means in the local councils and municipalities to carry out projects they want in their own localities. No need to come to Tehran, they can get it done through their local officials with funds made available to them."

I felt his interest and attention was so cordial and reciprocal, I launched into Khuzistan.

I reminded His Majesty that years ago—how many I couldn't recall, offhand—he had said to me that if I ran into problems that would result in delays in programs for which he held me responsible, I should waste no time bringing them directly to his attention rather than go through the channels of the Ministries. We had certainly had "problems" during the years.

However, believing that a good "servant" should solve problems himself rather than bring them to him, I had never done so. But this morning I was reporting on a failure that was clearly beyond me to do much about, but that he could.

The entire program of agricultural production has not succeeded. The country is importing more and more food and becoming less and less self-sufficient in food. There have been "promises" and vast programs announced but the fact is that agriculture is lagging, and urban people must meet higher prices and sometimes inadequate supplies of food.

He did not agree that no progress had been made. But he said there was discontent among city people about food prices and supplies. The lives of peasants were still largely untouched by the general prosperity due to oil revenues. "This could be dangerous," he said, but didn't elaborate.

I went on: the great plains of the Khuzistan region could provide much of the answer. That is what he said in 1964: the soil of Khuzistan could feed the whole of Iran. He broke in: "Much of our land is not fertile, but the soil and water and climate of Khuzistan are exceptional."

The basic facts have remained as we all understood them fifteen years ago: the water has been stored behind the Pahlavi Dam, the soil responds to good handling, is excellent considering how many centuries it has not been cultivated, the infrastructure is now in place—roads, amenities, labor supply is plentiful, and so on. The sugar cane operation at Haft Tapeh is one of the most profitable in the world, and is expanding.

The Shah broke in, in agreement, referring to future plans for sugar, including beets.

On my own initiative some ten or twelve years ago I proposed interesting foreign private investment of money and technology in the farming of these great flat areas. We had much to do with inducing large agribusiness corporations to take up leases, put their money in, bring in modern technology.

The owners of the agribusiness operations were told that they were taking on far too large areas in individual management than could be well operated—15,000 acres in a single unit. But these agribusiness corporations took no advice from anyone. They were "beset by greed," they expected to make a big profit from these leases in a very short time, not accepting the fact that agriculture is a much slower kind of business than industry, so far as results are concerned.

This result has been more than a financial disaster for these companies; it is a setback to Iran's need for the full productivity of this remarkable area, the best potential in the country, one of the best in the world.

I went on to my diagnosis of what should be done: to return to the "unified plan" for the region, by which a public agency, Khuzistan Water and Power Authority or its successor, should have more than a concession-giving role. It should be the public instrument for bringing to the farming lands the overall judgment of a public body having responsibility for making Khuzistan a great source of food for the country, rather than a means of providing financial returns to a few owners.

That had been the original concept, the one that His Majesty had approved long ago.

But as the years went along, KWPA, instead of having a comprehensive planning and execution role, drifted into being simply an electric power company, with no interest in agriculture, not even in the regional agricultural development center at Safiabad.

From this diagnosis of what might be done I got no response. Whether because of his long-time evidence of courtesy toward me and my ideas, whether he agreed or not, or because he was really thinking about what I said and reserved comment, I couldn't tell.

I am not going to make any friends in the official hierarchy by reminding them of the failure of agriculture in this country, or the downgrading of Khuzistan. I am not a great admirer of the way Rouhani, the Minister of Agriculture, has handled his job, though he is an extraordinarily dedicated and enthusiastic man. He is given to spinning off new formulae, some of them pretty way out—importing thousands and thousands of cattle, before there is forage, etc.—a sad story.

The Shah talked more about oil than at any time since long ago when he complained to me that "your country" buys more oil from Kuwait, an unimportant country of "crazy Arabs" than from Iran, a friend.

His expression during this part of the audience was one of intense concentration, measuring his words. The net effect: that he had been told by the oil companies and his own experts "that in thirty years oil will be finished" in Iran. He must begin at once to develop other sources of energy, and so he has begun a big atomic energy program. He didn't ask for any comment on this from me. I decided as he spoke not to inject my present views about atomic energy into the discussion.

But it gave me my cue to launch into my current chief enthusiasm, small (or intermediate) hydro. The point I hoped he would respond to most was that I was looking ahead for areas of energy that had been overlooked or not made use of because the experts' minds became fixed on their own concepts—i.e., that in the U.S. hydro was no longer of consequence. I characterized the mentality of those as inflexible, that this was the same kind of outlook (FAO etc.) that had dismissed Khuzistan twenty years ago as an area of no potential and had overlooked the site of the Pahlavi Dam.

This latter part of what I said about lack of imagination he followed closely, his head cocked to one side.

As we moved to the door I said Mr. Macy had been elected President of D&R. This remark the Shah greeted with lifted eyebrows of interest —surprise?—so I went on to say that I would continue as Chairman. I asked if John Macy, who had accompanied me and was waiting in the outer office, could step in to meet His Majesty. He didn't say aye or nay, so I opened the big door and beckoned to John, who came in while the Shah was standing waiting for me to depart. The Shah greeted John with graciousness and apparent pleasure, and John gave him the spirit of the Public Sector effort in a brief and very formal dignified way. It was obviously a big moment for John, and a great satisfaction for me.

As personal a reference to me and how he felt about my long years in Iran came as the exchange with John concluded—a matter of a few minutes. "Mr. Lilienthal knows Iran and was Iran's friend when no one knew much about us, as they today do. We were"—and his face was drawn with pain at the memory of this point—"miserable. He has always been a true friend from that day to this, and we have benefited from his advice and help."

OCTOBER 22, 1976
FLYING PAN AM TO LONDON

Coming through the dark padded doors, Minister Jamshid Amouzegar greeted me warmly, and his obvious delight in John Macy was evidence that they have become close friends in the past two and a half years.

John summarized some of the recent developments in decentralization, which has become the theme word and concept in our work in Iran as it was for so many years in TVA and Colombia. The Minister is chairman of what is called the Council on Decentralization, a national body under the Prime Minister. What a mark of acceptance of the principle and goal this is! Then D&R's PSM project recommendation of the merger of two Ministries in the field of education was touched upon, with some satisfaction.

I brought up the subject that above all is identified with Iran and Amouzegar: Oil.

Amouzegar's almost Mephistophelean features burst into life—this was indeed his "bag."

He gave a most remarkable critique of the hell-bent pace of development in Iran, a pace he stated clearly was more rapid and less orderly than he or anyone wanted—too fast to be based upon sober planning and careful execution, considering the shortage of skilled manpower and the other difficulties in a country moving ahead with such unprecedented speed.

Why does the Shah insist on such a pace? Because he has been advised that Iran's oil will be exhausted in thirty years, so no time can be lost to derive the revenues for development while the oil lasts.

But is it true that all the oil will be pumped out in that time; what about going back and recovering, by reprocessing methods, the 20% or so that was not and is not presently being extracted? At 75¢ a barrel, the very last 20% or 40% might not be "economic" to recover. But at $10 or $12 or now nearly $14 a barrel, isn't it worth the extra cost to squeeze out the billions of barrels not extracted in the earlier or even the current state of petroleum extraction?

He asked: How could he, not an expert, contest the opinion of oil experts?

An hour after we left Amouzegar, we were climbing the long red carpeted steps of the office of the Prime Minister. It was a beautiful day. Golden sun, a sky of such a glowing blue as to lift the heart, the mottled shadows cast by the great trees along Pasteur Avenue a delight to the eye and the senses.

The dark-visaged solemn woman who sits in on the Prime Minister's meetings, silently, expressionlessly, motioned us in. From behind his desk at the other side of the room (and not a very large room, at that) came a hail: "Hello, friend Lilienthal." This is Hoveyda's usual salutation to me whenever I meet him. Looking over his half-glasses, the perky orchid, his trademark, in the buttonhole of his coat, the gay, happy smile that he wears most of the time in contrast to the harassed look of most of his Ministers and indeed of his predecessor Prime Ministers I have known—it was a pleasant way to relax after the tense, frustrated, highly intellectual Minister of the Interior whose office we had just left.

"And how is your election going to come out? How about Carter and his chances? You, friend Lilienthal, ought to know if anyone does; you know everybody in America. Your *Journals*—I have read most of the latest one you gave me, and thank you for it, as I have read the earlier five volumes—everybody who is anybody in America is in there."

His mischievous face broke out into a grin: "I notice that we of Iran are a kind of issue; we were mentioned in the debates." So he keeps up with the campaign, probably more than any of his colleagues.

He said Iran wouldn't have oil or oil revenues forever: "We are told it will only be another thirty years, which is a pretty short time. So we are in need of other sources of energy and income when the oil does run out—and so are you; isn't that right?" (He had just returned from a trip to France to finalize contracts for a number of reactors to be produced by France with American know-how and Westinghouse licenses.)

I agreed, of course, and used this comment to give my spiel about neglected hydro and the troubles, in a cost sense, of atomic energy.

What I said about small hydro struck a spark of interest not shown by the Shah or Amouzegar. I said perhaps it would be worthwhile for Iran to consider a center of information about alternative new sources of energy, such as hydro.

"Send the memo directly to me. The Minister of Energy is too conservative for new ideas of that kind. He's not very sure of himself."

Two quite casual comments about atomic energy were made by this durable little man, neither of which gave me much reassurance about the level of understanding or seriousness with which this, to me, awesome subject is being treated by this apex (or next to apex) of power in the world.

"We don't want a bomb." But they do want the whole technology. Does he know what he is talking about?

And the match to this offhand remark. "A high-school boy proved that he could make an atomic bomb just from what he read in the public press." This is that same myth that we have heard—even in the Senate hearings—intended to prove that proliferation can't be stopped just by withholding information. On this one, I broke in, to say that anyone who tried to fabricate plutonium was dead right there. But of course, I made no impression, then or elsewhere.

OCTOBER 25, 1976
HEATHROW AIRPORT, LONDON

Here we have been sitting in a din and clatter, since 10 o'clock, and the latest word from Pan Am is that the plane is "delayed" until four. Five-hour delay, and more to come, no doubt.

The delights of foreign travel!

This morning the *New York Times* announced, on the best kind of reasoning, that it supports Carter.

7 P.M.

Here we are on a British Airways plane, "rebooked" in a flurry of excitement and recriminations, when it finally appeared at about six that Pan Am could not deliver.

A heartening start on hydro was confirmed most recently by Ken Fields and Tom Mead, reporting by telex about their meeting in York, Pennsylvania, with the Allis-Chalmers people, and Reuben Brown from the Polytechnic Institute in Brooklyn.

I have just had a devilishly painful experience: my cursed legs and feet. Had to walk and stand a good deal during the afternoon and to the plane. The pain was so ugly that before I had finished the walk to the plane, I was half faint.

Am I to let those damned leg muscles make a cripple out of me? Surely there is some doc who can do more than recommend exercises.

OCTOBER 31, 1976
PRINCETON

I am still in the process of pulling myself together, physically. I didn't realize it so much at the time, but there was a drain of energies and spirit in the long trip, and the accompanying illness, and angst, as well as strong affirmation and excitement packed into less than a three-week period.

This is intensified by the return of my super-energetic partner and President, John Macy. He began at once to beat the drums of action; what action? Never mind what, for him the important thing is to do something, set up appointments, write letters, speculate, go places.

At a low point in the depletion cycle, before I have recharged, the stubborn question keeps emerging: *When* do you call it quits? When and how do you give up this prodigious ambitious program and personal commitment through D&R? Surely there will be a time when you will want to say: I have had it, have had a full life, so stop where you are. But that time never seems to be now.

NOVEMBER 3, 1976
NEW YORK

At 3:30 this morning, Jimmy Carter was declared elected.

How pleased I was by the fact that the "apathy" didn't exist, apathy so freely predicted by the pundits for weeks.

I am such a partisan that I can detect partisanship by the TV voices when it probably only means that they are trying to keep a contest alive, when it is apparent that the contest is over.

Now, can Carter deliver? How many of his promises will he have to modify?

There will surely be a new spirit in the political scene. The stuffy people will be replaced in time by—by what? People less stuffy but perhaps more awkward.

In only one particular am I sure that this is indeed a great change, and a cosmic change. The humiliation of our treatment of Negroes (now called "blacks") which wounded me so when I first went to live in the South is definitely on its way out, by reason of this election.

NOVEMBER 4, 1976
NEW YORK

The painting for my office I "commissioned" Beatrice to do months ago is now hanging there, and I enjoy it so much. She is a very accomplished painter, that one.

This morning, while I am in a mood for complaining (or wincing) from the pain in my thigh muscles, making walking a second-class "ordeal," in comes John Macy. "I bring you greetings from a friend, Jim Webb, who I saw at breakfast. The poor guy has Parkinson's and it has changed his whole personality. Once so positive and aggressive, now with his hands shaking and so on, he has become tentative and negative."

The picture of Jim Webb faced with a future of living with that disease, all the worse for so outgiving and physically assertive of men. You and your thigh muscles!

Moving along on the hydro project, which looks more and more promising. Added to by the calling, by Governor Carey, of a regional conference of six state Governors, and others, for November 13 and 14. I'm at the moment the "only man alive" who has actually put together a regional enterprise embracing many states.

Will I speak up, or get crowded into a comfortable corner by those who have a special "angle," mostly rhetoric, about putting pressure on this Administration and Congress simply to get more funds from the Federal treasury in a united lobby? I should make a major TVA speech soon. The election results and this "conference" make it most timely.

NOVEMBER 9, 1976
PRINCETON

There will never be another day quite like this. There will never be another sunset quite like the gold and plum-blue that streaks through the bare branches from this upstairs living room. And there never was, nor will be, just this kind of today since I awoke.

So cherish it; cherish each day, each hour.

NOVEMBER 12, 1976
NEW YORK

Daniel Patrick Moynihan was the dinner guest and speaker at the Twentieth Century Fund last night. He proceeded to give us a classroom lecture. All he said was that the tension of frustration produced aggression. A crazy kind of hair-splitting evening it was.

The Senator-elect is a strange phenomenon. Very tall, the kind of figure that seems to be leaning way forward and could fall at any moment. A classroom manner. How he was elected I can't figure, but he was, decisively, and that proves something, proves a good deal. But *what* I am not sure. My preference for the earthy, honest, non-Ph.D.-ish uncomplicated Bella Abzug to whose primary campaign I contributed was confirmed.

Helen and I did a tourist "thing" together this afternoon, after the Twentieth Century board meeting. Went up 107 floors and then some more to the top of one of the Trade Center towers. A clear day: a princely view of a great, a unique city, and the empire that enfolds.

I was more than a quarter of a mile in the air because of the board meeting. Exciting subjects, alert competitive trustees, and idea-hungry staff group gathered about like predators ready to pounce on any lame idea or to adopt (and probably if necessary, subvert) criticism.

I had two high (more than one-quarter-mile high) moments. One, a proposal from a highly cleared scholar for a study and book about "regional development" in the U.S. A long-winded text explaining what he proposed to elucidate. Actually, his mind was on depressed cities and how we have gone about (miserably, actually) pulling them out of their doldrums by "regional economic development."

"Well," said Jim Rowe, presiding, "we have here on my right hand the world-famous expert on this subject." Invited me to comment.

I had read the proposal yesterday, noted that the fellow hadn't mentioned the only fully developed and going example of regional development, TVA.

How to make my point without seeming too prideful of my child, and too disdainful. So I read an opening sentence: The beginning of Federal commitment to regional development was in May 1961—citing a statute about something or other.

I stopped. "I think Franklin Roosevelt would find that sentence rather remarkable." I thought Charley Taft would laugh his head off.

I called the attention of the trustees to the fact that the subject of regional economic development was more than a study of laws or patch-work experience, but would be on the front pages of the papers, beginning tomorrow: the "Coalition of Governors" of the Northeast. Therefore, we had some responsibility to support a sound and objective report and book on the subject. The man's proposal was obviously too broad, and everyone, including the staff, agreed.

Another proposal dealt with nuclear proliferation—and here again I was referred (and deferred) to as "the pioneer in this field of public policy."

Over last weekend I had felt so fatigued and dispirited. "I am at the end of the line, and should not wait until others shake me off; get out while you can." Today's performance and warm reception throughout the meeting and the succeeding lunch—well, put off that recognition of "sad decline."

NOVEMBER 13, 1976
SARATOGA SPRINGS, NEW YORK

In my most wishful-thinking days, never would I ever expect to hear six or seven Governors of the northeastern states spend a day extolling regionalism. The tall, lanky Green Mountain Governor of *Vermont*(!) said, fervently: "I *believe* in regionalism."

NOVEMBER 15, 1976
PRINCETON

The strongest personality, appropriately, was the sponsor of the meeting, Hugh Carey, Governor of the dominant state. Whether on the podium guiding the Governor-speakers through their paces, or sitting across a small table from me at a breakfast meeting yesterday early morning, product of a far from blue-ribbon district near the Navy Yard in Brooklyn and of years in Congress, Carey has learned how to deal with equals.

Felix Rohatyn, who made up the fourth of our breakfast table, was very much in evidence throughout the weekend at Saratoga. He is living on his extraordinary success in saving New York City (temporarily, at least) from a default on its notes and a collapse of morale from very severe cuts in public services.

Rohatyn acknowledged that his proposal for a regional energy and development corporation for the Northeast was "just following in Dave's footsteps"; he was warm and generous. He seemed readily to acknowledge my criticism that a "compact" between the states would be the legal framework. When I praised him without qualification to Governor Carey, I meant it.

But I was concerned before the breakfast was over by a sense of the overdramatic on broad issues. I recognize both the thinness of a banking or financial background and temperament. A serious and sobering example:

Governor Carey, full of vehemence, repeated what he had said to the full audience about the effect of still another increase in OPEC prices. Felix leaned over the table and began to describe the precarious financial position of the New York City banks. He went on to condemn the banks —Rockefeller, and Wriston of Citibank particularly, and had to their face —for having loaned vast sums to European countries at a great profit, thus those countries—France, Britain, Italy, and Japan—would be likely to accept or acquiesce in further oil price increases. The effect of the latter on the American cities and states would be disastrous. He completed the picture by predicting a major crisis world-wide.

He said flatly: "If that happens, we should go through the Persian Gulf and take over the oil wells. A few parachute landings would do it."

Coming from a man with no particular responsibilities, that would be barbershop talk. But from Felix, talking to the Governor of a great state and, as it happened, to Senator Javits, a senior member of the Senate Committee on Foreign Relations, I thought this was more than show-off.

The Governor of the Commonwealth of Massachusetts, Michael Dukakis, was a very impressive fellow. Very dark hair and eyes, excellent speaking voice. In the lobby he stopped me, "When I was a student at Swarthmore, I read your speech on the regional administration of central national powers. That has stuck with me ever since and has a lot to do with my thinking about what I must consider here as a Governor." So ideas and words score again, I guess.

The substantive work of the conference was excellent, and some action resulted. Bill Miller, my new friend from Textron Corporation, headed a panel on energy that was an excellent summary of the situation not only for the Northeast but for the country.

The panel headed by Felix, on which I sat, did bring in a resolution favoring a regional energy and development corporation, and without detail, this was accepted by the Governors.

I enjoyed meeting new people. A group from Vermont, for example, who were quite excited by my fevered expressions about small hydro. Similarly, a youngish "power engineer," Bill Kelly, who knows gas turbines, and believes our ideas could be great for the whole electric supply problem, and illustrated it from his experience with gas turbines. I spread the concept of small hydros wherever I went.

NOVEMBER 17, 1976
NEW YORK

This is the day—mark it well—when my Energy Project for America was truly launched.

Today at a luncheon meeting with Rockefeller, Macy, Silveira, I laid out my ideas about how we take the next steps toward an energy program emphasizing waterpower. That I made it clear came through when Rodman, quite obviously geared up by the "presentation," said: "What you are talking about is a *consortium.*" Exactly.

NOVEMBER 20, 1976
PRINCETON

"Follow-up": one of John Macy's "principles." Thus, when you make a point or advance a step toward an objective, immediately *follow-up.* So when I suggested that the luncheon meeting with Rodman of the preceding day called for clarification, he said: "Let's see Rodman. Right now." Which we did. With a remarkable and unexpected result.

The energy plan as I had sketched it calls for a separate entity, separate from D&R. Apparently he understood this and had accepted it when he used the term "consortium."

Let me now try to report verbatim the next few minutes of this meeting.

Rodman said, turning to me, his face flushed and eyes quite bright: "There is another subject I want to take up with you, not in detail right now, but before long. Whatever comes out of this great new initiative, there must be some tangible way to recognize your achievements. Not only what has happened during the past five years since D&R and IBEC have been working together. But your children and your grandchildren should be benefited by a share in the profits of this latest plan of yours. A small percentage of the profits, perhaps, or shares. What you have devised and will work out is the very capstone of your career, and your children and grandchildren should be taken care of by the profits."

So, like a dope, I said that fortunately my children and grandchildren would receive from our estate more than would be "good for them," without anything from an idea that has yet to prove itself.

He was disappointed—as, so it turned out, was John Macy—by this prosaic response.

Whereupon we left his office. Macy said: "That was a remarkable thing that just happened. The fact that he expressed it in the only way a Rockefeller or other rich man can—that is, in money terms—hides the

'emotion' that impelled him to speak with such feeling, and so spontaneously. Don't underestimate the practical importance of what was said,
with such strong feeling. You think it is vague and expressed as a share
of an enterprise which he might have claimed belongs to him as owner
of all D&R common stock. It isn't that at all."

Thinking it over later, I found much in what Macy said and wrote a
longhand note to Rodman along that line.

NOVEMBER 23, 1976
NEW YORK

Have just had further evidence that my hydro orphan, after being
ignored, made to seem ridiculous, is now being embraced even by ERDA,
and is the subject of an interagency conference sponsored by the Federal
Power Commission.

I have yet to come up with a formula for making this issue seem as
important as I think it is. Such as a major consortium.

NOVEMBER 25, 1976
PRINCETON

A perfect Thanksgiving Day, family-style. Beatrice, Barney, David
and Nancy Tobey drove out for a mid-afternoon dinner, and a jolly time
around a fire. So impressed with the change in David over the years; how
confident and secure he is now, and more gracious with his family and
with us. Nancy seemed half withdrawn, but so lovely and so lively an
imagination.

A relaxed day it has been.

A long phone talk with Daniel. To listen to a young person who is full
of enthusiasm about his first months in college (Hampshire) is a tonic.
His interest in Latin America higher than ever, this time about Peru.
Asking me for any thoughts I have about the agricultural conditions and
the political and social circumstances affecting agriculture; wants me to
send full material about the Piura region which was too voluminous, we
thought, to be included in the published version of Volume VI.

DECEMBER 2, 1976
NEW YORK

André Meyer left me at the door of the elevator to his apartment at
the Carlyle.

The meeting was a happy one for me. It gave me a chance to say, in robust terms, how good it was to see him again, and to tell him what he knows, how much he did for me years ago.

I was glad Mrs. Meyer was present (and gave me tea).

André spoke of current events very little. Did I know Carter? Could he meet the terrible problems? "I have never been pessimistic before; but I am now, very. So much has been loaned against values that don't exist. I can't imagine how it will come out."

He was interested in drawing me out about D&R and about IBEC. He knows that IBEC isn't so much, but I said we were allowed to go our own way. "I am not sure," said I rather tactlessly, "whether IBEC has taken over D&R or the other way around." He understood that.

He asked about Helen, and said what an "intelligent and strong woman" she is. His last words as I left were, "Be sure to remember me to your wife."

I spoke highly of Felix Rohatyn's role in the Northeast Governors' Conference on energy and development. "Felix is very good in business," he said, with that glaze in his eyes I recall so well. "But he doesn't have time now for the work of the firm. And he thinks we should go to war because of oil. He put that idea in other people's minds—even Governor Carey's."

DECEMBER 3, 1976
NEW YORK

The *Times* this morning reports that Secretary of State Cyrus Vance is the first of the Cabinet about to be designated. Indeed, Johnson Administration retreads, experienced men and able, are being actively considered for the most responsible of the Carter posts. This is reassuring, since some of the names mentioned in the press are people with little experience of government or anything else.

I hope Carter keeps his hands off Macy, except part-time perhaps. The Johnson Administration, despite the Vietnam disaster, contained some exceptionally able men, and Macy as personnel advisor and talent scout had a lot to do with that.

DECEMBER 4, 1976
PRINCETON

"Rassling" with the horrible consequences of the splitting of the atom continues to be a heritage some of us can't shake off. The earliest chapter occupied me in the winter of 1946–47, thirty years ago. The most recent was my "statement" to the Senate Committee on Government

Operations calling for an embargo or moratorium on any further export of the critical stuff.

Thursday afternoon and evening—a year after that testimony of last January—I had the satisfaction of observing how seriously that testimony had forced a re-examination of a way to deal with the most recent baleful consequences of the exploding atom—the spread of nuclear weapons.

I sat with a group of perhaps thirty-five people at the Council on Foreign Relations, seeking to throw some light on the issue that I insisted was current, that we should not resign ourselves to the "inevitability" of the spread of these weapons, but set out to find, if not a solution, then an accommodation that would reduce the risk of world catastrophe.

The leading voice in the meeting was a wise-looking baldish fellow, new to me, but already famous among those names associated with atomic matters, Robert Fri. A senior associate of Robert Seamans', head of ERDA, he prepared a report for President Ford analyzing the picture, and coming up with proposals, the most significant of which was to stop the reprocessing activity for a period of three years, reprocessing of the spent fuel of atomic reactors, the product of which would be plutonium, the material for bombs.

This recommendation, approved by the President and not different from Carter's statement on the subject, is the substance of what I called for a year ago. It was in contrast to the testimony of the State Department witnesses (including Kissinger) before the same Committee, the essence of which was, "It is too late—the spread of weapons is inevitable; other countries can go ahead without American counsel or leadership."

Most of the ground covered by the discussion around the table at the Council was old stuff. A puzzlement. I recalled a comment made after a comparable fruitless discussion years ago, though then the issue was "control" of the weapons themselves. As we walked out, Robert Oppenheimer muttered to me, "Dave, that was a class B movie, but one we have seen three times before."

Macy and Chuck Luce, chairman of Con Ed, both new to this particular struggle, had a different view of this subject. They thought it was "useful" and productive.

Paul Leventhal was on hand, as former Committee counsel and spur of Senator Ribicoff's effort in this field. His comments didn't add much. He has been most generous to me, from the start, since he first saw the pre-release of my January testimony.

In a letter to me recently, he wrote: "Clearly, your testimony was the turning point in the battle to win the ear of the Congress. I believe that your statement was truly historic, and I am grateful beyond these inadequate words."

DECEMBER 5, 1976
PRINCETON

A long leading article in the *New York Times Magazine* this morning, condemning the dispersal of atomic technology and materials throughout the world, by someone who is reported to be a member of the California Public Utilities Commission.

DECEMBER 7, 1976
NEW YORK

Saigon revisited, this afternoon, in my office.

Among the crowd of sadistic newspapermen—several hundred—gathered for the Five O'Clock Saigon Follies, the official daily briefing from and hectoring of the American military officer, there had been a very short, tough-visaged little guy, one of the AP contingent. Today he sat across my desk and gave what can only be called a counter-interview. His name: Peter Arnett.

He asked to interview me about my latest *Journal* volume, the latter part of which, of course, is much about the Vietnam war as I saw it and reflected upon it. He explained that he had spent about eight years as the leading AP man out there in Saigon; that he had followed the troops in the field, knew and greatly respected the Vietnamese.

In the most energetic and eloquent way, he took over, and for at least twenty to thirty minutes I heard a firsthand story of how our military and civilian spokesmen in Vietnam and in Washington had dodged, evaded, and hid the truth about that war—hid it from themselves. "It was not so much deception as wishful thinking.

"The insights and the illustrative episodes in your *Journals* are the best—I think really the only—full disclosure of what it was that was really going on, filled with pictures of people, what they said, why they said it. Nowhere is there anything like what you have recorded, in direct quotation and in graphic language. Your *Journals* will be a major source for the coming history of the Vietnam war and its aftermath."

This was welcome comment.

Truth to tell (though I'm a bit ashamed of how I have begun to feel), I am more than a bit hurt that there has been so little by way of major reviews of Volume VI.

I said: "Why this chilly avoidance of the volume, if as you say, it does contain so much that is superior, even unique, recording such major events as the Guam Conference and the visit with Ambassador Porter and the false optimism of Bob Komer?"

His answer: "In the newspaper world, the Vietnam war is dead.

There is no interest in it now. But to the publishers of magazines and particularly of solid books, it is very much a live subject. Several major books are being written and will be published soon. Indeed, I am writing one myself after all those years out there."

My vignettes and appraisal of Johnson he thought highly of. And now that Lyndon Johnson's Administration is apparently (so the newspaper speculations go) producing much of the top-level personnel for the new Carter Administration, my favorable and graphic pictures of Johnson will be increasingly of interest, so he thought.

Maybe.

DECEMBER 8, 1976
NEW YORK

I am spending more and more time on the extraordinary set of memoranda from the Public Sector Management front. They are an excellent way to sense the nuances of one of the most significant public tasks in my whole public life. Tonight I found I was rather annotating them, here and there. An indication of how interesting they are, how they conjure up the people and the situations they report way out there in Iran's badly organized, rattling governmental machine.

DECEMBER 12, 1976
PRINCETON

An afternoon with Julian Boyd, from which we have just returned, is living in the 18th century; or better still, reliving the early days of this Republic. He and Grace live in an old and tasteful house, near those very stretches of countryside that are part of the Revolutionary story.

It is Jefferson that Julian brings alive, for he has spent years pursuing every fragment of that great man's life.

Helen turned out to be the star of a Jefferson story, in a most surprising way. Julian reminded us that Jefferson, when President, had written letters to all the American Indian tribal chiefs, recognizing their rights and the treaty obligations of the Republic. But Julian found some years ago that of all those very important letters, only one had been preserved; that it was in the possession of the chief of the Oto tribe in Oklahoma. A group of history buffs (including Arthur Houghton) went to Oklahoma to secure that letter as part of the Jefferson Papers.

Said Helen: "I was brought up in Perry, only a few miles from the Oto Reservation; I remember their coming into town, their papooses carried in a blanket by their mothers, the women with their hair hanging down in braids sitting in the town square. In Oklahoma at that time the Otos were not considered very much, not compared with the Cherokees and Osages, who were the aristocrats of the Indians of Oklahoma."

Good conversation is not easy to come by. This we find at the Boyd luncheon table, on our annual journeys, accompanied by Joe and Kitty Johnson. Thus: was George Washington as great as we have been taught to believe?—Julian uttering some minor but specific dissent. Who was the greater man, Washington or John Marshall? Citing examples that made me feel as if they were very much alive and part of current newspaper stories.

What was it that made Joe Johnson express such vast admiration for General George Marshall? Said Joe, defending his position against my query: just what had he done by way of great policy initiatives? Judgment, that is what Marshall had—and Joe would be explicit.

What was the turning point in the American Revolution? Julian and Joe agreed, spontaneously: the day that Washington, challenging a contrary view of his military leaders, decided against the idea of a monarchy as the only way in which a country could be governed.

DECEMBER 13, 1976
PRINCETON

On a starlit winter night such as this, a lavender fire popping, the delicate tones of a Horowitz recording, utterly quiet and peaceful. How serene, how secure. The "world" off there, and I not part of it. How comforting, pleasant, dreamlike.

Then why in hell do I keep going into the City, puzzling myself over problems once so exciting and new, now so much of a pattern?

That is my real world, not this. That's the answer to those questions, those apostrophes.

DECEMBER 17, 1976
NEW YORK

France announces that it will put an embargo on nuclear processing plants. Last January 21 when I had made such a proposal—though a broader one—for the U.S., I ran into McGeorge Bundy on the shuttle who —with that grin some people find condescending—said: "But how are you going to handle the French?" My bravado was showing: "We will find a way to handle the French."

And we'll "handle" the Germans, too.

DECEMBER 21, 1976
NEW YORK

A long phone call to Allis-Chalmers (Jim Meyers) tells me that that big hardboiled company has decided that the ideas I presented to them in Milwaukee early last fall have set them on a five-year plan for a *new* market for turbines—a new concept for a company that has been in that business for decades. The Allis-Chalmers' commitment, based, so Meyers declares, upon my notions, pretty largely, is not a paper-thin one from a promoter unwilling or unable to put funds and prestige into such a venture, but a seasoned company, among the more successful industrial companies in the company.

DECEMBER 22, 1976
NEW YORK

When I had described the Public Sector Project for Iran to Jonathan Daniels, he made his classic response of skepticism: "You'll never in the world get your high-falutin' technical ideas accepted and acted upon by the local tax collector and others in the Iranian equivalent of the grass roots." Then he shot his wonderful barb: "But good luck, Peter Pan."

Yesterday comes word that the Joint Committee on Atomic Energy, "the most powerful Committee on the Hill," appears to be approaching its end. Despite the roars of Pastore, the prestige of Chet Holifield, the maneuvering of Congressman Hosmer, my 1963 Stafford Little Lecture calling for an end to what I then called an anachronism seems about to become the will of the Congress—according to the latest word on Jonathan Bingham's bill.

It took from 1963 to 1976 for such a change, and other changes about the atom to take place. But the unraveling began with my testimony before the Senate Committee on proliferation last January, less than a year ago.

DECEMBER 24, 1976
PRINCETON

Yesterday Carter confirmed that he did intend to call for a reorganization of agencies of the Government dealing with energy. The evening TV news report was largely given over to the designation of James Schlesinger as head of a new Department of Energy and Natural Resources.

The most worthwhile part of the week's work, though, was that I produced a statement about a "new organization," a Consortium on Energy, which came out to be an understandable summary of what I have been kicking around in my mind, and extemporizing with Macy, Ken Fields, and Tom Mead for some time.

I came into the house yesterday noon to find Helen talking on the phone in the hall, saying, "I hear him coming right now." Said she, handing me the phone: "It's Senator Scoop Jackson to speak to you."

At John's insistence I had put in a call for Scoop, to tell him of our ideas about hydro and the reorganization.

Scoop's voice (from Everett, Washington, his hometown) had the boom of a man who has lost none of his self-assurance and fight.

He said it's been decided that there will be an Energy and Natural Resources Department, reporting to his Committee (Interior). Jim Schlesinger will head it; that was announced this morning. I didn't know Schlesinger except through correspondence while he was AEC Chairman.

Scoop said, "You will like him. I want you to phone him, and tell him you have talked to me. He is on the professor side, but he will do a good job.

"The Joint Committee is dead. And it should be."

I told him I was preoccupied with unused waterpower, and better organization of energy; had written a brief piece for the *Times*. He asked me to send it in manuscript; takes a long time to get the *Times* out there in Washington State. Gave me his address and phone number. "Wait a minute; let me give you Jim Schlesinger's phone number. Thought I had it here. Hold on while I go upstairs to get it."

Same informal, full-voiced Scoop.

"I have a man in my office now who will head the Energy Department staff, name of Daniel Dreyfus. Very good man."

DECEMBER 26, 1976
PRINCETON

A white cake frosting over everything. What yesterday was pine and rhodo and dogwood, this morning is delicious fluff, a professional confectioner's fantasy. Now the sun makes it all a glowing whiteness, a texture seen only in fantasies told to children.

DECEMBER 28, 1976
NEW YORK

I confess to a certain satisfaction in seeing my piece about energy from waters filling more than half the Op-Ed page of the *Times* this morning. I really thought the *Times* wouldn't print it at all; then that it would be "squoze down" in a corner. But what did appear was a splendid wood print of a waterfall, and my piece at the head of the page.

So this is a day when the venture of an "energy consortium" has carved its name too high and evident to be completely ignored. Another step on a new venture, and it could be one of the biggest ones I've ever attempted.

I *think* Lilienthal Luck continues, for in a mimeographed letter from the TVA power staff, I learned that Jim Watson, Power Manager of TVA, is "retiring" January 1. Lost no time phoning him: would he come up and discuss some kind of participation with us on a new energy venture? He certainly would. What he wants is to stay in the energy picture, in this country (doesn't want to work full-time; doesn't want to go abroad). So in a couple weeks he'll be here to see if he fits the bill we need to take some of the load off my back. For the fact is, I'm the only one who knows enough about electric energy, in a non-technical sense, to move these ideas forward.

DECEMBER 31, 1976
PRINCETON

Once again year's end. A day of beauty outside. In this home for two life-long companions and friends, there is clarity, calm, the doing of the day's "things."

The year was a year of exceptional activity, of not a little productivity, of happiness almost without a major blemish.

The year began with as important and consequential a statement on a public problem as any since my 1946 statement on international control of atomic energy, my statement before the Senate Committee on Government Operations, on January 19. By the end of the year it was evident that the position I took that day produced results, from the highest quarters —i.e., President Ford and President-elect Carter.

My speech to the Planners, in Washington on March 22, was productive too. It encouraged me to believe that not only did I have "something to say," but that people would listen.

The sixth volume of the *Journals* was certainly a mark of productivity.

I question seriously whether I should undertake to produce Volume VII. The material will be there for examination by those methodical creatures: "scholars." But if I must put out another book, shouldn't it be in something other than journal form?

Just this week I did write a 700-word article that was greeted well by

Oakes and the *Times,* published in a prominent place, and likely to be read and discussed.

This was the culmination of earlier expressions about the energy from waters, begun in a TV panel performance on Robert MacNeil's Channel 13 program back in May.

It was characteristic of me that I was not content to leave the subject of added energy to a series of speeches. I had to think of how to turn those words into action. I was not impressed with the paper studies about undeveloped waterpower. They seemed too academic and abstract to satisfy my craving for something that would actually produce a new chapter in the story of hydroelectric production, a story in which through TVA and Khuzistan I have participated over the years.

So now, I have thrown down the gage (to myself) and, with my Op-Ed piece, I have my work cut out for me for 1977.

Apparently professional work isn't enough to satisfy me. I have lived a long, long time, have seen great changes and have predicted many of them; have seen my own outlook as a man about personal and public things move and vibrate. I surely have something to say about that life.

Can I write a summing up that will be an exciting writing task, and have meaning for others, get a good reception now while I'm here to witness it?

X

1977

~~⚬~~

Vacation in Antigua—Development of small hydropower ideas and practical applications—Energy issues
and Appalachian Regional Commission—Trip to Iran

JANUARY 13, 1977
PRINCETON

Tuesday evening I left a five-hour meeting at the Council on Foreign
Relations with my spirits very low.

This was the second convening of a supposedly select group on how
to prevent the spread of atomic weapons. We listened to a 19th century
career Foreign Service Officer report on the "secret meetings of nuclear
supplier nations," being held over a period of several months, in London.
Our State Department was participating (being a nuclear "supplier"
nation, God knows), in what was described by Kissinger last year as an
effort to get agreements that would slow up or stop proliferation.

The net effect, so far as the outside world knew, was the explosion of
an atomic bomb by India, and agreements by Germany and France to
supply Brazil, Pakistan, and Korea (perhaps also Egypt and Israel, by the
U.S.) with the technology for producing plutonium from "spent" material from a nuclear power plant.

This State Department spokesman summed up the results of these
"secret" meetings this way: we have achieved a tacit moratorium, a period of quiet. What would come out of the moratorium he had no idea.
He made much of the intransigence of the French; they must not be
"pushed around," there must be a "consensus."

This means that the French, one of the "suppliers," had a *veto* over the concerns of the rest of the world, and particularly the U.S. One week they, the French, would not insist on their agreement to supply Pakistan a spent fuel reprocessing plant from which bombs could be made; the next week, they would go ahead with their contract, and continue to resist even signing a Non-Proliferation Treaty (much less live up to its important provisions).

I was called on to put questions or offer comments. I was deep in disgust with the confirmation of how weak-kneed is our American resolve, in dealing with the French in a pusillanimous way, we who had supplied the French with their technology in the first place (through license from Westinghouse, a *private* firm).

I made a loud-voiced warning: "Don't let anyone think that negotiations leading to agreements—in short, treaties, though called executive agreements—could be developed in secret. This would be a return to the very kind of discredited secret agreement system, on a subject of desperate importance.

"This is not a technical question, to be decided in these hallowed palaces; it will become a major political issue to be decided on the crossroads of every community in this country."

The assembled "experts" were shocked at such language. It is much more comfortable to debate points of the economics of the atom.

I stood outside the Council headquarters in a bitter cold wind, hailing a cab. But no more bitter and no colder than my heart. A dismal performance. Emphasized by the fact that the pale young man who "presided," a Professor Nye (yes, once more of the Harvard faculty), had that day been designated head of a State Department unit dealing with this very subject.

But the day came to a close with my enthusiasm and excitement at a very high peak. While Macy and General Fields and I were discussing what to do next about the waterpower project, I asked Miss Baron to get the president of Allis-Chalmers on the phone.

Macy had been suggesting it for several days; premature, I thought. I trust my sense of timing (but forget the times when my "impulses" have proved not too good, and remember only the times when the impulse and the timing worked out well). This time it was perfect.

David Scott, president of Allis-Chalmers, phoned me at home. All stirred up by my Op-Ed piece and information he has doubtless had from his Vice Presidents. Of course, he would see us, at once. Next Wednesday in Milwaukee was agreed on. I'm riding high again.

JANUARY 17, 1977
NEW YORK

It is almost a year since I started to persuade myself, and then the public et al., that the water in our smaller streams and rivers was a resource that was being wasted, that could be hitched to smallish turbines, made to supply enough electrical energy to make up, here and there, for the high cost of conventional sources in large dams, in large coal-burning plants, in nuclear plants.

The notion really didn't take hold, for months and months. It was really that piece of mine on the Op-Ed page of the *Times* that grabbed the imagination of the country. The evidence of support is coming in, but fast. It keeps coming in.

JANUARY 18, 1977
NEW YORK

Helen so animated and happy: Allen and Daniel with her last night, and off again this morning, heading for the West Coast in Allen's automobile, which is enjoying a second birth. I, unfortunately, here in New York. Said she over the phone, reporting on this happy event: "The boys are sometimes so amused by me and then the next moment, so protective."

Our visit session with Joe Flom was an education in how clear a business mind can be. He has absorbed the rudiments of my hydro concept in practically no time.

JANUARY 23, 1977
PRINCETON

The discomfort, sometimes genuine pain, in my thighs I have tried to suppress, as not being worth writing about nor thinking too much about. But a session last Monday with an orthopedist, Dr. Leon Root, confirmed for the first time that I must face the fact that I have developed arthritis in my hip joints to such an extent that I must take this into account; that it is "referred pain" in those joints that has caused the sometimes considerable discomfort in my thighs.

But if this is to continue to be a journal of truth, it is about time that some note be made of how walking a half-mile or standing for a long time has become a factor affecting my body (but not intolerably) and my spirits—particularly the latter.

Meeting with and exchanging ideas with a variety of people is an important part of the satisfaction I get out of my work (in addition to the fact that I, in effect, invented that work when I invented the enterprise that carries it out).

Last Wednesday's meeting in Milwaukee with the quite remarkable head of Allis-Chalmers and his executive and technical officers is the most recent instance of this observing of new people, in their working clothes, as one might say.

David Scott is a slight soft-voiced man, alert and concentrated. He took over management of an ailing but highly respected heavy manufacturing company with a conservative history in a cautious kind of community, Milwaukee. In something more than a mere five years, its earnings and market position have shown spectacular gains.

It has become very active overseas; half of its business is now "offshore," much of it due to his own toughness in getting out there and pushing things through.

When he took over Allis-Chalmers, he brought in his own "new team"—his description. They were all there, seven or eight of them, around a long table, where we sat from 9:30 until 1:30 (lunch served to us in the same room, the talk continuing).

Toward the end, Scott polled them: everyone reported a complete "consensus" that my concept and proposal, looking to a new and expanding market for their product, low head turbines, was sound and attractive, that the underlying concept of a revival of utilization of waterpower was attainable and in the interest not only of their business but of the country.

This meeting took place while the country, hit by extremely low temperatures, was in the midst of the first of the energy shortages since the oil embargo. The shortage in this case is one of natural gas, closing down industries, but the term "energy crisis" is again in the headlines and in the news. This contributed to the favorable view of adding hydroelectricity to the supply of electric energy—this being the focus of the notions I have been promoting these last ten months or so.

JANUARY 24, 1977
PRINCETON

Norman Clapp will take over as executive head of D&R's projected hydro company. His operating experience, as head of REA and chairmanship of the Wisconsin Public Service Commission, knowledge of government and of people, will be very much as I imagined.

Now *if* Allis-Chalmers—i.e., Scott—will come through with an affirmative response, we are on our way.

JANUARY 28, 1977
NEW YORK

To get the Lilienthal hydroelectric corporation off the ground requires a response "in writing" from David Scott of Allis-Chalmers, and from other prospective investors, notably the Rockefellers (because of IBEC, chiefly). Neither has responded, specifically.

A brief visit yesterday with the financial brains of The Family, Richardson "Dick" Dilworth, at his small office on the Fabulous Floor: "56" of Rockefeller Center.

Dilworth's profession as an investment banker with billions at his command is to be skeptical. What is "desirable" (i.e., an added source of electric energy from waterpower) and what is worth investing in or supporting (through IBEC) are two quite different things. So he can be open-minded and liberal, by saying it is desirable, and skeptical and negative when it comes to supporting something as new as my concept. Nice work if you can get it, and bankers do it all the time.

I am glad that Joe Flom is willing to "follow through" with Dilworth. I would have neither the patience nor the financial skills that the next step will require.

Each of the prospective parties to a new enterprise based on my concept has a quite different viewpoint. Flom is set and determined that I commit myself to setting up an electric producing enterprise that can be sold "as a package" and thereby increase the value of the common shares of the new company. I can see that this is an undertaking of a magnitude and a seriousness of the kind of negotiation not to my liking —though I did do this very thing years ago [in TVA] in the long duel with Wendell Willkie.

What the "deal" people are good at is shuffling finances around to make a deal, get a contract signed, a company restructured—on paper. That is their interest and that is really all they know.

The substance, making the "deal" amount to something in the real world, not just the world of corporate finance—that is not their trade. They dismiss that, and go on to cooking up another "deal," another shuffling of paper.

I have got to remember that I get so little *satisfaction* out of that kind of accomplishment. Such people deal in what in my book are the very kind of abstractions I find so unappealing among academics and economists and their ilk.

What is it I want?

During the night I thought: Why in hell get yourself, at this stage in life, in the middle of hard-nosed negotiations with utilities (as purchasers of an electric plant based on a hydro dam), with municipalities, with bankers? You have spawned an idea; why not leave it there, and enjoy a less complicated life that has more meaning to you?

JANUARY 30, 1977
PRINCETON

A phone talk with Mildred Baron, a source of good common sense and judgment. She agrees with the interim conclusion: to hold up on turning the deal people loose to shape my future and that of D&R.

This is reassuring, and a good note on which to take off for Antigua.

A splashy, trashy article about André Meyer and Lazard in the Sunday *Times* this morning. Of course, it was sparked by the publicity-thirsty Felix Rohatyn. Not a single affirmative word about André; all negative.

His great qualities I know so well. Who *built* Lazard, when it was almost on its last legs when Altschul was "running" it? Who taught these no longer young characters all they know? Who promoted art in this City? Not a word about that. Reading this article, and recognizing how such negative publicity is generated, I feel that Lazard may be on the skids.

My affection for André, what he did in making D&R possible and giving me an opportunity to become financially independent—I'm tempted strongly to write something about him.

FEBRUARY 2, 1977
ANTIGUA

This afternoon I talked out with Helen the problem of my future, that is, "what to do with Dave's energies."

In a half-hour of talking with her, the answer seemed clear: this is a time to concentrate on the new ideas and new work motivations you have developed in the past several months—and don't try to anticipate too much in detail *how* they will be worked out.

"Actually, you have little alternative. You live on driving toward something that means a good deal to you," she said. "When that approaches a goal, you find still another goal to try for."

FEBRUARY 5, 1977
ANTIGUA

Helen and I are so completely different. In nature, in temperament. The difference explains my susceptibility to frustration, my banging my head against what I construe as the inadequacy and shortcomings of people, my constant need for stimulation and the excitement of the new, the necessity for never letting well enough alone. This characteristic so upset Rodman Rockefeller that he said, some years ago, that there was no English word for that exasperating quality of mine, but there was a Spanish phrase for it.

Helen has the capacity to adjust. If things don't come out exactly as she wants, she accepts that as normal and to be expected. When people don't come up to full expectations—never extreme in any case—that, too, is to be expected and adjusted to.

What good fortune presided over me that I didn't try to live—permanently—with someone like myself.

Somehow this all seems clearer—the underlying reasons, I mean—than ever before, though the facts haven't changed one whit.

The single word "perfectionist" has often applied to me. The balancing quality Helen has, of acceptance and understanding—these two are what make this long love last.

I phoned my brother Ted in Clearwater to see how he has weathered this most recent heart attack that put him back in the hospital for six days. Still weak, he was recovering.

FEBRUARY 10, 1977
ANTIGUA

Coming out of the water after my midmorning swim, a notable conversation. "Good morning," said I. "Sir . . . ," said Richard Burton, he sunning himself, sprawled in a beach chair right outside our quarters. Even "sir" was spoken with that great organlike voice. Too bad I didn't bring my copy of *Richard II;* would ask him to read a few lines.

FEBRUARY 11, 1977
ANTIGUA

A two-hour visit with Archie and Ada MacLeish has become the event of an Antigua stay, so happy and "together" I feel when I am with him. True, the physical setting is so overwhelmingly beautiful it would make such a visit memorable in itself. The house at the tip of Mill Reef looks in all directions to the bluest of blue sea, far below. The house itself is a marvel of imaginative design.

The other guests were the Phil Reeds, he for many years chairman of General Electric. It was in that capacity that I knew him during my AEC days. He was always, in those days, one of the few men among younger industrialists who could be called progressive—a worthy successor to two of my heroes and friends, Owen Young and Gerard Swope.

He had heard of my new venture, electricity from existing dams in New England, and wanted to know more about it.

FEBRUARY 13, 1977
ANTIGUA

Never have I so utterly changed my picture of a person, by being close to him rather than depending on the images of the public prints, than tonight at a dinner as the guests of Richard Burton. After two entrancing hours of visit, it is as if Richard Burton, the great film and theatre star, never existed, he the center of many stories of high life and the on-again-off-again husband of Elizabeth Taylor.

A man of serious ideas, intensely interested and informed about the Tennessee Valley, for example, and capable of expressing deep insight into what is going on in the theatre. This was an entirely new picture of this extraordinarily handsome fellow who sat across a small dinner table with his very young new wife, conversing and listening with Helen and me, as good a discussion as I can remember in recent months.

The change in our picture of his new wife in a way was equally startling to us. Seeing her on the beach before our cottage, the contrast with the sexy Liz Taylor was evident: very thin, a soft gentle voice. And a comprehension of ideas. A beautiful non-theatrical smile and manner. Lived near Nairobi, where her father was a British Brigadier. Could this be the wife of the famous lover, Richard Burton?

The conversation ranged widely. Could solar energy or windmills provide electricity for a modest house they might want to build on Antigua? How tragic that government in Britain has bogged down so that nothing can be done. Explaining to his wife, Susan, about what TVA did. Why wasn't the radioactive waste problem solved after all these years?

I tried to turn the conversation to his special field, acting and the theatre. I had the impression that the theme of diffusion into many centers of vitality—decentralization—which was the theme of my own work, was beginning to evidence itself in the "performing arts." This was true, in his informed judgment.

He launched into a discussion of how the theatre is no longer just New York and Broadway. By no means. "Great stars are happy to perform in Edmonton in Canada, or in Minneapolis or Houston. For myself, I fully expect to undertake the one great role that every actor craves—Lear— and to perform it outside New York, although ten or fifteen years ago to put on Lear outside Broadway would be considered absurd."

In a pair of red bathing trunks, coming out of the water before our cottage in the early morning, Richard Burton is a man of slight build, and certainly not robust. He walks and carries himself with the grace of an athlete. Across a table for four, lighted only by a single candle, excited by the kind of things we four were talking about, he was more than a man —a kind of force. That *voice,* like the tone of an organ. (He said that he plays the organ; Susan is an accomplished pianist.)

"I smoke too much"—indeed he does, by the hour—"and in the end it will get me. But years ago Olivier told me that I should not try to cure my catarrh about which I was complaining: 'Catarrh gives your voice an edge that stands you in good stead.' "

FEBRUARY 14, 1977
ANTIGUA

This stimulating experience of last evening wouldn't have happened were it not for Helen. When she said the other night she had been asked by Ada MacLeish to "deliver a message" to Richard Burton, I tried to dissuade her going over to where they were sitting in the public dining room. Seemed too much like "invading the privacy of a noted movie star." But she did, was warmly received, and then we were invited to dine alone with them.

A footnote: "I'm on the wagon," said Burton. Susan ordered lime juice and water for him and herself, with a protective eye. Since I have stayed completely away from hard liquor on this trip, trying to lose some weight, I did likewise. But this brought back a vague recollection that at one time he was a hard drinker—which may be an understatement. Referring to Archie MacLeish, he said: "I haven't seen Archie for maybe ten years. Last time we got drunk together—anyway, I got drunk."

FEBRUARY 22, 1977
NEW YORK

Told Rodman that I had managed to find the man who could execute the energy program: Norman Clapp. And went on to state his qualifications.

Rockefeller was quite enthusiastic and understanding. Seemed quite willing to approve a vice presidency and membership on the board by Norman at our next board meeting.

I made a special point—General Fields with me backing up the point —that coal could be an important part of the D&R energy program, with the hydro as an "opener."

FEBRUARY 25, 1977
PRINCETON

The small hydro crusade is beginning to stir up the kind of emotional
commitment that has brought the strange, odd, no-growth environmental movement to a position where it can successfully challenge good
sense. I'm not one to deprecate emotional steaming, in public affairs.
An illustration:
The "deputy rector" of the most prestigious American church (excepting only St. Patrick's), Trinity, at the foot of Broadway and Wall
Street, is Jack Woodard—that's the way he signs himself.
After reading my Op-Ed *Times* piece, he wrote a warm letter of
agreement to the *Times,* which was published. Then a second one, answering a rather silly response from an officer of Niagara Mohawk
Power Co. After which he has been the center of "many phone calls and
much correspondence" from others who agree that hydro is being throt-
tled by the power companies. A prolific and able letter writer, he has kept
the hydro pot at a boil.
One of the protagonists of hydro is one Coleman, a New York City
union leader, of the Hatters Union. He called Tom Mead: he and others
of the labor movement would like to come in to see me, with some hydro
and anti-power company ideas (and to let off steam, no doubt). He had
been in touch with Father Woodard, who also wanted to see me. Emotionally committed people can be more helpful perhaps than economists and
power experts, at this point.

Dick Boss, librarian of Princeton, handed me the catalog of the D&R
Archive on Khuzistan in a handsomely offset-printed book, hard-cover
binding. Whether this is worth the nearly $75,000 Helen and I provided
for the work by Mead of compiling it, time will tell. (Frankly, I doubt it.)
But it was an idea and the idea is now a reality. It will be distributed by
the president of Princeton to libraries, etc. and gives an academic dignity
to the work of a private company that does not happen very often.

FEBRUARY 28, 1977
NEW YORK

S. David Freeman was director of the Ford Foundation's comprehensive energy study and report of several years ago.
The report predicted shortage, but was essentially based on a zero-
growth philosophy. The chief recommendation: don't use energy—i.e.,
"conservation." Now, several years later, an electricity and energy shortage is close at hand.

In comes a do-it President, Jimmy Carter, who says that energy suffi-
ciency is one of his major objectives.

Who does he select as head of his White House staff to prepare an
energy program—at last? S. David Freeman.

Today Freeman phoned me, from the White House Executive Offices,
saying that Norman Clapp had phoned him last week saying that Clapp
and I were working together on energy. Perhaps I had ideas that might
be useful to him. He is trying to prepare an Energy Message for President
Carter for transmission on April 24.

"I didn't get just what ideas you had; something about waterpower,
wasn't it? I tried all day Saturday to find something you had written or
said about this, but the American Public Power Association—usually
they know everything about power—didn't have anything of that kind."

"Well," said I, completely flabbergasted and not believing my ears.
"Don't you read the *New York Times*? I had an Op-Ed piece some weeks
ago, and before that, other things in the *Times* and in a TV panel discussion. Surely . . ."

So I said I would send it along, and then later talk to him about it,
with cases or numbers, if he wished.

He said: "Down here in Washington everybody thinks that waterpower is a thing of the past. I would call waterpower a form of solar
energy; that would be the only way I could attract any attention to it. You
know; the sun has produced the water, and so on; get it?"

No, I didn't get it. Then I remembered that ERDA had put waterpower under the man responsible for solar and geothermal energy.

This is a true and contemporaneous picture of Washington confronting the energy problem!!

MARCH 2, 1977
NEW YORK

A long and gratifying luncheon talk with John Oakes. He says he is
beginning to "adjust" to the idea that he no longer is responsible each
blessed day for what are clearly the most respected (and feared), and
certainly the most influential editorial pages in the whole world. (The
Times of London no longer is even a close competitor for that title.)

I was most pleased to see his great interest in my small hydro ideas,
the subject of the Op-Ed piece that he had asked me to write, quite a long
time ago. He was greatly pleased that the piece had had so much practical impact—this doesn't happen with every one of the many articles that
make up what has become an important new institution, the Op-Ed page
of the *Times*.

Says he went to an energy conference in Washington very recently.

Not one word at any time about waterpower—the same blindness that has so amazed me, and about which he says he would like to "do something" by way of a column in the *Times*. Wants me to supply some simple factual material, which, of course, I shall most certainly endeavor to do, pronto.

MARCH 5, 1977
PRINCETON

If I could curb my appetite of taking on new tasks, particularly writing chores, I would have more time for . . . for what?

Proposing that article for the *Smithsonian* magazine has kept me at it. Not just the writing—which is still ahead—but the ideas and the setting out of idea-notes. All day yesterday. And instead of a formal kind of letter to John Oakes about waterpower as an energy alternative, I spent literally several hours writing and rewriting, and digging through the memos that have piled up on the subject. I could avoid these things and sail along with a fair wind, but I don't.

MARCH 21, 1977
NEW YORK

The big conference room at IBEC was the scene of the "delivery" of a rather husky infant, the Lilienthal Electric Systems, Inc. Tom Dineen of Allis-Chalmers with five others, just in this morning from Milwaukee, provided the "Yes, we go along and will provide the seed money to the tune of perhaps as much as five million." I was the lady giving birth to a two-year idea.

A productive day it was. Happy my late Saturday night hunch, to expand the concept beyond simply hydro to a far broader one, proved to be what really brightened Dineen's eyes.

MARCH 23, 1977
NEW YORK

I am being given the standard runaround, Rockefeller-style. Long sessions at noon, and then with the charming Dick Dilworth, the chief poo-bah of the "Rockefeller Family" finances, sitting there in my little office. It is a low period for me. Like other genteel slaps, these defensively skilled guardians (of riches accumulated by great-grandfather long ago) lack enthusiasm and vision, and try to make up for it by not deciding, and using the tactic of "keeping the talk going."

I should tell them their problem is to persuade me that I should lend my energies to their efforts, rather than having the burden of proving that the new hydro company will make money.

The strength of their negative outlook is that they put me in the position of having to persuade them, with their money, on a basis of *numbers,* which have less than no meaning in the world of reality (one assumption based upon another assumption, coming out with figures that look definite but are just an alibi for doing nothing constructive).

Overtired.

Two solid weeks of seven days' work could certainly account for it. Bad night last night. Went to the board meeting ready to vomit, emotionally, over the Rockefeller prissiness about financing a really important idea, the small hydro concept.

Helen is reading the 1969 journal entries. Reminds me that at that time I was furious that D&R had no cash whatever, and little prospect from Iran. Today the report at the board meeting was of very large collections. Cash, and not just promises.

To me the big news of the day occurred at breakfast: John Oakes' column "Thinking Small," a stout endorsement of the small hydro concept, giving me full credit for originating it. Should produce some kind of favorable result.

MARCH 24, 1977
NEW YORK

Norman Clapp in today. What a big broad-shouldered handsome man, with a serenity of expression that will stand him in good stead—all of us, particularly me, the least (half the time) serene of men.

To the Century tonight, with Barney and Beatrice Tobey, to hear Benny Goodman, the magician of the clarinet, and Jean-Pierre Rampal, the French flutist, who is now the "hottest musician going," particularly among the young.

Cooled off about starting the "new energy company," certainly right now; try to begin it through D&R. The banker touch of the Rockefellers generally is a bit "too much for me." So far from the reality of what I want to do.

But this might turn around, in which case we must be flexible. But I want them—the whole damn caboodle of paper-pushers and stock-jobbers—to try to persuade *me;* I'm not going to try to persuade them. A big turnabout this is.

APRIL 2, 1977
PRINCETON

Drop the idea of the new energy company. Develop small hydro—or coal—through ideas, not big staffing. And ideas are what I can provide, without putting on my head a new set of worries.

This will maintain the balance between the need I have for activity and the need for time and an atmosphere in which to think ahead.

APRIL 5, 1977
NEW YORK

Celebrating Helen's 81st birthday was a happy event in every way. Plenty of laughter, no moaning about "age"; in fact, no consciousness of it.

A delightful part of the birthday occasion was dinner, the four of us, with the Tobeys at their home. What Beatrice can do with chicken, and salad, and applesauce!

Before dinner we spent a half-hour or so looking at the painting she has been doing in recent months. Color—rich, subtle, gay, warm, varied —is what she enjoys and does so wholeheartedly.

Both of us were very much taken with the vitality and originality of these "roughs," as she called them. Roughs being the term for early versions of what she has been submitting to the present art editor of *The New Yorker,* as proposed designs for *New Yorker* covers.

APRIL 7, 1977
PRINCETON

This is a day in which to take some considerable satisfaction: the President announced that the U.S. put an end to exporting plutonium and reprocessing technology that would produce plutonium. This was a "unilateral" position, with the hope that other nations would do the same, but without any agreement on their part (France, West Germany, etc.).

In short, his action supports my position of January, 1976, that this we should do "on our own" even though it would not thereby solve the whole problem.

APRIL 10, 1977
PRINCETON

There's that Helen, down on her knees in the kitchen garden so dear to her heart, putting in lily-of-the-valley roots, stray violets, and other of my "discards." Why in the kitchen garden along the north fence? Because no one else wants that desolate spot, and no one will disturb her orphans after she plants them there.

This is the way it is with this pair, Helen and me, she the one who conserves and I the one who wastes, but *talks* about "conservation." I am the one who earns the money—fair enough. But she sees to it that I don't spend quite all of it; this was true when we were poor, and is still true.

APRIL 13, 1977
NEW YORK

The non-secret of D&R (or, probably, of any significant enterprise) is the ability to attract exceptional people, to draw them in from other pursuits, to stimulate and cultivate their innate motivations and talents. John Macy, out of his long background of success in "personnel management," says that he has rarely seen such a quality of magnetism that brings, more and more, exceptional people of a certain kind.

"D&R is like a magnet drawing iron filings." He insists, time and again, that it is because of my record and personal convictions that this is true. Certainly my "leadership and record" have something to do with this, but he tends to exaggerate, and so do others who talk that way. It has been a cumulative process, a building step by step over the years, actually since the earliest days of TVA in the early thirties.

A great asset, human asset, was added yesterday afternoon: Jack Vaughn. A sturdy-looking, very sure, most articulate and driving kind of man, with an extraordinarily diversified record of work and achievement: Assistant Secretary of State for Latin America and Co-Director of the Alliance for Progress for Latin America; Director of the Peace Corps in its heyday; and so on.

He delighted me, in our long talk yesterday afternoon, by saying: "I am by nature and experience a manager." I liked that. The way he said it, with pride but with a recognition of what it means to be a professional manager. That is what I consider myself to be, first of all, so it was natural that my pulse quickened to hear this said without qualification.

He will take over the Iran operation, replacing Andrea Pampanini, who will have completed a two-year stint, come July. There could hardly be two more different "styles." Andrea is not a natural manager; intelligent, most articulate, but making hard decisions is not Andrea's forte.

Whether Jack will seem too direct, too tough, for the Persians will be something worth watching carefully.

But I think Iran needs "advisors" and fellow-workers who will be tough and forthright.

Don Straus, a veritable saint of a man, has spent many months speculating and devising methods he thinks can produce a process of discussion and reasoning that will bring opposing or differing viewpoints together. I assured him that anything that would contribute to minimizing the alarming degree of polarization on the environment issue should have everyone's support.

APRIL 15, 1977
PRINCETON

Looked out of my bedroom window early this morning with a broad smile, a happy satisfied grin. Reaching almost into the room was the ancient apple tree that has only part of a trunk, but is covered with bloom.

Today I gardened, on a perfect spring day, doing all the hard things that spell gardening to me: digging, dividing, planning ways of overcoming the problem places in the border, pouring bone meal and fertilizer on each of the hundred rose bushes, using a new cutting tool to clear away overhanging boughs over the Korean azaleas, just about ready for their brief but spectacular bloom.

How can I express to the Lord how grateful I am for this mark of a respite, to be able once more to be a real for-sure spring gardener?

APRIL 24, 1977
PRINCETON

This was Energy Week for the country. Also for me and my new D&R partner, Norman Clapp. Planning for a new future for D&R in furthering the energy needs of our own country—after so much attention given, for two decades, to the needs of Iran.

The interest in my special idea—small hydro—continues to grow. For example: John Oakes called me. He wants to do still another column on the subject, wants more "facts and figures."

Although the President did not include any reference to our idea in his message to the joint session of Congress, it was referred to (cautiously, I thought) in a supplement called Fact Sheet. Oakes thought it could be enough of a basis for further comment by him.

APRIL 28, 1977
NEW YORK

An hour with Governor Carey, the first of the several Governors that we are going to be seeing, or trying to see, about our ideas for a positive energy program.

The idea of a Federally-chartered corporation to buy power from Appalachian coal is roughly where we emerged after an hour's discussion. The Governor began looking for a structure for a regional enterprise that would mediate and conciliate and mute the state-eat-state competition that has been going on between the Northeast states.

What really ticked the meeting off was my referring to the point that Norman Clapp has made from the beginning—namely, that the important function for D&R, and the important function for the Northeast, is to "aggregate the market for electricity" coming from Appalachian coal.

The Governor picked this idea up and in a very practical way began to do some arithmetic that would make the idea acceptable to Congress —that is, come up with the value in dollars of the electricity or other production producible by the coal of eastern Kentucky, West Virginia, Pennsylvania, etc. and use that dollar total as the basis for financing the Appalachian regional enterprise, leaving the Northeast as the paying partner, without the Northeast becoming itself involved in the operation of an electricity system.

It is perfectly clear that the Governor has not settled on the kind of bill or the kind of program that he wants to place before the New York Legislature. The idea of institutionalizing an aggregate market either for coal by slurry (he threw that in) or by electricity carried by power lines, which he finds highly vulnerable to the environmentalists—but in any case, the concept of a series of projects by the Northeast states—"will not fly with Congress," says the Governor.

It was the Governor's view that we needed to have some projects in mind because people would say, "But what is this new corporation going to do?"

I said, of course, that I had selected the promotion of small hydroelectricity because it would incur the minimum of opposition from people concerned with the environment, and also from the private power companies, and a maximum of support from local communities.

The second specific project would be the utilization of Appalachian coal for the production of electricity and, on this, we plan to meet with not only the New York Governor but several of the Governors of the leading coal-producing states.

The upshot is that there was established in the first meeting at least a clear connection, organic, economic, and conceivably political, between the Northeast regional entity, whatever it is going to be, and the one entity that has the most prospect of being genuine and productive, and that is the Appalachian Regional Commission.

The question was asked: how would you restructure the Appalachian Regional Commission to fit this concept? I said we had been studying this and would be available to discuss it:

The Governor wound up the hour-long meeting by saying, "I have heard a new idea from Lilienthal about marketing as the key to the Northeast so far as energy is concerned."

APRIL 30, 1977
PRINCETON

Dizzy, dizzy, with the beauty of this perfect spring day, dizzy with the beauty of the garden in which we have been working all day, dizzy with gratitude for the quiet and serenity and heart-stopping sanctity of so utterly lovely a day and hour.

I have had a good life: my career, the people I have known, the events I have witnessed, the human beings I have loved and who have loved me.

Then such a day, such an hour as this last one has been, sitting out in the garden and luxuriating in the colors and forms and shapes of a spring garden, one that Helen and I have created—with an assist from the Lord of creation!

The joy I have had in the last half-hour from the color of a single scarlet tall tulip, or the dulcet blue of an anchusa's eye, or the completely overwhelming first rhodo, lavender and white. Remember all this when you are perplexed or overtired or up against what appears to be a wall of doubts and problems.

In point of fact, it is this garden, particular spots in it, which I have memorized, that strengthened and kept me when the going was tough or the path far from clear.

A happy note, too: a long talk with Ted, he in his hospital bed in the Thomas Jefferson in Philadelphia, me talking to him here. He enjoys visiting with me almost as much as I do with him. And praise the Lord for his deliverance after a year of pain and uncertainty.

MAY 3, 1977
NEW YORK

The luncheon conversation with Dick Dilworth yesterday was not confidential or even personal; he had initiated the idea of meeting to talk about IBEC and its relations to D&R. IBEC is one of his problems, as the Grand Vizier of "The Family."

Dilworth does not fit the picture of a man who has intimate knowledge of the Rockefeller family corporate and financial interests. He is the picture of a Yale Trustee of the Acheson–Vance–Kingman Brewster style. His manner is so courteous and almost deferential that he gives the picture not only of "good manners" (which I rate very highly in my business association), but when he spoke sharply and in a highly critical way, I had some moments of doubting what I was hearing.

I said that I had no current complaint to share with him; though there had been episodes rather painful for me and not particularly pleasant for Rodman, in which the issue was adherence, complete, unquestioned adherence, to the autonomy and independence of D&R, though all of its common shares, and therefore control, was in Rodman's hands. Deviation from this in recent weeks has been irritating but minor.

In fact, last week Rodman had said he was enthusiastic about D&R (as well he might be, considering our current position, both financially and in prestige) and had greeted the designation by me of Norman Clapp and Jack Vaughn as officers with the remark, "You D&R fellows have a kind of magic, getting people like that." Certainly this is a strong affirmation.

Mostly the problem is more symbolic and psychological than literal. But after the years since the merger, it still remains that the top management of D&R owns no shares whatever.

Dilworth leaned back away from the table with a pained expression on his face and said, "That is not right. It is a psychological matter." And then, showing that he understood the realities of the D&R picture in this respect, he said, "When the top four of you get on an elevator together to go down to the lobby, there goes the whole inventory." Which for a Yale Trustee is pretty good.

The only clear commitment Dick made was that *that* should be changed. I said it would not increase the loyalty or dedication or excitement of the top four or five members of the staff; to use Macy's terminology, "When you have got the accelerator down to the floorboards, you can't push it any further."

A problem in the relations between D&R and IBEC much more significant to me, and, I think, to the top staff of D&R, perhaps all of us, is one that I then laid out. I reminded Dick very briefly that the attraction that IBEC had for me as a home for D&R when we were in a serious cash problem was its history.

IBEC had been created by a genuinely great public servant, Nelson Rockefeller, to carry out a vision of helping in the development of underdeveloped countries, particularly in Latin America, through a non-governmental, non-foundation, private corporation, thus combining public interest objectives with the advantages of the structure and basic ideas of profit making through a private company. That, I thought, was a great idea, and through almost its first twenty-five years, that had been a guiding principle. That seemed a most appropriate home for D&R since I founded D&R with the same basic concept.

The sad fact is, however, that IBEC is not now recognized as the kind of company that Nelson Rockefeller had envisaged and had initiated.

The making of money as the sole and prime objective was now clearly the way IBEC was positioned and carried out. One could also say attempts to make money and the attempts to reduce losses by liquidation of assets mean that neither the initial idealistic objective exists nor is it a sound private enterprise idea.

I went on to say I thought for a while that Rodman shared the basic concept of public service through a private corporation and that he was trying to steer IBEC through some unfortunate investments, such as the Puerto Rico housing, and would return to the Nelson Rockefeller concept and the D&R concept when circumstances, financial and luck, permitted, but I had a rude awakening on this.

At the most recent board meeting, Rodman, speaking as he said, as "one director" (he did not refer to himself as the owner), criticized severely a disposition in D&R not to concentrate on charging fees that would make money; he spoke provocatively to the directors and staff that they should remember that the business of D&R is to make money.

I could not let this pass and so I took the floor to "remind the board meeting that D&R was based upon the same principle as Nelson Rockefeller had committed himself to in the founding of IBEC; if we were looking for enterprises that would make the most money, one could not exclude a chain of casinos or a chain of whorehouses, for that matter."

The outcome of all this will depend on whether there is a change in management in IBEC, whether Dilworth will take the initiative, or whether we will get more of the promises, promises, promises, without action, which have characterized the past. One thing I am sure of and that is that on both sides, the Rubicon has been crossed. And clearly there is no reason why any of us in D&R should or need retreat one millimeter from strict adherence to the proposition of autonomy and strict observance of the basic proposition on which D&R was founded, the combination of public interest and private capital.

MAY 7, 1977
PRINCETON

At my meeting last week with Governor Carey, he lost no time in taking a different course on the Northeast energy issue, after he heard me present an alternative to Felix Rohatyn's highly publicized banker's approach. Then, when I came to the office last Thursday morning, there was a *New York Daily News* story showing that what Carey said, Carey did.*

Also a *New York Times* stringer story, emphasizing the complete

*At a meeting of the Coalition of Northeast Governors, Carey proposed establishing a TVA-like energy corporation to help bring coal and other energy sources into the region.

change of strategy. Also the press release issued by Carey.

My real objective is to advance our hopes and aims for a role as advisors to the Appalachian Regional Commission, hopefully reconstituted. The concept I advanced, with great help from Norman Clapp, gave something workable for the Northeast Regional Corporation at the same time providing a tie to Appalachian coal. That our ideas will be given serious consideration—perhaps to the point of finally engaging D&R as "advisors"—is attested by receiving a message from Governor Shapp of Pennsylvania: he will come to see us Monday afternoon next. About Appalachia.

Wednesday I went with Norman Clapp and Tom Mead to Paterson, N.J. This is our first clear effort to *perform* and not just write and emote about small-size waterpower. It seems likely we will have a contract to rehabilitate the Great Falls of the Passaic River.

MAY 10, 1977
NEW YORK

Yesterday afternoon, our visitors had arrived. I pranced out, past my *New Yorker* cartoons displayed in the corridor, to greet a smallish man with a broad brow who gave me a big grin. Said I: "Welcome, Governor Shapp. I should tell you that it is not every day that the Governor of the great State of Pennsylvania comes to our office." Without losing a stitch, he came back: "And it isn't every day that the Governor of Pennsylvania gets to meet David Lilienthal."

That is what is known as graciousness, plus.

With Norman Clapp and two of the Governor's staff (a particularly impressive grey-headed fellow by the name of Wirth, very serious), we spent the best part of a couple hours talking about "energy" and in particular the proposed Northeast Energy Corporation, an idea now, a concept that in ten minutes of discussion was completely changed to fit Norman's and my ideas.

Shapp is an easy man to be with. Has a way of looking you hard in the eye when he is making a point, moves from one subject to another with the speed of light.

I remarked that his state was a chief producer of coal, that President Carter's energy program emphasized coal for energy, and particularly Appalachian coal. So we talked—or he did—about coal.

After all this rambling, I saw a pattern. He was trying to size me up as an advisor. He was trying to make up his mind about the proposal I made last week to Carey, of having the Northeast become the "guaranteed market" for Appalachian coal, using the revenues as the basis for a Federal guarantee of bonds. His doubts about me and my idea apparently resolved, he said: "You are right."

Signed a "firm proposal" to the Mayor of Paterson, for D&R's services to bring the Great Falls power plant back into service. I have personally underwritten the proposition that the power will be profitable and saleable. That is getting out on the edge of a cascade, one that looks like a minor-league Niagara Falls.

MAY 12, 1977
PRINCETON

My initial suggestion to Ed Thompson of *Smithsonian* magazine for an article and his approval of the idea was months ago. Good thing inertia and other demands intervened, for now we have Carter's much-touted national energy policy message, and D&R itself is closer than ever to specific cases of small hydro.

MAY 15, 1977
PRINCETON

A 187-pound guy, fully mature to say the least, peering hard at a new birdhouse he has put up in the fork of a dogwood on the edge of the garden. He lets out a whoop, unslings his binoculars: "The wren is inspecting the house. He's inside; now, sticking his head out. Now he is trying to fit a tiny twig into the opening. 'Turn it, turn it; it won't go in crossways.' There, he's made it."

You can't worry about D&R or anything else while you are trying to help a wren find a home.

MAY 19, 1977
NEW YORK

The interests of the Soviet Union are almost parallel to U.S. interests in seeking to control or limit the spread of nuclear weapons.

I have read an abstract of the Soviet position on the control of nuclear exports from the Soviet Union and the control that they impose on Communist countries to which they provide nuclear materials. They intend to proceed with the breeder reactor, which of course is plutonium-based and, therefore, is bound to increase the amount of bomb material, as indeed our own plutonium production for bombs has done and still does.

The long-term goal of the Carter program on proliferation is to seek a more stable world by limiting the number and the rate of spread of nuclear weapons. The rate of spread affects the expectations of every country in the world.

Proliferation is a process; it is not a matter of stopping it, but a phenomenon that "needs to be managed." The Carter program, dealing with this process, addresses two factors in the international scheme of things: (1) the motivations of nations and (2) their capabilities in the nuclear field, meaning of course, their capability of producing plutonium through power reactors, or the recycling of the reactors' rods to extract the plutonium.

Carter's program adds international incentives, presumably to make nations and their military establishments live within the existing safeguards. Incentives from the United States to presently non-nuclear-weapon states are illustrated by assuring and guaranteeing and covenanting for fuel supply for commercial peaceful reactors to states not now possessing (so far as we know) a nuclear weapons stockpile.

Of course, it occurred to me at once that this policy of weaning countries away from the development of nuclear weapons by providing incentives for commercial-use reactors was exactly the policy—the terribly mistaken, disastrous policy—that led the scientists under Seaborg and others and the politicians under Lewis Strauss and Eisenhower to propose the Atoms for Peace program. Partly as a public relations gimmick, partly out of a sincere and tragically naive notion that meetings in Geneva of scientists exchanging information and later providing nuclear materials would solve the problem of misuse of nuclear technology in the direction of weapons. Emotionally committed internationalists seem unable to see any connection between the earlier mistake and the current posture.

A third major segment of the Carter program is one which apparently the press did not report adequately until President Carter expounded it at the London economic summit meeting recently, a quite elaborate international conference for a multinational evaluation of the fuel cycling. It was evident that the Carter people held this out as what he called a "carrot"—that is, part of the incentive to other countries that might result in their renouncing the plutonium, the breeder reactor, the contracts for recycling, and so forth.

The fourth new policy of the Carter Administration calls for a renegotiation of contracts for cooperation, presumably with Euratom, with all the countries involved in the Atoms for Peace program.

The fifth point of the program dealt with incentives: a guarantee of a back-up supply of enriched uranium to countries in return for their confidence in the U.S.; perhaps a spent-fuel repository in the United

States. Such a notion rather shocked me. What state or what community would welcome this poisonous, highly radioactive junk, even if produced in our plants for their own protection, much less welcome this ghastly stuff in an international depository in a community of the U.S.? I am afraid this is one of the measures of the unreality of this highly intellectual process that has been going on in the Carter Administration in this respect.

MAY 21, 1977
PRINCETON

Felix Rohatyn, Wizard of Wall Street, came into Governor Carey's conference room in the MGM Building yesterday, and made a beeline for me. "Dave, you and I must see each other. It appears that you and I have diametrically opposite ideas of this regional corporation."

"Yes, we have," I said, without the precaution of asking him in what ways. "You think there is no need for Federal guarantees, that the investments will be made without guarantees. And all this talk of yours about 'aggregating revenues as a guarantee of the investments'—that is just pie in the sky.

"You were invited to the meeting with the Governor where I expressed my views to him, which he adopted at the meeting of the other Governors. You didn't attend the meeting."

Felix summarized (to his satisfaction, at least) the talks he and the Governor had earlier in the week with Secretary of the Treasury Blumenthal, and Jim Schlesinger and O'Leary of the White House advisory group on energy. "Blumenthal had agreed with me about the regional financing idea *before* he became Secretary," said Felix. "He has cooled off a bit now that he has the responsibility." Schlesinger obviously was not yet gung ho. He had his own ideas—and his own Mount Everest personal vanity, comparable to Felix's but with more justification on the record. Felix, who has become a master political strategist, beamed: "We can make Schlesinger believe that the regional corporation fits into his other ideas, that it is a tool he can use for his own program in energy; we should try to make him believe that."

Then Felix lighted into me, politely enough. "Dave is against all this." Said I: "I am honored that a banker should explain what I believe and don't believe, but I would prefer to state my position and reasons on my own."

Don Cook, who sat on my left, then described, in a quite soft voice and in considerable detail, the impossible situation the electric utilities were in because they could not finance additions and expansion of plants and facilities. "Within the next eighteen months, at a time of hot weather or of unusually cold weather, there will be shortage of a damaging kind. The need for added energy capacity is *now,* since it takes years before an authorized plant can come into use. So all the discussion of new technology, such as coal conversion, is beside the point. The need is now."

I suggested that there would be opposition to providing a subsidy (which is what the Federal guarantee actually is) for nuclear plants, particularly since their safety was being widely criticized and the subject of lengthy hearings and even "demonstrations"—the so-called Clam Shell picketing of a plant site at Seabrook, N.H.

Cook explained that it is not only nuclear but all electric plants that are in trouble, for the reasons he described—essentially, rates did not keep up with rising costs, and so the financial structure of most utilities was impaired, if not actually in default of their bond indentures, much less attracting new equity financing.

I commented that in the Tennessee Valley it was the users of energy in that region from the TVA system who provided the base for capital raising, through TVA revenue bonds. Very courteously Cook asked if he could comment on this reference to TVA.

"TVA sets its own rates, according to the dictates of its own conscience. There is no regulatory body that reviews them. So they can adjust their rates to meet the costs and needs of the system. TVA will never have any financing problem, for that reason."

What is standing in the way of new electric (and probably gas) plants is the lag between the need for higher rates to sustain earnings and action by the regulatory bodies to approve such increases. I puzzled over this through last night.

Just how does a subsidy to energy-related industries—the electric utilities particularly—speed up rate proceedings, or cut the rates to the consumer? Doesn't this subsidy, improving the earnings of a utility, benefit the investor? How can we assume that the subsidy will find its way into lower rates to the consumers—which is, I suppose, the purpose of this whole regional corporate energy proposal? I must try to figure this out.

I gathered that Governor Carey wasn't prepared to argue the position he had taken with the other Governors, following my discussions with him. But Felix's scoffing at my proposal about guaranteed contracts for electric supply from Appalachian coal probably was persuasive to the Governor. How he will reverse himself is his problem. The way he handled it at the meeting was to say that whatever charter terms are offered to the Congress, they will change them beyond recognition anyway, so why fuss now.

MAY 27, 1977
PRINCETON

Yesterday three typical Washington bureaucrats were dispatched to see me about what help D&R could provide to the Energy Research and Development Agency, now forced to recognize the idea I generated that small waterpower is indeed an appealing theme all over the country.

We explored the question of how D&R could contract to further ERDA's belatedly recognized role. For many months, the official line was that hydroelectricity was not within the charter purposes of ERDA, essentially a research and development undertaking. A strange picture this, since ERDA is the research splinter of what I once headed, a fission fragment of the old AEC. (And who, I may ask, caused AEC to fission into two parts?)

MAY 28, 1977
PRINCETON

I keep speculating on what the three ERDA emissaries will report to the acting agency head, Bob Fri, and what may come of this. We had definitely *not* counted on becoming involved, in our energy work, with anything requiring a money contract of any kind with a Federal agency, still nursing our wounds and our acute frustration over the dealings with AID, particularly during the Vietnam postwar project of unhappy memory.

But this time this may be the best alternative we have for getting definitely under way in the small hydro field. To become the acknowledged leaders, country-wide, in doing something affirmative about energy, would justify some financial shortcomings in dealing with the Federal Government, and the frustrations, too.

MAY 30, 1977
PRINCETON

I got a good deal of reassurance from reading, closely and slowly, a lengthy article in the current *Scientific American* by Bernard Cohen (now at the University of Pittsburgh) on the disposal of radioactive wastes.

Why reassurance? Not because he completely answered the question about the permanent disposal of high-level wastes, or completely satisfied all the concerns about the hazards of that long-lived poisonous stuff. Even the strictures of the Op-Ed article I wrote were not completely answered.

His article brought to the surface of my consciousness a concern, a fear perhaps, that must have been festering there for many years: was I responsible, as AEC Chairman, for failing to create one hell of a row over continued storage, in tanks at a shallow (forty feet) depth, of the wastes from the Hanford piles? As I read Cohen, that military or weapons-produced waste did leak—as I had feared—leaked badly, but happily not into the ground water that would seriously poison the Columbia River.

From Cohen's article, ERDA (AEC's successor) favors the deep (600-meter) permanent burial of wastes in glass canisters.

None of this meets the current temporary storage crisis. The stuff has to be "cooled off" in water pools before it can be considered ripe for permanent storage of the kind Cohen describes. And without a special place to store the stuff, in water tanks, the ongoing atomic program, the currently operating reactors, are in trouble.

The glory of the garden at 88 was never more resplendent than this spring. The rhododendron towered and glowed, in all shades, deep scarlet, in delicate orchid (the Scintillation fairly outdid themselves), pale lavender. The azaleas, beginning very early, with the eight-foot-high Royal; the whites, with ivory wide-open petals, became the spotless trumpets of Gabriel; the coral in sweet contrast to the neighboring white. The white iris, the falls crisp and smooth and nearly horizontal; the blue and purple became the robes of royalty, in a tapestry; the single siberica iris, a startling purple blossom, borne on extraordinarily tall slim staves, in erect groups of military stance; the doe-eyes of phlox, of the palest pale blue held in the air by filaments so innocent and fragile and wispy as to be invisible; the peonies, at first rubicund and healthy, the tips of robust breasts, then spilling open with carefree exuberance; the pale lemon columbine, clustering and fluttering and darting like tiny canaries, set off by the sedate deep blue hybrid aquilegia, their long spurs, or tiny tubes of cream, sprawling in all directions, breeze-stirred hair of wantons in a 17th century painting, pursued by satyrs—but not too far ahead; the slender stems which bore the tiniest of bells, the incomparable coral bell, high above the dark and compact and disapproving cluster of the plant that sent them out in all directions, mingling without permission with the blue of flax or the Chinese scarlet or delicate salmon of the sturdiest of Oriental Poppies, their centers an ominous black, their pods green and fuzzy and, before they broke, angry-seeming; the first of the clematis, the spread of petals so obvious and clownlike; and dotted, everywhere, all along the encircling arms of the border, the tiny blue stars of forget-me-not and anchusa, livened by the trustworthy solemn faces of the pansies, the gardener's patient, devoted Spaniels.

A week ago, at the time of our big garden party, this glory was at its supreme height, and this spring of springs, all at the same time, even some of the earliest, the lingering primula and decentra, the pink hearts "bursting with love" at the end of a green necklace outreaching from beneath the overhanging rhodo, and miracle of all, the memory of the earliest of all, the Virginia bluebell. (Quite impossible, this spring.)

Now the garden is "all"—(the Pennsylvania Dutch term meaning finished). When we return in the early fall there will be phlox, some cranes of digitalis stalking here and there perhaps, some absurdly tall nicotiana.

There will still be some roses then. The hundred roses in the front half-circle are of a profusion such as I have never seen, even in their homeland of Persia, or where they have been so wonderfully bred, France (the Meilands, the best).

But much as I enjoy watching each one unfurl—particularly the new golds and yellows—the real joy of gardening is the spring, when I can ingest them, as they first appear, and then display their incredible variety of shape and color and design.

It is a short life, this joy of a garden, but a merry one indeed.

JUNE 2, 1977
NEW YORK

Such a pleasant luncheon-chat with Rodman. He suggested we lunch at the "sunken" restaurant at Rockefeller Center. A sunny day, the gay umbrellas in the outdoor cafe. As we started down the steps from the street level, he paused at the plaque on which are engraved words from his grandfather about "the dignity of the individual." Pride written all over his face. I had quoted from this plaque in a speech to an IBEC gathering when we were both considering the corporation marriage which later ensued.

Spoke with pride about his daughter, now at Williams College. When she was just out of prep school at eighteen, the family proposed a "coming out" party for her. She scoffed at the idea; said it was old-fashioned, not done any more. The other day she proposed "a small party" for her friends; now it is a party for 150 and still growing. So at twenty-one, it is a deb party just the same.

JUNE 3, 1977
PRINCETON

At some time in the often discouraging course of getting up *traction* for a wholly new idea, there is a break, a turn. You can sense that you have made your case, persuaded yourself, and then others.

I felt yesterday, seeing a two-page article, plus a strong editorial, in the construction industry's top periodical, *Engineering News-Record*, that the turn had come. Could it be that the hurried, barely one-hour interview with Judith H. Dobrzynski of *Engineering News-Record* was that break? I think so today.

If we had written the article ourselves, it could hardly have been better as a promotion of my basic small hydro idea, developed initially, in a public sense, in the luncheon meeting at the University Club with Robert MacNeil, then part of his TV program in May of '76. That program served to commit me to the idea, but nothing much beyond that.

JUNE 10, 1977
PRINCETON

The stream of news stories and columns on small hydro has had an impact on Congressmen. Both the Senate and the House Committees' reports, just published, contain explicit authorization and directions to ERDA for a demonstration program. No wonder Fri yelled for our help.

JUNE 18, 1977
PRINCETON

The first three days of this past week—Monday, Tuesday, Wednesday —rank among the most creative and useful in many a day, for my long-time goals and purposes.

Met at the plane in Washington by Norman and Analoyce Clapp. We went almost immediately to luncheon with the newly appointed state director of staff of the lame and out-dated Appalachian Regional Commission, Leonard Schwartz, and with him, the representative of the Governor of Kentucky on the state-wide staff, Hausser. Schwartz was a kind of Assistant (N.Y.) Secretary of State, in the confidence of Governor Carey. I was told that the Governor insisted on putting Schwartz in this strategic spot as head of the staff of the several states because "the Governor feels that the lower-tier states—New York and Pennsylvania—should have more influence in the Appalachian region and its Commission."

Certainly Schwartz started right off: "I don't have any staff at all, in the energy field, none at all, and I know nothing about the subject. So we want you. We are open to any proposition that will make you our staff, you and Clapp and D&R. And we have ample money to finance what you think should be done."

Later in the day, Schwartz reported to Norman that he had been in touch with others of consequence; there was agreement that we should be "retained" for a preliminary period, enough to justify D&R putting forward a proposal for assistance, on energy issues, to the Regional Commission.

This is obviously an opportunity for D&R to become an important factor in our theme: bringing together the natural resources of Appalachia and the market for electricity-from-Appalachian-coal in the Northeast. This, in a different form, was Norman's original basic idea, and the Appalachian Regional Commission he thought could provide the best available vehicle.

Tuesday morning we spent forty-five minutes with two of the most powerful men in the Federal Government, the Chief of the Corps of Engineers, Lt. Gen. William Morris, and the Deputy, Maj. Gen. Ernest Graves. If they had said that the small hydro idea lacked substance, or even if they had shown no enthusiasm for it, this would have made the road from neglect (as of two years ago when I began to promote the idea) a real fizzle. That is how important they are, in Congress and among professional engineers.

But they—and that means the Corps—have taken the idea quite seriously. The President has directed that they take a look at the 49,000 existing small dams that are without electricity-producing facilities, and report within ninety days of the President's energy speech—that would be July 30 as a deadline.

General Graves was very open and candid about what could be expected from their "look"—certainly not an identification of particular sites or an evaluation of them. There would be really a computer print-out, of categories, perhaps. But this would be a good starting point. I even detected quite a bit of enthusiasm for my role in getting hydroelectricity considered again, after having been ignored and written off. The results of their "90-day wonder" look will be made available to us.

Much of this, of course, can be credited to Ken Fields' high standing with the Corps, who obviously greatly respect him as we do, and to his personal relation with General Graves. (A West Point classmate?)

Ken has been an excellent part-time consultant. In my initiatives against nuclear proliferation, Ken has been an enormous and substantive helper.

The greatest lift to my spirits was the reception I had in the old red brick nostalgic home of the *Smithsonian* magazine, squirreled away in one section of that historic castle on Jefferson Drive.

Publisher and editor Ed Thompson, the redoubtable creator of this new and extraordinary magazine, greeted me just inside the door. His enthusiasm for my article gave me great satisfaction. Perhaps I enjoy

UNFINISHED BUSINESS, 1977   [679

writing—or in any event, having my writing published—more than I am willing to admit, me with my frequent aspersions on the "word-people" vis-à-vis "us action people."

He took me to a big table, with light under it, on which he had put perhaps a dozen 35 mm. films of small dams or streams in New England, beautiful photography for which the *Smithsonian* is famous. It will be from among these that my article will be illustrated. Then I knew that the article *would* be published, and probably for the September issue. Equally satisfying was the remark of an assistant editor, Nancy Seaman, "It is just the right length."

Norman, Ken, and I spent a couple hours with Bob Fri, Acting Administrator of the Energy Research and Development Agency.

He assured me I need not really be too concerned about D&R being estopped by a conflict-of-interest problem should we accept a contract to help them "shape a small hydro program." It was evident they were candid about it—the small hydro idea has so taken hold of the imagination of people all over the country, and is so strongly reflected in the Congress, that they simply must have a demonstration program. Indeed, both in the report of the Senate Committee on Energy and the equivalent Committee in the House, there is a mandate (authorization) for such a program.

I found no enthusiasm for such a program from the five or six senior staff who sat with Bob Fri. When they said they knew nothing about small hydro—or any hydroelectricity—they meant it, and quickly proved the point.

JUNE 19, 1977
PRINCETON

At about 11, I "snuck" into the back of the Senate Energy Committee's hearing room, on Tuesday last, while Senator Jackson was presiding over a hearing, his office having said that he would try to see me. From his vantage point on the bench, he spotted me at once, raised his arm high, pointed to the door, a signal for me to come to his office. Which I did. Full of fire, shorter than I remembered him, and stockier.

He knows about my concept about small hydro, believes in it. "And Schlesinger is in-ner-rested. There needs to be an appropriation for planning and demonstration."

I told him apparently ERDA and Fri thought so too.

He asked his staff deputy to talk to me further, while he answered the call for a quorum. (This gambit is the traditional legislator's way of shortening the many, many calls from constituents or lobbyists—or such as me.)

The talented young men, as Scoop definitely was when I first knew him—what is it that sustains them in their wearing careers in elective public life?

That late afternoon and evening (Tuesday), I spent with Marguerite Owen, who influenced the course of TVA, particularly in its early days, about as much as any one single person, though her official designation was simply head of the Washington Office—i.e., relations to the Congress. We agreed in being rather outraged at David Freeman for his derogation of the present TVA leadership, Red Wagner.

I had spent a long and tiresome evening at the Clapps' with Freeman as one of two guests. (The other was a long-time member of the Federal Power Commission staff, Ronald Corso, who has mightily helped promote the small hydro idea.)

I had wanted to see Freeman because he is definitely part of the top White House staff on energy, close to Schlesinger. His Ford Foundation report of some years ago on energy has had an important effect, for it was there that the idea that somehow "conservation" should be a keystone of an energy program was furthered.

Freeman was a junior lawyer on the TVA staff of years ago. That he is a candidate for the vacancy on the TVA board stirred Marguerite's deep concern—and after listening to him for a whole evening, I came to share that concern.

A truly happy event yesterday: that big good-looking grandson Daniel arrived, with his backpack and a plaid six-inch-square patch on the seat of his jeans, a merry smile, and a serious outlook on life, on his education, on his special interest, which is agriculture, soil, land, and South America.

We sat at the card table on the back porch for our vegetarian dinner (he is definitely a committed non-meat-eater). Slowly he took off his huge shoes, peeled off his sweaty wool sox, deposited both at his side of the table, and we proceeded with dinner.

For the first time I can remember, he asked me a question about how I had gone about helping poor farmers to adopt better farming practices. I was so pleased, answered quite simply, and will show him the way I describe our methods in my book about the TVA.

JUNE 26, 1977
PRINCETON

The clan is gathering: Jack Vaughn, full of enthusiasm about what he found on his brief trip to Iran; John Silveira, full of problems, no doubt; John Macy, frazzled, I fear, and having his usual difficulty of allocating his time and vast energies, wanting naturally to get into the middle of the energy development that I, and Norman, have been pushing along; Norman, quite full of his new job and making a great beginning; Tom Mead, Ken Fields, and Andrea Pampanini. It should be quite a week.

JUNE 29, 1977
NEW YORK

Yesterday, the good feeling that comes when one can tell that one is functioning well, working at full capacity. A long day, very long and concentrated. What a happy state I am in.

We went over the main segments of the Iran operation, warts and all, troubles galore, but not all troubles, considerable achievements.

So there are ups and satisfactions, and there are evidences of fatigue and discouragement. That is the way it is today.

These big public dinners that are the mark of New York City I have come to abhor. I thought of several reasons why I should simply not go to the Asia Society dinner tonight—having done my duty by buying a ticket and contributing to its funds, for it is a very good Society indeed, and the hours I have enjoyed its gallery have been among the most treasured of my years in New York City.

But it was a good meeting, crowded, of course, but handsome. Secretary Vance made a speech about the Pacific that was admirable. One reason I thought so is that it so closely followed the theme and some of the terminology of the speech on the Pacific Basin and the U.S. that I made in Tokyo years ago.

Talked to John Rockefeller 3d and Blanchette, seated at an adjoining table—*not* on the waxworks dais—and leaving the spotlight to his willing extrovert brother David. John looks frail and even gaunt. I noticed that beside his chair was a shooting stick, the kind that opens up so one can sit on it. I don't need one of these right now, though the thought has occurred to me, particularly on trips where one has to stand a good deal. Blanchette beamed, seemed genuinely pleased to see me. She is a truly great lady, in the best tradition of quiet strength.

Hodding Carter III bore down on me before the meeting began. Said he was having the time of his life on his job of public affairs officer for the State Department, and he looked it too. Quite a change from the *Greenville Democrat* along the Mississippi.

Vance has had what is known as a "good press," as if this is something created by publicity rather than by being a good solid Secretary of State and a decent, modest man. Which he is.

JUNE 30, 1977
NEW YORK

Bob Fri called me this morning, early. He will leave ERDA by September 1. Does that mean that he, Fri, will not make a decision on our proposed program for "evaluating" small hydro, a proposition he had not yet seen? "Not at all. I intend to move ahead while I am here, and promptly."

Well, when he sees what we propose—or rather, when his "people down the line" see it, and wrap it in typical contract-officer barbed wire and time delays—that will be a different story.

JULY 4, 1977
MARTHA'S VINEYARD

How happy I am with the latest addition to "Topside." Helen's plans, impromptu sketches on paper, concerned and sometimes puzzled looks —these occupied much of her time through last summer; and the result, the reality, in wood, is such an achievement of good workmanship and imaginative planning. I am the beneficiary of her love and thoughtfulness, for the result is a suite, the large study (where I am writing this), a bathroom and separate shower, and a handsome good-sized bedroom, with drawers and closets galore. A loving birthday present.

The transformation of the tiny kitchen into a bedroom for Helen, and the new kitchen, are parsimonious in size compared to my quarters, but Helen seems to like both of the new additions—so that's right.

Terribly tired when I arrived Saturday late morning. It had been a week of driving myself and others around me, with some bumps and potholes on the road.

Now there is another effort at some kind of IBEC transfusion or "merger." What would be the consequences for D&R if this actually happened?

If I didn't feel so responsible for my colleagues in the company, it would be easy enough to pull out, set up a simple operation out of Princeton or New York, and keep myself occupied in that way—and let D&R's contracts be fulfilled by whoever would buy the shares from IBEC.

But that alternative, attractive in a way, just wouldn't do. I would be saving myself, but abandoning my partners and friends, which isn't like me.

The most serious bump of last week came out of a phone conversation with the geothermal man in ERDA, Dr. Bresee. He made it plain that the informal proposal D&R made last Tuesday for a program of "demonstrations of small hydro" would be long in considering, that it would be several months before they would make a decision.

Right now we might well be far better off to stay out of the gooey clutches of the Federal Government and go our way.

All that sense of urgency because Bob Fri wanted us to help shape a program which none of them at ERDA had any background for, was apparently wasted.

JULY 7, 1977
MARTHA'S VINEYARD

Helen's birthday present to me has somehow helped unravel me, after the accumulated wear and tear of weeks, months, of hard going. I doze off after lunch, and sometimes have a second nap before dinner. Now I can *feel* how fatigued I became—still am. But unlike other years —how many!!—I have *not* phoned the office "just to see how things are going."

I should be settling down to write about what it is like to be an aged man, still furious, or exulting, or planning big things against the future. The way I am now, in my "late seventies," would be a story worth reading by that increasing proportion of the population who lived beyond sixty (which used to be regarded as aged).

The past ten to fifteen years of my work hardly suggest that senility of any kind has overcome me. The "record" shows that I have come up with as many fresh, new concepts and approaches to public issues and how to deal with them as at any time in my life. The remarkable acceptance of my Public Sector Management improvement concept, with its contemporary adaptation of "decentralization" in a Mideastern country, or the small hydro idea, certainly are not marks of emotional or intellectual senility.

JULY 8, 1977
MARTHA'S VINEYARD

Well, I made it. Another birthday. As long as I *respond to life* with new ideas, new ventures, new appetites, fresh indignations, then having more "birthdays" is worthwhile (whatever the number: 28, 38—*or* 78).

JULY 10, 1977
MARTHA'S VINEYARD

My life consists of thousands of tiny visual episodes, tiny separate pictures. And one of the most pleasant added to the collection occurred today: Helen busy hemming a dress Nancy has just bought, Nancy seated at Helen's feet, both of them chattering away a mile a minute. Both looking so happy and content, in each other's company, for they do have such similar likes. Too bad, for Helen, that they don't see more of each other, through the year.

JULY 11, 1977
MARTHA'S VINEYARD

Such good news! Professor Thuc† has been told that he will be welcomed to France, with his family. Only this morning I spoke to Helen about my continuing concern about this little patriot, with the bright eyes, with whom I worked so hard when we tried to buck the forces of resignation and cynicism to achieve a plan for a future for Vietnam. He has been in prison twice, since the fall of Saigon. France is his second home.

JULY 16, 1977
MARTHA'S VINEYARD

It is what goes on *inside* of me that matters, that generates the ideas, the drive, the satisfactions and the frustrations—particularly the frustrations—and the solutions of the "problems" about which so much of my working life consists. And it is what goes on inside of me that is revealing, those intangible inward emotions—sometimes consciously, more often subconsciously—that explain what I am, and what I accomplish, or fail to accomplish. It is not the "episodes" (describing which I spend so much of my time), "problems," and energies which take up so much of the great volume of words I have written in the journals, year after year. By episodes I mean conflicts, business issues: "cash flow," "earnings," or lack of them, personnel matters.

Underneath the particular problems the past several months, there is this dual, largely subconscious fear of staying on too long, the fear of boredom and caving in, of being deprived, by my own act or that of others, of the fever and excitement of being in charge of an exacting life.

†Chief of the South Vietnam postwar economic planning and reconstruction group.

One of the functions of this journal has been, from time to time, to drag out many such concerns, fears, emotional debates within myself, put them into words, write them off.

I need to know *where* I am going. This troubled and disturbed period of recent weeks has now clarified the answer to that question. Sitting here on the deck, I let myself go, in one of those many, many memorable after-breakfast talks to Helen, my most perceptive, spirited, and understanding "audience."

I do know where I am going. Not the precise moves and responses to particular issues in the progress of my life and work, but the emotional response of a confident man, back of him a record of experience clearly unusual if not unique, a performance within the past eighteen months that took energy, talents, and a positive spirit.

I have here and now dedicated myself to the future. No half-hearted hedging. No fear that the capacity I have shown in the past will not be more than capable of meeting, one by one, the problems of how I can best apply my managerial and emotional talents.

This conclusion is not one I should constantly re-examine as new phases of my work and my personal life show up, as they will, as they do.

The theme: going ahead is what counts. No half-seeking a refuge, whether of retirement, or putting myself on the shelf, or showing lack of confidence, or too much attention to age.

JULY 17, 1977
MARTHA'S VINEYARD

Should I try to put together a book around the broad theme of energy? If I decide to do so, does this mean that we have to abandon the idea of a Volume VII of the *Journals?*

This morning I went over these interrelated questions with Helen in another of our post-breakfast sessions on the deck of "Topside."

Helen's approach to the book idea is conditioned by her having edited a collection of my speeches and essays, which became a well-received book: *This I Do Believe.* Well received, despite Harper's initial acute skepticism "about a market for a 'book of speeches.' "

She believes as a first step she can cull out of the published *Journals* and the enormous manuscript still unpublished all the material bearing on energy. She calls this "researching the material." In addition, our files show a good many speeches and articles, memoranda and letters, that could be the raw material out of which an energy book could be fashioned.

The theme is indeed a broad one, as an hour's vigorous talk on this foggy sticky morning made plain: atomic energy, environment, proliferation of nuclear materials, coal, and more recently, small hydro—or plain waterpower—here and abroad, for that matter.

The joint conclusion of this morning's talk was that she did not believe Volume VII should be abandoned, as I had suggested; that she would "research" the *Journals* for material specifically concerned with energy, and that I should ask Miss Baron to expand the listing of material she has already made, at my request, of office file material; and finally, that when I return from New York we take a look at what kind of mosaic her exploration produces.

JULY 20, 1977
NEW YORK

For a couple years I have been trying to ignore the recommendation that I have surgery to reduce the size of my prostate gland. The advice is not to procrastinate, to choose a time when this will interfere the least with my schedule. Yesterday afternoon I decided that I should ask Dr. Hoskins to arrange a time when this could be done, since recuperation this summer at the Vineyard would probably interfere least with getting ready for a very hefty program of work, which is opening up.

JULY 22, 1977
MARTHA'S VINEYARD

Teddy Roosevelt once said: "They say I am impulsive—act impulsively. Not so. I think a long time about things. But when I have made up my mind, I act right away."

That's me. It is so characteristic of me to be sitting at my desk discussing something I have been thinking about for a long time, and then, apparently suddenly (to others), grab the phone or yell to Miss Baron: Get so and so for me, please. And that looks impulsive—but it is only the acting that is impulsive, the thinking about it may be over a period of months.

JULY 23, 1977
MARTHA'S VINEYARD

A day of glory. From this hill the deep blue of the ocean to the south rivals the overreaching sky; to the north the sparkling green of the woods joins a great stretch of the blue waters of the Sound, and the tawny cliffs of Naushon. The air so crisp and inspiriting.

JULY 25, 1977
NEW YORK HOSPITAL
NEW YORK

So far except for some prodding and questions from young interns, male and female, black and white, there has been nothing to make it seem credible that tomorrow I will be wheeled out of here into an operating room.

How many times in one's lifetime does one go through the perfunctory EKGs and X-rays? I suppose I shouldn't complain: it is the way the hospitals take care of their overheads.

AUGUST 8, 1977
MARTHA'S VINEYARD

The Shah has named Jamshid Amouzegar as Prime Minister, to head a new Cabinet, replacing Hoveyda.

It is difficult to keep one's euphoric emotions under control with this news. Particularly when one thinks how closely our recent history in Iran has been tied to a special relationship with this strong and imaginative man.

A "blow" this morning: a bureaucrat named Charles DiBonna advised Norman Clapp that the "contract officers" of ERDA can't accept the idea that D&R is "unique" in the field of small hydro—that is, in a legal sense. So months of our initiative go down the drain.

AUGUST 9, 1977
MARTHA'S VINEYARD

With the warmth and generosity of spirit that is David Morse's outstanding characteristic, he spent more than an hour with Davey yesterday about our grandson's passion to create a life in the area that so completely dominates him: the restoration of antique objects of wood.

It happens—though this I had forgotten—that David Morse's father, beginning as a poor immigrant, was a cabinet maker—of particular talent—then a dealer in antiques. So David himself was brought up in a family where craftsmanship was part of its life as well as livelihood.

David Morse is often given to hyperbole and supergenerosity. Still, the impression David 3d made on him was obviously a stunner. He does have an assurance and a presence, and a beauty of person—and none of this was lost on our friend Morse.

The word about the new Amouzegar Cabinet in Iran continues to give me satisfaction. For example, the new Minister of Agriculture (replacing Rouhani) is Ahmad Ahmadi, first agricultural director of Khuzistan Development Service.

AUGUST 10, 1977
MARTHA'S VINEYARD

I was determined not to "complain" to Fri when he called to express himself as "chagrined." I respect him so much—and respect myself too —so I said not one word of our having been badly and unjustly treated by the termites of the "contract and procurement" division of ERDA— something that has grown up since I ran AEC.

Said Bob: "I thought you were right, and should have been selected on a 'sole source' basis. But I didn't want to go against a staff recommendation."

AUGUST 13, 1977
MARTHA'S VINEYARD

TVA now has a new member of the board: David Freeman. Now he will go through a transition: from being a report writer, an ideologue with extreme and arbitrary views about the primacy of the "environment," or conservation as a cure-all for the energy problem, or "no growth" as a philosophy—these will now be tested by the rigors of responsibility.

Freeman had his first test of this testing of "notions" against reality in two days of Senate Committee hearings. There he had to take a position on some of TVA's issues. The solace is that TVA is a concept so grand and its achievements so solid and visible that those who come to "turn it around" are soon absorbed in its support. At least this is what happened when Eisenhower named General Vogel to succeed Gordon Clapp in 1954, with orders to clean out those radicals in TVA. In no time at all, Vogel became a great advocate as Chairman of TVA. However, he was an open-minded and technically able engineer.

A slight family episode, but one that tells a good deal about Helen and me:

I had been showing concern and expressing it about Helen carrying too much of a burden here at "Topside" and "Yonside."

Helen put down my breakfast tray and delivered herself of the following:

"Dave, I wish you would stop talking like this. I sense that it is your concern for me and I appreciate that. But as long as I am physically able to run this place, including the driving and the rest, I intend to do it. The time will come when I can't. *That* is when I will be unhappy, not now when I am fully able to carry what I do, with the considerable amount of rest I do get.

"It will be the frustration of asking others to do my job because I can't do it, that is what will be hard for me. Until that time, please don't keep talking about it."

AUGUST 15, 1977
MARTHA'S VINEYARD

How delicious is our little visitor, Jerusha, still not four years old: golden curly hair, the bluest of merry eyes, floating one moment and dancing, bounding, pirouetting the next. We played together on the floor, and it came over me not too happily what an effort it was for me to get up from a floor-sitting position, while she fairly bounced. Does Nature have to make such a big deal of demonstrating to a great-grandfather what is meant by the "aging process"?

This place has so many reminders for us all, of other days, other years. Pamela, a fine figure of a young woman, with this delicious little child her greatest achievement—so I think. And just a few paces up the hill, beyond Mr. Mitty, the great rock outside this window, is the "hideaway" where Pam and her brother Mike and I used to create a world of our own, apart from the oldsters.

Part of the "Topside" ritual was duly observed: measuring Jerusha's height against the closet door where all the grandchildren's "historic" measurements were set out.

That door with its marks covering the many—and not so many— years means a lot to the now older children. The first thing Allen Bromberger and David 3d did on coming to the house some weeks ago was to walk past us and take a look at the door.

AUGUST 18, 1977
MARTHA'S VINEYARD

Norman Clapp phoned this morning reporting the results of the several hours of discussion he had yesterday, in Frankfort, Kentucky. Clearly, Governor Carroll and the staff people of the Appalachian Regional Commission (including the "Federal Co-Chairman") understood Norman's thesis for an undertaking by the Eastern coal states based upon a D&R report and proposal.

I said I was surprised (and pleased) that so much headway of agreement on principles and concept had been made; I thought it would take many more months to reach the point where they were asking D&R for an outline and a proposal for our services in developing an Appalachian Coal Authority—an operating mechanism for seeing to it that in the production and marketing of coal in those states, the social needs and objectives of the people of the region were a chief factor.

AUGUST 20, 1977
MARTHA'S VINEYARD

Four solid hours yesterday with John Macy of discussion and decision-making, about the many faces of today's D&R.

Macy will be off to Iran for a seven- or eight-week absence, when the Chief Executive Officer and the President will be reduced to being telex pals. The difference between face-to-face discussion—as yesterday—and mail, which is impossible (eight to ten days between the writing of ideas and a chance to read them and react). Though telex is instantaneous, it is a poor substitute. So my own chores are increased by his absence.

Then Norman has taken on new areas in which I must participate: the coal Governors, particularly Kentucky's Carroll, expect us to submit a proposal by October 18 which they can, in turn, present to the other Governors.

The real blow so far as my ability to handle the company's affairs in New York is that Norman is more or less committed to spend four days a week in Albany for the balance of the year, on his assignment from Governor Carey, growing out of the electric blackout. That almost eliminates him from helping me in the running of the company.

The Annual Love of Life Festival: Roger Baldwin's visit with D.E.L. this afternoon.

What exuberance, warmth of spirit, mirth—a distinctive man at any age; indeed, he carries his ninety-three years so well that one is not conscious of anything about years or aging. He has not "wasted" any of those years, or even moments. Something to give you heart about the possibilities, the almost infinite possibilities of living—as eager at the almost end as in the early years.

I asked Roger to inscribe a book about him by Peggy Lamson. He wrote, in a firm hand without a quaver: "To my good friends of many happy summers, and affection at all times. In kinship, Roger Baldwin."

Is living so worthwhile? Roger asked, then proceeded to answer the rhetorical question by an anecdote about Clarence Darrow. Of course, Darrow, like practically every public figure of the past seventy-five years, was a kind of intellectual colleague of Roger's.

Part of Darrow's lecture-platform repertoire was to ask the question: Is life worth living? And his answer: No, it is not.

Said Darrow: "What is it that makes people think it is, makes them keep on going? Dope, that is what. The dope of religion, the dope of mysticism, the dope of ambition. None of them really work. The real dope that makes life seem worth living is work."

AUGUST 21, 1977
MARTHA'S VINEYARD

Drove the car down the rutted narrow road to the shore, at the Daggetts'—as a pleasure, in itself, but chiefly as a way to rebuild my confidence, after the hospital experience [prostate operation]. It went well.

But what really gave my confidence and my self-esteem a boost was the affectionate greeting from Sparky, the Daggetts' watchdog, and Peter Daggett, one of the most delightful boys I have ever known.

Dogs and kids—if they go for you in a genuine way, you can't be all bad.

Golda Meir's autobiography, *My Life,* has shaken me with one emotion after another as I have read this passionate and intensely personal story, story of a life and story of an epic event, the establishment of a state based upon a concept I find impossible to accept—that is the idea of a political entity based upon a religion and a religious inheritance.

This is hard to square with my notions of political freedom and of democracy. It is evident that the extremist "Jewish religion bloc," as Golda Meir disposes of them, are unacceptable to me in terms of principles.

But against the background of human suffering and persecution, the story had me weeping. How could anyone feel distant or uninvolved in this story of the fight for survival and decent treatment of human beings?

Strangely enough, I found her account of the Israeli development programs for Africa almost as touching as anything in this story. It was because the thesis underlying Israeli development assistance to the newly independent and primitive African countries was so close to the philosophy I believe should permeate development effort from the "outside"—and which I believe in and try to get D&R to follow.

AUGUST 28, 1977
MARTHA'S VINEYARD

The *Smithsonian* September issue arrived at my desk last week. Stunning, beautiful pictures, beginning with the cover.

I put in a call to Ed Thompson. He came right on. Was greatly pleased, he said, that I called; agreed it was a good issue.

That something in a *monthly* magazine (necessarily written and prepared months ago) should be timely today is a mark of luck as much as anything else.

AUGUST 30, 1977
MARTHA'S VINEYARD

The Corps of Engineers has issued its ninety-day report on *existing* dams and has come up with the same number of megawatts we stated, in my *Smithsonian* article. Far from saying, as the President did in his Energy Message, that hydro isn't worth bothering with, the magnitude in the way of saving of oil makes solar look pretty feeble.

AUGUST 31, 1977
MARTHA'S VINEYARD

Have been dictating, by phone of course, long messages about and for Iran. To Ahmad Ahmadi, our early agricultural staffer in Khuzistan, recently made Minister of Agriculture, expressing great satisfaction in his appointment and confidence that he can move Iranian agriculture forward—it could stand it, goodness knows. And to [Ahmad] Aleyasin, a rugged engineer who was one of our early staff men, when D&R was running things, and afterward with KWPA—now just made Managing Director.

Can such changes bring KWPA out of its sleep and decline? Expressing confidence that these men and Jamshid Amouzegar, the new Prime Minister, can accomplish that may be only wishfulness: but it is the first real break in a long time toward effectiveness and toward a restoration of the broad concept of KWPA.

SEPTEMBER 3, 1977
MARTHA'S VINEYARD

The two-hour meeting here with Tom Lee, manager of General Electric's unit for strategic planning for power generation, went very well, I thought.

He agreed with me that small hydro must be taken seriously, but strictly on a comparison of economic factors with other sources. Still, he was rather impressed by the environmental advantage of the kind of additional energy I propose, from existing dams. Also he asserted, and I agreed, that ERDA funds aren't needed; the technology is complete and the advantage of "staying away from the Federal subsidy" route is considerable.

He asked me how D&R would expect to function in this picture. I suggested we join General Electric in examining a number of sites to see if they would qualify on the basis of comparative economics alone. He admitted that the environmental factor was important, but certainly we don't need Federal financing except in the most limited way.

He suggested that a member of our staff meet with the heads of their systems analysis group—which I'll suggest to Silveira.

Will we hear from this further? I don't know.

He gave me full credit for coming up with a concept that will have quite an impact. No reference to the *Smithsonian* article which I supplied him.

In the midst of our solemn deliberations, the place was turned into a clatter and hubbub of youthful enthusiasm and the whine of an electric tree-cutting saw. Davey and his cohorts, Allen and Daniel, were vigorously pruning the trees, cutting right and left, tasks that in years past I performed by hanging out of trees.

Helping in the tree-pruning exercise, and hauling the cut limbs up the hill, no easy task, was Allen's girl, Lisa Winick. She is delightful.

SEPTEMBER 4, 1977
MARTHA'S VINEYARD

Fifty-four years: difficult to believe. I don't remember clearly the wedding itself—it was in the morning. The night before I had a severe bellyache; that I do remember. I thought at the time it was indigestion; now I realize I was just scared. As soon became apparent, I had cause to be scared, me with only a $25-a-week job, and by Thanksgiving time Helen was down with a severe case of typhoid fever.

The picture of her at dinner here last evening will long remain in my mind: a happy woman, with the light of youth in her eyes as the grandsons tried to keep up with her joshing and wisecracking, she returning the volleys fast. My sole contribution was a word of warning to the young men: "Don't play leapfrog with a unicorn."

I have deliberately, and even cheerfully, accepted immobility this summer, here in this happy house, which has become in a very real sense more nearly *home* than 88 Battle Road in Princeton.

So I have done none of the physically active exploits of other years:

cutting back the trees, running (more than jogging), and of course, sailing. (My sailing days seem now as remote as the sand-lot baseball of my boyhood.)

One of the compensations of staying put has been much reading. (My intermittent quasi-nocturnal insomnia has helped on the reading too—almost always waking at or about two, *reading* for an hour or so, then back to sleep.)

Have just this hour finished a book I am surprised, in a way, I found so full of interest, so stimulating of personal identification: a full-scale biography of Ring Lardner.

Earlier I read a book by Liv Ullmann, the great Norwegian actress, whose portrayal of Anna Christie I enjoyed so this summer—far better than her better-known TV series. A biography of David Dubinsky, a fascinating illustrated book about Houdini—and so on.

Now I have begun the story of Sir Aurel Stein, the explorer and archeologist, created by our neighbor and friend, the incomparable Jeanette Mirsky.

Much reading, yes. But hours and hours here at the telephone to New York, Washington, and Albany at the table that is the centerpiece of my "study."

SEPTEMBER 5, 1977
MARTHA'S VINEYARD

A memorable hour-or-so visit with Davey, on the south-looking deck, the morning sun and the dark green of the surrounding trees the only witness. An intimate, personal kind of exchange.

"As Allen and you and I were together in the front seat of the car driving in to dinner the other evening, it came over both of us, as we said to each other, later, how strange it must be for you, being there with us, grown, with our problems as grownups. You have known us since we were [here he gestured] so high. And yet *you* haven't changed, but *we have*. Strange feeling."

SEPTEMBER 9, 1977
NEW YORK

One by one, the things that I once delighted in drop away, are gradually beyond me. (Is that what is meant by the phrase "growing old"?)

I am thinking of physical things. Boxing; had to give that up. Gave up riding without a saddle, bareback, then no riding at all. The calisthenics which I enjoyed, I suppose because I was vain about my shoulder development, diminished and now tapered to very little. The latest deprivation is quite recent, almost sudden. I can walk a distance now only with considerable pain—those cursed arthritic hips and the muscle spasms in my legs due, I'm told, to the condition of the thigh joints.

What is the mental parallel of this dropping away? And the emotional atrophy (for I assume there is such)? The physical dropping away is evident. I seem to have as much enthusiasm, emotional response, even creativity and intellectual ambition, as ever.

SEPTEMBER 10, 1977
NEW YORK

"Let me tell you something of the new Government." This was my oldest Iranian friend, Mehdi Samii, lunching with me at the Pierre, at his telegraphed request.

"I was glad and relieved to learn from John Macy that you have recovered some of your enthusiasm and confidence in Iran." This said tentatively, and looking at me out of the corners of his eyes.

"True," I said, "and the reason is that there is much recent evidence that the Iranian leadership now recognizes that having a lot of money— as you do—does not solve everything, doesn't solve the most critical of your problems, political or economic. Getting back to some sense of restraint—which you, Mehdi, were almost alone in advocating years ago—has been an important part of the change in my own feeling about Iran."

Before the two-and-a-half-hour luncheon was over, I demonstrated by my intensity and candor ("indiscretion," perhaps is the word) that I am every bit as committed to Iran now, as before.

Mehdi chatted for quite a while about how it happened that Hushang Ansary was not named Prime Minister, which almost everyone, Ansary particularly, had expected. In a picture of how a medieval court must have watched the sovereign's every gesture, so it was at a big shindig: "His Majesty sent word that he wanted to talk to Jamshid alone—and that was the signal."

Mehdi considers that the Amouzegar Prime Ministership may not last very long. He has offended members of the Majlis; it is well known that he can be quite harsh in dealing with the subordinates, that he has never before been able to build up strength in the Ministries he has occupied. (These negative things Mehdi had told me long ago.)

So what he said was no surprise. But his virtual prediction that Jamshid's enemies already have made inroads on him did surprise me.

Two strong and "very ambitious" men, Hushang and Jamshid. So strong that the Shah had to placate Hushang by agreeing that the Plan Organization's budget functions should be in the Ministry of Finance, his

Ministry, with the planning functions reporting independently to the Prime Minister.

Mehdi's comment: "Actually there has been no change [except that Majidi is no longer Managing Director] in the Plan Organization. No change whatever. That isn't understood, but you should know." I couldn't follow this, but I had better get Macy's reading on it.

Much of our time together was spent in my listening to him on the "specific matter Hoveyda wants your views about," what once he called the "bad image of Iran in America and what can be done about it."

Mehdi recalled, with his quiet little half-smile, that I had expressed myself on this very positively. In fact, he recalled a longhand note I wrote him, in 1974, for sharing with the then Prime Minister Hoveyda, which said, essentially: "Do you Iranians care what the American people think of you? If you don't, that's it. If you do, you have got to think about it carefully and take it seriously."

Mehdi was bringing a "message" to me from the now Minister of Court Hoveyda: get my advice about our "image" in America, how to improve it. A short-run reason: because the Shah is making a State visit in November. But Hoveyda is more interested in the long run, not just the November visit.

"How do we go about it? We just don't know. One thing we have done: set up a small Industrial Research Institute; prepared a series of meetings organized for us by Stanford Research Institute, for early October in Washington. Another similar meeting involving in both instances American industries, banks and investors, the regular Stanford one in San Francisco, the one that Ebtehaj always attends and will this year."

I sat silent for quite a while after hearing how they were going about explaining Iran (and "making America like Iran," I guess). All directed toward big shots in the American financial and business world. The assumption has long been that if the Robert Andersons and David Rockefellers and the Bechtels and Jack "Exxon" McCloys attend these meetings, speak to them, this will be a kind of "influencing American public opinion favorable to Iran."

The substance of my answer was that the money people—bankers, big-shot industrials—are very much on the defensive in America, many completely discredited, others just waiting for their retirement. If you rely upon their voices on behalf of Iran, you stir up skepticism and worse.

Today that lot has little support in the professional media, or among people, ordinary people, whose opinions count. America has changed completely in this respect in the past few years, completely.

Another group that your Ambassador thinks will help the "image" is the "society" crowd. Forget it. What good does *their* good opinion do you, or anyone?

Carter was pushed into this at the beginning of his campaign. Found himself at a lunch at "21," which is the kiss of death for a popular candidate, and equally so for a country like Iran, loaded with oil money at prices that are resented.

Any kind of ostentation, upper-class, financial or industrial or society, creates the very opposite impression that I happen still to have about Iran and the Shah, a sincere desire and program to improve the life of millions of very poor and illiterate people. The "21" restaurant and that kind of thing, in any form, simply confirms the opposite view. And Ambassador Zahedi's elaborate parties at the Embassy do the same.

And that new building being erected on Fifth Avenue: that is down the wrong track—right in the middle of the swankiest avenue in the world, built by Pahlavi riches. That's on the wrong road, and so is an investment in the Krupp industries of Germany.

Mehdi said, "I can see, by the way you talk to me now, that this is indeed the old Lilienthal speaking."

He will arrange—as an "advisor" to the Queen—that I have an "intimate exchange of views" with Her Majesty on this next trip; he agrees she is a remarkable and sensitive person. And that I will have an opportunity to meet most of the people who count, or who I consider are on the right track, as well as, I assume, those who are obviously people I take little comfort from seeing close to the center of things in the new Cabinet.

SEPTEMBER 12, 1977
NEW YORK

My interview in the *Engineering News-Record* led John Stetson of Utica to get in touch with the Niagara-Mohawk power company. This resulted in a D&R meeting with Niagara-Mohawk at Syracuse, the first half-hour of which was cold, lifeless, unrelieved by any favorable chemistry or lightness.

What was even worse, the presentation by their vice president for engineering was strictly about their hydro program. I felt that it must be broadened, that the problems of this great utility could not be limited to engineering or even environmental considerations revolving around their hydro program.

So I tried to provide them with my concept of how broad were the issues that a major utility must face in the next five to ten years.

I think this loosened things up—a bit. All of us D&R people became articulate then. John Silveira brought out many of the problems of water resources on a broad scale that would have to be faced, and that I daresay their own consultants would not even recognize.

I reminded them that New York State had in the past been a "battle-ground for attack on public utilities," and that this could be expected to happen again. It was well to see their position in the broadest perspective. And here would be one place where D&R would be uniquely qualified.

Well, it has been a long day, began at seven this morning. So I should summarize: we did make headway; we have been invited to submit more about our own capabilities that might have value to them, and with Stetson's help, may produce further discussion.

Come what may, it was a good way for D&R (and D.E.L.) to get closer to the thinking and agenda and (largely pedestrian) outlook of a great and diversified utility.

It is difficult to say to a technical group in the presence of their boss that they might need help from the outside.

SEPTEMBER 13, 1977
NEW YORK

The Shah's twin sister, the elegant Princess Ashraf, attacked by gunmen in the south of France, her companion killed. Part of the "Down with the Shah" crusade, so it is assumed.

Talked again to Mehdi about my attending the economics conference in Washington in early October. I am reluctant to go even for a day if it is not attended by Iranians of consequence—forget American businessmen who send their third-level staffers. I am not impressed with the line-up.

Mehdi was disturbed; insistent that I should participate. "I ask this as a personal favor, but more than that, those back home will appreciate it, will not quite understand if you don't attend." Well, I suppose I must. Some things one must do, however one feels, and perhaps this is one of them. My D&R companions rely heavily on me, for ceremonial purposes, as well as other reasons.

SEPTEMBER 17, 1977
MARTHA'S VINEYARD

What does cheer me is the increasing tangible evidence that some of my ideas, and the skills of my senior partners, are making headway. Not conventional ideas either, and such notions always run into the tangle-wood of resistance from those whose whole careers are built upon other concepts; to expect a man in mid- or late-career to have an open mind about new ideas is expecting too much.

So, my proposal that General Electric consider moving into the small and medium hydro field apparently is very much of interest to them.

First, a talk with Phil Reed, at Antigua, last winter; then a luncheon meeting with the head of their power-generation department, then the discussion with the brilliant analyst Tom Lee, here on this hilltop, then a meeting with John Silveira last week, arranged by Lee, with the four or five leading GE systems analysts, and now a call from Lee reporting a very positive enthusiasm by Picozzi, head of GE's hydroelectricity department, and a meeting being arranged with Picozzi in New York week after next.

New fresh concepts are what keep an organization alive and vital. Whether it also makes for a profitable operation is not so clear—not by any means.

John Stetson has called to say that Niagara-Mohawk is now definitely interested in finding a role for D&R. Of this message what most appealed to me is that (according to Stetson) it was my little lecture about the revolution going on in the electricity business that made the chief impact. "We are groping to understand what this changed electric industry will be like." That is what they want guidance on, as well as more specific engineering and hydrologic help from D&R.

The progress that John Macy is making in Iran, using the Public Sector Management project as the device for enlightenment so that Hushang Ansary, a very self-confident little man, should insist on "help" from us on the improvement of the administration of the tax system (a most delicate area, to be sure), is only the most recent sign of the impact on a set-in-its-way bureaucracy and tax system.

President Carter must be a very sad man. His dream is shattered of a happy partnership with the Congress (which is predominantly of his own party, but clearly not of his way of thinking).

When there is a struggle for power, does it pay (i.e., work) to be conciliatory with the opposition, or even with one's friends?

Congress can torture the President after the fuzz is off the peach. Woodrow Wilson tried to carry the fight for his "cause" to the people, by traveling until he was utterly exhausted, and terribly ill. F.D.R. didn't believe in conciliating if he thought he could prevail in some more forthright way—and he had the aid of a great radio voice and manner, and a war to help.

Does Carter have the flair for a fight? He could put the fear of God into the opposition—which is a leaderless group of soreheads—with his command of the TV and the media. But is that his style? Is that the way he reads history?

SEPTEMBER 26, 1977
NEW YORK

After years and years of being battered, in public, over the TVA and the AEC, my inclination to read an injury into almost anything is something I have been warned to watch out for. Being easily bruised, looking for slights when they weren't there, this is a characteristic of mine ever since those years of having to fight so hard to protect what I built and believed in. But it must be severely guarded against now that I am an "old man," for it is characteristic of many old people, and particularly men who carry on in the company of younger men.

Having Davey with us this summer was a great treat. And the past couple days in Princeton gave us a chance to talk, into the night, alone. He summed it up yesterday late afternoon: "Our long talk meant a lot to me, a very great deal. Now I see you as a human being. Before, you intimidated me."

As he explained, he and his cousins were "in awe" of what I had accomplished, whereas they were groping and not at all sure where they were going in their career. But admitting, and emphasizing, how often I had fumbled, how confused at times I am, too, made me a "human being."

OCTOBER 13, 1977
PRINCETON

Asked Dick Dilworth to give me a report on the condition of our "parent"—a misnomer if ever there was one—since it is so well known that IBEC is once more unloading properties, including the Bellows machinery enterprise.

I felt confident, after a fifteen-minute phone talk with Dick, that he understands our problem of retaining key staff and their morale, particularly after that Rodman memo "To the Staff" that has upset us, as a harbinger of trouble with IBEC.

OCTOBER 19, 1977
NEW YORK

Looking out over a great view of this absurd and magnificent city, Helen and I, at noon today, separately signed a "last will and testament." With it, a compilation of what are our "assets" to be divided with our children and their satellites.

Said Helen, "We have never thought about wealth, about wealth as an objective, have we?" and indeed we haven't.

Does it mean very much? Only when you are pinching pennies—as for years we did—or certainly kept track of every cent—can you judge whether it "means much" never to have to be concerned about having enough to continue to live in the "manner" we prefer.

OCTOBER 24, 1977
ROME

David, grey-bearded, white hair floating in all directions; his son, with a red beard and looking so very young, came into our hotel suite here, about noon yesterday.

Because I find that extensive walking and standing—as a sightseer —can be uncomfortable, we taxied to the piazza near the Pantheon, and became part of the Sunday crowd of Italians enjoying the sunshine. There is a liveliness about Romans, particularly the young ones, on a holiday, that is quite delightful to observe.

OCTOBER 27, 1977
TEHRAN

Began my latest "return to Tehran," as of Tuesday forenoon, with severe muscle and joint aching. Reminded me of the grippe I had recently, perhaps a relapse induced by the long flight.

This time is quite different because Helen is here. Such good care she took of me during the couple days when I was not doing well at all. She doesn't fuss over me, fortunately, but I always "know she is there."

OCTOBER 29, 1977
TEHRAN

This is the day I don my white shirt and put on my *new* store-bought suit, for the first time.

In short, this is the day I head for the Niavaran Palace and an audience with the Shah—and wish him a happy birthday.

The audience began as usual—i.e., exactly on time (11 o'clock) with His Majesty crossing the big room to shake my hand, welcome me, take me to a seat on a divan, while the tail-coated white-haired attendant brought him tea in a small glass, a brimming and beautiful cup for me. (Which, again, as usual, I drank only ceremonially, not wanting to interrupt the easy, almost comradely, human contact—as warm and casual as ever in the many past meetings.)

He opened the subject that was actually closest to my own thoughts and what I wanted to be discussed: Khuzistan. How are things going there? Am I making a trip to Khuzistan? I could affirm that we were indeed going to Khuzistan. He launched into a bit of nostalgia about how poor the people of that region had been "right after Mossadegh"—which is about when, in February, 1956, I made our first trip to what was then a miserable region.

Now is the time for another "unified plan," the original one presented to him in early 1959 having laid the groundwork for the developing of the region. But everything has changed. He said with satisfaction that the Japanese had just decided to invest $6 billion in a vast petrochemical project in the region.

I spun out a kind of twenty-year look *into the future,* a comprehensive survey that his new Khuzistan Governor General Namazi and the new head of KWPA (Aleyasin) together with the National Iranian Oil Company were favoring, and that we, my colleagues and I, were prepared to man with an experienced team drawn largely from veterans of the first unified plan.

Which reminded me, sadly, of the death just the other day of our former chief engineer, Bill Voorduin, and could I transmit His Majesty's condolence to his surviving daughter? Of course.

The fifty minutes of talk ranged very widely, including anecdotes told with relish by this very serious (and beset) man. But there were two subjects I wanted to have discussed, and on which I wanted the Shah's approval (or at least the absence of disapproval).

One was about a new plan for Khuzistan, what could be a major undertaking, and a most satisfying one, since it would tend to confirm our early initiative in this country, contrasting it with the situation we had found. The second was the future of the Public Sector Management program.

On Khuzistan, I thought his reaction was everything that I could have desired, and my own presentation restrained and relatively brief. After all, he knows the Khuzistan story from its beginning and has seen what has happened and is happening to the transformation of the region.

I wasn't too sure about how much he really knows about the improvement of public administration that has been stimulated and (not to be absurdly modest) designed by John Macy and the thirty consultants engaged on this enterprise over the past almost three years.

I began by referring back to the audience he tendered me almost exactly three years ago, when he approved a contract (actually written between Minister Amouzegar and me, personally).

By late March this contract will have expired by its own terms. Should it be continued? Macy and I are prepared to go on to further work in this field. We have been invited to provide "assistance" to half of the Ministries (nine out of sixteen, I believe) but there is much to be done. And much hinges on the theme of "decentralization."

He rared back in his chair and picked up the discourse from there.

"Decentralization is the cardinal idea of everything we are trying to do. Decentralization is the key to ever-increasing democratization."

Wow. To the ears of this ex-TVAer, and my 1944 book on that very theme and terminology, this really made my head swim.

He went on from there: not only decentralization in government—it is the "participation of the people in every area" that we are aiming for, in the factories and farms.

He repeated the story of worker ownership in the companies for which they work, treating this as an evidence of "people participation" as a mark of the "cardinal" theme of decentralization.

Could this be the ogre, the dictator, the authoritarian oppressor of the people, as he has been pictured? To what extent was the leaven of our presence out here responsible for adherence to (or in any case, fervent expression of) such ideas from an all-powerful ruler?

"The Crown Prince telephoned to the Mayor of Tehran asking a number of questions and expecting answers. Now that is what I mean: the Mayor is responsible for whatever goes on in the city, and this should be true in the towns and villages too."

I was hardly up to commenting that a phone call from the royal family was hardly to be ignored, but if he thought it was an earthy example of grass-roots activity, so be it.

A good deal of the time of the audience was spent in his elaboration of his theme, the "cardinal principle of decentralization," and how committed his country is to that principle. An alternative phrase, and oft repeated, was "the participation of the people" in the direction of their lives and of their country.

We talked about energy and oil. On oil, I recalled a meeting with Jamshid Amouzegar years ago, when he was, as I remembered, Minister of Finance. Iran was then forced (through the oil consortium) to sell its oil at less than a dollar a barrel. He broke in: 87¢ was what we received as our part; yes, you are right: less than a dollar a barrel. No one, I recalled, protested the "injustice" of such a price.

He picked up the theme: "I explained years ago that the oil would not always be there, that it would run out. Now, everywhere it is recognized that this is so. There must be other sources of energy. Yet President Carter can't exercise leadership toward other energy supplies; Congress won't listen to him. Your country is being run not by one leadership, but by a crowd—can't have a policy about energy that way."

I said the energy plan of Carter didn't appeal to me because it was made up of "tax gimmicks—nothing fundamental." I referred to my own efforts toward utilizing the small streams for energy, recognizing that this is only a small fraction of the country's needs, but it is specific, manageable, and encouraging to local initiative. He said that "we too" have small streams.

As His Majesty walked me to the door, the audience over, I remarked on how "fit" he appeared to be (he *is* trim, a light-colored close-fitting suit setting off his erect figure). Not only fit, "but you must be a happy man over the way in which your country and your leadership have prospered." He looked *so* sad, his glance cast to the floor. "Yes, happy perhaps," and then looked up: "but I am worried about the world—much."

Almost equally emphasized, as he looked hard at me, was reference to the illness of the West, except for Germany. The British won't work, Americans don't work hard. "Look at the Japanese: they have nothing, absolutely nothing, and yet by hard work they are pushing even the U.S. And your media is irresponsible." (A look of extreme distaste accompanied this remark.)

OCTOBER 31, 1977
TEHRAN

Events here are so lively and interesting—and demanding too—that "keeping a journal" currently and as a unit seems a bit too difficult. Time was when I would sit up half the night to record what had happened that day, if there had been happenings. The wisdom or prudence of getting or trying to get rest these days suggests that I prefer not to take too great chances, and journal writing suffers.

But the word that I do have the "discipline" of regular journal writing has spread pretty widely. At the Ebtehaj luncheon the other day, the oddity that I am a journal keeper was the subject of considerable talk, some joking, and on the whole, a good deal of respect. Said Ebtehaj, "We expect you to keep and publish another ten years of journals."

Yesterday noon, John and I called on the Minister of Court, Hoveyda, who was Prime Minister, continuously and very successfully, for twelve and a half years, until a new Cabinet under Jamshid Amouzegar was installed a couple months ago.

I had sent a warm and essentially personal message to Hoveyda when his replacement was announced. He appreciated this, but there is no note of sourness or feeling of being unjustly treated. A cheerful, eloquent man, earthy for a graduate of the London School of Economics.

He set a new and higher standard of conduct in referring to the new Cabinet and particularly his successor, Amouzegar. Sitting on a low chair beside me, not once during perhaps a half-hour did he "bad-mouth" the new Administration; on the contrary, he had words of praise and admiration for the new "rulers." He referred to Ahmad Ahmadi, the new Minister of Agriculture, in this fashion: "Not brilliant and full of fire like Rouhani" (whom he replaced). "But," said Hoveyda, "there are times when we need to pause, and Ahmadi is just the man to consolidate." As he referred to Ahmadi, he said, as an aside: "He is one of your boys." As indeed he is—or was. Quite a memory, Hoveyda has.

Hoveyda greeted us jauntily, his traditional miniature orchid spray in his coat lapel, the jovial manner that has carried him through so many crises and extended trips throughout the world.

"I hear you had a very good audience yesterday," he sang out. Found it encouraging that he had heard of the audience, and was told it was a "good one." At the time I thought it was not a bad one, but somehow not up to some of the many that preceded it.

There is something reminiscent of Alben Barkley, our own Kentucky "Veep," about this Iranian statesman and politician. Higher praise from me it would be difficult to come by.

NOVEMBER 1, 1977
AHWAZ, IRAN

A big (and unsuitable) suite in the Royal Astoria Hotel, no less.

I thought that in my Iran experience I had seen all the drama that could be squeezed into almost half a lifetime. But this 1977 return of the non-native has added scenes and chapters that fairly make my head bobble. Not the least, this opulent hotel ("Royal Astoria," *in Ahwaz*). Ahwaz, into the dusty, sleepy streets of which only twenty-odd years ago I walked under the arcades of a 15th century village, now sprouting this elegance. True, the business streets still carry the graceful Persian arches covering the entrances to the dozens of small artisan shops; but many of the shops are now fronted with clear glass.

As we flew in from Tehran, a severe kind of nostalgia, evoked by the yellow-gold gas flares leaping into the sable sky. That was my first impression of Khuzistan, in February 1956. It was that picture of waste and of natural wealth that warmed my imagination about what could be made to happen in this, at that time, desolate and forgotten region.

Another experience today drove home to me how great a change is my position in this fabulous country. Hushang Ansary, Minister of Economic Affairs and Finance, had Macy and me to lunch at his home. Such super-elegance, such evidence of wealth, combined with good taste in that house; one room after another dazzled us.

But most of all, the extraordinary assessment of what my presence in this country means both to the mighty and to the exceptionally capable younger public servants developed by conscious effort and deliberate design.

"David," Ansary said, "you began in one particular region, doing a particular and relatively limited piece of development—the Khuzistan. The results have been so good and so well known that now you are extending your help and influence to the whole of the country and into every segment, through the public sector program, which is more than that, actually." He nodded to John Macy. "In this way, your philosophy and style, begun in one region, have brought together in this most recent activity the various parts of the whole that *is* Iran. We in the Government must see the country as a whole and see its many parts *together.* That is what you are helping us do, through D&R. And this is but the beginning, not the least being the emphasis on decentralization and how to make it work."

NOVEMBER 6, 1977
FLYING TO MUNICH

In some ways the most special experience of my entire Iranian voyage of nearly twenty-two years was the forty-five minutes, alone, visiting with the slender young woman, with the severely backdrawn hair—a knot at the back of the neck, the broad brow accentuated by the tiniest of plucked pencilled eyebrows—the Empress Farah, now become a secure and accepted and, by Iranians, a much-loved figure.

I have seen Her Majesty several times, at close range. Indeed, the first time was in March 1960, at the beginning of her marriage. At an outdoor reception in the Railway Park at Ahwaz, she joined me at the inspection of one of the earliest of the big electric switchyards in the Khuzistan, and later, wearing a white hard hat (as I recall) when His Majesty visited the early (and exciting) stages of Pahlavi Dam, then under construction.

Then she was a girlish figure, in demeanor, an Iranian beauty. At Ahwaz, she spoke hardly at all, in tentative English. Now she is the mother of the young man who is being "trained" to succeed his greying but still trim and grim father, the Shah. Her English is fluent and at times even eloquent—as these notes will record.

Her voice was a surprise: reedy and thin, though quite audible. She has a delightfully shy one-sided smile, when something is said that is either amusing or ironic.

But the whole impression from this forty-five minutes of conversation is that of a deeply serious person, a human being with strong, patently sincere convictions. Convictions about her country, and about what "the King" has accomplished, and is planning for the future, to bring to "our people, particularly our poor people, what they want, and believe the King desires to bring for them."

Her references to the Shah as "the King" surprised but pleased me. I have avoided the term "Shah" in unpremeditated references to him, but most people say "Shah," and about her, the formal phrase is "Shahbanou." I find this strained, so I referred to her, yesterday, as "the Queen," which matches her term, "King."

I was late for the audience, by perhaps ten minutes, and for a "command" appearance this is not forgiven by the hovering Palace staff. I walked a long space from the outside gate, then the usual steps. At the portal of the family chambers, a huge very black Great Dane, who paid me no mind, I was glad to note. I was quite unprepared for the foyer (a poor word), a four-story-high entrance to a "modern" palace, such a happy contrast to the stuffy 19th century French palaces where I usually have my audiences with the King. Columns in the interior that take you in, rather than keep you out of the perspective and beauty of the whole establishment. Upstairs, into a very small room; on all sides, ancient pottery enclosed in glass doors.

Then I was directed to a door, held open, and into an even smaller room, with the Queen standing, with an outstretched hand. Happily, no protocol or others in attendance.

Mehdi Samii, one of her "advisors," had persuaded me to request this meeting, but I was by no means sure he had identified me to the Queen. I felt she needed to hear from me what serious purpose I had in having this audience, so I took off on that almost at once.

On November 15 she will be with His Majesty in Washington on a brief State visit. On January 12, the Asia Society is tendering her a public dinner, in New York City.

The Washington visit will be the King's first meeting with our new President; Carter will receive official reports about Iran.

I regret that in America there is a widespread lack of understanding of contemporary Iran and of the impact of the Shah's programs. In fact, there is considerable antagonism, due I think to ignorance. The Asia Society meeting in January could provide an opportunity through the Queen's presence to sense the humane goals of Iran today. Her sincerity and simplicity have already impressed many Americans, and her interest and concern, among her own people, particularly in the villages and slums, is a side of the Iranian program of the King's that she can bring to American attention, far, far better than any "brochures or books."

She confirmed her determination to meet as many of the poor as possible, all over Iran, and why she found this so important:

"They want to believe in the King. In Iran, the King is the one thing they can completely believe in, in the midst of their poverty and their personal troubles. And for the Queen to visit with them rather than just open and dedicate bridges or plants—this strengthens their faith."

She was particularly impressive in what she said about the "participation of the people," a phrase that the Shah repeated again and again during the almost hour of my audience of a week ago. She didn't use the term "decentralization," as he did—and, of course, as we do, perhaps too much.

One revealing insight came when I said, "Perhaps it is ungracious of me to say so, but I sometimes think I liked Iran and Iranians better when you were poor than now when you are rich." A wan one-sided smile—of understanding. "When people are poor, they are more considerate of each other, help each other more." A classic picture of a real Queen.

In speaking of her special position in portraying an important aspect of Iranian life today, I talked of another woman, the wife of my first boss in public life, Franklin Roosevelt; how Mrs. Roosevelt went everywhere in what corresponded to Iranian poor villages, coal mines, everywhere. At first criticized, even ridiculed, later she became the accepted First Lady of the land—and that is as near to a Queen as anything we Americans have.

I left the Palace, the bright sunlight filtered through the towering trees in startling patterns; a brown and white Springer Spaniel, no longer young, was curled up warming himself, and like the Great Dane earlier, paying no attention whatever to the stranger, on his way out.

NOVEMBER 7, 1977
MUNICH, GERMANY

To the hotel hall porter this morning: "Will you give us the address of the Roman and Greek Museum, so we can give it to the taxi driver, please?"

"Sorry; all the museums are closed on Mondays; too bad."

"The director of the museum, the Herr Professor Doktor Ohly,‡ is meeting us and opening the museum for us."

Frau Ohly, a sprightly, handsome lady, was waiting at the portico of the great Greek structure, waving and smiling and so glad to see us. And the director took us through his masterpiece, item by magnificent item.

What a happy experience this was, to be sure. Their eager friendliness, their pride in the temple of Agnia excavated largely through his efforts.

---

‡Ohly spent a year at the Institute for Advanced Study in Princeton.

NOVEMBER 8, 1977
FLYING TO NEW YORK

Never have I seen more heavy firearms, and determined-looking young men carrying them at the ready than in the airport in Munich, and even more obviously as we set down at Cologne. No mystery about this: three "terrorists," among those who captured a Lufthansa plane, with hostages, were killed recently by German commandos—and the German newspapers are filled with their comrades' threats of "retaliation" against Lufthansa planes.

A call soon after we reached the hotel from a favorite of Khuzistan days, the German doctor "Louie" Gremliza. And for us, a bowl of flowers. The visit with them was an utter delight. The bright-eyed little man was standing on the sidewalk as our taxi searched for the right address, arms high over his head. What a greeting!

Frau Gremliza is a tense little woman, speaking a readily understood English, presiding over a very comfortable apartment. It was filled with artifacts—shreds of pottery and figurines, gatherings from the surface (not "digs") during the years they lived under the most primitive conditions in the wasteland of Dasht-e-Mashed in the extreme western part of Khuzistan, ministering with extraordinary compassion to the black-robed Arab women of that God-forsaken region.

What warmhearted people they are. One evidence of this is a very handsome dark-eyed dark-skinned Iranian young woman, an orphan whom they adopted as a small child, and "brought up"—now a technical assistant in Gremliza's clinic in Munich.

I told the doctor something of our visit in Iran, and the prospect that a new and revised unified report might be coming out of Khuzistan. He has always had a concept and a vision of "development" quite unusual, distinctive and very much along lines that focus on the individual. Indeed, I thought it fit very well some of the things the Queen said just the other day. Of course, Gremliza was delighted.

The most consequential meeting of the whole period in Iran was with the new Prime Minister, Jamshid Amouzegar.

As I opened the handsome door to his office, he was standing just inside, hand outstretched. His handsome, distinctive, aristocratic visage lighted up with the warmest kind of smile of greeting. Characteristically, his head cocked to one side.

An hour of talk with Macy and myself in that familiar office—familiar except that the jocund Hoveyda was not now behind the distant desk.

This Prime Minister is in great contrast to Hoveyda. Amouzegar is impatient, tough, relentless in his demand for results, not charm. For example, speaking of his own selection to head the Public Sector Management improvement work, he said, "Alimard is too soft." A bill intended for the Majlis two years ago to amend the Civil Service Code has still not been presented finally to that body—a cause of stern irritation to the Prime Minister.

More concerned was he about the way in which the Shah had been "misled" about electric power. "We were told about how much power the hydroelectric dams could produce, without taking into account two things: the increase in demand and need for power because of the new industrial commitments, and a dry-water year. As if God would always provide the same amount of water year after year.

"The Shah can't be in charge of everything. He has to rely on someone. Why is it that so many quite intelligent men in this government fail? Vahidi—good education, intelligent, honorable man. But look at what happened to failure of power supply."

I broke in to say that something of the same kind will befall them about the predictions of production from atomic energy plants. "You can't depend upon the vendor's statements, as to cost or schedules of delivery." He remembered a discussion we had (it must be three years ago) on this very subject, including his request that I prepare a report to the Shah about the troubled state of the Reza Shah Kabir hydro.

"We need an outside impartial qualified judgment about the atomic energy program," he said. John leaned forward eagerly at this, implying that D.E.L. might provide that. D.E.L. wasn't so happy at the prospect of being asked to do this. Etemad, the Iranian in charge of the atomic energy program, is a very complacent—or extremely self-confident man —and disputing his conclusions would be a tough assignment—*until* the whole deck of atomic cards begins to sway and fall. Which it may well.

From a practical point of view, the most significant discussion was about the continuation—or otherwise—of the Public Sector Management program. John really dug in on this. The present contract, now more than two years old, is to end by its terms in March 1978. Should it continue, on the same basis as to funds and procedures?

Amouzegar seemed surprised that the question should be asked. "Of course," he said, and that was that. That would seem—it did to John, certainly—to settle the question he has been writing memos about for several months, suggesting alternatives of a truncated or limited kind of contract.

NOVEMBER 16, 1977
NEW YORK

Only two weeks ago I sat, alone, alongside the Shah of Iran, in almost an hour of discussion. It is startling to see his face in the U.S.—amid one of the most disgraceful episodes accompanying the appearance here of the Head of State of a friendly country.

The Ku Klux Klan wore sheets. The "protesting Iranian students" covered their faces in masks.

NOVEMBER 19, 1977
PRINCETON

Fifty years ago Helen gave me the signal; we squeezed into our little Chevy and drove, over icy streets, from Palos Park to the Osteopathic Hospital in Chicago. David, a chunky baby, was born soon after. I can remember that ride so vividly.

Now we have a fifty-year-old son.

NOVEMBER 20, 1977
PRINCETON

How I have ranted about TV. But after a deeply moving experience this forenoon, I must take back that scowling—much of it, at least.

Beginning at 8 o'clock, I saw the President of a nation at war with another nation speak to its Parliament. President Sadat, arriving alone, to be greeted warmly by his "enemies," the Israelis, and see them applaud him for his courage, candor, for a kind of patriotism that flies over national boundaries and age-old hatred.

It was an event so true and honest, speaking the very best of what man can do to save himself—and without two technical achievements this experience could not have been mine: the satellite which beamed it from Jerusalem, and the TV instrument in our living room.

The spectacle of two men honoring each other despite great differences can do what all the intellectual skill of professional diplomats and the God-pretentions of editorial writers and columnists cannot accomplish.

Both of these eloquent men risked a great deal. It was because both Begin and Sadat did not try to placate or give in to the more timid or "realistic" of their supporters or critics that this was an event that should put heart into those of us who believe that man should reach beyond his grasp.

It was this spirit that distinguished the five so-different men who served with me on the atomic-bomb consulting board in 1946, enabled us to come up with a radical plan that shook the world, the world of the sagacious and realistic.

What a different world it would be today if we "idealists" had prevailed. The pile-up of atomic armament chills the blood, and threatens bankruptcy to economic systems.

NOVEMBER 21, 1977
NEW YORK

John Macy and I made our decision about D&R and our future: he will tell Rodman tomorrow that he has decided to resign; I will retire. Both to take effect when we have fulfilled contracts in Iran, in April.

I would not have suggested this on my own. But John came up with this position as the simplest, cleanest solution least likely to provoke all sorts of discussion and "negotiation." We just don't want to continue to spend so much of our lives doing things that do not interest us all that much.

So, the question decided, now we face a new chapter, without knowing quite where it will lead; but change has always been a theme of my life, and adjusting to change a skill I have learned.

NOVEMBER 26, 1977
PRINCETON

Today was the first time Helen and I had seriously discussed the range of decisions that must be made, consequent upon my decision to resign from D&R and "terminate the relationship with IBEC."

Yesterday it was my tentative view that it might make sense for me to recognize that John Macy should "inherit" virtually the only part of D&R that is genuinely lively and definitely profitable: the Public Sector program in Iran. I conceded that three years ago the idea for such a program came from me, and the contract grew out of my standing in Iran. Also, that I contributed the idea of John Macy as a man capable of making it a success—which he has; it is really a Macy program, except for polite references by him and the Iranians that it was my past contributions to Iran that made it possible.

That doesn't leave anything of substance, except the domestic energy program which I have been carrying (but which is a long way from being self-supporting, financially); the Appalachian Regional coal project, similarly far from supporting itself financially yet, but which could be turned over to Norman Clapp, or Norman could decide that the prospects in D&R were not very favorable for him, after the year of trial.

True, this leaves me with nothing much to show for my past contributions to D&R, including its founding and twenty-two years of sitting in the chair of the Chairman. But it would leave me free to try to find other things that might interest me, or simply sink into writing or pro bono activities, if any.

The mild-mannered Helen spoke up:

It is your name, your record and reputation for coming up with ideas, your standing in this country and in Iran which is what makes D&R and is what would make a new company or partnership. You have a habit of down-grading yourself. Don't do it. It doesn't fit the facts.

I was reminded of another crucial episode, at the very beginning of TVA. I returned from Washington to tell Helen that Arthur Morgan had announced that if I was reappointed, he would resign. He being the "great engineer" and close to F.D.R., I felt I should not oppose him but tell the President that I should not be considered for reappointment.

She took me apart at that time, and I went on to fight A. E. Morgan with his way-out ideas, and it was he who lost that battle; TVA became what it was because I didn't knuckle under.

This is quite a different situation, except for one thing: that once more I am underestimating what my reputation and ability to come up with ideas would contribute to a new partnership or a new company.

NOVEMBER 27, 1977
PRINCETON

Macy brought back word of a conversation with Senator Ribicoff about my testimony of nearly two years ago before the Government Operations Committee. The Senator dwelt upon the effect of my "startling" testimony about proliferation of atomic weapons, crediting it with turning the issue from resignation to a firm step forward, in the new policy posture President Carter and his Administration have taken. It was my taking chances, risks, that made this possible.

This, and similar comment from Congressman Jonathan Bingham and Senator Percy, has stirred up in me an impulse to take a similarly way-out public position on the basic issue I addressed in the Stafford Little Lectures of years ago: the elimination of atomic weapons, rather than stimulating the arms race by what is called "disarmament negotiation." I can get up a big head of steam about this.

This has been stimulated by reading in the *New York Times Magazine* today a lengthy article by George Kistiakowsky, a review of the past arms events since 1950. It was then that as AEC Chairman I opposed the hydrogen bomb, as a decrease in "security" rather than an increase—for us and for the Soviets.

The daring of Sadat, with its shaking of conventional and disastrous courses in the Mideast confrontation, encourages me to believe that if one who has some credentials (which I do have still) would speak out to the Russian people as well as to our own arms warriors, it might not be "too late."

A fellow's personality, his outlook, his nature, have so much to do with decisions and plans and dispositions of his time such as I am now considering.

And there are plenty of risks and unproved assumptions in this situation. I shouldn't move into this new way of working and living without remembering, vividly, that I do like risks.

NOVEMBER 28, 1977
NEW YORK

Blair Butterworth is the son of a dear departed friend, Walton Butterworth. Rarely have I been more impressed by a combination of masculinity and shrewdness which was confirmed as, for over two hours, we talked together.

Blair managed Dixy Lee Ray's successful campaign for Governor of the state of Washington. He parted from her in the past few weeks. "She trusts no one, and particularly the press—she's paranoid about the press."

Blair was one of a group of perhaps a score of full-blooded, enthusiastic, and sometimes rowdy risk-taking young people. Retelling some of their exploits and plans, living together in Georgetown and full of talk, talk, talk about the country's future, reminded me, of course, of the same kind of phenomenon during the early New Deal. They now represent the secondary effect of that idealistic but hard-boiled Peace Corps crowd of the Kennedy days.

DECEMBER 3, 1977
PRINCETON

"Conferences on energy" are a dime a dozen these days, everywhere, and I have declined to take part in any of them. But I do have something I would like to say, *not* about the customary polarized subject (pro and no about atomic energy, mostly) but the equivalent of my life-long theme —a unified approach to energy, which is certainly precisely what we do not have today in all the welter of discussion, newspaper stories, and heated Congressional hearings on the President's Energy Bill.

Perspective is what I should be able to bring to this subject.

DECEMBER 5, 1977
NEW YORK

The "decision" to resign and set up a new company was reconsidered and reversed this morning. Largely the result of an intense, hard-headed conversation with Helen yesterday afternoon.

I recited to John early this morning the tribulations there would be for us should we start a new company. We agreed we could not decently face the ethical problem of our new company taking on present D&R contracts, on their expiration in April.

I think both of us were relieved that we had reconsidered. How to present this to Rodman?

DECEMBER 10, 1977
PRINCETON

I participated in a gathering of Governors last Thursday afternoon. This was the Energy Committee of the most absurd and misbegotten institution (for getting anything done, that is) in my experience: the Appalachian Regional Commission.

The chairman, Governor Carroll of Kentucky, knows the ways of committees, even committees made up of highly independent and self-important men, the Governors of nine or ten states.

The chairman called on Norman Clapp to summarize the report on an approach to the coal problem of the Appalachian region. Norman's long legislative experience, as an assistant to [Senator] Bob LaFollette and later as head of REA, for years, showed in his presentation— made from notes, not read, as so many Congressional witnesses these days do.

The chairman asked me if I wanted to add something. Most of the discussion in "our" plan, as presented by Norman, was about the "economics" of marketing coal, the importance of Appalachian coal for the Carter Energy Program. I hadn't really expected to make a statement, but felt impelled to.

I reminded the Committee (and the chock-full hearing room) that I was "not a stranger" to regional development, nor to the development of natural resources such as coal, but that our chief concern should be the people in the small towns in the coal-producing areas. I knew those small coal-miner towns from my earliest TVA days, and so far as I could observe, their condition now was about the same as it was in the thirties.

Unless our "plan" changed things for them, it was beside the point to add up the figures about coal production and marketing. I don't think my comment got over; certainly it was not anything Governor Rockefeller of West Virginia found appetizing.

The outcome of the Committee on Energy's hearing, as reported to me yesterday afternoon, was hardly inspiring. A Policy Committee of Governors' representatives was to be organized, and they in turn would consider our proposal along with others, with a fund of $100,000 available for costs.

During the week Norman expressed himself as pretty discouraged about his role in D&R, and indicated that at the end of the first year, in March, he would probably go on to something else. He said that he didn't think he, not being an "engineer," could move the small hydro program along; it was almost "entirely engineering." (I don't by any means agree with this assessment.)

In the late afternoon Thursday, we met with the geothermal people of ERDA, now part of the new Department of Energy. Dr. Bresee reported how much "pressure" was being put on them by communities all over the country wanting to install small hydro facilities. "You started all this," said the geothermal expert. (Hydroelectricity is still in the geothermal division of the Department!) They couldn't contract with D&R to advise them, just took our advice for free months ago. Their idea is to contract with me, as an individual. The obvious problem of a conflict of interest between me functioning for the Government as a consultant and D&R's intention to seek a government contract for a client who has a potential hydro site—that conflict could be resolved, so he thought. A proposal will come to us from them along that line.

I don't like that kind of arrangement. I don't see how I can function without relying on D&R staff, which would present the conflict in sharp focus. They thought there would be a way out of that, despite my statement that not only should there not be a conflict of interest, but there shouldn't *appear* to be one, with me as a consultant to the agency that would pass on D&R's clients' applications for a demonstration plant using government funds for a feasibility contract.

The bright spot was the appearance of a real character at the conference table, David McDonald, a bewhiskered giant of a man, actually an engineer with experience in hydro. It was he who prepared the "90-day-wonder" report for the Corps of Engineers, tabulating the number of *existing* dams in the country.

I tried out on McDonald the need to consider the effect of these 49,000 existing dams on the best and fullest development of streams—the basin or unified concept that made the Tennessee Valley an outstanding example of good water planning and execution. It appeared to be a somewhat new concept to him, so preoccupied has he and all others been on the dam-at-a-time approach which lies behind the current legislation for small hydro.

Both McDonald and Bresee are apparently overwhelmed with the *emotional* response to my small hydro concept. And as the demonstration phase gets under way—the Federal Government is so damned slow about everything that it may be a long time—they will be more than ever swamped by the response from communities needing power, as the shortages begin to be more and more apparent. An article in the *Wall Street Journal* the other day identifies these evidences of shortages, so that municipal authorities find that the big power systems can't assure them of added supply, except on a day-by-day basis.

DECEMBER 24, 1977
PRINCETON

I have committed myself to a "lecture" at Princeton, in late February, on my convictions about energy. Then suddenly (or so it seemed), I called Cass Canfield, agreed that I would do the "small" book he has been urging on me for some years (actually about "development"—which is roughly a synonym for my concept of energy) and, so I would feel fully "committed," wrote him a letter to make it firm.

I feel I can do it, and within a few months. The chief reasons I am reasonably confident are two: (1) I have been thinking about *"growth"* (which also equates with energy) for several years, going back to that speech at Geneva and (2) John Macy, the most considerate partner a man could have, has assured me that it is so important that I "speak out," and do it now, that he believes my work can be so arranged that I can devote myself part-time to this book without a feeling of guilt about time taken away from D&R. It occurs to both of us, I daresay, that such a book will add to D&R's stature, certainly to its visibility.

DECEMBER 25, 1977
CHRISTMAS
PRINCETON

It did seem like Christmas, last evening. A group of perhaps twenty carol singers, mostly quite young children, the tiny ones carrying little lanterns, gathered outside our front door, shepherded by three adults.

This touched off memories of other Christmases. Helen said: "Remember our first Christmas together, fifty-four years ago?" (1977 less 1923 equals 54!) "It was the happiest Christmas I have ever, ever known," said I. Helen still in the hospital, but her life no longer in danger, after weeks of typhoid fever. What a way to begin a marriage!

Other remembering: the Christmas a few days before Nancy's arrival, the Christmas Eve of Daniel's birth, he now twenty-one years old.

DECEMBER 26, 1977
PRINCETON

Long talk by phone last evening with Daniel, happy, full of himself, in the best way. Continues to have a conviction about wanting to "do something" about agriculture, farming, the soil, and the people who depend on it. So, he said, he would leave Hampshire College soon, go to Berkeley and join his brother Allen, and try to get admitted as a student at Davis, the Ag School of the University of California.

How his passionate interest in agriculture came about is one of those pleasant mysteries about young people. Of course, it pleases me, though that has nothing, really, to do with it.

DECEMBER 27, 1977
PRINCETON

This year of '77 has been a rough one. Physically rough, an operation and an erratic pattern of recovery, bringing disappointments and frustration at times. (This morning, with a couple good nights of sleep, I'm full of beans.)

Very formally, I asked Helen if she could spend an hour talking over Volume VII-to-be preparatory to my lunching with Canfield this week. The formality amused her, which means I still amuse her (unintentionally).

DECEMBER 31, 1977
PRINCETON

By the traditions of the calendar, the year 1977 is about to give way to what is euphemistically called a *New* Year. The Persians have a better idea: their new year, Now Ruz, is the beginning of spring, of flowering and the stirring of fresh life after the pause of winter.

But nonetheless, a good, a very *good* substantial year it has been.

Crises in my work there were. What a difference it makes in my emotional accounting that the work of D&R, which has meant so much to me, flourished during the year, is effective, and particularly that it is profitable and self-supporting.

XI

1978

⁓⁂⁓

New York visit of Empress Farah—Vacation in Antigua—
Cardiac problem—Revolution in Iran

JANUARY 2, 1978
PRINCETON

Starting the new year on an upbeat: a spirited all-morning give-and-
take with David about my a-borning new book (mostly take). In our
sun-swept living room. Outside, the clean, new, snow-dusted reborn landscape.

My son is by all odds the best collaborator I have ever known. I feel
always that he has a critical faculty about ideas designed to warn me of
the shakiness and vulnerability of some of my assertions. Out of that two
or three hours of discussion about development and growth, come affirmative new concepts.

JANUARY 7, 1978
PRINCETON

One writing prospect that appeals to me is not so much a didactic
book about energy and development, but rather seeing those themes as
part of my experience of life. An American walking through many
decades of the century, experiencing so many aspects of American and
international life. I have seen these changes, these consequences, with
my own eyes, have been a part of them.

To be present and a participant, shoulder to shoulder with so many
personalities—why wouldn't that semi-autobiographic style be the most

appropriate way of saying what I have to say on current policy about development?

This is what Dean Acheson did when he wrote his great book *Present at the Creation*—i.e., the creation of a new American international policy and its execution; a personal view.

JANUARY 11, 1978
NEW YORK

Never have I seen so many uniformed policeman, scores of them, helmeted, Park Avenue lined with police vehicles of all kinds, and to top it off, a squadron of eight mounted policemen.

All to "protect" one slender young woman: the Empress of Iran, visiting an exhibition of Sassanian art of the 6th and 7th centuries, at Asia House.

And, of course, a gaggle of TV cameramen, their umbilical cords running in all directions from their cameras and sound equipment, pursuing the Queen as she went from one part of the exhibit to another.

Phil Talbot called yesterday to invite me to be present. I expected to lose myself in the background, as is, regrettably, my custom. But after the Queen had greeted us, I was seated in the circle around her, and was called on for comment.

I said that it was assumed that a country "ruled by one man," as the story has it, was not moving rapidly toward democracy in important ways, and referred to my recent audience and the Shah's emphasis on decentralization, and the "participation of the people" in the government and affairs of the country. But it was also evident that very few of the group realized what we have been up to in the Public Sector Management project, now more than three years old.

The Queen's reference to my part in the development of the country, and the warm expressions, after my brief talk, from other Iranians, really quite made my day.

John Rockefeller 3rd was very much a participant. He looks very thin and drawn, but well—healthy. He carried a shooting stick as a cane. He said he had arranged with Dr. Stanchfield of Columbia Presbyterian to operate on one of his hips, and said he understood it was a highly successful operation. I refuse to consider that alternative.

JANUARY 14, 1978
PRINCETON

Thursday evening the young woman now known as the Shahbanou of Iran demonstrated brilliantly those rare qualities of leadership and personality that entitle her to be called "Your Majesty." Such composure in the face of shrieks of "She is a liar," etc., from "demonstrators" who somehow several times got into the gallery of the hall. Not once did she look up from the script from which she was delivering her address (a dull one, true, but well read), and then she responded to written questions from the audience, done impromptu and in a winning manner. She had indeed captured that audience.

Just before she went to the platform, I took Helen to greet Ambassador Zahedi, who then introduced my Queen to Iran's. They were equally regal, in the best sense. Empress Farah has a smile so fresh and glowing that it seems impossible to believe that the smile she gave Helen was not one she had reserved all day for just that occasion.

From three o'clock, most of the afternoon, a crowd of "Iranian students," led by one with a bullhorn, chanted, "Down with the Shah" on the corner opposite the Hilton.

There were hundreds of New York policemen lining the streets, with police vans everywhere. Her visit must have cost New York City a big sum.

I doubt whether anyone who witnessed her behavior and appearance (she is quite beautiful) would ever retain the picture of Iran harbored by so many Americans.

At the reception before the speaking, Helen and I met a good many old friends. Among them, George McGhee, one of the real stalwarts of the State Department of twenty years ago. Said George: "I read what you said about George Kennan in the latest volume of your *Journals*, and I agree, completely. George would lecture to us, but never *listen.*"

We sought out a table to take a load off my feet. All of a sudden a spark of energy and vitality overwhelmed us. "Hope you won't mind my breaking in on you; I'm Lady Bird Johnson." She pulled up a chair and we lived once more in the glow of one of the real figures of public life. Recalled our visits to the White House dinners of the past. "I am helping get electricity to rural people in our part of Texas. What a difference electricity does make to them," she said.

There is only one Lady Bird. She, too, has the personal qualities that make Farah so distinctive—and from such different backgrounds. Eleanor Roosevelt was of the same breed. Too rare.

JANUARY 18, 1978
PRINCETON

Genuine old-fashioned winter, such as we haven't seen here for some years: icing of the roads (and the trees—and how utterly beautiful this has been: a crystal fairyland). So I have, quite happily, decided to stay home.

Pressing hard to get my ideas for the Walter Edge Lecture, and the bare bones of a book. It hasn't come easily.

In the afternoon and evening, I luxuriate on casual reading. A novel of Virginia Woolf's *(Mrs. Dalloway)* in a single sitting. Her comments about the creative process in *A Writer's Diary,* with a preface by Leonard Woolf. Rereading *Vanity Fair.* A new casual "social history" of the period 1929–1941 by J. C. Furnas. Very flattering references to me, which I appreciate, of course, but what is best is that he has summarized the TVA story beautifully. Here again the long-time enduring value of writing to fortify what one has done is illustrated. The *Journals* are treated as a book of reference, not just the popular book of an hour.

JANUARY 22, 1978
PRINCETON

A great snowstorm; everyone snowbound for two days.

Helen Meyner is just back from an eleven-day visit to eight Mideast countries. A member of the House International Affairs Committee.

In Iran, the group was given lunch by the Shah. She said he had sent greetings to me, commented on the work I had done for Iran.

FEBRUARY 5, 1978
ANTIGUA, BRITISH WEST INDIES

The weather, the swimming, the view of the yacht-filled harbor from our two rooms, the "service" by these soft-voiced black girls—all this has been just the best.

But the discomfort—a mild word—in my hips and legs has been bad. Can't help worrying about the progress—in the wrong direction—of this ailment within a single year, since I was here only a year ago.

FEBRUARY 12, 1978
ANTIGUA

After breakfast I ran over with Helen the bare outline of my ideas for the energy lecture. Not particularly overenthusiastic, but thought I had the "structure."

I have been working on this set of ideas during most of this last week, and think I have it in fair shape for dictation and testing.

Yesterday we had the first real storm we remember on Antigua: high wind and ripsnorting tide. Peter Deeth's sloop, anchored just outside our cottages, plunged and twisted like a frightened horse. Now—at sundown —calm as glass.

FEBRUARY 15, 1978
FLYING INTO KENNEDY FROM MIAMI

I got a wheelchair when we learned that the long-delayed flight from Antigua would have to "go through Customs" at Miami, the most elaborate and frustrating airport we have ever traversed. The robust porter who was my motive power must have covered ten miles of turnings and twistings. Helen, walking the whole course, looked as fresh as the sunrise that will soon greet us.

What a way to finish off a splendid and most successful holiday. We were scheduled for Kennedy at 10:30 P.M.; we will arrive, God willing, by 3:30 A.M., if we're lucky.

FEBRUARY 19, 1978
PRINCETON

What an ordeal the writing (and perpetual rewriting) of this energy lecture has been. Four—almost five—consecutive days. Helen has stepped in this afternoon to save me from I don't know what: listening to my organization problems (nasty and badly handled) and the undue and boring length. And there she sits at the typewriter, pounding out the scarred and horrid pages.

Will it get any attention? Surely it will, for it is explosive and "provocative." But whether it makes any difference in public policy matters it addresses, it is something I simply had to do.

MARCH 4, 1978
PRINCETON

That gap between the agonizing completion of the energy manuscript and this hour is one of the strangest anticlimaxes of recent personal history. From feeling top-hole and pleased with the writing and thinking job, to ten days in a hospital bed—and that after a delightful holiday in the sun and sand of Antigua—what kind of absurdity is that? I didn't dream it all up; it happened, and the wobbliness of my legs is one evidence of those ten days in a spacious room in New York Hospital.

Monday morning, the 20th of February, I got into Tom Moore's car, and had an uncomfortable feeling across the chest. The discomfort in the chest was gone when I reached the office. Said I to Mildred: "I read so much these days about how to identify a heart attack, maybe I ought to call Dr. Hoskins and have him talk me out of any apprehension."

She went into action—I must not actually have looked quite as cocky as I felt. "Better come right over to the office," said Hoskins, "and let me check you out."

And soon after I reached his office, where I had a cardiograph taken, saw a smart-aleck young cardiologist for a few minutes, I found myself —of all places—in the "emergency room" of New York Hospital, and then into a bed which I didn't really "vacate" until Wednesday morning, the first of March.

I arrived home again full of resolutions about treating this as a "warning." Let's see.

MARCH 5, 1978
PRINCETON

I am a recorder of life, not a recorder of events, not even a commenter on events. David made the point long ago (and it found its way into some of my "prefaces") that this is the narrative of a life.

But what has come to me in the past few days is perhaps basically different from any of the previous self-interpretation, even now with the sand in the hourglass lower and lower, something quite different, so it seems in the past twenty-four hours.

Journal writing, like essay writing, is a *literary* activity, a dealing with words, phrases, paragraphs, to be judged by oneself and by others for their literary qualities. But a rereading of large segments of Volumes I and II the other day showed more clearly than I had previously recognized that this is not a literary exercise at all—bar a few exciting passages perhaps.

The writing is loose, sometimes disjointed, not literary in any sense. It is a contemporary, current living record in words, mostly in captured emotions, of a fragment of life.

MARCH 8, 1978
PRINCETON

The half-hour with Dr. William Haynes confirmed that there had been "damage" to the minor arteries of my heart, but gave me reassurance about the future. "The injury to your heart is mending beautifully."

So I am a lucky guy—again.

Had I ignored Mildred Baron's gentle but determined advice to me "to let Dr. Hoskins take a look," I might very readily have moved into more serious damage.

APRIL 5, 1978
PRINCETON

After more than a month of recuperation, and being cooped up at 88, yesterday's meeting with the doctor gives me assurance that no permanent harm has been done.

To my surprise, he suggested that I go into the office next week, for an hour at a time initially.

Great news.

MAY 25, 1978
PRINCETON

What could lift my heart and spirits more than the sight of the very first rose in bloom in my crescent-shaped rose border? And it is a sight —ivory John F. Kennedy.

Perhaps this will encourage me to resume an occasional journal writing, something I had almost given up—despaired of, is perhaps a better way of putting it.

A lack of zest is what I have missed most. As good a manifestation of it as any has been not turning to the shorthand notebooks and recording notions and "events."

MAY 27, 1978
PRINCETON

Yesterday a "call from the White House." A lady, Miss Baux, explaining that the President was taking very seriously the two appointments he has to make to the TVA board. A long conversation ensued: what was my perspective about the future course of TVA?

I got the impression that this call wasn't just "courtesy" to a former TVA Chairman; if it was courtesy, it was the first sign from Carter I have received of any kind.

JUNE 20, 1978
PRINCETON

Conservation of energy and emotion just isn't part of my nature. It is not what made it possible for me to get many things done—including some significant writing.

I have found of late that I tend to be discouraged about public issues, make cynical or even defeatist comments, about "how bad things are." This just isn't like me. I blame it on the "hold-back" regime I have been told I must submit to.

But not forever.

John Macy and David Morse both had much more severe "heart attacks," years ago, and certainly John shows no signs of holding back. So it is a matter of getting over the damned thing—and that I shall.

Moving the office to smaller quarters—which a contraction by IBEC of its own headquarters makes necessary—has contributed to this uneasiness. And the pain in my legs from the arthritic hips is part of a picture I deplore, but must overcome, somehow.

I have almost stopped writing journal entries in the recent period of concern about my body. That is a bad sign, too.

JULY 8, 1978
MARTHA'S VINEYARD

What a truly happy birthday. Happy for two reasons, one personal—a gladsome and noisy family reunion of three generations, returned to their roots on this hilltop. Second, happy because in recent days particularly, I am demonstrating, to myself and to my working associates, that I have resumed the kind of specific creative idea-style of leadership for a time recently I had doubted.

What a lucky family we are: the gathering of the clan, from Italy, from New Jersey, from California, from Massachusetts. This for most of us was "the place" where the young people brought their babies, now handsome giants, the kind of children and grandchildren that give us joy, pride, and are fun to be with.

A visit with David. Talked about his writing, and about the nature of my journal writing. Why had I very nearly stopped the habit of writing? He disposed of one reason I had advanced: that I would not "be around" when the entries now written would be edited and published.

"That reason has no merit," he said. "You write because the very writing has some meaning to you, now, the same reason that most writers have regardless of the time they are published—if ever they are. So whether you are alive when the journal entries of '78 are available for editing and publishing isn't relevant to the question whether you should continue.

"It is the need to write, to record, that matters, not what happens (or doesn't happen) to the pages, once written."

JULY 12, 1978
NEW YORK

John Rockefeller dead; killed in an automobile collision on the grounds of the great estate on the Hudson.

I only learned of this terrible news today; the accident and death occurred Monday night. Deeply grieved. Of all the Rockefeller men, I always thought John the most human, compassionate, and so friendly to me and to Helen. And we love Blanchette.

JULY 13, 1978
NEW YORK

A meeting with Ahmad Aleyasin, Managing Director of Khuzistan Water and Power Authority, and as guests, the top officials of the Power Authority of New York State, who seemed very much a cut above the average utility operator.

When I challenged the now conventional low projections of future power demand, they admitted that a swing back from the current economic recession could catch the whole electricity business very much short. The lamest response was the most candid. Said the general manager: "Well, if we are caught short because we have squeezed our projects to meet the furor of those who don't want added power plants, we can just drop load, not just voltage, but load."

This kind of dehumanized terminology reminds me of the way military men, planners, describe the human side by referring to "targets"—meaning cities filled with human beings doomed to be blown to death by bombs.

JULY 24, 1978
MARTHA'S VINEYARD

This island is so chock full of literary (writing) celebrities that when someone brings some of them together you wonder what the other 40,000 people do.

Henry Hough had such a gathering for an al fresco lunch yesterday. John Hersey, very tall, excessively erect, a narrow head and so pale (though he is a sailor), with Lillian Hellman. She is easily the most productive of recent literary people, certainly among the thirty or so people there under the trees.

AUGUST 7, 1978
MARTHA'S VINEYARD

I didn't fully realize or comprehend until the past few weeks how much of a Family Man I am. The grandchildren are among the most interesting adults I have ever known. And Nancy and Sylvain so devoted and understanding of their two sons, Allen and Daniel, and yet so fully committed to "letting them go"—a too-rare quality among parents, the absence of which has caused so much heartache—on both sides of the parent-child equation.

AUGUST 9, 1978
MARTHA'S VINEYARD

A call from Evan Thomas, now with W. W. Norton, the publishers. Said he is reading a book "by the Shah" which they are considering publishing. "But he is an absolute dictator, isn't he?"

Thomas has never heard, of course, of the move toward decentralization and other evidence of democratization. I told him he is like "all the other intellectuals," they have *their* concept of democracy; *we* could do with a President who runs the ship, makes decisions.

He is seeing Ambassador Hoveyda Monday. "The man at the Council on Foreign Relations who brought the Shah's book to me said Iran will buy 5000 copies of the book. That helps, doesn't it?"

I was shocked, but let it pass.

AUGUST 28, 1978
MARTHA'S VINEYARD

A pretty agitated John Macy called me from Washington early this morning. Had I read that the entire Amouzegar Cabinet had resigned? Following the horror of the terrorist fire in the Abadan movie theater; martial law in Abadan and elsewhere. The new Prime Minister was a former P.M., Sharif-Imami, whom I remember from years ago; how would this affect our work, and particularly the "liberalizing" of our decentralization thesis and program?

It will take some time—perhaps a month—to assess things after what is not the ordinary kind of Cabinet shake-up.

That the change will probably mean delays in decision, perhaps in funding, is highly probable; but a take-over of the Throne seems to me most unlikely.

SEPTEMBER 4, 1978
MARTHA'S VINEYARD

This is the fifty-fifth anniversary of our wedding. With all the quite visible evidence of the success of that marriage (children and grandchildren, and beautiful ones they are), this has been one of the best of celebrations.

SEPTEMBER 8, 1978
MARTHA'S VINEYARD

The turmoil and "demonstration" in Iran have reached what may well be the point of no return. Ordered to disperse, the demonstrators refused to do so, whereupon an order was given, and carried out, to shoot into the crowd. One hundred people dead.

If this report, conveyed to me by Miss Baron just now, proves to be correct, what future has D&R in such a country? And how can I go on lending my name, if nothing more, to such a country?

OCTOBER 2, 1978
NEW YORK

Exploring ideas, from their first glimmer, by writing about them, has been one of the chief reasons and products of journal writing. Recording on paper the ebbs and flows of emotion—discouragement, elation, and everything in between—has been a way of letting off steam, a harmless way, if the words go no further than the transcripts that are piling up in our files.

A phone conversation last evening with Daniel, in Palo Alto. At times so parsimonious of words, he was overflowing with excitement as a member (junior grade) of a "research" project intended to prove that X times more food could be raised on a small plot of ground than had been possible by other methods—whatever they are.

"Are you happy?" I asked; that is the decisive question, I thought. "Very happy"—there could be no mistaking that he is doing what he wants most to do. He had just got back from a long day at work: "Grandfather, my hands are still covered with dirt." Enough of theory study—that sort of reaction.

Because I made such a point last summer in our talks about the importance, in horticulture, of not only what happens in the soil, but *why*, which is what the science of soils is pretty much about, and because I nagged him about record keeping so others can benefit from their results, he told me of the professors of chemistry, et al., who are part of this "research," and that he is indeed concerned about record keeping.

OCTOBER 4, 1978
WASHINGTON

How did the speech* go today? "Restoration of Faith in the Energy
*To a conference of utility managers and regulators.

Industries"—the one I have been struggling with ever since last February, and most of the summer.

It was a professional piece of speaking, in the manner of so many in the past. But this time there was a difference: it was a test of my recovery from the physical troubles that have pursued me for a year and a half. And particularly it demonstrated that I can stand the pressure of speaking passionately for thirty minutes, holding the attention of an audience completely for that period.

OCTOBER 7, 1978
PRINCETON

Our years (1956–1978) of work and achievements in Iran appear to be near obliteration, judging from a sober factual letter from John Macy, just received. (Dated September 29—brought to Washington for mailing.)

Like my feeling about the disaster that overwhelmed our "Postwar Economic Development" efforts in Vietnam, I feel no personal regret that I threw so much into that effort in Iran. The forces of reaction by Moslem religious leaders will either destroy the future of that wonderful country or, like many other evil forces, will recede.

What this will mean for the future of D&R can better be put: does it have a future? But once again I say, as so many times in an introspective mood: D&R—and my work—are not the whole of life.

So glad I put so much into that energy speech, stirring up ideas and prospects for thought and action for many, whether in D&R or elsewhere. How lucky I was and am that years ago I turned to making enough "keeping" money so I have a choice not dictated solely by personal economic necessity.

OCTOBER 11, 1978
NEW YORK

It is a trial to see the Shah's years of improvement being turned into Persian self-hatred. All those years of hope and forward looking—are they to be swallowed up in one gulp by reaction?

I recall vividly the great extremes among the Persian people that I have seen: the arrogant displays of wealth on the one hand, and the continued poverty. Jamshid Amouzegar fears that the poor see little of the increased wealth from oil, and this may be a danger, and one that the Shah only vaguely understands or is prepared to do something about. When this kind of revulsion takes hold, it is a tide that sweeps moderates aside.

John's letters are so gloomy—what with strikes and arrests and mounting uncertainty.

OCTOBER 15, 1978
PRINCETON

Reliving the days of the atom—now twenty years ago—and the agonies of the "trial" of Robert Oppenheimer is something I avoid when I can. But yesterday, two members of the Princeton faculty were here for a couple hours doing just that. One, Professor Sherwin, is at work on a "political biography" (his phrase) of Robert. The other, Fred Greenstein (Henry Luce Professor of Politics), is almost a specialist on the Presidency and this led him into reading FBI files (now open to view, under new policies) that led to questioning me about the way Truman and, later, Eisenhower dealt with secrecy issues and the rights (or lack of them) of AEC people.

The refreshing part of these hours here in my study was on no such subject. Davey had said to me that he would like to sit in on the professors' questioning of me. Sprawled (all 6 ft. 4 inches of him) in the big gold easy chair, his eyes bugged out as he listened to a rerun of the night that J. Edgar Hoover called me, saying he was sending an FBI file to me (as Chairman) on the outstanding figure in the atomic world, Robert Oppenheimer.

I told my visitors of Davey's interest in American history, which he has been pretty well shut out of because of living in Italy since he was eleven years old.

OCTOBER 19, 1978
IN THE LOBBY OF THE HOTEL ROOSEVELT
WAITING FOR THE CAR TO PRINCETON

The Overseas Development Council's board meeting was ho-hum but for two events: an extraordinary man in action, the chairman, Father Ted Hesburgh, president of Notre Dame; and the opportunity I had to pay my non-respects to Walter Levy, oil economist, who predicted dire catastrophe because of oil scarcity and high prices.

I couldn't restrain myself, and cut loose on him. Walter isn't used to any kind of exchange except awe about his preeminence in the oil field. I said, sharply, "I profoundly disagree with this talk about the need for America to cut its energy consumption by 10% because of the oil shortage. I have lived long enough to discount predictions of catastrophe."

What stirred everybody was my closing impromptu remark: "Walter Levy is an oil economist, but he is not a humanist. In this world, you are

either an optimist—and therefore a fool—or a pessimist and dead. I prefer to be an optimist." Cheers from the other directors.

But the big event was "Father Ted." Curly head, close-cropped, sprinkled with grey, a most self-assured and robust man, a splendid voice and
a businesslike chairman, decisive and gracious. He manages and leads
many activities and still runs Notre Dame.

When John Diebold asked him to set aside two dates for "social
activities" by the ODC Board in late December, he swept this aside. No,
positively no; not at that time of year. "That's when C. R. Smith and I have
a vacation together; have for years. This time we're going to get into a
boat and go up the Amazon. C.R. doesn't walk too well now, so it will be
a boat. You know, the pins give out first." (Don't I know!)

Father Hesburgh and I exchanged reminiscences about "C.R.," the
founder of American Airlines. When I joked about Smith's profanity as
a way of conversation, Hesburgh picked it up with a smile, and quoted
Smith, including the God-damns. How popular this man must be with the
students at Notre Dame.

OCTOBER 26, 1978
NEW YORK

Attending a Century Club do—to hear Arthur Schlesinger on the
Imperial Presidency—tempts me to resume writing journal entries. For
what he said, in that superior lecture-style he has, was articulate and
"balanced." But despite the rather obvious effort to be "objective" before
such a basically conservative well-heeled Republican crowd, the coating
wore off at times. He criticized Carter as a non-leader more interested in
making the Government work than in shaping the thinking about America's goal and purpose (being an engineer, that would be natural for him,
said Arthur, in a great big dose of Carter deflation).

But I thought it obvious that the Kennedy wing—if "wing" is the
word, which it isn't, quite—is out to develop a more or less loyal opposition, of sorts, with the goal being Ted Kennedy for the nomination in 1984,
or sooner.

Arthur's balanced objectivity broke down completely at only one
point. What do you think of Governor Brown? he was asked, from the
audience. "We have accustomed ourselves to a Catholic as President, to
a twice-born Baptist, but I doubt if we are ready for a Zen Buddhist."

A brief encounter with one of the most handsome of our "statesmen"
—Congressman Jonathan Bingham. Looking puzzled, he asked me, "Tell
me; how in the world do you find time and energy to write your journals?
They are so carefully written, and cover so much ground. Where do you
find the time? It must take great discipline."

I should remember that my writing of journals is the most distinctive thing about me, in the eyes of many people, since the days when I was in controversial public life.

OCTOBER 29, 1978
PRINCETON

The voice of John Macy on the phone at 7:30 last evening, as resonant and alive as ever. Just returned from Iran. The story he summarized of chaos and anarchy there, even with his super-optimistic nature, dampened him down. When he said, "Our Public Sector Management work has been in vain," he wrote off one of the greatest achievements of his career in public service, with sadness but without whining.

Where does this leave D&R? In Iran, probably only the work in Khuzistan, and even that is questionable.

The country has been immobilized; even the sacred "autonomous" oil company (National Iranian Oil Company) is on strike, including the loading at Kharg Island. This he learned from Hushang Ansary, now head of NIOC.

OCTOBER 30, 1978
PRINCETON

Friday morning another one of those new interests that somehow I continue to invent—or that somehow happen to me. To the graphic arts department at the Firestone Library, for a lively and refreshing visit with the woman in charge, Sally Black Santosuosso. The occasion was to discuss the forthcoming exhibition of what is now called, portentously, "The David E. Lilienthal Collection of New Yorker Cartoons."

I brought with me from the city the latest acquisition of this "collection," a Barney Tobey drawing of a student at a very modern college saying, "This isn't my first choice; I wanted to go to an ivy-covered college" (the caption approximately in those words). As I unwrapped it, a tall dark-haired student, eyeing it, let out an explosive laugh. Said he: "This place doesn't have enough laughing." And went on to say that this exhibition of cartoons will be very "popular with the younger people." Sally is a likeable non-arty girl in about her mid-thirties.

NOVEMBER 3, 1978
PRINCETON

When John Macy came through the office early Wednesday morning, he was a worried man and, for the first time I can remember, low-key, lacking his usual exuberance and optimism. His stories about the utter disarray in Iran were dramatic, and without a touch of wishful thinking.

About D&R, he said neither he nor Jack Vaughn, holding the fort out there, was ready to give up; on the contrary, they thought the work should go forward as well as possible in a country where apparently about every-one is either on strike or "demonstrating" or just plain doing nothing but complain, demanding triple increases in salary or wages, completely ignoring what progress has been made under the aegis of the Shah.

He had a two-hour visit in Tehran, in his modest little home, with Jamshid Amouzegar, whose tenure as Prime Minister must have been a painful experience. John very carefully and objectively wrote a long record on this talk, which is an important bit of historical recording of events that not only turn the clock back in Iran but also may prove to be severe in consequence for the U.S.

John spent some time with Hushang Ansary, in his home. As head of NIOC, he was confronted with the most immediate threat to the West, a strike of oil industry workers, including those loading (or *not* loading) the tankers at Kharg Island. A serious stoppage of oil production and transportation is the latest blow—and it could be the one that will awaken the West, particularly the U.S., to the kind of collapse that the extremist Moslem religious leaders are and have been encouraging, com-bining—with exquisite, baleful irony—with the intellectuals and stu-dents.

I hit a positive note, for the first time since the crisis in Iran became evident, some weeks ago.

We, D&R, have done a good job in Iran, a constructive human and honest job. We should not become defensive. I believe in the Shah's leadership, because it is nothing but a miracle that he has been able to move that fundamentalist-ridden Islamic people along as far as he has.

As to the future of D&R, there was a bright spot of cheer. Rodman has decided that IBEC will become an agribusiness company, selling the profusion of enterprises that have been collected over the years. In that setting, D&R fits with IBEC. Which was the thesis of the merger with them.

NOVEMBER 8, 1978
NEW YORK

Jack Vaughn and I had a couple hours together: He is just in from the front line in Iran; his account of the demoralization and near collapse of that country—and its monarch—does not omit any of the dramatization —not to say overdramatization—which doubtless the actual situation calls for.

What people are saying, Jack told me, is the familiar refrain of almost any post-almost-mortem: 20/20 hindsight, and a plentiful portion of the blame *on the Shah* (or whoever is at the center of such a fire as this). The old story: the people who surround him screened him from what was going on.

Said Jack, "I could not believe that the position of the Shah could deteriorate so rapidly as it has."

Jack attributed the outbreaks of last Saturday to the "killing of the students" (by the Army); the students then rampaged through the main streets, burning banks, hotels, the British Embassy. I questioned him about who these "university students" were. Turns out the mob was largely youngsters between fourteen and eighteen—hardly an analogy to the *workers'* Russian Revolution.

NOVEMBER 9, 1978
NEW YORK

Yesterday Macy recommended that I write a message to the Shah. This morning I read that he has ordered the arrest of Hoveyda. I will wait and see about supporting the Shah at this juncture. Is he ready to do anything to save his Throne (or skin)?

What we did in Iran is good.

I urged John to carry a serious message to the Managing Director of KWPA: if there is a strike (as reported) in KWPA, Aleyasin should see to it that the powerhouse at Pahlavi Dam is not left without a qualified operating group, or there could be serious damage.

NOVEMBER 12, 1978
PRINCETON

A memorable post-breakfast hour's exchange of ideas with Helen. (She never fails me.)

What we did was to lay out a program for each of us, for the design of the book on "development." I had little conviction or enthusiasm about the book I thought she had in mind. Now I think—after this very collected discussion of an hour ago—we see the subject more clearly and the importance of the task.

Development is the most important theme in the world today. When I wrote *TVA: Democracy on the March* in 1944, TVA was a prototype of both technique and philosophy.

Now development reaches out beyond TVA, then the only example of a world-wide theme: the handling of change through the philosophy and the techniques of development rather than merely political or "economic" thinking and action.

A visit from two most personable young men, juniors at Princeton, and leaders in the "ancient and honorable Whig-Clio" Society. The Society wants me to make a speech at their interesting headquarters on campus, or engage in a seminar, or both.

Since my reason for being more than willing to participate is to be exposed to the ideas of students, rather than having an "audience," I found the idea of a seminar, with perhaps twenty to twenty-five students, most appealing, and I'll do it.

I gathered they hadn't much of an idea of what I had done in my lifetime, nor had they heard about the *Journals.* They were particularly interested in the *Journals* as a repository of my life's activities, the serious and public, and the personal and not serious. On the not serious side, they literally cheered when I told them that my collection of *New Yorker* cartoons would be in an exhibition at Firestone's graphic arts division beginning December 6.

NOVEMBER 14, 1978
PRINCETON

Two positive happenings about the Iranian debacle: (1) an article in the *New York Times Magazine* by Flora Lewis that provided the perspective and setting in which the Persian situation should be viewed—a transformation of a feudal, tradition-bound country—and (2) the "general strike" called by the long-whiskered Moslem leader, in Paris, was a flop, and even the oil company operations are beginning to be resumed.

NOVEMBER 18, 1978
PRINCETON

I had always thought Abba Eban one of the most felicitous and articulate of speakers—and writers. Listening intently to him lecturing for an hour the other evening at the Institute for Advanced Study added to my admiration for his forensic and literary brilliance.

But what he said—the substance—by no means persuaded me that he has the qualities of a world statesman.

He was talking, most critically but with British restraint, about the futility of the methods, the way in which the effort to reach a Mideast treaty, between Egypt and Israel, have been conducted. He traces his concerns back to Woodrow Wilson's "open covenants openly arrived at." But the media "intrusion" of the past days has made this worse, even though for thirteen days Prime Minister Begin and President Sadat were spared that by Carter's removal of the talks to the isolation of Camp David.

Eban's reservations and abhorrence go beyond the publicity given international negotiations. He doesn't believe in what he called the "parliamentary," as contrasted with the diplomatic, way of dealing with international conflicts.

I left the meeting with great envy of his skill as a speaker and analyst —logician, I might say. But he made me think: Here is an Israeli George Kennan. By which I meant that his professionalism, like Kennan's, about diplomacy, and sense of superiority, intellectually, to those in elected offices, make neither of them effective or persuasive in a world seeking to find democratic solutions to our troubles.

NOVEMBER 23, 1978
THANKSGIVING
PRINCETON

David Morse (looking terrible) in for a talk Wednesday. Told me that the former Prime Minister Amouzegar is in this country; his wife is undergoing medical treatment here in New York. The story Amouzegar told Morse was very much the same as he told John Macy, at such length (as recorded by John).

The future for the Shah is clouded at this point; the future of Iran also in doubt. How quickly all this broke into the open, though it has been "brewing" for years and years.

NOVEMBER 27, 1978
PRINCETON

More than once while I lived and worked in the South, I witnessed the price people pay for the orgies of fundamentalist religion, and their phony leaders.

But the whole world in the past few days has seen what these sects can lead to, almost the reverse of religion. The worst case of all—the mass suicide of the California sect in the primitive little country of Guyana on the north coast of South America—is a story literally beyond belief.

Yesterday I cut three beautiful roses. Today the border and all are covered with snow.

Never have I seen such a rose-growing season! We have been cutting roses right through November! And the foliage is so healthy, unmarked by black spot or fungus: deep, lustrous green.

NOVEMBER 28, 1978
PRINCETON

The explosion against the Shah is so thorough, so uncompromising, the reversal so complete, that even President Carter publicly complained that our "intelligence agencies" were derelict in not being aware of the widespread opposition, an opposition that could rock the country and paralyze it almost overnight, as it is said.

Here is Jamshid Amouzegar, so recently Prime Minister, now in a hotel room at the Watergate Hotel in Washington. And Hushang Ansary, in the New York Hospital, virtually a fugitive, so secure and unflappable when we saw him at his splendid home only a year ago.

What has impressed me and others, and saddened us, is that the violent demonstrations (i.e., burning and sacking) have been directed against Iranians and Iranian institutions. Violence against a foreigner's bank or embassy is familiar enough, but the mobs set out to destroy the National Iranian Oil Company building in the heart of Tehran, and are threatening, it is said, to destroy the oil wells in the South. Those oil wells don't belong to the hated British or the Consortium (as in Mossadegh's time) but belong to the people of Iran.

But is it all that "sudden"? Is the President right in decrying the negligence of the CIA in not recognizing the depth of the antagonism toward the Shah's regime?

I have just reread the account of the ceremonies at the University of California (Los Angeles) back in 1964—fourteen years ago. Outcries from the audience at the ceremony, a banner "Down with the Shah," security guards everywhere. We dismissed this at the time as being financed by the Soviets or East Germany: nothing significant. Jack Vaughn pointed out that the Shah didn't communicate with Iranian students, and that this was a sign of the blindness of the Shah and his regime. The chant "Down with the Shah" has continued for all these years. Then the other day the troops fired on students in Tehran, and the violence and sacking grew into a pintsize reproduction of a Russian Communist takeover.

The complaint about foreigners certainly doesn't apply to D&R: we began determined to train Iranians and to build Iranian institutions and organization, and we did. But did this make Iranians see D&R as being different from those Westerners who, like Bell Helicopter, set up enclaves and showed disdain for Iranians?

DECEMBER 10, 1978
PRINCETON

This is a tough time, the kind that tests whatever character the long earlier rugged years have produced in me. I can hardly believe the wreckage of so much I have worked to produce in Iran; but there it is, daily accounts of a whole nation committed to destruction.

What has particularly made this so chilling an experience is the effect on so many Iranians who were—and are—my friends. The cheap slurs on Amouzegar hurt particularly, but there are so many others of lesser "situation" who can see their country blazing in the eyes of the world, badly crippled.

DECEMBER 15, 1978
PRINCETON

The "holy" celebration of the 12th came and went without a blood-bath. What I think may be happening is that the Iran middle class (a growing number it is) has begun to realize that a mob can attract TV attention, but a mob can't run a country—that is, get the things done that the ordinary citizen has been counting on in his daily life. A mob so often turns on the leaders of the mob.

DECEMBER 26, 1978
PRINCETON

A telex from Jack Vaughn that our public sector work and contracts for Iran are not only cancelled (just like that) but we are not to expect payment for work we have done.

DECEMBER 29, 1978
PRINCETON

This is surely one of the saddest entries I have ever made in these journals: the Shah is leaving Iran; the long campaign has succeeded.

The Communists have registered one of their greatest gains.

This forenoon John Macy reported on a phone conversation with Jack Vaughn from Tehran: the city was at a standstill, no electricity, no automobiles, no gasoline, no water, the Central Bank closed, oil produc-tion shut down, no air service in or out, another general strike called for today.

John directed that all of our staff leave Iran (six in number now, with their families, about eighteen Americans for whom D&R is responsible) since the Embassy seems to have no ideas or facilities. Most of the Ameri-can employees of other companies, including those who supervise the oil operations, are being evacuated by charter plane.

I know I should have no remorse, should not say that all those twenty-three years of work and dedication to the people of Iran have been wasted. We did a good job and cut new paths for development. It was a great experience. Still, it comes hard, and difficult not to be somewhat bitter, particularly toward the "Iranian students" who kept this campaign against the Shah going all these many years, while they lived on American largesse.

Two thousand "students" demonstrated in San Francisco yesterday: "Down with the Shah," "Down with the U.S."

We should say: Iranians, go home.

XII

1979

~~⁓◗⁓~~

D&R employees evacuated from Iran—D&R Corporation liquidated—Three Mile Island nuclear plant
malfunction—Visit to TVA on occasion of its 46th anniversary celebration—Writing *Atomic Energy: A New
Start*—Visit to James Bay hydroelectric project in
Quebec

JANUARY 7, 1979
PRINCETON

John Macy's incorrigible optimism faded with word from his friend
Alimard that the Public Sector Management program and contract were
cancelled and furthermore that what was owed us would probably not be
paid.

Then Vaughn from Iran reported that our work in Khuzistan was
over, after all these years.

I took all this with a surprising calm. Not quite indifference, but close
to it. So D&R, after so many Hairbreadth Harry escapes from decease,
would have to be liquidated.

John set off Friday night to deliver the bad news to the Sacramento
group that most of them would be out of jobs in D&R. He might well have
suggested to me that since this was my company, in origin, I should face
them with the sad fact of virtually dissolving D&R. Not at all. He braced
himself and went out there.

A good man, strong, honorable, able, one of the best men I have ever
known.

JANUARY 15, 1979
PRINCETON

Our remaining staff people in Iran, nervous and frightened, trying to
find ways of getting to safety (as they saw it), began demanding all kinds
of financial assurances. So no work, no revenues, and contingent claims.
Jack Vaughn, a seasoned man for such a crisis, handled this very well.

JANUARY 19, 1979
PRINCETON

The Shah and the Queen have left Iran for a "vacation," and have left
Iran in a state of near collapse.

The day he took a plane, last Wednesday, I felt as if I had been
physically wounded.

I asked John Macy: "Would you go back to Iran if conditions change
and you were asked to?" Looking very solemn, the exuberance so characteristic of him completely drawn out of his face, he said without hesitation: "Never. I would never go back."

JANUARY 23, 1979
PRINCETON

How many times I have "retired" from D&R, because of financial
troubles of D&R or just plain boredom with what we were doing, in a
repetitive way—and so on.

Well, it is about to happen. D&R is truly on its last legs. I must say
it took a bloody revolution and a "holy war" by Moslem professionals to
bring on the decision to give D&R as decent a burial as possible.

It is far too early to try to sort out my ideas or emotions about the
death of so hopeful and useful an undertaking as Gordon and I began on
that first trip to Iran in the winter of 1956. It has been a major part of my
life; more than that, it has been a period in which American prestige and
standing have fallen to a dangerous point.

The chief victim of the collapse of Iran in the past few months has
been the ordinary Iranian people. But from my point of view, the injury
to my own country is what hurts the most.

JANUARY 26, 1979
NEW YORK

So, I'm free at last!
After so many efforts—fruitless and frustrating and futile—to disen-

gage myself from the less vital aspects of D&R, and the erosion that came from battering my head and spirit against management shortcomings and inadequacies on the financial side particularly, yesterday Macy and I resigned. Not only is our recommendation that D&R be liquidated in view of the bloodstained debacle in Iran, but the IBEC board has finally decided to liquidate IBEC itself!

There was, I admit, a strange feeling as I stopped by the office early this afternoon, realizing that I was in the ranks of the "unemployed" for the first time in a long, long time. But I refuse to permit that kind of let-down become chronic or even frequent.

JANUARY 27, 1979
PRINCETON

Nelson Rockefeller died last evening. Now Rodman is a senior heir, not a son who was always at odds with his father—and vice versa.

JANUARY 31, 1979
NEW YORK

I was so puzzled by Governor Rockefeller's sudden death: that a sturdy, husky man should simply collapse, he who took good care of himself and was relieved of the pressures of public life and business worries.

John and I repeated our expressions of sympathy to Rodman this morning. He must have noted my surprise about the suddenness of the death. Rodman said, "It really wasn't all that sudden. He really couldn't accept the failure of his Presidential ambitions, couldn't adjust to the idea at all, though he tried this art project, and getting the Saudis to support an energy project in this country, and that didn't go."

How could that affect his heart—cause sudden heart failure?

But I know that a broken heart isn't just a literary figure of speech.

John Macy, on our way to lunch, compared this state of lost direction, lost place, to those who were close to the Kennedys when they suddenly were struck down. They had no place in the world except surrounding Jack and Bobby, and when *they* disappeared, they didn't know where they were. This would be the kind of "study" of political life that I have never seen written about.

There is a kind of warning in all of this for me; the "disappearance" of D&R, now decided upon, after all the years of excitement, satisfaction, frustration, angst, could leave a gap, unfilled, that might have ill effects.

Rodman, a sensitive and quite kindly man, saw that I might be apply-ing the "diagnosis" of his famous father's death to my own case. Smiling at me wanly, he said, "But David, you have so many other interests, your writing, for example, that there's no chance the going of D&R would affect you that way."

I think he is right, but I mustn't take it completely for granted.

FEBRUARY 3, 1979
PRINCETON

How could there be a "transformation" of Iran if the mass of people haven't changed their views of the world? And how can that happen in a mullah-dominated village society?

FEBRUARY 4, 1979
PRINCETON

A delightful evening yesterday with Virginia Butterworth; her guests, Julian Boyd and Grace, and Joe Johnson.

Lively and witty conversation. We talked about what historians say: never destroy anything that might have historical value. This recalled the story about Bess Truman's love letters to Harry, which were in the process of being burned. Said a horrified observer: "You shouldn't burn those letters. Think of history." To which Bess responded: "That's what I was thinking about."

FEBRUARY 12, 1979
PRINCETON

The first chapter of the revolution in Iran is over, the part that is fun for the mob: burning and shouting and "demonstrating."

Now comes the test of the well-advertised "religious fervor." Can the shouters and ideologues and mullahs get people to go back to work—which isn't all that fun. And who now will replace the Shah, and more recently, Bakhtiar, in the chant: "Down with the _____!"?

FEBRUARY 13, 1979
PRINCETON

Difficult to keep out of my mind the horror stories of the morning newspapers—any morning these latter days.

The highly publicized violence in Tehran has set me to asking myself some stiff questions about myself. Could I be all that wrong, after all those years of experience in development and particularly in Iran, that such a blood-filled ugly disgrace could happen?

FEBRUARY 15, 1979
NEW YORK

The naive and mindless notion that the "revolution" in Iran is purely
a reaction from repression, that it has no economic radicalism roots but
is purely nationalistic, and that there is nothing anti-American about it,
took a great big beating day before last: the capture, with arms, of the
American Embassy compound and the Ambassador and perhaps a hundred Americans.

The Embassy is on American soil; our less than perceptive press
reports overlook that, and it is the one remaining element of extrater-
ritoriality. The American flag was disgraced. This was not by chance.
This was an extension of the fifteen or more years of extreme Communist
attacks on America and on the democratic capitalist system.

The America that I left on my first trip to Iran in February 1956 was,
by any comparison in the world, prosperous. The U.S. was a country in
which women not only had legal rights as persons and as wives, but had
open to them increasingly the privileges and responsibilities enjoyed by
men. It was a country in which the issue of the separation of the hierarchy of the church and the hierarchy of the state had long been accepted
and was beyond question. So-called religious leaders invaded the field of
government and politics at their peril as being contrary to a fundamental
constitutional and emotional tradition.

We in America have shown a high level of concern for the poor, the
protection of the rights of those accused of crime, and such other concerns as sanitary conditions in urban centers, protection of the public's
health and perhaps, above all, a respect for the role of education—not
mere literacy, but education available to almost all, and where not available, that inaccessibility to education was widely considered contrary to
American principles and practices. This latter was demonstrated most
dramatically by the growing concern for what came to be called "minori-
ties," meaning usually blacks.

This in capsule is what a more professorial type than I am would call
the "culture" of the United States of America in February 1956.

I was asked, with my late partner, Gordon Clapp, who had succeeded
me as Chairman of TVA, to go to Iran because the development of the
Valley of the Tennessee along the ideas of democracy was well known to
the monarch of Iran and to his Chief of Plans, a banker, Abolhassan
Ebtehaj. We were asked to provide the background of that TVA experience (which at another time I described as a living testament to my faith
in democratic principles) to a region of Iran encompassing the drainage
basin of five great rivers and referred to as the Khuzistan region.

The Khuzistan region had been in ancient times, in the time of the foundation of the Persian Empire, and for several centuries thereafter, the very heart of the great nation of Persia. At the time of its hegemony, it spread from Mesopotamia to Greece, even to India. But during the centuries the region had suffered neglect, invasion, domination by fanatic and retrogressive Islamic religious leaders. It had retrograded and gave the appearance of a desert, almost devoid of life and of a people devoid of spirit and enterprise. The inhabitants gained nothing from the rich oil resources, also within this province.

I had a general understanding of the region to which we were invited to apply our democratic ideas and our TVA methods of development.

But what I saw in February 1956 in the villages of Khuzistan and even in its principal city, Ahwaz (near the ruins of Susa, the ancient capital of Persia), was in such shocking and tragic and bitter contrast to the great though young country from which, a few days before, I had departed, that the sense of dismay and even horror I felt as I saw the condition of the region and the condition of the people of the region has remained a vivid scar on my mind ever since.

None of the esthetic joy of the Persian painting and sculpture of the Sassanian period in which I had taken such delight could erase or minimize the degradation of human beings in this potentially rich country (how rich I did not at that time realize, nor did the world). The physical degradation, as I saw my first villages of Khuzistan, was extreme. The larger towns, dominated by a profusion of mosques, and their religious leaders, the mullahs, compared to the filth, to the unwholesome conditions of life that I had seen in such cancerous places as Calcutta. What we call poverty in the United States, such as in parts of Harlem in New York City, was as nothing compared to the physical conditions of the villages.

I found nothing picturesque about all this. Including the well-advertised wild and untamed life of the nomads, with their black tents and sheep. The town of Dezful, in the heart of the region, I was told was the oldest organized community in the world. There I saw the flies over the faces of children, the marks of blindness because of trachoma, the wasted condition that follows endemic malaria and the snail-borne bilharzia.

The evidences of greed and the relation between the large owners of land and the peasants were equally startling, by any standards. The plowing of the fields with a wooden plow drawn by ill-assorted animals was about the same way plowing had been done thousands of years before. But it was the lack of freedom, the denial of manhood and womanhood, that I found in sharpest contrast to the America I had left, the abomination of the 14th century when we were, in fact, living in the 20th century.

As an example, in the early years our company employed peasants as laborers on a construction job. They were paid a low wage in currency. Early in this minor building operation, during the night, these men were attacked and brutally beaten; the next day they did not return to work. A representative of a sheik, a local landlord, explained their absence. These peasants were not free to work for anyone else than the sheik, who exacted a portion of their wages. They had been told this, but had nevertheless chosen to work and were beaten up as a warning of even worse punishment.

Another kind of example of the degradation of human beings of this region was the school system. In 1956 on my first exposure and for several years thereafter, as my wife and I visited these villages, we saw the kind of elementary school that the sons of peasants attended. No girls received any education. Schools were a single room. Not every village had a school. Instruction was below fourth-grade level. Only arithmetic, reading, and writing were taught. There was no instruction in even the most elementary forms of agriculture, in personal cleanliness or village sanitary methods.

All village boys also were given religious instruction by a mullah. As they squatted on the ground around him, he intoned passages from the Koran which the boys repeated, by rote, until they had memorized them.

A decade later, at the direction of the Shah, a strong effort was made to overcome this overwhelming illiteracy that dominated all rural Iran. Schools were established in hundreds more villages, girls were admitted to all schools, receiving the same instruction as the boys. Scores of teachers were being trained, both men and women.

While the mullahs continued their religious instruction, they were bitterly opposed to this "new" education. The mullahs were the chief deterrent for any hope for a successful and expanding rate of literacy in rural Iran.

One of the responsibilities for which the Government of Iran had brought us to this region was to put the waters of these five great snow-fed rivers to work for the people of the region and of the country. This being a region of low average rainfall—that is to say, arid, by most American standards—the damming of the streams to accumulate water later to be released for the irrigation of farm land was a very high priority. Our company did find a major damsite and was responsible for the building of one of the world's great dams and irrigation systems.

During our very first visit to the Khuzistan in 1956, we were taken to the only completed dam on any of the Khuzistan streams, known as the Karkheh Bongah, or irrigation district.

The dam was a disaster. It not only did not hold water, but because of faulty design and faulty workmanship, it performed no useful function for irrigation, to say nothing of electric power. Parallel to the failure to develop the copious waters of the region in its streams was the failure of having any organization equipped to deal with a faulty dam much less design a workable one.

To such failures with basic development was added failure to protect even the most limited forms of human rights against the exactions of the landlords, village sheiks, and mullahs.

All of this sad picture in February of 1956 was not only shocking in contrast to the pleasant and decent country from which I came but was in painful contrast to the stated objectives of the sovereign of this country.

It was because the monarch, the Shah, had expressed a determination to change these wretched conditions that my colleague and our associates agreed to make an all-out effort to provide these changes. The changes were not simply to be physical changes, though they were most obviously needed, but to change the mental furniture that permitted such conditions to go on.

FEBRUARY 18, 1979
PRINCETON

A year ago David wrote me a highly critical letter about Iran; the inference I drew—perhaps not so intended—was that I was once more lending my energies and good name to an unworthy cause, the military-dominated regime in Iran. To which I responded with perhaps unjustified vehemence, as I did about working for that *part* of the Vietnam story that I believed in.

David's letter of February 5th, received the 15th, was so much more understanding. And it contains a thought (also referred to in his mostly severe stricture of a year ago) that my efforts and that of D&R would support those "elements" of the Government ("people," "individuals," would have been better terms than "elements" of the Government) that were progressive, and in that way helping to move the country in directions in which I believed.

"In which I believe"—which prompted me this cold and grey winter's day to think about how decisive are ethics, one's convictions about democracy and the primacy of the individual in American political life and policies.

If you believe in democratic methods and goals, if your faith is in the Judeo-Christian precepts, then you are on one side of most public issues, and are opposed to those who don't so believe. This is the Great Divide —between faith in democratic precepts and those who find other beliefs persuade them.

FEBRUARY 19, 1979
PRINCETON

A great blizzard during the night, and fiercely blowing and snowing yesterday. Everything stands still till the noble mantle settles, and this sophisticated world begins to find itself again. New York, a phone call I have just had tells me, is like a city abandoned—nothing can move and there is a serenity over Central Park that brings out its beauty.

We are comfortable, warm, even cozy, in this house, in this home we have made, Helen and I, with the blizzard howling outside, ten inches of snow and more coming.

But what makes for that security and comfort is a man in a yellow slicker and cape, up to his hips in the drifted snow, digging out the place near the rose border where he can put down the hose connected to his huge fuel truck. These servicers make possible this comfort for those of us inside.

FEBRUARY 24, 1979
PRINCETON

A beautiful memorial service for a beautiful human being: Bill Lock-wood, a great scholar at Princeton and perhaps *the* authority on modern Japan.

As we came out, stopping to greet Ginny, his widow, and the two sons and a beautiful daughter, the lady next to me in the line referred to the Institute of Pacific Relations and the ugly period when that monster Joe McCarthy portrayed the Institute as a kind of Communist front. Gerard Swope, then head of General Electric, and I were among the directors (or trustees). But it was Bill Lockwood who got most of the flak.

Now China is the beacon of international Communism, and we do those "Reds" the highest honors. What a cockeyed world it is.

Stand up for what you believe, don't let cheap loud-mouthed punks like McCarthy scare you. It will be no time until positions are almost reversed.

The self-righteous characters who made a profession of being anti-war, that is anti–Vietnam war, and worshipers of Ho Chi Minh and Hanoi now are running for cover about how wonderful North Vietnam is—what with their invasion of Cambodia.

A young red-haired assistant professor from Yale spent a couple hours with me here this morning at his request. Finishing a book on the early political and military strategy period of this atom era. He was fascinated by the fact that in the pre–Lilienthal State Department Board period, no one knew anything, really, about uranium resources. Searls, Baruch's great expert on world minerals, swore that Russia had no significant uranium, and Groves estimated that the Soviets would not have an atomic bomb for many years because they had no uranium. Now it comes out of everyone's ears.

How could there be such a mountain of ignorance on what was an important part of the early strategy and the dictum that the U.S. had a monopoly?

MARCH 6, 1979
PRINCETON

Jane Martin, an engineering student at Vanderbilt University, came for three hours. I definitely enjoyed being "interviewed" on what TVA meant, for the future, in my eyes. What I said was full of the feeling about America that in my case wells up out of conviction and experience.

I found Jane highly intelligent, and she had certainly done her "homework." We went to the Mudd Manuscript Library, for a look at the D.E.L. personal papers, and the D&R Archives.

I committed myself—and happily—to a trip, with Helen, to the Tennessee Valley come April or early May.

I will have to get my ideas well in order on nuclear power plants, for that Valley is where the biggest single concentration of atomic power plants is being assembled.

The prospect of a return to the Valley comes at a very good time. For I have not, of course, recovered from the pain of burying my D&R child, nor adjusted to the cruel, bloody, and humiliating collapse of Iran, a country which I came to love and where many of my friends are being persecuted.

Yesterday another experience provided by a "seminar" with about fifteen students of Professor Greenstein of Princeton. What they found most interesting, judging by their questions, was my personal and anecdotal recollections of the several Presidents I served under. I rather relished telling them about these remarkable and oh so different men. What the net effect was on their understanding of the Presidency—the central topic of the course Greenstein is teaching—I'm not too sure. I think it was that one can't understand the Presidency as an institution apart from the highly diverse personalities of the human beings who occupied that pinnacle.

So I think I was able to make the point from what I said about the five Presidents (F.D.R., H.S.T., Ike, Kennedy and, particularly, L.B.J.) of how utterly different they were, and yet how the "Presidency" was something that was a reflection of their personal characteristics and even state of health, rather than giving a more formal "analysis," such as the scholars of the Presidency go in for.

MARCH 9, 1979
PRINCETON

All day yesterday I was in the special world of the physicist and mathematician. Celebrating the 100th anniversary of the birth of Albert Einstein, at the Institute for Advanced Study across the way.

How these superbrains, from all over the world and the U.S., *live* their equations and concepts!

One session was a panel of men who "had worked with Einstein" here in Princeton. This was largely anecdotal, and the anecdotes were salty, amusing, and in the setting of "in" jokes about physics, but all of this was understandable to me. The later sessions were too much for me.

MARCH 12, 1979
PRINCETON

The day at the Institute was stimulating in many ways. It is from this *mix* of humankind that I get my greatest satisfaction.

Sat at lunch with an officer of Bell Labs, W. O. Baker of the Cherry Hill lab. He said, "You people in the first AEC weren't like the present ones who are so timid and out of touch. You set up a truly great General Advisory Committee to the Commission, and other advisory committees, and you listened to them. That way you kept in touch with the potentials among the scientific and industrial people who could help. And they did."

The last two mornings' front-page stories from Iran carry a ray of hope: the women have organized their own protest demonstrations against Old Whiskers [Khomeini] and the Islamic "law" about women which makes them completely subservient to males, destroys the protection of property and marital rights, etc.

Think of the courage of 15,000 women, dressed *not* in chadours or veils but jeans, defying Old Whiskers, getting roundly defamed and brutally assaulted.

MARCH 22, 1979
PRINCETON

Late the other evening Helen, answering the phone, asked me if I would talk to "some lady calling from Palo Alto." Under my new regime, I took the receiver. "Are you the David Lilienthal who is an optimist? And are you really seventy-nine years old? What you write sounds so young." She said she had just read what I had "written" about optimism, in the *Palo Alto Times.* So I concluded that my recent interview by Cunniff had been sent out on the AP wire and had been published—at least in one newspaper.

MARCH 26, 1979
NEW YORK

In John Macy's remarkable record of a two-hour meeting with Jamshid Amouzegar during his last visit to Iran, Amouzegar reported events and views of the most critical kind, the full force and effect of which did not appear at the time John had this meeting. (Amouzegar had resigned six weeks before this meeting, which would mean that the "sudden" explosion which Washington and the media insisted came as such a "surprise" was actually no sudden explosion at all. The fuse had been lighted and was burning steadily long before the events of November.)

MARCH 28, 1979
NEW YORK

Lunch this noon with John Burnett, now head of Rockefeller Realty, handling the personal holdings in real estate of the Rockefeller family, including the Time & Life Building, Rockefeller Plaza, etc. A devoted internationalist, public servant (in AID), now just as excited and happy doing real-estate deals. He finds the problems tantalizing, and I'll bet he is very good at it.

It takes that kind of personal excitement over what one is doing, because one is doing it, to make a dent on some otherwise actually tiresome affairs.

That is what happened to me about Minerals and Chemicals: could anything be less stimulating to one who had just left the leadership of the atomic energy program of the U.S. than making mud more useful—and profitable? This is what I did for several years in the late fifties. Today, Engelhard Minerals & Chemicals, descendant of that early venture I had charge of and put so much zing into, is a $10 billion business.

APRIL 1, 1979
PRINCETON

The whole country upset by a malfunction of a big nuclear plant in Pennsylvania, in the region of Harrisburg.

Which led me to recall my strong statements on April 4, 1963, about nuclear safety before the Joint Committee and later the American Nuclear Society in November 1963.

The scientists—now the Union of Concerned Scientists—were furious with me—"hurt the program." Where were they then? Did they support me? Hell no.

The journal entries in Volume V (pp. 461, 489, 522) make interesting reading today.

APRIL 3, 1979
PRINCETON

A phone call from Florence: David wishing his mother a "happy birthday." He seemed so full of love and life.

And for good health and good spirits, at *any* age, one can be grateful and thankful for one's loved ones, and particularly a partner of so long a voyage as Helen and I have had.

And if the foregoing is sentimentality, so be it. Intended to be.

APRIL 8, 1979
PRINCETON

I try to keep my mind and emotions away from the barbarism that has descended upon Iran. Hoveyda being "tried" for offenses against Allah, according to Khomeini, tried before a lynching bee who announced in advance what the verdict will be: the firing squad. A nation that spawned great art and poetry, founded by Cyrus and now in the hands of savage turbaned hoodlums and American-educated (at Iranian expense) twirps.

Hard for me to get this ugliness out of my mind, knowing as I do better than most what splendid things that country can produce. This goes on without a word of protest from those outfits that made such an outcry about human rights when it was the Shah they were protesting about.

APRIL 17, 1979
PRINCETON

The malfunction of the atomic reactor at Harrisburg—the Three Mile Island plant, now a part of everyday speech—has projected me back into the atom, in a way I thought I had long since left behind.

The media grabbed this and ran with it, to the benefit of circulation and TV revenues. Some of the things that were said on nationwide programs were shocking and indecent. By that I mean, imaginings of what *might* happen but didn't were blown up to the point that panic might have resulted.

But there was no panic. That is reassuring about people's good sense. In fact, what little evidence we have indicates that the future of civil atomic energy is more secure in people's minds than before. Strange—but true.

APRIL 22, 1979
PRINCETON

Spring—at last. Digging and dividing, and drinking in Nature's softest colors: the petals of tulips. The rose border suffered from one of the coldest winters, but whispering sweet loving words to them seems to be producing dark shoots on the butchered stalks.

Quite excited by the prospect of the Tennessee Valley trip. A letter from Dave Freeman lays out a smorgasbord of briefings that will fill my mental gullet. How to see the people—that will come, too, once it is known that I am around.

APRIL 23, 1979
PRINCETON

Planning the trip to the Valley, talked to Barrett Shelton at Decatur about what kind of stop I might make there. Then it occurred to me that we should pay a courtesy call on Senator John Sparkman at Huntsville. That kind of "gesture" is what I used to be very sensitive to, in the years gone by. John is ill, but it may be possible to spend five minutes with him —and talk to the press afterward about what he has done for his country, including the Valley.

APRIL 26, 1979
PRINCETON

Walt Seymour died this morning. A long association in work and a many-year friendship comes to an end. A strong personality, with a well-organized if hardly imaginative mind.

Phoned Joe Swidler, who was very close to Walt, in the Interior Department, in TVA, and in some of Walt's D&R work. Joe will take this hard, though what he says is philosophical: Walt's number came up.

Joe and I talked at length about what he thinks I should do about "integrating" civil atomic energy into the total picture of America's energy needs. He thinks I am about the only one who can be objective, with no "conflict of interest" distractions. "Take this very seriously, Dave," said Joe. "People will listen to you; think over carefully what you have to say."

APRIL 28, 1979
PRINCETON

What would I have thought, years ago when the *Chicago Tribune* was denouncing me and TVA, if it had been predicted that "someday" WGN would send a senior writer all that way to do a story on me? I would guess it will be a thoughtful and favorable one too. For I have "come out of the closet of silence"—as I put it—about energy, and particularly atomic energy.

The writer—Charles Leroux—is a fairly young man, an acute fellow.

When he phoned some time ago, requesting an interview, I said I do give interviews now and then if the correspondent "did his homework." Leroux certainly had done just that. He quoted from my *Journals,* my book, *Change, Hope, and the Bomb,* and dug up questions from them.

He said he wanted some background to the day's news—which continues to be sweating (quite ignorantly for the most part) over the nuclear malfunction at Three Mile Island. Flattery or not, he said that I had a deeper history about energy than anyone in the country, and therefore should have perspective. "How does it happen that you haven't been interviewed about the Harrisburg reactor trouble?"

Leroux and I went at it for more than two hours. What he will make of our talk it is never safe to prophesy. But we did start on a philosophical and historical note—which was what he wanted and which pleased me.

I do feel *free* to do what interests me. And right now, with spring erupting gloriously all over in this beautiful community, gardening and admiring the garden are a big part of that occupation.

Because of my trouble with my hip and legs and because Helen is not quite as "spry" as thirty years ago, we had some serious doubts during the winter whether we could do gardening. Watching someone we might hire to do the work just wouldn't do, for us.

Helen has cast all that limitation aside. She plants dozens of pansies, petunias, etc., and I have managed to do a moderate but highly satisfying amount of planting and dividing.

Princeton today is beautiful beyond imagining. Such a glow of the flowering crab at the end of our street. The junior dogwood tree I planted between the giant gingus trees has spread its wavy arms, as the buds of that magic tree open.

Reading further in Peter Drucker's puzzling book: *Adventures of a Bystander.* He defines the term "bystander" as the opposite of "activist."

This is a hothouse European intellectual's intellectual speaking. The fact that he has written any number of books explaining management and American corporations doesn't change the fact—as a reading of this strange anecdotal book makes clear. This is Europe talking to an America that he can't possibly understand. We are so pragmatic; he is chock full of the abstract ideology (or anti-ideology) of middle-European high-brows.

I think we have developed something new under the sun, in this America of the 20th century, that one of the airborne intellectuals of Europe cannot possibly understand.

What I should do, dammit, is write (or speak) about this undogmatic dogma of doing what works, for us.

Come to think of it, I have written just such an explanation in some of my writing—in *This I Do Believe* and in the *Smithsonian* piece, for example. I should bring them together and up to date.

APRIL 30, 1979
PRINCETON

The other day I wrote a note to a truly great publisher, Alfred Knopf, complimenting him on a forthright "letter to the editor" of the book section of the *New York Times.* It was a bouncy kind of note, the kind I enjoy writing.

Today a phone call from him. He was greatly pleased; asked what he had done to deserve such a letter. (What indeed; more than fifty-five years of outstanding publishing, stimulating writers, setting new standards of excellence in the format of fine books).

He said: "Do you remember the Sunday afternoon we spent together years ago out here at Purchase, sitting under the old ash tree—it is still here—discussing TVA and the world? Elinore Herrick was with us."

Of course, I remembered. And was proud that he had.

But he is bitter and without illusions. "The bad things that have happened—are happening—are irreversible." (I had said that some things weren't so good but could be made better.) "No, some things are *irreversible.*"

The "old man of the tree"—the apple tree—with which I identify is covered with blossoms, making others in the town look bare. Its trunk is hollow, and it has only one limb—the others were severed. As I look out of my bedroom window and see what heart this tree has, I don't hear it say it is old or maimed, both of which it is. It just goes on blooming like anything.

MAY 1, 1979
NEW YORK

Yesterday John Macy saw the President and has accepted an appointment to head a new top-level agency to "coordinate" all the emergency activities of the Federal Government. He can provide to the whole establishment a quality of professionalism about management that it sadly lacks. But what Administration doesn't have such a weakness!

The Shah, poor deserted soul, thought that because he was "His Imperial Majesty" and King of Kings he needed only to give an order and it was carried out. How sadly off the mark *that* was. And not just about recent events—it was true all through the twenty-three years we were working for Iran.

MAY 6, 1979
PRINCETON

A phone call from Cass Canfield day before yesterday. Wants me to write a "short book" about nuclear energy. The occasion for this interest is obviously the nationwide—worldwide—anxiety and excitement about safety, induced in part by the exaggerated news stories about the Three Mile Island malfunction. (I wrote a brief letter to the *Times* saying that I thought we could not write the atom off, but should make this a "new beginning.")

This call has started me on a rather fevered sorting out of ideas. The first thing I thought about was a title. The one I came up with at once was: *How to Live with the Atom.*

The trip to TVA should give me some fresh material, since TVA is the largest producer at present of atomic energy (I am dropping the nuclear word in favor of the original terminology) and has a half-dozen new plants in various stages of construction.

MAY 13, 1979
KNOXVILLE

It is certainly a different Knoxville! A grubby city it was when we first set foot here in June of 1933. The swing toward apparent affluence at this fancy hotel is a bit too much.

As I looked around the dining hall—and at some of the people—I couldn't help remembering my remark to Queen Farah about the Iranians: "I liked you better when you were poor."

Dave Freeman had the equivalent of the town band out to greet us as we got out of the plane, after a storm-tossed ride. Big floodlights, cameras, TV—the works.

He is quite evidently counting on the interest in my visit here—and the aura that surrounds someone who has been away a long time—to help him strengthen his standing with the Valley people, and with some of his staff, a staff fully loyal to the ex-Chairman, Red Wagner, I would surmise.

Well, this is all to the good if, as I tentatively believe, Dave is just about what TVA and the Valley need right now—whether they know it or not. He is fluent, good with words and uses plenty of them, but he does have the drive to make things happen and bring TVA back into the *nation's* awareness. It had been almost forgotten except here in the Valley—and he is right: TVA is a national asset and to be so must be known—again—as in the days when I was battling and promoting TVA ideas all over the country.

MAY 16, 1979
KNOXVILLE

Two days of the long-planned "return of the adopted native" have been happy and exciting and personally rewarding.

A helicopter flight over the incredibly rugged country to the Northeast of Knoxville, to a new village, Clinchport, and then on to an old-fashioned hero's return to the historic and beautiful town of Jonesboro, not far physically from Bristol and Kingsport but a long way from those rather conventional industrial cities.

Wherever I have visited on Monday, and yesterday, Tuesday, a flock of photographers and TV movie cameramen. It is the local TV men who more or less take the place of a local newspaper reporter—a twist new to me.

On a good many of the smiling faces in Jonesboro, and in the corridors of the huge TVA offices (a far, far cry from the decrepit New Sprankle Building where I spent nearly fourteen years), there was a look almost of incredulity. Could this flesh-and-blood guy be the Lilienthal they had read about for so many years? A widely grinning man in Jonesboro —a town alderman—kept saying to me: "I have heard about you all these years, since I was a boy, and here you are in Jonesboro."

The point of Jonesboro is a serious one, to me, aside from the pleasure of being so warmly greeted—flags on the streets, etc. The renovation and preservation of a historic landmark of the whole cross-Appalachian region of pre-Revolutionary days has been planned and the character of the town been determined by a real democratic process of local "participation" and decentralization which are more than rhetoric here. I am given credit for the ideas that are being carried out, so many years later, by the people of this very American community. One man spoke with feeling about how the ideas of "your book" (meaning *Democracy on the March*) had much to do with how he and his fellow-townsmen set about to create that kind of "preserved town."

And a beautiful town it is. It wasn't a Rockefeller "from the outside" creation like Williamsburg.

Much impressed with Dave Freeman's accomplishments in the year or so he has been in charge. "A tough act to follow"—the sixteen years of Red Wagner—more than sixteen years actually, for he was a strong General Manager operating under Gordon's concept of strong centralization within TVA.

My guess is that, by and large, David Freeman has a strong following in the Valley and he works hard at it, visiting localities all the time, a practice he told Helen he is following because so many people say to him: "You are the first member of the TVA board we have seen in this county since Dave Lilienthal."

From this town that was the capital of the State of Franklin two hundred years ago to the future is the prospect for today: a carefully planned visit to the Sequoyah atomic energy plant, nearing completion at Chattanooga. And at a time when nuclear energy is the center of very emotional antagonism and opposition all over the country.

MAY 24, 1979
PRINCETON

The most important result of the week-long frenetic tour of the Valley was this: my confidence in my health and stamina was restored. It was a tough schedule by any standard for anyone, but I went through it —under close observation by a horde of reporters and photographers— without any slowing down.

The news and photographic coverage of the trip was greater than I could have expected, with press conferences—planned and impromptu —at almost every stop.

I got the greatest pleasure out of two occasions: a talk, brief and impromptu, to a gathering of perhaps three thousand TVA employees in the plaza before the new office quarters (TVA Towers, they call it) in Knoxville, on a beautiful sunny morning.

The second was a friendly folksy "reunion" at Norris Lake State Park. The faces who greeted me were older but recognizable. I didn't get to eat my fried chicken (for it was a "picnic") because of the crowds of oldtimers. "Do you remember?" was the key phrase.

JULY 4, 1979
NEW YORK

Yesterday, at this desk, was the real beginning of a beginning in the writing of the book about energy. For weeks I have been making notes, reading, stewing, gazing off into space. But yesterday I began to write an "introduction." The ideas, the stance, began to flow out of the pen. Doubtless the couple of pages will be tossed away in the coming weeks, but for the first time I had the feeling of creation. I was reminded of the day back in 1944 when I sat down in a Washington hotel and, almost in a single sitting, wrote the opening chapter of *Democracy on the March*.

Those words set the tone and manner of that book, and that book and that writing did as much as any single thing that I did to shape TVA and make it a presence and a force in American life.

The book I am working on will not have the same kind of influence, but it will be dealing with issues that are troubling and frustrating America almost as much as any single anxiety (and promise, hope, possibility) in recent years.

JULY 6, 1979
MARTHA'S VINEYARD

There is love in this house. Without a word being spoken or a gesture, I can feel it around me. Each of the three of us who are here has his work to do, David whanging away at the arthritic typewriter, Helen in her little—and much-loved—kitchen, getting ready for the big birthday bash come Sunday (my eightieth birthday), and me thinking over the atom book session David and I had, in the bright sunshine on the south deck for a couple of hours this morning. How satisfying it all is. It is as if the calendar and the clock stood still.

My huge grey-haired, whiskered son has once more been a guide and an intellectual catalyst. The best, the most sensitive, the most effective partner I have ever had. I'm happy about what he has been able to do in so brief a time in clarifying both the problems of structure for the book and understanding almost miraculously the substantive points that must be raised and answered about nuclear energy.

It is the back and forth of discussion with him that has put this tough piece of writing (and thinking through) so far forward, in just two days. This is the kind of stimulus and corrective that he supplied many summers ago, when I was working on the predecessor of this book, the

Stafford Little Lectures, and particularly the form those statements took when we put it together into *Change, Hope, and the Bomb.*

The more I reflect on what I saw at TVA, the stronger I feel that come what may about public reaction, the clearer it is to me at this time that reason—and the needs of America—will ultimately support a rational nonpolemic assertion: the atom is here to stay.

JULY 24, 1979
MARTHA'S VINEYARD

From early morning, David and I working away in this study.

Discussing, with vigor on my part, ideas about the "hazards" of atomic energy. "Suppose the very worst thing that could happened, despite the many safeguards you have described in this manuscript—then what?"

And so on to the broadest kind of issues: the fact that life is made up of the taking and assessment of risks of disaster and suffering and death.

When I got off on some of these philosophical excursions, David would wait till I had cooled off a bit and would say: "You don't need to go that far; something more commonplace would answer the issue for the purposes of this book." Or, he would say, "You have to meet that issue or you will lose a lot of people—lose me, probably."

JULY 31, 1979
MARTHA'S VINEYARD

It is beginning to roll. I have stopped being too constrained by David's insistence that I stick to the outline of the book we worked out. The net effect is good—i.e., more interesting—because I use so many episodes in my "life with the atom," from TVA days on.

One of the best things about having this book to write is that it keeps me so occupied that I have less time or inclination to suffer over the weather—which has been insufferably hot and incredibly humid, for days and days. Veterans like Erford Burt, my favorite sailing skipper, say this is the worst spell they can remember over many years.

AUGUST 8, 1979
MARTHA'S VINEYARD

More than five straight weeks of hard work on the Harper book— seven days a week. Yesterday took to the photocopier a big stack of manuscript. It begins to look like a book will come out of this. But there is much still to be done.

AUGUST 18, 1979
MARTHA'S VINEYARD

This has been a fabulous experience, these days since July 5 when David and I began a special kind of collaboration toward writing a book about energy, and particularly atomic energy and my experience with it, since its very beginning in August of 1946. It has been hard, exacting work, hard close thinking on a complex and sometimes unpleasant subject.

OCTOBER 17, 1979
NEW YORK

I have tried deliberately to erase Iran from my mind, even from my subconscious mind.

But when Abolhassan Ebtehaj phoned me last week asking to see me, I thought this would be carrying insulation too far; so day before yesterday, I spent a long and painful hour or more with him in this office.

I'm glad I did. After all, it was he who invited me and the fledgling D&R to Iran ("fledgling" meaning practically just Gordon Clapp and myself). It was he who told everyone that I knew what I could do for Khuzistan—and not to harass me, and to make it plain to the ever-present fixers that we would never even remotely consider any form of side-payments. Not once in all those twenty-three years did anyone make an "improper" proposal.

Listening to Ebtehaj the other day did confirm that the "revolution" was made almost inevitable by the blind greed of the "very best" of the Westernized Iranians. Ebtehaj built one of the most fabulous homes and styles of living I have ever seen, while the poor people of the country— well, they were to be the beneficiaries of "development," and development became for him a technical achievement, not a human goal.

I complained that no one had ever explained to me during all those many years that the 200,000 mullahs I now hear were functioning throughout the country had great political power. He spoke of those mullahs with the greatest disdain. They come from the "lowest" and most ignorant of Iran's people; they know nothing, can run nothing. Moreover, the mullahs, these begging dirty, turbaned characters, are much more corrupt than anything in the days of the Shah.

OCTOBER 24, 1979
NEW YORK

The tragedy of Iran grows, deepens.

Returning from the Oyster Bar last evening, I was greeted by a huge newspaper headline: the Shah is at New York Hospital, for treatment. "Cancer" was the word.

Well, whether the poor man has cancer or not, certainly his country has—an illness fatal to what Persia stood for through so many centuries.

DECEMBER 3, 1979
PRINCETON

When I first went to Iran, in February, 1956, not many people knew where Iran was or much about it. For the past six weeks, Iran has been the focus of most people's minds, and their apprehensions.

As I look back on my own Iranian experience, I am aware that I can hardly be completely objective about the bitter complaints and ugly revengeful howls of the mullahs and their followers, demanding the Shah's blood (and doubtless his dismemberment in a gruesome ritual execution).

I thought the Shah and the Iranians I dealt with were engaged in a constructive and well-motivated effort to improve the lives of the ordinary people of that historic country. So much so that I dedicated one of the volumes of my *Journals* to the Shah and to his efforts to improve the lot of his people.

Even as I now reflect on how impressed I was about what I was lending my efforts and reputation to furthering, shadows and doubts cross my mind, the shadows of the display of wealth of some of those close to the Shah, particularly the "Family," the Minister of Economics and his palatial home, and even Ebtehaj, the fighter against the Shah but beneficiary of the country's economic progress.

A further reflection about this fearsome story, now approaching the very brink of war against Iran by the U.S.: how ignorant I was, and most people were, about the potential power of the mullahs to assemble mobs and inflame mob violence.

Friday last Mildred Baron delivered, personally, to Harper's the manuscript of the book about the atom.

Working out and writing that book was literally my sole preoccupation for four months and more, day and night. The last piece of work was about the most difficult, a chapter on atomic weapons.

I have a lot of thinking to do about my future. In the past, what I do with myself was decided for me by events—often right out of the blue. I can't now expect this non-functional future.

I took on the invitation to join a group of public utility regulators from the New England states to visit the super-great James Bay hydroelectric project in northern Quebec. Coming on the heels of a bad cold, and the aftermath of a nasty fall that put me in the hospital for a couple days, to make this trip was a conscious dare. If I backed out I would be safe, but unsure of my endurance and stamina. So I went—and made it back.

But the ten-year developing arthritis in my hips has plagued me more lately than I like to admit. The last couple days have been particularly painful and in fact crippling.

DECEMBER 6, 1979
PRINCETON

Driving back from the City this morning with Tom Moore gave me a varied picture of Princeton, and was utterly fascinating. As the proprietor of a taxi service, Tom's interests and friendships are far-ranging, as I found when I encouraged him to talk.

He is a patient and high-ranking golfer.

I asked if he remembered Einstein, in Princeton. He said he used to see a lot of him, going to the railroad station to meet people who came to visit Einstein—and then named some of them, usually great physicists. Einstein would visit with him and the other "cabbies" at the station. I got a picture of a very relaxed "old gentleman" surrounded by the young men of the town who picked up their passengers while they exchanged stories with him.

This led to Tom's recollections about other passenger-"clients" of his cab. "No, I can't recall that Einstein smoked—saw some pictures of him once with a pipe. But Robert Oppenheimer—I would drive him and his daughter a lot. Oppenheimer had a pipe that smelled *awful.* After he left the cab, I would have to open the doors and freshen the air. Smelled to high heaven."

DECEMBER 10, 1979
NEW YORK

New York City was overwhelming tonight. The lights at Rockefeller Center, the great Christmas tree piercing a clear sky—a magnificent city. But what made it so moving for me, of course, were the families—the young children being held up by proud papas to see the animated window displays.

This topped off a moving-picture experience as delightful as almost any: *The Black Stallion.* Can there possibly be any animal, be he man or beast, as commanding, as wild with energy and beauty as a great horse?

The day began on quite another note: a consultation with two doctors.

That trip to Quebec did wonders for my morale, but the amount of walking and stair-climbing must have inflamed the arthritis in my hips —which shows up as considerable pain in the thighs, referred pain.

Both doctors made it clear that the "risks" of surgery ("hip joint replacement" operation) were too great—prolonged anesthesia—so I simply must face and somehow manage the formula "grin and bear it" or, in any event, "bear it." I have had pain before, but it was always of the kind the docs call "reversible." This is definitely not reversible.

DECEMBER II, 1979
NEW YORK

On my desk at the office the eye-popping jacket for *Atomic Energy: A New Start*—strong red and white letters against a black background.

I have a satisfied feeling, whether the critics will think so or not. Being dissatisfied and self-critical is the mood of today, particularly among the frustrated characters whose chief, perhaps only, talent is criticizing what someone else has done.

DECEMBER 12, 1979
NEW YORK

Hard to get out of my mind and sense of outrage the way the masters of television are threatening to take over sensitive public policy. They have made their cameras available to terrorists by showing to millions of Americans the filming made within the captured Embassy in Tehran!

The first "outside" test of the new book: a couple hours with Corona Machemer, who is editor for Harper.

Corona, I felt, would be a hard critic to satisfy. She is of the generation who have, as someone said, "been marinated" in the dyed-in-the-wool environment ideology. Among such, atomic energy is anathema. So when she said, in my office today, that she liked the book, agreed (however reluctantly, to be sure) that atomic energy is "probably less harmful environmentally" than any other source of energy for electricity, I was pleased. Corona is a reasonable sample of the younger audience.

It was evident in our conversation that she was much taken—for such a hardboiled editorial type, quite taken—with the point I make in the last chapter, and more specifically in the "Atoms for War" chapter: that with a new and safer source of atomic energy, as I proposed we develop, we have a "leverage" for the adoption of some form of real atomic arms elimination, some way to slow and perhaps stop the atomic arms race. That leverage we didn't have in 1946 and 1947 in the discussions of the Acheson-Lilienthal Plan.

DECEMBER 18, 1979
NEW YORK

I am full of indignation against the TV programs. The part they play in the lynching of the Shah, the damage they are doing to the President's efforts to get the fifty Americans out of the clutches of that band of hoodlums who invaded and have possession of the U.S. Embassy compound in Tehran, the way they have turned American television over to Iranian outlawry—all of this has emphasized again how irresponsible and powerful are the few men who decide what goes on the networks' broadcasts.

It is a sad chapter, all in all. The Security Council of the UN, the International Court, and American public opinion generally, "demand" that the prisoners of kidnappers be freed at once. But day after day, newscast after newscast, we are fed propaganda from the perpetrators on American television prime time.

DECEMBER 24, 1979
PRINCETON

Nancy and Sylvain arrived last evening, and we had a convivial dinner together. And today—Daniel's 23rd birthday—Nancy trimmed the tree with lights, with her father "in attendance." Phone calls to Allen and to Daniel, on the West Coast. I have just been permitted to see the Christmas turkey in the oven, tended by Helen.

But Grandfather isn't all that indomitable today. I have more pain and immobility than I have ever had. I am certainly worse off by far than a year ago, or six months ago. But happy and fulfilled in every other department.

DECEMBER 28, 1979
PRINCETON

Now that I have shed the day-to-day duties of "running something," I want very much to set off on a new career: that of a professional writer. After all, I have been writing, for publication, for many years.

Is this desire for a writing career realistic? It is not as if I don't know that writing is damned hard *work,* requires perseverance and concentration, is full of frustration. Do I have the ability to write, regularly, and as a pro?

DECEMBER 29, 1979
PRINCETON

It is about what I have *learned* that I want to write, in the coming months and years.

What I have learned is the product of experiences, and many of them I recorded in the six big fat volumes on the bookshelf behind me here. But at least as much, the lessons and judgments, even insights, came from thousands of men and women along the path of this often bumpy journey. Those thousands of individuals, friends, enemies, helpers, form the tapestry, the fabric of that life.

That array of people, separate individuals, could be the centerpiece of the writing I am so eager to set about doing.

This writing will not be fiction, in the conventional accepted meaning of "fiction"—the kind of story telling in which my son excels. Though after the passage of time and the gloss of imagination, what is fiction and what is "fact" becomes blurred.

What makes me what I am, today, at eighty, is a composite of the life experiences I had with those individuals. The mental stimulation of great minds reacting to my mind; the excitement—and the pain—of love; the fury and sleepless nights and tortured days during contests of will— for I was always a combative kind of guy—this catalog of encounters, could be the kind of thing I believe I should write about, as of this period of contemplating entry into writing.

DECEMBER 30, 1979
PRINCETON

The year 1979, now drawing quickly to an inglorious close, has not been a "good" one for most of the world's people, nor for me. But it has not been *dull*.

The end of the year used to be a time when I tried to sum up. This year these end-of-the-year entries should be more in the way of catching up with events or ideas that I didn't record.

At this time a year ago it did not seem possible that Iran, where a revolution had been going on for years under the guidance of the Shah —the White Revolution—would be shaken to its very foundations by a counter-revolution that would drive the Shah out of the country, and threaten not only his life and regime (and even the physical safety of the twenty-five or so Americans of the D&R staff).

In a single year, or less, Iran has become a danger to the peace of the world; not a day passes that the chief item in the media isn't of events in the country that for more than two decades was ignored by the rest of the world.

So Iran is the chief event of the year, for me, and for the whole world.

The happiest event was the trip to TVA in May, a fully recorded story.

The most affirmative part of the year was spending several months —the entire summer—thinking through and writing a book about my life with the atom. That occupied and still takes up much of my energy and attention, so much so that there has been not quite enough energy left for journal writing about it.

As the year ends, I am fighting the pain and unpleasantness of arthritis, determined, grimly determined, to lick it, and learn how to manage impaired mobility, and retain my spirits for the new career of writing.

I am far from dispirited; on the contrary, eager for new things as I come to the end of so full a year. A year of something I haven't had to meet for a long time, *two* health problems: a heart infarction and acute arthritis. I even have absorbed the "eighty-year syndrome," and the prospect, almost daily, of reading in the obit pages of the death of some friend of my vintage.

XIII

1980

~~⌒⌒~~

Surgery for bilateral hip replacement—Cataract operation—Opening a new office

JANUARY 11, 1980
PRINCETON

Yesterday evening, at the nearby Princeton Theological Seminary, a
meeting of the trustees of an invention of Dr. James McCord's, president
of the Seminary.

The seed idea of the Center for Theological Inquiry—the rather pretentious but descriptive sobriquet for the foundation—came from Jim
McCord, who selected the original members of the board of trustees.
McCord is a powerful man, a man of inner power. His skill in directing
a random group and perhaps welding it into something creative will be
tested by this enterprise.

He proposed the names of perhaps twenty "authorities" in theology,
and believes that these "advisory" people can find creative minds in this
field who can in turn propose members of a kind of "faculty" of the
Center.

This is vague, as one of the trustees, William Scheide, pointed out.
How can an advisory group meeting once a year come up with anything
without being in constant communication? The pragmatist McCord's
answer seemed to be: try it and see.

Finding financing for this foundation seems to be the least of the
problems.

The "moguls" are frantically looking for someplace—anyplace, apparently—to give large sums. Why? To cut down their Federal tax. (An-

other way of putting it is that by "giving" these big hunks of money rather than paying it to the Treasury, all the rest of us pay more taxes, and the "deficit" the moguls complain about is increased thereby.) Bob Meyner and I, he the former Governor of New Jersey, found this distasteful.

When you get so absorbed in working out deals that save the taxes of the wealthy, you squeeze out any other more constructive ideas, it would seem.

As I did at an earlier meeting, I made a strong point that the appeal of this Center to me was that it might throw some light on the practical problem facing the world, how to understand Islam and the misuse—as I saw it—of the political and military power of the Islamic religious leaders. It is a phenomenon common to Moslem countries, the taking over of political power by religious organizations, a reversal of the separation of Church and State that is so fundamental to our American Constitution and to English history since the 19th century.

McCord apparently thought my point over, and at the conclusion of the dinner meeting, as all of us were seated in a big circle, he asked me if I thought it was possible for the Center to bring together a "dialogue" between Christian, Jewish, and Islamic leaders. This, of course, is what I had thought he had in mind all along, but apparently not; he was preoccupied with a theologian's concern for scholarly studies.

JANUARY 15, 1980
NEW YORK

There was some happy irony in a letter from Dave Freeman just received. Referring to our visit to the Valley of last spring, he said, "You make all of us feel young and vital by your own personal yardstick which none of us measures up to. But we grow by trying."

Why is it that a strong fighting spirit is so often described as youthful? It is good to know that I have the capability of showing that youthful spirit that can infect others.

My beloved mentor and friend, "Dr. H.A." had that same effect on me*; it really isn't all that relevant that he was at that time younger than I am now by several years. But I sat with him as he lay dying of cancer, and his courage and good spirit even then was a "transfusion of courage" for me, and in memory, now.

Atomic energy, to my surprise and great satisfaction, continues to be current big news. News stories practically daily.

*Dr. Harcourt A. Morgan, a member of the original TVA board, and Chairman, 1938–41.

The latest deal with the grandiose plans and projects of the Soviet Union for major expansion of their program, and increasing signs that even their great resources of coal and waterpower aren't sufficient for their future energy needs. So they are giving atomic energy plants the highest kind of place in their overall energy program. What kind of reactors are they building or designing? Water-cooled, basically the very same design that I say, in the atom book, simply "isn't good enough"— i.e., isn't safe enough. And the UK is following suit with a Westinghouse water-cooled design for their expansion.

Added benefit of "retirement": reading novels and spy stories, in quantity. I would never have predicted this. But I'm enjoying it. Reading fiction "in the daytime"—really! And I read biography and history.

I don't, for the time being, feel that I have to be "saving the world" and solving or preaching about its problems.

However, I read the *Times* more carefully because there is so much atomic stuff in those pages.

I follow the weird turns and twists of the rudderless ugly chaos in Iran; those years of reasonable stability under the monarchy can't be forgotten by any citizen these days, least of all by me.

I feel free to accept or decline invitations that by long habit I would consider as "advancing my work" or being part of my job.

JANUARY 18, 1980
PRINCETON

IBEC has gone into a new transformation: acquired by a big British conglomerate, Booker's, but retaining its identity. From a company with revenues of $300 million, IBEC has been "divested" into a $66 million enterprise.

This must have been chewed over and "negotiated" till the cows came home before the deal was closed.

My surmise is that this is a way of getting better management in IBEC, which now will be run by an Englishman from Booker, with Rodman continuing as Chairman, but devoting himself to "policy and plans." I know what that phrase means when a company needs to be managed.

Rodman asked me to lunch with him yesterday. Once more I was impressed by (and grateful for) those human qualities of good manners and courtesy.

He is puzzled by why I need the office he has made available to me (an office in the IBEC suite) since I'm definitely not "in business." Don't know that I completely persuaded him. Myself, I'm sure I do need a New York spot, for the time being certainly.

Last night watched a one-hour "interview" with the Shah, conducted by David Frost, from the Shah's hideout on an island off Panama.

The photography was excellent, close up.

This man, whom I got to know so very well, has become the center of a fire-storm that has spread from his bedside in the New York Hospital to Afghanistan. In a sense, his presence in the U.S. ignited a world turbulence, which has gone on now for more than two months. The hooligans in Iran, howling for his blood, use his being in the U.S. as an excuse for their defiance of the U.S. and of world opinion.

The interview was mild enough. Like most of the "journalism" about Iran, it was almost entirely about the sins attributed to the Shah. Denying these stories of slaughter and torture fails to give a sensible picture of what constructive things took place in Iran during his regime. When will it be possible to tell that story?

JANUARY 19, 1980
PRINCETON

The humiliation—it is just that—of having to move, to walk, slowly and with distress, is in such contrast to the superactivity I have enjoyed, without thinking about it, for most of my life. This is what makes it so hard to take, I guess.

A musical program on TV swept away the discouragement. A magnificent tenor, Pavarotti, with the New York Philharmonic orchestra, pouring out glorious sounds. There, in our upstairs living room, I felt the clouds lift, and my spirits return to what is actually normal, for me, exuberance and confidence and zest.

There came over me a consciousness of the joy of fully living, of what richness and delight there is just in being alive.

There is so much more to living than freedom from pain. I know that I will overcome.

JANUARY 20, 1980
PRINCETON

Have just listened to the President, on *Meet the Press*.

Believing as I do that the Soviets are "on the move," with Afghanistan just the beginning, I didn't hear the word "war" either from the waxwork figures on the panel *or* explicitly from the President.

Evidence of the flavor of the time was the first question: what about boycotting the Moscow Olympics!!

JANUARY 21, 1980
NEW YORK

Over this tabletop is a big mirror in this little hotel room. For the first time I can recall, I stopped writing and looked at the face in that mirror. Time hasn't too greatly changed the face: a big nose, lines from the edge of the nose to the tight lips of concentration.

Then, without thinking, I raised my hands, fingers toward me, half-clenched my fists—and I saw the cords of the hands of an old man, tough, sinewed hands.

That old geezer there, in the big mirror, is two men. One is represented by those strong but corded hands. That man has seen a vast amount of living and of life, his own and others.

The old geezer can tell that image in the mirror another story. It is not one of looking back on those battles of yore, but an eagerness, an enthusiasm, a toughness, and a thirst for new experiences.

JANUARY 22, 1980
NEW YORK

What writing I do now need not be with publication during my lifetime in mind; if what I write, if the ideas have more than ephemeral importance, the writing itself will be recognized a decade, two decades, hence—or will fade into nothing.

I should write what pleases me, and leave out of consideration, as much as is possible, shaping the writing to suit the tastes or interests of today.

For the first time in my life I have the leisure to reflect and to write; I have the financial resources so I don't need to write for pay, or for prestige. It will take some time to accommodate myself to this new frame, this changed perspective.

FEBRUARY 9, 1980
PRINCETON

A long talk with David yesterday; he in Florence, of course.

It is not easy for David to accept graciously warm praise from his father. It has been equally difficult for him to praise his father, though I know that he is appreciative of what I have done—in fact, proud of me. He did tell me, though, that I must get great "satisfaction" from the atomic energy book. "It will have a very considerable impact," and my "pushing it through" was something he thought very highly of.

He is very possessive about the book. Greatly surprised, I think, that on a subject about which—as he asserts—he knew almost nothing, when we set down to begin work on July 4, he could become so engrossed, have strong feelings about it, and a paternal sense about the book itself. This is the kind of collaboration between two men that is so uncommon as to be notable; as between father and son quite rare.

FEBRUARY 10, 1980
PRINCETON

A footnote, and a specific one, about the "cure" for the energy crisis, conservation.

Don Koepp, the Princeton librarian, volunteered this. He found that in one of the university buildings, there was only one light switch. If you had the electric lights on in one room—or off—they would be on or off in all forty. When he complained about this, on conservation and horse-sense grounds, the answer was that it was easier to have one switch than forty, even though this meant that in thirty-nine rooms the lights would be on—or off—needlessly. So out of his own library budget, he installed thirty-nine switches, one for each room.

I complained the other day that my office was furiously overheated. Nothing can be done about any one room; all "centrally" controlled.

I remember a speech to an audience of an American advertising group by the then Minister of Finance, later Prime Minister, Amouzegar. He was making the point that Americans were wasteful of electricity, which meant of oil. The illustration he used was coming into a single office in a big office building in Manhattan (where he was making this speech). All the lights of the building were going full blast. He got the same answer as the Princeton librarian received.

The case is more impressive to me in Princeton because the Engineering School is talking a lot about their scientific plans for conservation on the campus—redesign, gadgets, etc., and yet such an elementary case as Koepp described is beneath the dignity of big-shot academic engineers.

FEBRUARY 16, 1980
PRINCETON

The "Notes and Comment" that opens this week's *New Yorker* magazine makes the point about Atoms for War that I made the theme for Chapter XIII of the atom book: that when our President and Secretary of Defense talk about "military action" to repel Soviet moves against the Persian Gulf oil, they don't have the wherewithal to carry out military action that far away from the U.S. *And* this big aggregation of nuclear weapons can't be used without bringing on a terrible destruction of civilization. Yet we keep pouring resources and rhetoric into the atomic weapons and "strategy" as if this made any sense.

My book continues to deal with current issues, months after I have finished writing it. This morning reports Senator Kennedy making an issue of atomic power plants—they should be closed down. He calls it "phased out."

The durability of what I write was again borne in on me this last week. A leading Japanese publisher has issued a handsome re-edition of a book I wrote in 1944 [*TVA: Democracy on the March*].

FEBRUARY 18, 1980
PRINCETON

Have spent an hour this forenoon skipping around in David Freeman's book, *Energy: A New Era*. The book was funded by the Twentieth Century Fund, but is published as a soft-cover.

The book, read today, is prophetic in almost every way.

I was particularly impressed, this morning, with the concluding pages. They are so reminiscent of the draft final chapter my son wrote last summer, and which appears, duly and severely edited by yours truly. He had insisted from the first discussions we had about the atom book that energy must be seen not as a domestic U.S. problem but a world issue. I didn't fully agree. Freeman made the same point, years ago, in his book.

I was also impressed with how much David Freeman knows about new technical sources, such as the fuel cell or using gas to produce electricity directly.

FEBRUARY 19, 1980
NEW YORK

The issue of the American "hostages" in Iran has been front-page for weeks. It has been as confused a question as can be imagined, a surrealist nightmare. A group of Iranians has turned the world's mind absolutely upside down.

The reason we have not been able to comprehend what has been happening is simply that these so-called militants (they used to be called "students") are not being regarded as kidnappers, but as a political force. They are being negotiated with by the Iranian "authorities," by the UN, the U.S., etc., not as kidnappers are usually dealt with, as criminals of the worst kind, but as a body politic.

Instead of being arrested and tried for a crime against innocent people, as kidnappers and terrorists are in Italy, for example, the U.S. will praise them for releasing diplomatic personnel, citizens of the U.S. It is about as topsy-turvy a mess as imaginable.

MARCH 3, 1980
NEW YORK

A call this morning from Professor George Lancowski of Berkeley. Jack McCloy and David Rockefeller had asked him to put together some of the facts about the constructive things that had been accomplished "by the preceding regime" in Iran.

When I saw the man had no designs on me or my time, I referred him to the *Journals* I had kept during those years. Of course, he had never heard of them, the old story. I referred him to the enormous archive of material about Khuzistan at Princeton and the catalog I financed.

I didn't disguise my sense of outrage about what is going on in that Allah-forsaken country. But I kept myself under control.

McGeorge Bundy's group at the Council on Foreign Relations deals with proliferation of atomic weapons, and in particular the issues about this touchy subject between India and Pakistan. That group is to meet tomorrow afternoon, and I plan to attend.

Chiefly, I would like to say that the real threat of atomic weapons these days is between the U.S. and the Soviets—that's what we should be chiefly concerned with. We and the Soviets have massive arsenals of these weapons *now,* and the prospect of using them is less remote than at any time in the last decade or so.

There are some constructive ways of achieving something like peace in the Indian subcontinent. Mac recalled my efforts in the 1950s to bring about a settlement of the division of the waters of the Indus River, and will expect me to make a statement about this. "It is distinctly relevant right now," he said.

MARCH 7, 1980
PRINCETON

Lunch meeting with Victor Gilinsky, a member of the Nuclear Regulatory Commission.

He had an interesting comment about President Carter. "He feels at home in nuclear energy; it brings out the engineer in him. He was furious about the way the media and particularly television handled the Three Mile Island accident. For the ten days while the Three Mile Island accident was front-page for the whole country, President Carter was on the phone to the NRC man, Denton, for fifteen minutes every day, wanting to know all the details. With all the problems a President has, to spend fifteen minutes every day about a nuclear plant?"

Last week I spent the afternoon at the baronial home of the Council on Foreign Relations in New York City. The meeting (on atomic proliferation) was held around a big oval table in what must have been the library of whatever robber baron built that house in the first place.

In one corner, in very white marble, is a massive head of Wendell Willkie. Willkie's fight against the TVA and me in the 1930s made him the hero of the New York intellectual and big-business establishment which had its spiritual home in the Council's headquarters. It was here that the shaggy "barefoot boy of Wall Street" (turned utility front man) acquired his following among the writers, academics, intellectuals who made him a national figure.

Willkie and I taught each other a lot during those years. I came to understand myself better because of that dead-earnest conflict, a contest for the minds of others. When we debated, during that period, before the Economic Club of New York, my throat was fiery sore; I considered asking to get out of the debate—I was constantly having sore throats and "flu" in those days of overwork and strain.

He clearly won the debate in that New York encounter, but I won it hands down among the people of the Tennessee Valley, and in Congress and the White House.

There was one member of the audience of big shots, cheering Wendell on, that night, who didn't miss the significance of my tough position. Floyd Carlisle, big, bluff upstate New York head of Niagara Hudson, came up to me after the meeting. "Years from now," he said, not argumentatively, just expressing his long-term judgment, "people will look back and see you were the man who socialized the electric industry." At the time he made this comment the future of the private utility industry seemed beyond questioning, and all the solid forces were set against me, and TVA.

MARCH 8, 1980
PRINCETON

One learns from illness about the meaning of life, the meaning of this one particular life which is my own. I am now—this moment—confronting one such lesson, am face to face with the strain, having to call upon all my resources of faith in the goodness of life, testing the rhetoric I resort to. This is happening now, today, and this has been a mounting burden in recent months, and weeks.

Now I have considerable mobility, so that—with determination, and the use of a cane—I do manage to walk, to come up and down the stairs here at 88. But not able to walk in a carefree way, or to walk freely in the city, which is the whole experience of New York City, which I have always cherished.

How can I understand the life of the people around me without some taste of what so many of them must contend with?

The way an individual deals with his own serious illness—perhaps this is one of the best measures of the quality and the strength—or weakness—of that individual. A negative way of measuring quality.

MARCH 9, 1980
PRINCETON

Under the glistening leaves of the dark-red azalea outside the dining-room window is the golden spread of winter aconite. No one can lose heart about a laggard spring when he remembers that these courageous little fellows have been blooming now for weeks, throughout very cold February days. And in the bed where last fall I planted bulbs, the first tulip leaf up through the inhospitable dark brown.

An illness today projects the imagination back to other days and other trials. Such as . . .

I had gone to New York to meet with Willkie, in his law office. My hotel room was a tiny one at the third-rate Barbizon Plaza. No fancy suite for the head of a big enterprise, his public service habits still with him. Upset by failure to make any decisive headway toward a settlement with Willkie that I could possibly recommend. The strangeness of New York and the wear and tear of a long battle. Then in the middle of the night, a sense of high fever and sweating, alternating with one wave of chills after another.

To Washington and Dr. Lewis Ecker, and in a room at Garfield Hospital. Undulant fever or Malta fever, he thought. No known cure, no sure understanding of where it comes from: raw milk?

Then came the terrible deep depression I had been warned would follow the acute fever and chill period. Weeks of lying in bed, in Norris, dejected and weak, before I began to take an interest in how Cap Krug and Joe Swidler were making out in the last stages of the negotiations with Willkie. Then a board meeting in our house at Norris, and a call to President Roosevelt. I got the President's approval of our "settlement" of the six- or seven-year war with Commonwealth and Southern.

Up there on the wall of this study, overshadowing all the other photographs, is a portrait of Senator Norris. On the floor of the Senate that sweet old boy described the state of TVA. He used a term that I so well remember: Lilienthal has a "lingering" illness.

Why is it that sickness—serious sickness that calls in question every plan, every value, tests every source of strength and plumbs every weakness of character—why are these chapters of an active man's life made so little of in biographies? There are exceptions: Robert Louis Stevenson's years of fighting consumption, sending him off to the South Sea island.

Another monumental exception: Franklin Roosevelt's sudden seizure with polio, and the struggle of Eleanor to keep him from being an "invalid."

Returning to my own serious illnesses, and how I "took" those confrontations:

A case of flu in 1958. Not uncommon for me. My face, in the mirror, as I shaved, seemed odd, strange somehow. Phoned Dana Atchley. He said: Stick a needle into the side of your face; if you can't feel it, get out here to Columbia Presbyterian Hospital right away. I think, he said, you have Bell's Palsy.

This was a nightmare of sheer naked pain—not ache, but sharp shattering pain, not in the face, where the paralysis had set in, but in the ear. Life consisted of trying to hold on until the next shot in the arm of morphine (or whatever it was), calling on a neurologist, deciding whether it was necessary to sever a nerve to stop the pain. The right side of my face was flat as a board.

After a long time and no change, Nate Greene called on me. My appearance hadn't improved but my spirit revived. I began asking him about D&R. Said he, "You are going to make it; I can tell that." It was evident that he had been "delegated" by André Meyer and Gordon Clapp to judge whether I was "through."

Luckily, there was no facial disfigurement, and soon I was able to carry on as before.

MARCH 31, 1980
PRINCETON

How many decisions I have had to make in my time. Now I have a decision to make that is personal in the extreme; the consequences, up or down, will not affect the fate of the Republic but will very specifically affect my life as a person, an individual.

Shall I have major surgery performed, replacing my hip joints with artificial ones?

APRIL 5, 1980
PRINCETON

It has often been said of me that Senator McKellar, who was such a violent "enemy," made me famous—the reference is to the impromptu statement referred to as "This I Do Believe."†

But Senator McKellar did far more than make me well known because of his unrestrained attacks on me: he made me strong and tough. I learned from his attacks what it was about public life and public policy that I did indeed "deeply believe."

So the roster of people I might write about will not be only of those I admired or who agreed with me, but as much those who opposed me. Only a few days of exposure to Arthur Morgan's ideas—and manner toward others—taught me what I believed, of an affirmative kind, about democracy, and its opposite, such as A. E. Morgan's paternalism and do-goodism.

More than anything, it was his personality (a strong one, too, God knows) that brought out of the wells of my being and my thinking process, the convictions that fueled my contest with him, and which became part of the basic precepts of an institution, the TVA.

It was not only famous or powerful people who "taught" me—forced me by conflict to find out what I believe, or taught me my limitations.

APRIL 6, 1980
EASTER SUNDAY
PRINCETON

A morning of full sun, the kind that warms the bones and encourages into bloom the apparently dead twigs of the ancient apple tree.

The glorious sun is not much help to the pain in my thighs. Hospital for Special Surgery, here I come.

What has been the purpose of the other books I have written?

First, the *Journals:* a current account of D.E.L.'s life, sometimes day to day, always chronological, usually concerned with issues, public issues, and how to advance them or explain them.

Other books were essays about impersonal issues—collective bargaining in the public service. Or my philosophy about democracy. This was *This I Do Believe,* a book of essays, put together by Helen, but written separately and impersonally.

Big Business: A New Era was built around several magazine articles. Not really personal.

†At the AEC Chairmanship confirmation hearings in 1947.

The new book *Atomic Energy: A New Start,* is about a public policy; the personal content is incidental.

Now, the "project" that fills my head with its prospects is quite different from these predecessors.

It will be about *people.*

People, individuals, will not be incidental to the discussion of policies, programs, events. The individuals in this new writing will be the centerpiece. The impact of these people on my growth will be the purpose of the work. It is this concept, that people shaped my life and my work and the policies and programs I espoused, that is the distinctive part of what I am trying to create as a literary product. I will describe these people (vignettes) partly because they are interesting in themselves, and therefore worth writing about and reading about. But the purpose of describing the people is that it is they who shaped the course of one particular life, my own.

APRIL 17, 1980
PRINCETON

Yesterday at twelve noon, in a cubicle at the Hospital for Special Surgery in New York, I made a decision of more than ordinary importance: I agreed with a distinguished orthopedic physician, Dr. Philip Wilson, that on June 3 he would replace, in both hips, bones and tissue that have been with me for lo these many years with metallic and plastic hip joints.

Helen was with me as Dr. Wilson explained what he found, and what I could expect as I recuperated. She pushed me in a wheelchair as we were picked up by Tom Moore. Both of us were "relieved."

APRIL 26, 1980
PRINCETON

Yesterday morning I turned on TV, at 9 o'clock, and there was Jimmy Carter, full face, talking softly as is his wont. What is he saying? He had cancelled *what?* And then I realized that what Harold Brown had said to the Council on Foreign Relations a couple weeks ago had been more than a speech: they really meant that they were sure they could pluck the hostages out of the U.S. Embassy in the middle of Tehran.

Recently I wrote David that I was persuaded that I couldn't write a reminiscent kind of story of my own boyhood, a subject he and I had discussed together.

He disagreed, and then said a highly relevant thing: the *material* creates the creation. "And goodness knows, you have the material." In other words, I have lived through so much that the skill of writing becomes secondary to the "material."

The satisfaction I am getting out of this exploration is that I can see far better than ever before that the passionate feeling I brought to TVA's power problems had little to do with my knowledge or even intellectual interest in a new kind of electricity schedule: the one I came up with at Madison that first summer of TVA, a schedule of rates that shook the electricity industry and the stock market, too, for that matter.

It was because I was the kind of person I was that produced that rate schedule, and the economic philosophy of promoting an improvement in people's lives in the Valley through greater use of electricity.

Coming out with those unique electric rates (a pretty dry subject to most people) was an expression of my personality, of my concern about people in that Valley, of my combative instincts, of my antagonism to the fat-cat power company people, of a creative impulse wanting to do something that hadn't been done before. Only David Lilienthal could produce just that result, that rate schedule, and the words I used to describe it to the country. So that kind of man determined that kind of rather prosaic result—i.e., an electric rate schedule.

APRIL 27, 1980
PRINCETON

Just as the sixties were colored for me by the black revolution in this country, and the seventies by the revulsion over the Vietnam war and the shooting of students at Kent State, so the rise and spread of patent homosexuality, even pride in homosexuality, marks this period, and is bound to affect my own thinking and observation of society in America.

This aspect of the sexual revolution is reflected in still another way: the frequency and casualness of divorce, and the avoidance of marriage, "living together" by couples who are, for the time being at least, in love but who prefer the freedom of living together (as "man and wife," as we used to say) but without marriage.

How much does this affect, consciously or unconsciously, the thinking and judgment and outlook of those of us who are much older and who grew up in a far different mode?

APRIL 28, 1980
PRINCETON

The unsuccessful attempt to rescue the Americans kidnapped by Iranian terrorists has cast gloom over most everyone. I think I feel it more than most; after all, we worked hard to be helpful to Iran, and both Helen and I became attached to the country. It is hard for me to suppress my emotions against them now, with their ghoulish display of the bodies of American soldiers burned to death or dismembered by the collision of the rescue planes.

Then I pull myself together, try to overlook the glee of American journalists and TV commentators at one more American "defeat"—and remember the Sunday morning of the attack on Pearl Harbor. That was no minor setback of a rescue expedition: practically our whole Pacific fleet of warships was sunk.

F.D.R. did not pull back. We began the long, painful effort to defeat the Japanese. And did just that. Lincoln had to contend with the Copperheads, at a dark hour of the Civil War.

APRIL 29, 1980
NEW YORK

The clan of newspaper writers is having a big to-do with the resignation of Cy Vance as Secretary of State. His reason: that he disapproved the hostage rescue mission. He will find that his influence on the Carter foreign policy could have been far greater if he had stayed on at his post. It is not too easy to judge a dismissing, a resignation offered on the grounds of "personal" principle, balanced against sticking it out and fighting for your position inside the fort.

Coming in the middle of a national political campaign, his judgment can be questioned, if he really means that he believes and supports most of Carter's other foreign policies and acts.

Newspaper writers are pretty short on *history*. This is by no means the first or the most important resignation. What was the story back of William Jennings Bryan's break with Wilson on a comparable issue: the issue of military force, on the sea? Bryan felt sure this would bring on a World War—which, of course, it did. Who would defend Bryan's "principle," then (seven Senators) or now?

I could not have disagreed more with the frantic crash program for an H-bomb. I was given a full opportunity to state my dissent before Truman, though because I foolishly classified the document and obeyed the rules about security, no one knew much about my views, at the time when it might have been useful to have those views known. I resigned some time afterward, for I thought it would be a fine display of principle, but a low blow against a President I believed in, to resign at the time of the H-bomb furor and Truman's decision.

Principle, personal integrity—these are wonderful words to toss around in editorial columns, but there is another principle, that of loyalty and decorum in high public trust.

The whole subject of personal principle in public life is a fascinating one, but it is too often dealt with, as in the Vance resignation case, without weighing fully against personal integrity and maintenance of personal principle a public officer's duty to the country when a decision or policy goes contrary to his own judgment or conviction. I faced that in the H-bomb case. That case could throw some light on the deeper question —how much must a public man's "conscience" (once he has expressed himself "within the official family") yield to the effect of the expression of his "conscience" on the public interest?

MAY 3, 1980
PRINCETON

Sitting in a lawn chair watching my wife do the active gardening—that is when I have the most acute sense of deprivation. The damned arthritis! Perhaps by this time next spring I can dig and transplant as of yore. This standing by while spring and gardening are in full tilt and I am on the sidelines—this is my worst pain.

My recollections of years past are closely woven into gardens I have made and tended and gloried in. This passion comes from my mother; Dad had no interest whatever in growing things, in gardening in any way. But Mina wanted always to get her hands into the soil, and her zest for picking flowers was one of our favorite family jokes.

Which was my favorite garden, of all the long string? The one I created on the hillside at our place in Norris, I suppose. "Created" is the word; I had to dig into the hillside and overcome the handicap of heavy shade, the enemy of flower gardening. But I had an advantage; I had the cooperation of Mac—the choicest kind of fertilizer, that from a beloved horse. A rare substance, and much better than cow manure.

When we were first married, living in an apartment, the prospect of staying in the city (Chicago) the whole week long without gardening was one I couldn't endure. I solved the problem by inviting myself to help Florence Richberg in her gardening—she the young and attractive new wife of my boss, Don, and a dedicated gardener.

The soil at Palos Park, where the Richbergs lived, was a stubborn one, so I had good hard digging to do creating soil—the part of gardening I have always liked most.

This meant that I spent my Sundays away from our apartment and Helen. My conscience for this indulgence still smarts at this thoughtlessness.

Later we leased a place in Palos Park and I had my own garden. At Palos I inherited a rock garden, developed by the lady from whom we rented that part of a farm. It was there that I tried English rock plant seeds. And in the sun-filled window of my study, I planted annual seeds in flat boxes, tilted up to get the most of the late winter sun. Helen still remembers my telephoning to her (she with a big house and a baby and small child to care for) that it was time to sprinkle the seeds, or turn the boxes.

The garden that has meant the most to me, from which I have learned the most, is the one here at 88 Battle Road. When I began laying it out, I discovered what must have been a dump by our predecessors. The yucca plants in the front, ugly beyond words, and persistent, took several seasons to eradicate. My dream of a half-circle rose garden in front of the house replaces them. The beginning of rhododendron plantings, some now standing more than twenty-five feet tall, the laying out of an informal curving perennial border—the enchantment of the awakening of a border in the spring—all of this is as much a part of my life as the public events or public figures involved in my career.

My life story—like that of almost everyone else—is the familiar one of choosing one road rather than another. The summing up is the familiar Robert Frost poem: "The Road Not Taken."

"I shall be telling this with a sigh somewhere ages and ages hence: Two roads diverged in a wood, and I, I took the one less traveled by, and that has made all the difference."

At the breakfast table this morning, Helen improved on the "less traveled road" note. With some pride she said, "You chose the *right* road." The choice I made, she concurring quietly but strongly, was to give up my life as an oncoming lawyer to go to Wisconsin on a public service career with no assurance of where that road led.

Where it led, as it turned out, was to an adventure with TVA—not then even a glint in my eye or F.D.R.'s for that matter—and from that "less traveled" road to other paths still less defined, in the mind of Albert Einstein, and later still André Meyer.

"But," said Helen, "think of it not as another road but the *right* road."

The other road, the road I was traveling as a "promising" young lawyer and expert on public utility law, would have made me a corporate lawyer, rich in money and repute, as happened to others of my law-school class and time.

It was because I was headed for financial success as a utility and corporate lawyer that the choice I made that night, in Madison, when Phil LaFollette asked me to become a Commissioner, was so dramatic, decisive, and adventuresome.

When I settle down to the actual writing of this "writing project," that part of my story should be told in detail. A vignette of Phil, the aggressive handsome young Wisconsin Governor, hardly settled into the old-fashioned "mansion"; his intellectual wife, Isen; and my shock when he pressed me to accept an important post in his government in 1931; my walking and walking and walking around the Capitol grounds most of the night, taking the 4 A.M. train back to Chicago, where Helen and I talked about what it would do to our life; how she took the financial deprivation without a bit of hesitation.

My law practice and my legal writing had already identified me as a "comer"; it was clear that this kind of career was opening up—and yet we decided to give up all that for a vague future. But it was the *right* road: I never had money-making as part of my goal; never; yet that was what I was heading for.

This recollection reminds me of the career of a classmate: Jim Nicely, top of our class, president of the Law Review, law secretary on graduation to Mr. Justice Holmes (practically God), a junior partnership at once in the most important law firm in New York, then on to George Baker's First National Bank. How bitterly disappointed when he was passed over for the presidency of Guaranty Trust Co., and his early death. What road did he take?

MAY 15, 1980
PRINCETON

Nancy was here for a couple days' visit. She is my idea of a splendid woman, adjusting herself beautifully to the "after the children have left the nest" period, enthusiastic about her free-lance proofreading and copyediting, and preparing for a year's sabbatical on the West Coast with Sylvain. Nancy never answered the description of many parents about their children: "a problem."

Now as a middle-aged and still very attractive person, she is a joy to be with.

In the summer-vacation period before my sophomore college year, I wrote the first drafts of an "oration," intending to compete in the oratorical contests that were then the vogue. What I wrote became "The Mission of the Jew," and a successful oration. "The unity of mankind" theme in that oration doesn't sound like an idea that an eighteen-year-old today could declaim about so confidently as I did back then.

MAY 18, 1980
PRINCETON

A phone call Friday afternoon from Dave Freeman, responding to a call I had made about the remarkable TVA Annual Report. He talked with enthusiasm, having just come from a picnic at Norris State Park, of 150 retired TVA-ers, on the anniversary date (47th) of the signing of the TVA Act (Helen and I attended last year's anniversary gathering).

The TVA Annual Report, like most such documents, has always been wholly factual, with emphasis on the management's achievements during the year reported. But not so the Annual Report I have just read. I read a good many such reports from companies in which I have a stock investment. Imagine any of them carrying a picture of a young boy on the cover —not the Chairman—and dedicating the report to the *future* of that boy, a lad living in a poor, drafty house not far from TVA's rather grand offices in Knoxville. And inside the cover of the report, a heart-stopping picture of a very poor family of children and their mother, a picture taken forty-six years ago, when TVA was founded.

When I saw this I wept, not only because of the image of those kids and what TVA has been able to do for so many of them but also because the report began with quotes from my speech to the TVA employees a year ago, and concluded, as an epilogue, with a quotation from *TVA: Democracy on the March.*

MAY 25, 1980
PRINCETON

Poverty: I have had little of it in my own life, but much of the meaning of my earlier working life—from the earliest TVA days on—is summed up by what to *do* about it—what can be done by you and those who listen to you, about poverty.

In 1933 I suddenly became an *operating* figure in the most depressed and poverty-stricken region of the country—the Southeast.

It was about that time that the whole country had a chance to see what rural poverty among true-blue white Americans looked like. Looked, because the poverty of sharecroppers and the "mountain whites" was photographed and written about.

I didn't see this poverty as an observer, a newspaperman, a social scientist. The poverty I saw was the worn-out cotton fields of northern Alabama and Mississippi, and the eroded hills and eroded lives of the hill country of eastern Tennessee.

There was the greatest difference possible: it was my job, my duty, my inner challenge to do things that would enable these people to stem that cancer of poverty of land and community. I had to *do* something, not just evoke sympathy, or *look* on these desperately poor people and this poor land as something picturesque and worthy of writing about or photographing.

That was the difference between my self-imposed role and that of the

Farm Security Administration's dramatic photographs, or the dreamy "planning" talk of Rex Tugwell and Eleanor Roosevelt.

Long ago, I was visiting New York. I asked Beatrice, then a teenage girl with heavy dark braids around her head, to tell me where I could buy fireplace andirons for our home.

She took me to a place on the Lower East Side where the streets and curbs were, then, lined with pushcarts, where everything was sold, in the open air, by people, freshly emigrated from the poor parts of Europe.

Said Beatrice: "Isn't this colorful, this picture of life?" I said perhaps colorful, but these are poor people, very poor. Instead of thinking of it as picturesque, I would hope to find ways to help them out of this obvious poverty.

This remark "shocked" her then. She remembered it years later, when I found that the poverty of the sharecroppers and coal-mine people was not colorful but something that should change.

MAY 29, 1980
PRINCETON

Word just received that Julian Boyd died last night. Like many others he has been been in what the papers call "failing health" for months and months. But Julian simply paid no mind to his health. He loved being with people; at parties he was voluble, spreading his famous Virginia charm. Then a relapse, but soon he was up and going again. No withdrawing to the shell that his parlous health would justify. Julian and I hit it off very well.

One chapter of my atom book discussed radiation. Some of the most ignorant and most easily scared critics of atomic energy insist, with their hearts in their throats, that *any* radiation is terribly harmful, produces cancer. I think the way I handled this issue, in the book, was quite sensible, and will stand up.

I think of this because yesterday at the hospital there was a concentration of X-ray machines as great as any I have seen. Though my lower body was twisted and contorted into most unnatural shapes (and damned painful it was), I could see the reason for this hour and a half of X-ray picture taking, since Dr. Wilson will need to know during the surgery just exactly how my bones fit together.

This would have been quite impossible without that form of radiation we call "X-rays." In the section where this was going on, there were displayed the yellow posters so familiar in my early traffic with the atom: Radiation Area—Danger.

In the tiny dressing room ("changing" room) preparatory to X-rays, I stared into a bold yellow sign on the door: "Attention: If You Are Pregnant, Advise the Technician."

A pregnant mother-to-be is the way I am being treated by my ever-loving spouse, as the days pass and I'm that much closer to surgical dissection. Helen doesn't fuss with me, but I'm not permitted to pick up things I have dropped, and the solicitude about when I want to have a meal grows.

I don't think she is really worried about how the operation will come out—quite—but like a late-pregnant woman my idiosyncrasies are catered to.

Now I have a whole summer ahead of me for reflection and summing up. I need to recover from a major operation, true; but I'm not ill, no disease, the only impediment being the getting over the not inconsiderable shock of the surgery and learning to walk with artificial joints.

I have long had a deep personal aversion to too much introspection, whether in private matters or public affairs. There is something in my nature that rejects the inward look, in contrast to action.

One reason for this is that I naturally look ahead, concern myself in imagination or in action with the future. What will happen in the future? How can I help shape that future?

But reflection such as I contemplate for the next several months—can it be directed not only to the past but have meaning for the future?

MAY 31, 1980
PRINCETON

A D.E.L. retrospective, on film—six reels of eleven minutes each. I was seated in the garden, with the eye of a professional motion-picture camera staring at me, a sound man cross-legged under the old apple tree, and Ross Spears, the director, asking me questions about my past, and how that past looks today.

I talked much too much. But he was the kind of interviewer who rather encourages loquacity. A film director has the advantage over a newsman in that he can, and does, cut the hell out of whatever one says, under the excuse of "editing."

This filming is to be part of a documentary about TVA which will be another year in the making.

Among many questions Spears put to me during the filming was one something like this: "With all of the punishment and worries you had to take, and did take, Mr. Lilienthal, what kept you going? How did you manage to put up with the harassment of Congressional investigations, attacks on your integrity, exhaustingly long days and nights without sleep; what kept you going?"

I said, "As my journals show, there were times when I seemed to question whether I could get through another day, another week. But *I did.*

"There is no one single answer, of course. TVA was so important and the TVA and Valley people, my friends, looked to me to persevere, not to abandon the struggle."

The deeper answer lies within me, the way I am put together, the genes I inherited from centuries ago.

"For at least the first ten years of my TVA life, overwhelmingly the press and radio as well as the Congress were dead set against me. During the row with A. E. Morgan, so widely read a commentator as Dorothy Thompson wrote a scathing personal attack on me, saying that this young Turk had induced a heart attack in 'an old ailing man, shortening A.E.'s life'—or words to this effect. A. E. died during just this last year at age ninety-three!

"My combativeness, pride, basic good health and constitution, love of adventure perhaps, could partially explain survival through crises."

"Weren't the toughest times the dull periods when you appeared to have lost your way toward anything worthwhile, toward what in your youth you had set your heart on achieving?" Spears asked.

"There were several such deadly doldrums. In the earliest period of my law practice," I said, "when I perversely would not go out to be visible as a lawyer needing clients, in the way well-trained young lawyers should. I didn't engage in Bar Association activities, didn't cultivate a law practice, and expended my energies writing one law-review article after another. I was a lost, unhappy young man.

"And long, long afterward in the 1950s, when I had firmly established the fact that I had tangible accomplishments of a high order that I could point to, after AEC, I was quite lost at Lazard Frères, one of the unhappiest, dullest periods of my life. Ultimately, I pulled out of each of these arid experiences.

"These trials, these strains, and, yes, agonies (for they were that) were not the consequence of fights and controversy and being in the limelight of adverse publicity."

JUNE 1, 1980
PRINCETON

Tomorrow afternoon Helen, Tom Moore, and I, with Beatrice joining us in New York, will deposit me at the hospital, at which time I will lose my freedom and turn it over to the doctors and nurses. The routine of life will be replaced by one dictated by the need to be carved up and restored —as I fully and unconditionally expect I shall be.

A most considerate phone call from David from Florence. He does have me in mind, for we have grown closer, bound more closely by last summer's working together day after long day on the atom book.

JUNE 17, 1980
NEW YORK HOSPITAL FOR SPECIAL SURGERY
NEW YORK

Exactly two weeks ago the educated butchers of this remarkable place sliced me way open, across both hips, and began a process that dawn that lasted until nearly 4 P.M.

Since that time I have learned to adjust myself to life with a walker, an aluminum frame that keeps me up, as I plow my way back to normal locomotion. This latter will take some weeks, but I am surprised at the progress I have made, and by the absence of real pain or weakness (except for the first day or so).

XIV

1981

JANUARY 2, 1981
PRINCETON

At year's end it has been my custom, even habit, to attempt a summary, a summing-up of the year just concluded, and almost always with a blast of exuberance about "looking ahead." The future is your concern, I thought, and wrote.

This was as tough a year as I have known for a long time. Two surgical operations: a "bilateral hip replacement" and a cataract eye operation. A hard year.

But a good one, too. For I got rid of the continued pain, and then fear of approaching invalidism or surgery was conquered. And the eye operation was without complications. I still wear a Hathaway piratical black patch over the left eye, and I shouldn't be writing or reading, which is frustrating to say the least.

So 1980 was a year in which I went through a risky major "ordeal" (Dr. Wilson's word, at last week's examination).

But the upbeat I found today in rereading journal entries of early 1980. That note of confidence is still there, otherwise how could it be that I have committed myself to a new and expensive office in the middle of Manhattan?

Other signs of confidence despite my griping about the disability imposed by the still-healing eye: I have committed myself to a trip to the University of Texas in mid-February and a statement at Brown University (call it a lecture) about Canadian waterpower and the future of an ailing New England.

If I could just get past this period of no reading and no writing. These journal notes are the first I have permitted myself for months and months.

EPILOGUE

This was the last journal entry my husband wrote. As he himself noted, it was one he should not have made at all, as he had been forbidden to read or write since his cataract operation in November, in order to avoid movement of the eye.

He had endured patiently these weeks of enforced inactivity. He was anxious to return to work again; at the same time he was concerned about his eye, wondering if in fact his vision would be fully restored.

Eleven days after this last entry—on Tuesday, January 13—his Princeton driver, Tom Moore, took him to New York for a late afternoon appointment with the specialist. The eye was found to be properly healed, and was fitted with a special contact lens. My husband's secretary, Mildred Baron, remembers how delighted he was as he came out into the doctor's waiting room. "Now I can really see you for the first time in months," he told her.

Mr. Moore drove him to his midtown hotel, where he was to spend the night. He planned to go to his new office at 1700 Broadway the next day to sign some papers, and then make another visit to the specialist to see how the eye was reacting to the new lens.

He telephoned me from the hotel to report the successful outcome of his examination.

His mood was jubilant. The many months of pain and physical disability had finally ended. He had fully recovered from his June operation for arthritis. He could walk without discomfort, without crutches or even a cane; now he could see again. Even the knowledge that he would soon have to undergo a cataract operation on the other eye did not daunt him. With characteristic eagerness he was looking forward to the projects he had been forced to set aside—chief among them being the editing of this volume of his Journals.

This last day of my husband's life was one of triumph and happiness.

He retired early that evening, and died peacefully in his sleep during the night.

—Helen M. Lilienthal

INDEX

(*L. means David E. Lilienthal*)

(*Prepared by Helen M. Lilienthal*)

[797]